PHILOSOPHY HERE AND NOW

WHAT PEOPLE ARE SAYING ABOUT
PHILOSOPHY HERE AND NOW:

"Most compelling is Lewis Vaughn's effort to connect the study of philosophy with the cultivation of general intellectual skills (critical thinking and writing about difficult, abstract ideas) that philosophy promotes and develops. I share his conviction that philosophy is a practical discipline—its enduring questions are ones that any person needs to reflect on, and the intellectual training it provides is crucial to both professional success and the development of a meaningful (or coherent) personal worldview."

—Nancy Matchett, *University of Northern Colorado*

"There is no doubt that *Philosophy Here and Now* is a creative, innovative, and very distinctive way to approach the problem of the basic philosophy textbook. Lewis Vaughn encourages students not only to think about philosophy and to critically evaluate their beliefs—he helps them learn to 'make philosophy' in a sophisticated and logically consistent fashion."

—Alexander Izrailevsky, *Salt Lake Community College*

"The goals of the text seem to be to enable students to see that philosophy is the activity of thinking clearly about matters that matter, and to introduce them to philosophy through selections of primary source material that is manageable for beginning students. I think the author achieves these goals. End-of-chapter stories and narratives are certainly one of the strengths of the book. . . . [The key strength of the book is] the clarity with which it presents philosophical issues."

—Robert M. Baird, *Baylor University*

"Lewis Vaughn attempts to introduce the student to the philosophical enterprise by making it relevant to their lives. He definitely succeeds in doing this by encouraging the students to engage (ponder, critique, evaluate) the philosophical arguments of the great philosophers instead of merely being passive readers. His emphasis on the importance of maintaining the high standards of critical thinking throughout the book was very impressive."

—Thi Lam, *San Jacinto College Central*

"Instead of insisting that [students] leave their familiar territory to discover philosophy elsewhere, this book ventures into their stomping ground and shows them that philosophy is already there. It wants them to think more clearly about the enduring puzzles of human life and it knows that the way to do this is through writing. . . . Lewis Vaughn's writing style is very accessible and a pleasure to read, making complicated ideas understandable."

—Sharon Kaye, *John Carroll University*

PHILOSOPHY HERE AND NOW

Powerful Ideas in Everyday Life

Second Edition

Lewis Vaughn

NEW YORK OXFORD
OXFORD UNIVERSITY PRESS

Oxford University Press is a department of the University of Oxford.
It furthers the University's objective of excellence in research,
scholarship, and education by publishing worldwide.

Oxford   New York
Auckland   Cape Town   Dar es Salaam   Hong Kong   Karachi
Kuala Lumpur   Madrid   Melbourne   Mexico City   Nairobi
New Delhi   Shanghai   Taipei   Toronto

With offices in
Argentina   Austria   Brazil   Chile   Czech Republic   France   Greece
Guatemala   Hungary   Italy   Japan   Poland   Portugal   Singapore
South Korea   Switzerland   Thailand   Turkey   Ukraine   Vietnam

For titles covered by Section 112 of the US Higher Education
Opportunity Act, please visit www.oup.com/us/he for the
latest information about pricing and alternate formats.

Published by Oxford University Press
198 Madison Ave, New York, NY 10016
http://www.oup.com

Oxford is a registered trade mark of Oxford University Press.

Library of Congress Cataloging-in-Publication Data
Vaughn, Lewis.
   Philosophy here and now : powerful ideas in everyday life / Lewis Vaughn. —
Second Edition.
      pages cm
   ISBN 978-0-19-020703-8
  1. Philosophy—Textbooks. I. Title.
   BD31.V38 2015
   100—dc23
                                                        2015027009

Printing number: 9 8 7 6 5 4 3 2

Printed in the United States of America
on acid-free paper

BRIEF CONTENTS

PREFACE   xxi

CHAPTER 1:   **PHILOSOPHY** AND **YOU**   1

CHAPTER 2:   **GOD** AND **RELIGION**   54

CHAPTER 3:   **MORALITY** AND THE **MORAL LIFE**   130

CHAPTER 4:   **MIND** AND **BODY**   196

CHAPTER 5:   **FREE WILL** AND **DETERMINISM**   228

CHAPTER 6:   **KNOWLEDGE** AND **SKEPTICISM**   262

CHAPTER 7:   **AESTHETICS**   320

CHAPTER 8:   **THE JUST SOCIETY**   337

CHAPTER 9:   **THE MEANING** OF **LIFE**   389

APPENDIX A: **ANSWERS** TO **EXERCISES**   411

APPENDIX B: **HOW** TO **WRITE** A **PHILOSOPHY PAPER**   415

NOTES   425

GLOSSARY   431

CREDITS   435

INDEX of MARGINAL
QUOTATIONS   437

GENERAL INDEX   439

CONTENTS

Preface   xxi

CHAPTER 1   PHILOSOPHY AND YOU   1

   1.1 PHILOSOPHY: THE QUEST FOR UNDERSTANDING   2

      The Good of Philosophy   2

      Philosophical Terrain   4

      What Do You Believe? Your Philosophical Beliefs   5

      Essay/Discussion Questions   7

   1.2 SOCRATES AND THE EXAMINED LIFE   8

      Philosophers at Work: Plato   9

      PLATO: The Republic   10

      Philosophy Now: Socrates Café   12

      Essay/Discussion Questions   13

   1.3 THINKING PHILOSOPHICALLY   13

      Reasons and Arguments   14

      Philosophy Lab   15

      Reading Philosophy   24

      Philosophers at Work: Hypatia   26

      Fallacious Reasoning   29

      Philosophy Now: Philosophy in the News   30

      Essay/Discussion Questions   36

   REVIEW NOTES   37

      Writing to Understand: Arguing Your Own Views   38

   KEY TERMS   39

   ARGUMENT EXERCISES   40

   NARRATIVE: Plato, *The Trial and Death of Socrates*   44

   PROBING QUESTIONS   52

   FOR FURTHER READING   52

CHAPTER 2 GOD AND RELIGION 54

2.1 OVERVIEW: GOD AND PHILOSOPHY 55

Why Religion Matters 55

Overview: The Philosopher's Quest 56

Philosophy Now: Who Believes in God? 57

What Do You Believe? Hard-Wired for God? 60

Belief and Disbelief 61

Writing to Understand: Critiquing Philosophical Views 63

2.2 ARGUMENTS FOR THE EXISTENCE OF GOD 63

Cosmological Arguments 63

AQUINAS: Summa Theologica 64

Philosophers at Work: St. Thomas Aquinas 65

Philosophy Now: Science and the Uncaused Universe 66

CRAIG: Reasonable Faith 67

Design Arguments 69

PALEY: Natural Theology 69

HUME: Dialogues Concerning Natural Religion 71

Ontological Arguments 75

ANSELM: Proslogium 75

Philosophy Now: Evolution and Intelligent Design 76

KANT: Critique of Pure Reason 79

Writing to Understand: Critiquing Philosophical Views 79

2.3 GOD AND THE PROBLEM OF EVIL 80

Rowe's Argument from Evil 80

ROWE: Philosophy of Religion 80

The Free Will Defense 83

SWINBURNE: Is There a God? 83

Philosophy Now: God and Hurricane Katrina 84

The Soul-Making Defense 85

HICK: Evil and the God of Love 85

Writing to Understand: Critiquing Philosophical Views 88

2.4 THEISM AND RELIGIOUS EXPERIENCE   89

ST. TERESA OF AVILA: The Life of
Teresa of Jesus   89

MACKIE: The Miracle of Theism   90

Philosophy Lab   91

ROWE: Philosophy of Religion   92

Philosophy Now: Proof of the Power of Prayer?   93

SWINBURNE: The Existence of God   94

Writing to Understand: Critiquing Philosophical
Views   95

2.5 BELIEF WITHOUT REASON   95

James: Pragmatic Faith   96

JAMES: "The Will to Believe"   97

MARTIN: Atheism: A Philosophical
Justification   103

Pascal: Betting on God   103

What Do You Believe? Do You Live by Faith?   104

PASCAL: Pensees and Other Writings   104

Writing to Understand: Critiquing Philosophical
Views   106

2.6 EASTERN RELIGIONS   106

Buddhism   106

SUMEDHO: Buddha-Nature   109

RAHULA: What the Buddha Taught   109

Hinduism   112

Philosophy Now: The Caste System   116

Daoism   118

CHUANG TZU: All Things Are One   119

LAO-TZU: Tao-te ching   119

Writing to Understand: Critiquing Philosophical
Views   121

REVIEW NOTES   122

Writing to Understand: Arguing Your Own
Views   124

KEY TERMS   125

FICTION: Arthur C. Clarke, "The Star"   **126**

PROBING QUESTIONS   128

FOR FURTHER READING   129

CHAPTER 3   MORALITY AND THE **MORAL LIFE   130**

3.1 OVERVIEW: ETHICS AND THE MORAL DOMAIN   131

Ethics and Morality   131

Moral Theories   134

> *Philosophy Now:* The Morality of Human Cloning   138

Religion and Morality   141

> *SHAFER-LANDAU: Whatever Happened to Good and Evil?*   141
>
> *Writing to Understand:* Critiquing Philosophical Views   142

3.2 MORAL RELATIVISM   143

Subjective Relativism   143

Cultural Relativism   145

> *What Do You Believe?* Cultural Relativism and Women's Rights   146
>
> *Writing to Understand:* Critiquing Philosophical Views   149

3.3 MORALITY BASED ON CONSEQUENCES   150

Utilitarianism   150

> *MILL:* "What Utilitarianism Is"   153
>
> *Philosophy Now:* Utilitarianism and the Death Penalty   154
>
> *Philosophy Lab*   158

Ethical Egoism   159

> *Philosophers at Work:* John Stuart Mill   160
>
> *Writing to Understand:* Critiquing Philosophical Views   162

3.4 MORALITY BASED ON DUTY AND RIGHTS   163

> *KANT: Groundwork of the Metaphysic of Morals*   163

Writing to Understand: Critiquing Philosophical
Views   168

3.5 MORALITY BASED ON CHARACTER   168

ARISTOTLE: Nicomachean Ethics   169

*SHAFER-LANDAU: The Fundamentals
of Ethics*   173

Writing to Understand: Critiquing Philosophical
Views   174

3.6 FEMINIST ETHICS AND THE ETHICS OF CARE   174

JAGGAR: "Feminist Ethics"   175

CROSTHWAITE: "Gender and Bioethics"   175

HELD: The Ethics of Care   177

BAIER: "The Need for More Than Justice"   179

Writing to Understand: Critiquing Philosophical
Views   179

3.7 ALBERT CAMUS: AN EXISTENTIALIST VOICE   180

CAMUS: The Myth of Sisyphus   181

Writing to Understand: Critiquing Philosophical
Views   183

3.8 CONFUCIANISM   183

CONFUCIUS: Analects   184

NOSS: A History of the World's Religions   186

Writing to Understand: Critiquing Philosophical
Views   186

REVIEW NOTES   187

Writing to Understand: Arguing Your Own
Views   189

KEY TERMS   189

FICTION: Ursula K. Le Guin, "The Ones Who Walk Away from Omelas"   191

PROBING QUESTIONS   194

FOR FURTHER READING   194

CHAPTER 4   MIND and BODY   196

4.1 OVERVIEW: THE MIND–BODY PROBLEM   197

Writing to Understand: Critiquing Philosophical Views   202

4.2 SUBSTANCE DUALISM   202

DESCARTES: Discourse on the Method of Rightly Conducting the Reason   203

SCHICK: Doing Philosophy   203

DESCARTES: Meditations on First Philosophy   204
What Do You Believe? The Immortal Soul   205

SEARLE: Mind   207
Writing to Understand: Critiquing Philosophical Views   208

4.3 MIND–BODY IDENTITY   208

SMART: "Sensations and Brain Processes"   208

CHALMERS: The Conscious Mind   209

NAGEL: "What Is It Like to Be a Bat?"   211
Writing to Understand: Critiquing Philosophical Views   212

4.4 THE MIND AS SOFTWARE   212

FODOR: "The Mind–Body Problem"   213

BLOCK: "Troubles with Functionalism"   214

SEARLE: Mind   215
Philosophers at Work: John R. Searle   216
Writing to Understand: Critiquing Philosophical Views   217
Philosophy Now: AI, Ethics, and War   218

4.5 THE MIND AS PROPERTIES   218

CHALMERS: The Conscious Mind   220
Philosophy Lab   221
Writing to Understand: Critiquing Philosophical Views   222

REVIEW NOTES   222

Writing to Understand: Arguing Your Own Views   223

KEY TERMS   224

FICTION: Terry Bisson, "They're Made out of Meat"   **225**

PROBING QUESTIONS   226

FOR FURTHER READING   226

CHAPTER 5   FREE WILL AND DETERMINISM   228

5.1 OVERVIEW: THE FREE WILL PROBLEM   229

What Do You Believe? Fate   233

Writing to Understand: Critiquing Philosophical Views   234

5.2 DETERMINISM AND INDETERMINISM   234

D'HOLBACH: "Of the System of Man's Free Agency"   234

Philosophers at Work: William James   236

JAMES: "The Dilemma of Determinism"   237

Writing to Understand: Critiquing Philosophical Views   238

5.3 COMPATIBILISM   238

LOCKE: An Essay Concerning Human Understanding   239

STACE: Religion and the Modern Mind   239

Philosophy Now: Does Belief in Free Will Matter?   240

ROWE: "Two Concepts of Freedom"   242

Writing to Understand: Critiquing Philosophical Views   243

5.4 LIBERTARIANISM   243

Philosophy Now: Science and Free Will   244

VAN INWAGEN: An Essay on Free Will   245

Philosophy Lab   246

TAYLOR: Metaphysics   246

Writing to Understand: Critiquing Philosophical Views   249

5.5 SARTRE'S PROFOUND FREEDOM   249

SARTRE: "Existentialism Is a Humanism"   250

Writing to Understand: Critiquing Philosophical
Views 254

REVIEW NOTES 254

Writing to Understand: Arguing Your Own
Views 256

KEY TERMS 256

FICTION: Thomas D. Davis, "A Little Omniscience
Goes a Long Way" **258**

PROBING QUESTIONS 261

FOR FURTHER READING 261

CHAPTER 6   KNOWLEDGE AND **SKEPTICISM   262**

**6.1 OVERVIEW: THE PROBLEM
OF KNOWLEDGE 263**

What Do You Believe? Cognitive Relativism
Undone 265
Writing to Understand: Critiquing Philosophical
Views 268

6.2 THE RATIONALIST ROAD 269

Plato's Rationalism 269

PLATO: Meno 271

Descartes' Doubt 272

*DESCARTES: Meditations on First
Philosophy* 273
Philosophy Now: Living in The Matrix 275
Philosophy Lab 276

Descartes' Certainty 276

DESCARTES: Meditations on First Philosophy 276
Philosophers at Work: René Descartes 278
Writing to Understand: Critiquing Philosophical
Views 280

6.3 THE EMPIRICIST TURN 281

Locke 281

*LOCKE: An Essay Concerning Human
Understanding* 281

Berkeley   287

    BERKELEY: Of the Principles of Human Knowledge   288

Hume   291

    Philosophers at Work: David Hume   292

    HUME: An Enquiry Concerning Human Understanding   293

    Writing to Understand: Critiquing Philosophical Views   298

6.4 THE KANTIAN COMPROMISE   299

    KANT: Critique of Pure Reason   300

    Philosophers at Work: Immanuel Kant   301

    Philosophy Now: Conceptualizing the World   304

    Writing to Understand: Critiquing Philosophical Views   307

6.5 A FEMINIST PERSPECTIVE ON KNOWLEDGE   307

    AINLEY: "Feminist Philosophy"   308

    ANTONY: "Embodiment and Epistemology"   308

    ANDERSON: "Feminist Epistemology and Philosophy of Science"   309

    COLE: Philosophy and Feminist Criticism   309

    Philosophers at Work: Mary Wollstonecraft   312

    Writing to Understand: Critiquing Philosophical Views   314

REVIEW NOTES   314

    Writing to Understand: Arguing Your Own Views   317

KEY TERMS   317

FICTION: Lewis Carroll, *Through the Looking-Glass*   318

PROBING QUESTIONS   318

FOR FURTHER READING   319

CHAPTER 7   AESTHETICS   320

7.1 OVERVIEW: PHILOSOPHY OF BEAUTY   321

Writing to Understand: Critiquing Philosophical
Views   321

7.2 WHAT IS ART?   321

Philosophy Now: Controversial Art   322

BELL: Art   323

Writing to Understand: Critiquing Philosophical
Views   323

7.3 AESTHETIC VALUE   323

What Do You Believe? Are There Objective
Standards in Art?   324
Philosophers at Work: Arthur C. Danto   325
Writing to Understand: Critiquing Philosophical
Views   326

7.4 PLATO, ARISTOTLE, AND HUME   326

ARISTOTLE: The Poetics   326
Philosophy Lab   327

HUME: Of the Standard of Taste   329
Writing to Understand: Critiquing Philosophical
Views   331

REVIEW NOTES   332

Writing to Understand: Arguing Your Own
Views   333

KEY TERMS   333

FICTION: Edgar Allan Poe, "The Oval Portrait"   334

PROBING QUESTIONS   335

FOR FURTHER READING   335

CHAPTER 8   THE JUST SOCIETY   337

8.1 OVERVIEW: JUSTICE AND POLITICAL PHILOSOPHY   338

What Do You Believe? Political Views in Flux   341
Writing to Understand: Critiquing Philosophical
Views   342

8.2 PLATO'S THEORY: JUSTICE AS MERIT   343

PLATO: The Republic   344

Philosophy Now: Merit or Equality: Who Gets to Live? 346

Writing to Understand: Critiquing Philosophical Views 347

8.3 SOCIAL CONTRACT THEORIES 347

Hobbes 348

Philosophers at Work: Thomas Hobbes 348

HOBBES: Leviathan 349

Locke 353

LOCKE: Second Treatise of Government 354

Rawls 358

Philosophers at Work: John Locke 358

RAWLS: A Theory of Justice 359

Writing to Understand: Critiquing Philosophical Views 361

8.4 SOCIALIST THEORIES 362

Philosophy Lab 363

Philosophy Now: Is the United States a Socialist Country? 364

MARX and ENGELS: Manifesto of the Communist Party 364

Writing to Understand: Critiquing Philosophical Views 370

8.5 FEMINISM AND SOCIAL JUSTICE 370

OKIN: Justice, Gender, and the Family 371

MILLER: Political Philosophy 375

Writing to Understand: Critiquing Philosophical Views 375

REVIEW NOTES 376

Writing to Understand: Arguing Your Own Views 378

KEY TERMS 378

FICTION: William Golding, "Lord of the Flies" **380**

PROBING QUESTIONS 388

FOR FURTHER READING 388

CHAPTER 9   THE MEANING OF LIFE   389

9.1 OVERVIEW: PHILOSOPHY AND THE MEANING
     OF LIFE   390
     Philosophy Lab   393

9.2 PESSIMISM: LIFE HAS NO MEANING   394
     TOLSTOY: My Confession   394
     SCHOPENHAUER: "On the Sufferings of the
         World"   396
     BAGGINI: What's It All About?   397
     Philosophy Now: Nietzsche: Reflections
         on Meaning   398

9.3 OPTIMISM: LIFE CAN HAVE MEANING   399
     Meaning from Above   399
         TOLSTOY: My Confession   399
         Philosophy Now: Is Religion Necessary
             for a Meaningful Life?   402
         BAGGINI: What's It All About?   403
     Meaning from Below   404
         EDWARDS: The Encyclopedia of Philosophy   404

REVIEW NOTES   405
     *What Do You Believe? What Can and Cannot Give
         Life Meaning?*   406
     Writing to Understand: Arguing Your Own
         Views   407

FICTION: Voltaire, "The Good Brahmin"   408

PROBING QUESTIONS   409

FOR FURTHER READING   409

     Appendix A: Answers to Exercises   411
     Appendix B: How to Write a Philosophy Paper   415
     Notes   425
     Glossary   431
     Credits   435
     Index of Marginal Quotations   437
     General Index   439

PREFACE

This second edition of *Philosophy Here and Now* stays true to the aspirations and character of the first. From the beginning the text has been designed to provide an extraordinary amount of encouragement and guidance to students who are encountering philosophy for the first (and perhaps last) time. Its ambitious aim is to get such students to take some big steps toward understanding, appreciating, and even doing philosophy. *Philosophy Here and Now* thus tries to do a great deal more than most other text readers. To foster a serious understanding of philosophy, it includes solid coverage of critical thinking skills and argument basics as well as guidance and practice in reading philosophical works. Students of course can appreciate the point and power of philosophy as they comprehend philosophical writings, but their appreciation blossoms when they see how philosophical issues and reasoning play out in contemporary society and how philosophical insights apply to their own lives. So the book's coverage and pedagogical features help students grasp philosophy's relevance and timeliness. Students learn how to *do* philosophy—to think and write philosophically—when they get encouragement and practice in analyzing and critiquing their own views and those of the philosophers they study. To this end, *Philosophy Here and Now* emphasizes philosophical writing, reinforced with step-by-step coaching in how to write argumentative essays and supported by multiple opportunities to hone basic skills.

In addition to these core elements, *Philosophy Here and Now* further engages today's learners with abundant illustrations and color graphics; marginal notes, questions, and quotes; profiles of a diverse array of philosophers; and ample representation of non-Western and nontraditional sources.

TOPICS AND READINGS

Nine chapters cover the existence of God, morality and the moral life, mind and body, free will and determinism, knowledge and skepticism, political philosophy, aesthetics, and the meaning of life. These topics are explored in seventy traditional and contemporary readings integrated into the main text, featuring both the indispensible standard readings and newer selections. The standards include writings by Plato, Aristotle, Aquinas, Pascal, Anselm, Descartes, Hume, Hobbes, Locke, Berkeley, Kant, d'Holbach, Paley, James, Sartre, Marx, and others. Among the more recent voices are those of Searle, Chalmers, Craig, Swinburne, Hick, Mackie, Rowe, Rahula, Jaggar, Held, Baier, Nagel, Block, Van Inwagen, Taylor, Cole, Ainley, Rawls, Okin, and Schopenhauer.

All these selections are juxtaposed with end-of-chapter pieces of fiction or narrative—stories meant to explore and dramatize the philosophical issues encountered in the chapters. They include some classic stories such as "The Good Brahmin" by Voltaire, "The Ones Who Walk Away from Omelas" by Ursula Le Guin, and "They're Made Out of Meat" by Terry Bisson, as well as lesser known fiction by notable writers like Arthur C. Clarke and William Golding. Each story is accompanied by discussion/essay questions designed to draw out its philosophical implications.

MAIN FEATURES

- **A comprehensive introductory chapter that lays the groundwork for philosophical thinking**—Through examples drawn from philosophical literature and everyday life, this chapter explains clearly the nature and scope of philosophy and how it relates to students' lives. This much, of course, is what any good text in this field should do. But this first chapter also shows how to devise and evaluate arguments and guides students in critically thinking, reading, and writing about philosophical issues.
- **Critical thinking questions that correspond to relevant passages in the main text or readings**—These questions, located in the margins of the text, invite students to ponder the implications of the material and to think critically about the assumptions and arguments found there. The questions are numbered and highlighted and easily lend themselves to both writing assignments and class discussion. The point of their marginal placement is to prompt students to think carefully and analytically as they read.
- **Six engaging types of text boxes demonstrate the value and relevance of philosophy:**
  - **"Philosophy Now"**—These boxes contain news items and research reports that illustrate how each chapter's philosophical issues permeate everyday life. They demonstrate that philosophical concerns arise continually in science, society, ethics, religion, politics, medicine, and more. Each box ends with questions that prompt critical thinking and philosophical reflection.
  - **"What Do You Believe?"**—Prompting student engagement and reflection, these boxes explore issues related to the chapter's topics and challenge students' beliefs.
  - **"Writing to Understand: Critiquing Philosophical Views"**—These boxes appear at the end of each section and consist of essay questions that prompt students to critically examine the strengths and weaknesses of the views discussed in the sections. Students can hark back to what they learned in answering the preceding marginal questions, and they can get plenty of writing help in Appendix B, "How to Write a Philosophy Paper."
  - **"Writing to Understand: Arguing Your Own Views"**—These boxes appear at the end of each chapter and ask students to explain and defend their own views on the chapter's topics in short essays.
  - **"Philosophers at Work"**—These boxes profile the lives and work of compelling figures in philosophy, past and present, Western and non-Western or

nontraditional, male and female. Some feature philosophers from the past whose story adds a human and historical dimension to the ideas discussed in the chapter, and some profile contemporary thinkers who are grappling with the important issues of the day. The point of these features is, of course, to show that philosophy is very much a living, relevant enterprise.

- **"Philosophy Lab"**—These boxes present simple thought experiments challenging students to think through scenarios that can reveal deeper philosophical insights or perspectives.
- **A final chapter, "The Meaning of Life"**—This chapter discusses how philosophers have clarified and explored the topic of life's meaning. It covers the main philosophical perspectives on the subject and samples the views of philosophers past and present.

All these features are supplemented with other elements to make the material even more engaging and accessible:

- **Marginal quotes**—These pithy, compelling quotes from an array of philosophers appear throughout the text, inviting students to join the ongoing conversation of philosophy.
- **Key terms, marginal definitions, and end-of-book glossary**—Key terms in each chapter appear in boldface at their first appearance in a chapter, and a marginal definition helps students learn the term within its immediate context. A list of the chapter's Key Terms appears at the end of each chapter, along with the page numbers on which the term and its definition first appear. Finally, a Glossary of those Key Terms and definitions provides an essential reference for students as they review and prepare for tests as well as draft their own philosophical essays and arguments.
- **Chapter objectives**—This list at the beginning of each chapter helps to scaffold student learning by providing both structure and support for previewing, note-taking, and retention of content.
- **End-of-chapter reviews**—Concluding each chapter, this feature revisits the Chapter Objectives, encouraging students to reflect and review.
- **An index of marginal quotes**—This supplemental index helps students locate the words of philosophers that seem especially insightful or inspiring to them.
- **"For Further Reading"**—Located at the end of each chapter, these useful references point students to sources that will enhance their understanding of chapter issues and arguments.
- **Timeline**—Featuring philosophers' lives and important events, this visual learning tool helps students appreciate the historic significance of philosophical ideas by placing them within a larger context.
- **Charts, tables, and color photos**—Appearing throughout the book, these have been selected or created to deepen student engagement with and understanding of complex ideas and abstract concepts. In addition, captions for these images include brief and open-ended questions to help students "read" visuals with the same critical attention they learn to bring to written texts.

NEW TO THIS EDITION

- **A new chapter on aesthetics (Chapter 7)**—In response to requests from teachers, this new edition includes a full chapter on aesthetics—a topic of great interest to students in a media-saturated environment. The chapter covers issues relating to the definition of art, objective and subjective standards, controversial artworks, and the philosophical examination of art (including explorations by Plato, Aristotle, Hume, and Danto). The end-of-chapter fiction selection, Edgar Allan Poe's "The Oval Portrait," should lead to rich classroom discussion of its disturbing themes, which still resonate in today's popular culture.
- **Expanded coverage of non-Western religions and perspectives**—Reflecting a call for more multicultural perspectives, Chapter 2 ("God and Religion") is now enhanced by coverage of Hinduism and Taoism as well as Buddhism. Chapter 3 ("Morality and the Moral Life") now covers Confucianism as a moral system.
- **Greater support for challenging readings**—While teachers who used the first edition praised the selection of primary sources as well as the supporting pedagogy, they suggested that some of the longer readings be made more accessible through careful excerpting as well as more frequent insertion of explanatory text. The second edition responds throughout to that excellent suggestion.
- **An important addition to Chapter 9 ("The Meaning of Life")**—The chapter now includes Nietzsche's reflections on life's meaning, the death of God, and the will to power.
- **Updated "For Further Reading" bibliographies**—These lists have been refreshed to include a wide range of contemporary perspectives and sources.

ANCILLARIES

- The Oxford University Press **Ancillary Resource Center (ARC)** (www.oup-arc.com/vaughn-philosophy-here-and-now) houses a wealth of Instructor Resources, including an Instructor's Manual with sample syllabi, reading summaries, essay/discussion questions, suggested Web links, and a glossary of key terms from the text; a Computerized Test Bank with fifty or more multiple-choice and true/false questions per chapter (also available as a traditional "pencil-and-paper" Test Bank in the Instructor's Manual); and PowerPoint lecture outlines.
- A **Companion Website** (www.oup.com/us/vaughn) contains study materials for students, including level-one and level-two practice quizzes with multiple-choice and true/false questions taken from the Test Bank, essay/discussion questions, reading summaries, flashcards of key terms from the text, and suggested Web links.
- Student resources are also available on **Dashboard** (www.oup.com/us/dashboard), an intuitive, integrated, auto-graded homework system that analyzes students' specific strengths and problem areas. The *Philosophy Here and Now* Dashboard includes the level-one and level-two self-quiz questions from the Companion Website, each linked to a specific chapter objective, flashcards of key terms from the text, and a glossary. Access to Dashboard can be packaged with the text at a

discount, stocked separately by your college bookstore, or purchased directly at the Dashboard site.
- All instructor and student resources are also available as cartridges for **Learning Management Systems**. For more information, please contact your Oxford University Press Sales Representative at 1-800-280-0280.

ACKNOWLEDGMENTS

A text like this is not possible without the help of a lot of talented and conscientious people. At the top of the list are my fine editors at Oxford University Press—most notably Robert Miller and Meg Botteon, as well as Marianne Paul and Kaitlin Coats. Throughout the formative stages of this text, many astute reviewers provided invaluable suggestions and criticisms, and the book is much the better for it. Many thanks to:

Donald Anderson
University of New Mexico, Los Alamos

Marcos Arandia
North Lake College

Gary Backhaus
Harford College

Robert Baird
Baylor University

Joseph A. Baltimore
West Virginia University

Carlos R. Bovell
Gloucester County College

Teresa Cantrell
University of Louisville

Stephen Capone
University of Utah

Sally Carey
Lakeland Community College

Glenn Chicoine
University of Dallas

Stephen H. Daniel
Texas A&M University

Miguel Endara
Los Angeles Pierce College

Paul Herrick
Shoreline Community College

Elaine Hurst
St. Francis College

Alexander M. Izrailevsky
Salt Lake Community College

Sharon Kaye
John Carroll University

Stephen D. Kovach
Dona Ana Community College

Thi Lam
San Jacinto College

David Lopez
American River College

Shannon Love
Old Dominion University

Sarah Lublink
Edison State College

Dennis Lucius
Columbia College

Michael Mardoyan
Wayne County Community College

Nancy Matchett
University of Northern Colorado

Tinola Mayfield-Guerrero
Monroe Cummunity College

Bruce McGraw
*Southwestern College, Cuyamaca
College, and Palomar College*

Alexander Miller
Piedmont Technical College

Gary London Pagels
*Northwest Mississippi Community
College*

Craig Payne
Indian Hills College

Christian Perring
Dowling College

Susan Purviance
University of Toledo

James E. Reed
*Northwest Mississippi Community
College*

Jordy Rocheleau
Austin Peay State University

Philip Robbins
University of Missouri

Srujesh Shah
College of Lake County

Timothy Shanahan
Loyola Marymount University

Michael Sturm
Kishwaukee College

Jesse Switzer
*University of Mississippi and
Mississippi State University*

William P. Thomas, Jr.,
*Pennsylvania Highlands
Community College*

Sandra Woien
Mesa Community College

Ruth E. Zollars
*Neosho County Community
College*

PHILOSOPHY HERE AND NOW

CHAPTER 1

PHILOSOPHY AND YOU

Chapter Objectives

1.1 PHILOSOPHY: THE QUEST FOR UNDERSTANDING

- Know the practical and theoretical benefits of studying philosophy.
- Take an inventory of your philosophical beliefs.
- Know the four main divisions of philosophy and the kinds of questions they examine.

1.2 SOCRATES AND THE EXAMINED LIFE

- Understand why Socrates declared that "the unexamined life is not worth living."
- Explain the Socratic method and how Socrates used it in search of understanding.
- Relate how Socrates showed that Thrasymachus's notion of justice was wrong.
- Explain how *reductio ad absurdum* arguments work.

1.3 THINKING PHILOSOPHICALLY

- Define *argument*, *statement*, *conclusion*, and *premise*.
- Know the two conditions that must be met for an argument to be *good*.
- Define *deductive argument*, *inductive argument*, *valid*, *sound*, *cogent*, *strong*, and *weak*. Understand inferences to the best explanation and how their strength is evaluated.
- Be able to identify arguments in the form of *modus ponens*, *modus tollens*, affirming the consequent, and denying the antecedent.
- Be able to identify arguments in various contexts and tell whether they are valid or invalid, sound or not sound, strong or weak, and cogent or not cogent.
- Understand the guidelines for reading and appreciating philosophy.
- Be aware of common fallacies and know how to identify them in various contexts.

1.1 PHILOSOPHY: THE QUEST FOR UNDERSTANDING

The title of this text, *Philosophy Here and Now*, is meant to emphasize that philosophy is, well, here and now—that is, *relevant* and *current*. This means that philosophy, even with its ancient lineage and seemingly remote concerns, applies to your life and your times and your world. Philosophy achieves this immediacy by being many good things at once: it is enlightening, thought-provoking, life-changing, liberating, theoretical, and practical. The world is full of students and teachers who can attest to these claims. More importantly, you will find proof of them in the remainder of this text—and in the writings of the great philosophers, in your grasping what they say and the reasons they give for saying it, and in your own honest attempts to apply philosophy to your life.

Philosophy is the name that philosophers have given to both a discipline and a process. As a discipline, philosophy is one of the humanities, a field of study out of which several other fields have evolved—physics, biology, political science, and many others. As a process, philosophy is a penetrating mode of reflection for understanding life's most important truths. This mode is what we may call the *philosophical method*—the systematic use of critical reasoning to try to find answers to fundamental questions about reality, morality, and knowledge. The method, however, is not a master key used exclusively by professional philosophers to unlock mysteries hidden from common folk. The philosophical method is the birthright of every person, for we are all born with the capacity to reason, to question, to discover. For thousands of years, great minds like Aristotle, Plato, Confucius, Descartes, Aquinas, and Sartre have used it in their search for wisdom, and what they found has changed countless lives. But amateur philosophers like you have also used it—and continue to use it—to achieve life-altering understanding that would have eluded them otherwise.

The Good of Philosophy

Philosophy is not just about ideas; it's about *fundamental* ideas, those upon which other ideas depend. A fundamental belief logically supports other beliefs, and the more beliefs it supports the more fundamental it is. Your belief or disbelief in God, for example, might support a host of other beliefs about morality, life after death, heaven, hell, free will, science, evolution, prayer, abortion, miracles, homosexuality, and more. Thanks to your upbringing, your culture, your peers, and other influences, you already have a head full of fundamental beliefs, some of them true, some false. Whether true or false, they constitute the framework of your whole belief system, and as such they help you make sense of a wide range of important issues in life—issues concerning what exists and what doesn't, what actions are right or wrong (or neither), and what kinds of things we can know and not know. Fundamental beliefs, therefore, make up your "philosophy of life," which informs your thinking and guides your actions.

Perhaps now you can better appreciate philosophy's greatest *practical* benefit: it gives us the intellectual wherewithal to improve our lives by improving our philosophy of life. A faulty philosophy of life—that is, one that comprises a great many false fundamental beliefs—can lead to a misspent or misdirected life, a life less meaningful than it could be. Philosophy is the most powerful instrument we have for evaluating the worth of our fundamental beliefs and for changing them for the better. Through philosophy we exert control over the trajectory of our lives, making major course corrections by reason and reflection.

The Greek philosopher Socrates (469–399 BCE), one of Western civilization's great intellectual heroes, says, "An unexamined life is not worth living." To examine your life is to scrutinize the core ideas that shape it, and the deepest form of scrutiny is exercised through philosophy. This search for answers goes to the heart of the traditional conception of philosophy as a search for wisdom (the term *philosophy* is derived from Greek words meaning "love of wisdom"). With the attainment of wisdom, we come to understand the true nature of reality and how to apply that understanding to living a good life.

Philosophy's chief *theoretical* benefit is the same one that most other fields of inquiry pursue: understanding for its own sake. Even if philosophy had no practical applications at all, it would still hold great value for us. We want to know how the world

Figure 1.1 Socrates (469–399 BCE).

works, what truths it hides, just for the sake of knowing. And philosophy obliges. Astronomers search the sky, physicists study subatomic particles, and archaeologists search for ancient ruins, all the while knowing that what they find may have no practical implications at all. We humans wonder, and that's often all the reason we need to search for answers. As the great philosopher Aristotle says, "For it is owing to their wonder that people both now begin and at first began to philosophize."

For many people, the quest for understanding through philosophy is a spiritual, transformative endeavor, an ennobling pursuit of truths at the core of life. Thus, several philosophers speak of philosophy as something that enriches or nurtures the soul or mind. Socrates, speaking to the jurors who condemned him for practicing philosophy on the streets of Athens, asked, "Are you not ashamed that, while you take care to acquire as much wealth as possible, with honor and glory as well, yet you take no care or thought for understanding or truth, or for the best possible state of your soul?" In a similar vein, the Greek philosopher Epicurus (341–270 BCE) said, "Let no young man delay the study of philosophy, and let no old man become weary of it; for it is never too early nor too late to care for the well-being of the soul." And in our own era, the philosopher Walter Kaufmann (1921–1980) declared, "Philosophy means liberation from the two dimensions of routine, soaring above the well known, seeing it in new perspectives, arousing wonder and the wish to fly."

Along with philosophical inquiry comes freedom. We begin our lives at a particular place and time, steeped in the ideas and values of a particular culture, fed ready-made beliefs that may or may not be true and that we may never think to question.

2 Is it possible to lead a meaningful life without self-examination?

Philosophy is the highest music.
—Plato

Figure 1.2 Aristotle (384–322 BCE).

To teach how to live without certainty and yet without being paralysed by hesitation is perhaps the chief thing that philosophy, in our age, can do for those who study it.
—Bertrand Russell

3 Has your thinking recently led you to reflect on philosophical questions? If so, how did the thought process begin, and what fundamental belief did you end up contemplating?

Metaphysics is the study of reality in the broadest sense, an inquiry into the elemental nature of the universe and the things in it.

If you passively accept such beliefs, then those beliefs are *not really yours*. If they are not really yours, and you let them guide your choices and actions, then they—not you—are in charge of your life. You thus forfeit your personal freedom. But philosophy helps us rise above this predicament, to transcend the narrow and obstructed standpoint from which we may view everything. It helps us sift our hand-me-down beliefs in the light of reason, look beyond the prejudices that blind us, and see what's real and true. By using the philosophical method, we may learn that some of our beliefs are on solid ground and some are not. In either case, through philosophy our beliefs become truly and authentically our own.

Philosophical Terrain

Philosophy's sphere of interest is vast, encompassing fundamental beliefs drawn from many places. Philosophical questions can arise anywhere. Part of the reason for this is that ordinary beliefs that seem to have no connection with philosophy can become philosophical in short order. A physiologist may want to know how our brains work, but she ventures into the philosophical arena when she wonders whether the brain is the same thing as the mind—a question that science alone cannot answer. A lawyer studies how the death penalty is administered in Texas, but he does philosophy when he considers whether capital punishment is ever morally permissible. A medical scientist wants to know how a human fetus develops, but she finds it difficult to avoid the philosophical query of what the moral status of the fetus is. An astrophysicist studies the Big Bang, the cataclysmic explosion thought to have brought the universe into being—but then asks whether the Big Bang shows that God caused the universe to exist. On CNN you see the horrors of war and famine, but then you find yourself grappling with whether they can be squared with the existence of an all-powerful, all-knowing, and all-good God. Or you wonder what your moral obligations are to the poor and hungry of the world. Or you ponder whether government should help people in need or leave them to fend for themselves.

We can divide philosophy's subject matter into four main divisions, each of which is a branch of inquiry in its own right with many subcategories. Here's a brief rundown of these divisions and a sampling of the kinds of questions that each asks.

Metaphysics is the study of reality in the broadest sense, an inquiry into the elemental nature of the universe and the things in it. Though it must take into account the findings of science, metaphysics generally focuses on basic questions that science cannot address. Questions of interest: Does the world consist only of matter, or is it made up of other basic things, such as ideas or minds? Is there a spiritual, ideal realm that exists beyond the material world? Is the mind the same thing as the

WHAT DO YOU BELIEVE?

Your Philosophical Beliefs

Where do you stand on the fundamental issues in philosophy? Here is your chance to take inventory of your views. After you finish this course, take the survey again to see if your perspective has changed or become more nuanced. Answer with these numbers: 5 = true; 4 = probably true; 3 = neither probable nor improbable; 2 = probably false; 1 = false.

1. At least some moral norms or principles are objectively true or valid for everyone. _____

2. Moral standards are relative to what individuals or cultures believe. _____
3. Mind and body consist of two fundamentally different kinds of stuff—nonphysical stuff and physical stuff. _____
4. The mind, or soul, can exist without the body. _____
5. Our mental states are nothing but brain states (mind states are identical to brain states). _____

6. No one has free will. _____
7. Persons have free will (some of our actions are free). _____
8. Although our actions are determined, they can still be free (free will and determinism are not in conflict). _____
9. The God of traditional Western religions (an all-knowing, all-powerful, all-good deity) exists. _____
10. The apparent design of the universe shows that it had an intelligent designer. _____
11. Right actions are those commanded by God; wrong actions are those forbidden by God. _____
12. God does not make actions right or wrong by commanding them to be so. _____
13. We can know some things about the external world. _____
14. We cannot know anything about the external world. _____
15. The theory of evolution is a better explanation of the apparent design of biological life than the theory of "intelligent design." _____
16. Truth about something depends on what a person or culture believes. _____
17. Libertarianism is the correct political theory. _____
18. Welfare liberalism is the correct moral theory. _____
19. Meaning in life comes from outside ourselves, from God or some other transcendent reality. _____
20. Meaning in life comes from within ourselves. _____

body? How are mind and body related? Do people have immortal souls? Do humans have free will, or are our actions determined by forces beyond our control? Can they be both free and determined? Does God exist? How can both a good God and evil exist simultaneously? What is the nature of causality? Can an effect ever precede its cause? What is the nature of time? Is time travel possible?

And what, Socrates, is the food of the soul? Surely, I said, knowledge is the food of the soul.
—Plato

MAIN DIVISIONS OF PHILOSOPHY

DIVISION	QUESTIONS
Metaphysics	Does the world consist only of matter, or is it made up of other basic things, such as ideas or mind? Is there a spiritual, ideal realm that exists beyond the material world? Is the mind the same thing as the body? How are mind and body related? Do people have immortal souls? Do humans have free will, or are our actions determined by forces beyond our control? Can they be both free and determined? Does God exist? How can both a good God and evil exist simultaneously? What is the nature of causality? Can an effect ever precede its cause? What is the nature of time? Is time travel possible?
Epistemology	What is knowledge? What is truth? Is knowledge possible—can we ever know anything? Does knowledge require certainty? What are the sources of knowledge? Is experience a source of knowledge? Is mysticism or faith a source? Can we gain knowledge of the empirical world through reason alone? If we have knowledge, how much do we have? When are we justified in saying that we know something? Do we have good reasons to believe that the world exists independently of our minds? Or do our minds constitute reality?
Axiology	What makes an action right (or wrong)? What things are intrinsically good? What is the good life? What gives life meaning? What makes someone good (or bad)? What moral principles should guide our actions and choices? Which is the best moral theory? Is killing ever morally permissible? If so, why? Are moral standards objective or subjective? Is an action right merely because a culture endorses it? Does morality depend on God? What makes a society just?
Logic	What are the rules for drawing correct inferences? What are the nature and structure of deductive arguments? How can propositional or predicate logic be used to evaluate arguments? Upon what logical principles does reasoning depend? Does logic describe how the world is—or just how our minds work? Can conclusions reached through inductive logic be rationally justified?

Epistemology is the study of knowledge.

Axiology is the study of value, including both aesthetic value and moral value. **Ethics** is the study of moral value using the methods of philosophy.

Epistemology is the study of knowledge. Questions of interest: What is knowledge? What is truth? Is knowledge possible—can we ever know anything? Does knowledge require certainty? What are the sources of knowledge? Is experience a source of knowledge? Is mysticism or faith a source? Can we gain knowledge of the empirical world through reason alone? If we have knowledge, how much do we have? When are we justified in saying that we know something? Do we have good reasons to believe that the world exists independently of our minds? Or do our minds constitute reality?

Axiology is the study of value, including both aesthetic value and moral value. The study of moral value is known as **ethics**. Ethics involves inquiries into the nature of moral judgments, virtues, values, obligations, and theories. Questions of interest: What makes an action right (or wrong)? What things are intrinsically good? What is the good life? What gives life meaning? What makes someone good (or bad)? What moral principles should guide our actions and choices? Which is the best moral theory? Is killing ever morally permissible? If so, why? Are moral standards objective or subjective? Is an action right merely because a culture endorses it? Does morality depend on God? What makes a society just?

Logic is the study of correct reasoning. Questions of interest: What are the rules for drawing correct inferences? What are the nature and structure of deductive arguments? How can propositional or predicate logic be used to evaluate arguments? Upon what logical principles does reasoning depend? Does logic describe how the world is—or just how our minds work? Can conclusions reached through inductive logic be rationally justified?

In addition to these divisions, there are subdivisions of philosophy whose job is to examine critically the assumptions and principles that underlie other fields. Thus we have the philosophy of science, the philosophy of law, the philosophy of mathematics, the philosophy of history, the philosophy of language, and many others. When those laboring in a discipline begin questioning its most basic ideas—ideas that define its subject matter and principles of inquiry—philosophy, the most elemental mode of investigation, steps in.

Figure 1.3 Plato, pointing upward toward the higher realm of ideas, and Aristotle, gesturing down toward the things of this earth.

Logic is the study of correct reasoning.

There's a difference between a philosophy and a bumper sticker.
—Charles M. Schulz

ESSAY/DISCUSSION QUESTIONS   Section 1.1

1. What is the philosophical method? Who can make use of this approach to important questions? Can only philosophers use it? Have you used it? How?

2. What are some fundamental beliefs that are part of your philosophy of life? How do these beliefs influence your life?

3. What is philosophy's greatest practical benefit? Do you think studying philosophy could change your life goals or your fundamental beliefs? Why or why not?

4. How can philosophy enhance your personal freedom? What are some of your fundamental beliefs that you have never fully examined? What might be the result of never examining a fundamental belief?

5. Which of the four main divisions of philosophy interests you the most? Why? What philosophical questions listed in this section would you most want to have answers to?

1.2 SOCRATES AND THE EXAMINED LIFE

The point of philosophy is to start with something so simple as not to seem worth stating, and to end with something so paradoxical that no one will believe it.
—Bertrand Russell

4 Socrates says that a good man can never be harmed. What do you think he means by this?

There is no better way to understand and appreciate the philosophical quest for knowledge than to study the life and work of Socrates, one of philosophy's greatest practitioners and the most revered figure in its history. Socrates wrote no philosophy, but we know about his thinking and character through his famous pupil Plato, who portrayed him in several dialogues, or conversations (notably in *Euthyphro*, *Crito*, and *Apology*). For two and a half millennia Socrates has been inspiring generations by his devotion to philosophical inquiry, his relentless search for wisdom, and his determination to live according to his own high standards. As mentioned earlier, he famously said that "the unexamined life is not worth living," and he became the best example of someone living his life by that maxim. Thus, at a time when most philosophy was directed at cosmological speculations, he turned to critically examining people's basic concepts, common beliefs, and moral thinking.

For Socrates, an unexamined life is a tragedy because it results in grievous harm to the soul, a person's true self or essence. The soul is harmed by lack of knowledge—ignorance of one's own self and of the most important values in life (the good). But knowledge of these things is a mark of the soul's excellence. A clear sign that a person has an unhealthy soul is her exclusive pursuit of social status, wealth, power, and pleasure instead of the good of the soul. The good of the soul is attained only through an uncompromising search for what's true and real, through the wisdom to see what is most vital in life. Such insight comes from rational self-examination and critical questioning of facile assumptions and unsupported beliefs. To get to the truth, Socrates thought, we must go around the false certitudes of custom, tradition, and superstition and let reason be our guide. Thus he played the role of philosophical gadfly, an annoying pest to the people of Athens, prodding them to wake up and seek the wisdom within their grasp.

We know very little about Socrates' life. He spent all his days in Athens except for a term of military service in which he soldiered in the Peloponnesian War. He was married and had three sons. He spent much of his time roaming the streets of Athens, speaking with anyone who would listen. His habit was to ask people seemingly simple questions about their views on virtue, religion, justice, or the good, challenging them to think critically about their basic assumptions. This sort of question-and-answer dialogue in which propositions are methodically scrutinized to uncover the truth has become known as the **Socratic method**. Usually when Socrates used it in conversations, or dialogues, with his fellow Athenians, their views would be exposed as false or confused. The main point of the exercise for Socrates, however, was not to win arguments but to get closer to the truth. He thought people who pursued this noble aim as he did should not be embarrassed by being shown to be wrong; they should be delighted to be weaned from a false opinion. Nevertheless, the Socratic conversations often ended in the humiliation of eminent Athenians. They were enraged by Socrates, while many youths gravitated to him.

Eventually Socrates was arrested and charged with disrespecting the gods and corrupting the youth of the city. He was tried before five hundred jurors, a majority

The **Socratic method** is a question-and-answer dialogue in which propositions are methodically scrutinized to uncover the truth.

The chief benefit, which results from philosophy, arises in an indirect manner, and proceeds more from its secret, insensible influence, than from its immediate application.
—David Hume

PHILOSOPHERS AT WORK

Plato

No philosopher—with the possible exception of Aristotle—has had a deeper and more lasting effect on Western thought than Plato (c. 427–347 BCE). He was born in Athens into an influential aristocratic family and grew up during the perilous years of the Peloponnesian War, a struggle between Athens and the Peloponnesian states. He was a student and admirer of Socrates, who turned Plato's

Figure 1.4 Plato (c. 427–347 BCE).

mind toward philosophy and the pursuit of wisdom. He was horrified by Socrates' execution in 399 for impiety and corruption of Athenian youth, so he left Athens and traveled widely, possibly to Sicily and Egypt. When he returned to Athens, he founded the Academy, a teaching college regarded as the first university, and devoted the rest of his life to teaching and writing philosophy. (The Academy endured for hundreds of years until it was abolished by the Eastern Roman emperor Justinian I.) The Academy's most renowned student was Aristotle, who entered the school at age seventeen and remained for twenty years.

Plato's thinking is embodied in his dialogues, twenty-five of which exist in their complete form. They were written during a span of fifty years and have been divided into three periods: early, middle, and late. The early dialogues include *Euthyphro*, *Apology*, *Crito*, *Meno*, and *Gorgias*. These early works portray Socrates as a brilliant and principled deflater of his contemporaries' bogus claims to knowledge. The middle dialogues include *Phaedo*, *Republic*, and *Theaetetus*; the late ones consist of *Critias*, *Parmenides*, *Sophist*, *Laws*, and others.

of whom voted to convict him. His sentence was death or exile; he chose death by poison rather than leave his beloved Athens. In his dialogues *Crito* and *Phaedo*, Plato recounts the events of the trial, including Socrates' address to the jurors. Socrates is portrayed as a man of brilliant intellect and unshakeable integrity who would not compromise his principles, even to escape death.

In one form or another, the Socratic method has been part of Western education for centuries. It is one of the ways that philosophy is done, a powerful procedure for applying critical thinking to many statements that seem out of reason's reach. As Socrates used it, the method typically would go like this: (1) someone poses a question about the meaning of a concept (for example, "What is justice?"); (2) Socrates' companion gives an answer; (3) Socrates raises questions about the answer, proving that the answer is inadequate; (4) to avoid the problems inherent in this answer, the companion offers a second answer; (5) steps (3) and (4) are repeated a

Figure 1.5 *The Death of Socrates* by Jacques-Louis David.

number of times, ultimately revealing that the companion does not know what he thought he knew. To Socrates, this negative outcome is actually a kind of progress. False answers are eliminated, opinions are improved, and perhaps the truth is a little closer than before.

Let's watch Socrates in action. Here is his conversation with Thrasymachus, a teacher eager to demonstrate that Socrates is not as wise as people say he is. The question is "What is justice?" and Thrasymachus insists that justice is whatever is in the interest of the strongest—that is, might makes right.

Plato, *The Republic*

Listen, then, he [Thrasymachus] said; I proclaim that justice is nothing else than the interest of the stronger. And now why do you not praise me? But of course you won't.

Let me first understand you, I [Socrates] replied. Justice, as you say, is the interest of the stronger. What, Thrasymachus, is the meaning of this? You can not mean to say that because Polydamas, the pancratiast [an athlete], is stronger than we are, and finds the *eating* of beef conducive to his bodily strength, that to eat beef is therefore equally for our good who are weaker than he is, and right and just for us?

That's abominable of you, Socrates; you take the words in the sense which is most damaging to the argument.

Not at all, my good sir, I said; I am trying to understand them; and I wish that you would be a little clearer.

Well, he said, have you never heard that forms of government differ; there are tyrannies, and there are democracies, and there are aristocracies?

Yes, I know.

And the government is the ruling power in each state?

Certainly.

And the different forms of government make laws democratical, aristocratical, tyrannical, with a view to their several interests; and these laws, which are made by them for their own interests, are the justice which they deliver to their subjects, and him who transgresses them they punish as a breaker of the law and unjust. And that is what I mean when I say that in all states there is the same principle of justice, which is the interest of the government; and as the government must be supposed to have power, the only reasonable conclusion is, that everywhere there is one principle of justice, which is the interest of the stronger.

Now I understand you, I said; and whether you are right or not I will try to discover. But let me remark, that in defining justice you have yourself used the word "interest" which you forbade me to use. It is true, however, that in your definition the words "of the stronger" are added.

A small addition, you must allow, he said.

Great or small, never mind about that: we must first inquire whether what you are saying is the truth. Now we are both agreed that justice is interest of some sort, but you go on to say "of the stronger"; about this addition I am not so sure, and must therefore consider further.

Proceed.

I will; and first tell me, Do you admit that it is just for subjects to obey their rulers?

I do.

But are the rulers of states absolutely infallible, or are they sometimes liable to err?

To be sure, he replied, they are liable to err.

Then in making their laws they may sometimes make them rightly, and sometimes not?

True.

When they make them rightly, they make them agreeably to their interest; when they are mistaken, contrary to their interest; you admit that?

Yes.

And the laws which they make must be obeyed by their subjects—and that is what you call justice?

Doubtless.

Then justice, according to your argument, is not only obedience to the interest of the stronger but the reverse?

What is that you are saying? he asked.

I am only repeating what you are saying, I believe. But let us consider: Have we not admitted that the rulers may be mistaken about their own interest in what they command, and also that to obey them is justice? Has not that been admitted?

Yes.

Then you must also have acknowledged justice not to be for the interest of the stronger, when the rulers unintentionally command things to be done which are to their own injury. For if, as you say, justice is the obedience which the subject renders to their commands, in that case, O wisest of men, is there any escape from the conclusion that the weaker are commanded to do, not what is for the interest, but what is for the injury of the stronger?[1]

> Astonishment is the root of philosophy.
> —Paul Tillich

5 Socrates never seems adversarial or combative in his dialogues. What effect do you think this approach has on those who enter into dialogue with him?

PHILOSOPHY NOW

Socrates Café

The Socratic method is alive and well in the twenty-first century—Christopher Phillips, author and educator, has seen to that. He has traveled from one end of the country to the other to facilitate philosophical discussions based on the Socratic method. These informal gatherings attract people of all ages from all sorts of backgrounds and life experiences. He calls the dialogues Socrates Cafés. They are held in coffeehouses, day care centers, senior centers, high schools, churches, and other places, and they have had a profound effect on him and on many people who have participated in such discussions. As Phillips says,

> For a long time, I'd had a notion that the demise of a certain type of philosophy has been to the detriment of our society. It is a type of philosophy that Socrates and other philosophers practiced in Athens in the sixth and fifth centuries B.C. A type that utilized a method of philosophical inquiry that "everyman" and "everywoman" could embrace and take for his or her own, and in the process rekindle the childlike—but by no means childish— sense of wonder. . . .
>
> The Socratic method of questioning aims to help people gain a better understanding of themselves and their nature and their potential for excellence. At times, it can help people make more well-informed life choices, because they now are in a better position to know themselves, to comprehend who they are and what they want. It can also enable a thoughtful person to articulate and then apply his or her unique philosophy of life. This in turn will better equip a questioning soul to engage in the endless and noble pursuit of wisdom.—*Socrates Café* (2001)

Phillips is the author of several books including *Socrates Café* and *Six Questions of Socrates: A Modern-Day Journey of Discovery through World Philosophy*. He is also co-founder of the Society for Philosophical Inquiry (www.philosopher.org), which supports the creation and development of Socrates Cafés around the world. He says there are now over six hundred Socrates Cafés worldwide.

Socrates Cafés usually begin with a question such as "What is sanity?" "When is life not worth living?" or "Is there such a thing as human nature?" The list of possible questions is long and varied. If you were to participate in a Socrates Café, what question would you most like to address?

Socrates uses his famous question-and-answer approach to prove that Thrasymachus's definition of justice is wrong. In particular, he applies a common form of argument called **reductio ad absurdum**. (Other argument forms are discussed in the following section.) The basic idea behind it is if you assume that a set of statements is true, and yet you can deduce a false or absurd statement from it, then the original set of statements as a whole must be false. So, in the preceding dialogue, Socrates says in effect, Let's assume that Thrasymachus is right that justice is whatever is in the interest of the powerful, and that people are just if they obey the laws made by the powerful. It is clear, however, that the powerful sometimes make mistakes and demand obedience to laws that are *not* in their best interest. So if Thrasymachus's definition of justice is correct, then it is right for people to do what is in the interest of the powerful, and it is also right to do what is *not* in the interest of the powerful. His idea of justice then leads to a logical contradiction and is therefore false.

> *Reductio ad absurdum* is an argument form in which a set of statements to be proved false is assumed, and absurd or false statements are deduced from the set as a whole, showing that the original statement must be false.

ESSAY/DISCUSSION QUESTIONS   Section 1.2

1. Could the execution of someone for saying unpopular things happen in this country? Why or why not? Are there countries in the world where such things happen regularly? Is the execution of someone for his or her offensive speech ever justified? Explain.

2. What do you think Socrates would think about modern consumer societies?

3. Socrates is often regarded as the noblest of the great philosophers. Is this opinion justified? Why or why not?

4. Write an imaginary Socratic dialogue between yourself and a friend. Imagine that your friend declares, "Everyone lies. No one ever tells the truth," and you want to show that those statements are false.

5. Write a Socratic dialogue between two fictional characters. Imagine that the opening statement is, "Courtesy to others is always a cynical attempt to serve your own interests. Respect for people has nothing to do with courtesy."

1.3 THINKING PHILOSOPHICALLY

As we have seen, to think philosophically is to bring your powers of critical reasoning to bear on fundamental questions. When you do this, you are usually clarifying the meaning of concepts, constructing and evaluating philosophical theories, or devising and evaluating logical arguments. This latter task constitutes the principal labor of philosophy. Socrates, Plato, Aristotle, Descartes, and other great thinkers do not deliver their philosophical insights to us without argument, as if we are automatically to accept their views with no questions asked. Philosophers provide *reasons* for thinking their ideas are plausible—that is, they give us arguments. And if we believe what they say, it should be because there are good reasons for doing so. Likewise, if we expect intelligent people to accept *our* philosophical views, we must argue our case. Since the philosophy we read will most likely contain arguments, our understanding of the text will hang on our ability to identify and understand those arguments.

Reasons and Arguments

As you might have guessed, the term *argument* does not refer to heated disagreements or emotional squabbles. An **argument** is a group of statements in which one of them is meant to be supported by the others. A **statement** (or **claim**) is an assertion that something is or is not the case and is therefore the kind of utterance that is either true or false. In an argument, the statement being supported is the **conclusion**, and the statements supporting the conclusion are the **premises**. The premises are meant to provide reasons for believing that the conclusion is true. A good argument gives us good reasons for accepting a conclusion; a bad argument fails to provide good reasons. In philosophy—and in any other kind of rational inquiry—accepting a conclusion (statement) without good reasons is an elementary mistake in reasoning. Believing a statement without good reasons is a recipe for error; believing a statement for good reasons increases your chances of uncovering the truth.

When we do philosophy, then, we are likely at some point to be grappling with arguments—we are trying to either (1) devise an argument to support a statement or (2) evaluate an argument to see if there really are good reasons for accepting its conclusion.

An **argument** is a statement coupled with other statements that are meant to support that statement. A **statement (claim)** is an assertion that something is or is not the case and is therefore the kind of utterance that is either true or false. A **conclusion** is the statement being supported. A **premise** is a statement supporting the conclusion.

Note that *argument* in the sense used here is not synonymous with *persuasion*. An argument provides us with reasons for accepting a claim; it is an attempted "proof" for an assertion. But persuasion does not necessarily involve giving any reasons at all for accepting a claim. To persuade is to influence people's opinions, which can be accomplished by offering a good argument but also by misleading with logical fallacies, exploiting emotions and prejudices, dazzling with rhetorical gimmicks, hiding or distorting the facts, threatening or coercing people—the list is long. Good arguments prove something whether or not they persuade. Persuasive ploys can change minds but do not necessarily prove anything.

Now consider these two simple arguments:

Argument 1
It's wrong to take the life of an innocent person.
Abortion takes the life of an innocent person.
Therefore abortion is wrong.

Argument 2
God does not exist. After all, most college students believe that that is the case.

Figure 1.6 Hitler was a master persuader, relying not on good arguments but on emotional rhetoric. How many people today would be persuaded by a contemporary politician with Hitler's rhetorical talents?

PHILOSOPHY LAB

Do you live an examined life? The following statements express some fundamental beliefs—beliefs that countless people have but may never have thought much about. Read each statement and select the ones that you sincerely believe. Then try to recall if you have ever seriously questioned these beliefs. (Passing thoughts and idle revelry do not count.) Be honest. This little experiment could be very revealing—and helpful as you think about your life and values.

1. God exists and watches over me.
2. God sometimes answers prayers.
3. There is a heaven.
4. I have both a body and an immortal soul.
5. My emotions are not under my control; they just happen.
6. It is wrong to criticize other cultures.
7. It is wrong to judge other people's actions.
8. The moral principles that I was raised to believe are the right ones.
9. Political conservatives are wrong about most issues.
10. Political liberals are wrong about most issues.
11. I make free choices; all my decisions are up to me.
12. I can come to know some things by faith alone.
13. My emotions are my best guide to what is morally right or wrong.
14. People are basically bad.
15. People are basically good.

In Argument 1, the conclusion is "abortion is wrong," and it is backed by two premises: "It's wrong to take the life of an innocent person" and "Abortion takes the life of an innocent person." In Argument 2, the conclusion is "God does not exist," which is supported by the premise "After all, most college students believe that that is the case." Despite the differences between these two passages (differences in content, the number of premises, and the order of their parts), they are both arguments because they exemplify basic argument structure: a conclusion supported by at least one premise.

Though the components of an argument seem clear enough, people often fail to distinguish between arguments and strong statements that contain no arguments at all. Suppose we change Argument 1 into this:

> Abortion is wrong. I can't believe how many people think it's morally okay. The world is insane.

Now there is no argument, just an expression of exasperation or anger. There are no statements giving us reasons to believe a conclusion. What we have are some unsupported assertions that may merely *appear* to make a case. If we ignore the

Philosophy asks the simple question, what is it all about?
—Alfred North Whitehead

distinction between genuine arguments and nonargumentative material, critical reasoning is undone.

The simplest way to locate an argument is to *find its conclusion first, then its premises*. Zeroing in on conclusions and premises can be a lot easier if you keep an eye out for *indicator words*. Indicator words often tag along with arguments and indicate that a conclusion or premise may be nearby.

Here are a few conclusion indicator words:

consequently	as a result
thus	hence
therefore	so
it follows that	which means that

Here are some premise indicator words:

in view of the fact	assuming that
because	since
due to the fact that	for
inasmuch as	given that

Just remember that indicator words do not *guarantee* the presence of conclusions and premises. They are simply telltale signs.

Assuming we can recognize an argument when we see it, how can we tell if it is a good one? Fortunately, the general criteria for judging the merits of an argument are simple and clear. A good argument—one that gives us good reasons for believing a claim—must have (1) solid logic and (2) true premises. Requirement (1) means that the conclusion should follow logically from the premises, that there must be a proper logical connection between the supporting statements and the statement supported. Requirement (2) says that what the premises assert must in fact be the case. An argument that fails in either respect is a bad argument.

There are two basic kinds of arguments—deductive and inductive—and our two requirements hold for both of them, even though the logical connections in each type are distinct. **Deductive arguments** are intended to give *logically conclusive* support to their conclusions so that if the premises are true, the conclusion absolutely must be true. Argument 1 is a deductive argument and is therefore supposed to be constructed so that if the two premises are true, its conclusion cannot possibly be false. Here it is with its structure laid bare:

Argument 1

1. It's wrong to take the life of an innocent person.
2. Abortion takes the life of an innocent person.
3. Therefore, abortion is wrong.

Do you see that, given the form or structure of this argument, if the premises are true, then the conclusion *has to be true*? It would be very strange—illogical, in fact—to agree that the two premises are true but that the conclusion is false.

One's philosophy is not best expressed in words; it is expressed in the choices one makes . . . and the choices we make are ultimately our responsibility.
—Eleanor Roosevelt

6 Recall some statements that you have heard or read in which strong assertions were made but no argument was presented. Did the assertions prove anything? What was your reaction at the time? Were you persuaded or impressed by them?

A deductive argument is an argument intended to give logically conclusive support to its conclusion.

Now look at this one:

Argument 3

1. All dogs are mammals.
2. Rex is a dog.
3. Therefore, Rex is a mammal.

Again, there is no way for the premises to be true while the conclusion is false. The deductive form of the argument guarantees this.

So a deductive argument is intended to have this sort of airtight structure. If it actually does have this structure, it is said to be *valid*. Argument 1 is deductive because it is intended to provide logically conclusive support to its conclusion. It is valid because, as a matter of fact, it does offer this kind of support. A deductive argument that fails to provide conclusive support to its conclusion is said to be *invalid*. In such an argument, it is possible for the premises to be true and the conclusion false. Argument 3 is intended to have a deductive form, and because it actually does have this form, the argument is also valid.

An elementary fact about deductive arguments is that their validity (or lack thereof) is a *separate issue* from the truth of the premises. Validity is a structural matter, depending on how an argument is put together. Truth concerns the nature of the claims made in the premises and conclusion. A deductive argument is supposed to be built so that *if* the premises are true, the conclusion must be true—but in a particular case, the premises might *not* be true. A valid argument can have true or false premises and a true or false conclusion. (By definition, of course, it cannot have true premises and a false conclusion.) In any case, being invalid or having false premises dooms a deductive argument.

Inductive arguments are supposed to give *probable* support to their conclusions. Unlike deductive arguments, they are not designed to support their conclusions decisively. They can establish only that, if their premises are true, their conclusions are probably true (more likely to be true than not). Argument 2 is an inductive argument meant to demonstrate the probable truth that "God does not exist." Like all inductive arguments (and unlike deductive ones), it can have true premises and a false conclusion. So it's possible for the sole premise—"After all, most college students believe that that is the case"—to be true while the conclusion is false.

If inductive arguments succeed in lending probable support to their conclusions, they are said to be *strong*. Strong arguments are such that if their premises are true, their conclusions are probably true. If they fail to provide this probable support, they are termed *weak*. Argument 2 is a weak argument because its premise, even if true, does not show that more likely than not God does not exist. What college students (or any other group) believe about God does not constitute good evidence for or against God's existence.

But consider this inductive argument:

Argument 4

1. Eighty-five percent of the students at this university are Republicans.
2. Sonia is a student at this university.
3. Therefore, Sonia is probably a Republican.

Philosophy, when superficially studied, excites doubt; when thoroughly explored, it dispels it.
—Francis Bacon

An **inductive argument** is an argument intended to give probable support to its conclusion.

This argument is strong. If its premises are true, its conclusion is likely to be true. If 85 percent of the university's students are Republicans, and Sonia is a university student, she is more likely than not to be a Republican too.

When a valid (deductive) argument has true premises, it is a good argument. A good deductive argument is said to be *sound*. Argument 1 is valid, but we cannot say whether it is sound until we determine the truth of the premises. Argument 3 is valid, and if its premises are true, it is sound. When a strong (inductive) argument has true premises, it is also a good argument. A good inductive argument is said to be *cogent*. Argument 2 is weak, so there is no way it can be cogent. Argument 4 is strong, and if its premises are true, it is cogent.

Checking the validity or strength of an argument is often a plain, commonsense undertaking. Using our natural reasoning ability, we can examine how the premises are linked to the conclusion and can see quickly whether the conclusion follows from the premises. We are most likely to make an easy job of it when the arguments are simple. Many times, however, we need some help, and help is available in the form of methods and guidelines for evaluating arguments.

Having a familiarity with common argument patterns, or forms, is especially useful when assessing the validity of deductive arguments. We are likely to encounter these forms again and again. Here is a prime example:

Argument 5

> 1. If the surgeon operates, then the patient will be cured.
> 2. The surgeon is operating.
> 3. Therefore, the patient will be cured.

> Philosophy is like trying to open a safe with a combination lock: each little adjustment of the dials seems to achieve nothing, only when everything is in place does the door open.
> —Ludwig Wittgenstein

This argument form contains a *conditional* premise—that is, a premise consisting of a conditional, or if-then, statement (actually a compound statement composed of two constituent statements). Premise 1 is a conditional statement. A conditional statement has two parts: the part beginning with *if* (called the *antecedent*), and the part beginning with *then* (known as the *consequent*). So the antecedent of Premise 1 is "If the surgeon operates," and the consequent is "then the patient will be cured."

The best way to appreciate the structure of such an argument (or any deductive argument, for that matter) is to translate it into traditional argument symbols in which each statement is symbolized by a letter. Here is the symbolization for Argument 5:

> 1. If p, then q.
> 2. p.
> 3. Therefore, q.

We can see that p represents "the surgeon operates," and q represents "the patient will be cured." But notice that we can use this same symbolized argument form to represent countless other arguments—arguments with different statements but having the same basic structure.

It just so happens that the underlying argument form for Argument 5 is extremely common—common enough to have a name, *modus ponens* (or affirming the antecedent). The truly useful fact about *modus ponens* is that any argument having this form is valid. We can plug any statements we want into the formula and the result will be a valid argument, a circumstance in which if the premises are true, the conclusion must be true.

An equally prevalent argument form is *modus tollens* (or denying the consequent). For example:

Argument 6

1. If the dose is low, then the healing is slow.
2. The healing is not slow.
3. Therefore, the dose is not low.

1. If *p*, then *q*.
2. Not *q*.
3. Therefore, not *p*.

Modus tollens is also a valid form, and any argument using this form must also be valid.

There are also common argument forms that are invalid. Here are two of them:

Argument 7 (Affirming the Consequent)

1. If the mind is an immaterial substance, then ESP is real.
2. ESP is real.
3. Therefore, the mind is an immaterial substance.

1. If *p*, then *q*.
2. *q*.
3. Therefore, *p*.

Argument 8 (Denying the Antecedent)

1. If morality is relative to persons (that is, if moral rightness or wrongness depends on what people believe), then moral disagreement between persons would be nearly impossible.
2. But morality is not relative to persons.
3. Therefore, moral disagreement between persons is not nearly impossible.

1. If *p*, then *q*.
2. Not *p*.
3. Therefore, not *q*.

The advantage of being able to recognize these and other common argument forms is that you can use that skill to readily determine the validity of many deductive arguments. You know, for example, that any argument having the same form as *modus ponens* or *modus tollens* must be valid, and any argument in one of the common invalid forms must be invalid.

Inductive arguments also have distinctive forms, and being familiar with the forms can help you evaluate the arguments. In *enumerative induction*, we arrive at a generalization about an entire group of things after observing just some members of the group. Consider these:

7 Before reading this chapter, would you have found any of the invalid argument forms persuasive? Why or why not?

Argument 9

Every formatted disk I have bought from the computer store is defective.

Therefore, all formatted disks sold at the computer store are probably defective.

Argument 10

All the hawks in this wildlife sanctuary that I have observed have had red tails.

Therefore, all the hawks in this sanctuary probably have red tails.

Argument 11

Sixty percent of the Bostonians I have interviewed in various parts of the city are pro-choice.

Therefore, 60 percent of all Bostonians are probably pro-choice.

As you can see, enumerative induction has this form:

X percent of the observed members of group A have property P.

Therefore, X percent of all members of group A probably have property P.

The observed members of the group are simply a sample of the entire group. So based on what we know about this sample, we can generalize to all the members. But how do we know whether such an argument is strong? Everything depends on the sample. If the sample is large enough and representative enough, we can safely assume that our generalization drawn from the sample is probably an accurate reflection of the whole group of members. A sample is representative of an entire group only if each member of the group has an equal chance of being included in the sample. In general, the larger the sample, the greater the probability that it accurately reflects the nature of the group as a whole. Often common sense tells us when a sample is too small.

We do not know how many formatted disks from the computer store are in the sample mentioned in Argument 9. But if the number is several dozen and the disks were bought over a period of weeks or months, the sample is probably sufficiently large and representative. If so, the argument is strong. Likewise, in Argument 10 we don't know the size of the sample or how it was obtained. But if the sample was taken from all the likely spots in the sanctuary where hawks live, and if several hawks were observed in each location, the sample is probably adequate—and the argument is strong. In Argument 11, if the sample consists of a handful of Bostonians interviewed on a few street corners, the sample is definitely inadequate and the argument is weak. But if the sample consists of several hundred people, and if every member of the whole group has an equal chance of being included in the sample, then the sample would be good enough to allow us to accurately generalize about the whole

---

VALID AND INVALID ARGUMENT FORMS

VALID ARGUMENT FORMS

Affirming the Antecedent (*Modus Ponens*)	Denying the Consequent (*Modus Tollens*)
If *p*, then *q*.	If *p*, then *q*.
p.	Not *q*.
Therefore, *q*.	Therefore, not *p*.
Example:	Example:
If Spot barks, a burglar is in the house.	If Spot barks, a burglar is in the house.
Spot is barking.	A burglar is not in the house.
Therefore, a burglar is in the house.	Therefore, Spot is not barking.

INVALID ARGUMENT FORMS

Affirming the Consequent	Denying the Antecedent
If *p*, then *q*.	If *p*, then *q*.
q.	Not *p*.
Therefore, *p*.	Therefore, not *q*.
Example:	Example:
If the cat is on the mat, she is asleep.	If the cat is on the mat, she is asleep.
She is asleep.	She is not on the mat.
Therefore, she is on the mat.	Therefore, she is not asleep.

---

population. Typically, selecting such a sample of a large population is done by professional polling organizations.

In the argument form known as *analogical induction* (or argument by analogy), we reason in this fashion: Two or more things are similar in several ways; therefore, they are probably similar in one further way. Consider this argument:

Argument 12

Humans can walk upright, use simple tools, learn new skills, and devise deductive arguments.

Chimpanzees can walk upright, use simple tools, and learn new skills.

Therefore, chimpanzees can probably devise deductive arguments.

Figure 1.7 How much is a watch like the universe? Everything depends on the relevant similarities and differences.

The object of studying philosophy is to know one's own mind, not other people's.
—Dean Inge

This argument says that because chimpanzees are similar to humans in several respects, they probably are similar to humans in one further respect.

Here's an argument by analogy that has become a classic in philosophy:

Argument 13

A watch is a complex mechanism with many parts that seem arranged to achieve a specific purpose—a purpose chosen by the watch's designer.

In similar fashion, the universe is a complex mechanism with many parts that seem arranged to achieve a specific purpose.

Therefore, the universe must also have a designer.

We can represent the form of an argument by analogy in this way:

X has properties P1, P2, P3, plus the property P4.

Y has properties P1, P2, and P3.

Therefore, Y probably has property P4.

The strength of an analogical induction depends on the relevant similarities between the two things compared. The more relevant similarities there are, the greater the probability that the conclusion is true. In Argument 12, several similarities are noted. But there are some unmentioned dissimilarities. The brain of a chimpanzee is smaller and more primitive than that of a human, a difference that probably inhibits higher intellectual functions such as logical argument. Argument 12, then, is weak. A common response to Argument 13 is that the argument is weak because although the universe resembles a watch in some ways, in other ways it does not resemble a watch. Specifically, the universe also resembles a living thing.

The third type of inductive argument is known as *inference to the best explanation* (or abduction), a kind of reasoning that we all use daily and that is at the heart of scientific investigations. Recall that an argument gives us reasons for believing *that* something is the case. An *explanation*, on the other hand, states *how* or *why* something is the case. It attempts to clarify or elucidate, not offer proof. For example:

1. Megan definitely understood the material, for she could answer every question on the test.
2. Megan understood the material because she has a good memory.

Sentence 1 is an argument. The conclusion is "Megan definitely understood the material," and the reason (premise) given for believing that the conclusion is true is "for she could answer every question on the test." Sentence 2, though, is an explanation. It does not try to present reasons for believing something; it has nothing to prove. Instead, it tries to show why something is the way it is (why Megan understood the material). Sentence 2 assumes that Megan understood the material then tries to explain why. Such explanations play a crucial role in inference to the best explanation.

In inference to the best explanation, we begin with premises about a phenomenon or state of affairs to be explained. Then we reason from those premises to an explanation for that state of affairs. We try to produce not just any old explanation, but the best explanation among several possibilities. The best explanation is the one most likely to be true. The conclusion of the argument is that the preferred explanation is indeed probably true. For example:

Argument 14

> Tariq flunked his philosophy course.
>
> The best explanation for his failure is that he didn't read the material.
>
> Therefore, he probably didn't read the material.

Argument 15

> Ladies and gentlemen of the jury, the defendant was found with the murder weapon in his hand, blood on his clothes, and the victim's wallet in his pocket. We have an eyewitness putting the defendant at the scene of the crime. The best explanation for all these facts is that the defendant committed the murder. There can be very little doubt—he's guilty.

Here's the form of inference to the best explanation:

> Phenomenon Q.
>
> E provides the best explanation for Q.
>
> Therefore, it is probable that E is true.

In any argument of this pattern, if the explanation given is really the best, then the argument is inductively strong. If the explanation is not the best, the argument is inductively weak. If the premises of the strong argument are true, then the argument is cogent. If the argument is cogent, then we have good reason to believe that the conclusion is true.

The biggest challenge in using inference to the best explanation is determining which explanation is the best. Sometimes this feat is easy. If our car has a flat tire, we may quickly uncover the best explanation for such a state of affairs. If we see a nail sticking out of the flat and there is no obvious evidence of tampering or of any other extraordinary cause (that is, there are no good alternative explanations), we may safely conclude that the best explanation is that a nail punctured the tire.

In more complicated situations, we may need to do what scientists do to evaluate explanations, or theories—use special criteria to sort through the possibilities. Scientists call these standards the *criteria of adequacy*. Despite this fancy name, these criteria are basically just common sense, standards that you have probably used yourself.

> The true function of philosophy is to educate us in the principles of reasoning and not to put an end to further reasoning by the introduction of fixed conclusions.
> —George Henry Lewes

One of these criteria is called *conservatism*. This criterion says that, all things being equal, the best explanation or theory is the one that fits best with what is already known or established. For example, if a friend of yours says—in all seriousness—that she can fly to the moon without using any kind of rocket or spaceship, you probably wouldn't believe her (and might even think that she needed psychiatric help). Your reasons for doubting her would probably rest on the criterion of conservatism—that what she says conflicts with everything science knows about spaceflight, human anatomy, aerodynamics, laws of nature, and much more. It is logically possible that she really can fly to the moon, but her claim's lack of conservatism (the fact that it conflicts with so much of what we already know about the world) casts serious doubt on it.

Here is another useful criterion for judging the worth of explanations: *simplicity*. Other things being equal, the best explanation is the one that is the simplest—that is, the one that rests on the fewest assumptions. The theory making the fewest assumptions is less likely to be false because there are fewer ways for it to go wrong. In the example about the flat tire, one possible (but strange) explanation is that space aliens punctured the tire. You probably wouldn't put much credence in this explanation because you would have to assume too many unknown entities and processes—namely, space aliens who have come from who-knows-where using who-knows-what methods to move about and puncture your tires. The nail-in-the-tire theory is much simpler (it assumes no unknown entities or processes) and is therefore much more likely to be true.

When you are carefully reading an argument (whether in an essay or some other context), you will be just as interested in whether the premises are true as in whether the conclusion follows from the premises. If the writer is conscientious, he or she will try to ensure that each premise is either well supported or in no need of support (because the premise is obvious or agreed to by all parties). The needed support will come from the citing of examples, statistics, research, expert opinion, and other kinds of evidence or reasons. This arrangement means that each premise of the primary argument may be a conclusion supported in turn by premises citing evidence or reasons. In any case, you as the reader will have to evaluate carefully the truth of all premises and the support behind them.

Reading Philosophy

Unfortunately, arguments in philosophical essays rarely come neatly labeled so you can find and evaluate them. You have to do that work yourself, a task that requires careful reading and thinking. The process can be challenging because in the real world, arguments can be simple or complex, clearly stated or perplexing, and apparent or hidden. This is true for philosophical essays as well as for any other kind of writing that contains arguments. In some philosophical prose, the relationship between the conclusion (or conclusions) and the premises can be complicated, and even good arguments can be surrounded by material irrelevant to the arguments at hand. The remedy for these difficulties is instructive examples and plenty of practice, some of which you can get in this chapter.

Let's begin by identifying and analyzing the argument in the following passage. The issue is whether humans have free will or are compelled by forces beyond their control to act as they do (a topic we take up in Chapter 5). The statements are numbered for ease of reference.

> (1) The famous trial lawyer Clarence Darrow (1857–1938) made a name for himself by using the "determinism defense" to get his clients acquitted of serious crimes. (2) The crux of this approach is the idea that humans are not really responsible for anything they do because they cannot choose freely—they are "determined," predestined, if you will, by nature (or God) to be the way they are. (3) So in a sense, Darrow says, humans are like wind-up toys with no control over any action or decision. (4) They have no free will. (5) Remember that Darrow was a renowned agnostic who was skeptical of all religious claims. (6) But Darrow is wrong about human free will for two reasons. (7) First, in our everyday moral life, our own commonsense experience suggests that sometimes people are free to make moral decisions. (8) We should not abandon what our commonsense experience tells us without good reason—and (9) Darrow has given us no good reason. (10) Second, Darrow's determinism is not confirmed by science, as he claims—but actually conflicts with science. (11) Modern science says that there are many things (at the subatomic level of matter) that are not determined at all: (12) they just happen.

Indicator words are scarce in this argument, unless you count the words "first" and "second" as signifying premises. But the conclusion is not hard to find; it's Statement 6: "Darrow is wrong about human free will for two reasons." Locating the conclusion enables us to see that some statements (Statements 1 through 4) are neither conclusion nor premises; they are just background information on Darrow's views. Most argumentative essays contain some supplemental information like this. Statement 5 is irrelevant to the argument; Darrow's agnosticism has no logical connection to the premises or conclusion. Statement 12 is just a rewording of Statement 11. After this elimination process, only the following premises and conclusion (Statement 6) remain:

> (6) But Darrow is wrong about human free will for two reasons.
>
> (7) First, in our everyday moral life, our own commonsense experience suggests that sometimes people are free to make moral decisions.
>
> (8) We should not abandon what our commonsense experience tells us without good reason.
>
> (9) Darrow has given us no good reason.
>
> (10) Darrow's determinism is not confirmed by science, as he claims—but actually conflicts with science.
>
> (11) Modern science says that there are many things (at the subatomic level) that are not determined at all.

Figure 1.8 Clarence Darrow (1857–1938).

Statements 7 through 11 are the premises. They are all meant to provide support to Statement 6, but their support is of unequal weight. Statement 10 gives independent support to the conclusion without the help of any other premises, so it is an *independent* premise. We can say the same thing about Statement 11; it too is an independent premise. But notice that Statements 7, 8, and 9 are *dependent* premises supporting the conclusion. That is, taken separately, they are weak, but together they constitute a plausible reason for accepting Statement 6. Statement 10 directly supports the conclusion, and in turn is supported by Premise 11.

Now take a look at this passage:

> (1) As the Islamic clerics cling to power in Iran, students there are agitating for greater freedom and less suppression of views that the clerics dislike. (2) Even though ultimate power in Iran rests with the mullahs, it is not at all certain where the nation is headed. Here's a radical suggestion: (3) the Islamic republic in Iran will fall within the

PHILOSOPHERS AT WORK

Hypatia

Hypatia (c. 370–415) was the greatest philosopher of her day. She lived in the Greek city of Alexandria, which in the fourth century was the intellectual epicenter of the world, excelling in scientific and philosophical learning. It also was the home of the famed Library, which contained thousands of scholarly manuscripts drawn from the best thinkers of ancient times, including the works of

Figure 1.9 Hypatia (c. 370–415).

Plato and Aristotle. In this rich environment, Hypatia achieved fame as a Neoplatonist philosophy teacher, an astronomer, and a mathematician. At around age twenty-five or thirty she became the director of the school of the renowned philosopher Plotinus—a very high honor, since women were traditionally not appointed to such offices. Another indication of her sterling reputation was that she was appointed by a Christian government even though she was known to be a pagan.

She taught the works of the "pagan" philosophers such as Plato and Aristotle, and students came from far-flung places for the privilege of being her students. She also is thought to have written three commentaries on noted mathematical treatises.

In 415, Cyril, the Bishop of Alexandria, arranged for Hypatia's brutal murder at the hands of a Christian mob. She was pulled from her chariot, hauled to a church, stripped naked, and skinned alive with oyster shells. Cyril, on the other hand, was later canonized.

next five years. Why do I say this? (4) <u>Because</u> the majority of Iranians are in favor of democratic reforms, (5) and no regime can stand for very long when citizens are demanding access to the political process. (6) Also, Iran today is a mirror image of the Soviet Union before it broke apart—there's widespread dissatisfaction and dissent at a time when the regime seems to be trying to hold the people's loyalty. (7) Every nation that has taken such a path has imploded within five years. (8) Finally, the old Iranian trick of gaining support for the government by fomenting hatred of America will not work anymore (9) <u>because</u> Iran is now trying to be friends with the United States.

The conclusion is Statement 3, and the premises are Statements 4 through 9. The first two statements are extraneous. Statements 4 and 5 are dependent premises and so are Statements 6 and 7. Statements 8 and 9 constitute an argument that gives support to the passage's main conclusion (Statement 3). Statement 8 is the conclusion; Statement 9, the premise. Notice also that the sentence "Why do I say this?" is not a statement.

So remember: When you read a philosophical essay, you are not simply trying to glean some facts from it as you might if you were reading a science text or technical report. Neither are you following a storyline as if you were reading a mystery novel (though philosophy papers sometimes contain their share of mysteries). In most cases, you are tracing the steps in an argument, trying to see what conclusion the writer wants to prove and whether she succeeds in proving it. Along the way, you may encounter several premises with their accompanying analyses, clarifications, explanations, and examples. You may even run into a whole chain of arguments. In the end, if you have read well and the writer has written well, you are left not with a new set of data or a story ending, but a realization—maybe even a revelation—that a conclusion is, or is not, worthy of belief.

The best way to learn how to read philosophy well is to read philosophy often. You will probably get plenty of chances to do that in your current philosophy course. Having a few rules to guide you in your reading, however, may help shorten the learning curve. As you read, keep the following in mind.

1. Approach the text with an open mind. If you are studying philosophy for the first time, you are likely—at least at first—to find a good bit of the material difficult, strange, or exasperating, sometimes all three at once. That's normal. Philosophy is an exploration of the rugged frontiers of our knowledge of fundamental things, so much of this new territory is likely to seem daunting or unfamiliar. There's also an excellent chance that your first visits to this terrain will be vexing, perhaps even infuriating, because you may sometimes disagree with what you read.

There is no shame in experiencing any of these reactions. They come with the territory. But if you are to make any headway in philosophy, you need to try your best to counteract these attitudes and feelings. Remember, philosophy at its best is a fair-minded, fearless search for truth. Anything that interferes with this noble quest must be overcome and cast aside.

Avoid making a judgment about an essay's ideas or arguments until you fully understand them and have fairly considered them. Make sure you are not reading with

8 Suppose you are presented with written material containing statements and arguments that strike you as irreverent or unorthodox. Would you be able to read such a text with an open mind? Can you recall a case in which you did just that?

the intent to prove the conclusions false (or true). Be open to the possibility that the essay could give you good reasons to change your mind about something.

Try to maintain a neutral attitude toward the writer, presuming neither that she is right nor wrong, neither sinner nor saint. Don't assume that everything a renowned philosopher says must be true, and don't presuppose that everything a philosopher you dislike says must be false. Give the writer the same attention and respect that you would give a friend who is discussing a serious issue with you.

If you are reading the work of a famous philosopher and you find yourself thinking that his or her ideas are obviously silly or ridiculous, think again. The odds are good that you are misunderstanding what you read. It is wiser to assume that the text offers something of value (even if you disagree with it) and that you need to read more carefully.

2. Read actively and critically. Philosophical reading is intense. It cannot be rushed. It cannot be crammed. It cannot be done while your mind is on automatic pilot.

Philosophical reading is *active* reading. Instead of reading just to get through a piece of writing, you must take your time and ask yourself what key terms and passages mean, how the argument is structured, what the central thesis is, where the premises are, how certain key ideas are related, whether the main conclusion conflicts with propositions you know are true, even how the material compares with other philosophical writing on the same subject.

Philosophical reading is also *critical* reading. In critical reading, you ask not just what something means but whether a statement is true and if the reasoning is solid. You ask if the conclusion really follows from the premises, whether the premises are true, if the analysis of a term really makes sense, if an argument has been overlooked, if an analogy is weak, whether there are counterexamples to key claims, and whether the claims agree with other things you have good reason to believe.

3. Identify the conclusion first, then the premises. When you first begin reading philosophical texts, they may seem to you like dark thickets of propositions into which you may not enter without losing your way. But your situation is really not that bad. In argumentative writing (the kind you are most likely to encounter in philosophy), you can depend on there being, well, an argument, a conclusion backed by premises. There could, of course, be several arguments that support the main argument, and the arguments could be complex, but these sets of conclusion-plus-premises will all serve as recognizable guideposts. If you want to penetrate the thicket, then, you must first identify the argument (or arguments). And the key to doing that is to find the conclusion first, then look for the premises.

When you find the main conclusion, you thereby identify the main point of the essay, and you then have the number-one clue to the function of all the rest of the text. Once you uncover the point that the writer is trying to prove, finding the supporting premises becomes much easier. And when you isolate the premises, locating the text that explains and amplifies the premises gets easier too. Therefore, the first—and most important—question you can ask about a philosophical essay is, "What claim is the writer trying to prove?"

4. Outline, paraphrase, or summarize the argument. Understanding an essay's argument is so important that testing whether you really "get it" is crucial. You can test your grasp of the argument by outlining, paraphrasing, or summarizing it. If you can lay out an argument's premises and conclusion in an outline, or if you can accurately paraphrase or summarize the argument, you probably have a pretty good understanding of it. Very often students who think they comprehend an argument are surprised to see that they cannot devise an adequate outline or summary of it. Such failures suggest that, although outlining, paraphrasing, or summarizing may seem to some to be unnecessary, they are not—at least not to those who are new to philosophy.

5. Evaluate the argument and formulate a tentative judgment. When you read philosophy, understanding it is just the first step. You also must do something that many beginners find both difficult and alien: you must make an informed judgment about what you read. Simply reiterating what the writer has said will not do. Your judgment is what matters here. Mainly, this judgment is your evaluation of the argument presented by the writer—an assessment of (1) whether the conclusion follows from the premises and (2) whether the premises are true. Only when the answer to both of these questions is yes can you say that the conclusion of the argument is worthy of acceptance. This kind of evaluation is precisely what your instructor expects when she asks you to critique an argumentative essay in philosophy.

Fallacious Reasoning

You can become more proficient in reading and writing philosophy if you know how to identify fallacies when you see them. **Fallacies** are common but bad arguments. They are defective arguments that appear so often in writing and speech that philosophers have given them names and offered instructions on how to recognize and avoid them.

> A **fallacy** is a common but bad argument.

Many fallacies are not just failed arguments—they are also deceptively plausible appeals. They can easily appear sound or cogent, misleading the reader. Their potential for slipperiness is another good reason to study fallacies. The best way to avoid being taken in by them is to study them until you can consistently pick them out of any random selection of prose. Here are some of the more prevalent ones.

> This is patently absurd; but whoever wishes to become a philosopher must learn not to be frightened by absurdities.
> —Bertrand Russell

Straw Man

The **straw man** fallacy is the misrepresentation of a person's views so they can be more easily attacked or dismissed. Let's say you argue that the war in Afghanistan is too costly in lives and money, and your opponent replies this way:

> My adversary argues that the war in Afghanistan is much too difficult for the United States, and that we ought to, in effect, cut and run while we can. But why must we take the coward's way out?

> The **straw man** is the fallacy of misrepresenting a person's views so they can be more easily attacked or dismissed.

Thus, your point has been distorted, made to look more extreme or radical than it really is; it is now an easy target. The notion that we ought to "cut and run"

PHILOSOPHY NOW

Philosophy in the News

Very often, behind the headlines we see every day there lurks a deeper philosophical issue. And when people reflect on the stories, they frequently find themselves pondering fundamental questions and beliefs. Philosophy is hard to avoid. Here is a sampling of possible headlines paired with the philosophical questions they raise.

Tea Party Rejects Entitlement and Welfare Programs	Is libertarianism a viable political theory?
Man Claims Out-of-Body Experience	Can the mind (soul) exist independently of the body?
Residents Demand Death Penalty for Child Killer	Is capital punishment ever morally permissible?
Christopher Hitchens Book Says "God Is Not Great"	Does God exist? Does religion do more harm than good?
Japan Tsunami Kills Thousands	Does natural evil show that there is no God?
Scientists Say "Big Bang" Uncaused	Is Aquinas's first-cause argument doomed?
Attorneys Say Hormones Caused Woman to Kill	Do we have free will? Are all our actions caused by factors beyond our control?
Stem Cell Research Banned	Is the fetus a person with full moral rights from the moment of conception?
China Says It Must Be Judged by Chinese Morality	Is morality relative to cultures? Does "human rights" apply only to the West?

Are most perennial debates in politics really about fundamental philosophical issues that are never discussed? Could these issues be resolved if people, in good faith, applied the Socratic method?

or "take the coward's way out" *does not follow* from the statement that the war in Afghanistan is too costly.

The straw man kind of distortion, of course, proves nothing, though many people fall for it every day. This fallacy is probably the most common type of fallacious reasoning used in politics. It is also popular in many other kinds of argumentation—including student philosophy papers.

Figure 1.10 Politics is rife with fallacies—especially straw man, appeal to the person, and slippery slope. What fallacies in politics have you heard or read lately?

Appeal to the Person

Closely related to the straw man fallacy is **appeal to the person** (also known as the *ad hominem* fallacy). Appeal to the person is the rejecting of a statement on the grounds that it comes from a particular person, not because the statement, or claim, itself is false or dubious. For example:

> You can safely discard anything that Susan has to say about government. She's a dyed-in-the-wool socialist.

> Johnson argues that our current welfare system is defective. But don't listen to him—he's a conservative.

Ad hominem arguments often creep into student philosophy papers. Part of the reason is that some appeals to the person are not so obvious. For example:

> Swinburne's cosmological argument is a serious attempt to show that God is the best explanation for the existence of the universe. However, he is a well-known theist, and this fact raises some doubts about the strength of his case.

> Dennett argues from the materialist standpoint, so he begins with a bias that we need to take into account.

> Some of the strongest arguments against the death penalty come from a few people who are actually on death row. They obviously have a vested interest in showing that capital punishment is morally wrong. We therefore are forced to take their arguments—however convincing—with a grain of salt.

Appeal to the person is the fallacy of rejecting a statement on the grounds that it comes from a particular person, not because the statement, or claim, itself is false or dubious.

Each of these arguments is defective because it asks us to reject or resist a claim solely because of a person's character, background, or circumstances—things that are generally irrelevant to the truth of claims. A statement must stand or fall *on its own merits*. The personal characteristics of the person espousing the view do not necessarily have a bearing on its truth. Only if we can show that someone's dubious traits somehow make the claim dubious are we justified in rejecting the claim because of a person's personal characteristics. Such a circumstance is rare.

Appeal to Popularity

The **appeal to popularity** (or appeal to the masses) is another extremely common fallacy. It is arguing that a claim must be true not because it is backed by good reasons, but simply because many people believe it. The idea is that, somehow, there is truth in numbers. For example:

> Of course there's a God. Everyone believes that.

> Seventy percent of Americans believe that the president's tax cuts are good for the economy. So don't try to tell me the tax cuts aren't good for the economy.

> Most people believe that Jones is guilty, so he's guilty.

In each of these arguments, the conclusion is thought to be true merely because it is believed by an impressive number of people. The number of people who believe a claim, however, is irrelevant to the claim's truth. What really matters is how much support the claim has from good reasons. Large groups of people have been—and are—wrong about many things. Many people once believed that Earth is flat, mermaids are real, and human sacrifices help crops grow. They were wrong.

Remember, however, that the number of people who accept a claim *can* be relevant to its truth if the people happen to be experts. Twenty professional astronomers who predict an eclipse are more reliable than one hundred nonexperts who swear that no such eclipse will occur.

Genetic Fallacy

A ploy like the appeal to the person is the **genetic fallacy**—arguing that a statement can be judged true or false based on its source. In an appeal to the person, someone's character or circumstance is thought to tell the tale. In the genetic fallacy, the truth of a statement is supposed to depend on origins other than an individual—organizations, political platforms, groups, schools of thought, even exceptional states of mind (like dreams and intuitions). Look:

> That new military reform idea has gotta be bunk. It comes from a liberal think tank.

> At the city council meeting Hernando said that he had a plan to curb the number of car crashes on Highway 19. But you can bet that whatever it is, it's half-baked—he said the plan came to him when he was stoned on marijuana.

Appeal to popularity is the fallacy of arguing that a claim must be true not because it is backed by good reasons, but simply because many people believe it.

Genetic fallacy is the fallacy of arguing that a statement can be judged true or false based on its source.

The U.S. Senate is considering a proposal to reform affirmative action, but you know their ideas must be ridiculous. What do they know about the rights of the disadvantaged? They're a bunch of rich, white guys.

Equivocation

The fallacy of **equivocation** is assigning two different meanings to the same significant word in an argument. The word is used in one sense in a premise and in a different sense in another place in the argument. The switch in meaning can deceive the reader and disrupt the argument, rendering it invalid or weaker than it would be otherwise. Here's a classic example:

Equivocation is the fallacy of assigning two different meanings to the same significant word in an argument.

> Only man is rational.
>
> No woman is a man.
>
> Therefore, no woman is rational.

And one other:

> You are a bad writer.
>
> If you are a bad writer, then you are a bad boy.
>
> Therefore, you are a bad boy.

The first argument equivocates on the word *man*. In the first premise, *man* means humankind; in the second, male. Thus, the argument seems to prove that women are not rational. You can see the trick better if you assign the same meaning to both instances of *man*. Like this:

> Only humans are rational.
>
> No woman is a human.
>
> Therefore, no woman is rational.

In the second argument, the equivocal term is *bad*. In the first premise, *bad* means incompetent; in the second, immoral.

Appeal to Ignorance

As its name implies, this fallacy tries to prove something by appealing to what we *don't* know. The **appeal to ignorance** is arguing that either (1) a claim is true because it hasn't been proven false or (2) a claim is false because it hasn't been proven true. For example:

Appeal to ignorance is the fallacy of arguing that either (1) a claim is true because it hasn't been proven false or (2) a claim is false because it hasn't been proven true.

> Try as they may, scientists have never been able to disprove the existence of an afterlife. The conclusion to be drawn from this is that there is in fact an afterlife.
>
> Super Green Algae can cure cancer. No scientific study has ever shown that it does not work.
>
> No one has ever shown that ESP (extrasensory perception) is real. Therefore, it does not exist.

> There is no evidence that people on welfare are hardworking and responsible. Therefore, they are not hardworking and responsible.

The first two arguments try to prove a claim by pointing out that it hasn't been proven false. The second two try to prove that a claim is false because it hasn't been proven true. Both kinds of arguments are bogus because they assume that a lack of evidence proves something. A lack of evidence, however, can prove nothing. Being ignorant of the facts does not enlighten us.

Notice that if a lack of evidence could prove something, then you could prove just about anything you wanted. You could reason, for instance, that since no one can prove that horses *can't* fly, horses must be able to fly. Since no one can disprove that you possess supernatural powers, you must possess supernatural powers.

False Dilemma

False dilemma is the fallacy of arguing erroneously that since there are only two alternatives to choose from and one of them is unacceptable, the other one must be true.

In a dilemma, you are forced to choose between two unattractive possibilities. The fallacy of **false dilemma** is arguing erroneously that since there are only two alternatives to choose from and one of them is unacceptable, the other one must be true. Consider these:

> You have to listen to reason. Either you must sell your car to pay your rent, or your landlord will throw you out on the street. You obviously aren't going to sell your car, so you will be evicted.

> You have to face the hard facts about the war on drugs. Either we must spend billions of dollars to increase military and law enforcement operations against drug cartels, or we must legalize all drugs. We obviously are not going to legalize all drugs, so we have to spend billions on anti-cartel operations.

Philosophy is at once the most sublime and the most trivial of human pursuits.
—William James

The first argument says that there are only two choices to consider: either sell your car or get evicted, and since you will not sell your car, you will get evicted. This argument is fallacious because (presumably) the first premise is false—there seem to be more than just two alternatives here. You could get a job, borrow money from a friend, or sell your DVD player and TV. If the argument seems convincing, it is because other possibilities are excluded.

The second argument asserts that there are only two ways to go: spend billions to attack drug cartels or legalize all drugs. Since we won't legalize all drugs, we must therefore spend billions to assault the cartels. The first (either/or) premise, however, is false; there are at least three other options. The billions could be spent to reduce and prevent drug use, drug producers could be given monetary incentives to switch to non-drug businesses, or only some drugs could be legalized.

Begging the question is the fallacy of trying to prove a conclusion by using that very same conclusion as support.

Begging the Question

The fallacy of **begging the question** is trying to prove a conclusion by using that very same conclusion as support. It is arguing in a circle. This way of trying to prove something says, in effect, "X is true because X is true." Few people would fall for this fallacy in such a simple form, but more subtle kinds can be beguiling. For example, here's the classic instance of begging the question:

> The Bible says that God exists.
>
> The Bible is true because God wrote it.
>
> Therefore, God exists.

The conclusion here ("God exists") is supported by premises that assume that very conclusion.

Here's another one:

> All citizens have the right to a fair trial because those whom the state is obliged to protect and give consideration are automatically due judicial criminal proceedings that are equitable by any reasonable standard.

This passage may at first seem like a good argument, but it isn't. It reduces to this unimpressive assertion: "All citizens have the right to a fair trial because all citizens have the right to a fair trial." The conclusion is "All citizens have the right to a fair trial," but that's more or less what the premise says. The premise—"those whom the state is obliged to protect and give consideration are automatically due judicial criminal proceedings that are equitable by any reasonable standard"—is equivalent to "All citizens have the right to a fair trial."

When circular reasoning is subtle, it can ensnare even its own creators. The fallacy can easily sneak into an argument if the premise and conclusion say the same thing but say it in different, complicated ways.

Slippery Slope

The metaphor behind this fallacy suggests the danger of stepping on a dicey incline, losing your footing, and sliding to disaster. The fallacy of **slippery slope**, then, is arguing erroneously that a particular action should not be taken because it will lead inevitably to other actions resulting in some dire outcome. The key word here is *erroneously*. A slippery slope scenario becomes fallacious when there is no reason to believe that the chain of events predicted will ever happen. For example:

> This trend toward gay marriage must be stopped. If gay marriage is permitted, then traditional marriage between a man and a woman will be debased and devalued, which will lead to an increase in divorces. And higher divorce rates can only harm our children.

Slippery slope is the fallacy of arguing erroneously that a particular action should not be taken because it will lead inevitably to other actions resulting in some dire outcome.

This argument is fallacious because there are no reasons for believing that gay marriage will ultimately result in the chain of events described. If good reasons could be given, the argument might be salvaged.

Composition

Sometimes what is true about the parts of a thing is also true of the whole—and sometimes not. The fallacy of **composition** is arguing erroneously that what can be said of the parts can also be said of the whole. Consider:

Composition is the fallacy of arguing erroneously that what can be said of the parts can also be said of the whole.

Each piece of wood that makes up this house is lightweight. Therefore, the whole house is lightweight.

Each soldier in the platoon is proficient. Therefore, the platoon as a whole is proficient.

The monthly payments on this car are low. Hence, the cost of the car is low.

Just remember, sometimes the whole does have the same properties as the parts. If each part of the rocket is made of steel, the whole rocket is made of steel.

Division

Division is the fallacy of arguing erroneously that what can be said of the whole can be said of the parts.

If you turn the fallacy of composition upside down, you get the fallacy of **division**—arguing erroneously that what can be said of the whole can be said of the parts:

The house is heavy. Therefore, every part of the house is heavy.

The platoon is very effective. Therefore, every member of the platoon is effective.

That herd of elephants eats an enormous amount of food each day. Therefore, each elephant in the herd eats an enormous amount of food each day.

ESSAY/DISCUSSION QUESTIONS Section 1.3

1. What is the difference between an argument and an explanation? What is the difference between an argument and a set of accusations? or expressions of outrage?

2. How is reading philosophy different from, say, reading a physics text? or reading a novel?

3. Think about the political commentators you've read or listened to. What fallacies have they been guilty of using?

4. The straw man fallacy is rampant in political debates. Give an example of such a tactic being used by commentators or politicians, or make up an example of your own.

5. Devise an argument in favor of the proposition that people should (or should not) be punished as Socrates was for speaking their minds.

Review Notes

1.1 PHILOSOPHY: THE QUEST FOR UNDERSTANDING

- Studying philosophy has both practical and theoretical benefits. To some, the pursuit of knowledge through philosophy is a spiritual quest.

- Taking an inventory of your philosophical beliefs at the beginning of this course will help you gauge your progress as you study.

- The four main divisions of philosophy are metaphysics, epistemology, axiology, and logic. There are also subdivisions of philosophy that examine basic issues found in other fields.

1.2 SOCRATES AND THE EXAMINED LIFE

- For Socrates, an unexamined life is a tragedy because it results in grievous harm to the soul, a person's true self or essence. The soul is harmed by lack of knowledge—ignorance of one's own self and of the most important values in life (the good).

- The Socratic method is a question-and-answer dialogue in which propositions are methodically scrutinized to uncover the truth. Usually when Socrates used it in conversations with his fellow Athenians, their views would be exposed as false or confused. The main point of the exercise for Socrates, however, was not to win arguments, but to get closer to the truth.

- Socrates says, in effect, Let's assume that Thrasymachus is right that justice is whatever is in the interest of the powerful, and that people are just if they obey the laws made by the powerful. But the powerful sometimes make mistakes and demand obedience to laws that are *not* in their best interest. So if Thrasymachus's definition of justice is correct, then it is right for people to do what is in the interest of the powerful, and it is also right to do what is *not* in the interest of the powerful. His idea of justice then leads to a logical contradiction.

- The basic idea behind *reductio ad absurdum* is if you assume that a set of statements is true, and yet you can deduce a false or absurd statement from it, then the original set of statements as a whole must be false.

1.3 THINKING PHILOSOPHICALLY

- An argument is a group of statements in which one of them is meant to be supported by the others. A statement (or claim) is an assertion that something is or is not the case and is therefore the kind of utterance that is either true or false. In an argument, the statement being supported is the conclusion, and the statements supporting the conclusion are the premises.

- A good argument must have (1) solid logic and (2) true premises. Requirement (1) means that the conclusion should follow logically from the premises. Requirement (2) says that what the premises assert must in fact be the case.

- A deductive argument is intended to give logically conclusive support to its conclusion. An inductive argument is intended to give probable support to its conclusion. A deductive argument with the proper structure is said to be valid; a deductive argument that fails to have this structure is said to be invalid. If inductive arguments succeed in lending probable support to their conclusions, they are said to be strong. If they fail to provide this probable support, they are termed weak. When a valid (deductive) argument has true premises, it is said to be sound. When a strong (inductive) argument has true premises, it is said to be cogent. In inference to the best explanation, we begin with premises about a phenomenon or state of affairs to be explained. Then we reason from those premises to an explanation for that state of affairs. We try to produce not just any explanation, but the best explanation among several possibilities. The best explanation is the one most likely to be true.

- The guidelines for reading philosophy are: (1) Approach the text with an open mind; (2) read actively and critically; (3) identify the conclusion first, then the premises; (4) outline, paraphrase, or summarize the argument; and (5) evaluate the argument and formulate a tentative judgment.

WRITING TO UNDERSTAND: ARGUING YOUR OWN VIEWS   Chapter 1

1. Do you believe, as Thrasymachus did, that might makes right, that morality is not about objective right and wrong but about who has the most power? Devise an argument to support your belief.

2. Choose one of your fundamental beliefs that you have not thought much about and write an argument defending it or rejecting it.

3. Socrates said to his jurors, "Are you not ashamed that, while you take care to acquire as much wealth as possible, with honor and glory as well, yet you take no care or thought for understanding or truth, or for the best possible state of your soul?" Do you agree with this attitude? Why or why not?

4. What is the difference between the way philosophy approaches important questions and the way that religion does?

5. Argue the case for using (or not using) the Socratic method in education.

Key Terms

appeal to ignorance The fallacy of arguing that either (1) a claim is true because it hasn't been proven false or (2) a claim is false because it hasn't been proven true. (33)

appeal to popularity The fallacy of arguing that a claim must be true not because it is backed by good reasons, but simply because many people believe it. (32)

appeal to the person The fallacy of rejecting a statement on the grounds that it comes from a particular person, not because the statement, or claim, itself is false or dubious. (31)

argument A statement coupled with other statements that are meant to support that statement. (14)

axiology The study of value, including both aesthetic value and moral value. (6)

begging the question The fallacy of trying to prove a conclusion by using that very same conclusion as support. (34)

composition The fallacy of arguing erroneously that what can be said of the parts can also be said of the whole. (35)

conclusion In an argument, the statement being supported. (14)

deductive argument An argument intended to give logically conclusive support to its conclusion. (16)

division The fallacy of arguing erroneously that what can be said of the whole can be said of the parts. (36)

epistemology The study of knowledge. (6)

equivocation The fallacy of assigning two different meanings to the same significant word in an argument. (33)

ethics (moral philosophy) The study of morality using the methods of philosophy. (6)

fallacy A common but bad argument. (29)

false dilemma The fallacy of arguing erroneously that since there are only two alternatives to choose from, and one of them is unacceptable, the other one must be true. (34)

genetic fallacy The fallacy of arguing that a statement can be judged true or false based on its source. (32)

inductive argument An argument intended to give probable support to its conclusion. (17)

logic The study of correct reasoning. (7)

metaphysics The study of reality, an inquiry into the fundamental nature of the universe and the things in it. (4)

premise In an argument, a statement supporting the conclusion. (14)

reductio ad absurdum An argument of this form: If you assume that a set of statements is true, and yet you can deduce a false or absurd statement from it, then the original set of statements as a whole must be false. (12)

slippery slope The fallacy of arguing erroneously that a particular action should not be taken because it will lead inevitably to other actions resulting in some dire outcome. (35)

Socratic method Question-and-answer dialogue in which propositions are methodically scrutinized to uncover the truth. (8)

statement (claim) An assertion that something is or is not the case and is therefore the kind of utterance that is either true or false. (14)

straw man The fallacy of misrepresenting a person's views so they can be more easily attacked or dismissed. (29)

Argument Exercises

(Answers in Appendix A)

Exercise 1.1

For each of the passages that follow, indicate whether it constitutes an argument. For each argument, specify both the conclusion and the premises.

1. Faster-than-light travel is not possible. It would violate a law of nature.
2. You have neglected your duty on several occasions, and you have been absent from work too many times. Therefore, you are not fit to serve in your current capacity.
3. Racial profiling is not an issue for white people, but it is an issue for blacks.
4. The flu epidemic on the East Coast is real. Government health officials say so. And I personally have read at least a dozen news stories that characterize the situation as a "flu epidemic."
5. Communism is bunk. Only naïve, impressionable pinheads believe that stuff.
6. Current-day Christians use violence to spread their right-to-life message. These Christians, often referred to as the religious right, are well known for violent demonstrations against Planned Parenthood and other abortion clinics. Doctors and other personnel are threatened with death, clinics have been bombed, there have even been cases of doctors being murdered.—Letter to the editor, *Arizona Daily Wildcat*
7. I am writing about the cost of concert tickets. I am outraged at how much ticket prices are increasing every year. A few years ago, one could attend a popular concert for a decent price. Now some musicians are asking as much as $200 to $300.—Letter to the editor, *Buffalo News*
8. Homeland security is a cruel charade for unborn children. Some 4,000 per day are killed in their mother's womb by abortion. This American holocaust was legalized by the Supreme Court in an exercise of raw judicial power.—Letter to the editor, *Buffalo News*
9. Witches are real. They are mentioned in the Bible. There are many people today who claim to be witches. And historical records reveal that there were witches in Salem.
10. Stretched upon the dark silk night, bracelets of city lights glisten brightly.

Exercise 1.2

For each passage that follows, list the conclusion and premises.

1. There are those who maintain . . . that even if God is not required as the author of the moral law, he is nevertheless required as the enforcer of it, for without the threat of divine punishment, people will not act morally. But this position is [not plausible]. In the first place, as an empirical hypothesis about the psychology of human beings, it is questionable. There is no unambiguous evidence that theists are more moral than nontheists. Not only have psychological studies failed to find a significant correlation between frequency of religious worship and moral conduct, but convicted criminals are much [more] likely to be theists than atheists. Second, the threat of divine punishment cannot impose a moral obligation, for might does not make right. Threats extort; they do not create a moral duty.—*Free Inquiry*, Summer 1997

2. I love *Reason* [magazine], but [regarding a previous article by Nick Gillespie] I'm wondering if all the illegal drugs that Nick Gillespie used to take are finally getting to him. He has a right to speak out against President Bush, but when he refers to him as "the millionaire president who waited out the Vietnam War in the Texas Air National Guard," it reminds me of the garbage rhetoric that I might see if I were reading Ted Rall, or Susan Sontag, or one of the other hate-mongering, America-bashing, leftist whiners. That kind of ad hominem attack is not only disrespectful to a man who is doing a damned good job as commander-in-chief (with approval ratings of more than 80 percent); it detracts from the whole point of the article.—Letter to the editor, *Reason*, July 2002

3. The fifth way [of proving that God exists] is taken from the governance of the world. We see that things which lack knowledge, such as natural bodies, act for an end, and this is evident from their acting always, or nearly always, in the same way, so as to obtain the best result. Hence it is plain that they achieve their end, not fortuitously, but designedly. Now whatever lacks knowledge cannot move towards an end, unless it be directed by some being endowed with knowledge and intelligence; as the arrow is directed by the archer. Therefore some intelligent being exists by whom all natural things are directed to their end; and this being we call God.—Thomas Aquinas, *Summa Theologica*

4. The first thing that must occur to anyone studying moral subjectivism [the view that the rightness or wrongness of an action depends on the beliefs of an individual or group] seriously is that the view allows the possibility that an action can be both right and not right, or wrong and not wrong, etc. This possibility exists because, as we have seen, the subjectivist claims that the moral character of an action is determined by individual subjective states; and these states can vary from person to person, even when directed toward the same action on the same occasion. Hence one and the same action can evidently be determined to have—simultaneously—radically different moral characters. . . . [If] subjectivism . . . does generate such contradictory conclusions,

the position is certainly untenable.—Phillip Montague, *Philosophy and Phenomenological Research,* June 1986

5. A Florida judge dismissed a lawsuit that accused the Vatican of hiding instances of sexual abuse by priests. The suit was thrown out because Florida's statute of limitations had run out on the case. I submit that the dismissal was proper and ethical considering the community stature and function of priests and the benefits that accrue to society in the aftermath of the decision. Let's consider community stature first. The community stature of priests must always be taken into account in these abuse cases. A priest is not just anybody; he performs a special role in society—namely, to provide spiritual guidance and to remind people that there is both a moral order and a divine order in the world. The priest's role is special because it helps to underpin and secure society itself. Anything that could undermine this role must be neutralized as soon as possible. Among those things that can weaken the priestly role are publicity, public debate, and legal actions. Abuse cases are better handled in private by those who are keenly aware of the importance of a positive public image of priests. And what of the benefits of curtailing the legal proceedings? The benefits to society of dismissing the legal case outweigh all the alleged disadvantages of continuing with public hearings. The primary benefit is the continued nurturing of the community's faith, without which the community would cease to function effectively.

Exercise 1.3

In the following passages, identify any fallacies. Some passages may contain more than one fallacy.

1. The *New York Times* reported that one-third of Republican senators have been guilty of Senate ethics violations. But you know that's false—the *Times* is a notorious liberal rag.
2. Geraldo says that students who cheat on exams should not automatically be expelled from school. But it's ridiculous to insist that students should never be punished for cheating.
3. My sweater is blue. Therefore, the atoms that make up the sweater are blue.
4. Kelly says that many women who live in predominantly Muslim countries are discriminated against. But how the heck would she know? She's not a Muslim.
5. The study found that 80 percent of women who took the drug daily had no recurrence of breast cancer. But that doesn't mean anything. The study was funded in part by the company that makes the drug.
6. The only proof capable of being given that an object is visible, is that people actually see it. The only proof that a sound is audible, is that people hear it: and so of the other sources of our experience. In like manner, I apprehend, the sole evidence it is possible to produce that anything is desirable, is that people actually desire it.—John Stuart Mill
7. Gremlins exist, that's for sure. No scientist has ever proved that they don't exist.

8. The former mayor was convicted of drug possession, and he spent time in jail. So you can safely ignore anything he has to say about legalizing drugs.

9. I believe that baby-carrying storks are real creatures. No one has ever proved that they don't exist.

10. Only man has morals. No woman is a man. Therefore, no woman has morals.

The Trial and Death of Socrates

Plato

> The ancient Greek philosopher Plato (c. 427–347 BCE) is one of the most influential thinkers of Western civilization. He was the student of Socrates, teacher of Aristotle, and timeless inspiration to all who sought wisdom through philosophy. In this narrative, one of his many dialogues, Plato relates Socrates' address to the jury at his famous trial for corrupting Athenian youth and disrespecting the gods.

How you, O Athenians, have been affected by my accusers, I cannot tell; but I know that they almost made me forget who I was—so persuasively did they speak; and yet they have hardly uttered a word of truth. But of the many falsehoods told by them, there was one which quite amazed me—I mean when they said that you should be upon your guard and not allow yourselves to be deceived by the force of my eloquence. To say this, when they were certain to be detected as soon as I opened my lips and proved myself to be anything but a great speaker, did indeed appear to me most shameless—unless by the force of eloquence they mean the force of truth; for if such is their meaning, I admit that I am eloquent. But in how different a way from theirs! Well, as I was saying, they have scarcely spoken the truth at all; but from me you shall hear the whole truth: not, however, delivered after their manner in a set oration duly ornamented with words and phrases. No, by heaven! but I shall use the words and arguments which occur to me at the moment; for I am confident in the justice of my cause: at my time of life I ought not to be appearing before you, O men of Athens, in the character of a juvenile orator—let no one expect it of me. And I must beg of you to grant me a favour: If I defend myself in my accustomed manner, and you hear me using the words which I have been in the habit of using in the [market], at the tables of the money-changers, or anywhere else, I would ask you not to be surprised, and not to interrupt me on this account. For I am more than seventy years of age, and appearing now for the first time in a court of law, I am quite a stranger to the language of the place; and therefore I would have you regard me as if I were really

a stranger, whom you would excuse if he spoke in his native tongue, and after the fashion of his country: Am I making an unfair request of you? Never mind the manner, which may or may not be good; but think only of the truth of my words, and give heed to that: let the speaker speak truly and the judge decide justly. . . .

Well, then, I must make my defence, and endeavor to clear away in a short time, a slander which has lasted a long time. May I succeed, if to succeed be for my good and yours, or likely to avail me in my cause! The task is not an easy one; I quite understand the nature of it. And so leaving the event with God, in obedience to the law I will now make my defence.

I will begin at the beginning, and ask what is the accusation which has given rise to the slander of me, and in fact has encouraged Meletus to prefer this charge against me. Well, what do the slanderers say? They shall be my prosecutors, and I will sum up their words in an affidavit: 'Socrates is an evil-doer, and a curious person, who searches into things under the earth and in heaven, and he makes the worse appear the better cause; and he teaches the aforesaid doctrines to others.' Such is the nature of the accusation: it is just what you have yourselves seen in the comedy of Aristophanes, who has introduced a man whom he calls Socrates, going about and saying that he walks in air, and talking a deal of nonsense concerning matters of which I do not pretend to know either much or little—not that I mean to speak disparagingly of any one who is a student of natural philosophy. I should be very sorry if Meletus could bring so grave a charge against me. But the simple truth is, O Athenians, that I have nothing to do with physical speculations. Very many of those here present are witnesses to the truth of this, and to them I appeal. Speak then, you who have heard me, and tell your neighbours whether any of you have ever known me hold forth in few words or

From Plato, *The Apology*, in *Dialogues of Plato*, trans. Benjamin Jowett, Oxford, 1896.

in many upon such matters. . . . You hear their answer. And from what they say of this part of the charge you will be able to judge of the truth of the rest.

As little foundation is there for the report that I am a teacher, and take money; this accusation has no more truth in it than the other. Although, if a man were really able to instruct mankind, to receive money for giving instruction would, in my opinion, be an honour to him. There is Gorgias of Leontium, and Prodicus of Ceos, and Hippias of Elis, who go the round of the cities, and are able to persuade the young men to leave their own citizens by whom they might be taught for nothing, and come to them whom they not only pay, but are thankful if they may be allowed to pay them. . . .

I dare say, Athenians, that some one among you will reply, 'Yes, Socrates, but what is the origin of these accusations which are brought against you; there must have been something strange which you have been doing? All these rumours and this talk about you would never have arisen if you had been like other men: tell us, then, what is the cause of them, for we should be sorry to judge hastily of you.' Now I regard this as a fair challenge, and I will endeavour to explain to you the reason why I am called wise and have such an evil fame. Please do attend then. And although some of you may think that I am joking, I declare that I will tell you the entire truth. Men of Athens, this reputation of mine has come of a certain sort of wisdom which I possess. If you ask me what kind of wisdom, I reply, wisdom such as may perhaps be attained by man, for to that extent I am inclined to believe that I am wise; whereas the persons of whom I was speaking have a superhuman wisdom, which I may fail to describe, because I have it not myself; and he who says that I have, speaks falsely, and is taking away my character. And here, O men of Athens, I must beg you not to interrupt me, even if I seem to say something extravagant. For the word which I will speak is not mine. I will refer you to a witness who is worthy of credit; that witness shall be the God of Delphi—he will tell you about my wisdom, if I have any, and of what sort it is. You must have known Chaerephon; he was early a friend of mine, and also a friend of yours, for he shared in the recent exile of the people, and returned with you. Well, Chaerephon, as you know, was very impetuous in all his doings, and he went to Delphi and boldly asked the oracle to tell him whether—as I was saying, I must beg you not to

interrupt—he asked the oracle to tell him whether any one was wiser than I was, and the Pythian prophetess answered, that there was no man wiser. Chaerephon is dead himself; but his brother, who is in court, will confirm the truth of what I am saying.

Why do I mention this? Because I am going to explain to you why I have such an evil name. When I heard the answer, I said to myself, What can the god mean? and what is the interpretation of his riddle? for I know that I have no wisdom, small or great. What then can he mean when he says that I am the wisest of men? And yet he is a god, and cannot lie; that would be against his nature. After long consideration, I thought of a method of trying the question. I reflected that if I could only find a man wiser than myself, then I might go to the god with a refutation in my hand. I should say to him, 'Here is a man who is wiser than I am; but you said that I was the wisest.' Accordingly I went to one who had the reputation of wisdom, and observed him—his name I need not mention; he was a politician whom I selected for examination—and the result was as follows: When I began to talk with him, I could not help thinking that he was not really wise, although he was thought wise by many, and still wiser by himself; and thereupon I tried to explain to him that he thought himself wise, but was not really wise; and the consequence was that he hated me, and his enmity was shared by several who were present and heard me. So I left him, saying to myself, as I went away: Well, although I do not suppose that either of us knows anything really beautiful and good, I am better off than he is—for he knows nothing, and thinks that he knows; I neither know nor think that I know. In this latter particular, then, I seem to have slightly the advantage of him.

Then I went to another who had still higher pretensions to wisdom, and my conclusion was exactly the same. Whereupon I made another enemy of him, and of many others besides him. Then I went to one man after another, being not unconscious of the enmity which I provoked, and I lamented and feared this: But necessity was laid upon me,—the word of God, I thought, ought to be considered first. And I said to myself, Go I must to all who appear to know, and find out the meaning of the oracle. And I swear to you, Athenians, by the dog I swear!—for I must tell you the truth—the result of my mission was just this: I found that the men most in repute were all but the most foolish; and that others less esteemed were really wiser and better. I will tell you the tale of my wanderings and of the "Herculean" labours, as I may call them, which I endured only to find at last the oracle irrefutable. After the politicians, I went to the poets; tragic, dithyrambic, and all sorts. And there, I said to myself, you will be instantly detected; now you will find out that you are more ignorant than they are. Accordingly, I took them some of the most elaborate passages in their own writings, and asked what was the meaning of them—thinking that they would teach me something. Will you believe me? I am almost ashamed to confess the truth, but I must say that there is hardly a person present who would not have talked better about their poetry than they did themselves. Then I knew that not by wisdom do poets write poetry, but by a sort of genius and inspiration; they are like diviners or soothsayers who also say many fine things, but do not understand the meaning of them. The poets appeared to me to be much in the same case; and I further observed that upon the strength of their poetry they believed themselves to be the wisest of men in other things in which they were not wise. So I departed, conceiving myself to be superior to them for the same reason that I was superior to the politicians.

At last I went to the artisans, for I was conscious that I knew nothing at all, as I may say, and I was sure that they knew many fine things; and here I was not mistaken, for they did know many things of which I was ignorant, and in this they certainly were wiser than I was. But I observed that even the good artisans fell into the same error as the poets;—because they were good workmen they thought that they also knew all sorts of high matters, and this defect in them overshadowed their wisdom; and therefore I asked myself on behalf of the oracle, whether I would like to be as I was, neither having their knowledge nor their ignorance, or like them in both; and I made answer to myself and to the oracle that I was better off as I was.

This inquisition has led to my having many enemies of the worst and most dangerous kind, and has given occasion also to many calumnies. And I am called wise, for my hearers always imagine that I myself possess the wisdom which I find wanting in others: but the truth is, O men of Athens, that God only is wise; and by his answer he intends to show that the wisdom of men is worth little or nothing; he is not speaking of Socrates, he is only using my name by way of illustration, as if he said, He, O men, is the wisest, who, like Socrates, knows that his wisdom is in truth worth nothing. And so I go about the world, obedient to the god, and search and make enquiry into the wisdom of any one, whether citizen or stranger, who appears to be wise; and if he is

not wise, then in vindication of the oracle I show him that he is not wise; and my occupation quite absorbs me, and I have no time to give either to any public matter of interest or to any concern of my own, but I am in utter poverty by reason of my devotion to the god.

There is another thing: Young men of the richer classes, who have not much to do, come about me of their own accord; they like to hear the pretenders examined, and they often imitate me, and proceed to examine others; there are plenty of persons, as they quickly discover, who think that they know something, but really know little or nothing; and then those who are examined by them instead of being angry with themselves are angry with me: This confounded Socrates, they say, this villainous misleader of youth!—and then if somebody asks them, Why, what evil does he practise or teach? they do not know, and cannot tell; but in order that they may not appear to be at a loss, they repeat the readymade charges which are used against all philosophers about teaching things up in the clouds and under the earth, and having no gods, and making the worse appear the better cause; for they do not like to confess that their pretence of knowledge has been detected—which is the truth; and as they are numerous and ambitious and energetic, and are drawn up in battle array and have persuasive tongues, they have filled your ears with their loud and inveterate calumnies. And this is the reason why my three accusers, Meletus and Anytus and Lycon, have set upon me; Meletus, who has a quarrel with me on behalf of the poets; Anytus, on behalf of the craftsmen and politicians; Lycon, on behalf of the rhetoricians: and as I said at the beginning, I cannot expect to get rid of such a mass of calumny all in a moment. And this, O men of Athens, is the truth and the whole truth; I have concealed nothing, I have dissembled nothing. And yet, I know that my plainness of speech makes them hate me, and what is their hatred but a proof that I am speaking the truth?—Hence has arisen the prejudice against me; and this is the reason of it, as you will find out either in this or in any future enquiry.

I have said enough in my defence against the first class of my accusers; I turn to the second class. They are headed by Meletus, that good man and true lover of his country, as he calls himself. . . . He says that I am a doer of evil, and corrupt the youth; but I say, O men of Athens, that Meletus is a doer of evil, in that he pretends to be in earnest when he is only in jest, and is so eager to bring men to trial from a pretended zeal and interest about matters in which he really never had the smallest interest. And the truth of this I will endeavour to prove to you.

Come hither, Meletus, and let me ask a question of you. You think a great deal about the improvement of youth?

Yes, I do.

Tell the judges, then, who is their improver; for you must know, as you have taken the pains to discover their corrupter, and are citing and accusing me before them. Speak, then, and tell the judges who their improver is.—Observe, Meletus, that you are silent, and have nothing to say. But is not this rather disgraceful, and a very considerable proof of what I was saying, that you have no interest in the matter? Speak up, friend, and tell us who their improver is.

The laws.

But that, my good sir, is not my meaning. I want to know who the person is, who, in the first place, knows the laws.

The judges, Socrates, who are present in court.

What, do you mean to say, Meletus, that they are able to instruct and improve youth?

Certainly they are.

What, all of them, or some only and not others?

All of them.

By the goddess Herè, that is good news! There are plenty of improvers, then. And what do you say of the audience—do they improve them?

Yes, they do.

And the senators?

Yes, the senators improve them.

But perhaps the members of the assembly corrupt them?—or do they too improve them?

They improve them.

Then every Athenian improves and elevates them; all with the exception of myself; and I alone am their corrupter? Is that what you affirm?

That is what I stoutly affirm.

I am very unfortunate if you are right. But suppose I ask you a question: How about horses? Does one man do them harm and all the world good? Is not the exact opposite the truth? One man is able to do them good, or at least not many—the trainer of horses, that is to say, does them good, and others who have to do with them rather injure them? Is not that true, Meletus, of horses, or of any other animals? Most assuredly it is; whether you and Anytus say yes or no. Happy indeed would be the condition of youth if they had one corrupter only, and all the rest of the world were their improvers. But you, Meletus, have sufficiently shown that you never had a thought about the young: your carelessness is seen in your not caring about the very things which you bring against me.

And now, Meletus, I will ask you another question—by Zeus I will: Which is better, to live among bad citizens, or among good ones? Answer, friend, I say; the question is one which may be easily answered. Do not the good do their neighbours good, and the bad do them evil?

Certainly.

And is there any one who would rather be injured than benefited by those who live with him? Answer, my good friend, the law requires you to answer—does any one like to be injured?

Certainly not.

And when you accuse me of corrupting and deteriorating the youth, do you allege that I corrupt them intentionally or unintentionally?

Intentionally, I say.

But you have just admitted that the good do their neighbours good, and evil do them evil. Now, is that a truth which your superior wisdom has recognized thus early in life, and am I, at my age, in such darkness and ignorance as not to know that if a man with whom I have to live is corrupted by me, I am very likely to be harmed by him; and yet I corrupt him, and intentionally, too—so you say, although neither I nor any other human being is ever likely to be convinced by you. But either I do not corrupt them, or I corrupt them unintentionally; and on either view of the case you lie. If my offence is unintentional, the law has no cognizance of unintentional offences: you ought to have taken me privately, and warned and admonished me; for if I had been better advised, I should have left off doing what I only did unintentionally—no doubt I should; but you would have nothing to say to me and refused to teach me. And now you bring me up in this court, which is a place not of instruction, but of punishment.

It will be very clear to you, Athenians, as I was saying, that Meletus has no care at all, great or small, about the matter. But still I should like to know, Meletus, in what I am affirmed to corrupt the young. I suppose you mean, as I infer from your indictment, that I teach them not to acknowledge the gods which the state acknowledges, but some other new divinities or spiritual agencies in their stead. These are the lessons by which I corrupt the youth, as you say.

Yes, that I say emphatically.

Then, by the gods, Meletus, of whom we are speaking, tell me and the court, in somewhat plainer terms, what you mean! for I do not as yet understand whether you affirm that I teach other men to acknowledge some gods, and therefore that I do believe in gods, and am not an entire atheist—this you do not lay to my charge—but only you say that they are not the same gods which the city recognizes—the charge is that they are different gods. Or, do you mean that I am an atheist simply, and a teacher of atheism?

I mean the latter—that you are a complete atheist.

What an extraordinary statement! Why do you think so, Meletus? Do you mean that I do not believe in the godhead of the sun or moon, like other men?

I assure you, judges, that he does not: for he says that the sun is stone, and the moon earth.

Friend Meletus, you think that you are accusing Anaxagoras: and you have but a bad opinion of the judges, if you fancy them illiterate to such a degree as not to know that these doctrines are found in the books of Anaxagoras the Clazomenian, which are full of them. And so, forsooth, the youth are said to be taught them by Socrates, when there are not infrequently exhibitions of them at the theatre (price of admission one drachma at the most); and they might pay their money, and laugh at Socrates if he pretends to father these extraordinary views. And so, Meletus, you really think that I do not believe in any god?

I swear by Zeus that you believe absolutely in none at all.

Nobody will believe you, Meletus, and I am pretty sure that you do not believe yourself. I cannot help thinking, men of Athens, that Meletus is reckless and impudent, and that he has written this indictment in a spirit of mere wantonness and youthful bravado. Has he not compounded a riddle, thinking to try me? He said to himself: I shall see whether the wise Socrates will discover my facetious contradiction, or whether I shall be able to deceive him and the rest of them. For he certainly does appear to me to contradict himself in the indictment as much as if he said that Socrates is guilty of not believing in the gods, and yet of believing them—but this is not like a person who is in earnest.

I should like you, O men of Athens, to join me in examining what I conceive to be his inconsistency; and do you, Meletus, answer. And I must remind the audience of my request that they would not make a disturbance if I speak in my accustomed manner:

Did ever man, Meletus, believe in the existence of human things, and not of human beings? . . . I wish, men of Athens, that he would answer, and not be always trying to get up an interruption. Did ever any man believe in horsemanship, and not in horses? or in flute-playing, and not flute-players? No, my friend; I will answer to you and to the court, as you refuse to answer for yourself. There is no man who ever did. But now please to answer the next question: Can a man believe in spiritual and divine agencies, and not in spirits or demigods?

He cannot.

How lucky I am to have extracted that answer, by the assistance of the court! But then you swear in the indictment that I teach and believe in divine or spiritual agencies (new or old, no matter for that); at any rate I believe in spiritual agencies—so you say and swear in the affidavit; and yet if I believe in divine beings, how can I help believing in spirits or demigods—must I not? To be sure I must; and therefore I may assume that your silence gives consent. Now what are spirits or demigods? are they not either gods or the sons of gods?

Certainly they are.

But this is what I call the facetious riddle invented by you: the demigods or spirits are gods, and you say first that I do not believe in gods, and then again that I do believe in gods; that is, if I believe in demigods. For if the demigods are the illegitimate sons of gods, whether by the nymphs or by any other mothers, of whom they are said to be the sons—what human being will ever believe that there are no gods if they are the sons of gods? You might as well affirm the existence of mules, and deny that of horses and asses. Such nonsense, Meletus, could only have been intended by you to make trial of me. You have put this into the indictment because you had nothing real of which to accuse me. But no one who has a particle of understanding will ever be convinced by you that the same men can believe in divine and superhuman things, and yet not believe that there are gods and demigods and heroes.

I have said enough in answer to the charge of Meletus: any elaborate defence is unnecessary; but I know only too well how many are the enmities which I have incurred, and this is what will be my destruction if I am destroyed—not Meletus, nor yet Anytus, but the envy and detraction of the world, which has been the death of many good men, and will probably be the death of many more; there is no danger of my being the last of them.

Some one will say: And are you not ashamed, Socrates, of a course of life which is likely to bring you to an untimely end? To him I may fairly answer: There you are mistaken: a man who is good for anything ought not to calculate the chance of living or dying; he ought only to consider whether in doing anything he is doing right or wrong—acting the part of a good man or of a bad. . . .

Strange, indeed, would be my conduct, O men of Athens, if I who, when I was ordered by the generals whom you chose to command me at Potidaea and Amphipolis and Delium, remained where they placed me, like any other man, facing death—if now, when, as I conceive and imagine, God orders me to fulfill the philosopher's mission of searching into myself and other men, I were to desert my post through fear of death, or any other fear; that would indeed be strange, and I might justly be arraigned in court for denying the existence of the gods, if I disobeyed the oracle because I was afraid of death, fancying that I was wise when I was not wise. For the fear of death is indeed the pretence of wisdom, and not real wisdom, being a pretence of knowing the unknown; and no one knows whether death, which men in their fear apprehend to be the greatest evil, may not be the greatest good. Is not this ignorance of a disgraceful sort, the ignorance which is the conceit that man knows what he does not know? And in this respect only I believe myself to differ from men in general, and may perhaps claim to be wiser than they are—that whereas I know but little of the world below, I do not suppose that I know: but I do know that injustice and disobedience to a better, whether God or man, is evil and dishonourable, and I will never fear or avoid a possible good rather than a certain evil. And therefore if you let me go now, and are not convinced by Anytus, who said that since I had been prosecuted I must be put to death . . . —if you say to me, Socrates, this time we will not mind Anytus, and you shall be let off, but upon one condition, that you are not to enquire and speculate in this way any more, and that if you are caught doing so again you shall die—if this was the condition on which you let me go, I should reply: Men of Athens, I honour and love you; but I shall obey God rather than you, and while I have life and strength I shall never cease from the practice and teaching of philosophy, exhorting any one whom I meet and saying to him after my manner: You, my friend—a citizen of the great and mighty and wise city of Athens—are you not ashamed of heaping up the greatest amount of money and honour and reputation, and caring so little about wisdom and truth and the greatest improvement of the soul, which you never regard or heed at all? And if the person with whom I am arguing, says: Yes, but I do care; then I do not leave him or let him go at once; but I proceed to interrogate and examine and cross-examine him, and if I think that he has no virtue in him, but only says that he has, I reproach him with undervaluing the greater, and overvaluing the less. And I shall repeat the same words to every one whom I meet, young and old, citizen and alien, but especially to the citizens, inasmuch as they are my brethren. For know that this is the command of God; and I believe that no greater good has ever happened in the state than my service to the God. For I do nothing but go about persuading you all, old and young alike, not to take thought for your persons or your properties, but first and chiefly to care about the greatest improvement of the soul. I tell you that virtue is not given by money, but that from virtue comes money and every other good of man, public as well as private. This is my teaching, and if this is the doctrine which corrupts the youth, I am a mischievous person. But if any one says that this is not my teaching, he is speaking an untruth. Wherefore, O men of Athens, I say to you, do as Anytus bids or not as Anytus bids, and either acquit me or not; but whichever you do, understand that I shall never alter my ways, not even if I have to die many times. . . .

And now, Athenians, I am not going to argue for my own sake, as you may think, but for yours, that you may not sin against the God by condemning me, who am his gift to you. For if you kill me you will not easily find a successor to me, who, if I may use such a ludicrous figure of speech, am a sort of gadfly, given to the state by God; and the state is a great and noble steed who is tardy in his motions owing to his very size, and requires to be stirred into life. I am that gadfly which God has attached to the state, and all day long and in all places am always fastening upon you, arousing and persuading and reproaching you. You will not easily find another like me, and therefore I would advise you to spare me. . . .

Now do you think that I could have remained alive all these years if I had taken part in public affairs, and had always maintained the cause of justice like an honest man, and had held it a paramount duty, as it is, to do so? Certainly not, Athenians, nor could any other man. But throughout my whole life, both in private and in public, whenever I have had to take part in public affairs, you will find I have always been the same and have never yielded unjustly to anyone; no, not to those whom my enemies falsely assert to have been my pupils. But

I was never anyone's teacher. I have never withheld myself from anyone, young or old, who was anxious to hear me discuss while I was making my investigation; neither do I discuss for payment, and refuse to discuss without payment. I am ready to ask questions of rich and poor alike, and if any man wishes to answer me, and then listen to what I have to say, he may. . . .

I believe in the gods as no one of my accusers believes in them: and to you and to God I commit my cause to be decided as is best for you and for me.

[The vote is taken and he is found guilty by 281 votes to 220.]

There are many reasons why I am not grieved, O men of Athens, at the vote of condemnation. I expected it, and am only surprised that the votes are so nearly equal; for I had thought that the majority against me would have been far larger; but now, had thirty votes gone over to the other side, I should have been acquitted. And I may say, I think, that I have escaped Meletus. I may say more; for without the assistance of Anytus and Lycon, any one may see that he would not have had a fifth part of the votes, as the law requires, in which case he would have incurred a fine of a thousand drachmae.

And so he proposes death as the penalty. And what shall I propose on my part, O men of Athens? Clearly that which is my due. And what is my due? What return shall be made to the man who has never had the wit to be idle during his whole life; but has been careless of what the many care for—wealth, and family interests, and military offices, and speaking in the assembly, and magistracies, and plots, and parties. Reflecting that I was really too honest a man to be a politician and live, I did not go where I could do no good to you or to myself; but where I could do the greatest good privately to every one of you, thither I went, and sought to persuade every man among you that he must look to himself, and seek virtue and wisdom before he looks to his private interests, and look to the state before he looks to the interests of the state; and that this should be the order which he observes in all his actions. What shall be done to such an one? Doubtless some good thing, O men of Athens, if he has his reward; and the good should be of a kind suitable to him. What would be a reward suitable to a poor man who is your benefactor, and who desires leisure that he may instruct you? There can be no reward so fitting as maintenance in the Prytaneum, O men of Athens, a reward which he deserves far more than the citizen who has won the prize at Olympia in the horse or chariot race, whether the chariots were drawn by two horses or by many. For I am in want, and he has enough; and he only gives you the appearance of happiness, and I give you the reality. And if I am to estimate the penalty fairly, I should say that maintenance in the Prytaneum is the just return.

Perhaps you think that I am braving you in what I am saying now, as in what I said before about the tears and prayers. But this is not so. I speak rather because I am convinced that I never intentionally wronged any one, although I cannot convince you—the time has been too short; if there were a law at Athens, as there is in other cities, that a capital cause should not be decided in one day, then I believe that I should have convinced you. But I cannot in a moment refute great slanders; and, as I am convinced that I never wronged another, I will assuredly not wrong myself. I will not say of myself that I deserve any evil, or propose any penalty. Why should I? Because I am afraid of the penalty of death which Meletus proposes? When I do not know whether death is a good or an evil, why should I propose a penalty which would certainly be an evil? Shall I say imprisonment? And why should I live in prison, and be the slave of the magistrates of the year—of the Eleven? Or shall the penalty be a fine, and imprisonment until the fine is paid? There is the same objection. I should have to lie in prison, for money I have none, and cannot pay. And if I say exile (and this may possibly be the penalty which you will affix), I must indeed be blinded by the love of life, if I am so irrational as to expect that when you, who are my own citizens, cannot endure my discourses and words, and have found them so grievous and odious that you will have no more of them, others are likely to endure me. No indeed, men of Athens, that is not very likely. And what a life should I lead, at my age, wandering from city to city, ever changing my place of exile, and always being driven out! For I am quite sure that wherever I go, there, as here, the young men will flock to me; and if I drive them away, their elders will drive me out at their request; and if I let them come, their fathers and friends will drive me out for their sakes.

Some one will say: Yes, Socrates, but cannot you hold your tongue, and then you may go into a foreign city, and no one will interfere with you? Now I have great difficulty in making you understand my answer to this. For if I tell you that to do as you say would be a disobedience to the God, and therefore that I cannot hold my tongue, you will not believe that I am serious; and if I say again that daily to discourse about virtue, and of those other things about which you hear me examining myself and others, is the greatest good of man, and that the unexamined life is not worth living, you are still less likely to believe me. Yet I say what is true, although a thing of which it is hard for me to persuade you. Also, I have never been accustomed to think that I deserve to suffer any harm. Had I money I might have estimated the offence at what I was able to pay, and not have been much the worse. But I have none, and therefore I must ask you to proportion the fine to my means. Well, perhaps I could afford a mina, and therefore I propose that penalty: Plato, Crito, Critobulus, and Apollodorus, my friends here, bid me say thirty minae, and they will be the sureties. Let thirty minae be the penalty; for which sum they will be ample security to you.

[2nd vote: The jury decides for the death penalty by a vote of 360 to 141.]

Not much time will be gained, O Athenians, in return for the evil name which you will get from the detractors of the city, who will say that you killed Socrates, a wise man; for they will call me wise, even although I am not wise, when they want to reproach you. If you had waited a little while, your desire would have been fulfilled in the course of nature. For I am far advanced in years, as you may perceive, and not far from death. . . .

The difficulty, my friends, is not to avoid death, but to avoid unrighteousness; for that runs faster than death. I am old and move slowly, and the slower runner has overtaken me, and my accusers are keen and quick, and the faster runner, who is unrighteousness, has overtaken them. And now I depart hence condemned by you to suffer the penalty of death—they too go their ways condemned by the truth to suffer the penalty of villainy and wrong; and I must abide by my award—let them abide by theirs. I suppose that these things may be regarded as fated—and I think that they are well. . . .

Friends, who would have acquitted me, I would like also to talk with you about the thing which has come to pass, while the magistrates are busy, and before I go to the place at which I must die. Stay then a little, for we may as well talk with one another while there is time. You are my friends, and I should like to show you the meaning of this event which has happened to me. O my judges—for you I may truly call judges—I should like to tell you of a wonderful circumstance. Hitherto the divine faculty of which the internal oracle is the source has constantly been in the habit of opposing me even about trifles, if I was going to make a slip or error in any

matter; and now as you see there has come upon me that which may be thought, and is generally believed to be, the last and worst evil. But the oracle made no sign of opposition, either when I was leaving my house in the morning, or when I was on my way to the court, or while I was speaking, at anything which I was going to say; and yet I have often been stopped in the middle of a speech, but now in nothing I either said or did touching the matter in hand has the oracle opposed me. What do I take to be the explanation of this silence? I will tell you. It is an intimation that what has happened to me is a good, and that those of us who think that death is an evil are in error. For the customary sign would surely have opposed me had I been going to evil and not to good.

Let us reflect in another way, and we shall see that there is great reason to hope that death is a good; for one of two things—either death is a state of nothingness and utter unconsciousness, or, as men say, there is a change and migration of the soul from this world to another. Now if you suppose that there is no consciousness, but a sleep like the sleep of him who is undisturbed even by dreams, death will be an unspeakable gain. For if a person were to select the night in which his sleep was undisturbed even by dreams, and were to compare with this the other days and nights of his life, and then were to tell us how many days and nights he had passed in the course of his life better and more pleasantly than this one, I think that any man, I will not say a private man, but even the great king will not find many such days or nights, when compared with the others. Now if death be of such a nature, I say that to die is gain; for eternity is then only a single night. But if death is the journey to another place, and there, as men say, all the dead abide, what good, O my friends and judges, can be greater than this? If indeed when the pilgrim arrives in the world below, he is delivered from the professors of justice in this world, and finds the true judges who are said to give judgment there, Minos and Rhadamanthus and Aeacus and Triptolemus, and other sons of God who were righteous in their own life, that pilgrimage will be worth making. What would not a man give if he might converse with Orpheus and Musaeus and Hesiod and Homer? Nay, if this be true, let me die again and again. I myself, too, shall have a wonderful interest in there meeting and conversing with Palamedes, and Ajax the son of Telamon, and any other ancient hero who has suffered death through an unjust judgment; and there will be no small pleasure, as I think, in comparing my own sufferings with theirs. Above all, I shall then be able to continue my search into true and false knowledge; as in this world, so also in the next; and I shall find out who is wise, and who pretends to be wise, and is not. What would not a man give, O judges, to be able to examine the leader of the great Trojan expedition; or Odysseus or Sisyphus, or numberless others, men and women too! What infinite delight would there be in conversing with them and asking them questions! In another world they do not put a man to death for asking questions: assuredly not. For besides being happier than we are, they will be immortal, if what is said is true.

Wherefore, O judges, be of good cheer about death, and know of a certainty, that no evil can happen to a good man, either in life or after death. He and his are not neglected by the gods; nor has my own approaching end happened by mere chance. But I see clearly that the time had arrived when it was better for me to die and be released from trouble; wherefore the oracle gave no sign. For which reason, also, I am not angry with my condemners, or with my accusers; they have done me no harm, although they did not mean to do me any good; and for this I may gently blame them.

Still I have a favour to ask of them. When my sons are grown up, I would ask you, O my friends, to punish them; and I would have you trouble them, as I have troubled you, if they seem to care about riches, or anything, more than about virtue; or if they pretend to be something when they are really nothing,—then reprove them, as I have reproved you, for not caring about that for which they ought to care, and thinking that they are something when they are really nothing. And if you do this, both I and my sons will have received justice at your hands.

The hour of departure has arrived, and we go our ways—I to die, and you to live. Which is better God only knows.

Probing Questions

1. What does Socrates mean by "The unexamined life is not worth living"? How does this view relate to Socrates' activity as the city's intellectual gadfly? Socrates seems to think that many of his jurors lead unexamined lives. Why does he think this?

2. Socrates was executed because he dealt in offensive and dangerous ideas. Have there been others in history who have also suffered because society thought their ideas were unacceptable? Is a society ever justified in punishing people for expressing such ideas?

3. Socrates died for his principles. What ideas in your life would you be willing to die for?

For Further Reading

Simon Blackburn, *Oxford Dictionary of Philosophy* (Oxford: Oxford University Press, 1994, 2005). A concise guide to hundreds of philosophy topics, with many of the entries being of substantial length.

Nicholas Bunnin and E. P. Tsui-James, ed., *The Blackwell Companion to Philosophy* (Cambridge, MA: Blackwell, 1969). A one-volume student reference covering the major divisions of philosophy.

Eliot D. Cohen, *Philosophers at Work* (New York: Holt, Rinehart, and Winston, 1989). Reports of how people in different professions use philosophy.

Edward Craig, ed., *Routledge Encyclopedia of Philosophy*, 10 vols. (New York: Routledge, 1998). A fine source of information on a vast number of philosophical topics.

Ted Honderich, ed., *The Oxford Companion to Philosophy* (Oxford: Oxford University Press, 1995). A good one-volume philosophy reference featuring many excellent articles on philosophical issues.

Brooke Moore and Richard Parker, *Critical Thinking*, 8th edition (New York: McGraw-Hill, 2007). A comprehensive and readable treatment of critical thinking skills.

Louis P. Pojman and Lewis Vaughn, eds., *Classics of Philosophy*, 3rd edition (New York: Oxford University Press, 2010). The most comprehensive anthology of Western philosophy available.

Bertrand Russell, *The Problems of Philosophy* (New York: Oxford University Press, 1959). A very readable classic work by an eminent philosopher. Focuses mostly on issues in epistemology.

Lewis Vaughn, *Great Philosophical Arguments: An Introduction to Philosophy* (New York: Oxford University Press, 2012). A text with readings organized by topic and by the standard arguments that have occupied thinkers throughout the centuries.

CHAPTER 2

GOD AND RELIGION

Chapter Objectives

2.1 OVERVIEW: GOD AND PHILOSOPHY

- Understand the importance of religious beliefs in the world and how they can influence what people think, do, and value.
- Know how philosophy tries to understand and evaluate religious claims.
- Give an overview of the traditional arguments for the existence of God and objections to them.
- Define *theism*, *atheism*, *agnosticism*, *monotheism*, *polytheism*, *deism*, *pantheism*, and *panentheism*.

2.2 ARGUMENTS FOR THE EXISTENCE OF GOD

- Explain and evaluate Aquinas's first-cause argument and Craig's Kalam cosmological argument.
- Explain and evaluate Paley's analogical design argument and the best-explanation design argument.
- Explain and evaluate Anselm's ontological argument.

2.3 GOD AND THE PROBLEM OF EVIL

- Understand Rowe's argument from evil and some major criticisms of it.
- Critically examine the free will defense.
- Explain and evaluate Hick's soul-making theodicy.

2.4 THEISM AND RELIGIOUS EXPERIENCE

- State and evaluate the argument from religious experience.
- Summarize Swinburne's argument from religious experience and assess criticisms of it.
- Assess the claim that the argument from religious experience fails because religious experiences are incompatible.

2.5 BELIEF WITHOUT REASON

- Summarize and evaluate James's pragmatic argument for believing the religious hypothesis.
- State and evaluate Pascal's wager.

2.6 EASTERN RELIGIONS

- Explain how Buddhism differs from Western religious traditions.
- State and explain the Buddha's Four Noble Truths.
- Define *samsara, atman, brahmin,* and *Brahman.*
- Explain the nature and significance of the *Vedas,* the *Upanishads,* and the *Bhagavad-Gita.*
- Know how the *Chuang Tzu* characterizes the Dao.
- Identify the parallels to the Dao in Western philosophy.

2.1 OVERVIEW: GOD AND PHILOSOPHY

What does philosophy have to do with religion? Throughout history they have often been intertwined. At times the two have bowed respectfully to each other (although sometimes from a distance), thrown stones at each other's conceptual temples, worked in each other's backyards, and chased wisdom along divergent paths that often crossed. For Socrates, Plato, and Aristotle, doing philosophy is not merely a search for truth; it is a spiritual quest, a journey to higher, invaluable things. From the Eastern religious traditions of Buddhism, Hinduism, Confucianism, and Taoism come philosophical insights that have influenced millions and earned the respect of Western thinkers. To the great philosophers of the medieval period—Augustine, Boethius, Avicenna, Anselm, Maimonides, Aquinas, and others—reason is a gift from God, and philosophy can reveal hidden knowledge and sacred truths. In modern philosophy, from Descartes to the present, philosophers (both religious and secular) examine claims about God, immortality, good and evil, and ultimate reality. Many contemporary thinkers would insist that philosophy, using its own distinctive methods of inquiry, seeks truth and, through truth, transcendence.

What some of the great philosophers have to say about God and religion is the subject of this chapter. Of course, being philosophers, they do not simply declare their views to be correct—they argue their cases. It is then up to us to evaluate their arguments to see if their claims are worthy of our acceptance. To embrace a view merely because it is comfortable, familiar, and emotionally satisfying is to violate the spirit of philosophical inquiry, which asks us to believe for good reasons.

> God is not what you imagine or what you think you understand. If you understand, you have failed.
> —Augustine

1 Are reasons or arguments relevant to your current religious beliefs? If so, how? If not, do you think your beliefs are nonetheless rational? Explain.

Why Religion Matters

Belief in God or in a spiritual reality has shaped civilizations and altered history. In the name of the divine, devotees have raised up and laid low mighty empires. They

2 How has your belief or nonbelief in God influenced the major choices you've made in your life? How has your belief or nonbelief affected your attitude toward science, morality, your education, people who don't share your beliefs, atheists, abortion, and terrorist acts?

have built temples, created art, produced sacred texts, and crafted ceremony and song. They have bequeathed to the world moral and legal codes, explanations of how the universe works, and conceptual maps showing where individuals belong in a divine plan. From such things, countless millions have drawn a sense of purpose, meaning, and courage in the face of loss.

But there is also a dark side of the religious realm. Faith has often engendered moral blindness, intolerance, narrow-mindedness, and cruelty. With unshakeable confidence in a transcendent power, believers have burned places of worship, books, heretics, and unbelievers. In the name of their gods they have trampled on human rights, blocked scientific inquiry, oppressed women, waged holy wars, and inflicted terrorism on innocents.

It seems that however we tally these lists of good and evil, we must conclude that the impact of religion on earth is incalculably large. This fact alone is reason enough to examine the claims of religion critically and dispassionately—that is, philosophically.

Religious belief or disbelief moves not just societies, but also individual lives. Whatever your ideas about God and religion, they will surely influence your thinking about some very important matters. Based on these beliefs, you may decide what sort of entities exist in the universe, what claims are true or false, and what things are good or bad. And from such views, your choices flow, and from your choices, your life is made.

I do not feel obliged to believe that the same God who has endowed us with sense, reason, and intellect has intended us to forgo their use.
—Galileo Galilei

Overview: The Philosopher's Quest

You may already have strong views about the existence of God and about the merits of a specific religious tradition. Where did those views come from? Chances are good that you believe what you do because you were raised that way, trained in a particular faith by your parents or culture. If so, you came by your religious beliefs accidentally. Out of the many religions of the world (and the thousands of faith groups), you found yourself in one of them. And the mere fact that your parents or your society handed those beliefs to you does not mean they are true. The point is not that the religious views we inherit are false, but that blindly accepting them is a poor way to discover the truth about them.

To judge the worth of any religious claims, to decide among the many competing assertions, we need the objective stance and critical reasoning of philosophical inquiry. The way of the philosopher is not to ask how you came to have a belief, but *whether the belief is supported by good reasons.* She knows that to judge a religious view from the standpoint of the religious tradition that spawned it is to beg the question and to bias her inquiry from the start. She strives instead for the philosophical ideal of unbiased evaluation in the court of reason.

This court has been in session for hundreds of years as philosophers and theologians debate religious issues, particularly the existence or nonexistence of God. They have put forth a number of arguments to try to demonstrate the latter, several of which are discussed in this chapter and its readings. The arguments concern the God of the three main Western religious traditions—Christianity, Judaism, and

3 Suppose you, like many people, have come by your beliefs about religion accidentally (because you were born at a particular place and time). How do you think you should respond to this fact? Should you (1) still assume your beliefs are true, (2) reject all your current beliefs, (3) suspend judgment about the beliefs, or (4) evaluate your beliefs using reason and evidence?

PHILOSOPHY NOW

Who Believes in God?

According to many surveys, belief in God, or gods, is widespread on the planet but is neither universal nor unchanging.

Belief in God over time in the United States

1944	96%
1981	95%
1997	94%
2006	89%

NORC/University of Chicago, 2009

"Absolutely certain" belief in God over time in the United States

1952	87%
1965	81%
1996	72%

NORC/University of Chicago, 2009

Belief in any form of God or supreme being vs. atheism

Italy	62%	7%
Spain	48%	11%
Germany	41%	20%
Great Britain	35%	17%
France	27%	32%

Harris Poll, 2006

People in the United States claiming no religion

1990	8.2%
2001	14.2%

(Those claiming no religion make up the only "religious" tradition growing in all fifty states.)

Pew Forum Survey, 2007

Why do you think belief in God in the United States has declined slightly in the last sixty years? Does the fact that the vast majority of Americans believe in God provide evidence for God's existence? Why or why not? European countries have much lower rates of belief in God (and higher rates of atheism) than the United States does. What conclusions can you draw from this?

[C]riticism of religious beliefs is often considered impolite or even unconstitutional (although it isn't). Religion is treated like a senile relative whose bizarre statements are not to be questioned.
—Walter Sinnott-Armstrong

Figure 2.1 Most people probably acquire their religious beliefs in childhood. Did you come by your current religious beliefs that way? If so, do you think you should critically examine them in adulthood? Why or why not?

Islam. This being is thought to be the creator of the universe, a person (as opposed to an impersonal force or substance, as in some Eastern religions) who is all-powerful (omnipotent), all-knowing (omniscient), and all-good (omnibenevolent).

Cosmological arguments are arguments that try to show that from the fact that the universe exists, God exists.

To try to prove the existence of this God, many thinkers have advanced **cosmological arguments**, which reason from the existence of the universe, or cosmos (or some fundamental feature of it), to the conclusion that God exists. For example, St. Thomas Aquinas (1225–1274) argues that some things in the universe are caused to exist, and that nothing can cause itself to exist or come into being through an infinite series of causes. So there must be a first uncaused cause of everything—and this first uncaused cause is God.

Philosophers, of course, aren't the only ones who argue this way. Many people—perhaps you are one of them—have thought or said something along these lines: "If God doesn't exist, how did the universe come into being? How did *we* come into being? To say that the world wasn't caused by anyone or that it was the result of an accident makes no sense. Only a supreme being could have caused it to exist." Philosophers have simply given this kind of argument more precision and coherence, as well as more critical scrutiny.

Teleological arguments are arguments that try to show that God must exist because features of the universe show signs of purpose or design.

Many try to make their case for God through **teleological arguments**, which reason from apparent signs of design or purposeful creation in the world to the existence of a supreme designer. William Paley (1743–1805), English theologian and moral philosopher, presents a classic version of this approach. Arguing by analogy, he asserts that a watch is devised by an intelligent designer; the universe resembles a watch in that it too looks as if it were designed by some intelligent being; therefore, the universe was probably also created by an intelligent designer—in other words, by God.

Some philosophers have cast the design argument as an inference to the best explanation. This version begins by pointing to some impressive features of the universe such as the intricate workings of biological systems or the just-so calibration of physical properties that allows the universe to exist. It then claims that the best explanation of such amazing facts is that God designed the universe. God must be the best explanation for these facts because it seems utterly improbable that they could have *just happened* without the intervention of a deity. So if God is the best explanation, then God must exist.

Ontological arguments appeal not to the empirical facts about the cosmos, but to the concept of God itself. From the definition of God, we prove with logic alone that a supreme deity is a reality. St. Anselm (1033–1109) was the first to articulate such an argument, and ever since, other philosophers have been offering their own versions. He first posits a definition of God as the greatest possible being. This assertion, Anselm says, implies that God must actually exist, because if he did not exist in reality (and only existed in our minds), he would not be the greatest possible being. (Existing in reality is thought to make something greater than if it exists merely in someone's mind.) Therefore, God exists.

Anselm's argument is not easy to grasp on a quick reading. To appreciate it, you may need to read it several times and spend some extra time with it. Just keep this in mind: There are good reasons why intrigued philosophers have been examining and reexamining Anselm's argument for the past nine hundred years. (We will take a closer look at the argument later in this chapter.)

For Anselm and others, the strongest arguments for God's existence spring from pure reason. But for many people, definitive evidence that God exists comes from personal experience—from direct awareness of what seems to be God's divine presence. People experience something that they believe is God or is of God, and this apparent encounter forms the basis of an **argument from religious experience**. The argument says that a person seems to have experienced God; the experience must have actually been a genuine encounter with God; therefore, God probably exists. This way of arguing is essentially an inference to the best explanation. The best explanation of the person's experience is that God's presence was somehow sensed, and if so, God likely exists.

Philosophers have subjected all the preceding arguments to critical examination, questioning both their conclusions and the truth of their premises. In the following sections, we

An **ontological argument** is an argument that tries to demonstrate God's existence by logical analysis of the concept of God.

I think we must attack—wherever we meet it—the nonsensical idea that mutually exclusive propositions about God can both be true.
—C. S. Lewis

An **argument from religious experience** is an argument of this form: A person seems to have experienced God; the experience must have actually been a genuine encounter with God; therefore, God probably exists.

Figure 2.2 Some people think the world so wondrous that a divine Designer must have brought it forth, but others have thought the world so thoroughly flawed in its design that we might well conclude that the Designer was incompetent. Which view are you more sympathetic to?

An **argument from evil** is an argument purporting to show that since there is unnecessary evil, an all-powerful, all-knowing, and all-good God must not exist.

will review some of these criticisms as well as reasoned responses to them. For now, it is important to understand that even if the arguments fail to prove their case, that doesn't demonstrate the *nonexistence* of God. If scientists have so far failed to find evidence for life outside our solar system, that doesn't prove that life doesn't exist somewhere out there. The failure of these arguments would show only that they give us no good reasons to believe in the traditional God of Western religion.

But there is another kind of argument that does purport to establish God's nonexistence: the **argument from evil**. You have probably heard this argument, or the complaint that inspires it, before. When you have seen people confronted with unbearable evil—pain, suffering, and injustice—you may have heard them say something like this: "Why did this tragedy happen? Why did God allow my mother—a

WHAT DO YOU BELIEVE?

Hard-Wired for God?

Do you believe in God? If so, why? Some scientists think they know why. Here is a recent report on the issue:

> Humans are programmed to believe in God because it gives them a better chance of survival, researchers claim. A study into the way children's brains develop suggests that during the process of evolution those with religious tendencies began to benefit from their beliefs—possibly by working in groups to ensure the future of their community.
>
> The findings of Bruce Hood, professor of developmental psychology at Bristol University, suggest that magical and supernatural beliefs are hard-wired into our brains from birth, and that religions are therefore tapping into a powerful psychological force. His work is supported by other researchers who have found evidence linking religious feelings and experience to particular regions of the brain. They suggest people are programmed to receive a feeling of spirituality from electrical activity in these areas.
>
> The findings challenge atheists such as Richard Dawkins, the author of *The God Delusion*, who has long argued that religious beliefs result from poor education and childhood "indoctrination."—*Daily Mail*, September 7, 2009

Suppose it is true that we are all programmed to believe in God. Would this fact support or undermine the proposition that God exists? If theism has evolutionary advantages, would this fact constitute a good reason for believing in God? Why or why not?

devout and loving person—to suffer so horribly for so long and then die so young? If there is a God, why does he permit such evils?" Believers in every age have struggled to reconcile the existence of evil with their belief in an all-powerful, all-knowing, and all-good God. The argument from evil asserts that these two things *cannot* be reconciled, and we are therefore forced by reason to abandon our belief.

Stated more precisely, the argument from evil says that if an all-powerful, all-knowing, and all-good God existed, unnecessary evil would not exist. (Some evil is deemed *necessary*, as when a child is given a painful injection to save her life, or when a farmer endures months of backbreaking work to assure a good harvest to feed his family. *Unnecessary* evil is thought to have no such excuses for occurring.) An all-powerful and all-knowing God would know about, and be able to prevent, evil, and an all-good God would want to prevent it. But there is in fact unnecessary evil in the world. Therefore, an all-powerful, all-knowing, and all-good God does not exist.

Philosophers have tried to answer the argument from evil in a variety of ways. Probably the most dramatic response is that unnecessary evil exists because God cannot or will not prevent it; that is, he is a finite deity, lacking one or more of the traditional divine attributes. This line, however, would seem to most people to make God unworthy of worship.

Other approaches try to defend against the argument from evil while retaining all the attributes in the traditional notion of God. These counterarguments are known as **theodicies**. They admit that evil exists but claim that it is *necessary* evil, required to achieve some greater good. So they deny that *unnecessary* evil exists in the world, which is the crucial premise in the argument from evil. The point of a theodicy is not to prove that God exists, but to show that the argument from evil does not succeed. It tries to demonstrate that there may be good reasons to think that the crucial premise is false—that is, to think that all the evil in the world is necessary. Among the possibilities are that evil is necessary to effect the moral improvement of individuals, to better the human race, to punish humans for sin, or to help people understand the true nature of evil.

Perhaps the most promising theodicy is the *free will defense*. It maintains that evil is a necessary result of humans having free will. God created people with the freedom to choose between good and evil, but he could not give people free will and at the same time ensure that they would never do evil. That's impossible even for God. So the evil produced by humans is a necessary result of their enjoying God's gift of freedom.

Belief and Disbelief

A wide spectrum of beliefs regarding the existence of God is possible, and fortunately there is some standard terminology to help us sort them out. A person who believes in the existence of God is a **theist,** and belief in the existence of God is **theism.** Someone who denies the existence of God is an **atheist**, and such denial is **atheism.** A person who neither believes nor disbelieves in God is known as an **agnostic.** If you are an agnostic, you may think that the evidence for or against theism is inconclusive, that you do not know what is the case. Or you may take the

4 Think about the four types of arguments for the existence of God glossed here. At this point in your reading of this chapter, which type do you think makes the strongest case for God? Why? Which do you think makes the weakest?

5 If you were to have a religious experience that seemed to be of God, would your experience be strong evidence for God's existence? Why or why not? Would you be able to distinguish a genuine experience of God from a false one— say, instances of wishful thinking, hallucination, or fantasy? If so, how? If not, would this fact change your degree of confidence that the experience was genuine?

I don't want a God that would go around killing people's little girls. Neither do I want a God who would kill his own son.
—Bishop John Spong

A **theodicy** is a defense of the traditional conception of God in light of the existence of evil.

A **theist** is someone who believes in God.

Theism is belief in the existence of God.

An **atheist** is someone who denies God's existence.

Atheism is the denial of the existence of God.

An **agnostic** is someone who neither accepts nor denies God's existence.

A man can no more diminish God's glory by refusing to worship Him than a lunatic can put out the sun by scribbling the word, 'darkness' on the walls of his cell.
—C. S. Lewis

6 Do you think the argument from evil is a strong argument for the nonexistence of God? Why or why not? If you believe in God, how do you reconcile that belief with the existence of evil? If you don't believe in God, is the argument from evil a factor in your nonbelief?

Monotheism is a belief in one God.

Polytheism is a belief in many gods.

Deism is a belief in one God who created the world but left it unattended to run on its own.

Pantheism is the view that God and the universe are one and the same thing, a divine Whole.

Panentheism is the view that although God and the world are distinct, the world is part of God.

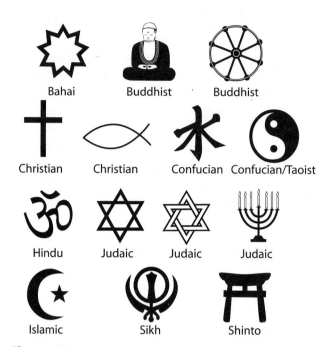

Bahai   Buddhist   Buddhist

Christian   Christian   Confucian   Confucian/Taoist

Hindu   Judaic   Judaic   Judaic

Islamic   Sikh   Shinto

Figure 2.3 There are thousands of religious groups in the world, worshiping thousands of gods in countless ways. Do you believe that one of these groups is the true one? Is one of these gods the right god?

more radical agnostic view that knowledge of the existence or nonexistence of God is impossible. That is, the truth about God is unknowable.

Belief in God or the divine can take different forms, and there are terms to reflect that fact. The view taken by many religions, including Christianity, Judaism, and Islam, is **monotheism**, belief in one God. Belief in several gods is **polytheism**, also prevalent throughout the world. A doctrine that arose among prominent thinkers in France and England in the seventeenth and eighteenth centuries is **deism**, the notion that there is one God who is essentially an "absentee landlord." This God created the universe but put it on autopilot and now ignores it, taking no interest in human affairs. Prominent deists of the past include George Washington, Thomas Paine, Thomas Jefferson, and Voltaire. **Pantheism** is the view that God and the universe are one and the same, a divine Whole. God and the world are basically identical. The great philosopher Baruch Spinoza (1632–1677) held this view, and other thinkers, including Albert Einstein (1879–1955), were sympathetic to it. Pantheism is distinct from **panentheism**, the idea that the universe is part of God rather than being identical with God.

Some thinkers have questioned the basic approach to the God question that most philosophers have taken. They reject the notion that has guided much of traditional philosophical inquiry—the view that rational belief in God requires reasons or evidence. They insist that we may rationally believe in the existence of God even though we have no good reasons for doing so. Others believe that faith and reason are incompatible, and that we can legitimately come to know religious truths, including the existence of God, only through a leap of faith.

WRITING TO UNDERSTAND:
CRITIQUING PHILOSOPHICAL VIEWS   Section 2.1

1. Do you believe in God? If so, can you state reasons for your belief? Do you think your belief is rational? Would you believe in God whether or not you had good reasons? Explain your position on these questions.

2. Would you consider yourself an agnostic or atheist? If so, do you have reasons for your lack of belief in God? Is your lack of belief rational? Do you think that believers are irrational? Explain.

3. What is William Paley's teleological argument? Do you think the analogy between a watch and the universe is strong enough to prove the existence of a Designer?

4. What is the argument from evil? Do you think the existence of evil shows that God doesn't exist? Why or why not?

5. Some philosophers and theologians believe that reason is a gift from God and should be used in the search for truth about God. Do you agree?

2.2 ARGUMENTS FOR THE EXISTENCE OF GOD

We can sort the arguments for God's existence into two categories: (1) those that appeal to the evidence of experience (what philosophers call *a posteriori* arguments) and (2) those that appeal to logical relations (called *a priori* arguments). *A posteriori* arguments reason from empirical facts about the world to the conclusion that God exists. Cosmological, teleological, and religious-experience arguments are of this kind. *A priori* arguments logically derive the conclusion that God exists from concepts of God. Ontological arguments take this form.

Cosmological Arguments

Cosmological arguments can boast a long lineage, having been set out by many theorists from Aristotle, Plato, Ghazali, Averroës, Aquinas, and Spinoza to contemporary philosophers such as Richard Swinburne and William Lane Craig. They all begin with the empirical fact that the universe, or one of its essential properties, exists—and end with the conclusion that only God could be responsible for this fact. In his masterpiece *Summa Theologica*, the Roman Catholic scholar Thomas Aquinas

---

If God lived on earth, people would break his windows.
—Jewish Proverb

7 Rabbi Harold Kushner, author of *When Bad Things Happen to Good People*, argues that unnecessary evil exists in the world because God is not able to prevent it. That is, God is finite, a less powerful deity than the traditional God. Do you think this is a good explanation of unnecessary evil? Why or why not? Would a finite God deserve your respect and devotion?

A God that can be understood is no God. Who can explain the Infinite in words?
—W. Somerset Maugham

Reason in man is rather like God in the world.
—Thomas Aquinas

offers five "proofs" (his famous "Five Ways") of God's existence, the first three of which are cosmological arguments. This is how Aquinas lays out the first two:

Thomas Aquinas, *Summa Theologica*

The existence of God can be shown in five ways.

The first and more manifest way is the argument from motion. It is certain, and evident to our senses, that in the world some things are in motion. Now whatever is in motion is put in motion by another, for nothing can be in motion except it is in potentiality to that towards which it is in motion; whereas a thing moves inasmuch as it is in actuality.

For motion is nothing else than the reduction of something from potentiality to actuality. But nothing can be reduced from potentiality to actuality, except by something in a state of actuality. Thus that which is actually hot, as fire, makes wood, which is potentially hot, to be actually hot, and thereby moves and changes it. Now it is not possible that the same thing should be at once in actuality and potentiality in the same respect, but only in different respects. For what is actually hot cannot simultaneously be potentially hot; but it is simultaneously potentially cold. It is therefore impossible that in the same respect and in the same way a thing should be both mover and moved, i.e. that it should move itself. Therefore, whatever is in motion must be put in motion by another. If that by which it is put in motion be itself put in motion, then this also must needs be put in motion by another, and that by another again. But this cannot go on to infinity, because then there would be no first mover, and, consequently, no other mover; seeing that subsequent movers move only inasmuch as they are put in motion by the first mover; as the staff moves only because it is put in motion by the hand. Therefore it is necessary to arrive at a first mover, put in motion by no other; and this everyone understands to be God.

The second way is from the nature of the efficient cause. In the world of sense we find there is an order of efficient causes. There is no case known (neither is it, indeed, possible) in which a thing is found to be the efficient cause of itself; for so it would be prior to itself, which is impossible. Now in efficient causes it is not possible to go on to infinity, because in all efficient causes following in order, the first is the cause of the intermediate cause, and the intermediate is the cause of the ultimate cause, whether the intermediate cause be several, or only one. Now to take away the cause is to take away the effect. Therefore, if there be no first cause among efficient causes, there will be no ultimate, nor any intermediate cause. But if in efficient causes it is possible to go on to infinity, there will be no first efficient cause, neither will there be an ultimate effect, nor any intermediate efficient causes; all of which is plainly false. Therefore it is necessary to admit a first efficient cause, to which everyone gives the name of God.[1]

8 Why does Aquinas think there cannot be an infinite chain of movers? Do you accept his reasons for this? Can you conceive of a series of movers stretching infinitely into the past? If so, can you detect any contradictions inherent in your conception?

9 Why does Aquinas insist that there must be a first cause? Does his argument show that the first cause is in fact God? Does it show, for example, that the first cause could not be an evil demon or an impersonal force?

Aquinas's *argument from motion* (his first way) goes like this: It is obvious that some things in the universe are moving (that is, changing), and if they are moving, something else must have caused them to move. And this "something else" must also have been moving, set in motion by yet another thing that was moving, and this thing set in motion by another moving thing, and so on. But this series of things-moving-other-things cannot go on forever, to infinity, because then there would not

PHILOSOPHERS AT WORK

St. Thomas Aquinas

Thomas Aquinas (1225–1274) was born into a noble family in southern Italy to eventually become the greatest philosopher of the medieval period and, to this day, the official theologian of the Roman Catholic church. Because his family had decided that he should be a great church leader, they packed him off before the age of six to the Benedictine monastery of Monte Cassino for training. At fourteen, he was sent to the University of Naples for further study, and there his life took what his family considered a radical turn. At age twenty, he joined the scholarly Dominican order and pursued, not a leadership position in the church, but the rarefied life of the intellect.

Figure 2.4 Thomas Aquinas, the philosopher who fused Aristotle with Christianity.

Becoming alarmed at Aquinas's change of plans, his family had him kidnapped and locked in the family castle for several months. When it became clear that he was not going to relinquish his scholarly ambitions, they released him, and he continued his studies and his writing at the University of Paris and in Cologne, Rome, Naples, Viterbo, and Orvieto.

Aquinas's great contribution to both philosophy and Christianity was his fusion of Aristotle's philosophy with Christian doctrines. In theology he distinguished between reason and faith, giving each its own domain of inquiry. Reason can be used to prove the existence of God, he says, but only through faith can we know such mysteries as the incarnation and the trinity.

be something that started all the moving. There must therefore be an initial mover (a "First Mover"), an extraordinary being that started the universe moving but is not itself moved by anything else—and this being we call God.

Aquinas's second way is his famous *first-cause argument*. He maintains that everything we can observe has a cause, and it is clear that nothing can cause itself. For something to cause itself, it would have to exist *prior to* itself, which is impossible. Neither can something be caused by an infinite regress of causes—that is, a series of causes stretching to infinity. In any series of causes, Aquinas says, there must be a first cause, which causes the second, which causes the third, and so on. But in an infinite series of causes, there would be no first cause and thus no subsequent causes, including causes existing now. So infinite regresses make no sense. Therefore, there must be a first cause of everything, and this first cause we call God. (Here Aquinas is not thinking of a first cause of a *temporal* series of causes, as in a sequence of falling

> Believe nothing, no matter where you read it, or who said it, no matter if I said it, unless it agrees with your own reason and your own common sense.
> —The Buddha

My religion consists of a humble admiration of the illimitable superior spirit who reveals himself (or herself) in the slight details we are able to perceive with our frail and feeble minds.

—Albert Einstein

dominoes, but of a first cause that sustains the whole series of causes, like the bottom building block that holds up all the others in a stack.)

Against these two arguments, philosophers have lodged several criticisms. One of the strongest takes aim at Aquinas's claim that an infinite regress is not possible. Aquinas thinks that a chain of causes must have a first cause; otherwise there would be no subsequent causes in the world. In an infinite regress of causes, he contends, there would be no first cause and therefore no subsequent causes. Critics reply that just because an infinite chain of causes has no first cause, that doesn't mean that the chain of causes has no cause at all: in an infinite chain of causes, *every* link has a cause. Many philosophers, including David Hume (1711–1776), see no logical contradiction in the idea of an infinite regress. They hold that the universe need not have

PHILOSOPHY NOW

Science and the Uncaused Universe

The notion that some events in the universe are entirely uncaused is now widely accepted among quantum physicists, the scientists who study the realm of subatomic particles (such as electrons, positrons, and quarks). According to quantum physics, subatomic particles frequently pop in and out of existence randomly—that is, they appear and disappear uncaused out of a perfect vacuum. From these findings, some scientists have speculated that the universe itself may have arisen uncaused. This is how two physicists describe the phenomenon:

[T]he idea of a First Cause sounds somewhat fishy in light of the modern theory of quantum mechanics. According to the most commonly accepted interpretation of quantum mechanics, individual subatomic particles can behave in unpredictable ways and there are numerous random, uncaused events.—Richard Morris, *Achilles in the Quantum World*, 1997

[Q]uantum electrodynamics reveals that an electron, positron, and photon occasionally emerge spontaneously in a perfect vacuum. When this happens, the three particles exist for a brief time, and then annihilate each other, leaving no trace behind. . . . The spontaneous, temporary emergence of particles from a vacuum is called a vacuum fluctuation, and it is utterly commonplace in quantum field theory.—Edward Tryon, "Is the Universe a Vacuum Fluctuation?" *Nature*, 1973

Suppose some subatomic events are uncaused. Does this show that the universe is uncaused? What bearing does the phenomenon have on the cosmological arguments of Aquinas and Craig? How might Craig reply to the physicists quoted above?

had a beginning; it may be eternal, without beginning, and without a first cause or a first mover. The universe may have simply *always been*.

Some claim that the worst problem with Aquinas's arguments is that at best they prove only that the universe had a first mover or first cause—but not that the first mover or first cause is God. For all the arguments show, the first mover or first cause could be an impersonal substance or energy, or several minor deities, or a supreme but evil demon. Perhaps the universe is, as many scientists and philosophers allege, simply an eternal, uncaused brute fact.

Inspired by recent findings in scientific cosmology (the study of the origin and structure of the universe), some philosophers have been interested in another kind of cosmological argument. Scientific evidence suggests that the universe suddenly came into existence about fourteen billion years ago in an unimaginably massive explosion known as the "Big Bang." Until that moment, the universe that we experience today simply *was not*. Using this fact as a starting point, William Lane Craig defends the *Kalam cosmological argument* (a name derived from medieval Islamic scholars):

William Lane Craig, *Reasonable Faith*

In particular, I find the *kalam* cosmological argument for a temporal first cause of the universe to be one of the most plausible arguments for God's existence. . . . The argument is basically this: both philosophical reasoning and scientific evidence show that the universe began to exist. Anything that begins to exist must have a cause that brings it into being. So the universe must have a cause. Philosophical analysis reveals that such a cause must have several of the principle theistic attributes.

10 Does the Big Bang prove that the universe must have had a beginning? Some scientists have thought that the Big Bang was not the beginning of the universe, because the universe is "oscillating"—that is, it expands and contracts continually in an eternal cycle of a Big Bang followed by periods of expansion then contraction and another Big Bang. There is now reason to think that the universe is not oscillating, but if oscillation were a plausible possibility, would this undermine the claim that the universe began to exist?

Figure 2.5 Was the Big Bang the beginning of the universe? Did the Big Bang have a cause?

William Lane Craig,
Reasonable Faith

11 Is it obvious to you, as it is to Craig, that nothing starts to exist without a cause? Do you think that the universe could be uncaused? Why or why not?

12 Can you conceive of a series of events stretching infinitely into the future? Can you conceive of a series of events continuing infinitely into the past? Do you think there is a contradiction lurking in the idea of an infinite series of causes? Does the weirdness of infinity in mathematics show that infinities in the empirical world cannot exist?

What we need is not the will to believe, but the will to find out.
—Bertrand Russell

The argument may be formulated in three simple steps.

1. Whatever begins to exist has a cause.
2. The universe began to exist.
3. Therefore, the universe has a cause.

The logic of the argument is valid and very simple; the argument has the same logical structure as the argument: "All men are mortal; Socrates is a man; therefore, Socrates is mortal." So the question is, are there good reasons to believe that each of the steps is true? I think there are.[2]

Craig thinks the first premise is obviously true: Nothing starts to exist without a cause. But many dispute this, insisting that there is no logical reason why the universe could not be uncaused. They ask why the notion of an uncaused origination of things makes no sense while the idea of a god creating things out of nothing does.

Some argue against Premise 1 on empirical grounds, pointing to findings in quantum physics suggesting that some events involving subatomic particles are uncaused. This evidence has prompted theorists to speculate that the universe itself may be uncaused. At the very least, they say, it proves that something's coming into existence uncaused is not impossible. (See the box "Philosophy Now: Science and the Uncaused Universe.")

Craig argues for Premise 2 ("The universe began to exist") in much the same way that Aquinas argues for a first cause: The universe must have begun to exist because the alternative is an infinite regress of past events, which is impossible. He maintains that the very idea of an actual infinity of things involves logical contradictions:

[W]hat is infinity minus infinity? Well, mathematically, you get self-contradictory answers. . . . [I]nfinity minus infinity is infinity. But suppose instead you subtract all the numbers greater than 2—how many are left? Three. So infinity minus infinity is 3! . . . This implies that infinity is just an idea in your mind, not something that exists in reality.[3]

Many philosophers reject this understanding of infinity. They agree that infinity can be perplexing, but they point out that mathematicians know how to work with infinity without inviting contradictions. More to the point, they hold that there is no logical absurdity in the notion of a series of events stretching into an infinite future. We can easily conceive of this. Likewise, they say, there is no logical absurdity in the idea of a series of events continuing into an infinite past. We can straightforwardly conceive of this as well.

Craig says that infinities may exist in mathematics (as in the series 0, 1, 2, 3, . . .), but that they are merely *potential* infinities, not *actual* infinities. Potential infinities "approach infinity as a limit, but they never actually get there. . . . [E]xistence in the mathematical realm does not imply existence in the real world."[4] Others reply that we may not be able to actually count to infinity or measure an infinite number of segments between two points, but that does not mean that the numbers or segments are nonexistent.

Figure 2.6 In his latest book, *The Grand Design*, world-renowned physicist Stephen Hawking declares, "Because there is a law such as gravity, the Universe can and will create itself from nothing. Spontaneous creation is the reason there is something rather than nothing, why the Universe exists, why we exist. . . . It is not necessary to invoke God to light the blue touch paper and set the Universe going." Is Hawking's view plausible? Why or why not?

Design Arguments

Teleological, or design, arguments for the existence of God are straightforward, the gist being that since the world seems to show signs of purposeful design, it most likely *was* purposefully designed—that is, intentionally made by an intelligent being, which we call God. A popular version takes the form of an argument from analogy and was famously laid down by the eighteenth-century Anglican clergyman William Paley:

William Paley, *Natural Theology*

In crossing a heath, suppose I pitched my foot against a *stone*, and were asked how the stone came to be there, I might possibly answer that, for anything I knew to the contrary, it had lain there forever; nor would it, perhaps, be very easy to show the absurdity of this answer. But suppose I found a *watch* upon the ground, and it should be inquired how the watch happened to be in that place, I should hardly think of the answer which I had given—that, for anything I knew, the watch might have always been there. Yet why should not this answer serve for the watch as well as for the stone? Why is it not as admissible in the second case as in the first? For this reason and for no

William Paley,
Natural Theology

As the poet said, "Only God can make a tree"—probably because it's so hard to figure out how to get the bark on.
—Woody Allen

other; viz., that, when we come to inspect the watch, we perceive (what we could not discover in the stone) that its several parts are framed and put together for a purpose, e.g., that they are so formed and adjusted as to produce motion, and that motion so regulated as to point out the hour of the day; that, if the different parts had been differently shaped from what they are, if a different size from what they are, or placed after any other manner, or in any other order than that in which they are placed, either no motion at all would have been carried on in the machine, or none which would have answered the use that is now served by it. To reckon up a few of the plainest of these parts, and of their offices, all tending to one result: We see a cylindrical box containing a coiled elastic spring, which, by its endeavor to relax itself, turns round the box. We next observe a flexible chain (artificially wrought for the sake of flexure) communicating the action of the spring from the box to the fuse. We then find a series of wheels, the teeth of which catch in, and apply to, each other, conducting the motion from the fuse to the balance, and from the balance to the pointer, and, at the same time, by the size and shape of those wheels, so regulating that motion as to terminate in causing an index, by an equable and measured progression, to pass over a given space in a given time. We take notice that the wheels are made of brass, in order to keep them from rust; the springs of steel, no other metal being so elastic; that over the face of the watch there is placed a glass, a material employed in no other part of the work, but in the room of which, if there had been any other than a transparent substance, the hour could not be seen without opening the case. This mechanism being observed (it requires indeed an examination of the instrument, and perhaps some previous knowledge of the subject, to perceive and understand it; but being once, as we have said, observed and understood), the inference, we think, is inevitable, that the watch must have had a maker; that there must have existed, at some time, and at some place or other, an artificer or artificers who formed it for the purpose which we find it answer; who comprehended its construction, and designed its use. . . .

Every indication of contrivance, every manifestation of design, which existed in the watch, exists in the works of nature; with the difference, on the side of nature, of being greater and more, and that in a degree which exceeds all computation. I mean that the contrivances of nature surpass the contrivances of art, in the complexity, subtlety, and curiosity of the mechanism; and still more, if possible, do they go beyond them in number and variety; yet in a multitude of cases, are not less evidently mechanical, not less evidently contrivances, not less evidently accommodated to their end, or suited to their office, than are the most perfect productions of human ingenuity. . . .[5]

It is obvious, Paley says, that the "several parts [of the watch] are framed and put together for a purpose," which suggests that it had an intelligent designer. Likewise, the universe manifests countless parts, all seemingly formed and arranged to achieve various ends. From this he concludes that the universe also probably has an intelligent designer, but one that surpasses immeasurably the power and understanding of humans. This great Designer must be God.

Before Paley made his case in *Natural Theology* (1802), David Hume (1711–1776) had launched a famous critique of design arguments in his *Dialogues Concerning Natural Religion* (1779), and it has been echoed and amplified by thinkers ever since. In *Dialogues*, Hume presents a discussion of the issues among three fictional characters—Demea, the orthodox believer; Cleanthes, the theologian; and Philo, the skeptic. Using Philo as his mouthpiece, Hume assaults the design argument from analogy on two broad fronts. He first contends that the argument fails because the analogy is weak, hampered by too few relevant similarities and too many dissimilarities. He then reasons that even if the argument demonstrates that the universe has a designer, the designer may not be the traditional God of theism. Here is Philo arguing the first point:

David Hume, *Dialogues Concerning Natural Religion*

If we see a house, *Cleanthes*, we conclude, with the greatest certainty, that it had an architect or builder because this is precisely that species of effect which we have experienced to proceed from that species of cause. But surely you will not affirm that the universe bears such a resemblance to a house that we can with the same certainty infer a similar cause, or that the analogy is here entire and perfect. The dissimilitude is so striking that the utmost you can here pretend to is a guess, a conjecture, a presumption concerning a similar cause; and how that precision will be received in the world, I leave you to consider. . . .

But can you think, *Cleanthes*, that your usual phlegm and philosophy have been preserved in so wide a step as you have taken when you compared to the universe houses, ships, furniture, machines; and, from their similarity in some circumstances, inferred a similarity in their causes? Thought, design, intelligence, such as we discover in men and other animals, is no more than one of the springs and principles of the universe, as well as heat or cold, attraction or repulsion, and a hundred others which fall under daily observation. It is an active cause by which some particular parts of nature, we find, produce alterations on other parts. But can a conclusion, with any propriety, be transferred from parts to the whole? Does not the great disproportion bar all comparison and inference? From observing the growth of a hair, can we learn anything concerning the generation of a man? Would the manner of a leaf's blowing, even though perfectly known, afford us any instruction concerning the vegetation of a tree? . . .

When two *species* of objects have always been observed to be conjoined together, I can *infer*, by custom, the existence of one wherever I see the existence of the other; and this I call an argument from experience. But how this argument can have place where the objects, as in the present case, are single, individual, without parallel or specific resemblance, may be difficult to explain. And will any man tell me with serious countenance that an orderly universe must arise from some thought and art like the human because we have experience of it? To ascertain this reasoning it were requisite that we had experience of the origin of worlds; and it is not sufficient, surely, that we have seen ships and cities arise from human art and contrivance. . . .

Now, if we survey the universe, so far as it falls under our knowledge, it bears a great resemblance to an animal or organized body, and seems actuated with a like principle of life and motion. A continual circulation of matter in it produces no disorder; a continual waste in every part is incessantly repaired; the closest sympathy is perceived throughout the entire system; and each part or member, in performing its proper offices, operates both to its own preservation and to that of the whole. The world, therefore, I infer, is an animal; and the Deity is the *soul* of the world, actuating it, and actuated by it.[6]

Philo asserts that trying to draw a conclusion about the cause of the universe based on what we know about the cause of, say, a house is pointless because the dissimilarities

13 Is Hume's argument about reasoning from parts to the whole correct? We certainly can't reason that because the bricks of a house are light in weight, the whole house is light in weight. But can't we legitimately argue that, say, because a bucket of water from a pond is polluted, the whole pond is polluted?

14 Do you agree with Hume that we can draw no conclusions about the cause of phenomena that are "single, individual, without parallel or specific resemblance"? Would contemporary scientists accept Hume's view?

15 Is Hume's suggestion that the universe is like a living thing at least as plausible as the view that it is like a machine? Why or why not? Suppose Hume is right. What would the implications be for Paley's argument?

16 If there are many imperfections in nature, as Hume suggests, would we necessarily be forced to conclude that the Designer was also imperfect?

between the two phenomena are enormous. We cannot make any firm inferences about the architect of the universe from what we know about the architects of houses. Further, he says, the intelligence that we observe in mankind is just one of the many forces that produce changes in the world. We therefore have no reason to presume that intelligence is the one thing that is responsible for the universe as a whole. If we contend that it is, we commit the logical fallacy of arguing from the part to the whole: because a part of a system has a particular characteristic, the entire system must have that characteristic too. As Philo puts it, "From observing the growth of a hair, can we learn anything concerning the generation of a man?" In a similar way, he says, we err if we conclude that one event always causes another just because we observe a single instance of such a pairing. We would need to encounter many instances of headaches preceded by a change in the weather before we could plausibly infer that the latter caused the former. Likewise, we can establish no firm conclusions about the cause of the universe, because we have only a single universe to examine. Finally, Philo tries to undermine the machine-universe analogy by offering what he considers a better comparison. The universe, he argues, is more like a living thing than a machine. In the world, as in living things, there is a continual circulation of matter, damage and waste are remedied, and each part operates to preserve itself and the whole. Living things create and regulate themselves, unlike machines, which require designers and technicians.

On the second point—that even if the universe has a designer, he may not be God—Philo has this to say:

David Hume,
Dialogues Concerning Natural Religion

Now, *Cleanthes*, said *Philo*, with an air of alacrity and triumph, mark the consequences. *First*, by this method of reasoning you renounce all claim to infinity in any of the attributes of the Deity. For, as the cause ought only to be proportioned to the effect, and the effect, so far as it falls under our cognizance, is not infinite: What pretensions have we, upon your suppositions, to ascribe that attribute to the Divine Being? You will insist that, by removing him so much from all similarity to human creatures, we give in to the most arbitrary hypothesis, and at the same time weaken all proofs of his existence.

Secondly, you have no reason, on your theory, for ascribing perfection to the Deity, even in his finite capacity; or for supposing him free from every error, mistake, or incoherence in his undertakings. There are many inexplicable difficulties in the works of Nature which if we allow a perfect author to be proved *a priori*, are easily solved, and become only seeming difficulties from the narrow capacity of man, who cannot trace infinite relations. But according to your method of reasoning, these difficulties become all real; and, perhaps, will be insisted on as new instances of likeness to human art and contrivance. At least, you must acknowledge that it is impossible for us to tell, from our limited views, whether this system contains any great faults or deserves any considerable praise if compared to other possible and even

Figure 2.7 Was the world designed by God with humans in mind? If so, some have claimed, God must have erred, because the earth seems more hospitable to insects than to humans. The famous agnostic and trial lawyer Clarence Darrow once said, "There are some millions of different species of animals on this earth, and one-half of these are insects. . . . If the land of the earth was made for life, it seems as if it was intended for insect life, which can exist almost anywhere." Do you agree?

real systems. Could a peasant, if the *Aeneid* were read to him, pronounce that poem to be absolutely faultless, or even assign to it its proper rank among the productions of human wit, he who had never seen any other production?

But were this world ever so perfect a production, it must still remain uncertain whether all the excellences of the work can justly be ascribed to the workman. If we survey a ship, what an exalted idea must we form of the ingenuity of the carpenter who framed so complicated, useful, and beautiful a machine? And what surprise must we feel when we find him a stupid mechanic who imitated others, and copied an art which, through a long succession of ages, after multiplied trials, mistakes, corrections, deliberations, and controversies, had been gradually improving? Many worlds might have been botched and bungled, throughout an eternity, ere this system was struck out; much labor lost; many fruitless trials made; and a slow but continued improvement carried on during infinite ages in the art of world-making. In such subjects, who can determine where the truth, nay, who can conjecture where the probability lies, amidst a great number of hypotheses which may be proposed, and a still greater which may be imagined?

And what shadow of an argument, continued *Philo*, can you produce from your hypothesis to prove the unity of the Deity? A great number of men join in building a house or ship, in rearing a city, in framing a commonwealth; why may not several deities combine in contriving and framing a world? This is only so much greater similarity to human affairs. By sharing the work among several, we may so much further limit the attributes of each, and get rid of that extensive power and knowledge which must be supposed in one deity, and which, according to you, can only serve to weaken the proof of his existence. And if such foolish, such vicious creatures as man can yet often unite in framing and executing one plan, how much more those deities or demons, whom we may suppose several degrees more perfect? . . .

And why not become a perfect anthropomorphite? Why not assert the deity or deities to be corporeal, and to have eyes, a nose, mouth, ears, etc.? *Epicurus* maintained that no man had ever seen reason but in a human figure; therefore, the gods must have a human figure. And this argument, which is deservedly so much ridiculed by *Cicero*, becomes, according to you, solid and philosophical.

In a word, *Cleanthes*, a man who follows your hypothesis is able, perhaps, to assert or conjecture the universe sometime arose from something like design. But beyond that position he cannot ascertain one single circumstance and is left afterwards to fix every point of his theology by the utmost license of fancy and hypothesis. This world, for aught he knows, is very faulty and imperfect, compared to a superior standard, and was only the first rude essay of some infant deity who afterwards abandoned it, ashamed of his lame performance. It is the work only of some dependent, inferior deity, and is the object of derision to his superiors. It is the production of old age and dotage in some superannuated deity; and ever since his death has run on at adventures, from the first impulse and active force which it received from him. . . .[7]

17 Hume suggests that, for all we know, there could have been many designers of the universe instead of one supreme deity. Is it reasonable to suppose that this is a genuine possibility?

Philo declares that if we carefully and consistently apply the kind of reasoning used in the design argument (as Cleanthes would have us do), we would have to accept some uncomfortable conclusions about the nature of the Designer. According to Cleanthes, we are supposed to judge the nature of the cause by the nature of the effect, and we are to reason from the attributes of human designers to the attributes of God. By this logic, Philo says, we would have to conclude that God (the cause) may not be infinite, because the universe (the effect) is not infinite. We would be forced to admit that God may not be perfect, because the universe is itself not perfect—an example, some say, of very poor design. And even if the world is perfect, we would not be able to conclude that the divine workman is perfect, for perhaps he is incompetent and achieved the present result only by trial and error through an eternity of lame attempts. Based on what we know of human designers, we would have to surmise that there may not be one designer, but many, for it usually takes many people to build a ship or a city. And just as humans have bodies, maybe the deity or deities are corporeal as well.

Hume's dissection of the design argument is not the last word on the subject. Many contemporary philosophers take Hume's side on the issue, while others try to counter his criticisms. His detractors, for example, challenge his contention that, because the universe is unique, design arguments do not work. They point out that we often draw conclusions about the nature and origin of unique objects. Scientists have discovered many things about the cosmos even though it is, for all we know, one of a kind. Defenders of the design argument also reject Hume's claim that the universe could very well have been built by a multitude of designers. They appeal to Ockham's razor, a principle of reasoning that says we should not posit more entities than necessary to explain a phenomenon. Why assume many designing gods when one will do?

Not all design arguments are arguments from analogy. Some are framed as inferences to the best explanation. They ask, What is the best explanation of the existence and nature of the world we experience? Their answer is that the workings of a supreme being or superintelligence explain these facts better than any alternative theory. Because this theory is best, it is the most likely be true.

As discussed in Chapter 1, we judge the worth of theories by the criteria of adequacy, the conceptual standards used by scientists, philosophers, and others to assess competing explanations. Richard Swinburne argues that by applying such criteria, "We find that the view that there is a God explains everything we observe. . . . It explains the fact that there is a universe at all, that scientific laws operate within it, that it contains conscious animals and humans with very complex intricately organized bodies, that we have abundant opportunities for developing ourselves and the world, as well as the more particular data that humans report miracles and have religious experiences."[8]

Most of the weight of his argument rests on the criterion of simplicity, which he defines as a matter of the number of components something has. By this definition, naturalistic (nontheistic) explanations of the world's existence and properties are not simple, because they postulate that "the ultimate explanation of things behaving as they do now is provided by the powers and liabilities of an immense (possibly infinite) number of material objects."[9] The theistic theory, on the other hand, is much simpler, because it posits just one thing—God—and this simplicity makes the theory more likely to be true.

Critics reply that Swinburne's argument fails because he misconstrues the criteria of adequacy, especially simplicity. They point out that often in the history of science, the most complex theory (in Swinburne's sense) has turned out to be the correct one. They contend that the criterion of simplicity is more plausibly understood as a measure of the number of assumptions a theory makes. By this standard, the God theory is inferior to naturalistic theories because it, by definition, assumes an unknown entity (God) with unknown powers and unknown properties. Naturalistic theories do not leap to such assumptions.

Ontological Arguments

Cosmological and teleological appeals rest ultimately on the evidence of experience. Ontological arguments rest on logic alone. Logic tells us that some things cannot possibly exist—round squares and married bachelors, for example. They cannot exist because they involve logical contradictions. And logic tells us that it is (logically) possible that golden mountains and flying horses exist (though they are not actual), for they involve no logical contradictions. So isn't it at least plausible that with logic alone we could somehow prove the existence of God? Anselm thought so. He was the first to articulate a precise statement of an ontological argument, and other thinkers since him have offered their own versions. He reasons that since God by definition is the greatest possible being, God must actually exist, because if he did not exist in reality (and merely existed in our minds), he would not be the greatest possible being. Here is the argument in Anselm's own words:

18 Does existence always add greatness to an entity? That is, is it always greater to exist than not to exist? Why or why not?

Anselm, *Proslogium*

And so, Lord, do thou, who dost give understanding to faith, give me, so far as thou knowest it to be profitable, to understand that thou art as we believe; and that thou art that which we believe. And, indeed, we believe that thou art a being than which nothing greater can be conceived. Or is there no such nature, since the fool hath said in his heart, there is no God? (Psalms xiv.1). But, at any rate, this very fool, when he hears of this being of which I speak—a being than which nothing greater can be conceived—understands what he hears, and what he understands is in his understanding; although he does not understand it to exist.

For, it is one thing for an object to be in the understanding, and another to understand that the object exists. When a painter first conceives of what he will afterwards perform, he has it in his understanding, but he does not yet understand it to be, because he has not yet performed it. But after he has made the painting, he both has it in his understanding, and he understands that it exists, because he has made it.

Hence, even the fool is convinced that something exists in the understanding, at least, than which nothing greater can be conceived. For, when he hears of this, he understands it. And whatever is understood, exists in the understanding. And assuredly that, than which nothing greater can be conceived, cannot exist in the understanding alone. For, suppose it exists in the understanding alone: then it can be conceived to exist in reality; which is greater.

Therefore, if that, than which nothing greater can be conceived, exists in the understanding alone, the very being, than which nothing greater can be conceived, is one, than which a greater can be conceived. But obviously this is impossible. Hence, there is no doubt that there exists a being, than which nothing greater can be conceived, and it exists both in the understanding and in reality.

And it assuredly exists so truly, that it cannot be conceived not to exist. For, it is possible to conceive of a being which cannot be conceived not to exist; and this is greater than one which can be conceived not to exist. Hence,

Figure 2.8 St. Anselm (1033–1109), medieval philosopher and theologian and the Archbishop of Canterbury. He held that reason was a friend of faith, not a source of religious skepticism.

PHILOSOPHY NOW

Evolution and Intelligent Design

Science maintains that the best explanation for the apparent design of biological life is the theory of evolution, which says that living things, in all their variety and complexity, arose through natural processes. But some claim that life on earth is best explained by the intervention of a supreme intelligence. Michael Behe famously argues that some biological systems are so profoundly intricate—so "irreducibly complex"—that they could not have been produced by gradual evolutionary changes. Only an intelligent designer can account for such complexity.

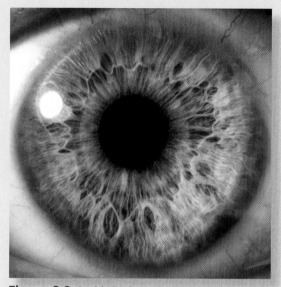

Figure 2.9 Could the human eye—a very complex system—have evolved through natural selection?

The consensus among scientists is that evolution operates through what Darwin called "natural selection." The basic idea is that offspring of organisms differ physically from their parents in various ways, and these differences can be passed on genetically to their offspring. If an offspring has an inherited trait (such as sharper vision or a larger brain) that increases its chances of surviving long enough to reproduce, the individual is more likely to survive and pass the trait on to the next generation. After several generations, this useful trait, or adaptation, spreads throughout a whole population of individuals, differentiating the population from its ancestors. Behe's claim is that it is impossible for irreducibly complex systems to be produced through natural selection. He says that an irreducibly complex system (for example, the eye) is composed of several interconnected, perfectly matched parts such that if even one part is missing, the system will not function. An eye can improve the survival prospects of organisms only if it

---

Anselm,
Proslogium

if that, than which nothing greater can be conceived, can be conceived not to exist, it is not that, than which nothing greater can be conceived. But this is an irreconcilable contradiction. There is, then, so truly a being than which nothing greater can be conceived to exist, that it cannot even be conceived not to exist; and this being thou art, O Lord, our God.

So truly, therefore, dost thou exist, O Lord, my God, that thou canst not be conceived not to exist; and rightly. For, if a mind could conceive of a being better than thee, the creature would rise above the Creator; and this is most absurd. And, indeed, whatever else there is, except thee alone, can be conceived not to exist. To thee alone, therefore, it belongs to exist more truly than all other beings, and hence in a higher functions, and proper functioning requires that each of its parts is there to do its job. According to evolution, the eye came about through slow, incremental changes. But, Behe asks, how can an unfinished, nonfunctioning eye improve survival? This shows, he argues, that the eye and all other irreducibly complex systems were created whole—not through evolution, but by some great intelligence.

But most biologists deny that the development of irreducibly complex systems through natural selection is physically impossible. Behe thinks natural selection requires that a complex system be formed by gradual addition of components until a functioning model is achieved. But critics point out that the components can be present all along or arise at different times, performing tasks that improve various processes. Then, because of a change in the genome, the parts may be put to new uses, forming an irreducibly complex structure.

From the fact that biologists generally do not know precisely how each step of such a process happens, it does not follow that the process is impossible or unknowable. Philip Kitcher thinks that the remedy for our ignorance of these matters is more and better research, not the presumption of an intelligent designer:

> Even if intelligent designers were right in supposing that the phenomena they indicate couldn't have evolved by natural selection, only a more explicit identification of the causal mechanism that was at work could justify the conclusion that that mechanism is intelligent.—Philip Kitcher, *Living With Darwin*, 2007

Suppose evolution is true and intelligent design theory is false. Would this mean that there is no supreme being who made biological life possible? Can someone consistently believe in both evolution and God?

degree than all others. For, whatever else exists does not exist so truly, and hence in a less degree it belongs to it to exist. Why, then, has the fool said in his heart, there is no God (Psalms xiv.1r), since it is so evident, to a rational mind, that thou dost exist in the highest degree of all? Why, except that he is dull and a fool?[10]

Here's the argument stated more formally:

1. God, by definition, is the greatest being possible.
2. Suppose the greatest being possible exists only in the understanding (in the mind, as a mental object).

19 What is the most plausible meaning of "exists in the understanding alone"? Could it mean that the concept of the greatest being possible is not actually exemplified, that it does not refer to anything existing in reality? If so, how would such an interpretation affect Anselm's argument?

If God did not exist, it would be necessary to invent him.
—Voltaire

I cannot conceive of a God who rewards and punishes his creatures, or has a will of the kind that we experience in ourselves. Neither can I nor would I want to conceive of an individual that survives his physical death; let feeble souls, from fear or absurd egoism, cherish such thoughts. I am satisfied with the mystery of the eternity of life and with the awareness and a glimpse of the marvelous structure of the existing world, together with the devoted striving to comprehend a portion, be it ever so tiny, of the Reason that manifests itself in nature.
—Albert Einstein

3. Then a greater being than the greatest being possible can be conceived, one existing not just in the understanding, but also in reality (for a being is greater if it exists in reality than if it exists only in the understanding).
4. But this yields a contradiction, for a being greater than the greatest being possible is impossible.
5. Therefore, God, the greatest being possible, must exist in reality, not just in the understanding.

Many have found fault with this line of reasoning. The first major criticism came from an eleventh-century monk named Gaunilo, who thought that Anselm was trying to define God into existence. He maintained that if Anselm's argument were a good piece of reasoning, we could use it to prove the existence of many things that obviously do not exist—for instance, the greatest island possible. We could argue that the greatest island possible must actually exist because if it existed only in the understanding, there could conceivably be an island that is greater, namely, one that exists in reality as well as in the understanding.

Anselm replied that his reasoning does not pertain to things like Gaunilo's island, but only to God, the greatest being possible. Others have suggested that Gaunilo's critique fails because his island is not a possibility. To them it seems that for any island thought to be the greatest possible, we can always imagine how it can be greater by enhancing its properties. Such an island could therefore never be the greatest. Critics have rejected both of these suggestions, and some have countered that Anselm's line could prove the existence of absurd things other than a perfect island—like a supremely evil superbeing.

In putting forth his argument, Anselm makes two assumptions: (1) existence makes something greater (that is, something is greater if it exists in the world than if it exists only in the mind as an idea) and (2) existence can be a defining property. Critics have questioned both of these. On the first count, they contend that there is no good reason to think that existence adds to the value of an entity. After all, it is not obvious that it is better for, say, a thoroughly evil being to exist than not to exist. On the second count, they doubt that existence can be any kind of defining property at all. Anselm assumes that one thing can be greater than another thing even though they have exactly the same properties, differing only in that the first thing exists and the second does not. In his view, existence is another defining property—the essential attribute that the one thing has and the other lacks. But is this plausible? Suppose you imagine an incredibly beautiful beach, detailing in your mind its every property (white sand,

Figure 2.10 Could there be such a thing as the greatest possible beach?

lovely palm trees, blue water, etc.). Then you add one more attribute—actual existence. Does this last step change the defining properties of your beach—or does it simply indicate that the beach with all its defining properties is actual? Many philosophers, including Immanuel Kant (1724–1804), would choose the latter. As Kant says,

> If triangles made a god, they would give him three sides.
>
> —Charles de Montesquieu

Immanuel Kant, *Critique of Pure Reason*

"*Being*" is obviously not a real predicate [term designating a property]; that is, it is not a concept of something which could be added to the concept of a thing. It is merely the positing of a thing, or of certain determinations, as existing in themselves. . . . By whatever and by however many predicates we may think a thing—even if we completely determine it—we do not make the least addition to the thing when we further declare that this thing *is*.[11]

In any case, some detractors think the weakest link in Anselm's chain of reasoning is Premise 2, the supposition that the greatest being possible exists only in the understanding. This claim gives rise to the contradiction that a greater being than the greatest being possible can be conceived (one existing in reality). But they argue that the contradiction dissolves if we take Premise 2 to mean not that the greatest being possible exists in some sense in the mind (the view that Anselm seems to take), but simply that the concept of the greatest being possible does not refer to any actually existing thing. The latter, they insist, is the more reasonable reading of "exists only in the understanding," and it does not yield any contradictions about the nature of God. With this reading of Premise 2, Anselm's argument does not go through.

WRITING TO UNDERSTAND:
CRITIQUING PHILOSOPHICAL VIEWS   Section 2.2

1. What is Aquinas's first-cause argument? Does it prove the existence of the traditional God of theism? Does it prove that the universe had a first cause?

2. What is Craig's cosmological argument? Critique its two premises. Are they true? Explain why you think they are true (or false). If the argument is sound, what does it prove? Does it prove that God exists?

3. What are the relevant similarities and differences between Paley's watch and the universe? Is the watch analogy a good one?

4. Are Hume's criticisms of the design argument cogent? Does he successfully refute it?

5. Are the assumptions behind Anselm's argument justified? That is, are there good reasons for accepting them?

2.3 GOD AND THE PROBLEM OF EVIL

Some people doubt the existence of God because they believe that the traditional arguments for theism fall short and that no other evidence in God's favor seems forthcoming. Others take a stronger stand against theism by setting forth the argument from evil. They ask, in effect, "If God exists, how can there be so much unnecessary evil in the world? An all-powerful, all-knowing, and all-good God might allow some evils because they are necessary to bring about some greater good. But much of the world's evils seem to be entirely and blatantly gratuitous. So how can we conclude anything other than that there must be no such God?"

Philosophers and theologians have generally concerned themselves with two types of evil. **Moral evil** comes from human choices and actions and the bad things that arise from them. Injustice, murder, deceit, theft, and torture are moral evils from which flow pain, suffering, injury, loss, and death. **Natural evil** results from the workings of nature. From hurricanes, floods, earthquakes, fires, disease, and drought come vast sums of evil in the form of human and animal suffering. To make their case, atheists have usually appealed to both kinds of evil, challenging theists to explain why a perfectly good and powerful God would allow such horrors.

Moral evil is evil that comes from human choices and actions and the bad things that arise from them.

Natural evil is evil that results from the workings of nature.

Rowe's Argument from Evil

One of the more influential versions of the argument from evil is provided by philosopher William L. Rowe, who focuses on evil as "intense human and animal suffering":

William L. Rowe, *Philosophy of Religion*

Taking human and animal suffering as a clear instance of evil which occurs with great frequency in our world, the . . . problem of evil can be stated in terms of the following argument for atheism.

1. There exist instances of intense suffering which an omnipotent, omniscient being could have prevented without thereby preventing the occurrence of any greater good.
2. An omniscient, wholly good being would prevent the occurrence of any intense suffering it could, unless it could not do so without thereby preventing the occurrence of some greater good.

Therefore,

3. There does not exist an omnipotent, omniscient, wholly good being.

What are we to say about this argument for atheism, an argument based on the profusion of one sort of evil in the world? The argument is valid; therefore, if we have rational grounds for accepting its premises, to that extent we have rational grounds for accepting atheism. Do we, however, have rational grounds for accepting the premises of this argument?

Figure 2.11 Does a fawn's suffering alone in the forest lead to a greater good? Could an omnipotent God obtain this greater good some other way?

The second premise of the argument expresses a belief about what a morally good being would do under certain circumstances. According to this belief, if a morally good being knew of some intense suffering that was about to occur and he was in a position to prevent its occurrence, he would prevent it *unless* he could not do so without thereby losing some greater good of which he was aware. This belief (or something very close to it) is, I think, held in common by theists and nontheists. Of course, there may be disagreement about whether something is good, and whether, if it is good, one would be morally justified in permitting some intense suffering to occur in order to obtain it. Someone might hold, for example, that no good is great enough to justify permitting an innocent child to suffer terribly. To hold such a view, however, is not to deny premise 2 which claims only that *if* an omniscient, wholly good being permits intense suffering *then* there must be some greater good (a good which outweighs the suffering in question) which the good being could not obtain without permitting the intense suffering. So stated, 2 seems to express a belief that accords with our basic moral principles, principles shared by both theists and nontheists. If we are to fault this argument, therefore, we must find some fault with its first premise.

Suppose in some distant forest lightning strikes a dead tree, resulting in a forest fire. In the fire a fawn is trapped, horribly burned, and lies in terrible agony for several days before death relieves its suffering. So far as we can see, the fawn's intense suffering is pointless, leading to no greater good. Could an omnipotent, omniscient being have prevented the fawn's apparently pointless suffering? The answer is obvious, as even the theist will insist. An omnipotent, omniscient being could easily have prevented the fawn from being horribly burned, or, given the burning, could have spared the fawn the intense suffering by quickly ending its life, rather than allowing the fawn to lie in terrible agony for several days. Since no greater good, so far as we can see, would have been lost had the fawn's intense suffering been prevented, doesn't it appear that premise 1 of the argument is true, that there exist instances of intense suffering which an omnipotent, omniscient being could have prevented without thereby preventing the occurrence of any greater good? . . .

20 Do you agree with Rowe that it seems unlikely that all instances of intense human and animal suffering lead to greater goods? And do you think that if all that suffering does lead to greater goods, that "an omnipotent, omniscient being could not have achieved at least some of those goods without permitting the instances of suffering that lead to them"?

William L. Rowe, *Philosophy of Religion*

The truth is that we are not in a position to *prove* that 1 is true. We cannot *know* with certainty that instances of suffering of the sort described in 1 do occur in our world. But it is one thing to *know* or *prove* that 1 is true and quite another thing to have *rational grounds* for believing 1 to be true. We are often in the position where in the light of our experience and knowledge it is rational to believe that a certain statement is true, even though we are not in a position to prove or to know with certainty that the statement is true. In the light of our past experience and knowledge it is, for example, very reasonable to believe that neither Goldwater nor McGovern will ever be elected president, but we are scarcely in the position of knowing with certainty that neither will be elected president. So, too, with 1, although we cannot know with certainty that it is true, it perhaps can be rationally supported, shown to be a rational belief.

Consider again the case of the fawn's suffering. There are two distinct questions we need to raise: "Does the fawn's suffering lead to some greater good?" and "Is the greater good to which it might lead such that an omnipotent, omniscient being could not obtain it without permitting the fawn's suffering?" It may strike us as unlikely that the answer to the first question is yes. And it may strike us as quite a bit more unlikely that the answer to the second question is yes. But even if we should think it is reasonable to believe that the fawn's suffering leads to a greater good unobtainable without that suffering, we must then ask whether it is reasonable to believe that *all* the instances of profound, seemingly pointless human and animal suffering lead to greater goods. And, if they should somehow all lead to greater goods, is it reasonable to believe that an omnipotent, omniscient being *could not* have brought about *any* of those goods without permitting the instances of suffering which supposedly lead to them? When we consider these more general questions in the light of our experience and knowledge of the variety and profusion of human and animal suffering occurring daily in our world, it seems that the answer must be *no*. It seems quite unlikely that all the instances of intense human and animal suffering occurring daily in our world lead to greater goods, and even more unlikely that if they all do, an omnipotent, omniscient being could not have achieved at least some of those goods without permitting the instances of suffering that lead to them. In the light of our experience and knowledge of the variety and scale of human and animal suffering in our world, the idea that none of those instances of suffering could have been prevented by an omnipotent being without the loss of a greater good seems an extraordinary, absurd idea, quite beyond our belief. It seems then that although we cannot *prove* that premise 1 is true, it is, nevertheless, altogether *reasonable* to believe that 1 is true, that it is a *rational* belief.[12]

Some theists reject Premise 1 by appealing to human ignorance. They argue that there could be goods unknown to us that justify the evil we see—goods comprehended by God but beyond our ken. Or our concept of good may not be God's, for his morality is of a higher, purer kind than ours. In God's eyes, then, what we believe is evil might be good, or what we think is good might be evil.

Defenders of Premise 1 reply that we may indeed be unaware of goods that God discerns, but none of the goods we do know about could ever compensate for life's vast burden of seemingly gratuitous evil. We need not know what God knows to be justified in believing Premise 1. As Rowe says,

> That things appear to us to be a certain way is itself justification for thinking things are this way. Of course, this justification may be defeated. But apart from such defeat, the fact that things appear to us

to be a certain way renders us rationally justified in believing that they are that way.[13]

And to assert that God's morality is higher than ours, some argue, is to cast doubt on all our moral judgments and to render meaningless our terms *good* and *evil*. J. L. Mackie observes that on this higher-morality view, "When the theist says that God is wholly good he does not mean that God has anything like the purposes and tendencies that would count as good in a human being. But then why call him good? Is not this description misleading?"[14]

The Free Will Defense

To many theists, the best way to counter the argument from evil is to present a theodicy, an explanation of why God permits evil. The point is to provide good reasons why evil may be a necessary part of God's creation, thereby showing that the argument from evil fails. Chief among such approaches is the free will defense, which is usually offered as an explanation of moral evil. It says that human free will is an enormous good, so much so that a universe where humans have free will is better than one where they don't, even if their exercise of freedom brings about much evil. Moral evil is the unavoidable byproduct of God's gift of free will. According to Richard Swinburne,

Richard Swinburne, *Is There a God?*

The free-will defence claims that it is a great good that humans have a certain sort of free will which I shall call free and responsible choice, but that, if they do, then necessarily there will be the natural possibility of moral evil. . . . A God who gives humans such free will necessarily brings about the possibility, and puts outside his own control whether or not that evil occurs. It is not logically possible—that is, it would be self-contradictory to suppose—that God could give us such free will and yet ensure that we always use it in the right way.[15]

21 Is Mackie correct in saying that an omnipotent God could have created people with free will who always choose the good? Is such a state of affairs logically possible?

Here free will may sound like a serious restriction of God's power (a denial of his omnipotence), but most philosophers, whether theistic or not, have not taken that view. They have interpreted God's omnipotence not as the power to do anything whatsoever, but the power to do anything that is logically possible. They have acknowledged that God cannot make a square circle or a married bachelor, cause 2 + 2 to equal 5, or create a triangle with four sides. But logical impossibilities are fundamental facts about reality and are not thought to set any restrictions on God's power.

Against the free will defense, two main objections have been raised. The first is the contention that there is no reason why an omnipotent God could not have created free agents who always choose the good. As Mackie says, "If God has made men such that in their free choices they sometimes prefer what is good and sometimes what is evil, why could he not have made men such that they always freely choose

PHILOSOPHY NOW

God and Hurricane Katrina

In 2005 Hurricane Katrina devastated New Orleans and other parts of Louisiana and Mississippi, killing over one thousand people and forcing hundreds of thousands from their homes. It seemed a prime example of natural evil, which prompted many to ask why God would allow it. Some noted religious conservatives asserted that Katrina was God's punishment for sin—the sin of abortion, homosexuality, gay marriage, the war in Iraq, occult practices, or Mardi Gras. Among those reported to have taken this line are John Hagee, a prominent evangelical leader and author; Louis Farrakhan, leader of the Nation of Islam; Chuck Baldwin, a conservative Christian commentator; and Reverend Bill Shanks, pastor of New Covenant Fellowship of New Orleans.

Figure 2.12 After hurricane Katrina smashed into the Gulf states, some people declared that it was punishment from God, some said it was the result of chance and natural forces, and some praised God for sparing them. What would your response have been?

Do you accept this "God's punishment" explanation for the evil that Katrina wrought? If so, what are your reasons? If not, why not? Is there a more plausible explanation?

the good?"[16] But many theists assert that to ensure people always freely do what is right, God would have to *force* them to do so—and forcing people to act freely is logically impossible.

The second objection is that even if God could not have made humans so they always freely choose the good, he could have at least made people such that they do less evil than they actually do. In this view, God could have given people better moral character so their desire to do good would be stronger and their desire to do evil would be weaker. Such an alteration in their character would not diminish their capacity to act freely, and even a slight change would reduce the amount of evil in the world. Many theists would object to this line, however, charging that such manipulation of character by God would indeed curtail free will. God's tinkering with people's psychological makeup would be analogous to controlling a person's behavior through hypnosis or drugs.

The Soul-Making Defense

In any case, free will is not the only good that has been offered as a justification for God's permitting evil. The philosopher John Hick says that the greatest good is "soul-making." In his theodicy, he argues that evil in the form of suffering is necessary to provide humans with a world where moral and spiritual progress is possible. Personal growth—soul-making—can take place only when people make free choices in response to the pain and anguish of living. Hick explains:

John Hick, *Evil and the God of Love*

Instead of regarding man as having been created by God in a finished state, as a finitely perfect being fulfilling the divine intention for our human level of existence, and then falling disastrously away from this, the [minority view] sees man as still in process of creation. Irenaeus himself expressed the point in terms of the (exegetically dubious) distinction between the 'image' and the 'likeness' of God referred to in Genesis i.26: 'Then God said, Let us make man in our image, after our likeness.' His view was that man as a personal and moral being already exists in the image, but has not yet been formed into the finite likeness of God. By this 'likeness' Irenaeus means something more than personal existence as such; he means a certain valuable quality of personal life which reflects finitely the divine life. This represents the perfecting of man, the fulfilment of God's purpose for humanity, the 'bringing of many sons to glory', the creating of 'children of God' who are 'fellow heirs with Christ' of his glory.

And so man, created as a personal being in the image of God, is only the raw material for a further and more difficult stage of God's creative work. This is the leading of men as relatively free and autonomous persons, through their own dealings with life in the world in which He has placed them, towards that quality of personal existence that is the finite likeness of God....

In the light of modern anthropological knowledge some form of two-stage conception of the creation of man has become an almost unavoidable Christian tenet. At the very least we must acknowledge as two distinguishable stages the fashioning of *homo*

John Hick,
Evil and the God of Love

22 According to Hick, what is the "soul-making process"? Is it, as he says, of such great value that it justifies all the human and animal suffering involved in it?

sapiens as a product of the long evolutionary process, and his sudden or gradual spiritualization as a child of God. But we may well extend the first stage to include the development of man as a rational and responsible person capable of personal relationship with the personal Infinite who has created him. This first stage of the creative process was, to our anthropomorphic imaginations, easy for divine omnipotence. By an exercise of creative power God caused the physical universe to exist, and in the course of countless ages to bring forth within it organic life, and finally to produce out of organic life personal life; and when man had thus emerged out of the evolution of the forms of organic life, a creature had been made who has the possibility of existing in conscious fellowship with God. But the second stage of the creative process is of a different kind altogether. It cannot be performed by omnipotent power as such. For personal life is essentially free and self-directing. It cannot be perfected by divine fiat, but only through the uncompelled responses and willing co-operation of human individuals in their actions and reactions in the world in which God has placed them. Men may eventually become the perfected persons whom the New Testament calls 'children of God', but they cannot be created ready-made as this.

The value-judgement that is implicitly being invoked here is that one who has attained to goodness by meeting and eventually mastering temptations, and thus by rightly making responsible choices in concrete situations, is good in a richer and more valuable sense than would be one created *ab initio* in a state either of innocence or of virtue. In the former case, which is that of the actual moral achievements of mankind, the individual's goodness has within it the strength of temptations overcome, a stability based upon an accumulation of right choices, and a positive and responsible character that comes from the investment of costly personal effort. I suggest, then, that it is an ethically reasonable judgement, even though in the nature of the case not one that is capable of demonstrative proof, that human goodness slowly built up through personal histories of moral effort has a value in the eyes of the Creator which justifies even the long travail of the soul-making process. . . .

If, then, God's aim in making the world is 'the bringing of many sons to glory', that aim will naturally determine the kind of world that He has created. Antitheistic writers almost invariably assume a conception of the divine purpose which is contrary to the Christian conception. They assume that the purpose of a loving God must be to create a hedonistic paradise; and therefore to the extent that the world is other than this, it proves to them that God is either not loving enough or not powerful enough to create such a world. They think of God's relation to the earth on the model of a human being building a cage for a pet animal to dwell in. If he is humane he will naturally make his pet's quarters as pleasant and healthful as he can. Any respect in which the cage falls short of the veterinarian's ideal, and contains possibilities of accident or disease, is evidence of either limited benevolence or limited means, or both. Those who use the problem of evil as an argument against belief in God almost invariably think of the world in this kind of way. David Hume, for example, speaks of an architect who is trying to plan a house that is to be as comfortable and convenient as possible. If we find that 'the windows, doors, fires, passages, stairs, and the whole economy of the building were the source of noise, confusion, fatigue, darkness, and the extremes of heat and cold' we should have no hesitation in blaming the architect. It would be in vain for him to prove that if this or that defect were corrected greater ills would result: 'still you would assert in general, that, if the architect had had skill and good intentions, he might have formed such a plan of the whole, and might have adjusted the parts in such a manner, as would have remedied all or most of these inconveniences'.

But if we are right in supposing that God's purpose for man is to lead him from human *Bios*, or the biological life of man, to that quality of *Zoe*, or the personal life of eternal worth, which we see in Christ, then the question that we have to ask is not, Is this the kind of world that an all-powerful and infinitely loving being would create as an environment for his human pets? or, Is the architecture of the world the most pleasant and convenient possible? The question that we have to ask is rather, Is this the kind of world that God might make as an environment in which moral beings may be fashioned, through their own free insights and responses, into 'children of God'?

Such critics as Hume are confusing what heaven ought to be, as an environment for perfected finite beings, with what this world ought to be, as an environment for beings who are in process of becoming perfected. For if our general conception of God's purpose is correct the world is not intended to be a paradise, but rather the scene of a history in which human personality may be formed towards the pattern of Christ. Men are not to be thought of on the analogy of animal pets, whose life is to be made as agreeable as possible, but rather on the analogy of human children, who are to grow to adulthood in an environment whose primary and overriding purpose is not immediate pleasure but the realizing of the most valuable potentialities of human personality.

Needless to say, this characterization of God as the heavenly Father is not a merely random illustration but an analogy that lies at the heart of the Christian faith. Jesus treated the likeness between the attitude of God to man and the attitude of human parents at their best towards their children, as providing the most adequate way for us to think about God. And so it is altogether relevant to a Christian understanding of this world to ask, How does the best parental love express itself in its influence upon the environment in which children are to grow up? I think it is clear that a parent who loves his children, and wants them to become the best human beings that they are capable of becoming, does not treat pleasure as the sole and supreme value. Certainly we seek pleasure for our children, and take great delight in obtaining it for them; but we do not desire for them unalloyed pleasure at the expense of their growth in such even greater values as moral integrity, unselfishness, compassion, courage, humour, reverence for the truth, and perhaps above all the capacity for love. We do not act on the premise that pleasure is the supreme end of life; and if the development of these other values sometimes clashes with the provision of pleasure, then we are willing to have our children miss a certain amount of this, rather than fail to come to possess and to be possessed by the finer and more precious qualities that are possible to the human personality. A child brought up on the principle that the only or the supreme value is pleasure would not be likely to become an ethically mature adult or an attractive or happy personality. And to most parents it seems more important to try to foster quality and strength of character in their children than to fill their lives at all times with the utmost possible degree of pleasure. If, then, there is any true analogy between God's purpose for his human creatures, and the purpose of loving and wise parents for their children, we have to recognize that the presence of pleasure and the absence of pain cannot be the supreme and overriding end for which the world exists. Rather, this world must be a place of soul-making. And its value is to be judged, not primarily by the quantity of pleasure and pain occurring in it at any particular moment, but by its fitness for its primary purpose, the purpose of soul-making. . . .

If, then, the evil in human life finally reveals its nature according as it becomes or fails to become a phase in the fulfilment of God's purpose, we must conclude, so far as the present life is concerned, that there are both good and evil suffering, and that there are redeemed and unredeemed sinners. Any revision of the verdict must depend upon lengthening the perspective out until it reaches a new and better conclusion.

Woe unto them that call evil good, and good evil.
—Isaiah 5:20 (King James Version)

23 Do you think Rowe's criticism of the soul-making theodicy is cogent? Can you conceive of a world that has slightly less suffering than our world has, yet in which plenty of soul-making takes place?

If there is any eventual resolution of the interplay between good and evil, any decisive bringing of good out of evil, it must lie beyond this world and beyond the enigma of death. Therefore we cannot hope to state a Christian theodicy without taking seriously the doctrine of a life beyond the grave. This doctrine is not, of course, based upon any theory of natural immortality, but upon the hope that beyond death God will resurrect or re-create or reconstitute the human personality in both its inner and its outer aspects. The Christian claim is that the ultimate life of man—after what further scenes of 'soul-making' we do not know—lies in that Kingdom of God which is depicted in the teaching of Jesus as a state of exultant and blissful happiness, symbolized as a joyous banquet in which all and sundry, having accepted God's gracious invitation, rejoice together. And Christian theodicy must point forward to that final blessedness, and claim that this infinite future good will render worthwhile all the pain and travail and wickedness that has occurred on the way to it. Theodicy cannot be content to look to the past, seeking an explanation of evil in its origins, but must look towards the future, expecting a triumphant resolution in the eventual perfect fulfilment of God's good purpose.[17]

Critics have assailed Hick's view on several fronts, arguing that suffering can warp character as well as build it, that God's allowing people to suffer for their own good constitutes morally repugnant paternalism, and that Hick's theodicy has the bizarre implication that our trying to eradicate evil would be wrong. Rowe's main criticism is that far more evil afflicts people than is required for soul-making:

> The problem Hick's theodicy leaves us is that it is altogether reasonable to believe that some of the evils that occur could have been prevented without either diminishing our moral and spiritual development or undermining our confidence that the world operates according to natural laws.[18]

WRITING TO UNDERSTAND:
CRITIQUING PHILOSOPHICAL VIEWS   Section 2.3

1. Do you think Hick's soul-making theodicy is an adequate response to the argument from evil? Explain.

2. Do you believe that Rowe's argument from evil is sound? Do you accept his first premise? Why or why not?

3. Consider this view: The evil experienced on this earth is nil when compared to the infinite and eternal happiness that Christians will experience after death. If this assertion is true, does it successfully rebut the argument from evil?

4. Some say that what humans might consider evil is actually good in the eyes of an omniscient God with infinite wisdom. Evaluate this claim.

5. Do you believe that physical good is impossible without physical evil? That is, is evil necessary for good to exist? Alternatively, is evil needed so we can understand and appreciate the good?

2.4 THEISM AND RELIGIOUS EXPERIENCE

Many people affirm that their belief in God does not rest on the kinds of appeals we have just examined. The cosmological, teleological, and ontological arguments carry no weight with them. They believe in God because they have had a religious experience that they think gives them knowledge of God's existence. For them, it is this religious experience that justifies their theism.

Some maintain that their encounters with the divine involve sensory content—they hear a voice, feel a touch, or see a light or a face or a form. Many biblical accounts—such as St. Paul's encounter on the road to Damascus and Moses' hearing a voice from a burning bush—are like this. Other people report having no sensations at all but nonetheless sensing a divine presence. Here is one such description from St. Teresa of Avila:

St. Teresa of Avila, *The Life of Teresa of Jesus*

I was at prayer on a festival of the glorious Saint Peter when I saw Christ at my side—or, to put it better, I was conscious of Him, for neither with the eyes of the body nor with those of the soul did I see anything. I thought He was quite close to me and I saw that it was He Who, as I thought, was speaking to me.[19]

And here, from William James, is another:

> [A]ll at once I experienced a feeling of being raised above myself, I felt the presence of God—I tell of the thing just as I was conscious of it—as if his goodness and his power were penetrating me altogether. The throb of emotion was so violent that I could barely tell the boys to pass on and not wait for me. . . . Then, slowly, the ecstasy left my heart; that is, I felt that God had withdrawn the communion which he had granted, and I was able to walk on, but very slowly, so strongly was I still possessed by the interior emotion. . . . I think it well to add that in this ecstasy of mine God had neither form, color, odor, nor taste; moreover, that the feeling of his presence was accompanied with no determinate localization. It was rather as if my personality had been transformed by the presence of a *spiritual spirit*. . . . At bottom the expression most apt to render what I felt is this: God was present, though invisible; he fell under no one of my senses, yet my consciousness perceived him.[20]

Since such occurrences are thought to justify belief in God, we can devise an argument from religious experience that looks like this:

1. Religious experiences occur in which God seems to be sensed.
2. The best explanation for these experiences is that God is indeed sensed (God caused the experience).
3. Therefore, God probably exists.

24 Can all religious experiences be explained in naturalistic terms? Are the naturalistic explanations better than the theistic one? What criteria would you use to decide?

God is real since he produces real effects.
—William James

Premise 1 is true. Few deny that people have experiences that they take to be of God. Premise 2, however, is not obviously true and is often contested. Some critics reject it on the grounds that naturalistic explanations of religious experiences are as good as, or better than, theistic explanations. J. L. Mackie, for example, points out that religious experiences are generally indistinguishable from experiences with a known psychological or physical cause.

J. L. Mackie, *The Miracle of Theism*

We are all familiar with dreams. Waking visions and hallucinations are relatively infrequent, but still common enough. Many people have occasionally had the impression of hearing words spoken when there have been no such physical sounds in the neighbourhood. Many religious experiences closely resemble, even in their sequences of contrasting phases, the almost universal human experience of being in love. Hysteria, delusions, cycles of mania and depression are known and reasonably well understood psychopathic phenomena in innumerable cases where there is no religious component; but experiences which have such components, which count as religious *par excellence*, share many features with these pathological ones. Experiences of the mystical kind are often induced by certain drugs. Some of the experiences reported by mystics almost irresistibly invite interpretation as expressions of violent sexual passion. From a psychological point of view, as [William] James himself makes clear, the phenomena of conversion, 'mind-cure', sensory or motor automatisms (such as hearing voices), inspiration, mysticism, and so on lend themselves very readily to being understood in terms of the operation of unconscious or subconscious parts of the mind. . . . Theologians themselves have long recognized that it is not easy to decide, about particular visions and messages, whether they come from God or from the devil. As James says . . . 'No appearances whatever are infallible proofs of grace. . . . The good dispositions that a vision, a voice, or other apparently heavenly favor leave behind them are the only marks by which we may be sure that they are not possible deceptions of the tempter'. Admittedly these alternatives, God and the devil, would both fall under the broad heading of 'some supernatural source'. But it will be fairly readily admitted today that the experiences initially ascribed to the devil are fully explicable in terms of purely human but subconscious motives; since it is also admitted that those which the theologian would ascribe to God are not intrinsically distinguishable from those which he would initially ascribe to the devil, it follows that even what he classes as genuinely religious experiences do not intrinsically resist explanation in purely human terms. And this in itself seems fatal to any argument *from* religious experience *to* any supernatural conclusions whatever.[21]

Figure 2.13 The Bible tells of Paul's conversion to Christianity after being struck blind during an encounter with God on the road to Damascus. Was it possible for Paul to *know* that he experienced God instead of, say, a very powerful Greek or Roman deity?

Still, some contend that a religious experience can give us good reasons for believing that God exists, just as ordinary sense experience can give us good reasons for believing that a cat is on the mat. Richard Swinburne takes this line. He maintains that by applying a basic principle of rationality (what he calls the "principle of credulity"), we can

PHILOSOPHY LAB

Read the two sets of statements below. On the left is a list of sensory or perceptual experiences that people have from time to time. There is no question about the reality of these experiences; both common sense and science show that they do in fact occur. On the right is a list of experiences that religious people often report. Not everyone agrees that these experiences have a spiritual or religious cause.

They sometimes feel a "sense of presence," a psychological state that engenders a feeling that someone unseen is nearby, even though no one is really there.	They sometimes feel the presence of God.
They sometimes feel certain about an idea or claim even when they are factually wrong. This sense of certainty often arises from strong emotions.	They sometimes have a strong feeling of certainty about religious matters.
They sometimes feel that something or someone unseen is touching them even when nothing is there—a known psychological or physiological reaction.	They sometimes have seemingly physical sensations that suggest that God is touching them.

Suppose you are religious and you have the experiences listed on the right. How do you distinguish these from the natural occurrences on the left? Saying that you "just know" does not answer the question. Do you have a special faculty unknown to science that helps you distinguish the two? What exactly allows you to separate the natural phenomena from the genuinely spiritual? Does faith enable you to tell the difference between the two kinds of events? Is it possible to misidentify your sensations?

be justified in believing that our experience reveals God's presence. The principle is roughly this: In the absence of reasons to the contrary, if something *seems* to be present, then it probably *is* present. When applied to religious experiences, the principle tells us that "in the absence of special considerations, all religious experiences ought to be taken by their subjects as genuine, and hence as substantial grounds for belief in the existence of their apparent object—God, Mary, or Ultimate Reality, or Poseidon."[22] The special considerations include doubts about the reliability of the perception (for example, when the person involved is known to hallucinate or to be under the influence of alcohol or drugs) and strong evidence that the object of the perception does not exist.

Clearly, to make sense of our ordinary experience and to acquire true beliefs, we must apply an epistemological rule like Swinburne's principle of credulity. But his principle is faulty, some say, inclining us to believe that an object is present when it isn't. Others doubt that any such principle could ever justify us in believing that a religious experience accurately reveals reality. As William L. Rowe says,

William L. Rowe, *Philosophy of Religion*

[T]he Principle of Credulity presupposes that we have some understanding of what reasons there might be for questioning our experiences and some way of telling whether or not these reasons are present. Consider again our example of your experience which you take to be a perception of a large, coiled snake. Like other physical objects that make up the world we perceive by our five senses, snakes are public objects that are observable by others who satisfy certain conditions. That is, we can predict that people with good eyesight will see a snake (if one is there) provided there is good light and they look in the right direction. It is because physical objects are subject to such predictions that we can understand what reasons there might be for questioning an experience which seems to be a perception of a snake and can often tell whether such reasons are present. In the case of divine beings, however, matters are quite different. Presumably, it is entirely up to God whether to reveal his presence to some human being. If God does so, he may or may not disclose himself to others who are in a similar situation. What this means is that it is quite difficult to discover reasons for thinking that someone's ordinary religious experience is delusive. But since the Principle of Credulity supposes that we understand what reasons there might be to question an experience, some doubt exists as to whether the principle can be fairly applied to experiences whose subjects take them be perceptions of the presence of a divine being.[23]

25 Why does Rowe doubt that Swinburne's principle of credulity can be successfully applied to religious experience? Do you agree with him?

By the lights of any adequate principle of rationality, we generally have good reason to doubt the truth of an experience if those who have it disagree about it. That is, we rightfully doubt experiences if they are not reliable. Many point to the apparent incompatibility of religious experiences as proof that they are indeed unreliable. Generally, religious experiences in Western traditions are of a God who is a divine person separate from the world. But experiences in Eastern traditions are often of a divine something that is entirely impersonal or identical with the world. Believers may have an experience of God as one being, God as a trinity of persons, God as many, God as emptiness or nothingness, or God as an ultimate reality. If someone experiences God as a person and another experiences God as impersonal, how can both of these experiences be true? How can both of them provide a window on reality? Religious experiences tend to arise out of and support specific religious traditions—traditions that differ drastically and disagree substantially in their views of spiritual reality. Conflicts among experiences or traditions that spawn experiences seem to cast doubt on the trustworthiness of all alleged encounters with the divine.

PHILOSOPHY NOW

Proof of the Power of Prayer?

Praying for others (intercessory prayer) is a common practice of millions worldwide, and its efficacy is an article of faith for numerous religious groups. For most, it isn't necessary to prove somehow that prayer works; they have faith that it does, and that's that. But a few have sought proof through science, hoping to uncover evidence that praying for sick people can make them well.

A famous 1988 study by cardiologist Randolph Byrd looked at medical complications in heart patients, some of whom were prayed for and some not. Those who were prayed for seemed to do better than the others. In 1999, a larger, similar study of heart patients found that the prayed-for group had fewer medical problems than a group not prayed for. In a 2001 study of 800 heart patients, researchers found no significant effect of intercessory prayer on the patients' health. In 2006, researchers studied 1,800 people who had undergone heart surgery and discovered that prayer had no effect on their recovery.

Figure 2.14 Can science prove that prayer works?

Unfortunately, most prayer studies have been too flawed for their results to be taken seriously. The upshot is that so far, science has not shown that intercessory prayer can improve people's health.

Many critics (both religious and nonreligious) think this kind of research is hopelessly misguided. To them, since intercessory prayer is neither well defined nor explained, studying it seems like chasing shadows. Some ask, Do the effects of prayer depend on the number or the faith of the people praying? If a deity can intervene in human affairs at any time, how can researchers ever trust study results? How can scientists take into account the influence of prayers from people not involved in the studies?

Do you believe that intercessory prayer works? What are your grounds for believing or not believing? Could science ever prove that prayer has real effects?

Swinburne, however, thinks otherwise:

Richard Swinburne, *The Existence of God*

Now, of course, devotees of different religions describe their religious experiences in the religious vocabulary with which they are familiar. But in itself this does not mean that their different descriptions are in conflict—God may be known under different names to different cultures (as both Old and New Testaments acknowledge—see Exodus 6:2–3 and Acts 17:23). Likewise a Greek's claim to have talked to Poseidon is not necessarily in conflict with a Jew's claim to have talked to the angel who watches over the sea; it is so only if to admit the existence of Poseidon is to commit one to a whole polytheistic theology, and there is no need to suppose that generally it is.

Admittedly, sometimes the giving of one description to the object of religious experience does carry commitment to a doctrine regarded as false by devotees of another religion. Claiming to have experienced the heavenly Christ commits one to a belief in an Incarnation that an orthodox Jew would not admit. But in these cases, if the opponent of the doctrine can produce good grounds for regarding the doctrine as false, that is reason for the subject of the experience to withdraw his original claim. Among those grounds may be that others have had conflicting experiences and that their experiences are more numerous and better authenticated; but there may be many grounds of other kinds as well. The subject of the religious experience need not in such a case withdraw his original claim totally; he need only describe it in a less committed way—for example, claim to have been aware of some supernatural being, not necessarily Dionysus (as originally claimed). The fact that sometimes . . . descriptions of the object of a religious experience are in conflict with descriptions of the object of another religious experience means only that we have a source of challenge to a particular detailed claim, not a source of scepticism about all claims of religious experience.[24]

> In many areas of understanding, none so much as in our understanding of God, we bump up against a simplicity so profound that we must assign complexities to it to comprehend it at all. It is mindful of how we paste decals to a sliding glass door to keep from bumping our nose against it.
> —Robert Brault

Suppose, then, that religious experiences did not clash in any important way. Could we then conclude that such experiences show that God exists? Perhaps, but agreement among experiences in itself cannot show that they yield knowledge of the divine, for we know that people can have the same sensory experience that turns out to be illusory (such as seeing a mirage).

Skeptics give another reason for denying that harmony among religious experiences attests to divine presence: the difficulty of recognizing God. They ask, How can you ever be sure that you are perceiving or experiencing God? Can you recognize an all-powerful, all-knowing, and all-good being when you encounter it? How can you distinguish such a being from one that is incredibly powerful but finite, or one that is enormously powerful and knowledgeable but demonic? In any case, how can we use our senses to detect God, since he presumably cannot be sensed? Some say their experiences come with a feeling of certainty that God is present. But how can such feelings give us knowledge? Feelings are not a reliable source of knowledge, for we can feel certain about many things and still be wrong. Some think we can recognize God through a kind of spiritual sixth sense. But unlike our ordinary senses, which have been tested again and again for reliability, no extra sense has been shown to be trustworthy. So how can we rely on it?

Theists have tried in various ways to answer these questions. One frequently heard defense is that the validity of religious experience does not depend on agreement or disagreement among various descriptions of it, for the true religious experience cannot be described at all. The experience is the same for everyone, but it gives rise to different descriptions because it is ineffable. It simply is not possible to put into words an encounter with the divine.

Perhaps an experience of God is indeed ineffable, but if so then nothing at all can be truthfully asserted about it, including the claim that religious experience can give us knowledge of God's existence. If nothing can be truthfully stated about something, then any statement about it would be false. So to affirm that ineffable religious experience gives us knowledge of God is to likewise assert something false.

WRITING TO UNDERSTAND:
CRITIQUING PHILOSOPHICAL VIEWS   Section 2.4

1. Some argue that the truth of religious experiences is corroborated by positive effects in the lives of those who have them—such as leading a morally better life. But consider: People can be inspired to be more virtuous by reading compelling works of fiction, but that doesn't show that the works are true. If an alleged experience of God inspires someone to lead a better life, is that reason enough to conclude that the experience is indeed of God?

2. What is the best explanation of religious experiences? Evaluate these two rival hypotheses: (1) religious experiences are caused by God; (2) religious experiences arise from people's own minds (due to hallucinations, wishful thinking, drugs, etc.). Which explanation is better? Why?

3. What is Swinburne's principle of credulity? What is Rowe's criticism of it? Do you agree with Rowe?

4. Do disagreements among religious experiences cast doubt on the trustworthiness of those experiences? Do you agree with Swinburne's view that such disagreements do not necessarily undermine the truth of the experiences?

5. Is it possible for someone to distinguish between an experience of an omnipotent God and an experience of a being that is extremely powerful but finite?

2.5 BELIEF WITHOUT REASON

The point of the arguments we've considered so far is to provide *epistemic* justification for believing (or not believing) in God—that is, reasons for believing that theism is true (or false). But there are also arguments intended to offer *pragmatic* justification for belief—reasons to think that believing in God offers practical advantages. Many who make pragmatic appeals deny that there can be any rational grounds for theism. They are convinced that the best-made arguments for God's existence are doomed to fail, but that we should believe anyway because belief brings with it certain invaluable benefits. In this way they can maintain that even though the truth of theism is not backed by reasons, belief in God can nevertheless be rational.

The best examples of such arguments come from William James (1842–1910), the distinguished American philosopher and psychologist, and Blaise Pascal (1623–1662), the French philosopher and mathematician who devised what we now call "Pascal's wager."

James: Pragmatic Faith

Contrary to his scientifically minded colleagues, James argues that sometimes we may be justified in making a leap of faith to embrace a belief that is entirely unsupported by evidence. In the absence of any evidence that could help us decide an issue, when we are presented with a true choice between opposing beliefs (a "genuine option"), believing on faith may be the rational thing to do. To James, a genuine option is one that is *live*, *forced*, and *momentous*. A live option presents someone with alternatives that he believes could possibly be actualized. A forced option is one that is unavoidable because the two possibilities are mutually exclusive, and not deciding is the same as choosing one of the alternatives. (An example from James is, "Either accept this truth or go without it.") A momentous option is one that really matters, because the stakes are high, the decision is irreversible, or the choice offers a once-in-a-lifetime opportunity. When we are confronted with a genuine option with no evidence to go by, James says, we have the right to let our "passional nature"—our feelings and desires—decide.

Evidentialism is the view that we are justified in believing something only if it is supported by sufficient evidence.

James thus repudiates **evidentialism**, the view that we are justified in believing something only if it is supported by sufficient evidence. In James's day, the foremost champion of evidentialism was W. K. Clifford, who declared, "It is wrong always, everywhere, and for anyone, to believe anything upon insufficient evidence."[25] In other words, it is *morally wrong* to believe beyond the evidence. Against this position James asserts, "Our passional nature not only lawfully may, but must, decide an option between propositions, whenever it is a genuine option that cannot by its nature be decided on intellectual grounds."[26]

To James, the decision to believe or not to believe in a divine reality (the "religious hypothesis") is a genuine option that the intellect cannot help us decide. It is indeed momentous, for "we are supposed to gain, even now, by our belief, and to lose by our nonbelief, a certain vital good."[27] The skeptic, out of fear of being wrong, would have us refrain from believing and wait until evidence tilts one way or the other. But James insists that the wiser choice—and the more advantageous—is to believe the religious hypothesis, to refuse to forfeit your "sole chance in life of getting upon the winning side." Moreover, to discover whether a divine being exists, we may first have to have faith that it does. Unless we first believe, we may not be able to confirm the truth through our own experience. One who insists on evidence before belief "might cut himself off forever from his only opportunity of making the gods' acquaintance."

This is how James makes his case:

William James, "The Will to Believe"

I

Let us give the name of *hypothesis* to anything that may be proposed to our belief; and just as the electricians speak of live and dead wires, let us speak of any hypothesis as either *live* or *dead*. A live hypothesis is one which appeals as a real possibility to him to whom it is proposed. If I ask you to believe in the Mahdi, the notion makes no electric connection with your nature—it refuses to scintillate with any credibility at all. As an hypothesis it is completely dead. To an Arab, however (even if he be not one of the Mahdi's followers), the hypothesis is among the mind's possibilities: it is alive. This shows that deadness and liveness in an hypothesis are not intrinsic properties, but relations to the individual thinker. They are measured by his willingness to act. The maximum of liveness in an hypothesis means willingness to act irrevocably. Practically, that means belief; but there is some believing tendency wherever there is willingness to act at all.

Next, let us call the decision between two hypotheses an *option*. Options may be of several kinds. They may be—1, *living* or *dead*; 2, *forced* or *avoidable*; 3, *momentous* or *trivial*; and for our purposes we may call an option a *genuine* option when it is of the forced, living and momentous kind.

1. A living option is one in which both hypotheses are live ones. If I say to you: "Be a theosophist or be a Mohammedan," it is probably a dead option, because for you neither hypothesis is likely to be alive. But if I say "Be an agnostic or be a Christian" it is otherwise: trained as you are, each hypothesis makes some appeal, however small, to your belief.

2. Next, if I say to you: "Choose between going out with your umbrella or without it," I do not offer you a genuine option for it is not forced. You can easily avoid it by not going out at all. Similarly, if I say "Either love me or hate me," "Either call my theory true or call it false," your option is avoidable. You may remain indifferent to me, neither loving nor hating, and you may decline to offer any judgment as to my theory. But if I say "Either accept this truth or go without it," I put on you a forced option for there is no standing place outside of the alternative. Every dilemma based on a complete logical disjunction, with no possibility of not choosing, is an option of this forced kind.

3. Finally, if I were Dr. Nansen and proposed to you to join my North Pole expedition, your option would be momentous; for this would probably be your only similar opportunity, and your choice now would either exclude you from the North Pole sort of immortality altogether or put at least the chance of it into your hands. He who refuses to embrace a unique opportunity loses the prize as surely as if he tried and failed. *Per contra*, the option is trivial when the opportunity is not unique, when the stake is insignificant, or when the decision is reversible if it later proves unwise. Such trivial options abound in the scientific life. A chemist finds an hypothesis live enough to spend a year in its verification: he believes in it to that extent. But if his experiments prove inconclusive either way, he is quit for his loss of time, no vital harm being done.

William James,
"The Will to Believe"

"Faith" means not wanting
to know.
—Friedrich Nietzsche

26 Do you agree
with Clifford that it is
immoral to believe any-
thing on insufficient
evidence? Why or why
not?

It will facilitate our discussion if we keep all these distinctions well in mind.

II

. . . It fortifies my soul to know
　　That, though I perish, Truth is so—

sings Clough, whilst Huxley exclaims: "My only consolation lies in the reflection that, however bad our posterity may become, so long as they hold by the plain rule of not pretending to believe what they have no reason to believe because it may be to their advantage so to pretend [the word 'pretend' is surely here redundant], they will not have reached the lowest depths of immorality." And that delicious *enfant terrible* Clifford writes: "Belief is desecrated when given to unproved and unquestioned statements, for the solace and private pleasure of the believer. . . . Whoso would deserve well of his fellows in this matter will guard the purity of his belief with a very fanaticism of jealous care, lest at any time it should rest on an unworthy object, and catch a stain which can never be wiped away. . . . If [a] belief has been accepted on insufficient evidence [even though the belief be true, as Clifford on the same page explains], the pleasure is a sto-len one. . . . It is sinful, because it is stolen in defiance of our duty to mankind. That duty is to guard ourselves from such beliefs as from a pestilence, which may shortly master our own body and then spread to the rest of the town. . . . It is wrong always, everywhere, and for every one to believe anything upon insufficient evidence."

III

All this strikes one as healthy, even when expressed, as by Clifford, with somewhat too much of robustious pathos in the voice. Free-will and simple wishing do seem, in the matter of our credences, to be only fifth wheels to the coach. Yet if anyone should thereupon assume that intellectual insight is what remains after wish and will and sentimental preference have taken wing, or that pure reason is what then settles our opinions, he would fly quite as directly in the teeth of the facts. . . .

Here in this room, we all of us believe in molecules and the conservation of energy, in democracy and necessary progress, in protestant Christianity and the duty of fight-ing for "the doctrine of the immortal Monroe," all for no reasons worthy of the name. We see into these matters with no more inner clearness, and probably with much less, than any disbeliever in them might possess. . . . Our reason is quite satisfied, in nine hundred and ninety-nine cases out of every thousand of us, if it can find a few argu-ments that will do to recite in case our credulity is criticized by some one else. Our faith is faith in someone else's faith, and in the greatest matters this is most the case. Our belief in truth itself, for instance, that there is a truth, and that our minds and it are made for each other,—what is it but a passionate affirmation of desire, in which our social system backs us up? We want to have a truth; we want to believe that our experiments and studies and discussions must put us in a continually better and better position towards it; and on this line we agree to fight out our thinking lives. But if a pyr-rhonistic sceptic asks us *how we know* all this, can our logic find a reply? No! Certainly it cannot. It is just one volition against another,—we are willing to go in for life upon a trust or assumption which he, for his part, does not care to make. . . . As a rule we disbelieve all facts and theories for which we have no use. . . .

Evidently, then, our nonintellectual nature does influence our convictions. There are passional tendencies and volitions which run before and others which come after belief, and it is only the latter that are too late for the fair; and they are not too late when the previous passional work has been already in their own direction. Pascal's argument, instead of being powerless, then seems a regular clincher, and is the last stroke needed to make our faith in masses and holy water complete. The state of things is evidently far from simple; and pure insight and logic, whatever they might do ideally, are not the only things that really do produce our creeds.

IV

Our next duty, having recognized this mixed up state of affairs, is to ask whether it be simply reprehensible and pathological, or whether, on the contrary, we must treat it as a normal element in making up our minds. The thesis I defend is, briefly stated, this: *Our passional nature not only lawfully may, but must, decide an option between propositions, whenever it is a genuine option that cannot by its nature be decided on intellectual grounds; for to say, under such circumstances, "Do not decide, but leave the question open," is itself a passional decision just like deciding yes or no,—and is attended with the same risk of losing the truth. . . .*

VII

. . . There are two ways of looking at our duty in the matter of opinion,—ways entirely different, and yet ways about whose difference the theory of knowledge seems hitherto to have shown very little concern. *We must know the truth*; and *we must avoid error,—* these are our first and great commandments as would-be knowers; but they are not two ways of stating an identical commandment, they are two separable laws. Although it may indeed happen that when we believe the truth A, we escape as an incidental consequence from believing the falsehood B, it hardly ever happens that by merely disbelieving B we necessarily believe A. We may in escaping B fall into believing other falsehoods, C or D, just as bad as B; or we may escape B by not believing anything at all, not even A.

Believe truth! Shun error!—these, we see, are two materially different laws; and by choosing between them we may end by colouring differently our whole intellectual life. We may regard the chase for truth as paramount, and the avoidance of error as secondary; or we may, on the other hand, treat the avoidance of error as more imperative, and let truth take its chance. Clifford, in the instructive passage which I have quoted, exhorts us to the latter course. Believe nothing, he tells us, keep your mind in suspense forever, rather than by closing it on insufficient evidence incur the awful risk of believing lies. You, on the other hand, may think that the risk of being in error is a very small matter when compared with the blessings of real knowledge, and be ready to be duped many times in your investigation rather than postpone indefinitely the chance of guessing true. I myself find it impossible to go with Clifford. We must remember that these feelings of our duty about either truth or error are in any case only expressions of our passional life. Biologically considered, our minds are as ready to grind out falsehood as veracity, and he who says "Better go without belief forever than believe a lie!" merely shows his own preponderant private horror of becoming a dupe. He may be critical of many of his desires and fears, but this fear he slavishly obeys. He cannot imagine anyone questioning its binding force. For my own part, I have also a horror of being duped; but I can believe that worse things than being duped may happen to a man in this world: so Clifford's exhortation has to my ears a thoroughly fantastic sound. It is like a general informing his soldiers that it is better to keep out of battle forever than to risk a single wound. Not so are victories either over enemies or over nature gained. Our errors are surely not such awfully solemn things.

27 Is it ever rational to believe something without evidence? James says yes; Clifford says no. Who is right?

William James,
"The Will to Believe"

In a world where we are so certain to incur them in spite of all our caution, a certain lightness of heart seems healthier than this excessive nervousness on their behalf. At any rate, it seems the fittest thing for the empiricist philosopher.

VIII

. . .The question next arises: Are there not somewhere forced options in our speculative questions, and can we (as men who may be interested at least as much in positively gaining truth as in merely escaping dupery) always wait with impunity till the coercive evidence shall have arrived? It seems *a priori* improbable that the truth should be so nicely adjusted to our needs and powers as that. In the great boardinghouse of nature, the cakes and the butter and the syrup seldom come out so even and leave the plates so clean. Indeed, we should view them with scientific suspicion if they did.

IX

I respect faith, but doubt is what gets you an education.
—Wilson Mizner

Moral questions immediately present themselves as questions whose solution cannot wait for sensible proof. A moral question is a question not of what sensibly exists, but of what is good, or would be good if it did exist. Science can tell us what exists; but to compare the worths, both of what exists and of what does not exist, we must consult not science, but what Pascal calls our heart. Science herself consults her heart when she lays it down that the infinite ascertainment of fact and correction of false belief are the supreme goods for man. Challenge the statement and science can only repeat it oracularly, or else prove it by showing that such ascertainment and correction bring man all sorts of other goods which man's heart in turn declares. The question of having moral beliefs at all or not having them is decided by our will. Are our moral preferences true or false, or are they only odd biological phenomena, making things good or bad for us, but in themselves indifferent? How can your pure intellect decide? If your heart does not want a world of moral reality, your head will assuredly never make you believe in one. Mephistophelian scepticism, indeed, will satisfy the head's play-instincts much better than any rigorous idealism can. Some men (even at the student age) are so naturally cool-hearted that the moralistic hypothesis never has for them any pungent life, and in their supercilious presence the hot young moralist always feels strangely ill at ease. The appearance of knowingness is on their side, of naiveté and gullibility on his. Yet, in the inarticulate heart of him, he clings to it that he is not a dupe, and that there is a realm in which (as Emerson says) all their wit and intellectual superiority is no better than the cunning of a fox. Moral scepticism can no more be refuted or proved by logic than intellectual scepticism can. When we stick to it that there is truth (be it of either kind), we do so with our whole nature, and resolve to stand or fall by the results. The sceptic with his whole nature adopts the doubting attitude; but which of us is the wiser, Omniscience only knows.

28 Are the beliefs involved in James's do-you-like-me example really groundless? Or are they backed by basic principles of human psychology?

Turn now from these wide questions of good to a certain class of questions of fact, questions concerning personal relations, states of mind between one man and another. *Do you like me or not?*—for example. Whether you do or not depends, in countless instances, on whether I meet you halfway, am willing to assume that you must like me, and show you trust and expectation. The previous faith on my part in your liking's existence is in such cases what makes your liking come. But if I stand aloof, and refuse to budge an inch until I have objective evidence, until you shall have done something apt, as the absolutists say, *ad extorquendum assensum meum*, ten to one your liking never comes. How many women's hearts are vanquished by the mere sanguine insistence of some man that they *must* love him! He will not consent to the hypothesis that they cannot. The desire for a certain kind of truth here brings about that special truth's existence; and so it is in innumerable cases of other sorts. Who gains promotions, boons, appointments, but the man in whose life they are seen to play the part of live hypotheses, who discounts them, sacrifices other things for their sake before they have come, and takes risks for them in advance? His faith acts on the powers above him as a claim, and creates its own verification. . . .

There are, then, cases where a fact cannot come at all unless a preliminary faith exists in it coming. *And where faith in a fact can help create the fact*, that would be an insane logic which should say that faith running ahead of scientific evidence is the "lowest kind of immorality" into which a thinking being can fall. Yet such is the logic by which our scientific absolutists pretend to regulate our lives!

X

In truths dependent on our personal action, then, faith based on desire is certainly a lawful and possibly an indispensable thing.

But now, it will be said, these are all childish human cases, and have nothing to do with great cosmical matters, like the question of religious faith. Let us then pass on to that. Religions differ so much in their accidents that in discussing the religious question we must make it very generic and broad. What then do we now mean by the religious hypothesis? Science says things are; morality says some things are better than other things; and religion says essentially two things.

First, she says that the best things are the more eternal things, the overlapping things, the things in the universe that throw the last stone, so to speak, and say the final word. "Perfection is eternal"—this phrase of Charles Secrétan seems a good way of putting this first affirmation of religion, an affirmation which obviously cannot yet be verified scientifically at all.

The second affirmation of religion is that we are better off even now if we believe her first affirmation to be true.

Now let us consider what the logical elements of this situation are *in case the religious hypothesis in both its branches be really true.* (Of course, we must admit that possibility at the outset. If we are to discuss the question at all, it must involve a living option. If for any of you religion be a hypothesis that cannot, by any living possibility be true, then you need go no farther. I speak to the 'saving remnant' alone.) So proceeding, we see, first, that religion offers itself as *a momentous* option. We are supposed to gain, even now, by our belief, and to lose by our nonbelief, a certain vital good. Secondly, religion is a *forced* option so far as that good goes. We cannot escape the issue by remaining sceptical and waiting for more light, because, although we do avoid error in that way *if religion be untrue*, we lose the good, *if it be true*, just as certainly as if we positively chose to disbelieve. It is as if a man should hesitate indefinitely to ask a certain woman to marry him because he was not perfectly sure that she would prove an angel after he brought her home. Would he not cut himself off from that particular angel-possibility as decisively as if he went and married someone else? Scepticism, then, is

Figure 2.15 Is it your faith that can change others' attitudes, or is it your behavior?

29 James assumes that we are better off in this life if we believe the religious hypothesis than if we don't. Is this assumption correct? What evidence can you bring to bear on this question?

William James,
"The Will to Believe"

not avoidance of option; it is option of a certain particular kind of risk. *Better risk loss of truth than chance of error,*—that is your faith-vetoer's exact position. He is actively playing his stake as much as the believer is; he is backing the field against the religious hypothesis, just as the believer is backing the religious hypothesis against the field. To preach scepticism to us as a duty until 'sufficient evidence' for religion be found, is tantamount therefore to telling us, when in presence of the religious hypothesis, that to yield to our fear of its being error is wiser and better than to yield to our hope that it may be true. It is not intellect against all passions, then; it is only intellect with one passion laying down its law. And by what, forsooth, is the supreme wisdom of this passion warranted? Dupery for dupery, what proof is there that dupery through hope is so much worse than dupery through fear? I, for one, can see no proof; and I simply refuse obedience to the scientist's command to imitate his kind of option, in a case where my own stake is important enough to give me the right to choose my own form of risk. If religion be true and the evidence for it be still insufficient, I do not wish, by putting your extinguisher upon my nature (which feels to me as if it had after all some business in this matter), to forfeit my sole chance in life of getting upon the winning side,—that chance depending, of course, on my willingness to run the risk of acting as if my passional need of taking the world religiously might be prophetic and right.

All this is on the supposition that it really may be prophetic and right, and that, even to us who are discussing the matter, religion is a live hypothesis which may be true. Now to most of us religion comes in a still farther way that makes a veto on our active faith even more illogical. The more perfect and more eternal aspect of the universe is represented in our religions as having personal form. The universe is no longer a mere *It* to us, but a *Thou*, if we are religious; and any relation that may be possible from person to person might be possible here. For instance, although in one sense we are passive portions of the universe, in another we show a curious autonomy, as if we were small active centers on our own account. We feel, too, as if the appeal of religion to us were made to our own active good-will as if evidence might be forever withheld from us unless we met the hypothesis halfway. To take a trivial illustration: just as a man who in a company of gentlemen made no advances, asked a warrant for every concession, and believed no one's word without proof, would cut himself off by such churlishness from all the social rewards that a more trusting spirit would earn,—so here, one who should shut himself up in snarling logicality and try to make the gods extort his recognition willy-nilly, or not get it at all, might cut himself off forever from his only opportunity of making the gods' acquaintance. This feeling, forced on us we know not whence, that by obstinately believing that there are gods (although not to do so would be so easy both for our logic and our life) we are doing the universe the deepest service we can, seems part of the living essence of the religious hypothesis. If the hypothesis *were* true in all its parts, including this one, then pure intellectualism, with its veto on our making willing advances, would be an absurdity; and some participation of our sympathetic nature would be logically required. I therefore, for one, cannot see my way to accepting the agnostic rules for truth-seeking, or willfully agree to keep my willing nature out of the game. I cannot do so for this plain reason, *that a rule of thinking which would absolutely prevent me from acknowledging certain kinds of truth if those kinds of truth were really there, would be an irrational rule.* That for me is the long and short of the formal logic of the situation, no matter what the kinds of truth might materially be.[28]

30 Is it reasonable to expect that by first having faith in God you can *confirm* his existence in your experience? Would having faith before you get confirmation distort this method of inquiry and bias the results?

Despite the eloquence of James's argument, it has many detractors. For starters, they deny his assumption that the claims of religion cannot be decided by argument and evidence. As we have seen, many theists and atheists think that reason can indeed decide the issue of God's existence, and the traditional arguments that we've examined are attempts to do just that.

Others doubt James's assertion that it is better to believe the religious hypothesis than not to believe it because by believing we acquire "even now . . . a certain vital good." He doesn't say what this vital good is, but if he means something like a better life, happiness, or spiritual satisfaction in this life, he seems to be on shaky ground. It is not obvious that religious believers of any sort lead better, happier, or more satisfying lives than nonbelievers.

Some have also taken issue with James's notion of verifying through our experiences the religious hypothesis by first believing it. Faith is supposed to be the prerequisite for experiences that will enable us to confirm some divine reality. But critics say that having faith first is not likely to corroborate anything. Michael Martin explains the point this way:

> Faith indeed tells what the senses do not tell, but not the contrary of what they see. It is above them and not contrary to them.
> —Blaise Pascal

Michael Martin, *Atheism: A Philosophical Justification*

James talks as if believing in God and seeing whether the hypothesis that God exists is confirmed in one's experience is like an experiment. But his procedure lacks an essential element of standard experimental procedure: he does not seem to allow for the *disconfirmation* of the hypothesis by the results of the experiment. Suppose one believes in some god and yet no evidence of his existence is revealed in one's experience. James does not entertain the possibility that this failure would count against the hypothesis that this god exists.[29]

Pascal: Betting on God

Pascal thinks that reason is impotent in helping us discern whether God exists. "If there is a God," he declares, "he is infinitely beyond our comprehension. . . . We are therefore incapable of knowing either what he is, or if he is."[30] So Pascal insists that we can have only a pragmatic justification for believing in God. We should believe because believing is advantageous; it is our best bet. "Pascal's wager" then says that if we believe in God and he really does exist, we win infinite happiness; if we believe and he doesn't exist, we lose nothing. On the other hand, if we don't believe and he exists, we lose the infinite happiness that believing leads to; if we don't believe and he doesn't exist, we lose nothing. Thus, by believing in God, we have everything to gain and nothing to lose—a bet that only an irrational person would turn down.

Figure 2.16 Blaise Pascal (1623–1662).

WHAT DO YOU BELIEVE?

Do You Live by Faith?

In urging others to accept the existence of God on faith rather than evidence, many contend that all of us—theists, atheists, and agnostics—live by faith every day. Here is a typical statement of this view:

> In this physical world that we live in, we all live by faith, whether we know it or not. For instance, we trust that our cars will start every morning to take us to work. We trust that we will get paid on payday. Am I right? Well, you know what, on the spiritual side of things, the Christian SHOULD live by faith, too! . . . [As the scripture says] "Behold, his soul [which] is lifted up is not upright in him: but the just shall live by his faith."

Is it accurate to say that we have *faith* that these everyday events will occur? Or are we merely expecting them to occur based on good evidence—our many previous experiences with the events?

But what if you are an agnostic or atheist who wants to go along with this bet? Can you believe in God simply by deciding to? Not likely. Pascal's answer to this problem is that those who want to believe can develop faith by behaving *as if* they believe, by taking holy water, having masses said, and undertaking other religious practices.

Here is Pascal laying out the wagering options:

Blaise Pascal, *Pensees and Other Writings*

31 Is it morally permissible to believe in God just because it is to your advantage to believe? Why or why not?

Let us therefore examine this point, and say: God is, or is not. But towards which side will we lean? Reason cannot decide anything. There is an infinite chaos separating us. At the far end of this infinite distance a game is being played and the coin will come down heads or tails. How will you wager? Reason cannot make you choose one way or the other, reason cannot make you defend either of the two choices.

So do not accuse those who have made a choice of being wrong, for you know nothing about it! "No, but I will blame them not for having made this choice, but for having made any choice. For, though the one who chooses heads and the other one are equally wrong, they are both wrong. The right thing is not to wager at all."

Yes, but you have to wager. It is not up to you, you are already committed. Which then will you choose? Let us see. Since you have to choose, let us see which interests you the least. You have two things to lose: the truth and the good, and two things to stake: your reason and will, your knowledge and beatitude; and your nature has two things to avoid: error and wretchedness. Your reason is not hurt more by choosing one rather than the other, since you do have to make the choice. That is one point disposed of. But your beatitude? Let us weigh up the gain and the loss by calling heads that God exists. Let us assess the two cases: if you win, you win everything; if you lose, you lose nothing. Wager that he exists then, without hesitating! "This is wonderful. Yes, I must wager. But perhaps I am betting too much." Let us see. Since there is an equal chance of gain and loss, if you won only two lives instead of one, you could still put on a bet. But if there were three lives to win, you would have to play (since you must necessarily play), and you would be unwise, once forced to play, not to chance your life to win three in a game where there is an equal chance of losing and winning. But there is an eternity of life and happiness. And that being so, even though there were an infinite number of chances of which only one were in your favour, you would still be right to wager one in order to win two, and you would be acting wrongly, since you are obliged to play, by refusing to stake one life against three in a game where out of an infinite number of chances there is one in your favour, if there were an infinitely happy infinity of life to be won. But here there is an infinitely happy infinity of life to be won, one chance of winning against a finite number of chances of losing, and what you are staking is finite. That removes all choice: wherever there is infinity and where there is no infinity of chances of losing against one of winning, there is no scope for wavering, you have to chance everything. And thus, as you are forced to gamble, you have to have discarded reason if you cling onto your life, rather than risk it for the infinite prize which is just as likely to happen as the loss of nothingness.[31]

Would you take this bet? Many philosophers would not. They fault Pascal for assuming only two alternatives (that his God exists and will bestow eternal happiness on believers, or that his God does not exist) and ignoring countless other possibilities. By his own lights, Pascal should take these other possibilities seriously if we are as ignorant of God's nature as he says. Consider: (1) that God ignores or punishes those who believe for self-serving reasons; (2) that God favors honest doubters who use their God-given power of reasoning to believe only according to the evidence; (3) that nothing people do or believe matters because they are predestined by God to go to heaven or hell; (4) that God hates people who gamble; (5) that people are rewarded for believing not in Pascal's Christian God, but in Yahweh, Apollo, Krishna, Ammon, Odin, or Shiva; or (6) that God is malicious, withholding eternal happiness from both nonbelievers and believers alike. Critics say that if we take such prospects into account, Pascal's wager loses its force and cultivating faith for pragmatic reasons seems unreasonable.

32 Is it plausible that God would look kindly on atheists and agnostics because they refuse to believe without evidence? After all, aren't they simply using God's gift of reason to arrive at their decision?

The reason Pascal's wager does not work is the same reason why you should never plan your retirement on winning the lotto.
—Massimo Pigliucci

> **WRITING TO UNDERSTAND:**
> **CRITIQUING PHILOSOPHICAL VIEWS** Section 2.5
>
> 1. Do you agree with James that faith in the religious hypothesis can bring about a "vital good" in one's life now? What evidence can you cite to back up your answer? For example, is there evidence showing that those who accept the religious hypothesis are happier than those who don't?
> 2. Suppose it is true that sometimes, as James says, "faith in a fact can help create the fact." Is the existence of God one of the facts that we can create by believing it?
> 3. Is evidentialism true? Are we sometimes justified in believing something even if it is unsupported by evidence? If so, in what situations? If not, why not?
> 4. Suppose God is a vicious deity who inflicts eternal punishment on anyone who believes in him and grants eternal bliss to anyone who refuses to believe in him. How would Pascal's wager apply to belief regarding such a deity?
> 5. Evaluate this quotation from Alan Dershowitz: "I have always considered 'Pascal's Wager' as a questionable bet to place, since any God worth believing in would prefer an honest agnostic to a calculating hypocrite."

2.6 EASTERN RELIGIONS

Eastern religious traditions—including Buddhism, Hinduism, Confucianism, Taoism, Jainism, and many others—diverge from Western religions in ways that both shock and intrigue those who trace their faith back to Moses, Muhammad, or Christ. But both domains of religious belief are rich in philosophical thought. While the West has used reason to defend or critique its religious doctrines, the East has built philosophical systems that try to plumb the depths of physical and spiritual reality. In the expanse of Eastern religious thought, Western philosophers see both drastically different conceptions of the world and many of their own ideas in new form staring back at them.

Buddhism

In its own fashion, Buddhism typifies the ways that most Eastern traditions differ from Western ones. Buddhism posits no creator God, no all-powerful, all-knowing deity who rules the universe, takes an interest in humans, or answers prayers. It teaches that the Buddha himself was neither God nor the child of a god. He was instead the ultimate teacher and an example for all Buddhists to follow. In accordance with the Buddha's wishes, Buddhism has no central religious authority. There is no Buddhist pope; there are only the Buddha's teachings. An individual achieves salvation not through faith in God, but primarily through his or her own efforts, by self-discipline and self-transformation. Buddhists must work out their own salvation.

The term *Buddhism* disguises the religion's complexities. Although Buddhists everywhere may hold in common some teachings of the Buddha, these core beliefs are few, allowing a great many meandering trails within a broad doctrinal highway. Buddhism therefore has no single set of authorized practices or a common rulebook or a universal statement of the articles of faith. Instead there are many schools of thought and practice in Buddhism (some would say *Buddhisms*), Zen Buddhism and Tibetan Buddhism being only the most familiar.

During a time of wrenching social change and clashing religious viewpoints, Buddhism arose in northern India (now southern Nepal) in the sixth century BCE. The spiritual landscape was dotted by religious and philosophical worldviews of all sorts, with each one competing for recognition and the allegiance of devotees.

Figure 2.17 Siddhartha Gautama, the Buddha (c. 563–483 BCE).

The practices advocated by various groups included meditation, celibacy, animal sacrifices, vegetarianism, nonviolence, worship of numerous gods, and asceticism (the denial of physical comfort or pleasures for religious ends). Some believed in rebirth and **karma** (the universal principle that our actions result in deserved pleasure or pain in this life or the next); some did not. Some accepted the notion of spiritual progress through one's own efforts; others denied it. Some thought that the actions of humans are never done freely but are fated to occur; some insisted that humans have free will. Into this chaos comes the man destined to become the Buddha (a title meaning "The Enlightened One"), born a prince in the tiny kingdom of Sakya in northern India and given the name Siddhartha Gautama (c. 563–483 BCE). After many years of reflection and searching for ultimate wisdom, he attains enlightenment—what he believes is a perfect understanding of the true nature of the universe, of life and death, and of suffering and liberation.

The teachings of the Buddha astonished many of his day who were used to the doctrines and practices of Indian religions. In contrast to the orthodoxies of the time, the Buddha rejected the caste system, extreme asceticism, the practice of animal sacrifice, the authority of the Vedas (Hindu scriptures), submission to the Brahmins (members of the Hindu priestly caste), and the existence of the soul (a permanent, unchanging identity). Contradicting the Hindu social conventions, he taught that women should not be barred from the spiritual life he proposed—they

Karma is the universal principle that our actions result in deserved pleasure or pain in this life or the next.

too could attain enlightenment. Contrary to doctrines of the major Western religious traditions, he was nontheistic in the sense that he had no use for the idea of a personal creator God. He believed that gods, goddesses, and demons exist, but that they are—like all other living things—finite, vulnerable, and mortal. They are trapped in the cycle of death and rebirth just as humans are. He therefore renounced religious devotion to any deity.

On some deep questions about the nature of reality—questions that most religions try to address—the Buddha was silent. He refused to conjecture about what happens after death, whether the universe is eternal, whether it is infinite, whether body and soul are the same thing, and what constitutes the divine. He taught that such speculations are pointless, since they overlook what is truly important in existence: the fact of suffering and the path of liberation from it. A person who spends his time trying to answer these imponderable questions, he said, is like a man struck by an arrow who will not pull it out until he has determined all the mundane facts about the arrow, bow, and archer—and dies needlessly while gathering the information.

The Buddha meant his teachings to be useful—a realistic, accurate appraisal of our burdensome existence and how to rise above it. To an unusual extent, his approach was also rational and empirical. He tried to provide a reasonable explanation for the problem of existence and offer a plausible solution. He thought that people should not accept his views on faith but test them out through their own experience in everyday life.

The Buddha's system of teachings about the true nature of reality and how to live correctly to transcend it is known as the **dharma**, the heart of which is the Four Noble Truths:

The **dharma** is the Buddha's system of teachings about the true nature of reality and how to live correctly to transcend it.

1. Life is suffering.
2. Suffering is caused by desires ("craving" or "thirst").
3. To banish suffering, banish desires.
4. Banish desires and end suffering by following the Noble Eightfold Path.

The First Noble Truth is that living brings suffering, or *dukkha*. In the traditional Buddhist way of putting it, "birth is painful, old age is painful, sickness is painful, death is painful, sorrow, lamentation, dejection, and despair are painful. Contact with unpleasant things is painful, not getting what one wishes is painful."[32] *Dukkha* comes in small and large doses—from mild stress and frustration to the agonies of devastating disease and the heartbreak of overwhelming loss and grief. But in any dose, suffering is inherent to living: an inescapable cost of existence. Another aspect of *dukkha* is impermanence (*anicca*)—the fact that things do not last, that whatever pleasures we enjoy soon fade, that whatever we possess we eventually lose, that whatever we do will be undone by time. The very transitory nature of life brings suffering, dissatisfaction, and pain.

Dukkha also arises because of another fact of life: *anatta*, the impermanence of the self, or not-self, or no-soul. A person—the "I" that we each refer to—is merely an ever-changing, fleeting assemblage of mental states or processes. (The Western philosopher David Hume argued for the same view of the self.) And if there is no permanent self, there is no way for any "I" to grope for happiness, satisfaction, pleasure, contentment, or anything else. The thought of not-self frightens people, but to most Buddhists, *anatta* is a very soothing doctrine. As one Buddhist monk says,

Ajahn Sumedho, *Buddha-Nature*

When you open the mind to the truth, then you realize there is nothing to fear. What arises passes away, what is born dies, and is not self—so that our sense of being caught in an identity with this human body fades out. We don't see ourselves as some isolated, alienated entity lost in a mysterious and frightening universe. We don't feel overwhelmed by it, trying to find a little piece of it that we can grasp and feel safe with, because we feel at peace with it. Then we have merged with the Truth.[33]

This focus on *dukkha* may seem like a dreary perspective on life, but it sets the stage for the Buddha's more optimistic views on the ultimate conquest of suffering. His message is not that we are doomed to unremitting suffering, but that there is a way to escape our torment, to attain true and lasting happiness.

The Second Noble Truth is that the cause of *dukkha* is selfish desire ("craving" or "thirst")—desire for things that we can never obtain, no matter how hard we try. We desire possessions, pleasures, power, money, life, and more. We want things to be different from what they are or to remain the way they are forever. But we can never have any of these for long because everything is ephemeral, constantly changing. We have no distinct, permanent identity; the "self" is no more than a locus of shifting, flowing energy. Such an insubstantial, transient thing can never acquire anything permanent, even if permanent objects exist. We desire this or that, but our desires are continually frustrated. The result is discontent, unhappiness, and pain—*dukkha*.

The Third Noble Truth is that suffering can be extinguished if desire is extinguished. *Dukkha* will end if desire ends. To quench selfish desires and therefore to end *dukkha* is to attain **nirvana**, the ultimate aim of all Buddhist practice and the final liberation to which all the Buddha's teachings point. It is the extinguishing of the flames of attachment, delusion, and hatred; it is also the blossoming of contentment and inner peace, the "quietude of the heart." The Buddhist scholar and monk Walpola Rahula describes it like this:

Do not dwell in the past, do not dream of the future, concentrate the mind on the present moment. —The Buddha

33 Contrast the Buddhist and Christian views of the cause of human suffering. Which seems to you more plausible?

Nirvana, or Enlightenment, is the ultimate aim of all Buddhist practice and the final liberation to which all the Buddha's teachings point.

Walpola Rahula, *What the Buddha Taught*

He who has realized the Truth, Nirvana, is the happiest being in the world. He is free from all 'complexes' and obsessions, the worries and troubles that torment others. His mental health is perfect. He does not repent the past, nor does he brood over the future. He lives fully in the present. Therefore he appreciates and enjoys things in the purest sense without self-projections. He is joyful, exultant, enjoying the pure life, his

Walpola Rahula,
*What the Buddha
Taught*

faculties pleased, free from anxiety, serene and peaceful. As he is free from selfish desire, hatred, ignorance, conceit, pride, and all such 'defilements', he is pure and gentle, full of universal love, compassion, kindness, sympathy, understanding and tolerance. His service to others is of the purest, for he has no thought of self. He gains nothing, accumulates nothing, not even anything spiritual, because he is free from the illusion of Self, and the 'thirst' for becoming.[34]

Nirvana is manifested both in life and at death. In life, it is—as Rahula suggests—a psychological and moral transformation and, ultimately, an enlightened way of living. At death, for an enlightened one, the continuing cycle, or wheel, of death and rebirth ends. *Dukkha*, the ever-recurring pain of existence, stops. And the controlling force behind the turning wheel—karma—ceases. So nirvana's quenching of "defilements" not only quenches *dukkha* in life, but it also terminates the repeating pattern of death–rebirth. Beyond this profound release, what nirvana entails at one's death is uncertain. The Buddha insisted that nirvana is beyond description and impossible to imagine, for it is neither annihilation nor survival of a soul. He said that people should devote themselves to attaining it rather than trying to plumb its depths. Buddhist sources, however, refer to nirvana with words such as *freedom*, *absolute truth*, *peace*, and *bliss*.

In Buddhism, one's cycle of repeated deaths and rebirths—called *samsara*, or "wandering"—is a painful process that can go on for millennia unless there is release from it through nirvana. The thing that wanders from one life to the next (what we refer to as "I") is not an eternally existing, permanent soul, self, or *atman*, but an ever-changing mix of personality fragments that recombine in each new life. The Buddha's classic illustration of this point is a flame (the "I") that is transferred from one candle to another. Only one flame is passed among multiple candles, so there is some continuity from one candle to the next. But the flame itself is also different from moment to moment.

Karma is the universal principle that governs the characteristics and quality of each rebirth, or future life. In the sense used in Buddhism, karma is not a system of justice decreed by a God; nor is it a cosmic force driven toward some purpose or goal. It is essentially a law of nature, a universal fact about the effects of a being's past actions. Karma dictates that people's deeds—their acts of will or intentions—form their present character *and* determine the general nature of their future lives. Good deeds (good karma) tend to lead to more pleasant rebirths; bad deeds (bad karma) are likely to yield less pleasant, even horrific, rebirths. Depending on karma, then, a rebirth may occur at any one of several different levels— from life in various hells to existence as an animal, ghost, human, or god. Karma can also affect the *quality* of life at each level.

In the Buddha's view of karma, through their own moral choices and acts people are free to try to change their karma and its associated results, and no one is trapped in a given level of existence

Figure 2.18 Buddhist Temple of the Dawn in Bangkok, Thailand.

forever. There is always the hope of rising to a higher point through spiritual effort or of halting the cycle of rebirths altogether through nirvana.

The notions of rebirth and karma lead naturally to the Buddhist attitude of compassion, tolerance, and kindness for all living things. After all, every being must follow the karmic current, being reborn as many different creatures from the lowest to the highest. Each human being has an implied empathetic connection with all other beings (humans, animals, and others) because he or she is likely to have *been* such beings at one time or another and to have endured the same kind of pain and grief they have.

The Fourth Noble Truth says that the way to end *dukkha* and to attain nirvana is to follow the Noble Eightfold Path. The Path consists of eight factors, or modes of practice, whose purpose is the development, or perfection, of the three fundamental aspects of Buddhist life: *wisdom*, *moral conduct*, and *mental discipline* or focus. The eight factors have been described as "steps," as if they should be done in order, but they are actually intended to be implemented in concert. Each one complements and enhances the others, and a complete life cultivates them all. Together they constitute a way of purposeful living that the Buddha is said to have discovered through his own experience—the "Middle Way" or "Middle Path" between the extremes of brutal asceticism and sensual self-indulgence. (Aristotle also taught that the good life is a virtuous one balanced between having too much and not having enough.) Here are the eight factors sorted into their three basic categories:

For the perfection of wisdom:
1. *Right understanding* is a deep understanding of the true nature of reality as revealed in the Four Noble Truths. This kind of wisdom refers not just to an intellectual grasp of the facts, but, more importantly, to profound insight that penetrates to how things really are in themselves, insight gleaned experientially through a trained mind free of spiritual impediments.
2. *Right thought* refers to the proper motivations underlying our thoughts and actions. Right motivations are selflessness, compassion, nonviolence, gentleness, and love. They are directed not toward a few, but toward all living things. Selfishness, hatred, violence, and malice undermine spiritual progress and impede true wisdom.

For the perfection of moral conduct:
3. *Right speech* means refraining from lying, slander, gossip, unkind or rude words, malicious or abusive talk, and idle or misleading assertions. Right speech, then, is truthful, kind, and constructive, fostering harmony, trust, and honesty.
4. *Right action* involves following the Buddha's Five Precepts: refraining from (1) harming living beings (a principle known as *ahimsa*, "non-harm" or "nonviolence"), (2) taking what is not given (stealing), (3) engaging in misconduct regarding sexual or sensual pleasures, (4) lying or speaking falsely, and (5) impairing the mind with intoxicating substances. To the Buddhist, these precepts are not moral laws or commandments that demand strict adherence as

I've developed a new philosophy. . . . I only dread one day at a time.
—Charles M. Schulz

34 The Buddha assumes the doctrine of reincarnation (the transmigration of the soul at death into a new body). Is this view plausible? Why or why not?

Life must be understood backward. But it must be lived forward.
—Søren Kierkegaard

if they were laid down by divine authority. They are moral ideals to strive for, affirmations to oneself for living a more compassionate, mindful life.

5. *Right livelihood* means avoiding jobs or professions that involve harming other living beings. These include occupations that traffic in weapons of war, intoxicants, and poisons; that entail the buying and selling of human beings; that cause harm or death to animals; and that involve greed, dishonesty, or deception.

For the perfection of mental discipline:

6. *Right effort* is cultivating wholesome states of mind and eliminating or minimizing unwholesome ones. It means fostering compassion, selflessness, empathy, and understanding and banishing selfish desire, hatred, attachment, and self-delusion.

7. *Right mindfulness* refers to the development through meditation of an extraordinary awareness of the functioning of one's own body and mind. It yields clear understanding of, and keen sensitivity to, one's bodily processes, emotional states, the attitudes and tendencies of the mind, and mental concepts that may help or hinder spiritual progress.

8. *Right concentration* is the development through meditation of a sublime inner peace and profound mental tranquility. Such inner calm is thought to yield insight.

Hinduism

Hinduism can claim to be the world's oldest living religion (dating back 3,000 years) and the third largest (with about 1 billion adherents). Many observers are amazed that it boasts of no common creed, founder, text, or deity. It comprises not one mode of devotion but a confounding diversity of them. Offerings to deity images, the chanting of mantras, temple worship, sensual rites, mystical experiences, ascetic privations, animal sacrifices—such practices may be embraced by some Hindus and ignored by others, but the broad tent of Hinduism accommodates them all. The sacred texts range from hymns to instructions for conducting rituals to philosophical treatises, and these are revered or disregarded to varying degrees by thousands of discrete religious groups. A Hindu may bow to many gods (polytheism), one supreme God (monotheism), one god among a whole pantheon (henotheism), or no gods whatsoever (atheism). And Hinduism's gods are said to number over a million.

The Western traditions of Christianity, Judaism, and Islam are generally faithful to a core of more or less coherent doctrines. Hinduism is different. It's a large, unwieldy family of beliefs and practices that seem reasonable and practical to Hindus but perplexing and contradictory to outsiders. Yet in the twenty-first century this family thrives both in its mother country (India) and on foreign soil, has devotees in both the East and the West, and influences the worldviews of persons high and low. And among this cacophony of views, systems of philosophical reflection and even scriptures containing philosophical speculation have their say.

Figure 2.19 Stone carving of one of India's more popular deities—Ganesha, the elephant-headed god.

Hinduism began in northwest India, emerging from a blend of native religions and the religious traditions of an Indo-European people who migrated there from central Asia. The indigenous populace established an advanced civilization that flourished in the Indus River region and beyond as early as 2500 BC. This Indus Valley civilization, as it is called, rivaled in many ways the Roman Empire, which was to come later. It devised a writing system, erected planned cities, and built impressive structures small and large—two-story houses, civic centers, porticos, baths, bathrooms, stairways, drainage systems, and worship halls.

Around 1500 BCE, the migrating Indo-Europeans, called Aryans, moved into northwest India, carrying their distinctive culture with them. Most importantly, they brought their speech, from which was derived the ancient language of Sanskrit, the medium of Hindu scripture. They were polytheistic, worshiping gods that were thought to embody powerful elements of nature such as the sun, moon, and fire. And they sacrificed animals (including horses) and proffered animal byproducts (such as butter and milk) as offerings to these gods.

Aryan culture was partitioned into four social classes called *varnas*. From these, the hereditary *caste system* was developed in Hindu society and still holds sway in modern India, although it has been refined into thousands of subdivisions based on social and occupational criteria. Traditionally the dominant class consisted of *brahmins*, the priests and teachers who alone could study and teach scripture. Brahmins still play a priestly role and are prevalent among India's professionals and civil servants.

For Hinduism, the most important result of the melding of the Aryan and Indus River cultures was a set of sacred compositions known as the **Vedas** ("knowledge"), regarded by almost all Hindus as eternal scripture and the essential reference point for all forms of Hinduism. They were produced by the Aryans between 1500 and 600 BCE (what has been called the Vedic era), which makes these compositions India's oldest existing literature. For thousands of years the *Vedas* were transmitted orally from brahmin to brahmin until they were finally put into writing. They are said to be *sruti* ("that which was heard")—revealed directly to Hindu seers (*rishis*) and presumed to be of neither human nor divine authorship. Later scriptures are thought to be *smriti* ("what is remembered")—of human authorship. These consist of commentaries and elaborations on the *sruti*. Hindus revere the *Vedas*, even though the majority of adherents are ignorant of their content, and their meanings are studied mostly by the educated. In fact, most Hindu devotional practices are derived not from the *Vedas*, but from the sacred texts that came later.

The *Vedas* consist of four collections, or books, of writings, each made up of four sections. The four books are the *Rig-Veda*, the *Yajur-Veda*, the *Sama-Veda*, and the *Atharva-Veda*. The sections are (1) *samhitas*: hymns, or chants, of praise or invocation to the gods (including many Aryan deities), mostly to be uttered publicly during sacrifices; (2) *brahmanas*: treatises on, and how-to instructions for, rituals; (3) *Aranyakas*: "forest treatises" for those who seek a reclusive religious life; and (4) the **Upanishads**: philosophical and religious speculations.

The oldest book is the *Rig-Veda*, which contains a section of over 1,000 ancient hymns, each one invoking a particular god or goddess—for example, Indra (the

The great secret of true success, of true happiness, is this: the man or woman who asks for no return, the perfectly unselfish person, is the most successful.
—Swami Vivekananda

In the morning I bathe my intellect in the stupendous and cosmogonal philosophy of the *Bhagavad-Gita*, in comparison with which our modern world and its literature seems puny and trivial.
—Henry David Thoreau

35 What is the caste system? Why is its existence in modern India controversial?

The **Vedas** are early Hindu scriptures, developed between 1500 and 600 BC.

36 What is the difference between *sruti* and *smriti*? Does the difference matter much to Hindus?

The **Upanishads** are Vedic literature concerning the self, Brahman, samsara, and liberation.

ruler of heaven), Agni (the god of fire), and Varuna (the god of moral order in the universe). Most of the hymns in the other books are taken from the *Rig-Veda*.

There are 123 *Upanishads*, but only thirteen or fourteen (called the principal *Upanishads*) are revered by all Hindus. The *Upanishads* were the latest additions to the *Vedas*, composed primarily from about 900 to 400 BCE during a time of intellectual and religious unease. The ancient certainties—the authority of the brahmins, the status of the *Vedas*, the caste system, the sacrificial rites, and the nature of the deities—were being called into question. The *Upanishads* put these issues in a different light and worked out some philosophical doctrines that became fundamental to Hinduism right up to the twenty-first century.

In the early *Vedas*, there is an emphasis on improving one's lot in life through religious practice and faith in the gods. But in the *Upanishads,* the central aim is release from this world. Specifically, the goal is liberation from **samsara**, one's repeating cycle of deaths and rebirths. The essential Hindu belief is that at death, one's soul or self (**atman**) departs from the lifeless body and is reborn into a new body, residing for a time until death, then being reborn in yet another physical form—a dreary sequence that may be repeated for thousands of lifetimes. (Westerners call this the doctrine of *reincarnation*.) And with each new incarnation comes the pain of living and reliving all the miseries of mortal existence.

The force that regulates *samsara* is karma, the universal principle that governs the characteristics and quality of each rebirth, or future life. Karma is like a law of nature; it is simply the way the world works. It dictates that people's actions and intentions form their present character and determine the general nature of their future lives. Good deeds (good karma) lead to more pleasant rebirths; bad deeds (bad karma) beget less pleasant, even appalling, rebirths. Depending on karma, the *atman* may be reborn into a human, an animal, an insect, or some other lowly creature. This repeating pattern of rebirth–death–rebirth continues because humans are ignorant of the true nature of reality, of what is real and what is merely appearance. They are enslaved by illusion (*maya*) and act accordingly, with predictable results.

According to the Upanishads, this ignorance and its painful consequences can only be ended, and liberation (*moksa*) from *samsara* and karma can only be won, through the freeing power of an ultimate, transcendent wisdom. This wisdom comes when an *atman* realizes that the soul is not separate from the world or from other souls but is one with the impersonal, all-pervading Spirit known as **Brahman**. Brahman is the universe, yet Brahman transcends all space and time.

Brahman is eternal and thus so is the *atman*. Brahman is Absolute Reality, and the *atman* is Brahman—a fact expressed in the famous adage "You are that [Brahman]," or "You are divine." The essential realization, then, is the oneness of Brahman and *atman*. Once an individual fully understands this ultimate unity, *moksha* occurs, *samsara* stops, and the *atman* attains full union with Brahman.

Achieving *moksha* is difficult, requiring great effort and involving many lifetimes through long expanses of time. The *Upanishads* stress that Brahman is ineffable—it cannot be described in words and must therefore be experienced directly through several means: meditation, various forms of yoga (both mental and physical disciplines), and asceticism. The aim of these practices is to look inward and discern the

Samsara is one's cycle of repeated deaths and rebirths.

Atman is one's soul or self.

I must confess to you that when doubt haunts me, when disappointments stare me in the face, and when I see not one ray of light on the horizon, I turn to the *Bhagavad Gita* and find a verse to comfort me; and I immediately begin to smile in the midst of overwhelming sorrow.
—Mahatma Gandhi

Brahman is the impersonal, all-pervading spirit that is the universe yet transcends all space and time. A **Brahmin** is a priest or teacher; a man of the priestly caste.

true nature of *atman* and its unity with Brahman. The rituals and sacrifices of the early *Vedas* are deemed superfluous.

As noted earlier, the *sruti* scriptures of the Vedic period (written roughly 1500 to 600 BCE) are thought to be of divine origin, revealed to the *rishis*, who received them via an intuitive or mystical experience. Hindus regard the *Vedas* as authoritative, eternal, and fixed. This canon remains as it was written, without further revelations or later emendations. But after the Vedic period, the human-authored *smriti* scriptures appeared. They too are venerated yet are considered less authoritative than the *Vedas*. They are also open-ended, a sacred work in progress. Over the centuries revered figures have added to them and continue to do so. But these facts have not diminished the influence of the *smriti* scriptures, which have probably had a greater impact on Hindu life than the *Vedas* have.

In Hindu scripture, newer writings generally do not supersede the old; they are added to the ever-expanding canon. Thus many ideas and practices found in both the *Vedas* and the post-Vedic scriptures are still relevant to contemporary Hinduism. Likewise, the ancient Vedic gods and goddesses were never entirely replaced by deities that arose later in history. The pantheon was simply enlarged. Today many of the old gods are ignored or deemphasized, while some of them are still revered.

The *smriti* material is voluminous and wide-ranging. It consists mainly of (1) the epics (the *Mahabharata* and the *Ramayana*), (2) myths and legends (the *Puranas*), and legal and moral codes (the *Laws of Manu*).

The great epics have served Indian and Hindu civilization much as Homer's *Iliad* and *Odyssey* served the ancient Greek and Hellenistic world: the stories express the culture's virtues, heroes, philosophy, and spiritual lessons. With eighteen voluminous chapters (or books) and 100,000 verses, the *Mahabharata* is the longest poem in existence, many times more extensive than the Christian Bible. Composed between 400 BCE and 400 CE, the epic recounts the ancient conflict between two great families, both of which are descendants of the ruler of Bharata (northern India). Their struggle culminates in a fateful battle at Kurukshetra. Among the warriors who are to fight there is the war hero Arjuna, who has serious misgivings about a battle that will pit brothers against brothers and cousins against cousins. Before the fight begins, as Arjuna contemplates the bloody fratricide to come, he throws down his bow in anguish and despair. He turns to his charioteer, Krishna—who in fact is God incarnate—and asks whether it is right to fight against his own kin in such a massive bloodletting. The conversation that then takes place between Krishna and Arjuna constitutes the most famous part of the *Mahabharata*: the *Bhagavad-Gita*, the most highly venerated and influential book in Hinduism.

The seven-hundred-verse **Bhagavad-Gita** (*Song of the Lord*) is no mere war story. In dramatic fashion, it confronts the moral and philosophical questions and conflicts that arise in Hindu concepts and practice—in devotion to the gods, the caste system, obligations to family, duties in time of war, the nature of the soul, the concept of Brahman, and the correct paths toward *moksha*.

In the *Gita*, we get a new account of the nature of God. In the *Upanishads*, Brahman is the impersonal Ultimate Reality, or World-Soul, pervading and constituting the universe but aloof from humans and their concerns. But Krishna turns out to be

37 What is the difference between the main goal in life as presented in the early *Vedas* and life's central aim as discussed in the *Upanishads*?

The apparent multiplication of gods is bewildering at the first glance, but you soon discover that they are the same GOD. There is always one uttermost God who defies personification. This makes Hinduism the most tolerant religion in the world, because its one transcendent God includes all possible gods. In fact Hinduism is so elastic and so subtle that the most profound Methodist, and crudest idolater, are equally at home with it.
—George Bernard Shaw

38 What is the relationship between Brahman and *atman*? How are *moksha* and *samsara* related to Brahman?

The **Bhagavad-Gita** is the most highly venerated and influential scripture in Hinduism.

PHILOSOPHY NOW

The Caste System

Much of the social and religious landscape of modern India has been shaped by 2,000-year-old Hindu treatises on religious, legal, and moral duty (*dharma*), the most famous being the *Laws of Manu*. (According to legend, all humans are descended from Manu, the original man.) Completed by around the first century of the Common Era, the *Laws* provided the basic outlines of India's *caste system*, laid down a code of conduct for each social class, and marked out the four stages of life for upper-class Indian men. The *Laws*, in effect, defined the ideal Hindu society, a framework that served as a reference point for modern laws and social rules in India today.

Figure 2.20 Sisters who belong to the Dalit caste in India.

India's premodern Aryan culture was divided into four hierarchical classes called *varnas*, which became the basis of the four main castes of Hinduism. In later eras these divisions were refined into myriad subdivisions and hardened to forbid social movement in one's lifetime from one class to another. In modern India both the four classes and the hundreds of subdivisions are referred to as *castes*; the subdivisions are also sometimes called *jatis*. These subcastes are based on occupation, kinship, geography, and even sectarian affiliation, and they are especially influential in rural areas of India. In general, caste protocol forbids members of one caste to marry members of another, and interactions with people from another caste are often restricted.

> In the great books of India, an empire spoke to us, nothing small or unworthy, but large, serene, consistent, the voice of an old intelligence, which in another age and climate had pondered and thus disposed of the questions that exercise us.
> —Ralph Waldo Emerson

the Supreme Being incarnate, a personal deity who loves and cares for humans and who often takes human form to help them.

Throughout history, many Hindus have believed there is only one path to liberation—solely through meditation or only through asceticism, for example. But in the *Gita*, Krishna insists that several paths (*marga*) can lead to *moksha*, a view that fits well with modern Hinduism. (Since these paths amount to spiritual disciplines, they are also referred to as forms of *yoga*.) Today there is a general awareness of multiple paths to liberation, each appropriate for a particular kind of person.

The path to liberation that Krishna speaks of most often is devotion to a personal god (*bhakti-marga*), the path chosen by most Hindus. *Bhakti-marga* entails overwhelming love and adoration of one's favored manifestation of God. The candidates for adoration are many—Krishna, Vishnu, Shiva, Varuna, Indra, Ganesha, Kali,

In ancient India the concepts of *dharma* and karma were central to the caste system, and the same is true today. Each caste is prescribed a *dharma*, a set of duties mandated for that caste. Theoretically no upward movement is possible during one's lifetime, but diligently performing one's *dharma* could lead to better karma and a higher-level rebirth in the next life.

Eventually the caste system was modified to include a fifth group—the "untouchables," or *dalits* ("oppressed ones"), who are thought to be "too polluting" to be included in any of the higher castes. This group comprises those who do "polluting" work such as sweeping streets; cleaning toilets; and handling leather, human waste, or dead bodies. The term "untouchables" comes from the traditional Hindu idea that upper-class persons who touch someone from the lowest class will be polluted and must therefore perform rituals to cleanse themselves. For generations *dalits* have been subjected to violence and discrimination—and they still are even in modern India, even though the untouchable class has been officially outlawed. Mohandas Gandhi called the *dalits* the "children of God" and advocated for their rights and their equal status in society.

In recent years the caste system has drawn fire from many critics. The main complaint is that the system is inherently unfair. The plight of the *dalits* is just one example. The *Laws of Manu* mandate a lower status for the lowest class, and caste hierarchy itself implies that some people are inherently less worthy than others, or that some deserve better treatment under the law than others, or that the highest classes are privileged and therefore should get special treatment. In practice, caste rules are not as rigid, and adherence to caste rules is not as widespread, as their advocates might prefer. The influence of caste in people's daily lives is weak in urban areas and much stronger in the countryside.

What do you think the civil rights leader Martin Luther King would say about India's caste system and the treatment of the *dalits*? Do you think the caste system is morally wrong? If so, what are your reasons?

and many other deities. The Hindu view of *bhakti* is that to love one of these finite manifestations of God is to move closer to the infinite God of everything. Brahman is supreme but impersonal. It is difficult to adore the all-encompassing essence of all that is; it is easier to love one of God's incarnations represented in countless earthly images. Thus a Hindu may bring an offering of flowers to a stone image of Krishna and pray for help or healing, expecting that Krishna himself will be pleased and perhaps answer the plea. The devotee will feel that *moksha* is a little closer and that Brahman is a little nearer.

Hinduism contains complex systems, or schools (*darshana*), of philosophical reflection offered by ancient sages and commentators. To immerse oneself in one of these is to follow the path of knowledge (*jnana-marga*), a route taken by only a minority of Hindus. The schools include six major orthodox ones, some of which

Figure 2.21 Reading the Vedic texts.

India has two million gods, and worships them all. In religion all other countries are paupers; India is the only millionaire.
—Mark Twain

appeared as far back as 500 BCE: *Samkhya* (probably the oldest), *Yoga*, *Nyaya*, *Vaisesika*, *Mimamsa*, and *Vedanta*. They all differ in important ways but presuppose the authority of the *Vedas*; accept the doctrines of reincarnation (the cycle of birth and death) and *moksha* (liberation); and set forth their doctrines in discourses, or books (*sutras*).

The *Nyaya* school focuses on developing a theory of knowledge (epistemology) and a system of logical proof that can yield indubitable truths. Some early Nyaya scholars were atheistic (as was Gautama), but later ones added the concept of a supreme divinity. The *Vedanta* school maintains a thoroughgoing monism (nondualism, *advaita*), claiming that reality consists not of two kinds of essential stuff (as the dualistic *Samkhya* school holds), but of only one kind, and this kind is Brahman, who alone is real. Brahman is all, and the self is identical to Brahman. The most influential proponent of this view was Shankara (788–820 CE). He argued that people persist in believing they are separate from Brahman because of *maya*—illusion. Only by shattering this ignorance with knowledge of true reality can they escape the torturous cycle of death and rebirth. The *Samkhya* school, in contrast, sees the world as dualistic—that is, consisting of two kinds of stuff or essences: spirit and matter. In its earlier forms, the school was atheistic in that it rejected the notion of a personal god; theistic elements were introduced later. The central belief of this view is that myriad souls are lodged in matter, and to be dislodged is to attain blissful liberation. The Yoga school accepts the philosophical outlook of *Samkhya* regarding spirit, matter, and liberation but goes further in emphasizing meditative and physical techniques for binding the spirit to Brahman and thus achieving *moksha*. It also makes room for a qualified theism.

Daoism

For 2,000 years *Daoism* (or *Taoism*) has been molding Chinese culture and changing the character of religions in the East. It has both philosophical and religious sides, and each of these has many permutations. It gets its name from the impossible-to-define notion of **Dao**, which has been translated as the "Way" or the "Way of Nature." Daoism is said to have been founded by Lao-Tzu, the supposed author of the classical Daoist text the *Tao-te ching* (*Classic of the Way and Its Power*), destined to become, along with Confucius's *Analects*, one of the two most respected books in Chinese writings. Scholars are unsure whether Lao-Tzu is a historical figure or a product of legend, but most agree that if Lao-Tzu was real, he probably lived in the sixth century BCE and may have been a contemporary of Confucius. The second most important text in philosophical Daoism is the *Chuang Tzu*, named after its presumed author. Regardless of their authorship, these two books laid the groundwork for a Daoism philosophy that influenced Chinese thinkers and nobles and has shaped the worldviews of the Chinese right up to the present.

Key Terms

agnostic Someone who neither accepts nor denies God's existence. (61)

argument from evil An argument purporting to show that since there is unnecessary evil, an all-powerful, all-knowing, and all-good God must not exist. (60)

argument from religious experience An argument of this form: a person seems to have experienced God; the experience must have actually been a genuine encounter with God; therefore, God probably exists. (59)

atheism The denial of the existence of God. (61)

atheist Someone who denies God's existence. (61)

atman One's soul or self. (114)

Bhagavad-Gita The most highly venerated and influential scriptures in Hinduism. (115)

Brahman The impersonal, all-pervading Spirit that is the universe yet transcends all space and time. (114)

brahmin A priest or teacher; a man of the priestly caste. (114)

cosmological arguments Arguments that try to show that from the fact that the universe exists, God exists. (58)

deism Belief in one God who created the world but left it unattended to run on its own. (62)

dharma The Buddha's system of teachings about the true nature of reality and how to live correctly to transcend it. (108)

evidentialism The view that we are justified in believing something only if it is supported by sufficient evidence. (96)

karma The universal principle that our actions result in deserved pleasure or pain in this life or the next. (107)

monotheism Belief in one God. (62)

moral evil Evil that comes from human choices and actions and the bad things that arise from them. (80)

natural evil Evil that results from the workings of nature. (80)

nirvana Enlightenment: the ultimate aim of all Buddhist practice and the final liberation to which all the Buddha's teachings point. (109)

ontological argument An argument that tries to demonstrate God's existence by logical analysis of the concept of God. (59)

panentheism The view that although God and the world are distinct, the world is part of God. (62)

pantheism The view that God and the universe are one and the same thing, a divine Whole. (62)

polytheism Belief in many gods. (62)

samsara One's cycle of repeated deaths and rebirths. (114)

teleological arguments Arguments that try to show that God must exist because features of the universe show signs of purpose or design. (58)

theism Belief in the existence of God. (61)

theist Someone who believes in God. (61)

theodicy A defense of the traditional conception of God in light of the existence of evil. (61)

Upanishads Vedic literature concerning the self, Brahman, *samsara*, and liberation. (113)

Vedas Early Hindu scriptures, developed between 1500 and 600 BCE. (113)

The Star

Arthur C. Clarke

Sir Arthur C. Clarke (1917–2008) was one of the world's great masters of science fiction. He is probably most famous for his novel *Childhood's End* and his screenplay for the movie *2001: A Space Odyssey*.

It is three thousand light-years to the Vatican. Once, I believed that space could have no power over faith, just as I believed the heavens declared the glory of God's handiwork. Now I have seen that handiwork, and my faith is sorely troubled. I stare at the crucifix that hangs on the cabin wall above the Mark VI Computer, and for the first time in my life I wonder if it is no more than an empty symbol.

I have told no one yet, but the truth cannot be concealed. The facts are there for all to read, recorded on the countless miles of magnetic tape and the thousands of photographs we are carrying back to Earth. Other scientists can interpret them as easily as I can, and I am not one who would condone that tampering with the truth which often gave my order a bad name in the olden days.

The crew were already sufficiently depressed: I wonder how they will take this ultimate irony. Few of them have any religious faith, yet they will not relish using this final weapon in their campaign against me—that private, good-natured, but fundamentally serious war which lasted all the way from Earth. It amused them to have a Jesuit as chief astrophysicist: Dr. Chandler, for instance, could never get over it. (Why are medical men such notorious atheists?) Sometimes he would meet me on the observation deck, where the lights are always low so that the stars shine with undiminished glory. He would come up to me in the gloom and stand staring out of the great oval port, while the heavens crawled slowly around us as the ship turned over and over with the residual spin we had never bothered to correct.

"Well, Father," he would say at last, "it goes on forever and forever, and perhaps *Something* made it. But how you can believe that Something has a special interest in us and our miserable little world—that just beats me." Then the argument would start, while the stars and

nebulae would swing around us in silent, endless arcs beyond the flawlessly clear plastic of the observation port.

It was, I think, the apparent incongruity of my position that caused most amusement among the crew. In vain I pointed to my three papers in the *Astrophysical Journal*, my five in the *Monthly Notices of the Royal Astronomical Society*. I would remind them that my order has long been famous for its scientific works. We may be few now, but ever since the eighteenth century we have made contributions to astronomy and geophysics out of all proportion to our numbers. Will my report on the Phoenix Nebula end our thousand years of history? It will end, I fear, much more than that.

I do not know who gave the nebula its name, which seems to me a very bad one. If it contains a prophecy, it is one that cannot be verified for several billion years. Even the word "nebula" is misleading; this is a far smaller object than those stupendous clouds of mist—the stuff of unborn stars—that are scattered throughout the length of the Milky Way. On the cosmic scale, indeed, the Phoenix Nebula is a tiny thing—a tenuous shell of gas surrounding a single star.

Or what is left of a star. . . .

The Rubens engraving of Loyola seems to mock me as it hangs there above the spectrophotometer tracings. What would *you*, Father, have made of this knowledge that has come into my keeping, so far from the little world that was all the Universe you knew? Would your faith have risen to the challenge, as mine has failed to do?

You gaze into the distance, Father, but I have traveled a distance beyond any that you could have imagined when you founded our order a thousand years ago. No other survey ship has been so far from Earth: we are at the very frontiers of the explored Universe. We set out to reach the Phoenix Nebula, we succeeded, and we are homeward bound with our burden of knowledge. I wish I could lift that burden from my shoulders, but I call to you in vain across the centuries and the light-years that lie between us.

On the book you are holding the words are plain to read. AD MAIOREM DEI GLORIAM, the message runs,

From *The Nine Billion Names of God: The Best Short Stories of Arthur C. Clarke* (New York: Signet/NAL, 1974), 235–240; full text from http://faculty.winthrop.edu/kosterj/engl510/star.htm

but it is a message I can no longer believe. Would you still believe it, if you could see what we have found?

We knew, of course, what the Phoenix Nebula was. Every year, in our Galaxy alone, more than a hundred stars explode, blazing for a few hours or days with hundreds of times their normal brilliance until they sink back into death and obscurity. Such are the ordinary novas—the commonplace disasters of the Universe. I have recorded the spectrograms and light curves of dozens since I started working at the Lunar Observatory.

But three or four times in every thousand years occurs something beside which even a nova pales into total insignificance.

When a star becomes a *supernova*, it may for a little while outshine all the massed suns of the Galaxy. The Chinese astronomers watched this happen in A.D. 1054, not knowing what it was they saw. Five centuries later, in 1572, a supernova blazed in Cassiopeia so brilliantly that it was visible in the daylight sky. There have been three more in the thousand years that have passed since then.

Our mission was to visit the remnants of such a catastrophe, to reconstruct the events that led up to it, and, if possible, to learn its cause. We came slowly in through the concentric shells of gas that had been blasted out six thousand years before, yet were expanding still. They were immensely hot, radiating even now with a fierce violet light, but were far too tenuous to do us any damage. When the star had exploded, its outer layers had been driven upward with such speed that they had escaped completely from its gravitational field. Now they formed a hollow shell large enough to engulf a thousand solar systems, and at its center burned the tiny, fantastic object which the star had now become—a White Dwarf, smaller than earth, yet weighing a million times as much.

The glowing gas shells were all around us, banishing the normal night of interstellar space. We were flying into the center of the cosmic bomb that had detonated millennia ago and whose incandescent fragments were still hurtling apart. The immense scale of the explosion, and the fact that the debris already covered a volume of space many millions of miles across, robbed the scene of any visible movement. It would take decades before the unaided eye could detect any motion in these tortured wisps and eddies of gas, yet the sense of turbulent expansion was overwhelming.

We had checked our primary drive hours before, and were drifting slowly toward the fierce little star ahead. Once it had been a sun like our own, but it had squandered in a few hours the energy that should have kept it shining for a million years. Now it was a shrunken miser, hoarding its resources as if trying to make amends for its prodigal youth.

No one seriously expected to find planets. If there had been any before the explosion, they would have been boiled into puffs of vapor, and their substance lost in the greater wreckage of the star itself. But we made the automatic search, as we always do when approaching an unknown sun, and presently we found a single small world circling the star at an immense distance. It must have been the Pluto of this vanished Solar System, orbiting on the frontiers of the night. Too far from the central sun ever to have known life, its remoteness had saved it from the fate of all its lost companions.

The passing fires had seared its rocks and burned away the mantle of frozen gas that must have covered it in the days before the disaster. We landed, and we found the Vault.

Its builders had made sure that we should. The monolithic marker that stood above the entrance was now a fused stump, but even the first long-range photographs told us that here was the work of intelligence. A little later we detected the continent-wide pattern of radioactivity that had been buried in the rock. Even if the pylon above the Vault had been destroyed, this would have remained, an immovable and all-but eternal beacon calling to the stars. Our ship fell toward this gigantic bull's eye like an arrow into its target.

The pylon must have been a mile high when it was built, but now it looked like a candle that had melted down into a puddle of wax. It took us a week to drill through the fused rock, since we did not have the proper tools for a task like this. We were astronomers, not archaeologists, but we could improvise. Our original purpose was forgotten: this lonely monument, reared with such labor at the greatest possible distance from the doomed sun, could have only one meaning. A civilization that knew it was about to die had made its last bid for immortality.

It will take us generations to examine all the treasures that were placed in the Vault. They had plenty of time to prepare, for their sun must have given its first warnings many years before the final detonation. Everything that they wished to preserve, all the fruits of their genius, they brought here to this distant world in the days before the end, hoping that some other race would find it and that they would not be utterly forgotten. Would we have done as well, or would we have been too lost in our own misery to give thought to a future we could never see or share?

If only they had had a little more time! They could travel freely enough between the planets of their own sun, but they had not yet learned to cross the interstellar gulfs, and the nearest Solar System was a hundred light-years away. Yet even had they possessed the secret of the Transfinite Drive, no more than a few millions could have been saved. Perhaps it was better thus.

Even if they had not been so disturbingly human as their sculpture shows, we could not have helped admiring them and grieving for their fate. They left thousands of visual records and the machines for projecting them, together with elaborate pictorial instructions from which it will not be difficult to learn their written language. We have examined many of these records, and brought to life for the first time in six thousand years the warmth and beauty of a civilization that in many ways must have been superior to our own. Perhaps they only showed us the best, and one can hardly blame them. But their worlds were very lovely, and their cities were built with a grace that matches anything of man's. We have watched them at work and play, and listened to their musical speech sounding across the centuries. One scene is still before my eyes—a group of children on a beach of strange blue sand, playing in the waves as children play on Earth. Curious whiplike trees line the shore, and some very large animal is wading in the shallows, yet attracting no attention at all.

And sinking into the sea, still warm and friendly and life-giving, is the sun that will soon turn traitor and obliterate all this innocent happiness.

Perhaps if we had not been so far from home and so vulnerable to loneliness, we should not have been so deeply moved. Many of us had seen the ruins of ancient civilizations on other worlds, but they had never affected us so profoundly. This tragedy was unique. It is one thing for a race to fail and die, as nations and cultures have done on Earth. But to be destroyed so completely in the full flower of its achievement, leaving no survivors—how could that be reconciled with the mercy of God?

My colleagues have asked me that, and I have given what answers I can. Perhaps you could have done better, Father Loyola, but I have found nothing in the *Exercitia Spiritualia* that helps me here. They were not an evil people: I do not know what gods they worshiped, if indeed they worshiped any. But I have looked back at them across the centuries, and have watched while the loveliness they used their last strength to preserve was brought forth again into the light of their shrunken sun. They could have taught us much: why were they destroyed?

I know the answers that my colleagues will give when they get back to Earth. They will say that the Universe has no purpose and no plan, that since a hundred suns explode every year in our Galaxy, at this very moment some race is dying in the depths of space. Whether that race has done good or evil during its lifetime will make no difference in the end: there is no divine justice, for there is no God.

Yet, of course, what we have seen proves nothing of the sort. Anyone who argues thus is being swayed by emotion, not logic. God has no need to justify His actions to man. He who built the Universe can destroy it when He chooses. It is arrogance—it is perilously near blasphemy—for us to say what He may or may not do.

This I could have accepted, hard though it is to look upon whole worlds and peoples thrown into the furnace. But there comes a point when even the deepest faith must falter, and now, as I look at the calculations lying before me, I have reached that point at last.

We could not tell, before we reached the nebula, how long ago the explosion took place. Now, from the astronomical evidence and the record in the rocks of that one surviving planet, I have been able to date it very exactly. I know in what year the light of this colossal conflagration reached the Earth. I know how brilliantly the supernova whose corpse now dwindles behind our speeding ship once shone in terrestrial skies. I know how it must have blazed low in the east before sunrise, like a beacon in that oriental dawn.

There can be no reasonable doubt: the ancient mystery is solved at last. Yet, oh God, there were so many stars you could have used. What was the need to give these people to the fire, that the symbol of their passing might shine above Bethlehem?

Probing Questions

1. What is the terrible irony revealed in the last sentence of this story? Could this irony arise in real life? That is, could the events recounted actually happen?

2. Why is the Jesuit astrophysicist's faith shaken? If you were in his position and knew what he did, would your faith falter?

3. What does this story suggest about the design of the universe? Do the events in the story imply that there is a designer God—or that there isn't? Explain.

For Further Reading

William Lane Craig, *Reasonable Faith: Christian Truth and Apologetics*, revised edition (Wheaton, IL: Crossway Books, 1994). A readable theistic defense of the existence of God.

William Lane Craig and Walter Sinnott-Armstrong, *God? A Debate Between a Christian and an Atheist* (New York: Oxford University Press, 2004). An informative give-and-take about the existence of God between a scholarly Christian and a knowledgeable atheist.

Richard M. Gale, *On the Nature and Existence of God* (Cambridge: Cambridge University Press, 1991). A sophisticated but readable examination of arguments for the existence of God.

Peter Harvey, *An Introduction to Buddhism: Teachings, History and Practices* (Cambridge: Cambridge University Press, 1990).

B. C. Johnson, *The Atheist Debater's Handbook* (Amherst, NY: Prometheus, 1983). A lucid, concise dismantling of major arguments for God's existence.

W. J. Johnson, trans., *The Bhagavad Gita* (Oxford: Oxford University Press, 1994).

Philip Kitcher, *Living with Darwin* (New York: Oxford University Press, 2007). A careful, even-handed examination of evolution and religion.

Kim Knott, *Hinduism: A Very Short Introduction* (Oxford: Oxford University Press, 1998).

J. L. Mackie, *The Miracle of Theism*, 3rd edition (Oxford: Oxford University Press, 1982). An atheistic philosopher's classic, readable assessment of arguments for God's existence.

Michael Martin, *Atheism: A Philosophical Justification* (Philadelphia: Temple University Press, 1990). A scholarly but accessible guide to major arguments for and against theism.

Willard G. Oxtoby, ed., *World Religions: Eastern Traditions* (Oxford: Oxford University Press, 2002).

Michael Peterson, William Hasker, Bruce Reichenbach, and David Basinger, *Reason and Religious Belief* (New York: Oxford University Press, 2003). Theistic philosophers assess the case for and against God's existence.

Alvin Plantinga, *God, Freedom, and Evil* (Grand Rapids, MI: Eerdmans, 1974). A very accessible, theistic rebuttal of the argument from evil.

Walpola Rahula, *What the Buddha Taught* (New York: Grove Press, 1979).

William L. Rowe, *Philosophy of Religion* (Belmont, CA: Wadsworth, 2001). A thorough, accessible survey of the main issues in the philosophy of religion.

Richard Swinburne, *The Existence of God*, 2nd edition (Oxford: Oxford University Press, 2004). A comprehensive defense of theism by a leading theistic philosopher.

CHAPTER 3

MORALITY AND THE MORAL LIFE

Chapter Objectives

3.1 OVERVIEW: ETHICS AND THE MORAL DOMAIN

- Understand the distinction between ethics and morality, and know the basic elements that make morality a unique normative enterprise.
- Understand the nature of moral theories and explain how the moral criteria of adequacy are used to evaluate them.
- Define *consequentialist, deontological, utilitarianism, ethical egoism, Kant's theory, virtue ethics, ethics of care, considered moral judgments,* and *divine command theory.*
- State the divine command theory and explain the arbitrariness argument against it.

3.2 MORAL RELATIVISM

- Define *moral objectivism, moral absolutism, moral relativism, subjective relativism,* and *cultural relativism.*
- Explain the main objections to subjective and cultural relativism, evaluate the standard argument for cultural relativism, and understand the relationship between cultural relativism and tolerance.

3.3 MORALITY BASED ON CONSEQUENCES

- State the central features of utilitarianism and describe Bentham's and Mill's different conceptions of happiness.
- Evaluate utilitarianism's strengths and weakness.
- Explain the distinction between ethical egoism and psychological egoism, and evaluate ethical egoism's strengths and weaknesses.

3.4 MORALITY BASED ON DUTY AND RIGHTS

- Describe the differences between the theories of Mill and Kant.
- Articulate the main features of Kant's theory and of his two versions of the categorical imperative.
- Evaluate the strengths and weaknesses of Kant's theory.

3.5 MORALITY BASED ON CHARACTER

- State the main features of virtue ethics and of Aristotle's view on the virtuous life.
- Describe the differences between virtue ethics and most other moral theories.
- Evaluate the strengths and weaknesses of virtue ethics.

3.6 FEMINIST ETHICS AND THE ETHICS OF CARE

- Explain how feminist ethics differs from both utilitarianism and Kant's theory.
- Describe the nature of the ethics of care, its most attractive features, and some of the criticisms that have been lodged against it.
- Articulate and defend your own moral theory—that is, your own view of the nature of right and wrong actions.

3.7 ALBERT CAMUS: AN EXISTENTIALIST VOICE

- Explain some of the main themes of existentialism.
- Summarize the points that Camus makes in his interpretation of the myth of Sisyphus

3.8 CONFUCIANISM

- Understand the main aim of Confucius's teaching.
- Know what *li* and *ren* mean and how Confucius thought they could be used to help someone become a "superior person."
- Define the obligation of filial piety and understand why Confucius thought it so important.

3.1 OVERVIEW: ETHICS AND THE MORAL DOMAIN

Ethics is part of philosophy; it is also part of life—a very large, vital, inevitable part of life. You cannot avoid thinking about right and wrong, judging people to be good or bad, wondering what kind of life is worthwhile, debating with others about moral issues, accepting or rejecting the moral beliefs of your family or culture, or coming to some general understanding (a moral theory) about the nature of morality itself. When you do these things, you are in the realm of ethics and will need philosophy's resources to sort out good answers from bad, justified beliefs from nonsense.

Ethics (moral philosophy) is the study of morality using the methods of philosophy.

Ethics and Morality

Ethics, or **moral philosophy**, is the study of morality using the methods of philosophy, and **morality** consists of our beliefs about right and wrong actions and good and bad persons or character. Morality has to do with our moral judgments, principles, values, and theories; ethics is the careful, philosophical examination of these.

Morality consists of our beliefs about right and wrong actions and good and bad persons or character.

Morality is not properly the doctrine of how we may make ourselves happy, but how we may make ourselves worthy of happiness.
—Immanuel Kant

Ethics applies critical reasoning to questions about what we should do and what is of value, questions that pervade our lives and demand reasonable answers.

In everyday language, people often blur the distinction between *ethics* and *morality*, using the terms as synonyms for moral beliefs or practices generally (as in "Morality is the foundation of civilization" or "Ethics cannot be ignored"). Or they may use the words to refer to the moral beliefs or practices of specific groups or persons ("Muslim morality," "Puritan ethics," "the ethics of Gandhi"). Those who maintain the distinction that we draw here will generally apply the adjective forms *moral* and *ethical* accordingly. But it is also common (including in this text) to use these words as equivalent to right and good ("That was the ethical thing to do"), and to use *immoral* or *unethical* as synonyms for wrong or bad ("abortion is immoral," "cheating on an exam is unethical").

Morality is a *normative* enterprise, which means that it provides us with norms, or standards, for judging actions and persons—standards usually in the form of moral principles or theories. With moral standards in hand, we decide whether an action is morally right or wrong, whether a person is morally good or bad, and whether we are living a good or bad life. The main business of morality is therefore not to describe how things are, but *to prescribe how things should be*. There are, of course, other normative spheres (art and law, for example), but these are interested in applying *nonmoral* norms (aesthetic and legal norms, for instance) to judge the worth or correctness of things. When we participate in ethics, we are typically either applying or evaluating moral norms and using the tools of philosophy to do it.

Morality stands out among other normative spheres because of its distinctive set of properties. One of these is that moral norms have a much stronger hold on us than nonmoral ones do. The former are thought to dominate the latter, possessing a property that philosophers call *overridingness*. For example, we would think that a moral norm mandating that everyone be treated fairly should override a legal norm (a law) that enjoined one group to discriminate against another. If a law commanded us to commit a seriously immoral act, we would probably think the law illegitimate and might even flout it in an act of civil disobedience. Moral norms are generally stronger and more important than nonmoral norms.

1 How is discrimination against a group of people contrary to morality's demand for impartiality? Can there ever be reasons for treating equals *unequally*? If so, what kind of reasons?

In addition, moral norms have *impartiality*: they apply to everyone equally. Morality demands that everyone be considered of equal moral worth, and that each person's interests be given equal weight. Morality, in other words, says that equals should be treated equally unless there is a morally relevant reason to treat them differently. We would consider it unjust to apply a moral norm to some people but not to others when there is no morally relevant difference between them.

Moral norms, like nonmoral ones, also possess the property of *universality*: they apply not just in a single case, but in all cases that are relevantly similar. Logic tells us that we cannot reasonably regard an action performed by one person as morally wrong while believing that the same action performed in an almost identical situation by another person is morally right. Morality demands consistency among similar cases.

Finally, morality is *reason based*. To be fully involved in the moral life and to make informed moral judgments is to engage in moral reasoning. To do moral reasoning

Figure 3.1 Moral issues are forced upon us throughout our lives. When they are, to what system of morality do you appeal—the one you were taught as a child, a code derived from your preferred religion, or some other moral theory?

is to try to ensure that our moral judgments are not wrought out of thin air or concocted from prejudice or blind emotion—but are supported by good reasons. We would think it preposterous for someone to assert that killing innocent children is morally permissible (or impermissible)—and that he has no reasons whatsoever for believing this. In science, medicine, law, business, and every other area of intellectual life, we want and expect claims to be backed by good reasons. Morality is no different. And ethics—the systematic search for moral understanding—can be successful only through careful reflection and the sifting of reasons for belief. Critical reasoning is the main engine that drives ethical inquiry.

But what about emotions—what role do they play in ethics? Feelings are an essential and inevitable part of the moral life. They can help us empathize with others and enlarge our understanding of the stakes involved in moral decisions. But they can also blind us. Our feelings are too often the product of our psychological needs, cultural conditioning, and selfish motivations. Critical reasoning is the corrective, giving us the power to examine and guide our feelings to achieve a more balanced view.

Some people believe that conscience, not ethics, is the best guide to plausible moral judgments. At times, it seems to speak to us in an imaginary though authoritative voice, telling us to do or not to do something. But conscience is no infallible indicator of moral truth. It is conditioned by our upbringing, cultural background,

2 Can you think of examples in history or literature in which people let their conscience be their guide and ended up committing immoral acts? Is it possible that Hitler's conscience told him to murder six million Jews?

and other factors and, like our feelings, it may be the result of irrelevant influences. Nevertheless, the voice of conscience should not be ignored; it can often alert us to something of moral importance. But we must submit its promptings to critical examination before we can have any confidence in them.

The moral life, then, is about grappling with a distinctive class of norms, which can include moral principles, rules, theories, and judgments. We apply these norms to two distinct spheres of our moral experience—to both moral *obligations* and moral *values*. Moral obligations concern our duty, what we are obligated to do. That is, obligations are about conduct, how we ought or ought not to behave. In this sphere, we talk primarily about *actions*. We may look to moral principles or rules to guide our actions, or study a moral theory that purports to explain right actions, or make judgments about right or wrong actions. Moral values, on the other hand, generally concern those things that we judge to be morally good, bad, praiseworthy, or blameworthy. Normally we use such words to describe persons (as in "He is a good person" or "She is to blame for hurting them"), their character ("He is virtuous"; "She is honest"), or their motives ("She did wrong but did not mean to"). Note that we also attribute *nonmoral* value to things. If we say that a book or bicycle or vacation is good, we mean good in a nonmoral sense. Such things in themselves cannot have *moral* value.

Strictly speaking, only actions are morally *right* or *wrong*, but persons are morally *good* or *bad* (or some degree of goodness or badness). With this distinction we can acknowledge a simple fact of the moral life: a good person can do something wrong, and a bad person can do something right.

Moral Theories

A large part of ethics and the moral life consists of devising and evaluating moral theories. That is, we do moral theorizing. In science, theories help us understand the empirical world by explaining the causes of events, why things are the way they are. The germ theory of disease explains how particular diseases arise and spread in a human population. The heliocentric (sun-centered) theory of planetary motion explains why the planets in our solar system behave the way they do. In ethics, moral theories have a similar explanatory role. A **moral theory** explains not why one event causes another, but why an action is right or wrong or why a person or a person's character is good or bad. A moral theory tells us what it is about an action that *makes it right*, or what it is about a person that *makes him or her good*. The divine command theory of morality, for example, says that right actions are those commanded or willed by God. Traditional utilitarianism says that right actions are those that produce the best balance of happiness over unhappiness for all concerned. These and other moral theories are attempts to define rightness or goodness. In this way, they are both more general and more basic than moral principles or other general norms.

Moral theorizing comes naturally to almost everyone. Whenever we try to understand what a moral property such as rightness or goodness means, or justify a moral principle or other norm, or resolve a conflict between two credible principles, or explain why a particular action or practice is right or wrong, or evaluate the

A **moral theory** is a theory that explains why an action is right or wrong or why a person or a person's character is good or bad.

I say that a man must be certain of his morality for the simple reason that he has to suffer for it.
—G. K. Chesterton

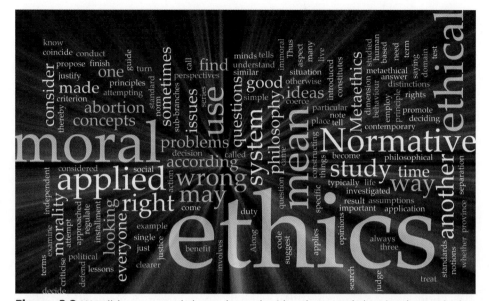

Figure 3.2 We all have a moral theory (even the idea that moral theories don't exist is a theoretical view about ethics). The important question is not whether you have a theory, but whether the theory you have is a good one.

A system of morality which is based on relative emotional values is a mere illusion, a thoroughly vulgar conception which has nothing sound in it and nothing true.
—Socrates

plausibility of specific moral intuitions or assumptions, we do moral theorizing. In fact, we *must* theorize if we are to make headway in such investigations. We must stand back from the situation at hand and try to grasp the larger pattern that only theory can reveal.

Two types of theories have been of the greatest interest to philosophers. **Consequentialist theories** insist that the rightness of actions depends solely on their consequences or results. The key question is what or how much good the actions produce, however *good* is defined. **Deontological** (or **nonconsequentialist**) **theories** say that the rightness of actions is determined not solely by their consequences, but partly or entirely by their intrinsic nature. For some or all actions, rightness depends on the kind of actions they are, not on how much good they produce. A consequentialist theory, then, may say that stealing is wrong because it causes more harm than good. But a deontological theory may contend that stealing is inherently wrong regardless of its consequences, good or bad.

The most influential consequentialist theory is **utilitarianism**, the view that right actions are those that maximize the overall well-being of everyone involved. Or, to put it another way, we should do what results in the greatest balance of good over bad, everyone considered. Various forms of utilitarianism differ in how they define the good, with some equating it with happiness or pleasure (the hedonistic view), others with satisfaction of preferences or desires or some other intrinsically valuable things or states, such as knowledge or perfection.

Another consequentialist theory is **ethical egoism**, the view that right actions are those that further one's own best interests. Your duty is to look out for yourself by doing what yields the most favorable consequences for you, even if the interests

A **consequentialist theory** is a moral theory in which the rightness of actions depends solely on their consequences or results.

A **deontological** (or **non-consequentialist**) **theory** is a moral theory in which the rightness of actions is determined not solely by their consequences, but partly or entirely by their intrinsic nature.

Utilitarianism is the view that right actions are those that result in the most beneficial balance of good over bad consequences for everyone involved.

Ethical egoism is the view that right actions are those that further one's own best interests.

Kant's theory is the theory that right actions are those that accord with the categorical imperative.

3 Do you generally judge the rightness or wrongness of an action by its consequences? By the nature of the action itself? By some other measure of rightness?

Virtue ethics is a moral theory that focuses on the development of virtuous character.

Ethics of care is a moral perspective that emphasizes the unique demands of specific situations and the virtues and feelings that are central to close personal relationships.

of others are ignored or thwarted. Ethical egoists may equate their interests with pleasure, happiness, self-realization, or other valued states, but they all agree that promoting these things for oneself is the essence of morality. Selfishness and wild abandon, however, are not entailed by ethical egoism, for ignoring the needs of others or acting without restraint may not be in one's best interests.

The most sophisticated and influential deontological theory comes from the German philosopher Immanuel Kant (1724–1804). **Kant's theory** is the very antithesis of utilitarianism, holding that right actions do not depend in the least on consequences, the production of happiness, or the desires and needs of human beings. For Kant, the core of morality consists in following a rational and universally applicable moral rule and doing so solely out of a sense of duty. An action is right only if it conforms to such a rule, and we are morally praiseworthy only if we perform it for duty's sake alone.

The preceding theories are what philosophers call theories of obligation, which emphasize the rightness or wrongness of actions and the duties of persons. Their main concern is knowing and doing what's right, and their chief guide to these aims is moral principles. An altogether different kind of moral theory is **virtue ethics**, which focuses not on rules and right actions, but on the development of virtuous character. According to virtue ethics, character is the key to the moral life, for it is from a virtuous character that moral conduct and values naturally arise. Virtues are engrained dispositions to act by standards of excellence, so having the proper virtues leads as a matter of course to right actions properly motivated. The central task in morality, then, is not knowing and applying principles, but being and becoming a good person, someone possessing the virtues that define moral excellence. In virtue ethics, one determines right action not by consulting rules, but by asking what a truly virtuous person would do or whether an action would accord with the relevant virtues.

The **ethics of care** is a distinctive moral perspective that arose out of feminist concerns and grew to challenge core elements of most other moral theories. Generally, those theories emphasize abstract principles, general duties, individual rights, impartial judgments, and deliberative reasoning. But the ethics of care shifts the focus to the unique demands of specific situations and to the virtues and feelings that are central to close personal relationships—empathy, compassion, love, sympathy, and fidelity. The heart of the moral life is feeling for and caring for those with whom you have a special, intimate connection.

None of these theories is perfect. Each one is an attempt to identify the true determinants of rightness or goodness, and each has grasped at least a piece of the truth about morality. But no theory manages to fully account for all our intuitions about the moral life.

That is not to say that all moral theories are created equal. Some are better than others, and a vital task in ethics is to try to tell which is which. Moral theories can be useful and valuable to us only if there are criteria for judging their worth—and fortunately there are such standards and straightforward ways of applying them.

Recall that moral theories are analogous to scientific theories. Scientists devise theories to explain the causes of events. For each phenomenon to be explained, scientists usually have several possible theories to consider, and the challenge is to determine which one is best (and is therefore most likely to be correct). The superior theory is the one that fares best when judged by generally accepted yardsticks known as the *scientific criteria of adequacy*. One criterion often invoked is *fruitfulness*—whether the theory makes successful predictions of previously unknown phenomena. All things being equal, a theory that makes successful predictions of novel phenomena is more likely to be true than one that does not. Another important criterion is *conservatism*—how well a theory fits with established facts, with what scientists already know. All things being equal, a theory that conflicts with what scientists already have good reasons to believe is less likely to be true than a theory that has no such conflicts. Of course, an unconservative theory can turn out to be correct, and a conservative theory wrong, but the odds are against this outcome. Analogously, moral theories are meant to explain what makes an action right or a person good. And to try to determine which moral theory is most likely correct, we apply conceptual yardsticks—the *moral criteria of adequacy*. Any plausible moral theory must measure up to these critical standards.

An important criterion of adequacy for moral theories is *consistency with our considered moral judgments*. Any plausible scientific theory must be consistent with the data that the theory is supposed to explain; there should be no conflicts between the theory and the relevant facts. Likewise, a moral theory must also be consistent with the data it is supposed to explain: our *considered moral judgments*, what some call our moral common sense. We arrive at them after careful deliberation that is as free of bias, self-interest, and other distorting influences as possible. Moral philosophers grant them considerable respect and try to take them into account in their moral theorizing. These judgments are fallible, and they are often revised under pressure from trustworthy principles or theories. But we are entitled to trust them unless we have good reason to doubt them. Therefore, any moral theory that is seriously inconsistent with our most

> All sects are different, because they come from men; morality is everywhere the same, because it comes from God.
> —Voltaire

IMPORTANT MORAL THEORIES

CONSEQUENTIALIST

utilitarianism The view that right actions are those that result in the most beneficial balance of good over bad consequences for everyone involved.

ethical egoism The view that right actions are those that further one's own best interests.

DEONTOLOGICAL

Kant's theory The theory that right actions are those that accord with the categorical imperative.

VIRTUE ORIENTED

virtue ethics A moral theory that focuses on the development of virtuous character.

ethics of care A moral perspective that emphasizes the unique demands of specific situations and the virtues and feelings that are central to close personal relationships.

PHILOSOPHY NOW

The Morality of Human Cloning

Modern technology is constantly presenting us with moral quandaries that would have been unthinkable to previous generations. A prime example is human reproductive cloning. Cloning is the asexual production of a genetically identical entity from an existing one. Cloning an individual animal or human is a matter of extracting the nucleus from an ordinary body cell, in-

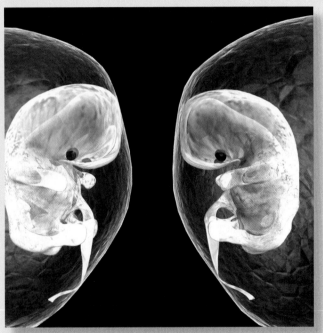

serting the nucleus into a "blank" egg cell (one without a nucleus), and stimulating the reconfigured cell to start cell division and development into an embryo. To date, no human has been successfully cloned (though many species of animals have), and for technical and moral reasons none is likely to be cloned any time soon. But the prospect of human cloning in the future has jump-started the moral debate over whether it should ever be done, even if feasible.

A typical response to the prospect of human cloning is moral outrage, which too often is based on misunderstandings. Chief among these is the notion that a human clone would be identical to an existing person, the clone's "parent." This idea has led to a host of silly fantasies played out in movies, literature, and the popular mind: an army of Hitler clones spawned from one of the führer's

Figure 3.3 If human reproductive cloning were feasible, should people be permitted to use this technology? Suppose the only way a childless couple could have a baby genetically related to them was through cloning. Would cloning be a morally permissible option for them?

basic considered judgments must generally be regarded as flawed, perhaps fatally so, and in need of revision. Our considered judgments, for example, tell us that slavery, murder, rape, and genocide are wrong. A moral theory that implies otherwise fails to meet this criterion and is a candidate for rejection. That equals should be treated equally, that there must be good reasons to deliberately cause harm to others, that justice is an essential part of the moral life—these and other considered judgments are among the many that good moral theories must account for.

cells, or a laboratory of Albert Einsteins discovering the secrets of the universe. The underlying fallacy is that genes make the person, that genetics ordains all of an individual's characteristics. This view is known as genetic determinism, and it is a myth. Einstein's clone would have Einstein's genes but would not and could not be Einstein. The clone would be unique and probably not much like his famous progenitor at all.

Many who favor the use of cloning rest their case on its likely benefits. For some people, their only hope of having a child to whom they are genetically related would be through cloning. Some men have no sperm; some women, no eggs; cloning could get around these problems. For couples who value this genetic connection and also want to avoid passing on a genetic disease or health risk to their child, cloning would be an attractive option—perhaps the only option. Parents whose only child dies could have her cloned from a cell harvested from her body, ensuring that some part of her would live on.

Some critics of cloning have charged that it violates the rights of the resulting clone—specifically, the right to a unique identity. A clone by definition is not genetically unique; his genome is iterated in his "parent." Aside from doubts about whether such a right exists, the strongest reply to this worry is that genetic uniqueness is neither necessary nor sufficient for personal uniqueness.

Many oppose the use of cloning technology because it is unnatural, a deviant way of bringing children into the world. This view is criticized as narrowly dogmatic, for some natural processes are bad (such as bacterial infection), and some unnatural ones are good (such as medical treatment).

A kindred objection holds that cloning replaces natural procreation with the artificial *manufacture* of children as products—a demeaning process that erodes our respect for human beings. Cloning is thus profoundly dehumanizing. But some reject this criticism, declaring that the value and worth of a being does not depend on how it is created, but on what that being is like (its nature).

Is human reproductive cloning morally permissible? Why or why not? Upon what moral principles do you base your view?

In applying this standard, we must keep in mind that in both science and ethics, there is tension between theory and data. A good theory explains the data, which in turn influence the shape of the theory. Particularly strong data can compel scientists to alter a theory to account for the information, but a good theory can also give scientists reasons to question or reject particular data. In the same way, there is a kind of give-and-take between a moral theory and the relevant data. Our considered moral judgments may give us good reasons for altering or even rejecting our moral theory.

But if our moral theory is coherent and well supported, it may oblige us to rethink or reject our considered judgments. In both science and ethics, the goal is to ensure that agreement between theory and data is as close as possible. The agreement is acceptably close when no further changes in the theory or the data are necessary—when there is a kind of balance between the two that moral philosophers call "reflective equilibrium."

Another test of adequacy is *consistency with the facts of the moral life*. In science, good theories are consistent with scientific background knowledge, with what scientists already have good reasons to believe. Such theories are, as mentioned earlier, conservative. This background knowledge includes other well-founded theories, highly reliable findings, and scientific (natural) laws. Moral theories should also be consistent with background knowledge—the *moral* background knowledge, the basic, inescapable experiences of the moral life. These experiences include making moral judgments, disagreeing with others on moral issues, being mistaken in our moral beliefs, and giving reasons for accepting moral beliefs. That we do in fact experience these things from time to time is a matter of moral common sense—seemingly obvious facts of the moral life. Thus, any moral theory that is inconsistent with these aspects of the moral life is deeply problematic. If a theory implies that disagreement on a moral issue is impossible, for example, we must suspect that there is something seriously wrong with it. It is possible that we are deluded about the moral life—that we, for example, merely think we are disagreeing with others on moral issues but are actually just venting our feelings. But our experience gives us good grounds for taking the commonsense view until we are given good reasons to believe otherwise.

Finally, we have this criterion: *resourcefulness in moral problem-solving*. If a scientific theory helps scientists answer questions, solve problems, and control events in the natural world, it demonstrates both its plausibility and its usefulness. All things being equal, such a resourceful theory is better than one that has none of these advantages. Much the same is true for moral theories. A resourceful moral theory helps us solve moral problems. It can help us identify morally relevant aspects of conduct, judge the rightness of actions, resolve conflicts among moral principles and judgments, test and correct our moral intuitions, and understand the underlying point of morality itself. Any moral theory that lacks problem-solving resourcefulness is neither useful nor credible.

Evaluating moral theories using these yardsticks is not a rote process. There is no standard procedure for applying the criteria to a theory and no set of instructions for assigning conceptual weight to each criterion as we judge a theory's worth. But the criteria do help us make broad judgments on rational grounds about a theory's strengths and weaknesses. We must use them as guides, relying on our best judgment in applying them, just as scientists must use their own educated judgment in wielding their kind of criteria of adequacy. In neither case is there a neat algorithm for theory assessment, but nonetheless, in both arenas the process is objective, reasonable, and essential.

Later in this chapter, we will look at how philosophers use these criteria to test major moral theories.

Religion and Morality

Morality and religion have always been closely intertwined. Historically, every religion has offered its adherents moral content in the form of commandments or precepts. Christianity, Judaism, Islam, Hinduism, and others all contain normative standards for right conduct. But many think that the connection between moral values and religious belief is even closer than these facts suggest: they believe that religion is the *source* of morality. The idea is that God *makes* morality; right and wrong are constituted by the will of God. Right actions are those commanded by God; wrong actions are those prohibited by God. This doctrine is known as the **divine command theory**, a view that has been taken to task in ethics by religious and nonreligious thinkers alike.

The problem as most philosophers see it is that the doctrine forces a troubling dilemma on us, one outlined by Socrates many centuries ago. In Plato's dialogue *Euthyphro*, Socrates asks, in effect, Are actions right because God commands them, or does God command them because they are right? To choose the first option is to say that God makes morality and to accept the divine command theory. To choose the second is to say that morality exists independently of God's will and even he must obey it. For many theists, the second option (the denial of the divine command theory) is far more palatable than the first, for the first one implies that morality is completely arbitrary.

These critics argue that if an action is morally right only because God says so, then any action at all could be morally right. If God so willed, the torture and slaughter of innocents would be morally right. As the divine command theory would have it, there could be no reasons for God's willing one way or the other. He just commands, and that makes an action right (or wrong). But if God has no reasons for his commands, no standards other than his say-so, his commands are arbitrary. This arbitrariness makes morality a cruel joke and reveals God as less than perfect.

A divine command theorist might reply that God would never command something as evil as the torture and slaughter of innocents because God is all-good. But this response appears to make the idea of the goodness of God meaningless. Russ Shafer-Landau makes the point like this:

Figure 3.4 Is morality constituted by the will of God?

Divine command theory is the doctrine that God is the creator of morality.

Russ Shafer-Landau, *Whatever Happened to Good and Evil?*

No, you say, such a thing is impossible. A good God would never allow such a thing [wicked deeds]. Right enough. But what does it mean to be good? If the Divine Command Theory is correct, then something is good just in case it is favored by God. But then look what happens: to say that God is good is just to say that God is favored by God. Is that really what we mean when we say that God is good?[1]

4 If the divine command theory were true, people would need to identify a reliable source of pronouncements about God's will (scriptures or some religious authority, for example). But there are many sources purporting to be the true one. How can believers discover which is the right one? Is it possible to choose in a nonarbitrary way?

The arbitrariness problem has led both theists and nontheists to reject the divine command theory and accept the second option of the dilemma, the view that morality is not dependent on God's will. Right and wrong must then exist independently of God and are binding on everyone, including God himself. In this way, the notion of God's goodness has real meaning, and the religious can coherently claim that God is good, that he unerringly observes the moral law, and that he urges his children to strive to do the same.

Some theists hold that even if God is not the source of the moral law, he provides the motivation to abide by it. The fear of God's disfavor in this life or everlasting torment in the next makes people want to be good. A desire for his blessings here and now or eternal bliss in the hereafter has the same effect. Thus, believers have reason to be moral, and unbelievers do not.

This contention can be viewed as an empirical claim about the psychological tendencies of theists and nontheists. If it's true, we would expect theists generally to be more moral than nontheists. But no evidence clearly substantiates this.

Many believers and nonbelievers think they have a deeper reason for rejecting the religious explanation of moral motivation. Suppose you do your best to always act morally—not because acting morally is your duty, but because you want to avoid God's wrath and incur his blessings. Your motives for being good then are self-serving and cynical, signs of poor moral character and disrespect for the moral law. People with good moral character do good for the sake of the good; they do their duty for duty's sake. Thus it seems that if the expectation of reward or punishment is what motivates people to act morally, moral character is undermined and morality itself becomes a hollow ideal.

WRITING TO UNDERSTAND:
CRITIQUING PHILOSOPHICAL VIEWS   Section 3.1

1. Where did your moral values come from? Did you arrive at them through critical reasoning—or did you absorb them from your family, peers, or culture?

2. Of the several moral theories mentioned in this chapter, which one are you most sympathetic to? Why?

3. How do you think a utilitarian would view the morality of human cloning (discussed in the accompanying box)? A divine command theorist?

4. Do you accept or reject the divine command theory? Why?

5. Is the hope for a heavenly reward a good reason to obey the moral law? Why or why not?

3.2 MORAL RELATIVISM

Without thinking much about it, most people accept a view of morality known as **moral objectivism**, the idea that at least some moral norms or principles are objectively valid or true for everyone. In this view, moral standards are valid or true regardless of whether people believe them, ignore them, agree about them, or have never heard of them. Just as some statements about physics or carpentry are objectively true regardless of people's beliefs on the subject, so some moral statements are objectively true no matter what people think. Moral objectivism, however, is distinct from **moral absolutism**, the belief that objective moral principles allow no exceptions or must be applied the same way in all cases and cultures. A moral objectivist can be absolutist about moral principles, or she can avoid absolutism by accepting that moral principles are *prima facie*—applicable unless exceptions are warranted (as when two principles conflict and one must be given more weight than the other). In any case, most people probably assume some form of moral objectivism and would not take seriously any claim implying that correct moral norms can be whatever we want them to be.

But some (including many college undergraduates) reject moral objectivism in favor of a doctrine that they find much more appealing: **moral relativism.** According to this view, moral standards are not objective, but are relative to what individuals or cultures believe. There simply are no objective moral truths, only relative ones. An action is morally right if endorsed by a person or culture and morally wrong if condemned by a person or culture. Morality is not an objective fact; it's a human invention, dependent entirely on what people believe. So an action is right for Person A if he approves of it but wrong for Person B if she disapproves of it, and the same would go for cultures with similarly diverging views. In this way, moral norms are not discovered but made; the individual or culture makes right and wrong. Moral relativism pertaining to individuals is known as **subjective relativism**, more precisely stated as the view that right actions are those sanctioned by a person. Moral relativism regarding cultures is called **cultural relativism**, the view that right actions are those sanctioned by one's culture.

Subjective Relativism

In some ways, subjective relativism is a comforting moral theory. It relieves individuals of the burden of serious critical reasoning about morality. After all, determining right and wrong is a matter of inventorying one's beliefs, and any sincerely held beliefs will do. Morality is essentially a matter of personal taste, which is an extremely easy thing to establish. Determining what one's moral views are may indeed involve deliberation and analysis—but neither of these is a necessary requirement for the job. Subjective relativism also helps people short-circuit the unpleasantness of moral debate. The subjective relativist's familiar refrain—"That may be *your* truth, but it's not *my* truth"—has a way of stopping conversations and putting an end to reasoned arguments.

Moral objectivism is the view that there are moral standards that are true or correct for everyone.

Moral absolutism is the belief that objective moral principles allow no exceptions or must be applied the same way in all cases and cultures.

What is morality in any given time or place? It is what the majority then and there happen to like, and immorality is what they dislike.
—Alfred North Whitehead

Moral relativism is the view that moral standards do not have independent status but are relative to what individuals or cultures believe.

Subjective relativism is the view that right actions are those endorsed by an individual.

Cultural relativism is the view that right actions are those endorsed by one's culture.

5 When you discuss moral issues with others, what moral theory do you assume—objectivism or relativism? Why?

There is nothing either good or bad, But thinking makes it so.
—William Shakespeare

6 Is moral disagreement possible? When you seem to be disagreeing with someone on a moral issue, what are you really doing? Are you disagreeing about an objective moral fact, or are you merely expressing your likes and dislikes?

But critics of the theory charge that in many ways it runs afoul of the moral criteria of adequacy, especially the one demanding consistency with the facts of the moral life. For starters, the doctrine implies that each person is morally infallible. An action is morally right for someone if he approves of it—if he sincerely believes it to be right. His approval makes the action right, and—if his approval is genuine—he cannot be mistaken. His believing it to be right makes it right, and that's the end of it. If he endorses infanticide as a method of population control, then infanticide is morally permissible. His sincere approval settles the issue, and he cannot be in error. But our commonsense moral experience suggests that this relativist account must be mistaken. Our judgments about moral matters—actions, principles, and people—are often wide of the mark. We are morally fallible, and we are rightly suspicious of anyone who claims to be otherwise.

There is a more disturbing way to frame this point. Suppose Hitler approved of killing millions of Jews during World War II. Suppose American serial killer and cannibal Jeffrey Dahmer approved of his murdering seventeen men and boys. Then by the lights of subjective relativism, all these mass killings were morally right because their perpetrators sincerely deemed them so. But we would find this conclusion almost impossible to swallow. We would think these actions morally wrong whether the killers approved of their own actions or not.

Figure 3.5 Subjective relativism implies that Hitler's slaughter of millions of Jews was morally right. Is this reason enough to reject the doctrine?

Subjective relativism also implies that all sincerely held moral opinions are created equal. If you sincerely approve of equal rights for women, and someone else sincerely disapproves, your view of the matter is as good or as true as his. If Jeffrey Dahmer honestly thought his vicious murders were morally justified, and you sincerely believe they were not, his view is no better or worse than yours. This equality of moral judgments seems incredible.

Something that seems an obvious fact of the moral life is that sometimes people have moral disagreements. But subjective relativism implies that moral disagreement is virtually impossible. Suppose a friend tells you that the terrorists who perpetrated the September 11 attacks on the United States were morally justified in doing so. And you respond that the terrorists were not morally justified. This would seem like an obvious example of two people having a disagreement about an important moral matter. But no disagreement at all is taking place, according to subjective relativism. You and your friend are merely expressing your approval and disapproval, your respective likes and dislikes. And because the two of you are just expressing your personal tastes, you are not really disagreeing on an issue—just as you would not be disagreeing if you said you like chocolate ice cream and your friend said she likes vanilla. The two of you are literally discussing different subjects. The notion that we can never have a moral disagreement with anyone is difficult to take seriously.

Cultural Relativism

These inconsistencies with the facts of the moral life raise serious doubts about subjective relativism. Many believe cultural relativism is a much more plausible view of morality. In fact, many think it obviously true, and they assume it without question. But the doctrine undermines itself in many of the same ways that subjective relativism does.

Like subjective relativism, cultural relativism implies moral infallibility, a very hard implication to take seriously. As the doctrine would have it, if a culture genuinely approves of an action, then there can be no question about the action's moral rightness: it is right, and that's that. Cultures make moral rightness, so they cannot be mistaken about it. But is it at all plausible that cultures cannot be wrong about morality? Throughout history, cultures have approved of ethnic cleansing, slavery, racism, holocausts, massacres, mass rape, torture of innocents, burning of heretics, and much more. Is it reasonable to conclude that the cultures that approved of such deeds could not have been mistaken? Is it plausible that such repugnant acts could become moral duties if a culture sees them as such?

Related to the infallibility problem is this difficulty: cultural relativism implies that we cannot legitimately criticize

7 Do you believe that your culture has made moral progress? Why or why not?

Figure 3.6 The fact that we no longer condone slavery seems like an obvious case of moral progress. But cultural relativism cannot countenance any progress in our moral views. Does this show that the doctrine is false?

WHAT DO YOU BELIEVE?

Cultural Relativism and Women's Rights

Debates about cultural relativism are not just academic exercises, for they have practical implications for women's rights throughout the world. Cultural relativists insist that cultures should be preserved, and that the moral values of specific cultures take precedence over universal human rights, including the rights of women. This means respecting the moral beliefs and practices of all cultures—even those that sanction abusive treatment of women. Critics find this view abhorrent because it, in effect, endorses such cultural practices as domestic

Figure 3.7 Are women's rights objective moral values?

> Custom is the law of fools.
> —Sir John Vanbrugh

other cultures. They are all beyond criticism. If a culture approves of its actions, then those actions are morally right—and it does not matter one bit whether another culture disapproves of them. Remember, there is no objective moral code to appeal to. Each society is its own maker of the moral law. It makes no sense for Society X to accuse Society Y of immorality, for what Society Y approves of *is* moral. Some may be willing to accept this consequence of cultural relativism, but look at what it would mean. What if the people of Germany approved of the extermination of millions of Jews, Gypsies, and others during World War II? Then the extermination was morally right. Suppose the people of Libya approved of the terrorist bombing of Pan Am Flight 103 over Lockerbie, Scotland, killing 270 people (a tragedy for which the Libyan government eventually took responsibility). Then the bombing was morally right, and those who placed the bomb on board did no wrong. But all this appears very much at odds with our moral experience. We think it makes perfect sense sometimes to condemn other cultures for morally wrong actions.

Cultural relativism also seems to rule out the possibility of moral progress. We sometimes compare our past moral beliefs with those of the present and judge our abuse, rape, polygamy, honor killings (the slaying of daughters and wives to restore honor to a family), and "female circumcision" (female genital cutting, the removal of all or part of the female genitals). They condemn these customs on the grounds that they violate universal, objective moral principles. For example, rights activist and commentator Maryam Namazie vigorously denounces the relativist doctrine:

> Let us be clear about what cultural relativism is. It is a profoundly racist phenomenon, which values and respects all cultural and religious practices, irrespective of their consequences for women. It asserts that the rights of people, women and girls are relative to where they are born, "their" cultures and religions. There is no right or wrong according to cultural relativists. As a result, cultural relativism supports and maintains sexual apartheid and violence against women in Islam-stricken societies like Iran because it is "their culture and religion" and it creates ghettoized, regressive "minority" communities in the West where women and girls continue to face apartheid and Islamic laws and customs.—From a speech at a panel discussion organized by the Action Committee on Women's Rights in Iran and Amnesty International's Women's Action Network, August 14, 2001

Are there universal human rights, including women's rights? Is it important to preserve cultural values, including those that are abhorrent to most people in the West? Do you agree with Namazie? Why or why not?

views to be morally better than they used to be. We no longer countenance such horrors as massacres of native peoples, slavery, lynchings, racial discrimination, sexism, and wanton destruction of the environment, and we think these changes are signs of moral progress. But cultural relativism implies that there can be no such thing. To legitimately claim that there has been moral progress, there must be an objective, transcultural standard for comparing cultures of the past and present. But according to cultural relativism, there are no objective moral standards, just norms relative to each culture. If over time a culture goes from condoning racial discrimination to condemning it, that does not represent moral progress. That is just a change from one set of moral attitudes to another, each one just as plausible as the other. The two are different, but one is not superior to the other. On the other hand, if there is such a thing as moral progress, then there must be objective moral standards.

Another problem for cultural relativism is that it has a difficult time explaining the moral status of social reformers. We tend to believe they are at least sometimes right and society is wrong. When we contemplate social reform, we think of such moral exemplars as Martin Luther King, Jr., Mahatma Gandhi, and Susan B. Anthony, all of whom agitated for justice and moral progress. But one of the consequences of cultural relativism is that social reformers can *never* be morally right. By definition, what society judges to be morally right is morally right, and since social reformers disagree with society, they cannot be right—ever. But surely on occasion it's the reformers who are right and society that is wrong.

Despite its serious difficulties, cultural relativism is an attractive moral theory to many, partly because it seems well supported by a common argument. The argument goes like this:

1. If people's moral judgments differ from culture to culture, moral standards are relative to culture (there are no objective moral standards).
2. People's moral judgments do differ from culture to culture.
3. Therefore, moral standards are relative to culture (there are no objective moral standards).

The argument is valid (the conclusion follows logically from the premises), but are the premises true? Look first at Premise 2. All sorts of empirical evidence—including a trove of anthropological and sociological data—show that the premise is in fact true. Clearly, the moral beliefs of people from diverse cultures often do differ drastically on the same moral issue. Some societies condone infanticide; others condemn it. Some approve of the killing of wives and daughters to protect a family's honor; others think this tradition evil. Some bury their dead; others cremate them. Some consider it a solemn duty to surgically remove the clitorises of young girls; others say this is immoral and cruel. Some commend the killing of people who practice a different religion; others believe such intolerance is morally reprehensible. We are forced to conclude that diversity of moral judgments among cultures is a reality.

But what of Premise 1—is it also true? It says that because cultures have different moral beliefs, they must also have different moral standards, which means morality is relative to cultures. This premise, however, is false. First, from the fact that cultures have divergent moral beliefs on an issue, it does not logically follow that there is no objective moral truth to be sought, that there is no opinion that is objectively correct. People may disagree about the existence of biological life on Mars, but the disagreement does not demonstrate that there is no fact of the matter, or that no statement on the subject could be objectively true. Disagreements on a moral question may simply indicate that there is an objective fact of the matter but that someone (or everyone) is wrong about it.

Second, a conflict between moral beliefs does not necessarily indicate a fundamental conflict between basic moral norms. Moral disagreements between cultures can arise not just because their basic moral principles clash, but because they have differing nonmoral beliefs that put those principles in very different lights. From the annals of anthropology, for example, we have the classic story of a culture that sanctions the killing of parents when they become elderly but not yet enfeebled. Our society would condemn such a practice, no doubt appealing to moral precepts urging respect for parents and for human life. But consider: This strange (to us) culture believes that people enter heaven when they die and spend eternity in the same physical condition they were in when they passed away. Those who kill their parents are doing so because they do not want their elders to spend eternity in a state of senility, but rather in good health. This culture's way is not our way; we are unlikely to share these people's nonmoral beliefs. But it is probable that they embrace the same moral principles of respect for parents and life that we do. According to some anthropologists, diverse cultures often share basic moral standards while seeming to have little or nothing in common. Thus the argument for cultural relativism founders because its key premise is false.

Many cultural relativists may not be bothered too much by the failure of this argument and by the doctrine's troubling implications mentioned earlier. That's because they think that cultural relativism strongly supports their belief in the important virtue of tolerance toward other cultures, and that moral objectivism does not. The idea is that if the values of one culture are no better or worse than those of another, then there is no basis for hatred or hostility toward any culture anywhere.

Tolerance is, of course, both morally praiseworthy and beneficial to our fractured planet of conflicting values. But cultural relativism has no advantage over moral objectivism in promoting tolerance—and may have a critical disadvantage.

First, note that moral objectivism does not entail intolerance. It says only that some moral beliefs are better than others; it does not imply anything about how objectivists should behave toward those they think are in moral error. Some objectivists are intolerant; many are not. But cultural relativism can easily justify intolerance and cannot consistently advocate tolerance. If there are intolerant cultures (and there surely are), then since cultures make rightness, intolerance in those cultures is morally right. For sincerely intolerant societies, the persecution of minorities and the killing of dissidents may be the height of moral rectitude. In addition, cultural relativists who insist that everyone should embrace tolerance are contradicting themselves. To say that tolerant behavior is right for everyone is to assert an objective moral norm—but cultural relativism says there are no objective moral norms. The moral objectivist, however, can plausibly claim that the moral requirement of tolerance is universal.

> Morality is largely a matter of geography.
> —Elbert Hubbard

WRITING TO UNDERSTAND:
CRITIQUING PHILOSOPHICAL VIEWS   Section 3.2

1. What is the difference between moral objectivism and moral relativism? Which view makes the most sense to you? Why?

2. Think about an argument that you have made on a moral issue. From which perspective were you arguing—moral objectivism, moral relativism, or some other theory? Why?

3. How is disagreement a problem for moral relativism? Is the problem fatal to the theory? Why or why not?

4. How would you judge the morality of the September 11 terrorist attacks on the United States—as a moral objectivist or a moral relativist? Why?

5. Is the oppression of women objectively wrong? Give reasons for your answer.

3.3 MORALITY BASED ON CONSEQUENCES

In deontological theories, the rightness or wrongness of an action is based on its nature, not on the consequences that follow from it. But consequentialist theories say the effects of an action are all that matter; our only duty is to ensure that the effects are a maximization of the good. The good is whatever has intrinsic value—whatever is valuable for its own sake—which can include such things as pleasure, happiness, virtue, knowledge, autonomy, and the satisfaction of desires. In consequentialist ethics, then, the ends (the results) justify the means (the actions).

For utilitarianism, the foremost consequentialist theory, the only thing of intrinsic value is well-being. For ethical egoism, it's self-interest. In either case, the rightness or wrongness of an action is to be judged by its impact on the people involved.

Utilitarianism

Utilitarians judge the morality of conduct by a single standard, the *principle of utility*: Right actions are those that result in greater overall well-being (or *utility*) for the people involved than any other possible actions. We are duty bound to maximize the utility of everyone affected, regardless of the contrary urgings of moral rules or unbending moral principles. In some moral theories, moral rules are absolute, allowing no exceptions even in exceptional cases. But in utilitarianism, there are no absolute prohibitions or mandates (except for the principle of utility itself). There is only the goal of maximizing well-being. Thus, utilitarianism is not bothered by unusual circumstances, nor is it hobbled by conflicting moral principles or rules that demand a uniform response to extraordinary situations.

In applying the utilitarian moral standard, some moral philosophers concentrate on specific acts and some on rules covering kinds of acts. The former approach is called **act-utilitarianism**, the idea that the rightness of actions depends solely on the overall well-being produced by *individual actions*. An act is right if in a particular situation it produces a greater balance of well-being over suffering than any alternative acts; determining rightness is a matter of weighing the effects of each possible act. The latter approach, known as **rule-utilitarianism**, avoids judging rightness by specific acts and focuses instead on *rules governing categories of acts*. It says a right action is one that conforms to a rule that, if followed consistently, would create for everyone involved the most beneficial balance of well-being over suffering. We are to adhere to the rules because, in the long run, they maximize well-being for everyone considered—even though a given act may produce bad effects in a particular situation.

Consider how these two forms of utilitarianism could apply to the moral issue of euthanasia, or mercy killing, the taking of someone's life for his or her own sake. Suppose a woman is terminally ill and is suffering horrible, inescapable pain, and she asks to be put out of her misery. An act-utilitarian might conclude that euthanasia would be the right course of action because it would result in the least amount of suffering for everyone concerned. Allowing the current situation to continue would cause enormous pain and anguish—the woman's own physical agony, the misery of

Act-utilitarianism is the idea that the rightness of actions depends solely on the overall well-being produced by *individual actions.*

Rule-utilitarianism is the doctrine that a right action is one that conforms to a rule that, if followed consistently, would create for everyone involved the most beneficial balance of well-being over suffering.

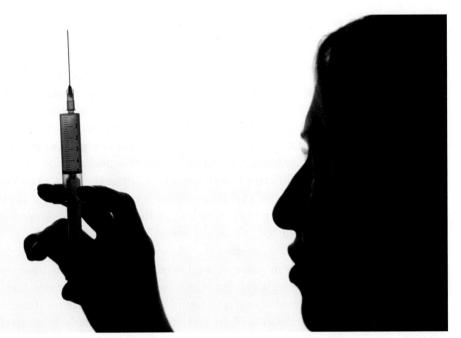

Figure 3.8 Should the morality of euthanasia depend on the act's consequences?

her distraught family, and the distress and frustration of the physician and nurses who can do little more than stand by as she withers away. Administering a lethal injection to her, however, would immediately end her pain and prevent future suffering. Her family would grieve for her but would at least find some relief—and perhaps peace—in knowing that her torture was over. The medical staff would probably also be relieved for the same reason. There would, of course, also be possible negative consequences to take into account. In administering the lethal injection, her physician would be risking both professional censure and criminal prosecution. If his actions were to become known publicly, people might begin to mistrust physicians who treat severely impaired children, undermining the whole medical profession. Perhaps the physician's action would lead to a general devaluing of the lives of disabled or elderly people everywhere. These dire consequences, however, would probably not be very likely if the physician acted discreetly. On balance, the act-utilitarian might say, greater net well-being (positive amounts of well-being minus negative influences on well-being) would result from the mercy killing, which would therefore be the morally right course. On the other hand, a rule-utilitarian might insist that more net well-being would be produced by consistently following a rule that disallowed euthanasia. The argument would be that permitting mercy killings would have terrible consequences overall—increases in involuntary euthanasia (mercy killing without the patient's consent), erosion of respect for the medical profession, and a weakening of society's abhorrence of homicide.

Notice that in either kind of utilitarianism, getting direct answers to a difficult moral problem is straightforward. The facts of the case may be difficult to ascertain, but the procedure for discerning the morally right course of action is theoretically

8 How might a deontological theorist judge a case of euthanasia? Do you think this approach is better than the utilitarian's? Why or why not?

9 Which view of the nature of happiness seems more plausible to you—Bentham's or Mill's?

simple: determine which action best maximizes well-being. Such simplicity makes utilitarianism an appealing theory, especially when compared to others that require the use of abstract principles or elusive moral concepts.

The classic version of utilitarianism was devised by English philosopher Jeremy Bentham (1748–1832) and given more detail and plausibility by another English philosopher, John Stuart Mill (1806–1873). Classic utilitarianism is hedonistic in that the utility to be maximized is pleasure, broadly termed happiness, the only intrinsic good. A right action produces more net happiness (amounts of happiness minus unhappiness) than any alternative action, everyone considered.

Bentham and Mill have different ideas about what happiness entails, as do many philosophers today. Bentham thinks that happiness is one-dimensional: it is pleasure, pure and simple, something that varies only in the amount that an agent can experience. In this scheme, it seems that the moral ideal would be to experience maximum amounts of pleasure, as does the glutton or the debauchee. But Mill thinks that pleasures can vary in quality as well as quantity. For him, there are lower and higher pleasures—the lower and inferior ones indulged in by the glutton and his ilk and the higher and more satisfying ones found in such experiences as the search for knowledge and the appreciation of art and music. Mill famously sums up this contrast by saying, "It is better to be a human being dissatisfied than a pig satisfied; better to be Socrates dissatisfied than a fool satisfied." [2]

Like all forms of utilitarianism, the classic formulation demands a strong sense of impartiality. When promoting happiness, we must not only take into account the happiness of everyone affected, but also give everyone's needs or interests equal weight. Mill explains:

> [The] happiness which forms the utilitarian standard of what is right conduct, is not the agent's own happiness, but that of all concerned. As between his own happiness and that of others, utilitarianism requires him to be as strictly impartial as a disinterested and benevolent spectator. [3]

This moral evenhandedness is an attractive feature of utilitarianism. As we have seen, impartiality is a fundamental characteristic of morality itself. Despite our differences in social status, race, gender, religion, and wealth, we are all equal before the moral law. Early utilitarians such as Bentham and Mill took moral equality seriously, crusading for social changes that were shockingly radical for the times: the abolition of slavery, humane treatment of prisoners, and women's rights.

In classic utilitarianism, the emphasis is on maximizing the total quantity of net happiness, not ensuring that it is rationed in any particular amounts among the people involved. This means that an action resulting in one thousand units of happiness for ten people is better than an action yielding only nine hundred units of happiness for those same ten people—regardless of how the units of happiness are distributed among them. Classic utilitarians do want to allocate the total amount of happiness among as many people as possible (thus their motto, "the greatest happiness for the greatest number"). But maximizing total happiness is the fundamental concern, whether everyone gets an equal portion or one person gets the lion's share.

This is how Mill defends his brand of utilitarianism:

John Stuart Mill, "What Utilitarianism Is"

. . . The creed which accepts as the foundation of morals, Utility, or the Greatest Happiness Principle, holds that actions are right in proportion as they tend to promote happiness, wrong as they tend to produce the reverse of happiness. By happiness is intended pleasure, and the absence of pain; by unhappiness, pain, and the privation of pleasure. To give a clear view of the moral standard set up by the theory, much more requires to be said; in particular, what things it includes in the ideas of pain and pleasure; and to what extent this is left an open question. But these supplementary explanations do not affect the theory of life on which this theory of morality is grounded—namely, that pleasure, and freedom from pain, are the only things desirable as ends; and that all desirable things (which are as numerous in the utilitarian as in any other scheme) are desirable either for the pleasure inherent in themselves, or as a means to the promotion of pleasure and the prevention of pain.

Now, such a theory of life excites in many minds, and among them in some of the most estimable in feeling and purpose, inveterate dislike. To suppose that life has (as they express it) no higher end than pleasure—no better and nobler object of desire and pursuit—they designate as utterly mean and groveling; as a doctrine worthy only of swine, to whom the followers of Epicurus were, at a very early period, contemptuously likened; and modern holders of the doctrine are occasionally made the subject of equally polite comparisons by its German, French, and English assailants.

When thus attacked, the Epicureans have always answered, that it is not they, but their accusers, who represent human nature in a degrading light; since the accusation supposes human beings to be capable of no pleasures except those of which swine are capable. If this supposition were true, the charge could not be gainsaid, but would then be no longer an imputation; for if the sources of pleasure were precisely the same to human beings and to swine, the rule of life which is good enough for the one would be good enough for the other. The comparison of the Epicurean life to that of beasts is felt as degrading, precisely because a beast's pleasures do not satisfy a human being's conception of happiness. Human beings have faculties more elevated than the animal appetites, and when once made conscious of them, do not regard anything as happiness which does not include their gratification. I do not, indeed, consider the Epicureans to have been by any means faultless in drawing out their scheme of consequences from the utilitarian principle. To do this in any sufficient manner, many Stoic, as well as Christian elements require to be included. But there is no known Epicurean theory of life which does not assign to the pleasures of the intellect, of the feelings and imagination, and of the moral sentiments, a much higher value as pleasures than to those of mere sensation. It must be admitted, however, that utilitarian writers in general have placed the superiority of mental over bodily pleasures chiefly in the greater permanency, safety, uncostliness, etc., of the former—that is, in their circumstantial advantages rather than in their intrinsic nature. And on all these points utilitarians have fully proved their case; but they might have taken the other, and, as it may be called, higher ground, with entire consistency. It is quite compatible with the principle of utility to recognise the fact, that some *kinds* of pleasure are more desirable and more valuable

PHILOSOPHY NOW

Utilitarianism and the Death Penalty

Utilitarianism is alive and well in contemporary debates about personal morality, institutional policy, and government programs. It plays an especially big role in arguments over capital punishment—officially sanctioned punishment by death for very grievous (capital) crimes. On one side of this dispute are the *abolitionists*, those who want to do away with capital punishment, who believe the death penalty is never justified. On the other side are the *retentionists*, those who want to retain the death penalty as part of a system of legal punishment, who believe that sometimes capital punishment is warranted. Both camps in the debate argue their cases on utilitarian grounds (as well as on the basis of deontological principles).

Many retentionists take the utilitarian path by arguing that the death penalty has positive effects on society—specifically, that it either *prevents* criminals from harming others again or *deters* would-be offenders from capital crimes. Executing hardened murderers, say retentionists, is the best way to prevent them from killing other inmates or escaping and killing innocent people. Abolitionists respond that life in prison without parole (and with appropriate security measures) is as effective as execution in preventing inmates from repeating their crimes. To make their arguments stick, both sides in this dispute have to support their nonmoral claims with empirical evidence, but definitive evidence for the effectiveness of the two prevention strategies is hard to come by. Each side can challenge the other to produce evidence to back their assertions.

Figure 3.9 In debates on capital punishment, which matters most: utility or rights?

John Stuart Mill, "What Utilitarianism Is"

than others. It would be absurd that while, in estimating all other things, quality is considered as well as quantity, the estimation of pleasures should be supposed to depend on quantity alone.

If I am asked, what I mean by difference of quality in pleasures, or what makes one pleasure more valuable than another, merely as a pleasure, except its being greater in amount, there is but one possible answer. Of two pleasures, if there be one which all or almost all who have experience of both give a decided preference, irrespective of any feeling of moral obligation to prefer it, that is the more desirable pleasure.

Retentionists often maintain that the most powerful deterrent against murders is the threat of the ultimate punishment, death. Several sociological studies seem to support this claim, but they have been the subject of a good deal of critical scrutiny and debate, a fact that abolitionists are quick to point out. Some retentionists argue that common sense tells us that the death penalty is a better deterrent than life in prison. It seems obvious, they say, that the more severe the punishment, the more it deters potential offenders. Abolitionists reply that there are reasons to think the commonsense view is mistaken.

Some retentionists take the deontological path through *retributivism*, the doctrine that people should be punished simply because they deserve it, and that the punishment should be proportional to the crime. Many abolitionists reject the retributivist theory of punishment and thus reject the retentionist argument that it supports. But some of them accept it, arguing that although offenders should get the punishment they deserve, no one deserves the death penalty.

Like retentionists, abolitionists also try to make their case on utilitarian grounds. They may contend that life in prison for murderers results in greater overall happiness or goodness for society than sentencing them to death. For one thing, if human life has great value, then preserving it by forgoing the death penalty must maximize the good. Abolitionists also insist that the death penalty brings with it some drawbacks that life sentences avoid. They may assert that the monetary costs involved in capital punishment exceed the costs of life sentences without parole, that the chances of unintentionally executing the innocent are great, or that the execution of offenders may actually provoke murders or have an overall dehumanizing effect on society. Retentionists may dispute these claims by questioning the evidence for them, or they may take a retributivist line by arguing that the consequences are beside the point.

Do you accept or reject the use of the death penalty? What are your grounds for doing so? Are your grounds utilitarian, deontological, or both?

If one of the two is, by those who are competently acquainted with both, placed so far above the other that they prefer it, even though knowing it to be attended with a great amount of discontent, and would not resign it for any quantity of the other pleasure which their nature is capable of, we are justified in ascribing to the preferred enjoyment a superiority in quality, so far outweighing quantity as to render it, in comparison, of small account.

Now it is an unquestionable fact that those who are equally acquainted with, and equally capable of appreciating and enjoying, both, do give a most marked preference

John Stuart Mill,
"What Utilitarianism Is"

10 Is the utilitarian view of morality based on the promotion of happiness demeaning? Is there more to life than the pursuit of happiness (as Mill defines it)?

to the manner of existence which employs their higher faculties. Few human creatures would consent to be changed into any of the lower animals, for a promise of the fullest allowance of a beast's pleasures; no intelligent human being would consent to be a fool, no instructed person would be an ignoramus, no person of feeling and conscience would be selfish and base, even though they should be persuaded that the fool, the dunce, or the rascal is better satisfied with his lot than they are with theirs. They would not resign what they possess more than he for the most complete satisfaction of all the desires which they have in common with him. If they ever fancy they would, it is only in cases of unhappiness so extreme, that to escape from it they would exchange their lot for almost any other, however undesirable in their own eyes. A being of higher faculties requires more to make him happy, is capable probably of more acute suffering, and certainly accessible to it at more points, than one of an inferior type; but in spite of these liabilities, he can never really wish to sink into what he feels to be a lower grade of existence. We may give what explanation we please of this unwillingness; we may attribute it to pride, a name which is given indiscriminately to some of the most and to some of the least estimable feelings of which mankind are capable; we may refer it to the love of liberty and personal independence, an appeal to which was with the Stoics one of the most effective means for the inculcation of it; to the love of power, or to the love of excitement, both of which do really enter into and contribute to it: but its most appropriate appellation is a sense of dignity, which all human beings possess in one form or another, and in some, though by no means in exact, proportion to their higher faculties, and which is so essential a part of the happiness of those in whom it is strong, that nothing which conflicts with it could be, otherwise than momentarily, an object of desire to them. Whoever supposes that this preference takes place at a sacrifice of happiness—that the superior being, in anything like equal circumstances, is not happier than the inferior—confounds the two very different ideas, of happiness, and content. It is indisputable that the being whose capacities of enjoyment are low, has the greatest chance of having them fully satisfied; and a highly endowed being will always feel that any happiness which he can look for, as the world is constituted, is imperfect. But he can learn to bear its imperfections, if they are at all bearable; and they will not make him envy the being who is indeed unconscious of the imperfections, but only because he feels not at all the good which those imperfections qualify. It is better to be a human being dissatisfied than a pig satisfied; better to be Socrates dissatisfied than a fool satisfied. And if the fool, or the pig, are of a different opinion, it is because they only know their own side of the question. The other party to the comparison knows both sides. . . .

From this verdict of the only competent judges, I apprehend there can be no appeal. On a question which is the best worth having of two pleasures, or which of two modes of existence is the most grateful to the feelings, apart from its moral attributes and from its consequences, the judgment of those who are qualified by knowledge of both, or, if they differ, that of the majority among them, must be admitted as final. And there needs to be the less hesitation to accept this judgment respecting the quality of pleasures, since there is no other tribunal to be referred to even on the question of quantity. What means are there of determining which is the acutest of two pains, or the intensest of two pleasurable sensations, except the general suffrage of those who are familiar with both? Neither pains nor pleasures are homogeneous, and pain is always heterogeneous with pleasure. What is there to decide whether a particular pleasure is worth purchasing at the cost of a particular pain, except the feelings and judgment of the experienced? When, therefore, those feelings and judgment declare the pleasures derived from the higher faculties to be preferable in *kind*, apart from the question of intensity, to those of which the animal nature, disjoined from the higher faculties, is susceptible, they are entitled on this subject to the same regard.

I have dwelt on this point, as being a necessary part of a perfectly just conception of Utility or Happiness, considered as the directive rule of human conduct. But it is by no means an indispensable condition to the acceptance of the utilitarian standard; for that standard is not the agent's own greatest happiness, but the greatest amount of happiness altogether; and if it may possibly be doubted whether a noble character is always the happier for its nobleness, there can be no doubt that it makes other people happier, and that the world in general is immensely a gainer by it. Utilitarianism, therefore, could only attain its end by the general cultivation of nobleness of character, even if each individual were only benefited by the nobleness of others, and his own, so far as happiness is concerned, were a sheer deduction from the benefit. But the bare enunciation of such an absurdity as this last, renders refutation superfluous.

According to the Greatest Happiness Principle, as above explained, the ultimate end, with reference to and for the sake of which all other things are desirable (whether we are considering our own good or that of other people), is an existence exempt as far as possible from pain, and as rich as possible in enjoyments, both in point of quantity and quality; the test of quality, and the rule for measuring it against quantity, being the preference felt by those who in their opportunities of experience, to which must be added their habits of self-consciousness and self-observation, are best furnished with the means of comparison. This, being, according to the utilitarian opinion, the end of human action, is necessarily also the standard of morality; which may accordingly be defined, the rules and precepts for human conduct, by the observance of which an existence such as has been described might be, to the greatest extent possible, secured to all mankind; and not to them only, but, so far as the nature of things admits, to the whole sentient creation. . . .

We have now, then, an answer to the question, of what sort of proof the principle of utility is susceptible. If the opinion which I have now stated is psychologically true—if human nature is so constituted as to desire nothing which is not either a part of happiness or a means of happiness, we can have no other proof, and we require no other, that these are the only things desirable. If so, happiness is the sole end of human action, and the promotion of it the test by which to judge of all human conduct; from whence it necessarily follows that it must be the criterion of morality, since a part is included in the whole.

And now to decide whether this is really so; whether mankind does desire nothing for itself but that which is a pleasure to them, or of which the absence is a pain; we have evidently arrived at a question of fact and experience, dependent, like all similar questions, upon evidence. It can only be determined by practised self-consciousness and self-observation, assisted by observation of others. I believe that these sources of evidence, impartially consulted, will declare that desiring a thing and finding it pleasant, aversion to it and thinking of it as painful, are phenomena entirely inseparable, or rather two parts of the same phenomenon; in strictness of language, two different modes of naming the same psychological fact: that to think of an object as desirable (unless for the sake of its consequences), and to think of it as pleasant, are one and the same thing; and that to desire anything, except in proportion as the idea of it is pleasant, is a physical and metaphysical possibility.[4]

11 Does the fact that people desire happiness prove that it should be desired, that achieving it should be the ultimate goal of the moral life?

So there is much to like about utilitarianism. Its simplicity, its straightforward application to moral problems, and its insistence on moral impartiality have helped to make it one of the most influential moral theories in modern history. Still, it has drawn many criticisms, the most serious one being that the theory flies in the face of our considered moral judgments, especially regarding issues of duty, rights, and justice.

Suppose you promise a friend that you will help her prepare for a big exam. You know the subject inside and out, but she constantly struggles with it. At the last minute, you decide that you would rather stay home and watch a movie. You calculate that the satisfaction you get from watching the movie outweighs whatever dissatisfaction your friend feels because you broke your promise. By utilitarian lights, you should stay home and watch the movie, for your only obligation is to maximize utility. But this view of the matter seems mistaken. When we make a promise, we impose a duty on ourselves, and such duties seem to carry weight in our moral deliberations that is independent of considerations of utility. Sometimes, when a large measure of well-being hangs in the balance, breaking a promise or forsaking some other duty seems justified. But our considered judgments suggest that duties cannot be automatically overridden by calculations of utility.

Now consider the case of a man arrested for murder who is in fact innocent of the crime. Angry citizens demand that he be lynched immediately, and they threaten riots and reprisal killings against the man's family. The local police chief knows that by lynching the man, the overall happiness of the people would be increased far more than if the man got a fair trial—the mob would be satisfied, lives would be

> Happiness is a pig's philosophy.
> —Friedrich Nietzsche

PHILOSOPHY LAB

Imagine that the great ocean liner *Titanic* has sunk after smashing into an iceberg in the cold North Atlantic. You are a member of the crew, now commanding a lifeboat filled to capacity with thirty of the ship's passengers. You know that the boat is overloaded with one passenger too many, and that unless one passenger leaves the boat, it will sink within an hour, killing all aboard. To leave the boat is to die within twenty minutes. To push someone into the water is to kill her. No passenger will get out of the boat voluntarily, not the good pastor, the elderly women, the teenage girls, the gambler, the alcoholic, or the thief. So you must make some decisions: Do you throw one person overboard? Do you refuse to commit such an act and thus allow everyone to die? And if you do decide to toss a person into the sea, who will you choose? One of the social outcasts? An elderly person who has already lived a full life? Any random passenger?

This scenario is fiction, but it is based on an actual event. In both cases, the questions are: What is the morally right action? and How do you justify it?

saved, and property would be spared destruction. So the chief lets the town string the man up. Does the chief do right? The utilitarian seems obliged to say yes. But our considered judgment would likely be that the chief did wrong by violating the man's rights and perpetrating an injustice. According to utilitarianism's critics, this shows that the theory is inadequate. The requirements of justice and individual rights must be taken into account; utility is not the only thing that matters.

Some utilitarians have replied to such criticisms by saying that scenarios like the one just presented are unrealistic and misleading. In the real world, they say, actions that seem to conflict with our moral intuitions almost always produce such bad consequences that the actions cannot be justified even on utilitarian grounds. Once *all* the possible consequences are taken into account, it becomes clear that the proposed actions do not maximize happiness, and that commonsense morality and utilitarianism coincide.

Critics reply that many times the judgments of commonsense morality and utilitarianism do in fact coincide when all the facts are known—but not always. They insist that even the utilitarian must admit that there could be cases in which actions that maximize utility do clash with our considered moral judgments, and this possibility raises doubts about the utilitarian standard.

Ethical Egoism

Ethical egoism, though consequentialist, is a conceptual mile away from utilitarianism. The utilitarian says we have a duty to maximize the well-being of everyone within our reach, and that we must treat everyone (including ourselves) impartially and with equal regard. Ethical egoism says that you have a moral obligation to maximize the well-being of just one person—yourself—and that you act morally only when you play favorites and give special treatment to number one. Whether you help or harm others, cooperate with them or oppose them, you must always do what produces the most favorable consequences for *you*. Doing what is in your own best interest is the essence of the moral life.

Ethical egoists have argued that the theory is on solid ground because it reflects what they believe is an obvious psychological fact about human nature: *people always act out of self-interest.* Altruism—the unselfish concern for the well-being of others—is never a motive for action. This claim about human motives is an empirical theory called **psychological egoism**. It is the starting point for the ethical egoist's main argument, which says that (1) we are obligated to act only if we *can* act; (2) we can act only when motivated by self-interest; (3) therefore, we are obligated to act only when motivated by self-interest. The argument is based on a simple fact about the moral life: We are not morally obligated to do the impossible. We have no duty to make our loved ones live two hundred years, because that is beyond our power. We have no obligation to ensure that everyone is healthy, because that feat is not possible. Likewise, we are not capable of acting altruistically, so we have no obligation to do so. We are duty bound to do only what we can do—which is to act purely out of self-interest.

Critics have rebutted this argument by rejecting psychological egoism (Premise 2). They point out that our experience suggests that we don't always act out of self-interest. We often look out for number one, but we also sometimes choose to

12 Is breaking the promise really wrong in this case? What would you do? Why?

The despotism of custom is everywhere the standing hindrance to human advancement.
—John Stuart Mill

Human history is the sad result of each one looking out for himself.
—Julio Cortazar

Psychological egoism is the theory that people always act out of self-interest.

13 Do people always act out of self-interest? Do *you* always act out of self-interest?

PHILOSOPHERS AT WORK

John Stuart Mill

John Stuart Mill (1806–1873) was one of the most influential minds of the nineteenth century. He was both an empiricist philosopher and a social reformer, dedicated to seeing that his liberal and utilitarian ideals were used for the betterment of society. He was born in London and given a rigorous education by his father, James Mill, a philosopher in his own right.

Figure 3.10 John Stuart Mill, philosopher, ethicist, and reformer.

James was a strong proponent of Jeremy Bentham's utilitarianism, and he was determined to raise John Stuart according to utilitarian principles. John Stuart turned out to be an extremely precocious and bright student, beginning the study of Greek at age three and Plato and Latin at eight. In his teens, he dutifully absorbed his father's philosophical and political views, worked for the East India Company, and went abroad to learn French and study chemistry and mathematics.

At age twenty, his life took an unexpected turn. He suffered a mental breakdown and fell into a dark depression, a condition that he later said was due to his strict upbringing and exacting education. After a few months, he recovered, having gained a new perspective on his life and his previous way of thinking. He remained a utilitarian, but he left behind many of the less desirable features of Bentham's theory. He developed a deep friendship with the feminist Mrs. Harriet Taylor, whom he married years later, after her husband died. She had a profound effect on his view of the world and was a major influence on the ideas he expressed in *The Subjection of Women* (1869).

Mill went on to earn a prestigious place in the pantheon of respected philosophers for his work in epistemology (the study of knowledge), deductive and inductive logic, political thought, and ethics. Among other works, he wrote *System of Logic* (1843), *On Liberty* (1860), and *Utilitarianism* (1861).

Mill is notable not only for his theory of ethics, but for his efforts to see it put into practice. He thus became one of the greatest social reformers of his day, advocating individual liberty, freedom of expression, social tolerance, aid to the poor, and women's rights.

inconvenience ourselves, incur serious disadvantages, or put ourselves at risk—to help someone else. People rush into burning buildings to save complete strangers. Mothers starve themselves so their children will have food. Husbands and wives sell everything they own to pay for their spouse's urgent medical care.

Ethical egoists are likely to respond to this line by declaring that such experiences are deceptive, for actions that seem purely altruistic are in fact done to achieve social advantage, to feel personal satisfaction, or to prevent some future calamity.

3.4 MORALITY BASED ON DUTY AND RIGHTS

The moral theory of Immanuel Kant is profoundly opposed to consequentialism on numerous counts. Utilitarians insist that the morality of an action depends entirely on its effects—whether it maximizes human well-being. No action whatsoever is *inherently* right or wrong; only its costs and benefits make it so. Kant will have none of this. He maintains that right actions do not depend on their consequences, the production of happiness, people's aims, or their desires and feelings. Right actions are those that are right *in themselves* because they are consistent with universal moral rules derived from reason, and the actions have moral worth only if we do them out of a sense of duty, simply because *they are our duty.* For Kant, the moral law cannot be something contingent, changeable, or relative. The moral law is absolute, unchangeable, and universal, a rock-solid structure built on eternal reason.

Here is Kant on the subject:

> Two things fill the mind with ever new and increasing admiration and awe: the starry heavens above and the moral law within.
> —Immanuel Kant

Immanuel Kant, *Groundwork of the Metaphysic of Morals*

As my concern here is with moral philosophy, I limit the question suggested to this: Whether it is not of the utmost necessity to construct a pure moral philosophy, perfectly cleared of everything which is only empirical, and which belongs to anthropology? For that such a philosophy must be possible is evident from the common idea of duty and of the moral laws. Everyone must admit that if a law is to have moral force, *i.e.,* to be the basis of an obligation, it must carry with it absolute necessity; that, for example, the precept, "Thou shall not lie," is not valid for men alone, as if other rational beings had no need to observe it; and so with all the other moral laws properly so called; that, therefore, the basis of obligation must not be sought in the nature of man, or in the circumstances in the world in which he is placed, but *a priori* simply in the conception of pure reason; and although any other precept which is founded on principles of mere experience may be in certain respects universal, yet in as far as it rests even in the least degree on an empirical basis, perhaps only as to a motive, such a precept, while it may be a practical rule, can never be called a moral law. . . .

15 What does Kant mean by his assertion that morality cannot have an empirical basis? Is he right about this?

   Nothing can possibly be conceived in the world, or even out of it, which can be called good, without qualification, except a Good Will. Intelligence, wit, judgment, and the other *talents* of the mind, however they may be named, or courage, resolution, perseverance, as qualities of temperament, are undoubtedly good and desirable in many respects; but these gifts of nature may also become extremely bad and mischievous if the will which is to make use of them, and which, therefore, constitutes what is called *character*, is not good. It is the same with the *gifts of fortune.* Power, riches, honour, even health, and the general well-being and contentment with one's conditions which is called *happiness*, inspire pride, and, often presumption, if there is not a good will to correct the influence of these on the mind, and with this also to rectify the whole principle of acting, and adapt it to its end. The sight of a being who is not adorned with a single feature of a pure and good will, enjoying unbroken prosperity, can never give pleasure to an impartial rational spectator. Thus a good will appears to constitute the indispensable condition even of being worthy of happiness.

16 What is Kant's argument for his view that nothing can be good without qualification except a good will? Is his argument sound?

All that any of us has to do in this world is his simple duty.

—H. C. Trumbull

The **categorical imperative** is Kant's fundamental moral principle, which he formulates as (1) "I am never to act otherwise than so *that I could also will that my maxim should become a universal law*," and (2) "So act as to treat humanity, whether in thine own person or in that of any other, in every case as an end withal, never as a means only."

Do not do unto others as you would they should do unto you. Their tastes may not be the same.

—George Bernard Shaw

There are even some qualities which are of service to this good will itself, and may facilitate its action, yet which have no intrinsic unconditional value, but always presuppose a good will, and this qualifies the esteem that we justly have for them, and does not permit us to regard them as absolutely good. Moderation in the affections and passions, self-control, and calm deliberation are not only good in many respects, but even seem to constitute part of the intrinsic worth of the person; but they are far from deserving to be called good without qualification, although they have been so unconditionally praised by the ancients. For without the principles of a good will, they may become extremely bad; and the coolness of a villain not only makes him far more dangerous, but also directly makes him more abominable in our eyes than he would have been without it.

A good will is good not because of what it performs or effects, not by its aptness for the attainment of some proposed end, but simply by virtue of the volition, that is, it is good in itself, and considered by itself to be esteemed much higher than all that can be brought about by it in favour of any inclination, nay, even of the sum-total of all inclinations. Even if it should happen that, owing to special disfavour of fortune, or the niggardly provision of a step-motherly nature, this will should wholly lack power to accomplish its purpose, if with its greatest efforts it should yet achieve nothing, and there should remain only the good will (not, to be sure, a mere wish, but the summoning of all means in our power), then, like a jewel, it would still shine by its own light, as a thing which has its whole value in itself. Its usefulness or fruitlessness can neither add to nor take away anything from this value. It would be, as it were, only the setting to enable us to handle it the more conveniently in common commerce, or to attract to it the attention of those who are not yet connoisseurs, but not to recommend it to true connoisseurs, or to determine its value. . . .[5]

In Kant's system, all our moral duties are expressed in the form of *categorical imperatives*. An imperative is a command to do something; it is categorical if it applies without exception and without regard for particular needs or purposes. A categorical imperative says, "Do this—regardless." In contrast, a *hypothetical imperative* is a command to do something if we want to achieve particular aims, as in "If you want good pay, work hard." The moral law, then, rests on absolute directives that do not depend on the contingencies of desire or utility.

Kant says that through reason and reflection we can derive our duties from a single moral principle, what he calls *the* **categorical imperative**. He formulates it in different ways, the first one being: "I am never to act otherwise than so *that I could also will that my maxim should become a universal law*."[6] For Kant, our actions have logical implications—they imply general rules, or maxims, of conduct. If you tell a lie for financial gain, you are in effect acting according to a maxim like "It's okay to lie to someone when doing so benefits you financially." The question is whether the maxim corresponding to an action is a legitimate moral law. To find out, we must ask if we could consistently will that the maxim become a universal law applicable to everyone—that is, if everyone could consistently act on the maxim and we would be willing to have them do so. If we could do this, then the action described by the maxim is morally permissible; if not, it is prohibited. Thus, moral laws embody two characteristics thought to be essential to morality itself: universality and impartiality.

To show us how to apply this formulation of the categorical imperative to a specific situation, Kant uses the example of a lying promise. Suppose you need to borrow money from a friend, but you know you could never pay her back. So, to get the loan, you decide to lie, falsely promising to repay the money. To find out if such a lying promise is morally permissible, Kant would have you ask if you could consistently will the maxim of your action to become a universal law, to ask, in effect, "What would happen if everyone did this?" The maxim is "Whenever you need to borrow money you cannot pay back, make a lying promise to repay." So what *would* happen if everyone in need of a loan acted in accordance with this maxim? People would make lying promises to obtain loans, but everyone would also know that such promises were worthless, and the custom of loaning money on promises would disappear. So willing the maxim to be a universal law involves a contradiction: If everyone made lying promises, promise-making itself would be no more; you cannot consistently will the maxim to become a universal law. Therefore, your duty is clear: Making a lying promise to borrow money is morally wrong.

Figure 3.12 An old canceled German stamp with Kant's image.

Kant's first formulation of the categorical imperative yields several other important duties. He argues that there is an absolute moral prohibition against killing the innocent, lying, committing suicide, and failing to help others when feasible.

Perhaps the most renowned formulation of the categorical imperative is the principle of respect for persons (a formulation distinct from the first one, though Kant thought them equivalent). As he expresses it, "So act as to treat humanity, whether in thine own person or in that of any other, in every case as an end withal, never as a means only." [7] People must never be treated as if they were mere instruments for achieving some further end, for people are ends in themselves, possessors of ultimate inherent worth. People have ultimate value because they are the ultimate source of value for other things. They bestow value; they do not have it bestowed upon them. So we should treat both ourselves and other persons with the respect that all inherently valuable beings deserve.

17 In Kant's view, is lying to someone to spare her feelings morally permissible? Do you think it is permissible?

. . . Now I say: man and generally any rational being *exists* as an end in himself, *not merely as a means* to be arbitrarily used by this or that will, but in all his actions, whether they concern himself or other rational beings, must be always regarded at the same time as an end. All objects of the inclinations have only a conditional worth; for if the inclinations and the wants founded on them did not exist, then their object would be without value. But the inclinations themselves being sources of want are so far from having an absolute worth for which they should be desired, that, on the contrary, it must be the universal wish of every rational being to be wholly free from them. Thus the worth of any object which is *to be acquired* by our action is always conditional. Beings whose existence depends not on our will but on nature's, have nevertheless, if they are nonrational beings, only a relative value as means, and are therefore called *things*; rational beings, on the contrary, are called *persons*, because their very nature

Immanuel Kant, *Groundwork of the Metaphysic of Morals*

Immanuel Kant, *Groundwork of the Metaphysic of Morals*

18 In these passages, does Kant make clear how we are supposed to apply his principle of respect for persons? For example, how exactly do you show respect for a person who is terminally ill and in great pain who begs you to help him end his life?

History is a voice forever sounding across the centuries the laws of right and wrong. Opinions alter, manners change, creeds rise and fall, but the moral law is written on the tablets of eternity.

—James A. Froude

19 Is Kant's view clearly superior to utilitarianism? Or is utilitarianism the superior one? Or does each theory offer something of value that should be part of any adequate system of morality?

points them out as ends in themselves, that is as something which must not be used merely as means, and so far therefore restricts freedom of action (and is an object of respect). These, therefore, are not merely subjective ends whose existence has a worth *for us* as an effect of our action, but *objective ends*, that is things whose existence is an end in itself: an end moreover for which no other can be substituted, which they should subserve *merely* as means, for otherwise nothing whatever would possess *absolute worth*; but if all worth were conditioned and therefore contingent, then there would be no supreme practical principle of reason whatever.

If then there is a supreme practical principle or, in respect of the human will, a categorical imperative, it must be one which, being drawn from the conception of that which is necessarily an end for everyone because it is *an end in itself*, constitutes an *objective* principle of will, and can therefore serve as a universal practical law. The foundation of this principle is: *rational nature exists as an end in itself*. Man necessarily conceives his own existence as being so: so far then this is a *subjective* principle of human actions. But every other rational being regards its existence similarly, just on the same rational principle that holds for me: so that it is at the same time an objective principle, from which as a supreme practical law all laws of the will must be capable of being deduced. Accordingly the practical imperative will be as follows: *So act as to treat humanity, whether in thine own person or in that of any other, in every case as an end withal, never as a means only. . . .*[8]

According to Kant, the inherent worth of persons derives from their nature as autonomous, rational beings capable of directing their own lives, determining their own ends, and decreeing their own rules by which to live. Thus, the inherent value of persons does not depend in any way on their social status, wealth, talent, race, or culture. Moreover, inherent value is something that all persons possess equally. Each person deserves the same measure of respect as any other.

Kant explains that we treat people merely as a means instead of an end-in-themselves if we disregard these characteristics of personhood—if we thwart people's freely chosen actions by coercing them, undermine their rational decision-making by lying to them, or discount their equality by discriminating against them.

Notice that this formulation of the categorical imperative does not actually prohibit treating a person as a means but forbids treating a person *simply*, or *merely*, as a means—as nothing but a means. Kant recognizes that in daily life we often must use people to achieve our various ends. To buy milk we use the cashier; to find books we use the librarian; to get well we use the doctor. But because their actions are freely chosen and we do not undermine their status as persons, we do not use them *solely* as instruments of our will.

Kant's principle of respect for persons captures what seems to most people an essential part of morality itself—the notion that some things must not be done to a person even if they increase the well-being of others. People have certain rights, and these rights cannot be violated merely for the sake of an overall increase in utility. We tend to think that there is something terribly wrong with jailing an innocent person just because her imprisonment would make a lot of other people very happy; or with seizing a person's possessions and giving them to the poor to maximize overall happiness; or with enslaving a race of people so the rest of the world can have a higher standard of living. Over the principle of respect for persons, Kantians and utilitarians part company. Utilitarians reject the concept of rights, or they define rights in terms of utility. Kantians see respect for rights as central to the moral life.

Kant's theory, however, does have its detractors. Many philosophers argue that it is not consistent with our considered moral judgments. A major cause of the problem, they say, is Kant's insistence that we have absolute (or "perfect") duties—obligations that must be honored without exception. Thus, in Kantian ethics, we have an absolute duty not to lie or to break a promise or to kill the innocent, come what may. Imagine that a band of killers wants to murder an innocent man who has taken refuge in your house, and the killers come to your door and ask you point-blank if he is in your house. To say no is to lie; to answer truthfully is to guarantee the man's death. What should you do? In a case like this, says Kant, you must *do your duty*—you must tell the truth, though murder will be the result and a lie would save a life. But in this case such devotion to moral absolutes seems completely askew, for saving an innocent life seems far more important morally than blindly obeying a rule. Moral common sense suggests that sometimes the consequences of our actions do matter more than adherence to the letter of the law, even if the law is generally worthy of our respect and obedience.

Some have thought that Kant's theory can yield implausible results for another reason. Recall that the first formulation of the categorical imperative says that an action is permissible if persons could consistently act on the relevant maxim, and

> Do not be too moral. You may cheat yourself out of much life. Aim above morality. Be not simply good; be good for something.
> —Henry David Thoreau

Figure 3.13 Imagine that in 1944 you own the house where the young Anne Frank and her family are hiding from the Nazis, and the Nazis ask you if anyone lives there. You can lie and save Anne and her family from death in a concentration camp, or you can tell the truth and doom them. Kant would have you tell the truth no matter what. Is he right? (In 1944 in the Netherlands, the authorities did in fact discover the hiding place of Anne and the other members of her family. They were all shipped off to concentration camps; only Anne's father survived.)

we would be willing to have them do so. This requirement seems to make sense if the maxim in question is something like "Do not kill the innocent" or "Treat equals equally." But what if the maxim is "Enslave all Christians" or "Kill all Ethiopians"? We could—without contradiction—will either one of these precepts to become a universal law. And if we were so inclined, we could be willing for everyone to act accordingly, even if we ourselves were Christians or Ethiopians. So, by Kantian lights, these actions could very well be morally permissible, and their permissibility would depend on whether someone was willing to have them apply universally. Critics conclude that because the first formulation of the categorical imperative seems to sanction such obviously immoral acts, the theory is deeply flawed. Defenders of Kant's theory, on the other hand, view the problems as repairable and have proposed revisions.

This apparent arbitrariness in the first formulation can significantly lessen the theory's usefulness. The categorical imperative is supposed to help us discern moral directives that are rational, universal, and objective. But if it is subjective in the way just described, its helpfulness as a guide for living morally is dubious. There may be remedies for this difficulty, but Kant's theory in its original form seems problematic.

WRITING TO UNDERSTAND:
CRITIQUING PHILOSOPHICAL VIEWS   Section 3.4

1. Is Kantian ethics too rigid because it fails to take consequences into account? Or is Kant correct that consequences are irrelevant? Explain.

2. Is it possible to universalize any of the following maxims—and if so, does that fact raise doubts about Kant's theory? (1) All senile people (including me, if I should become senile) should be executed by the state; (2) Anyone who is not a Christian (including me) should be killed; (3) Anyone (including me) who damages my car should be shot.

3. Is Kant right not to make any exceptions in applying categorical imperatives? Are there times when an exception should be made? For example, would you lie to save an innocent person's life?

4. Suppose two people save a friend from drowning. The first person acts only because she thinks it is her duty. The second person acts out of sincere compassion for his friend. Is Kant right that the first person would be morally superior to the second? Why or why not?

5. Kant seems to assume that our moral duties cannot conflict. Is he right?

3.5 MORALITY BASED ON CHARACTER

The moral theories just discussed are theories of obligation. They mainly are concerned with providing an answer to this question: *What should we do?* That is, what is our moral duty? What actions are we morally obligated to perform or not perform? These theories therefore emphasize knowing and doing what's right, and their chief guide to these aims is moral principles or directives.

Virtue ethics, however, is a different kind of moral theory altogether. It focuses not on duty, but on the development of virtuous character—not on what to do, but on what to *be*. According to virtue ethics, character is the key to the moral life, for it is from a virtuous character that moral conduct and values naturally arise. Virtues are engrained dispositions to act by standards of excellence, so having the proper virtues leads as a matter of course to right actions properly motivated. The central task in morality, then, is not knowing and applying principles, but being and becoming a good person, someone possessing the virtues that define moral excellence. In virtue ethics, someone determines right action not by consulting rules, but by asking what a truly virtuous person would do or whether an action would accord with the relevant virtues.

Virtue ethicists have a ready answer to the age-old question, Why be moral? We should strive to be moral—to be virtuous persons—because developing virtues is the key to living a good life. Virtues help us fare better in life; they enable us to attain what is truly valuable. Thus, virtues are both the traits that make us good persons and the dispositions that enable us to live good lives.

Aristotle (384–322 BCE) is the primary inspiration for contemporary versions of virtue ethics. For him, as for many modern virtue ethicists, the highest goal of humanity is the good life, or "human flourishing" (what he calls *eudaimonia*, or happiness), and developing virtues is the way to achieve such a rich and satisfying life. The good life is the virtuous life.

Aristotle defends this view in his masterpiece on morality, *Nicomachean Ethics* (named after his son Nicomachus):

> **Virtue ethics** is a moral theory that focuses on the development of virtuous character.

> With virtue you can't be entirely poor; without virtue you can't really be rich.
> —Chinese Proverb

Aristotle, *Nicomachean Ethics*

Every art and every inquiry, and similarly every action and choice, is thought to aim at some good; and for this reason the good has rightly been declared to be that at which all things aim. . . . If, then, there is some end of the things we do, which we desire for its own sake (everything else being desired for the sake of this), and if we do not choose everything for the sake of something else (for at that rate the process would go on to infinity, so that our desire would be empty and vain), clearly this must be the good and the chief good. Will not the knowledge of it, then, have a great influence on life? Shall we not, like archers who have a mark to aim at, be more likely to hit upon what we should? If so, we must try, in outline at least, to determine what it is. . . .

Now we call that which is in itself worthy of pursuit more complete than that which is worthy of pursuit for the sake of something else, and that which is never desirable for the sake of something else more complete than the things that are desirable both in themselves and for the sake of that other thing, and therefore we call complete without qualification that which is always desirable in itself and never for the sake of something else.

Now such a thing happiness, above all else, is held to be; for this we choose always for itself and never for the sake of something else, but honour, pleasure, reason, and

20 To Aristotle, is happiness subjective (something only in one's mind) or objective (something that has characteristics regardless of how one feels)?

21 What does Aristotle mean by "human good turns out to be activity of soul in conformity with excellence"?

every excellence we choose indeed for themselves (for if nothing resulted from them we should still choose each of them), but we choose them also for the sake of happiness, judging that through them we shall be happy. Happiness, on the other hand, no one chooses for the sake of these, nor, in general, for anything other than itself. . . .

Happiness, then, is something complete and self-sufficient, and is the end of action. . . .

Presumably, however, to say that happiness is the chief good seems a platitude, and a clearer account of what it is is still desired. This might perhaps be given, if we could first ascertain the function of man. For just as for a flute-player, a sculptor, or any artist, and, in general, for all things that have a function or activity, the good and the 'well' is thought to reside in the function, so would it seem to be for man, if he has a function. Have the carpenter, then, and the tanner certain functions or activities, and has man none? Is he naturally functionless? Or as eye, hand, foot, and in general each of the parts evidently has a function, may one lay it down that man similarly has a function apart from all these? What then can this be? Life seems to be common even to plants, but we are seeking what is peculiar to man. Let us exclude, therefore, the life of nutrition and growth. Next there would be a life of perception, but it also seems to be common even to the horse, the ox, and every animal. There remains, then, an active life of the element that has a rational principle. . . . Now if the function of man is an activity of soul in accordance with, or not without, rational principle, and if we say a so-and-so and a good so-and-so have a function which is the same in kind, e.g. a lyre-player and a good lyre-player, and so without qualification in all cases, eminence in respect of excellence being added to the function (for the function of a lyre-player is to play the lyre, and that of a good lyre-player is to do so well): if this is the case, and we state the function of man to be a certain kind of life, and this to be an activity or actions of the soul implying a rational principle, and the function of a good man to be the good and noble performance of these, and if any action is well performed when it is performed in accordance with the appropriate excellence: if this is the case, human good turns out to be activity of soul in conformity with excellence. . . .

In everything that is continuous and divisible it is possible to take more, less, or an equal amount, and that either in terms of the thing itself or relatively to us; and the equal is an intermediate between excess and defect. By the intermediate in the object I mean that which is equidistant from each of the extremes, which is one and the same for all men; by the intermediate relatively to us that which is neither too much nor too little—and this is not one, nor the same for all. . . .

Thus a master of any art avoids excess and defect, but seeks the intermediate and chooses this—the intermediate not in the object but relatively to us.

22 Is Aristotle's notion of virtue (the mean between two extremes) coherent? Can all virtues be considered a mean?

If it is thus, then, that every art does its work well—by looking to the intermediate and judging its works by this standard (so that we often say of good works of art that it is not possible either to take away or to add anything, implying that excess and defect destroy the goodness of works of art, while the mean preserves it; and good artists, as we say, look to this in their work), and if, further, excellence is more exact and better than any art, as nature also is, then it must have the quality of aiming at the intermediate. I mean moral excellence; for it is this that is concerned with passions and actions, and in these there is excess, defect, and the intermediate. For instance, both fear and confidence and appetite and anger and pity and in general pleasure and pain may be felt both too much and too little, and in both cases not well; but to feel them at the right times, with reference to the right objects, towards the right people, with the right aim, and in the right way, is what is both intermediate and best, and this is characteristic of excellence. Similarly with regard to actions also there is excess, defect, and the intermediate. Now excellence is concerned with passions and actions, in which excess is a form of failure, and so is defect, while the intermediate is praised and is a form of success; and both these things are characteristics of excellence. Therefore excellence is a kind of mean, since it aims at what is intermediate. . . .

We must, however, not only make this general statement, but also apply it to the individual facts. . . . With regard to feelings of fear and confidence courage is the mean; of the people who exceed, he who exceeds in fearlessness has no name (many of the states have no name), while the man who exceeds in confidence is rash, and he who exceeds in fear and falls short in confidence is a coward. With regard to pleasures and pains—not all of them, and not so much with regard to the pains—the mean is temperance, the excess self-indulgence. Persons deficient with regard to the pleasures are not often found; hence such persons also have received no name. But let us call them 'insensible.' [9]

> We are not concerned to know what goodness is, but how we are to become good men, for this alone gives the study [of ethics] its practical value.
> —Aristotle

Aristotle argues that the good life is one of happiness—a life not merely of pleasure, but of optimal well-being. Happiness is the one thing that is good in itself and not, like wealth or power, just instrumentally good (good as a means to something else). Happiness is about doing what is inherently valuable, which means fulfilling the function unique to human beings: acting through reason. To excel in the use of reason in all of life's endeavors is to possess the virtues in full, and the virtues are the key to a flourishing, happy life. For Aristotle, a virtue is the midpoint (the "golden mean") between the extremes of excess and deficit, and the extremes are the vices. Courage, for example, is the virtue that comes midway between the vices of cowardice (too much fear) and rashness (too little fear).

Figure 3.14 Raphael's renowned painting *The School of Athens* shows an array of great moral exemplars, including Aristotle (center, in blue robe), Plato (conversing with Aristotle), Socrates, Epicurus, Hypatia, and Pythagoras. Who is *your* moral exemplar?

It has been my experience that folks who have no vices have very few virtues.
—Abraham Lincoln

23 Do statements about virtues really give us adequate guidance in deciding what actions to perform?

Unlike theories of obligation, virtue ethics asks us to do much more than just observe minimal moral rules—it insists that we *aspire to moral excellence*, that we cultivate the virtues that will make us better persons. In this sense, virtue ethics is goal-directed, not rule-guided. The moral virtues—benevolence, honesty, loyalty, compassion, fairness, and the like—are ideals that we must ever strive to attain. By the lights of both Aristotle and modern virtue ethicists, character is not static. We can become more virtuous by reflecting on our lives and those of others, practicing virtuous behavior, or imitating moral exemplars such as Gandhi, Buddha, Jesus, Muhammad, Hypatia, and Socrates. We can—and should—be better than we are.

To the virtue ethicist, possessing the right virtues means having the proper motivations that naturally accompany those virtues. To act morally, we must act from virtue, and acting from virtue means acting with the appropriate motives. It is not enough to do right; we must do right for the right motivating reasons. If we save a drowning friend, we should do so out of genuine feelings of compassion, kindness, or loyalty—not merely because of the prodding of moral rules or social expectations. In contrast, some moral theories (notably Kant's) maintain that acting morally is solely a matter of acting for duty's sake—performing an action simply because duty requires it. Virtuous motives are irrelevant; we act morally if we do our duty regardless of our motivations. But this notion seems to many to offer a barren picture of the moral life. Surely, they say, motivations for acting are often relevant to our evaluations of people's character and actions. The friend we save from drowning would probably be appalled if we declared that we saved her out of duty, even though we did not really care whether she lived or died. Many moral philosophers agree that motivations are indeed important considerations in moral judgments, and they have incorporated virtues into their theories of obligation.

Little wonder, then, that virtue ethics has been lauded for emphasizing what duty-based theories neglect. Many theorists say it deserves a great deal of credit for containing a more plausible conception of motivation in moral conduct, for doing a better job of explaining the role of virtue in the moral life, and for focusing on the goal of living a good life.

But philosophers have also accused virtue ethics of harboring defects that limit its usefulness. For one thing, some critics argue that the theory doesn't give us nearly enough help in deciding what to do. They say, for example, that a woman may possess all the right virtues—and still not know whether to try *in vitro* fertilization, or help an illegal immigrant hide from the authorities, or be tested for a genetic defect.

On the contrary, virtue ethicists contend, the theory gives much more guidance to moral decision-making than critics assume. Embedded in statements about virtues and vices are directives about performing or refraining from certain actions. As the virtue ethicist Rosalind Hursthouse says, "[A] great deal of specific action guidance could be found in rules employing the virtue and vice terms ('v-rules') such as 'Do what is honest/charitable; do not do what is dishonest /uncharitable.'" [10]

A related difficulty is that virtue ethics seems to be hobbled by conflicts that arise among virtues. Suppose you see a coworker, a good friend, steal money from your company. You know that he desperately needs money to pay for medicine for his daughter, and you are sure that if his theft is discovered, he will be fired and likely prosecuted.

Your employer asks you point-blank if your friend is guilty of theft, and your answer will determine his fate. Should you tell the truth or lie? To tell the truth is to be honest yet disloyal (to your friend); to lie is to be dishonest yet loyal. Virtue ethics expects you to be both honest and loyal, but you cannot be both in this situation—and the theory gives very little guidance in resolving the conflict.

But, the virtue ethicist says, every theory is confronted with such conflicts. Duty-based theories must deal with conflicts among rules or principles, but the existence of such clashes does not show the theories to be defective beyond repair.

Another kind of conflict appears when virtuous people—those moral exemplars after whom we are to model ourselves—disagree about the correct action in the same circumstances. Virtue ethics says that right actions are those that virtuous people would do. But even moral exemplars sometimes differ on what to do in the same situation. When that happens, how are we to decide which model of virtue we are to follow? Even more worrisome is that such a difference of opinion among moral exemplars seems to reveal a logical contradiction within the theory. If in the same situation one virtuous person would perform a particular action while another virtuous person would not perform it, then the same behavior would seem to be simultaneously right and wrong. After all, right actions are by definition what moral exemplars do. But if virtuous people would do different things in the same circumstances, the action would appear to be both permissible and not permissible. Detractors say that the possibility of such contradictions casts serious doubt on the coherence of the theory. If so, it's open to virtue ethicists to somehow modify the theory to avoid the problem.

As critics see it, the most serious weakness in virtue ethics is that it cannot help us decide what to do because it focuses exclusively on virtues and leaves notions of duty out of account. We can see the difficulty by first noting that the theory claims both that right actions are those done by virtuous persons and that virtuous persons are those who do right actions. If we ask what is the right thing to do, the answer is that it is whatever the virtuous person does. And if we ask who the virtuous person is, the answer is that she's the one who does right actions. But this is circular reasoning. If virtue is defined in terms of action, we cannot then define action in terms of virtue. The result, theorists say, is that virtue ethics cannot tell us which actions are right or wrong. To avoid such circular reasoning, we have to introduce some independent moral standards of conduct.

Russ Shafer-Landau thinks this problem is similar to the one faced by the divine command theory (Section 3.1):

> Vices are sometimes only virtues carried to excess!
> —Charles Dickens

Russ Shafer-Landau, *The Fundamentals of Ethics*

Virtue ethics and the divine command theory share a basic structure. And they share a basic weakness. We can see this by posing a familiar dilemma. Virtuous people either have, or don't have, good reasons for their actions. (1) If they lack good reasons, then their actions are arbitrary, and can't possibly serve as the standard of morality. (2) If they do have good reasons to support their actions, then these reasons, and not the actions themselves, determine what is right and wrong.

Russ Shafer-Landau,
The Fundamentals of Ethics

The second option is the better one. We must suppose that virtuous people act on good reasons, or else they wouldn't really be virtuous. Consider again the immorality of rape, and the many reasons why it is wrong. A virtuous person is one who is aware of these reasons and takes them to heart. Rape is not wrong because good people oppose it. They oppose it because it is wrong.

This approach preserves the integrity, the wisdom, and the goodness of the virtuous person. But there is naturally a cost. And it is steep. The cost is that the virtue ethicist's account of right action is directly threatened. That account tells us that acts are morally right *just because* all virtuous people would perform them in the circumstances, and wrong just because such people would refrain. But as we have seen, the choices of virtuous people do not make actions right or wrong.[11]

WRITING TO UNDERSTAND:
CRITIQUING PHILOSOPHICAL VIEWS   Section 3.5

1. Aristotle argues that because every action aims at some end, there must be an end to which all actions aim. Is this a good argument? Why or why not?

2. Is virtue ethics sufficiently action guiding? Explain.

3. Do you think that morality is a matter of both duty and virtues? Why or why not?

4. What are the advantages and disadvantages of virtue ethics? Could virtue ethics be integrated into a duty-based theory like Kant's to produce a more plausible theory? If so, how would you merge the two?

5. Can virtue ethics be used to guide your actions? If so, how?

3.6 FEMINIST ETHICS AND THE ETHICS OF CARE

Feminist ethics is an approach to morality aimed at advancing women's interests, underscoring their distinctive experiences and characteristics, and advancing the obvious truth that women and men are morally equal.

All virtue is summed up in dealing justly.
—Aristotle

In recent decades, an important development has challenged the traditional theories and concepts of moral philosophy: the rise of **feminist ethics**. Feminist ethics is an approach to morality aimed at advancing women's interests, underscoring their distinctive experiences and characteristics, and advancing the obvious truth that women and men are morally equal. It is defined by a distinctive focus on these issues, rather than by a set of doctrines or common ideology among feminists, many of whom may disagree on the nature of feminist ethics or on particular moral issues.

Feminist ethics generally downplays the role of moral principles and traditional ethical concepts, insisting instead that moral reflection must take into account the social realities—the relevant social practices, relationships, institutions, and power arrangements. Many feminists think that the familiar principles of Western ethics—autonomy, utility, freedom, equality, and the like—are too broad and abstract to help us make moral judgments about specific persons who are enmeshed in concrete social situations. It is not enough, for example, to respect a woman's decision to have an abortion if she is too poor to have one, or if her culture is so oppressive (or oppressed) as to make abortion impossible to obtain, or if social conditioning leads her to believe that she has no choice or her views don't count. Theoretical autonomy does not mean much if it is so thoroughly undermined in reality.

Many feminist writers maintain that the values and virtues inherent in most traditional moral theories reflect a typically masculine perspective—and thus offer a one-sided (or wrong-sided) view of the moral life. What's needed, they say, is a moral outlook that takes into account values and experiences that usually have been identified with women. According to Alison Jaggar, a feminist philosopher, feminists claim that traditional ethics favors the

24 Is there such a thing as "the female perspective"? That is, do all women have the same basic outlook or style of reasoning?

Alison Jaggar, "Feminist Ethics"

supposedly masculine or male-associated values of independence, autonomy, intellect, will, wariness, hierarchy, domination, culture, transcendence, product, asceticism, war and death over the supposedly feminine or female-associated values of interdependence, community, connection, sharing, emotion, body, trust, absence of hierarchy, nature, immanence, process, joy, peace and life.[12]

Some proponents of feminist ethics also reject the traditional concept of the moral agent. Jan Crosthwaite says that the old notion is that of "abstract individuals as fundamentally autonomous agents, aware of their own preferences and values, and motivated by rational self-interest (though not necessarily selfish)."[13] But, she says, many feminists

Jan Crosthwaite, "Gender and Bioethics"

present a richer conception of persons as historically and culturally located, socially related and essentially embodied. Individuals are located in and formed by specific relationships (chosen and unchosen) and ties of affection and responsibility. . . . Such a conception of socially embedded selves refocuses thinking about autonomy, shifting the emphasis from independent self-determination towards ideals of integrity within relatedness. . . . Respecting autonomy becomes less a matter of protecting individuals from 'coercive' influences than one of positive empowerment, recognizing people's interdependence and supporting individuals' development of their own understanding of their situation and options.[14]

Many of these themes run through the **ethics of care**, a moral perspective that arose out of feminist concerns and grew to challenge core elements of most other moral theories. Generally, those theories emphasize abstract principles, general

Ethics of care is a moral perspective that emphasizes the unique demands of specific situations and the virtues and feelings that are central to close personal relationships.

Figure 3.15 Virginia Held, feminist, author, and distinguished professor of philosophy at City University of New York Graduate School.

The ethics of care confirms the priority that we naturally give to our family and friends, and so it seems a more plausible conception.
—James Rachels

duties, individual rights, justice, utility, impartial judgments, and deliberative reasoning. But the ethics of care shifts the focus to the unique demands of specific situations and to the virtues and feelings that are central to close personal relationships—empathy, compassion, love, sympathy, and fidelity. The heart of the moral life is feeling for and caring for those with whom you have a special, intimate connection.

Early on, the ethics of care drew inspiration from the notion that men and women have dramatically different styles of moral decision-making, with men seizing on principles, duties, and rights, and women homing in on personal relationships, caring, and empathy. This difference was highlighted in research done by psychologist Carol Gilligan and published in her 1982 book *In a Different Voice*.[15] Typically, men recognize an ethic of justice and rights, she says, and women are guided by an ethic of compassion and care. In her view, the latter is as legitimate as the former, and both have their place in ethics.

Other research has suggested that the differences between men and women in styles of moral thinking may not be as great as Gilligan suggests. But the credibility of the empirical claim does not affect the larger insight that the research seems to some writers to suggest: Caring is an essential part of morality, and the most influential theories have not fully taken it into account.

These points get support along several lines. First, virtue ethics reminds us that virtues are part of the moral life. If caring is viewed as a virtue—in the form of compassion, empathy, or kindness—then caring too must be an element of morality. A moral theory then would be deficient if it made no room for care.

Moreover, many argue that unlike the ethics of care, most moral theories push the principle of impartiality too far. Recall that impartiality in morality requires us to consider everyone as equal, counting everyone's interests the same. The principle applies widely, especially in matters of public justice, but less so in personal relationships of love, family, friendship, and the like. We seem to have special obligations (partiality) to close friends, family members, and others we care for, duties that we do not have to strangers or to universal humanity.

Most moral theories emphasize duties and downplay the role of emotions, attitudes, and motivations. Kant, for example, would have us do our duty for duty's sake, whatever our feelings. For him, to be a morally good parent, we need only act from duty. But taking care of our children as a matter of moral obligation alone seems an empty exercise. Surely, being a morally good parent also involves having feelings of love and attitudes of caring. The ethics of care eagerly takes these emotional elements into account.

The feminist philosopher Virginia Held offers this synopsis of the main elements of the ethics of care:

Virginia Held, *The Ethics of Care*

. . . I think one can discern among various versions of the ethics of care a number of major features.

First, the central focus of the ethics of care is on the compelling moral salience of attending to and meeting the needs of the particular others for whom we take responsibility. Caring for one's child, for instance, may well and defensibly be at the forefront of a person's moral concerns. The ethics of care recognizes that human beings are dependent for many years of their lives, that the moral claim of those dependent on us for the care they need is pressing, and that there are highly important moral aspects in developing the relations of caring that enable human beings to live and progress. All persons need care for at least their early years. Prospects for human progress and flourishing hinge fundamentally on the care that those needing it receive, and the ethics of care stresses the moral force of the responsibility to respond to the needs of the dependent. Many persons will become ill and dependent for some periods of their later lives, including in frail old age, and some who are permanently disabled will need care the whole of their lives. Moralities built on the image of the independent, autonomous, rational individual largely overlook the reality of human dependence and the morality for which it calls. The ethics of care attends to this central concern of human life and delineates the moral values involved. It refuses to relegate care to a realm "outside morality." . . .

Second, in the epistemological process of trying to understand what morality would recommend and what it would be morally best for us to do and to be, the ethics of care values emotion rather than rejects it. Not all emotion is valued, of course, but in contrast with the dominant rationalist approaches, such emotions as sympathy, empathy, sensitivity, and responsiveness are seen as the kind of moral emotions that need to be cultivated not only to help in the implementation of the dictates of reason but to better ascertain what morality recommends. Even anger may be a component of the moral indignation that should be felt when people are treated unjustly or inhumanely, and it may contribute to (rather than interfere with) an appropriate interpretation of the moral wrong. This is not to say that raw emotion can be a guide to morality; feelings need to be reflected on and educated. But from the care perspective, moral inquiries that rely entirely on reason and rationalistic deductions or calculations are seen as deficient. . . .

Third, the ethics of care rejects the view of the dominant moral theories that the more abstract the reasoning about a moral problem the better because the more likely to avoid bias and arbitrariness, the more nearly to achieve impartiality. The ethics of care respects rather than removes itself from the claims of particular others with whom we share actual relationships. It calls into question the universalistic and abstract rules of the dominant theories. When the latter consider such actual relations as between a parent and child, if they say anything about them at all, they may see them as permitted and cultivating them a preference that a person may have. Or they may recognize a universal obligation for all parents to care for their children. But they do not permit actual relations ever to take priority over the requirements of impartiality. . . .

To most advocates of the ethics of care, the compelling moral claim of the particular other may be valid even when it conflicts with the requirement usually made by

25 Does Held suggest a way to decide which emotions to heed and which to ignore? If the ethics of care cannot help us sort out our emotions, should we consider it a bad theory?

A man's ethical behavior should be based effectively on sympathy, education, and social relationships; no religious basis is necessary. Man would indeed be in a poor way if he had to be restrained by fear of punishment and hope of reward after death.
—Albert Einstein

Virginia Held,
The Ethics of Care

I reject the notion of universal caring—that is, caring for everyone—on the grounds that it is impossible to actualize and leads us to substitute abstract problem solving and mere talk for genuine caring.

—Nel Noddings

moral theories that moral judgments be universalizeable, and this is of fundamental moral importance.

Dominant moral theories tend to interpret moral problems as if they were conflicts between egoistic individual interests on the one hand, and universal moral principles on the other. The extremes of "selfish individual" and "humanity" are recognized, but what lies between these is often overlooked. The ethics of care, in contrast, focuses especially on the area between these extremes. Those who conscientiously care for others are not seeking primarily to further their own *individual* interests; their interests are intertwined with the persons they care for. Neither are they acting for the sake of *all others* or *humanity in general*; they seek instead to preserve or promote an actual human relation between themselves and *particular others*. Persons in caring relations are acting for self-and-other together. Their characteristic stance is neither egoistic nor altruistic; these are the options in a conflictual situation, but the well-being of a caring relation involves the cooperative well-being of those in the relation and the well-being of the relation itself. . . .

A fourth characteristic of the ethics of care is that like much feminist thought in many areas, it reconceptualizes traditional notions about the public and the private. The traditional view, built into the dominant moral theories, is that the household is a private sphere beyond politics into which government, based on consent, should not intrude. . . .

Dominant moral theories have seen "public" life as relevant to morality while missing the moral significance of the "private" domains of family and friendship. Thus the dominant theories have assumed that morality should be sought for unrelated, independent, and mutually indifferent individuals assumed to be equal. They have posited an abstract, fully rational "agent as such" from which to construct morality, while missing the moral issues that arise between interconnected persons in the contexts of family, friendship, and social groups. In the context of the family, it is typical for relations to be between persons with highly unequal power who did not choose the ties and obligations in which they find themselves enmeshed. For instance, no child can choose her parents yet she may well have obligations to care for them. Relations of this kind are standardly noncontractual, and conceptualizing them as contractual would often undermine or at least obscure the trust on which their worth depends. The ethics of care addresses rather than neglects moral issues arising in relations among the unequal and dependent, relations that are often laden with emotion and involuntary, and then notices how often these attributes apply not only in the household but in the wider society as well. . . .

A fifth characteristic of the ethics of care is the conception of persons with which it begins. . . . The ethics of care usually works with a conception of persons as relational, rather than as the self-sufficient independent individuals of the dominant moral theories.[16]

Many philosophers, including some who favor traditional theories, think the ethics of care is surely right about certain aspects of the moral life. Caring, they say, is indeed a vital part of morality. Sometimes the most important factor in moral decision-making is not justice, utility, or rights, but compassionate consideration. Impartiality is a basic requirement of morality, an ideal that guides us to fairness and justice and away from prejudice and inequality. But it often does not apply in our relationships with friends and loved ones, for to those close to us we may have special obligations that we do not have toward others. And, contrary to Kant, feelings do matter. They can alert us to important moral issues and give us a deeper understanding of morality's point and purpose. True, reason must hold the reins of our emotions, but there can be no denying that emotions have a legitimate place in the moral life.

To these concessions many moral philosophers would add a cautionary note: the ethics of care is not the whole of morality, and to view it that way is a mistake. To decide on the right action, we often cannot avoid applying the concepts of justice and rights. Sometimes impartiality is the best (or only) policy, without which our moral decisions would be misguided, even tragic. And abstract principles or rules, though unwieldy in many cases, may be essential to reconciling conflicting obligations or intuitions.

So should plausible moral theories try to accommodate *both* an ethic of obligation and an ethic of care? Many theorists, including several writing from a feminist perspective, think so. Annette Baier, for example, says that

Annette C. Baier, "The Need for More Than Justice"

[T]he best moral theory has to be a cooperative product of women and men, has to harmonize justice and care. The morality it theorizes about is after all for all persons, for men and for women, and will need their combined insights. As Gilligan said, what we need now is a 'marriage' of the old male and the newly articulated female insights.[17]

WRITING TO UNDERSTAND:
CRITIQUING PHILOSOPHICAL VIEWS   Section 3.6

1. Is it possible to combine Kant's theory with the ethics of care? If so, how?
2. Do you think there are *innate* differences between men and women in the ways they think about morality or moral issues? Are there *culturally engrained* differences in moral thinking?
3. Do you think it possible to arrive at plausible moral judgments based entirely on emotion and personal experience? Explain.
4. What features of the ethics of care do you find plausible? Are there any important elements missing? If so, what elements?
5. What role do you think emotions play in the moral life and moral thinking?

3.7 ALBERT CAMUS: AN EXISTENTIALIST VOICE

Long before the ethics of care and feminist ethics began to strongly challenge traditional moral theories, an even more influential and revolutionary moral outlook arose in post–World War II Europe. This view came to be known as *existentialism*, a perspective that quickly spread throughout the intellectual world and is still compelling to many thoughtful people in the twenty-first century. Several noted thinkers have been identified as existentialist, including Jean-Paul Sartre (1905–1980), Søren Kierkegaard (1813–1855), Albert Camus (1913–1960), Friedrich Nietzsche (1844–1900), and Simone de Beauvoir (1908–1986). These and other existentialist writers differ dramatically on some major issues (for example, some are atheists, like Sartre, Camus, and Nietzsche; and some, like Kierkegaard, are Christians). But most of them also address common themes that are characteristic of existentialism, which itself is difficult to straightforwardly define.

Unlike deontological and consequentialist theories, existentialism does not offer rules or principles to guide moral action. Instead it provides a broad analysis of the individual's predicament in an uncaring universe and explains how to find meaning in such a forlorn world. Thus, a central existentialist theme is that our existence is *absurd*: There is an unbearable conflict between our need for meaning and purpose in life and the meaningless, indifferent universe. Our situation is impossible, and there is no higher power or governing principle to help us make sense of it. There is just us and the cold, silent universe, which cares nothing about our needs and desires. Moreover, our condition is terminal; our death is guaranteed. So we must live an absurd existence, and at the last we get no answers, just an ending. What makes this predicament even more intolerable is brought out by another theme—*existence precedes essence*. The traditional view is that we come into existence with an essence, a human nature, that is in a sense already set before we come into the world. And we have no say in this; what we are as individuals is predetermined. But existentialists argue that reality is the other way around. We first come into existence, and then we define ourselves (establish our essence) through the choices we make. It is we who are totally responsible for what we become. We are totally responsible because we have *absolute freedom* to do as we will. We are radically and painfully free to choose what we will be and how we will respond to the absurdity of living. As Sartre says, "We are condemned to be free." The responsibility of self-definition rests heavily upon us. To many, the weight is terrifying. But those who accept their responsibility and freedom, who recognize that they alone are the ultimate designers of their lives, who are brave enough to make the best of an absurd existence—they are living *authentically*. Those who allow society, religion, history, mass culture, or their own fear to define them are living inauthentically.

In his famous essay "The Myth of Sisyphus," Camus dramatizes the absurdity of human existence by likening it to that of the mythical Sisyphus, who is forced by the gods to repeat a pointless task for all eternity: to push a boulder to the top of a mountain only to have it tumble down again to the bottom. Yet Sisyphus finds meaning in this seemingly meaningless burden by courageously embracing it and refusing to be overwhelmed by despair. The implication for humans is that we too can live meaningfully and bravely by accepting our freedom and shaping our own lives through free choices. To Camus, Sisyphus is a hero because he accepts his fate and valiantly pushes on anyway. Likewise, humans too can be heroic by carrying on with life even though it has no inherent meaning and will soon be over.

Albert Camus, *The Myth of Sisyphus*

The gods had condemned Sisyphus to ceaselessly rolling a rock to the top of a mountain, whence the stone would fall back of its own weight. They had thought with some reason that there is no more dreadful punishment than futile and hopeless labor.

If one believes Homer, Sisyphus was the wisest and most prudent of mortals. According to another tradition, however, he was disposed to practice the profession of highwayman. I see no contradiction in this. Opinions differ as to the reasons why he became the futile laborer of the underworld. To begin with, he is accused of a certain levity in regard to the gods. He stole their secrets. Ægina, the daughter of Æsopus, was carried off by Jupiter. The father was shocked by that disappearance and complained to Sisyphus. He, who knew of the abduction, offered to tell about it on condition that Æsopus would give water to the citadel of Corinth. To the celestial thunderbolts he preferred the benediction of water. He was punished for this in the underworld. Homer tells us also that Sisyphus had put Death in chains. Pluto could not endure the sight of his deserted, silent empire. He dispatched the god of war, who liberated Death from the hands of her conqueror.

It is said also that Sisyphus, being near to death, rashly wanted to test his wife's love. He ordered her to cast his unburied body into the middle of the public square. Sisyphus woke up in the underworld. And there, annoyed by an obedience so contrary to human love, he obtained from Pluto permission to return to earth in order to chastise his wife. But when he had seen again the face of this world, enjoyed water and sun, warm stones and the sea, he no longer wanted to go back to the infernal darkness. Recalls, signs of anger, warnings were of no avail. Many years more he lived facing the curve of the gulf, the sparkling sea, and the smiles of earth. A decree of the gods was necessary. Mercury came and seized the impudent man by the collar and, snatching him from his joys, led him forcibly back to the underworld, where his rock was ready for him.

You have already grasped that Sisyphus is the absurd hero. He is, as much through his passions as through his torture. His scorn of the gods, his hatred of death, and his passion for life won him that unspeakable penalty in which the whole being is exerted toward accomplishing nothing. This is the price that must be paid for the passions of this earth. Nothing is told us about Sisyphus in the underworld. Myths are made for the imagination to breathe life into them. As for this myth, one sees merely the whole effort of a body straining to raise the huge stone, to roll it and push it up a slope a hundred times over; one sees the face screwed up, the cheek tight against the stone, the shoulder bracing the clay-covered mass, the foot wedging it, the fresh start with arms outstretched, the wholly human security of two earth-clotted hands. At the very end of his long effort measured by skyless space and time without depth, the purpose is achieved. Then Sisyphus watches the stone rush down in a few moments toward that lower world whence he will have to push it up again towards the summit. He goes back down to the plain.

It is during that return, that pause, that Sisyphus interests me. A face that toils so close to stones is already stone itself! I see that man going back down with a heavy yet measured step toward that torment of which he will never know the end. That hour like a breathing-space which returns as surely as his suffering, that is the hour of

26 Does Camus' perspective leave open the possibility of moral relativism? If we have absolute freedom of choice, does that mean we can make any moral choice at all? Does Camus set any limits on moral decisions?

consciousness. At each of those moments when he leaves the heights and gradually sinks toward the lairs of the gods, he is superior to his fate. He is stronger than his rock.

If this myth is tragic, that is because its hero is conscious. Where would his torture be, indeed, if at every step the hope of succeeding upheld him? The workman of today works every day in his life at the same tasks, and this fate is no less absurd. But it is tragic only at the rare moments when it becomes conscious. Sisyphus, proletarian of the gods, powerless and rebellious, knows the whole extent of his wretched condition: it is what he thinks of during his descent. The lucidity that was to constitute his torture at the same time crowns his victory. There is no fate that cannot be surmounted by scorn.

If the descent is thus sometimes performed in sorrow, it can also take place in joy. This word is not too much. Again I fancy Sisyphus returning toward his rock, and the sorrow was in the beginning. When the images of earth cling too tightly to memory, when the call of happiness becomes too insistent, it happens that melancholy rises in man's heart: this is the rock's victory, this is the rock itself. The boundless grief is too heavy to bear. These are our nights of Gethsemane. But crushing truths perish from being acknowledged. Thus, Œdipus at the outset obeys fate without knowing it. But from the moment he knows, his tragedy begins. Yet at the same moment, blind and desperate, he realizes that the only bond linking him to the world is the cool hand of a girl. Then a tremendous remark rings out: "Despite so many ordeals, my advanced age and the nobility of my soul make me conclude that all is well." Sophocles' Œdipus, like Dostoevsky's Kirilov, thus gives the recipe for the absurd victory. Ancient wisdom confirms modern heroism.

One does not discover the absurd without being tempted to write a manual of happiness. "What! by such narrow ways—?" There is but one world, however. Happiness and the absurd are two sons of the same earth. They are inseparable. It would be a mistake to say that happiness necessarily springs from the absurd discovery. It happens as well that the feeling of the absurd springs from happiness. "I conclude that all is well," says Œdipus, and that remark is sacred. It echoes in the wild and limited universe of man. It teaches that all is not, has not been, exhausted. It drives out of this world a god who had come into it with dissatisfaction and a preference for futile sufferings. It makes of fate a human matter, which must be settled among men.

All Sisyphus' silent joy is contained therein. His fate belongs to him. His rock is his thing. Likewise, the absurd man when he contemplates his torment, silences all the idols. In the universe suddenly restored to its silence, the myriad wondering little voices of the earth rise up. Unconscious, secret calls, invitations from all the faces, they are the necessary reverse and price of victory. There is no sun without shadow, and it is essential to know the night. The absurd man says yes and his effort will henceforth be unceasing. If there is a personal fate, there is no higher destiny, or at least there is but one which he concludes is inevitable and despicable. For the rest, he knows himself to be the master of his days. At that subtle moment when man glances backward over his life, Sisyphus returning toward his rock, in that slight pivoting he contemplates that series of unrelated actions which becomes his fate, created by him, combined under his memory's eye and soon sealed by his death. Thus, convinced of the wholly human origin of all that is human, a blind man eager to see who knows that the night has no end, he is still on the go. The rock is still rolling.

I leave Sisyphus at the foot of the mountain! One always finds one's burden again. But Sisyphus teaches the higher fidelity that negates the gods and raises rocks. He too concludes that all is well. This universe henceforth without a master seems to him neither sterile nor futile. Each atom of that stone, each mineral flake of that night-filled mountain, in itself forms a world. The struggle itself toward the heights is enough to fill a man's heart. One must imagine Sisyphus happy.[18]

WRITING TO UNDERSTAND:
CRITIQUING PHILOSOPHICAL VIEWS   Section 3.7

1. What are some of the main themes of existentialism? Are they an accurate depiction of the human predicament? Why or why not?

2. Can life have meaning even if there is no God? Support your answer.

3. Are we absolutely free to live our lives according to our own preferences? Are we "condemned to be free"? Explain.

4. How does the myth of Sisyphus dramatize the absurdity of the human condition? Do you agree with Camus' assessment of human existence?

5. According to Camus, how can life be lived meaningfully in a meaningless world? Can *your* life be lived meaningfully? If so, how?

3.8 CONFUCIANISM

Confucianism is a school of thought that arose out of ancient China and, along with Taoism, has been a dominant philosophical system there for hundreds of years. Its effect on Chinese and East Asian life, culture, and government has been enormous—comparable to the influence of Christianity, Judaism, and Islam in the West. Until the early twentieth century, Confucian virtues and training were required of anyone entering Chinese civil service, and even now under Communist rule China holds to its Confucian roots in everyday life. Elsewhere in the East (especially in Korea, Japan, and Vietnam), Confucian ethics and ideals have remodeled society, providing moral underpinning and guidance to social relationships at all levels.

Part of the appeal of Confucianism is that in times of ideological confusion it has offered plausible answers to essential philosophical questions: What kind of person should I be? What kind of society is best? What are my moral obligations to my family, those who rule, and the rest of humanity? In the twenty-first century, millions of people are attracted to the answers supplied by this 2,000-year-old tradition.

Many of the elements of Confucianism were part of Chinese culture long before Confucius arrived on the scene. In fact, he claimed merely to transmit the wisdom of the ancients to new generations, but what he transmitted plus what he added became the distinctive Confucian worldview. From early Chinese civilization came the Confucian emphasis on rituals and their correct performance; the veneration of ancestors; social and cosmic harmony; virtuous behavior and ideals; and the will of Heaven (or *Tian*), the ultimate power and organizing principle in the universe.

Into this mix of characteristically Eastern ideas and practices there appeared in 551 BCE the renowned thinker we call Confucius (the Westernized spelling), otherwise known as K'ung Ch'iu or as K'ung Fu-tzu (Master K'ung). According to legend and very sketchy information about his life,

Figure 3.16 Confucius (551–479 BCE).

By three methods we may learn wisdom: First, by reflection, which is noblest; second, by imitation, which is easiest; and third, by experience, which is the bitterest.
—Confucius

27 Consider the Confucian emphasis on the noble or superior person. Do you think striving to become such a person is a laudable goal? Would it decrease or increase the enjoyment of life?

Li In early Confucianism, ritual, etiquette, principle, and propriety; conscientious behavior and right action.

Ren The essential Confucian virtues, including benevolence, sympathy, kindness, generosity, respect for others, and human-heartedness.

To be wealthy and honored in an unjust society is a disgrace.
—Confucius

he was born to a poor family in the tiny Chinese state of Lu. He served briefly at age fifty in the Lu government as police commissioner, and during the next thirteen years he visited other Chinese states trying to persuade their rulers to implement his philosophy of wise government. One leader after another turned him down. He spent the rest of his life teaching his philosophy and contributing to the Confucian works known as the *Five Classics*. He died in 479 BCE without his ideas having achieved wide acceptance. Only later did his views become a major influence.

Confucianism, especially later forms of it, has always featured some religious or divine aspects. Confucius himself believed in the supreme deity Heaven, asserting that we should align ourselves with its will. But in general he veered away from the supernatural beliefs of the past, for his main interest was teaching a humanistic doctrine centered on social relationships. His aim was the creation of harmony and virtue in the world—specifically in individuals, in the way they interacted with one another, and in how they were treated by the state. He saw his teachings as a remedy for the social disorder, corruption, and inhumanity existing all around him, from the lowest levels of society to the highest.

In Confucianism, the ideal world is generated through the practice of *li* and *ren*. **Li** has several meanings, including ritual, etiquette, principle, and propriety, but its essence is conscientious behavior and right action. To follow *li* is to conduct yourself in your dealings with others according to moral and customary norms, and to act in this way is to contribute to social stability and harmony. **Ren** is about social virtues; it encompasses benevolence, sympathy, kindness, generosity, respect for others, and human-heartedness. At its core is the imperative to work for the common good and to recognize the essential worth of others regardless of their social status. The expression of these virtues is governed by the notion of reciprocity (*shu*), what has been called Confucius's (negative) golden rule: "Never do to others what you would not like them to do to you." (The Christian golden rule is stated positively: "Do unto others as you would have them do unto you.")

Confucius urges people not merely to try to live according to *li* and *ren* but to excel at such a life, to become a "superior person" (a *junzi*), a noble. Contrary to history and custom, Confucius's idea of nobility has nothing to do with noble blood; true nobility, he says, comes from noble virtues and wisdom, and these anyone can acquire. He refers to a man who embodies this kind of nobility as a *gentleman*. We get a glimpse of the gentleman in the *Analects*, the main Confucian text:

Confucius, *Analects*

Tzu-kung asked about the true gentleman. The Master [Confucius] said, He does not preach what he practises till he has practised what he preaches. . . .

The Master said, A gentleman can see a question from all sides without bias. The small man is biased and can see a question only from one side.

The Master said, the Ways of the true gentleman are three. I myself have met with success in none of them. For he that is really Good is never unhappy, he that is really wise is never perplexed, he that is really brave is never afraid. Tzu-kung said, That, Master, is your own Way!

Tzu-kung asked about the qualities of a true gentleman. The Master said, He cultivates in himself the capacity to be diligent in his tasks. . . . The Master said, He cultivates in himself the capacity to ease the lot of other people. . . . The Master said, He cultivates in himself the capacity to ease the lot of the whole populace.[19]

So living by *li* and *ren* requires self-cultivation and action—learning the moral norms, understanding the virtues, and acting to apply these to the real world. Being a superior person, then, demands knowledge and judgment as well as devotion to the noblest values and virtues.

In Confucianism, individuals are not like atoms: They are not discrete, isolated units of stuff defined only by what they're made of. Individuals are part of a complex lattice of social relationships that must be taken into account. So in Confucian ethics, *ren* tells us what virtues apply to social relationships generally, and the text called the "Five Relationships" details the most important connections and the specific duties and virtues associated with particular relationships. These relationships are between parent and child, elder brother and younger brother, husband and wife, elder and junior, and ruler and subject. Harmony will pervade society, says Confucius, when (1) parents provide for their children, and children respect and obey their parents and care for them in their old age; (2) elder brothers look after younger brothers, and the younger show deference to the elder; (3) husbands support and protect wives, and wives obey husbands and tend to children and household; (4) elders show consideration for the younger, and the younger respect and heed elders; and (5) rulers care for and protect subjects, and subjects are loyal to rulers.

The relationship on which all others are based is that of parent and child, or, as Confucius would have it, father and son. The son owes the father respect, obedience, and support—an obligation that Confucianism calls "filial piety." The central feature of this relationship is that it is hierarchical. Father and son are not equal partners; the son is subordinate. The other four relationships are also hierarchical, with the wife subordinate to the husband, the younger brother to the older, the elder to the junior, and the subject to the ruler. And as in filial piety, the subordinates have a duty of obedience and respect, and the superiors are obligated to treat the subordinates with kindness and authority, as a father would. Confucius believes that if everyone conscientiously assumes his or her proper role, harmony, happiness, and goodness will reign in the land.

At fifteen I set my heart upon learning.

At thirty, I had planted my feet firm upon the ground.

At forty, I no longer suffered from perplexities.

At fifty, I knew what were the biddings of Heaven.

At sixty, I heard them with docile ear.

At seventy, I could follow the dictates of my own heart; for what I desired no longer overstepped the boundaries of right.
—Confucius

28 Is the Confucian prescription for harmony likely to be fully implemented in Western countries? That is, could there ever be a democratic, capitalist, consumer society that was also strictly Confucian?

The noble-minded are calm and steady. Little people are forever fussing and fretting.
—Confucius

Confucius, *Analects*

On filial piety, Confucius had this to say:

Meng I Tzu asked about the treatment of parents. The Master said, Never disobey! When Ch'ih was driving his carriage for him, the Master said, Meng asked me about the treatment of parents and I said, Never disobey! Fan Ch'ih said, In what sense did you mean it? The Master said, While they are alive, serve them according to ritual. When they die, bury them according to ritual and sacrifice to them according to ritual. . . .

Confucius, *Analects*

Tzu-yu asked about the treatment of parents. The Master said, "Filial sons" nowadays are people who see to it that their parents get enough to eat. But even dogs and horses are cared for to that extent. If there is no feeling of respect, wherein lies the difference?[20]

The virtue of filial piety is still a strong force in China today, as this scholar explains:

John B. Noss, *A History of the World's Religions*

In China, loyalty to the family has been one's first loyalty. No lad in China ever comes of age, in the Western sense. It is still true that his whole service is expected to be devoted to the family until death, and he is expected to obey his father and, when his father dies, his eldest brother, with a perfect compliance. This has meant in the past that every father has a great and grave responsibility to fulfill toward his family. He must seek to produce virtue in his sons by being himself the best example of it. The fact that the present communist government speaks of making itself "father and elder brother" and claims for itself the first loyalty of every citizen has not totally invalidated the personal virtue of filial piety in the context of family life.[21]

Today the influence of the Confucian virtue of filial piety helps to explain why there is in much of Asia a greater emphasis on meeting obligations to family, community, and state than on ensuring individual rights and personal freedom.

WRITING TO UNDERSTAND:

CRITIQUING PHILOSOPHICAL VIEWS   Section 3.8

1. What are *li* and *ren*? How would society change if everyone acted according to these two virtues?
2. If you always strived to become a superior person, would your life be better than it is now or worse?
3. Confucianism downplays individual liberty and emphasizes the importance of yielding to the group in many matters. Is this an attractive aspect of Confucianism? Why or why not?
4. Does Confucianism fit easily with a Western society that has a strong respect for individual rights? Explain.
5. Would you prefer to live in a strict Confucian culture rather than the culture you live in now? Why or why not?

Review Notes

3.1 OVERVIEW: ETHICS AND THE MORAL DOMAIN

- Ethics, or moral philosophy, is the study of morality using the methods of philosophy, and morality consists of our beliefs about right and wrong actions and good and bad persons or character. Morality has to do with our moral judgments, principles, values, and theories; ethics is the careful, philosophical examination of these.

- Morality is a normative enterprise with a distinctive set of properties: overridingness, impartiality, universality, and reasonableness.

- A moral theory explains not why one event causes another, but why an action is right or wrong or why a person or a person's character is good or bad. Some theories are consequentialist (like utilitarianism and ethical egoism), and some theories are deontological (like Kant's theory).

- We can evaluate the worth of moral theories by applying the moral criteria of adequacy—consistency with our considered moral judgments, consistency with the facts of the moral life, and resourcefulness in moral problem-solving.

- The doctrine that right and wrong are constituted by God's will is known as the divine command theory. It raises the specter of the *Euthyphro* dilemma and implies that the doctrine is guilty of arbitrariness.

3.2 MORAL RELATIVISM

- Moral objectivism is the view that at least some moral norms or principles are objectively valid or true for everyone. Moral relativism says that moral standards are not objective but are relative to what individuals or cultures believe. Moral relativism pertaining to individuals is known as subjective relativism, more precisely stated as the view that right actions are those sanctioned by a person. Moral relativism regarding cultures is called cultural relativism, the view that right actions are those sanctioned by one's culture. Both forms of relativism face serious difficulties.

3.3 MORALITY BASED ON CONSEQUENCES

- Utilitarianism judges the morality of conduct by a single standard, the principle of utility—right actions are those that result in greater overall well-being (or utility) for the people involved than any other possible actions. The theory has many attractive features but also some problems, the most serious being that it seems to conflict with our considered moral judgments.

- Ethical egoism says that right actions are those that maximize one's own well-being. It is thought to be supported by the empirical theory called psychological egoism. Both theories have been subjected to intense criticism.

3.4 MORALITY BASED ON DUTY AND RIGHTS

• Kant's theory says that right actions are those that are right in themselves because they are consistent with universal moral rules derived from reason, and the actions have moral worth only if we do them out of a sense of duty. Kant's central moral tenet is the categorical imperative. Like utilitarianism, the theory has been accused of flying in the face of our considered moral judgments.

3.5 MORALITY BASED ON CHARACTER

• Virtue ethics focuses not on duty but on the development of virtuous character—not on what to do but what to be. According to virtue ethics, character is the key to the moral life, for it is from a virtuous character that moral conduct and values naturally arise.

3.6 FEMINIST ETHICS AND THE ETHICS OF CARE

• The ethics of care is a moral perspective that arose out of feminist concerns and grew to challenge core elements of most other moral theories. This approach shifts the focus from abstract principles and rules to the unique demands of specific situations and to the virtues and feelings that are central to close personal relationships. The heart of the moral life is feeling for and caring for those with whom you have a special, intimate connection.

3.7 ALBERT CAMUS: AN EXISTENTIALIST VOICE

• Several themes are prominent in existentialism, including the absurdity of human existence; existence precedes essence; we are totally responsible for how we live our lives; and we are radically and painfully free to choose what we will be and how we will respond to the absurdity of living.

3.8 CONFUCIANISM

• Confucianism is a school of thought that arose out of ancient China and, along with Taoism, has been a dominant philosophical system there for hundreds of years. Its effect on Chinese and East Asian life, culture, and government has been enormous—comparable to the influence of Christianity, Judaism, and Islam in the West.

• Confucius veered away from the supernatural beliefs of the past, for his main interest was teaching a humanistic doctrine centered on social relationships. His aim was the creation of harmony and virtue in the world—specifically in individuals, in the way they interact with one another, and in how they are treated by the state.

• *Li* has several meanings, including ritual, etiquette, principle, and propriety, but its essence is conscientious behavior and right action. To follow *li* is to conduct yourself in your dealings with others according to moral and customary norms. *Ren* is about social virtues; it encompasses benevolence, sympathy, kindness, generosity, respect for others, and human-heartedness. At its core is the imperative to work for the common good and to recognize the essential worth of others regardless of their social status.

WRITING TO UNDERSTAND: ARGUING YOUR OWN VIEWS — Chapter 3

1. According to Kant, right actions do not depend on consequences. He says, for example, that telling a lie is wrong even if it will save someone's life. But many people think that in this case *not* lying is wrong, because it's more important to preserve life than to blindly follow a moral rule. Do you agree with this assessment or with Kant? Give reasons for your answer.

2. Does it make sense to use utilitarian reasoning in deciding how to fight a war? How might a deontologist and a utilitarian differ in deciding on the morality of dropping the A-bomb on Hiroshima during World War II? Which approach seems more plausible? Why?

3. Is Aristotle's ethics sufficiently action guiding? Does it help us make decisions? If we ask what we should do in situation X, Aristotle would seem to say, "Do what the virtuous person would do." But if I ask how I am to recognize the virtuous person, he would seem to say, "He is one who acts justly." Is there something circular about this reasoning? Does virtue ethics need supplementation from other ethical systems, or can it solve this problem?

4. Is it plausible that we have duties only to those we care about? Don't we have duties to some people we don't care about? Don't we have obligations to deal justly with others and respect their rights, even if they are not part of our family or community? Give reasons for your answers.

5. What is your own view of what makes actions right or wrong? What reasons support this position?

Key Terms

act-utilitarianism The idea that the rightness of actions depends solely on the overall well-being produced by *individual actions*. (150)

Analects Confucian text containing the conversations of Confucius and his followers. (184)

categorical imperative Kant's fundamental moral principle, which he formulates as (1) "I am never to act otherwise than so *that I could also will that my maxim should become a universal law*," and (2) "So act as to treat humanity, whether in thine own person or in that of any other, in every case as an end withal, never as a means only." (164)

consequentialist theory A moral theory in which the rightness of actions depends solely on their consequences or results. (135)

cultural relativism The view that right actions are those endorsed by one's culture. (143)

deontological (nonconsequentialist) theory A moral theory in which the rightness of actions is determined not solely by their consequences, but partly or entirely by their intrinsic nature. (135)

divine command theory The doctrine that God is the creator of morality. (141)

ethical egoism The view that right actions are those that further one's own best interests. (135)

ethics (moral philosophy) The study of morality using the methods of philosophy. (131)

ethics of care A moral perspective that emphasizes the unique demands of specific situations and the virtues and feelings that are central to close personal relationships. (136, 175)

feminist ethics An approach to morality aimed at advancing women's interests, underscoring their distinctive experiences and characteristics, and advancing the obvious truth that women and men are morally equal. (174)

Kant's theory The theory that right actions are those that accord with the categorical imperative. (136)

li In early Confucianism, ritual, etiquette, principle, and propriety; conscientious behavior and right action. (184)

moral absolutism The belief that objective moral principles allow no exceptions or must be applied the same way in all cases and cultures. (143)

moral objectivism The view that there are moral standards that are true or correct for everyone. (143)

moral relativism The view that moral standards do not have independent status but are relative to what individuals or cultures believe. (143)

moral theory A theory that explains why an action is right or wrong or why a person or a person's character is good or bad. (134)

morality Beliefs about right and wrong actions and good and bad persons or character. (131)

psychological egoism The theory that people always act out of self-interest. (159)

ren The essential Confucian virtues, including benevolence, sympathy, kindness, generosity, respect for others, and human-heartedness. (184)

rule-utilitarianism The doctrine that a right action is one that conforms to a rule that, if followed consistently, would create for everyone involved the most beneficial balance of well-being over suffering. (150)

subjective relativism The view that right actions are those endorsed by an individual. (143)

utilitarianism The view that right actions are those that result in the most beneficial balance of good over bad consequences for everyone involved. (135)

virtue ethics A moral theory that focuses on the development of virtuous character. (136, 169)

FICTION

The Ones Who Walk Away from Omelas

Ursula K. Le Guin

> Born in 1929, Ursula K. Le Guin is an award-winning author of several genres, most notably realistic fiction, science fiction, and fantasy. Her best-known works include the six *Books of Earthsea*, the science fiction masterpiece *The Left Hand of Darkness*, and the novels *The Dispossessed* and *Always Coming Home*.

With a clamor of bells that set the swallows soaring, the Festival of Summer came to the city Omelas, bright-towered by the sea. The rigging of the boats in harbor sparkled with flags. In the streets between houses with red roofs and painted walls, between old moss-grown gardens and under avenues of trees, past great parks and public buildings, processions moved. Some were decorous: old people in long stiff robes of mauve and grey, grave master work-men, quiet, merry women carrying their babies and chatting as they walked. In other streets the music beat faster, a shimmering of gong and tambourine, and the people went dancing, the procession was a dance. Children dodged in and out, their high calls rising like the swallows' crossing flights over the music and the singing. All the processions wound towards the north side of the city, where on the great water-meadow called the Green Fields boys and girls, naked in the bright air, with mud-stained feet and ankles and long, lithe arms, exercised their restive horses before the race. The horses wore no gear at all but a halter without bit. Their manes were braided with streamers of silver, gold, and green. They flared their nostrils and pranced and boasted to one another; they were vastly excited, the horse being the only animal who has adopted our ceremonies as his own. Far off to the north and west the mountains stood up half encircling Omelas on her bay. The air of morning was so clear that the snow still crowning the Eighteen Peaks burned with white-gold fire across the miles of sunlit air, under the dark blue of the sky. There was just enough wind to make the banners that marked the racecourse snap and flutter now and then. In the silence of the broad green meadows one could hear the music winding through the city streets, farther and nearer and ever approaching, a cheerful faint sweetness of the air that from time to time trembled and gathered together and broke out into the great joyous clanging of the bells.

Joyous! How is one to tell about joy? How describe the citizens of Omelas?

They were not simple folk, you see, though they were happy. But we do not say the words of cheer much any more. All smiles have become archaic. Given a description such as this one tends to make certain assumptions. Given a description such as this one tends to look next for the King, mounted on a splendid stallion and surrounded by his noble knights, or perhaps in a golden litter borne by great-muscled slaves. But there was no king. They did not use swords, or keep slaves. They were not barbarians. I do not know the rules and laws of their society, but I suspect that they were singularly few. As they did without monarchy and slavery, so they also got on without the stock exchange, the advertisement, the secret police, and the bomb. Yet I repeat that these were not simple folk, not dulcet shepherds, noble savages, bland utopians. They were not less complex than us. The trouble is that we have a bad habit, encouraged by pedants and sophisticates, of considering happiness as something rather stupid. Only pain is intellectual, only evil interesting. This is the treason of the artist: a refusal to admit the banality of evil and the terrible boredom of pain. If you can't lick 'em, join 'em. If it hurts, repeat it. But to praise despair is to condemn delight, to embrace violence is to lose hold of everything else. We have almost lost hold; we can no longer describe a happy man, nor make any celebration of joy. How can I tell you about the people of Omelas? They were not naive and happy children—though their children were, in fact, happy. They were mature, intelligent, passionate adults whose lives were not wretched. O miracle! but I wish I could describe it better. I wish I could convince you. Omelas sounds in my words like a

Ursula K. Le Guin, 1973; first appeared in *New Dimensions 3*; from *The Wind's Twelve Quarters*; reprinted by permission of the author and the author's agent, the Virginia Kidd Agency, Inc.

city in a fairy tale, long ago and far away, once upon a time. Perhaps it would be best if you imagined it as your own fancy bids, assuming it will rise to the occasion, for certainly I cannot suit you all. For instance, how about technology? I think that there would be no cars or helicopters in and above the streets; this follows from the fact that the people of Omelas are happy people. Happiness is based on a just discrimination of what is necessary, what is neither necessary nor destructive, and what is destructive. In the middle category, however—that of the unnecessary but undestructive, that of comfort, luxury, exuberance, etc.—they could perfectly well have central heating, subway trains, washing machines, and all kinds of marvelous devices not yet invented here, floating light-sources, fuelless power, a cure for the common cold. Or they could have none of that: it doesn't matter. As you like it. I incline to think that people from towns up and down the coast have been coming in to Omelas during the last days before the Festival on very fast little trains and double-decked trams, and that the train station of Omelas is actually the handsomest building in town, though plainer than the magnificent Farmers' Market. But even granted trains, I fear that Omelas so far strikes some of you as goody-goody. Smiles, bells, parades, horses, blah. If so, please add an orgy. If an orgy would help, don't hesitate. Let us not, however, have temples from which issue beautiful nude priests and priestesses already half in ecstasy and ready to copulate with any man or woman, lover or stranger, who desires union with the deep godhead of the blood, although that was my first idea. But really it would be better not to have any temples in Omelas—at least, not manned temples. Religion yes, clergy no. Surely the beautiful nudes can just wander about, offering themselves like divine soufflés to the hunger of the needy and the rapture of the flesh. Let them join the processions. Let tambourines be struck above the copulations, and the glory of desire be proclaimed upon the gongs, and (a not unimportant point) let the offspring of these delightful rituals be beloved and looked after by all. One thing I know there is none of in Omelas is guilt. But what else should there be? I thought at first there were no drugs, but that is puritanical. For those who like it, the faint insistent sweetness of *drooz* may perfume the ways of the city, *drooz* which first brings a great lightness and brilliance to the mind and limbs, and then after some hours a dreamy languor, and wonderful visions at last of the very arcana and inmost secrets of the Universe, as well as exciting the pleasure of sex beyond all belief; and it is not habit-forming. For more modest tastes I think there ought to be beer. What else, what else belongs in the joyous city? The sense of victory, surely, the celebration of courage. But as we did without clergy, let us do without soldiers. The joy built upon successful slaughter is not the right kind of joy; it will not do; it is fearful and it is trivial. A boundless and generous contentment, a magnanimous triumph felt not against some outer enemy but in communion with the finest and fairest in the souls of all men everywhere and the splendor of the world's summer: this is what swells the hearts of the people of Omelas, and the victory they celebrate is that of life. I really don't think many of them need to take *drooz*.

Most of the processions have reached the Green Fields by now. A marvelous smell of cooking goes forth from the red and blue tents of the provisioners. The faces of small children are amiably sticky; in the benign grey beard of a man a couple of crumbs of rich pastry are entangled. The youths and girls have mounted their horses and are beginning to group around the starting line of the course. An old woman, small, fat, and laughing, is passing out flowers from a basket, and tall young men wear her flowers in their shining hair. A child of nine or ten sits at the edge of the crowd, alone, playing on a wooden flute. People pause to listen, and they smile, but they do not speak to him, for he never ceases playing and never sees them, his dark eyes wholly rapt in the sweet, thin magic of the tune.

He finishes, and slowly lowers his hands holding the wooden flute.

As if that little private silence were the signal, all at once a trumpet sounds from the pavilion near the starting line: imperious, melancholy, piercing. The horses rear on their slender legs, and some of them neigh in answer. Sober-faced, the young riders stroke the horses' necks and soothe them, whispering, "Quiet, quiet, there my beauty, my hope. . . ." They begin to form in rank along the starting line. The crowds along the racecourse are like a field of grass and flowers in the wind. The Festival of Summer has begun.

Do you believe? Do you accept the festival, the city, the joy? No? Then let me describe one more thing.

In a basement under one of the beautiful public buildings of Omelas, or perhaps in the cellar of one of its spacious private homes, there is a room. It has one locked door, and no window. A little light seeps in dustily between cracks in the boards, secondhand from a cobwebbed window somewhere across the cellar. In one corner of the little room a couple of mops, with stiff, clotted, foul-smelling heads, stand near a rusty bucket. The floor is dirt, a little damp to the touch, as cellar dirt usually is. The room is about three paces long and two wide: a mere broom closet or disused tool room. In the room a child is sitting. It could be a boy or a girl. It looks about six, but actually is nearly ten. It is feeble-minded. Perhaps it was born defective, or perhaps it has become imbecile through fear, malnutrition, and neglect. It picks its nose and occasionally fumbles vaguely with its toes or genitals, as it sits hunched in the corner farthest from the bucket and the two mops. It is afraid of the mops. It finds them horrible. It shuts its eyes, but it knows the mops are still standing there; and the door is locked; and nobody will come. The door is always locked; and nobody ever comes, except that sometimes—the child has no understanding of time or interval—sometimes the door rattles terribly and opens, and a person, or several people, are there. One of them may come in and kick the child to make it stand up. The others never come close, but peer in at it with frightened, disgusted eyes. The food bowl and the water jug are hastily filled, the door is locked, the eyes disappear. The people at the door never say anything, but the child, who has not always lived in the tool room, and can remember sunlight and its mother's voice, sometimes speaks. "I will be good," it says. "Please let me out. I will be good!" They never answer. The child used to scream for help at night, and cry a good deal, but now it only makes a kind of whining, "eh-haa, eh-haa," and it speaks less and less often. It is so thin there are no calves to its legs; its belly protrudes; it lives on a half-bowl of cornmeal and grease a day. It is naked. Its buttocks and thighs are a mass of festered sores, as it sits in its own excrement continually.

They all know it is there, all the people of Omelas. Some of them have come to see it, others are content merely to know it is there. They all know that it has to be there. Some of them understand why, and some do not, but they all understand that their happiness, the beauty of their city, the tenderness of their friendships, the health of their children, the wisdom of their scholars, the skill of their makers, even the abundance of their harvest and the kindly weathers of their skies, depend wholly on this child's abominable misery.

This is usually explained to children when they are between eight and twelve, whenever they seem capable of understanding; and most of those who come to see the child are young people, though often enough an adult comes, or comes back, to see the child. No matter how well the matter has been explained to them, these young spectators are always shocked and sickened at the sight. They feel disgust, which they had thought themselves superior to. They feel anger, outrage, impotence, despite all the explanations. They would like to do something for the child. But there is nothing they can do. If the child were brought up into the sunlight out of that vile place, if it were cleaned and fed and comforted, that would be a good thing, indeed; but if it were done, in that day and hour all the prosperity and beauty and delight of Omelas would wither and be destroyed. Those are the terms. To exchange all the goodness and grace of every life in Omelas for that single, small improvement: to throw away the happiness of thousands for the chance of the happiness of one: that would be to let guilt within the walls indeed.

The terms are strict and absolute; there may not even be a kind word spoken to the child.

Often the young people go home in tears, or in a tearless rage, when they have seen the child and faced this terrible paradox. They may brood over it for weeks or years. But as time goes on they begin to realize that even if the child could be released, it would not get much good of its freedom: a little vague pleasure of warmth and food, no doubt, but little more. It is too degraded and imbecile to know any real joy. It has been afraid too long ever to be free of fear. Its habits are too uncouth for it to respond to humane treatment. Indeed, after so long it would probably be wretched without walls about it to protect it, and darkness for its eyes, and its own excrement to sit in. Their tears at the bitter injustice dry when they begin to perceive the terrible justice of reality, and to accept it. Yet it is their tears and anger, the trying of their generosity and the acceptance of their helplessness, which are perhaps the true source of the splendor of their lives. Theirs is no vapid, irresponsible happiness. They know that they, like the child, are not free. They know compassion. It is the existence of the child, and their knowledge of its existence, that makes possible the nobility of their architecture, the poignancy of their music, the profundity of their science. It is because of the child that they are so gentle with children. They know that if the wretched one were not there snivelling in the dark, the other one, the flute-player, could make no joyful music as the young riders line up in their beauty for the race in the sunlight of the first morning of summer.

Now do you believe in them? Are they not more credible? But there is one more thing to tell, and this is quite incredible.

At times one of the adolescent girls or boys who go to see the child does not go home to weep or rage, does not, in fact, go home at all. Sometimes also a man or woman much older falls silent for a day or two, and then leaves home. These people go out into the street, and walk down the street alone. They keep walking, and walk straight out of the city of Omelas, through the beautiful gates. They keep walking across the farmlands of Omelas. Each one goes alone, youth or girl, man or woman. Night falls; the traveler must pass down village streets, between the houses with yellow-lit windows, and on out into the darkness of the fields. Each alone, they go west or north, towards the mountains. They go on. They leave Omelas, they walk ahead into the darkness, and they do not come back. The place they go towards is a place even less imaginable to most of us than the city of happiness. I cannot describe it at all. It is possible that it does not exist. But they seem to know where they are going, the ones who walk away from Omelas.

Probing Questions

1. How does this story apply to utilitarian moral theories? Does it put these theories in a good light or bad—or something in between?

2. Does our happiness in a relatively prosperous nation depend on the suffering of the poorer people of the world who work for low wages to support our consumer society?

3. If you were a citizen of Omelas, would you walk away from it as a few have done? Would you think that the suffering of one child, though regrettable, was justified to create a utopia for so many to enjoy? Explain.

For Further Reading

Robert Audi, *Moral Knowledge and Ethical Character* (New York: Oxford University Press, 1997). A carefully argued defense of a moral theory that integrates naturalist and rationalistic elements.

Steven M. Cahn and Joram G. Haber, *Twentieth Century Ethical Theory* (Upper Saddle River, NJ: Prentice-Hall, 1995). A comprehensive anthology of some of the most influential moral theorizing of the twentieth century.

William K. Frankena, *Ethics*, 2nd edition (Englewood Cliffs, NJ: Prentice-Hall, 1973). A highly regarded concise introduction to ethics.

C. E. Harris, *Applying Moral Theories* (Belmont, CA: Wadsworth, 1997). An introduction to ethics that covers moral theories and how they can be applied to real issues.

Kai Nielsen, *Ethics Without God* (Buffalo, NY: Prometheus, 1973). A concise, readable defense of the proposition that ethics does not require theism.

Onora O'Neill, "Kantian Ethics," in *A Companion to Ethics*, ed. Peter Singer (Cambridge: Blackwell, 1993), 175–185. An informative perspective on Kant's ethical theory.

Jennifer Oldstone-Moore, *Confucianism: Origins, Beliefs, Practices, Holy Texts, and Sacred Places* (New York: Oxford University Press, 2002).

Louis P. Pojman, *Ethics: Discovering Right and Wrong*, 4th edition (Belmont, CA: Wadsworth, 2002). An introduction to ethics that lays out a case for objective morality.

James Rachels, *The Elements of Moral Philosophy*, 4th edition (New York: McGraw-Hill, 2003). A concise guide to ethics and ethical theories.

Russ Shafer-Landau, *Whatever Happened to Good and Evil?* (New York: Oxford University Press, 2004). A readable, carefully crafted defense of objective ethics.

Peter Singer, ed., *A Companion to Ethics* (Cambridge: Blackwell, 1993). A topical anthology covering many issues, including moral theory, theory applications, and challenges to commonsense ethics.

Lewis Vaughn, *Contemporary Moral Arguments: Readings in Ethical Issues* (New York: Oxford University Press, 2010). A moral-issues anthology organized by topic and by influential, classic arguments.

Lewis Vaughn, *Doing Ethics: Moral Reasoning and Contemporary Issues*, 4th edition (New York: W. W. Norton, 2010). An introduction to ethical issues featuring a wide range of readings and thorough coverage of moral reasoning and ethical theory.

CHAPTER 4

MIND AND BODY

Chapter Objectives

4.1 OVERVIEW: THE MIND–BODY PROBLEM

- Understand the nature and importance of the mind–body problem.
- Define *substance dualism, Cartesian dualism, materialism, logical behaviorism, identity theory, multiple realizability, functionalism, epiphenomenalism,* and *property dualism.*

4.2 SUBSTANCE DUALISM

- Articulate Descartes' conceivability and divisibility arguments and the main objections to them.
- Explain why the issue of mind–body interaction is a problem for Cartesian dualism.
- Understand why Descartes' theory seems to violate the principle of the causal closure of the physical and the law of the conservation of mass-energy and be able to explain why such violations would render the theory implausible.

4.3 MIND–BODY IDENTITY

- Articulate the advantages of the identity theory over Cartesian dualism.
- Understand Chalmers's zombie argument and why it seems to pose a threat to the identity theory.
- Understand Nagel's bat argument and how it seems to undermine materialist theories.

4.4 THE MIND AS SOFTWARE

- Explain functionalism and how the theory differs from substance dualism and the identity theory.
- Describe Ned Block's absent qualia argument, explain how it is supposed to show functionalism to be false, and articulate possible responses to the argument from functionalists.
- Define strong AI and explain how functionalism is supposed to make it possible.

- Understand Searle's Chinese room thought experiment, his distinction between syntax and semantics, and how his argument is supposed to show that strong AI is not possible.

4.5 THE MIND AS PROPERTIES

- Understand how philosophers have reasoned from the failure of prominent mind–body theories to the plausibility of property dualism.
- Explain the main philosophical challenge to property dualism.

4.1 OVERVIEW: THE MIND–BODY PROBLEM

Philosophy is notorious for intruding into facets of life that seem at first glance to get along just fine without philosophical inquiry. People may very well wonder, Why do we need philosophy to help us understand what already seems obvious? Why does philosophy see problems where nothing seems problematic? A prime example of a subject matter that may appear to many not to need any philosophical help (but gets it anyway) is mind and body. After all, if there is anything that we seem directly and intimately acquainted with, it's our own minds and our own bodies. And our commonplace theory about these things (usually derived from our culture or religion) seems to be perfectly consistent with our personal experience. So what's the problem?

Well, several hundred years of philosophical work have shown that many of our commonplace notions about mind and body are suspect or wrong, and that, for many reasons, we very much need to get them right. The commonplace view goes like this: You have a *physical* body, a thing that has shape, size, and weight, an entity with a physical structure running physical processes subject to physical laws like any rock, tree, or star. You also have a *nonphysical* mind (or soul), a mental thing that cannot be weighed, measured, or dissected, an entity that thinks, feels, and senses. Your body (brain) is nothing like your mind; your mind is nothing like your body. Yet somehow your physical body affects your nonphysical mind, as when your dropping a brick on your foot causes you to feel a sharp pain and to ask yourself how you could be so clumsy. And your mind affects your body, as when you experience thirst and then decide to walk to the kitchen for a drink of water. Moreover, according to this view, your mind and body are independent of one another, so it's possible for your mind or soul to continue existing after your body dies.

But how are interactions between body and mind (or soul) possible? How can our physical brains cause something to happen in our seemingly nonphysical minds and vice versa? How can something entirely physical have anything to do with an entity without any physical characteristics? This is like asking how smoke could interact with a rock—except that the problem is worse than that, because, unlike smoke, the mind is supposed to have no physical properties at all. Has the nature of mind been

Tis true, tis certain; man though dead retains, Part of himself: the immortal mind remains.
—Alexander Pope

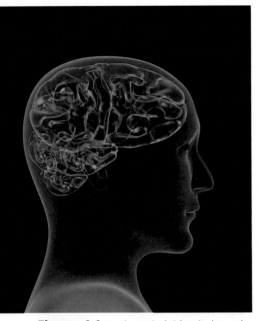

Figure 4.1 Is the mind identical to the brain? Or are they two entirely different things, as Descartes thought? If so, how do they interact?

The **mind–body problem** is the issue of what mental phenomena are and how they relate to the physical world.

Substance dualism is the notion that mind and body consist of two fundamentally different kinds of stuff, or substances.

Consciousness is the glory of creation.
—James Broughton

Cartesian dualism is the view that mind (or soul) and body are completely independent of one another and interact causally.

Materialism (or **physicalism**) is the doctrine that every object and event in the world is physical.

entirely misconceived? Are the widely accepted ideas about the relationship between mind and body drastically mistaken?

These are the central concerns in what is called the **mind–body problem**—the issue of what mental phenomena really are and how they relate to the physical world. The most important responses to it constitute the foremost theories of mind in Western thought.

The commonplace theory—the one that you likely hold and may never have doubted—is known as **substance dualism**. It says that mind and body consist of two fundamentally different kinds of stuff, or substances—the mind being of nonphysical stuff, and the body of physical stuff. The mind's mental states—desires, sensations, emotions, and thoughts—are states of nonphysical (or immaterial) stuff. The body's physical states—electrochemical and biomechanical—are states of physical (material) stuff. Together these two substances—this dualism of stuff—make up a person. In fact, for substance dualists, the entire universe is constituted by just these two substances.

Beginning with Plato, many great thinkers have been substance dualists, but the most influential proponent of the theory in the modern period (beginning in the seventeenth century) is René Descartes (1596–1650). He argues not only that the body and soul are composed of two distinct and independent substances (mental and physical), but that these two parts of a person interact causally. (Like many other substance dualists, Descartes uses the word *soul* instead of *mind*, but both terms refer roughly to the nonphysical, mental aspect of a person.) The mind, though immaterial, can influence the material body, and the body can affect the mind. This doctrine of distinct but interacting substances is known, for obvious reasons, as **Cartesian dualism** or interactionism. It underpins belief in an immortal soul that lives on after death.

Among contemporary philosophers, however, Descartes' dualism has very little credibility (for reasons discussed in the next section). Most of them hold instead to various forms of **materialism** (or **physicalism**), the doctrine that every object and event in the world is physical. So mental states must be physical states or somehow reducible to physical states.

One materialist theory is **logical behaviorism**, the idea that mental states are dispositions to behave in particular ways in certain circumstances. To be in a mental state is just to be disposed to certain kinds of behavior. So to have a headache is to be disposed to wincing and taking an aspirin. To be afraid of thunder is to be disposed to crying out and covering your head with a blanket when the sky rumbles. The central claim is not that we come to know about a person's mental states by taking note of her behavior, but that her mental states *are* dispositions to behavior.

To its credit, logical behaviorism avoids Cartesian dualism's problem of explaining mind–body interaction. But to critics, the theory seems to be in denial about the nature of our mental states, for many of our mental states have a particular subjective feel or quality to them (what philosophers call *qualitative content* or *qualia*). It feels a certain way to us to be in pain, to be thirsty, to want a chocolate sundae, to see and smell a rose, or to experience happiness. Logical behaviorism, however, says that mental states have nothing to do with our interior feelings; dispositions to behave are all that matter. But this seems to many people to deny the obvious.

Similarly, logical behaviorism is at odds with our commonsense intuition that mental states often *cause* behavior. We feel hungry, so we eat lunch. We fantasize about a dream vacation in Aruba, so we look up Aruba on a map. But because the logical behaviorist recognizes only behavior and essentially discounts the existence of subjective mental states, he cannot countenance any cause-and-effect relationship between our inner life and our outer behavior.

A more widely accepted materialist approach to the mind–body problem is the **identity theory**, the view that mental states are identical to physical brain states. The central claim is not that the meaning of mental terms can be expressed or defined in physical (brain) terms, but rather that it is an empirical fact that *mental states are nothing but brain states*. The mind and body (brain) are not distinct substances as substance dualism holds; the mind *is* the brain.

Thus the identity theory offers a better explanation of mind–body interaction than Cartesian dualism does because the mind is the body. It provides a better account of mental causation than logical behaviorism does, because mental states are brain states and brain states cause behavior. It also fits well with a massive amount of scientific evidence showing correlations between brain states and mental function. Brain research has shown in countless ways that if a person's brain is damaged

1 At this point in your reading, does Cartesian dualism strike you as a plausible theory of mind? Is it obvious to you that people have both a physical body and a nonphysical mind? What reasons do you have for your views?

Logical behaviorism is the idea that mental states are dispositions to behave in particular ways in certain circumstances.

Consciousness is what makes the mind–body problem really intractable.
—Thomas Nagel

Identity theory is the view that mental states are identical to physical brain states.

2 Do you think it is possible to know everything about a person's mental states just by knowing all the facts regarding his physical states? Do physical states and mental states amount to the same thing?

Figure 4.2 Could a space alien have a mind without having a brain like ours?

Brain: an apparatus with
which we think we think.
—Ambrose Bierce

or physically stimulated, there are corresponding changes in psychological activity.
And when a person engages in some psychological activity (remembering or imagining, for example), there are predictable alterations in brain activity.

But several arguments have been lodged against the identity theory, most of
them being attempts to show that mental states cannot possibly be brain states. The
common argument pattern is this: If the identity theory is true, then we can know
or explain everything about a person's mental states by knowing or explaining everything about the person's brain states. But it is not possible to know or explain mental
states by knowing or explaining brain states. Therefore, the identity theory is false.

Another kind of argument appeals to our intuitions about the possibility of non-
humans having minds. The identity theory claims that since the mind is identical to
the brain, no being can have a mind unless it has a brain. But to some critics, this
conclusion is implausible. It seems possible, they argue, that a being (an alien life-
form, for example) could possess a mind (have desires, ideas, emotions, sensations,
etc.) without having a brain (the human organ). Consider the fictional alien E.T. or
Star Trek's android Mr. Data. It is conceivable that such creatures could have minds
but be made of an entirely different kind of stuff than we are. If so, there must be
something wrong with the identity theory.

Multiple realizability is
the capacity to be realized
or instantiated in a variety
of forms and materials.

Functionalism is the
view that the mind is the
functions that the brain
performs.

The assumption behind this argument is that mental states have what philosophers call **multiple realizability**, the capacity to be realized or instantiated in a
variety of forms and materials. In the theory of mind known as **functionalism**,
multiple realizability is a core doctrine. Logical behaviorism claims that the mind
is behavioral dispositions; the identity theory holds that the mind is the brain; but
functionalism asserts that the mind is the *functions* that the brain performs. The
theory maintains that a mental state is defined by its causal role—by the stimuli that
initiate it, the resulting interactions with other mental states, and the behavior that
is subsequently produced. A mental state, then, is just a distinctive set of inputs and
outputs. Thus functionalism says that the material or substance that gives rise to a
mind is unimportant; the stuff that produces a mind can be almost anything. What
matters are the functional relations embodied in the stuff. So functionalism can be
cast as a materialist view (and usually is) or given a nonmaterialist interpretation.

3 Is it conceivable that
a space alien could
have a mind (feel pain,
perceive colors, etc.)
despite his being made
out of stuff that is
nothing like our brain
stuff? Suppose, for
example, he is not a
carbon-based life-form
like us, but a silicon-
based creature.

Inspired by the insight behind functionalism, some theorists have come to think
of the mind as a sophisticated computer that's running some sort of software. Functionalism holds that the mind is the performance of functions, the processing of
inputs and outputs—which is what any computer does. A computer runs software
that determines what and how the inputs and outputs are processed. So some functionalists claim that to have a mind is just to run the appropriate type of software.
The brain is hardware; the mind software. If so, it is possible for computers to have
minds as long as they process inputs and outputs in the right way.

This view has come to be known as *strong artificial intelligence*, or strong AI.
(*Weak artificial intelligence* refers not to the making of a mind but to the use of computer simulations to study the mind.) Many assume that it is only a matter of time
before scientists develop a computer so sophisticated that it will be able to think on
its own, to have what we would describe as a mind. After all, don't we already have
computers that can do astounding calculations, simulations, and problem solving?

Hasn't an IBM computer called Deep Blue already defeated the world's best chess player, Garry Kasparov? And hasn't a computer called Watson beaten two human opponents in a game of Jeopardy? But although such feats are indeed impressive, many philosophers remain unconvinced that a computer mind is possible.

These theorists take issue with functionalism on the grounds that it does not do justice to the subjective, qualitative nature of our experience—to what is called phenomenal consciousness. They argue that it is possible to be in a mental state that does not correspond at all with a specific functional state. For example, consider the mental state of being in pain. It has a certain qualitative feel to be sure, but it does not seem to be equivalent to any particular functional situation. Many times pain doesn't seem to have a causal role at all; it just hurts.

Some critics put forth what are called *absent qualia* objections to functionalism. These arguments try to demonstrate that it is possible for a

Figure 4.3 World chess champion Garry Kasparov playing Deep Blue. The computer beat him. Does this show that Deep Blue has a mind or that it could eventually become conscious?

system to be in a particular functional state and yet be in no mental, qualitative state at all. The system has the right inputs and outputs, but no mental state seems to be present. If such arguments are correct, then the notion that an appropriately programmed computer is a mind (the central claim of strong AI) is mistaken.

Many philosophers draw a similar conclusion about all materialist theories: materialism is false. If that is the case, they contend, the world must have both physical and nonphysical features, and the latter cannot be reduced to the former.

But if the world contains both physical and nonphysical things, aren't we led back to Cartesian dualism, a reality consisting of two substances that may or may not interact? Not necessarily. Some theorists defend a different kind of dualism—not Descartes' dualism but **property dualism**, the view that mental properties, or features, are nonphysical properties arising from, but not reducible to, physical properties. The idea is that there are properties of individuals—mental, experiential properties—that do not constitute an independent substance and that cannot be reduced to physical properties, even though they may somehow depend on physical properties. We may see the color red, feel a pain, or remember our first kiss, and none of these is the same thing as a physical process, although the latter may give rise to the former.

Property dualism, however, has been accused of having some of the same weaknesses as substance dualism and raising some of the same questions. How can a physical property give rise to a mental property? How can mental events interact with physical events? If mental events produce physical events, doesn't this fly in the face of the laws of physics? Modern physics says that physical matter/energy in the universe cannot be added to or subtracted from. But this seems to rule out any

Curiously enough man's body and his mind appear to differ in their climatic adaptations.
—Ellsworth Huntington

Property dualism is the view that mental properties are nonphysical properties arising from, but not reducible to, physical properties.

Minds are simply what brains do.
—Marvin Minsky

Epiphenomenalism is the notion that mental properties do not cause anything, but merely accompany physical processes.

addition of nonphysical energy. If mental events do not cause physical events, we are left with **epiphenomenalism**, the notion that mental properties do not cause anything, but merely accompany physical processes. This theory suggests, for instance, that thinking about being late for an appointment is not what causes you to run. But epiphenomenalism seems to conflict with our commonsense intuitions about how our minds and bodies are related.

WRITING TO UNDERSTAND:
CRITIQUING PHILOSOPHICAL VIEWS   Section 4.1

1. Is Cartesian dualism plausible? Can you think of a way that a non-physical mind and physical body could influence each other—that is, interact causally?

2. How do you think scientists view the notion of mind–body interaction? Are they likely to be skeptical of physical things causally interacting with nonphysical entities? If so, why?

3. Is multiple realizability a genuine property of minds? That is, do you think it plausible that a mind can be realized in a variety of physical systems?

4. Do you think the mind is essentially software running on a physical system like the human brain? Why or why not?

5. Is epiphenomenalism a credible theory of mind? Does it make sense, for example, that every time you decide to cross the street, your body walks across the street—and yet your deciding to walk has nothing to do with your actually walking?

4.2 SUBSTANCE DUALISM

For Descartes, the universe consists not merely of the kind of stuff that science studies, the physical, but also of the nonphysical. The chief characteristic of physical things, he says, is that they have *extension*—they have length, width, and height and are located in physical space. They are things like pebbles, molecules, water, desks, and stars. But nonphysical entities have no molecules, no physical dimensions, and no location in space. Our bodies are physical things, matter extended in space. Our minds are nonphysical, mental things—consciousness. Our true selves consist entirely of this mental stuff; our bodies are adjuncts. Despite the profound difference between the mental and physical, they interact causally. The body collects sensory data, which cause the mind to experience sights, sounds, textures, and odors; and the choices, beliefs, and desires of the mind cause the body to respond to the world. A human being, then, is a fusion of body and mind, but the essential person, the self, is pure mind, an immortal soul. You are, in the famous phrase, a "ghost in the machine."

Descartes formulated his type of dualism in the seventeenth century when the findings of science and the doctrines of traditional religion seemed to be in conflict. His dualism helped to ease the tension between them by placing science and religion in different, noncompeting realms. Science could concern itself with the physical—with biology, physics, astronomy, and the like. Religion could focus on the mental, on the domain of immortal souls and religious morality.

You don't have a soul. You are a Soul. You have a body.
—C. S. Lewis

Descartes offers several arguments to support his theory of mind, including what philosophers call his *conceivability argument*. In it Descartes contends that we cannot be just physical bodies, as the materialists believe. We must be *distinct* from our bodies—we must be nonphysical minds. This is how Descartes lays out the argument:

René Descartes, *Discourse on the Method of Rightly Conducting the Reason*

And then, examining attentively that which I was, I saw that I could conceive that I had no body, and that there was no world nor place where I might be; but yet that I could not for all that conceive that I was not. On the contrary, I saw from the very fact that I thought of doubting the truth of other things, it very evidently and certainly followed that I was; on the other hand if I had only ceased from thinking, even if all the rest of what I had ever imagined had really existed, I should have no reason for thinking that I had existed. From that I knew that I was a substance the whole essence or nature of which is to think, and that for its existence there is no need of any place, nor does it depend on any material thing; so that this 'me,' that is to say, the soul by which I am what I am, is entirely distinct from body, and is even more easy to know than is the latter; and even if body were not, the soul would not cease to be what it is.[1]

Descartes reasons that it is conceivable that he could exist without his body, and that whatever is conceivable is logically possible. (For example, silver unicorns are conceivable and thus logically possible; square circles are inconceivable and therefore logically impossible.) So it is logically possible that he could exist without his body. If it is logically possible that he could exist without his body, then he is not identical to his body. His nonphysical mind and his physical body are distinct; he is therefore an immaterial, thinking thing. Dualism is true.

4 Is your existing without a body really conceivable? That is, can you conceive of your mind existing without any physical properties at all, without even a ghostlike quasi-physical presence?

Philosophers have taken issue with this argument. Their main criticism is that Descartes' first premise (that it is conceivable that he could exist without his body) is dubious. Theodore Schick, Jr., states the complaint like this:

Theodore Schick, Jr., *Doing Philosophy*

The crucial premise here is that disembodied existence is conceivable. Is it? Try the thought experiment yourself. Imagine you have no body—no arms, no legs, no hands, no eyes, no ears, and so on. Can you do it? If so, are you really imagining existing

Theodore Schick, Jr.,
Doing Philosophy

without a body, or are you imagining existing in a ghostlike quasi-physical body? Remember, Cartesian minds have no physical attributes, not even a location in space. You wouldn't be able to do anything (besides think) or feel anything because you wouldn't have a body. You wouldn't be able to communicate with others unless you were given some sort of telepathic ability. But, even then, it's unclear how you would identify them, for they, too, would have neither a body nor a location in space.[2]

My mind is incapable of conceiving such a thing as a soul. I may be in error, and man may have a soul; but I simply do not believe it.
—Thomas A. Edison

If disembodied existence is not conceivable, then it is not logically possible and Descartes' argument fails.

Descartes also tries to prove his dualist theory using the *divisibility argument*. The crux of this reasoning is that bodies and minds must be different things (and thus dualism is true) because bodies can be divided into parts but minds cannot. As Descartes says,

René Descartes, *Meditations on First Philosophy*

In order to begin this examination, then, I here say, in the first place, that there is a great difference between mind and body, inasmuch as body is by nature always divisible, and the mind is entirely indivisible. For, as a matter of fact, when I consider the mind, that is to say, myself inasmuch as I am only a thinking thing, I cannot distinguish in myself any parts, but apprehend myself to be clearly one and entire; and although the whole mind seems to be united to the whole body, yet if a foot, or an arm, or some other part, is separated from my body, I am aware that nothing has been taken away from my mind. And the faculties of willing, feeling, conceiving, etc. cannot be properly speaking said to be its parts, for it is one and the same mind which employs itself in willing and in feeling and understanding. But it is quite otherwise with corporeal or extended objects, for there is not one of these imaginable by me which my mind cannot easily divide into parts, and which consequently I do not recognise as being divisible; this would be sufficient to teach me that the mind or soul of man is entirely different from the body, if I had not already learned it from other sources.[3]

Thought is a secretion of the brain.
—Pierre-Jean Georges Cabanis

5 Is Descartes correct that the mind is indivisible? Do the counterexamples of multiple personalities and cerebral commissurotomy show that the mind can in fact be divided?

Here Descartes uses the logical principle that if two things are one and the same, then they must have exactly the same properties; conversely, if they have different properties, they must not be one and the same. So he argues that if minds are not divisible into parts, and if bodies are divisible into parts (since they are spatially extended), then minds and bodies do not have the same properties. They are therefore distinct, and dualism is true.

Bodies are divisible, but is it really true that minds are indivisible? Two facts give critics reason to think that minds are actually divisible. First, psychiatrists have identified a form of mental illness known as *multiple personality disorder* in which a person has at least one alternate personality that can direct behavior. Those who have this disorder are said to lack the normal unity of consciousness; their minds appear to be divided. Second, a person's consciousness can apparently be divided through a kind of brain surgery known as cerebral commissurotomy. The procedure,

WHAT DO YOU BELIEVE?

The Immortal Soul

Notions about the soul and its possible immortality have changed through the centuries and have been subject to intense debate and philosophical inquiry. Many ancient Greeks thought that the soul is a material thing that animates bodies and is dispersed (and thus destroyed) like smoke after the body dies. Plato taught that the soul is an essential, nonphysical part of an organism and, unlike material things, is not subject to dissolution. The soul then is immortal, although it is fused with the body for awhile. But souls are not restricted to persons; living things of all kinds can also have souls.

Aristotle had very different ideas about souls. To him, the soul is the form of the body—that is, the abilities or capacities manifested through the living body. And since the soul requires a body to manifest itself, the soul perishes when the body dies. Aristotle therefore rejects the possibility of immortality, the transmigration of souls, and disembodied existence.

The biblical account of the soul is at odds with the soul–body dualism of much contemporary thought. Biblical scholars generally agree that the scriptural view of body and soul is monistic, not dualistic. The

Figure 4.4 A depiction of the soul leaving the body—a dualism at odds with the biblical account of the soul.

person is a single, undivided entity—a unity of soul and body. It is not the case that the soul takes up residence in the body then departs at death to live a separate, immortal existence. Body and soul are one, both therefore being subject to disintegration when a person dies.

The prevailing Christian view closely follows Plato's and Descartes' dualistic notion: The soul is the essential component of a human being, a substance both immaterial and immortal, while the body is material and inessential.

Most contemporary philosophers are materialists regarding mind and body and therefore reject the substance dualism of Descartes and Western religion. They are also skeptical of any claims of immortality.

Do you believe that you have an immortal soul? If so, on what grounds? If you do not, why not? Of the theories of soul just mentioned, which do you think is most plausible? Why?

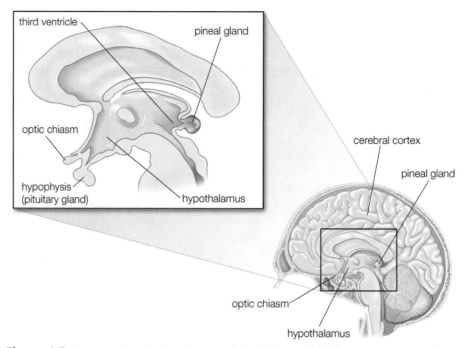

Figure 4.5 Descartes thought that the material and immaterial substances came together in the pineal gland. Does this notion remove the mystery of how interaction happens?

often performed to treat epilepsy, severs the cord of nerves linking the brain's two hemispheres. The result is a breakdown in communication between the hemispheres, which in turn leaves the patient with two distinct domains of consciousness. This seems to show that the mind is indeed divisible.

In addition to trying to undermine Descartes' arguments for his theory of mind, philosophers have also launched some strong arguments against it. The primary attack of this kind concerns the problem of mind–body interaction. In Cartesian dualism, mind and body are thought to be two radically different kinds of substances that somehow interact causally. But how is such interaction possible? How can an object with physical properties affect something with no physical properties whatsoever? How can a mysterious, nonphysical reality influence any event involving atoms, cells, blood, and bone? Descartes' theory doesn't explain how mind–body interaction occurs and is therefore regarded by many philosophers as inadequate. He does posit a weak explanation of the causal connection between mind and body by claiming that the two substances intermingle in a small appendage of the brain known as the pineal gland. But many find this incredible. Whatever the gland's function (which was unknown in Descartes' day), it still is a physical thing, and proposing it as the site of physical/nonphysical interaction does not banish the mystery of how the material can affect the immaterial.

Another common charge against Cartesian dualism (or any kind of dualism in which the physical and nonphysical affect each other) is that it is incompatible with science. For example, the theory is said to violate the scientific principle of

6 Is it possible that nonphysical (mental) causes do not exist, that the world contains only physical causes and physical effects?

the **causal closure of the physical**, which affirms a physical cause for every physical effect. The world is a closed system of physical causes and effects; nonphysical (mental) causes are superfluous. It seems that we can explain every event without reference to the immaterial. For any physical effect, scientists can in principle map out a detailed series of physical causes leading up to that effect. If so, there seems to be no need for mental causes.

Causal closure of the physical is the principle that the world is a closed system of physical causes and effects.

In addition, substance dualism, with its insistence on nonphysical causes of physical events, seems to conflict with a basic law of science—the law of the conservation of mass-energy. John Searle explains the problem like this:

John R. Searle, *Mind*

All forms of substance dualism inherit Descartes' problem of how to give a coherent account of the causal relations between the soul and the body, but recent versions have an additional problem. It seems impossible to make substance dualism consistent with modern physics. Physics says that the amount of matter/energy in the universe is constant; but substance dualism seems to imply that there is another kind of energy, mental energy or spiritual energy, that is not fixed by physics. So if substance dualism is true then it seems that one of the most fundamental laws of physics, the law of conservation, must be false.[4]

One way that dualists of any stripe can respond to criticisms concerning mind–body interaction and incompatibility with science is to embrace epiphenomenalism, the view that mental properties do not affect physical properties. If the body impacts the mind, but the mind does not impact the body, then there is no problem with how the mind and body interact, and the principle of the causal closure of the physical is not violated.

But epiphenomenalism seems to many theorists to be a denial of common sense. Searle is one of them:

Among the facts of the universe to be accounted for, it may be said, is Mind; and it is self evident that nothing can have produced Mind but Mind.
—John Stuart Mill

On this view [epiphenomenalism] consciousness exists alright, but it is like the froth on the wave or the flash of sunlight reflected off the surface of the water. It is there but it does not really matter. It is an epiphenomenon. But this seems too counterintuitive. Every time I decide to raise my arm, it goes up. I do not say, "Well, that's the thing about the old arm. Some days she goes up and some days she doesn't."[5]

John R. Searle, *Mind*

WRITING TO UNDERSTAND:
CRITIQUING PHILOSOPHICAL VIEWS   Section 4.2

---

1. What is Descartes' conceivability argument? Do you think it is successful in showing that some form of dualism must be true? Why or why not?

2. Evaluate Descartes' divisibility argument. Are its premises true? Does it show that bodies are divisible but minds are not?

3. What is Descartes' explanation of how mind and body interact? Is it plausible?

4. Suppose Descartes is right that bodies are divisible and minds are not. Would this show that minds can exist independently from bodies? Why or why not?

5. What is epiphenomenalism? Is it an adequate explanation of the relationship between mind and body? Is it a better or worse explanation than Cartesian dualism?

4.3 MIND–BODY IDENTITY

The favorite view among materialists is the identity theory, which says that mind states are brain states. Our apparent sensations, thoughts, perceptions, and emotions (so-called phenomenal consciousness) are not immaterial phenomena distinct from the material brain. These mental states are *identical to* physical brain states, just as lightning is identical to an electrical discharge. A pain or a perception is nothing more than a certain process going on in the brain's neurons. J. J. C. Smart, one of the first philosophers to articulate the identity theory, explains it like this:

J. J. C. Smart, "Sensations and Brain Processes"

Let me first try to state more accurately the thesis that sensations are brain processes. It is not the thesis that, for example, "after-image" or "ache" means the same as "brain process of sort X" (where "X" is replaced by a description of a certain sort of brain process). It is that, in so far as "afterimage" or "ache" is a report of a process, it is a report of a process that *happens to be* a brain process. It follows that the thesis does not claim that sensation statements can be *translated* into statements about brain processes. Nor does it claim that the logic of a sensation statement is the same as that of a brain-process statement. All it claims is that in so far as a sensation statement is a report of something, that something is in fact a brain process. Sensations are nothing over and above brain processes. Nations are nothing "over and above" citizens, but this does not prevent the logic of nation statements being very different from the logic of citizen statements, nor does it insure the translatability of nation statements into citizen statements. (I do not, however, wish to assert that the relation of sensation statements to brain-process statements is very like that of nation statements to citizen statements. Nations do not just *happen to be* nothing over and above citizens, for example. I bring in the "nations" example merely to make a negative point: that the fact that the logic of A-statements is different from that of B-statements does not insure that A's are anything over and above B's.)

When I say that a sensation is a brain process or that lightning is an electric discharge, I am using "is" in the sense of strict identity. (Just as in the—in this case necessary—proposition "7 is identical with the smallest prime number greater than 5.") When I say that a sensation is a brain process or that lightning is an electric discharge I do not mean just that the sensation is somehow spatially or temporally continuous with the brain process or that the lightning is just spatially or temporally continuous with the discharge.[6]

> **7** It seems that thoughts and mental images are not located in physical space. Does this show that Smart is mistaken about thoughts and mental images being brain processes?

The identity theory avoids some of the criticisms directed at Cartesian dualism (that mind–body interaction is mysterious and that the causal closure principle is violated) and at logical behaviorism (that mental causation is ignored or denied). And it explains how mental states affect behavior, how mental states can cause other mental states, and why many mental states are known to be correlated with brain processes.

But some philosophers reject the theory using *conceivability arguments* (à la Descartes) to try to show that the theory is deeply flawed. A well-known version of such an argument comes from David Chalmers, who wields it against all materialist views, not just the identity theory. His argument is based on, strangely enough, the possibility of zombies:

David J. Chalmers, *The Conscious Mind*

. . . [C]onsider the logical possibility of a *zombie*: someone or something physically identical to me (or to any other conscious being), but lacking conscious experiences altogether. At the global level, we can consider the logical possibility of a *zombie world*: a world physically identical to ours, but in which there are no conscious experiences at all. In such a world, everybody is a zombie.

So let us consider my zombie twin. This creature is molecule for molecule identical to me, and identical in all the low-level properties postulated by a completed physics, but he lacks conscious experience entirely. (Some might prefer to call a zombie "it," but I use the personal pronoun; I have grown quite fond of my zombie twin.) To fix ideas, we can imagine that right now I am gazing out the window, experiencing some nice green sensations from seeing the trees outside, having pleasant taste experiences through munching on a chocolate bar, and feeling a dull aching sensation in my right shoulder.

What is going on in my zombie twin? He is physically identical to me, and we may as well suppose that he is embedded in an identical environment. He will certainly be identical to me *functionally*: he will be processing the same sort of information, reacting

David J. Chalmers,
The Conscious Mind

8 Can you conceive of your zombie twin? If so, what does that prove?

If the human mind was simple enough to understand, we'd be too simple to understand it.
—Emerson Pugh

in a similar way to inputs, with his internal configurations being modified appropriately and with indistinguishable behavior resulting. He will be *psychologically* identical to me. . . . He will be perceiving the trees outside, in the functional sense, and tasting the chocolate, in the psychological sense. All of this follows logically from the fact that he is physically identical to me, by virtue of the functional analyses of psychological notions. He will even be "conscious" in the functional senses described earlier—he will be awake, able to report the contents of his internal states, able to focus attention in various places, and so on. It is just that none of this functioning will be accompanied by any real conscious experience. There will be no phenomenal feel. There is nothing it is like to be a zombie.[7]

Chalmers asserts that it is conceivable that such a zombie could exist. That is, it is conceivable that there could be a creature physically identical to him in every way but lacking the mental states that constitute conscious experience. If this zombie is conceivable, he says, then it is logically possible that the zombie could exist. If it is logically possible that the zombie could exist, then physical states must not be essential to conscious experience. Materialism, therefore, must be false.

This is how Chalmers outlines the argument:

1. It is conceivable that there be zombies.
2. If it is conceivable that there be zombies, it is metaphysically possible that there be zombies.
3. If it is metaphysically possible that there be zombies, then consciousness is nonphysical.
4. Consciousness is nonphysical.[8]

How might a materialist respond to this argument? One way is to charge that Chalmers is mistaken, that his zombies are actually inconceivable and therefore not logically possible. Many people, however, would probably disagree. Can you imagine an android like *Star Trek*'s Mr. Data that is physically identical to you but lacking any trace of internal conscious experience?

Another kind of attack against the identity theory (as well as other materialist views) comes in the form of *knowledge arguments*. The basic line is that brains have the property of being known through empirical investigation, but mental states cannot be known this way. The qualitative content of mental states has to be experienced subjectively, from the inside. And since brain states and mental states have different properties in this way, brain states and mental states are not identical. So the identity theory is false.

Thomas Nagel makes such an argument using a provocative thought experiment about bats. Presumably bats have experience (some level of consciousness), he says, although it is radically different from our own. To say that bats have experience is to say that "there is something that it is like to be a bat." Through scientific study, we could come to

Figure 4.6 David Chalmers, distinguished professor of philosophy and director of the Centre for Consciousness at the Australian National University.

Figure 4.7 Hollywood zombies like these are a far cry from Chalmers's kind of zombies, which are physically identical to normal people. Does the possibility of such zombies show that materialism is false?

Aristotle was famous for knowing everything. He taught that the brain exists merely to cool the blood and is not involved in the process of thinking. This is true only of certain persons.
—Will Cuppy

know everything there is to know about bat neurophysiology and all the other facts of bat biology. Nevertheless, there would still be something that we would not and could not know: *what it feels like to be a bat.* The bat's conscious experience would be beyond our ken. We could say the same about humans. If we knew all the facts about their physical states we still would not know all there is to know about their mental states. Therefore, it cannot be the case that physical states and mental states are identical. Nagel declares,

Thomas Nagel, "What Is It Like to Be a Bat?"

Whatever may be the status of facts about what it is like to be a human being, or a bat, or a Martian, these appear to be facts that embody a particular point of view. . . . This bears directly on the mind–body problem. For if the facts of experience—facts about what it is like *for* the experiencing organism—are accessible only from one point of view, then it is a mystery how the true character of experiences could be revealed in the physical operation of that organism.[9]

Some materialists rebut this kind of argument by insisting that, contrary to Nagel and others, consciousness is not a kind of experience (qualia) that is over and above the brain's cognitive or behavioral functions. Consciousness just *is* the brain's cognitive or behavioral functions. Once we know all about the brain's basic functions—how it

accesses information, discriminates stimuli, controls behavior, monitors its internal states, and the like—we know all there is to know about consciousness. And we can know about these things through objective, third-person investigations.

Figure 4.8 Is there something that it is like to be a bat? If there is and we nonbats could never know what it feels like to be a bat despite our expert knowledge of objective bat facts, what does that prove about the plausibility of materialism?

9 Do bats have conscious experience? Why or why not?

WRITING TO UNDERSTAND: CRITIQUING PHILOSOPHICAL VIEWS   Section 4.3

1. If Nagel thinks that bats have minds (that is, conscious experience), what other creatures must he admit have minds? Do wrens have minds? Grasshoppers? Lobsters?

2. Must humans have immaterial minds in order to fall in love, write a song, or remember smelling a rose? Smart thinks not. Do you agree?

3. Imagine a space alien coming to earth and scientists being able to examine its internal organs. And suppose nothing resembling the human brain could be found. According to the identity theory, would this being have a mind? Imagine that its behavior was in most ways indistinguishable from human behavior. Would you conclude that it had a mind?

4. Brain phenomena have a location in space, but thoughts and perceptions seem not to have a location in space. Does this show that the identity theory is false? Why or why not?

5. When your body dies, will your mind still exist? How would identity theorists answer this? Is their answer plausible?

4.4 THE MIND AS SOFTWARE

The brain may be regarded as a kind of parasite of the organism, a pensioner, as it were, who dwells with the body.
—Arthur Schopenhauer

Functionalism says that mental states are neither brain states nor behavioral states. They are states that have causal functions, and it's possible for these functions to play out in just about any kind of stuff, physical or nonphysical (although contemporary functionalists say the stuff is physical). That is, a mind is the *functions* that the brain carries out, a system of causal relationships that is multiply realizable. A mental state is therefore a causal sequence of inputs and outputs—initial stimuli that cause certain internal events or states (such as beliefs or desires) that in turn cause external behavior. For example, pain is what is caused by some kind of unpleasant stimuli (such as a burn to Rosa's hand), which causes other mental states (such as Rosa's believing that she should put ice on the burn), which causes external behavior (as when she reaches for ice in the freezer). Pain is whatever manifests such typical functional roles in an organism, and anything that exhibits these kinds of functions is a mind.

Here is Jerry Fodor explaining the theory and the reasons why he thinks it is superior to both logical behaviorism and the identity theory:

Jerry A. Fodor, "The Mind–Body Problem"

In the past fifteen years a philosophy of mind called functionalism that is neither dualist nor materialist has emerged from philosophical reflection on developments in artificial intelligence, computational theory, linguistics, cybernetics and psychology. All these fields, which are collectively known as the cognitive sciences, have in common a certain level of abstraction and a concern with systems that process information. Functionalism, which seeks to provide a philosophical account of this level of abstraction, recognizes the possibility that systems as diverse as human beings, calculating machines and disembodied spirits could all have mental states. In the functionalist view the psychology of a system depends not on the stuff it is made of (living cells, mental or spiritual energy) but on how the stuff is put together. . . .

All of this emerged ten or fifteen years ago as a nasty dilemma for the materialist program in the philosophy of mind. On the one hand the identity theorist (and not the logical behaviorist) had got right the causal character of the interactions of mind and body. On the other the logical behaviorist (and not the identity theorist) had got right the relational character of mental properties. Functionalism has apparently been able to resolve the dilemma. By stressing the distinction computer science draws between hardware and software the functionalist can make sense of both the causal and the relational character of the mental.

The intuition underlying functionalism is that what determines the psychological type to which a mental particular belongs is the causal role of the particular in the mental life of the organism. Functional individuation is differentiation with respect to causal role. A headache, for example, is identified with the type of mental state that among other things causes a disposition for taking aspirin in people who believe aspirin relieves a headache, causes a desire to rid oneself of the pain one is feeling, often causes someone who speaks English to say such things as "I have a headache" and is brought on by overwork, eyestrain, and tension. This list is presumably not complete. More will be known about the nature of a headache as psychological and physiological research discover more about its causal role.

Functionalism construes the concept of causal role in such a way that a mental state can be defined by its causal relations to other mental states. In this respect functionalism is completely different from logical behaviorism. Another major difference is that functionalism is not a reductionist thesis. It does not foresee, even in principle, the elimination of mentalistic concepts from the explanatory apparatus of psychological theories.[10]

Despite these advantages of functionalism, critics claim that it has a fatal flaw: it fails to account for the subjective, qualitative feel of consciousness. Thus, the most common arguments against it (absent qualia arguments) try to show that the theory leaves out conscious experience, or qualia, the seemingly obvious, essential feature of mind. The gist of these arguments is that functionalism must be false because it is possible to introduce an appropriate functional organization into some system and yet,

10 Is functionalism really a better theory of mind than logical behaviorism and the identity theory, as Fodor says?

contrary to functionalist claims, no mental states are brought into existence. Consider Ned Block's absent qualia argument in the form of a famous thought experiment:

Ned Block, "Troubles with Functionalism"

Suppose we convert the government of China to functionalism, and we convince its officials that it would enormously enhance their international prestige to realize a human mind for an hour. We provide each of the billion people in China (I chose China because it has a billion inhabitants) with a specially designed two-way radio that connects them in the appropriate way to other persons and to [an] artificial body. . . . [W]e . . . arrange to have letters displayed on a series of satellites placed so that they can be seen from anywhere in China. Surely such a system is not physically impossible. It could be functionally equivalent to you for a short time, say an hour. . . .

What makes the homunculi-headed [many-headed] system . . . just described a prima facie counter example to (machine) functionalism is that there is prima facie doubt whether it has any mental states at all—especially whether it has what philosophers have variously called "qualitative states," "raw feels," or "immediate phenomenological qualities." (You ask: What is it that philosophers have called qualitative states? I answer, only half in jest. As Louis Armstrong said when asked what jazz is, "If you got to ask, you ain't never gonna get to know.") In Nagel's terms, there is a prima facie doubt whether there is anything which it is like to be the homunculi-headed system.[11]

11 Does it seem to you that the Chinese brain lacks qualitative states? If not, why not?

I have a theory about the human mind. A brain is a lot like a computer. It will only take so many facts, and then it will go on overload and blow up.
—Erma Bombeck

If functionalism is true, the proper arrangement of inputs and outputs among the billion people should produce a mind having qualitative mental states. That is, from the one billion Chinese people there should arise one more person—the one brought forth by the whole system's functional organization. But, says Block, what makes the Chinese brain a counterexample to functionalism is that it is logically possible that this "brain" has no qualitative mental states at all. If this is the case, then merely being in certain functional states does not guarantee being in any qualitative mental states, and functionalism is false.

It is open to opponents of this argument to show that it is somehow incoherent, harboring a crippling contradiction. They would need to establish that the conditions set forth in the Chinese brain scenario (and similar thought experiments) are not possible. They can also allege bias: they can claim that the intuition behind Block's thought experiment seems strong only because we are prejudiced in favor of minds like ours that arise naturally from human brains.

Figure 4.9 Could a billion Chinese people connected in the right way constitute a mind?

The doctrine of functionalism has led many philosophers and researchers to see the mind as computer software. John Searle describes the early days of heady speculation about this new perspective:

John R. Searle, *Mind*

It seemed that we knew the answer to the question that faced us: the way the system works is that the brain is a digital computer and what we call the "mind" is a digital computer program or set of programs. . . . [M]ental states are computational states of the brain. . . . A principle that formed the foundation for any number of textbooks was this: the mind is to the brain as the program is to the hardware.[12]

Searle dubbed this view of the mind strong *artificial intelligence* (strong AI). "On the strong AI view," he says, "the appropriately programmed digital computer does not just simulate having a mind; it literally has a mind."[13] The appropriately programmed computer can demonstrate genuine intelligence, achieving any cognitive capacity such as understanding and believing. It was this astonishing possibility that engendered the field of cognitive science.

Many in the discipline also believed there was a way to test whether a programmed computer had attained true intelligence. This test is derived from the work of Alan Turing (1912–1954), the father of contemporary computer science and the genius behind today's computers. He invented the Turing machine, a theoretical model that became the blueprint for modern digital computers (which are all basically Turing machines), and then he devised the Turing test, a method that he thought could determine whether the machines are intelligent. Searle explains:

Figure 4.10 Alan Turing (1912–1954), father of the modern computer, inventor of the Turing machine, and breaker of the "unbreakable" codes produced by the German Enigma cipher machine in World War II.

John R. Searle, *Mind*

There are different versions of [the test], but the basic idea is this: we can side-step all the great debates about the other minds problem, about whether or not there really is any thinking going on in the machine, whether the machine is really intelligent, by simply asking ourselves, Can the machine perform in such a way that an expert cannot distinguish its performance from a human performance? If the machine responds to questions put to it in Chinese as well as a native Chinese speaker, so that other native Chinese speakers could not tell the difference between the machine and a native Chinese speaker, then we would have to say that the machine understood Chinese.[14]

Those who took the strong AI position believed that eventually a digital computer would be able to pass the Turing test and thus prove that it had a mind. Searle, however, rejects strong AI and tries to refute it with his classic thought experiment known as the "Chinese Room." The idea is that if strong AI is true, then a person should be able to attain a cognitive capacity (thinking, understanding, believing, etc.) simply by implementing an appropriate computer program. Searle thinks the thought experiment shows that no such capacities are achieved. Consider:

I do not, as a matter of fact, understand any Chinese at all. I cannot even tell Chinese writing from Japanese writing. But, we imagine that I am locked in a room with

PHILOSOPHERS AT WORK

John R. Searle

John Searle (b. 1932), an American philosopher, has had an extraordinary influence on the philosophy of language, the philosophy of mind, and philosophical ideas about social reality. He was born in Denver, Colorado, but was educated mostly at the University of Oxford, where he obtained his first teaching position at Christ Church. For over forty years he has been a philosophy professor at the University of California, Berkeley, while occasionally serving as a visiting professor at many other universities both in the United States and abroad.

Figure 4.11 John Searle, professor of the philosophy of mind and language at the University of California, Berkeley.

In the philosophy of mind, Searle has made his mark by offering a widely read and debated criticism of strong AI and by developing innovative theories of consciousness and intentionality. Against strong AI, he launched his most famous salvo—the Chinese Room argument. Through it, he argues that an appropriately programmed computer cannot acquire a cognitive capacity such as understanding and believing. That is, strong AI is false. A programmed computer, he says, works by manipulating the syntax of formal symbols, but that is a far cry from semantics, which concerns the meaning of the symbols.

His view of consciousness is that it cannot be reduced to the physical (brains or neurons). It is a phenomenon that can only be observed from a subjective, first-person perspective. It has a qualitative feel to it that may emerge from the physical but cannot be reduced to it.

Searle is the author of *Mind: A Brief Introduction (2004), The Rediscovery of the Mind (1994), The Mystery of Consciousness* (2002), *Mind, Language, and Society: Philosophy in the Real World* (1998), and *Intentionality: An Essay in the Philosophy of Mind* (1983).

John R. Searle, *Mind*

boxes full of Chinese symbols, and I have a rule book, in effect, a computer program, that enables me to answer questions put to me in Chinese. I receive symbols that, unknown to me, are questions; I look up in the rule book what I am supposed to do; I pick up symbols from the boxes, manipulate them according to the rules in the program, and hand out the required symbols, which are interpreted as answers. We can suppose that I pass the Turing test for understanding Chinese, but, all the same, I do not understand a word of Chinese. And if I do not understand Chinese on the basis of implementing the right computer program, then neither does any other computer just on the basis of implementing the program, because no computer has anything that I do not have.

You can see the difference between computation and real understanding if you imagine what it is like for me also to answer questions in English. Imagine that in the same room I am given questions in English, which I then answer. From the outside my answers to the English and the Chinese questions are equally good. I pass the Turing test for both. But from the inside, there is a tremendous difference. What is the difference exactly? In English, I understand what the words mean; in Chinese, I understand nothing. In Chinese, I am just a computer.[15]

For Searle, the reason a computer cannot think or understand (and why people can) is that a computer processes symbols by their physical properties (like shape, size, and order), and people process symbols by their meaning. That is, computers manipulate symbols *syntactically*, according to what they look like or where they are positioned; people use symbols *semantically*, according to what they mean. "Having the symbols by themselves—just having the syntax—is not sufficient for having the semantics," Searle says. "Merely manipulating symbols is not enough to guarantee knowledge of what they mean."[16]

Searle's influential thought experiment has drawn both praise and censure. The objections are many, and he has responded to several of them. Some say that the man in the room doesn't understand Chinese, but he would if the system were connected appropriately to the rest of the world. Many others argue that the program would understand Chinese if it simulated the brain processes of a Chinese speaker. Probably the most common counterargument is this: In the scenario, the man doesn't understand Chinese, but the whole room (the entire computational system) does. In other words, the man is merely part of the whole system made up of the man, the room, the boxes of Chinese symbols, the rule book, and everything else. The man doesn't understand Chinese, but the *whole system* does understand. Searle replies that whether we consider just the man in the room or the whole system, the result is the same: The man doesn't have access to semantics (the meaning of symbols), just syntax (the physical form of symbols). And if the man doesn't have any semantics, neither does the whole room. Without semantics, the system doesn't understand anything.

12 If a computer passed the Turing test, would that demonstrate that the computer had genuine intelligence? If not, would passing the test be *evidence* that the computer might have genuine intelligence?

13 Does this thought experiment show that functionalism is false?

WRITING TO UNDERSTAND:
CRITIQUING PHILOSOPHICAL VIEWS   Section 4.4

1. Does the Chinese brain thought experiment show that functionalism is false? If so, how? If not, where does it go wrong?

2. Searle thinks that even if a computer passed the Turing test, that wouldn't prove that the machine had cognitive capacities. Why does he think this? Do you agree with his reasoning?

3. Is it possible for a computer to process symbols semantically the way people do? Why or why not?

4. Does Searle claim that no machine of any kind can think? Is it physically possible to build a machine that is so advanced that it has conscious experience?

5. Suppose that instead of handling symbols, the man in the Chinese room somehow simulated nerve firings like the kind in the human brain. Would the man then understand Chinese?

PHILOSOPHY NOW

AI, Ethics, and War

Whether strong AI (artificial intelligence) is true, and whether advanced AI systems will prove it true, is an open question. But *autonomous* AI systems—those that can decide and act on their own—are already close at hand. They are expected to proliferate rapidly in the future, especially for military purposes. Patrick Lin, an expert on the military uses of autonomous robots, declares, "Robots are now replacing human soldiers in dull, dirty and dangerous missions, like searching tunnels and caves for terrorists, rescuing wounded soldiers, spying on enemies and even killing humans. In Iraq, robots have defused over 10,000 roadside bombs, which are responsible for 40% of U.S. casualties there. In 2003, the U.S. had no ground robots in Iraq or

Figure 4.12 An Explosive Ordnance Disposal Robot gripping a mortar round.

Afghanistan; now we have over 12,000 robots on the ground and 7,000 in the air in those conflict areas. By all accounts, the Robotic Revolution is here."

And with the revolution, Lin says, comes a host of ethical questions that were almost unthinkable a few years ago:

- Who should be blamed and punished for improper robotic conduct, such as illegal or accidental killings, if a robot can make its own attack decisions?

- Does the option of military robots make it easier for one nation to wage war, since they help reduce risk and friendly casualties, which both bear a heavy political cost? Just-war theory, which dates back to Aristotle and

4.5 THE MIND AS PROPERTIES

After pondering the full range of mind–body theories (including those covered in the preceding sections), some philosophers reason like this: Whatever the mind is, it cannot be a Cartesian immaterial substance that interacts causally with the physical world. For it seems profoundly puzzling (not to mention highly improbable) that these two could affect one another. In addition, Descartes' dualism violates the principle of the causal closure of the physical and the law of the conservation of mass-energy. The main alternative to Descartes' view is the identity theory, which other ancient philosophers, requires war to be the very last option, since it is so terrible.

- Should we allow robots to make some attack decisions by themselves—choices that would lead to human deaths?

- If we seek to guide robots in an ethical framework, which ethical theory should we use? The obvious choices have both advantages and serious liabilities. Should we let a robot decide that it is permissible to sacrifice one innocent person (for instance, a child) to save 10 or 100 others?

- If robots advance to the point of having animal-level intelligence, or can mimic human decision-making capabilities, or perhaps satisfy conditions for personhood, would we be morally required to give rights to these thinking machines? After all, we already count as legal persons, and give rights to, such things as corporations and ships. And some animals, such as dolphins and chimpanzees, arguably deserve rights, especially since they may be more capable than some rights-endowed humans who are born with or suffer severe cognitive impairments.

Patrick Lin, "The Ethical War Machine," Forbes.com, *June 29, 2009, http://www.forbes. com/2009/06/18/military-robots-ethics-opinions-contributors-artificial-intelligence-09-patrick-lin.html.*

Do you think autonomous robots should be trusted to make life-and-death decisions on the battlefield without human supervision? Is it possible to build good moral decision-making into them?

tells us that mental states are identical to physical brain states. But thought experiments featuring Chalmers's zombie and Nagel's bat suggest that mind–brain identity is implausible. Likewise, arguments using scenarios like Ned Block's Chinese brain and John Searle's Chinese room show that functionalism is also dubious, for it seems possible to introduce an appropriate functional organization into a system and still not attain conscious experience or a cognitive capacity. According to these philosophers, the failure of these views suggests an alternative theory of mind, one that posits no mysterious immaterial substance, denies no scientific principles, and is neither materialist nor functionalist. We are driven, they say, to the hypothesis that

It seems impossible to make substance dualism consistent with modern physics.
—John R. Searle

the mind is an arrangement of nonphysical *properties* arising from—yet dependent on—physical properties. We are led, in other words, to property dualism (or nonreductive materialism). As Chalmers says,

David J. Chalmers, *The Conscious Mind*

The best evidence of contemporary science tells us that the physical world is more or less causally closed: for every physical event, there is a physical sufficient cause. If so, there is no room for a mental "ghost in the machine" to do any extra causal work. . . . In any case . . . it remains plausible that *physical* events can be explained in physical terms, so a move to a Cartesian dualism would be a stronger reaction than is warranted.

The dualism implied here is instead a kind of *property* dualism: conscious experience involves properties of an individual that are not entailed by the physical properties of that individual, although they may depend lawfully on those properties. Consciousness is a *feature* of the world over and above the physical features of the world. This is not to say it is a separate "substance"; the issue of what it would take to constitute a dualism of substances seems quite unclear to me. All we know is that there are properties of individuals in this world—the phenomenal properties—that are ontologically independent of physical properties.[17]

The biggest challenge facing property dualism is how to explain the relationship between the mental and the physical. The main worry is that how mental properties could ever cause any changes in the physical world is extremely puzzling. If the mind is entirely physical (that is, if the mind is the brain), how it causes physical movements of the body is no mystery: the physical brain causes effects in the physical body. But how are nerves, blood, and bone supposed to be altered by nonphysical properties of the mind? (This problem is essentially the same one that Descartes faced in explaining how a nonphysical, spiritual substance could affect a physical, extended substance.)

Some property dualists avoid these difficulties by accepting epiphenomenalism, the doctrine that the mental does not influence the physical. But others reject epiphenomenalism because it conflicts with commonsense intuitions about the nature of human actions. It seems obvious to them that the mind does indeed bring about changes in the body—that, for example, thinking about a friend causes you to call her on the phone, or that having a headache leads you to reach for aspirin. So these theorists usually embrace what is called *downward causation*, the view that causal sequences can run from mind to body (from higher levels down to lower ones) as well as from body to mind (from lower levels up to higher ones). Their task, then, is to explain how downward causation can occur without running afoul of the causal closure of the physical or the conservation of mass-energy.

Much is riding on the outcome of the debate between materialists and property dualists. If the materialists are right, human beings are physical through and through; there is no immaterial essence or soul or self. Survival after death is impossible. If

14 Do you agree that there is no room for a "'ghost in the machine' to do any extra causal work"? Why or why not?

No explanation given wholly in physical terms can ever account for the emergence of conscious experience.
—David J. Chalmers

PHILOSOPHY LAB

Imagine that all the critics have been wrong, and Bigfoot lives! One specimen—which appears to be the only one on the planet—is locked away in a government laboratory. You, however, have full access to Bigfoot because you are the scientist who must decide how the world is supposed to treat the creature. If he has roughly the same physical and mental makeup as an ape, you will recommend that we treat him accordingly—keep him in captivity, perhaps in a zoo, and maybe do some experiments on him. He would have the same rights that an ape does. But if he is obviously intelligent (even able to reason), self-conscious, self-aware, and self-motivated, you will recommend—what? He has all the high-level characteristics that we see in humans, the same traits that oblige us to treat humans with respect, to grant them full moral rights—to call them *persons*. But Bigfoot is not a human, though he seems to be a person.

You are faced with deep philosophical questions: Can a nonhuman be a person? Do only humans have full moral rights? To answer no to the first question and yes to the second is to take the traditional view embraced by many cultures and religions. To answer yes to the first question and no to the second is to say that personhood does not depend on what species a creature is. So what are you going to do with Bigfoot?

epiphenomenalism is true, then our mental states can cause nothing; our thoughts have no effect on our behavior. If property dualism is true, then the world is more complicated than most scientists believe. In addition to physical objects, the universe contains nonphysical consciousness, a mysterious something that we barely understand. And how this immaterial reality relates to material things such as human bodies and the external world is almost as baffling as Descartes' interacting substances.

WRITING TO UNDERSTAND:
CRITIQUING PHILOSOPHICAL VIEWS   Section 4.5

---

1. Which is the better theory of mind—property dualism or substance dualism? Why?

2. Is property dualism a better theory than identity theory? Why or why not?

3. Is epiphenomenalism an adequate theory of mind? What considerations count against it?

4. Is downward causation possible? Can you think of a way that the mind could affect behavior without violating the causal closure of the physical or the conservation of mass-energy?

5. What would be the religious or scientific implications of the identity theory?

Review Notes

4.1 OVERVIEW: THE MIND–BODY PROBLEM

- The mind–body problem is the issue of what mental phenomena really are and how they relate to the physical world. The most important responses to it constitute the foremost theories of mind in Western thought.

- Substance dualism is the doctrine that mind and body consist of two fundamentally different kinds of stuff, or substances. The most influential form of this view is Cartesian dualism, which says that the separate substances interact. Most philosophers hold to various forms of materialism (or physicalism), the view that every object and event in the world is physical. Major materialistic theories include logical behaviorism (the idea that mental states are dispositions to behave in a particular way in certain circumstances) and identity theory (the view that mental states are identical to physical brain states). Functionalism (the doctrine that the mind is the functions that the brain performs) is usually interpreted as a materialist theory. Property dualism is the view that mental properties, or features, are nonphysical properties arising from, but not reducible to, physical properties.

4.2 SUBSTANCE DUALISM

- To defend his brand of substance dualism, Descartes offers arguments based on conceivability and divisibility. Critics have found fault with both of these and charge that Cartesian dualism violates the principle of the causal closure of the physical and the law of conservation of mass-energy.

4.3 MIND–BODY IDENTITY

• The identity theory avoids some of the problems that beset Cartesian dualism, but theorists have rejected it using conceivability arguments (such as Chalmers's zombie thought experiment) and knowledge arguments (such as Nagel's bat scenario).

4.4 THE MIND AS SOFTWARE

• Functionalism has been accused of failing to account for the subjective, qualitative feel of consciousness. Absent qualia arguments (such as Ned Block's Chinese brain thought argument) try to demonstrate this. Searle's Chinese room argument tries to debunk the functionalist view that the mind is essentially software.

4.5 THE MIND AS PROPERTIES

• For some philosophers, property dualism is the most plausible theory of mind, in light of the failures of substance dualism, identity theory, and functionalism. Its biggest challenge is explaining the relationship between the mental and the physical.

WRITING TO UNDERSTAND:
ARGUING YOUR OWN VIEWS   Chapter 4

1. Critique Descartes' substance dualism. Explain the theory, discuss the strengths and weaknesses of Descartes' conceivability and divisibility arguments, and defend your verdict regarding the theory's adequacy.

2. Examine Chalmers's zombie argument against the identity theory. Do you think the argument is successful? Why or why not?

3. Do you think the brain is a computer running some sort of software? Defend your view by evaluating the standard arguments for and against functionalism.

4. Do you think epiphenomenalism is true? Evaluate what you take to be the strongest arguments for and against it and then render your verdict.

5. Do you believe that you have an immortal soul? Explain and defend your view, taking into account the principle of the causal closure of the physical, the law of conservation of mass-energy, and the brain research showing countless correlations between mental properties (beliefs, perceptions, etc.) and physiological activity.

Key Terms

Cartesian dualism The view that mind (or soul) and body are completely independent of one another and interact causally. (198)

causal closure of the physical The principle that the world is a closed system of physical causes and effects. (207)

epiphenomenalism The notion that mental properties do not cause anything, but merely accompany physical processes. (202)

functionalism The view that the mind is the functions that the brain performs. (200)

identity theory The view that mental states are identical to physical brain states. (199)

logical behaviorism The idea that mental states are dispositions to behave in particular ways in certain circumstances. (198)

materialism (or **physicalism**) The doctrine that every object and event in the world is physical. (198)

mind–body problem The issue of what mental phenomena are and how they relate to the physical world. (198)

multiple realizability The capacity to be realized or instantiated in a variety of forms and materials. (200)

property dualism The view that mental properties are nonphysical properties arising from, but not reducible to, physical properties. (201)

substance dualism The notion that mind and body consist of two fundamentally different kinds of stuff, or substances. (198)

FICTION

They're Made out of Meat

Terry Bisson

Terry Bisson is a much-lauded science fiction writer, author of seven novels (including *Talking Man*, *Fire on the Mountain*, and *Voyage to the Red Planet*) and numerous short stories (including "Bears Discover Fire" and the following selection).

"They're made out of meat."

"Meat?"

"Meat. They're made out of meat."

"Meat?"

"There's no doubt about it. We picked up several from different parts of the planet, took them aboard our recon vessels, and probed them all the way through. They're completely meat."

"That's impossible. What about the radio signals? The messages to the stars?"

"They use the radio waves to talk, but the signals don't come from them. The signals come from machines."

"So who made the machines? That's who we want to contact."

"They made the machines. That's what I'm trying to tell you. Meat made the machines."

"That's ridiculous. How can meat make a machine? You're asking me to believe in sentient meat."

"I'm not asking you, I'm telling you. These creatures are the only sentient race in that sector and they're made out of meat."

"Maybe they're like the orfolei. You know, a carbon-based intelligence that goes through a meat stage."

"Nope. They're born meat and they die meat. We studied them for several of their life spans, which didn't take long. Do you have any idea what's the life span of meat?"

"Spare me. Okay, maybe they're only part meat. You know, like the weddilei. A meat head with an electron plasma brain inside."

"Nope. We thought of that, since they do have meat heads, like the weddilei. But I told you, we probed them. They're meat all the way through."

"No brain?"

"Oh, there's a brain all right. It's just that the brain is made out of meat! That's what I've been trying to tell you."

"So . . . what does the thinking?"

"You're not understanding, are you? You're refusing to deal with what I'm telling you. The brain does the thinking. The meat."

"Thinking meat! You're asking me to believe in thinking meat!"

"Yes, thinking meat! Conscious meat! Loving meat. Dreaming meat. The meat is the whole deal! Are you beginning to get the picture or do I have to start all over?"

"Omigod. You're serious then. They're made out of meat."

"Thank you. Finally. Yes. They are indeed made out of meat. And they've been trying to get in touch with us for almost a hundred of their years."

"Omigod. So what does this meat have in mind?"

"First it wants to talk to us. Then I imagine it wants to explore the Universe, contact other sentiences, swap ideas and information. The usual."

"We're supposed to talk to meat."

"That's the idea. That's the message they're sending out by radio. 'Hello. Anyone out there. Anybody home.' That sort of thing."

"They actually do talk, then. They use words, ideas, concepts?"

"Oh, yes. Except they do it with meat."

"I thought you just told me they used radio."

"They do, but what do you think is on the radio? Meat sounds. You know how when you slap or flap meat, it makes a noise? They talk by flapping their meat at each other. They can even sing by squirting air through their meat."

"Omigod. Singing meat. This is altogether too much. So what do you advise?"

"Officially or unofficially?"

Terry Bisson, *Omni*, 1990. From http://www.terrybisson.com/page6/page6.html.

"Both."

"Officially, we are required to contact, welcome and log in any and all sentient races or multibeings in this quadrant of the Universe, without prejudice, fear or favor. Unofficially, I advise that we erase the records and forget the whole thing."

"I was hoping you would say that."

"It seems harsh, but there is a limit. Do we really want to make contact with meat?"

"I agree one hundred percent. What's there to say? 'Hello, meat. How's it going?' But will this work? How many planets are we dealing with here?"

"Just one. They can travel to other planets in special meat containers, but they can't live on them. And being meat, they can only travel through C space. Which limits them to the speed of light and makes the possibility of their ever making contact pretty slim. Infinitesimal, in fact."

"So we just pretend there's no one home in the Universe."

"That's it."

"Cruel. But you said it yourself, who wants to meet meat? And the ones who have been aboard our vessels, the ones you probed? You're sure they won't remember?"

"They'll be considered crackpots if they do. We went into their heads and smoothed out their meat so that we're just a dream to them."

"A dream to meat! How strangely appropriate, that we should be meat's dream."

"And we marked the entire sector unoccupied."

"Good. Agreed, officially and unofficially. Case closed. Any others? Anyone interesting on that side of the galaxy?"

"Yes, a rather shy but sweet hydrogen core cluster intelligence in a class nine star in G445 zone. Was in contact two galactic rotations ago, wants to be friendly again."

"They always come around."

"And why not? Imagine how unbearably, how unutterably cold the Universe would be if one were all alone . . ."

Probing Questions

1. Why is this story told from the perspective of intelligent but alien (to us) beings? What can you learn about minds from this way of looking at reality?

2. What point does this story make about the relationship between mental stuff and physical stuff?

3. Are alien but intelligent beings without brains conceivable? That is, is it logically possible that such creatures exist?

For Further Reading

David J. Chalmers, ed., *Philosophy of Mind: Classical and Contemporary Readings* (New York: Oxford University Press, 2002). A comprehensive collection of readings covering all the key issues.

David J. Chalmers, *The Conscious Mind* (New York: Oxford University Press, 1996). A clear introduction to issues regarding consciousness by one of the leading thinkers in the field. Offers a sustained critique of physicalism.

James Cornman and Keith Lehrer, "The Mind–Body Problem," in *Philosophical Problems and Arguments* (New York: Macmillan, 1982). A straightforward examination of many of the main arguments in philosophy of mind.

Daniel C. Dennett, *Consciousness Explained* (Boston: Little, Brown, and Company, 1991). A plainspoken discussion of consciousness as a physicalist phenomenon.

Brian P. McLaughlin, with Ansgar Beckermann and Sven Walter, *The Oxford Handbook of Philosophy of Mind* (Oxford: Oxford University Press, 2009). A large, comprehensive set of readings.

Ian Ravenscroft, *Philosophy of Mind: A Beginner's Guide* (Oxford: Oxford University Press, 2005). A clear and concise introduction to the central theories in the philosophy of mind.

John R. Searle, *Mind: A Brief Introduction* (New York: Oxford University Press, 2004). A fine introduction for beginners to all the leading theories of mind.

FREE WILL AND DETERMINISM

Chapter Objectives

5.1 OVERVIEW: THE FREE WILL PROBLEM

- Understand the nature and importance of the free will problem.
- Define *determinism*, *hard determinism*, *incompatibilism*, *indeterminism*, *compatibilism*, and *libertarianism*.
- Give an overview of the three major philosophical responses to the free will problem.
- Understand the main reasons why people think the issue of free will matters.

5.2 DETERMINISM AND INDETERMINISM

- Understand d'Holbach's position on free will and the main reason he takes it.
- Explain how science is used to argue for determinism.
- Understand how quantum physics seems to provide a counterexample to determinism.
- Summarize James's indeterminist view and why some philosophers have rejected it.

5.3 COMPATIBILISM

- Explain the compatibilist position on free will.
- Understand how compatibilists define "could do otherwise."
- Summarize Rowe's objection to compatibilism.
- Critically examine Stace's compatibilism.

5.4 LIBERTARIANISM

- Understand the three types of arguments that libertarians have put forth to support their view.
- Understand the Consequence Argument.
- State and evaluate the libertarian's argument from experience.
- Explain agent causation and know the main arguments for and against it.

5.5 SARTRE'S PROFOUND FREEDOM
• Understand Sartre's existentialist freedom.
• Explain his notion of "existence precedes essence."
• Evaluate his idea of radical freedom.

5.1 OVERVIEW: THE FREE WILL PROBLEM

Few things in life are more valuable to us than freedom. We want it, we demand it, we say we cannot live without it. We yearn for and expect social or political freedom, the freedom to go where we want, say what we please, and do as we may within broad legal and social limits. But we also want—and usually assume we have—a more profound kind of freedom, what philosophers call free will. This type of freedom is the power of self-determination: If we possess it, then at least some of our choices are not decided for us or forced upon us but are *up to us.* If we don't possess it, our social and political freedoms would seem to be considerably less valuable. If our actions are not our own because, say, someone has brainwashed or drugged us to control how we vote, then being free to vote would seem to be an empty liberty. So the central question in free will debates is whether we in fact have this more fundamental form of freedom.

The question arises because, as in many other issues in philosophy, two of our basic beliefs about ourselves and the world seem to conflict. On one hand, we tend to think we have free will in the sense just described. On the other, we also usually assume that every event has a cause. Or, as philosophers would say, we accept **determinism**, the doctrine that every event is determined or necessitated by preceding events and the laws of nature. Determinism says that all events—including our choices and actions—are produced inexorably by previous events, which are caused by still earlier events, which are caused by still others, the chain of causes leading back into the indefinite past. Since every cause always results in the same effect, the future can unfold in only one way. Everything that happens *must happen* in an unalterable, preset fashion. But if determinism is true, how can any

Figure 5.1 Are all of our actions produced by a chain of events that stretches back into the indefinite past?

choices we make or any actions we perform be up to us? How can we do anything "of our own free will"? If determinism is true, your reading this book right now was caused by prior events such as certain states in your brain, body, and environment, and these events were in turn caused by still others, and the causal sequence must stretch back countless years to a time before you existed. You had no say in the movement or direction of this causal train, no control over how it went. Your reading this book right now could not have turned out any other way. You could not have done otherwise. How, then, could your actions be free?

From this conflict comes the **problem of free will**—the challenge of reconciling determinism with our intuitions or ideas about personal freedom. The problem seems all the sharper because both horns of this apparent dilemma are endorsed by common sense. In our lives we recognize the work of deterministic forces: Every cause does seem to regularly and lawfully produce an effect, and every effect seems to have a cause. Baseballs obey gravity, bread nourishes, fire burns, electronics work, human bodies are shaped by genetics, and human personalities are molded by experience. All this is reinforced by science, which tirelessly traces the universe's myriad links between cause and effect. Our everyday experience also suggests that sometimes it is indeed up to us how we choose and act, and that we could have chosen and acted otherwise than we did.

But who cares whether all our actions are determined by forces beyond our control? Well, we do. Most of us are unsettled by the thought that our choices and actions may not be our own, that everything we do is inevitable, preset, or necessary. This fear of a predetermined existence is reflected in movies, books, and popular culture. In the films *Gattaca*, *A Clockwork Orange*, and *The Truman Show*, deterministic forces in various guises are part of what makes these movies so disturbing. The novel *Brave New World* by Aldous Huxley shows us a futuristic society of contented citizens who are happy with their lot in life—but only because social engineers manipulate and dampen the people's desires with a mind-numbing drug called *soma*. B. F. Skinner's novel *Walden II* depicts another community of happy folk who want only what they can readily acquire or achieve. They are perfectly satisfied with their lives because they have been programmed through lifelong behavioral conditioning (the kind that Skinner himself advocated) to desire only what is attainable. Skinner portrays his vision as a utopia, but many think it is a dystopia in which social freedom is a reality but free will is nonexistent.

People also care about the issue of free will because upon it hang momentous questions about moral responsibility, legal punishment, praise and blame, and social and political control. If our actions are not free in any important sense, it is difficult to see how we could be held morally responsible for what we do. If our actions are fully determined, how could we be legitimately subjected to punishment, praise, or blame for our actions? Punishing us for something we did would be like penalizing us for having red hair or brown eyes. As you might expect, many who reject the notion of free will think that punishing people for crimes makes no sense. Instead of punishing criminals, they say, we should try to modify their behavior. Instead of imprisoning or executing them, we should train them through behavioral conditioning and other techniques to be law-abiding.

The issues of determinism and free will often come up in court when someone is being tried for a serious crime such as rape or murder. The defense attorney argues that the defendant is not responsible for his actions, for his character was warped by abusive parents, an impoverished or brutal environment, or bad genes. His life was programmed—determined—to turn out a certain way, and he had no say in any of it. The prosecutor insists that despite the influence of these factors, the defendant deserves most of the blame for his crime because ultimately he acted freely. The jury then must decide where determinism ends and free will begins.

Philosophers both ancient and modern have proposed three solutions to the free will problem. The first is known as **hard determinism**, the view that no one has free will. Hard determinists accept these three propositions: (1) determinism is true; (2) determinism and free will are incompatible; and (3) we never act freely. Proposition 2 is a statement of the doctrine of **incompatibilism**: Determinism and free will are incompatible doctrines; they both cannot be true. That is, if every

Figure 5.2 A teenager on death row, 1986. To many, if determinism is true, criminals should not be punished, just trained. Does this way of dealing with criminals make sense to you?

event is determined, there can be no free will; if free will exists, determinism cannot be actual. Hard determinists argue that given the truth of determinism and the truth of incompatibilism, the assertion of free will must be false.

To support Proposition 1, determinists typically appeal to the deliverances of science. They point out that scientific research in many fields, from astrophysics to zoology, is forever uncovering causal connections, seeming to confirm a deterministic picture of the world. Scientists now know that human behavior is shaped to a remarkable degree by heredity, the brain's biochemistry, behavioral conditioning, and evolution. All these facts reinforce the notion that human choices and actions are brought about deterministically.

Strangely enough, science—specifically quantum physics—has also provided evidence that determinism is false. Or, to put it another way, some scientific evidence supports **indeterminism**, the view that not every event is determined by preceding events and the laws of nature. The standard view among quantum physicists is that many events on the quantum level (the domain of subatomic particles) are uncaused. Among philosophers, however, debate still continues over what this quantum indeterminacy means for the problem of free will.

The second proposed solution to the free will problem is **compatibilism**, or soft determinism. Compatibilists believe that (1) determinism is true; (2) determinism and free will are compatible; and (3) we sometimes act freely. So compatibilism claims that although determinism is true, our actions can still be free because

Hard determinism is the view that free will does not exist, that no one acts freely.

Incompatibilism is the view that if determinism is true, no one can act freely.

Indeterminism is the view that not every event is determined by preceding events and the laws of nature.

Compatibilism is the view that although determinism is true, our actions can still be free.

Life is like a game of cards. The hand you are dealt is determinism; the way you play it is free will.
—Jawaharlal Nehru

2 How would a personal belief in determinism affect your view of crime and punishment? Do you think that people are generally responsible for their crimes, or are they not responsible due to deterministic forces beyond their control?

One of the annoying things about believing in free will and individual responsibility is the difficulty of finding somebody to blame your problems on. And when you do find somebody, it's remarkable how often his picture turns up on your driver's license.
—P. J. O'Rourke

Libertarianism (not political) is the view that some actions are free, for they are caused or controlled by the person or agent.

3 At this point in your reading, which doctrine are you more sympathetic to—hard determinism, compatibilism, or libertarianism?

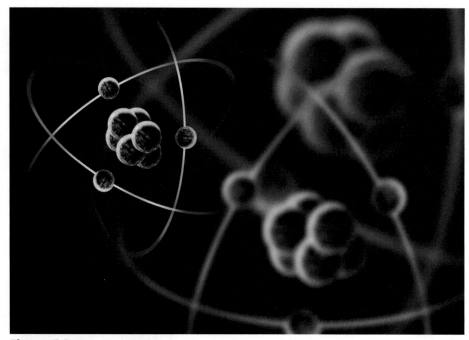

Figure 5.3 Physicists think that some events on the quantum level are uncaused. Does this mean that some events on the macro level (the level inhabited by rocks, stars, and people) are also uncaused? If so, would this indeterminism give us free will?

determinism and free will are not in conflict (incompatibilism is false). It is possible for every event to be caused by preceding events plus the laws of nature—*and* for us to still act freely. But how is such a thing possible?

Traditional compatibilism holds that your action is free if (1) it is caused by your own choices or desires and (2) it is not impeded or constrained by anything. You act in complete freedom when you give money to a charity—*if* you really do want to give your money and *if* nothing prevents you from doing so (for example, no physical obstacles stand in your way, no one is coercing you, and no inner compulsion restrains you). You act freely when you are able to do what you desire to do; you do not act freely when you are not able to do what you desire to do. This would be true, according to traditional compatibilism, even if your desires were themselves determined by forces beyond your control. Your will itself may be determined by preceding events and the laws of nature, but if you are able to do what you will, you act freely. In this way, says the compatibilist, free will is compatible with determinism.

But some critics reject the compatibilist's notion of freedom. They maintain that merely being able to act according to your desires without constraints is not real freedom *if your desires are determined for you in the first place.*

The third answer to the problem of free will is **libertarianism** (not to be confused with the political doctrine of the same name). It asserts that some actions are free, for they are ultimately caused, or controlled, by the person, or agent. So libertarians believe that (1) determinism is false (indeterminism is true); (2) determinism

WHAT DO YOU BELIEVE?

Fate

Are you a fatalist? Do you believe that fate rules your life so that your future will unfold in a certain way *regardless of what you do*? Soldiers in battle sometimes take a fatalistic attitude. They say, "If a bullet is meant to kill you, you will die, and there's nothing you can do about it. If a bullet is meant to spare you, you will live no matter what you do. Either way, whatever happens, fate will decide, and there's no point in worrying about it or trying to avoid your destiny." Have you ever had similar thoughts about death, failure, love relationships, or—heaven forbid—final exams?

Fatalism is the view that what will be, will be, and no human actions can change it. It says that any actions you might take to alter your fate are futile. Determinism is different. It says that events happen because of preceding events, but these preceding events can include *things that we do*.

So is fatalism true? Apparently not. It seems obvious that many events happen because our actions help bring them about. Sometimes events occur *because of what we do*, not regardless of what we do. Whether the soldier is killed by the bullet may depend on whether he tries to avoid getting hit.

Do you believe in fate? If so, why? What evidence supports your belief? Why do you think some people take a fatalist view of life?

and free will are incompatible; and (3) we sometimes act freely. They hold that indeterminism is necessary for free will, that free actions can occur only in a world where not all events are determined by prior events and natural laws. Note how libertarianism differs from the other two positions on free will. Both libertarians and hard determinists accept incompatibilism, but they take opposing views on determinism and free action. And, contrary to compatibilists, libertarians reject determinism and embrace incompatibilism.

Like the other free will theories, libertarianism has its detractors. For example, some have objected that it is incoherent, mysterious, or both. They ask, How can an agent cause event A when there is no previous event B in the agent that causes event A, and no prior event C that causes event B, and so on? Because libertarians accept indeterminism, they are committed to denying such a causal sequence. But explaining how free will is possible while rejecting deterministic causal chains has been a challenge for libertarians, and some of their solutions have provoked considerable skepticism.

> **WRITING TO UNDERSTAND:**
> **CRITIQUING PHILOSOPHICAL VIEWS**   Section 5.1
>
> 1. Does science really show that determinism is true? Why or why not?
> 2. Does quantum indeterminacy prove that determinism is false (that indeterminism is true)? Some philosophers say that the breakdown of determinism on the quantum level isn't relevant to the free will issue, because the indeterminacy is confined mostly to subatomic particles and generally doesn't affect human actions. Do you agree? Explain.
> 3. Do you believe that the compatibilist's concept of free will is plausible? If you were free to act on any of your desires but your desires were controlled by God, would you have free will?
> 4. Suppose hard determinism were true. Would that mean we are not responsible for our actions? If hard determinism did make responsibility impossible, would that fact show that the theory is false?
> 5. Which theory of free will seems to agree best with your own experience of making choices and taking action?

5.2 DETERMINISM AND INDETERMINISM

The hard determinist believes that determinism is a fact about the universe and that incompatibilism is true (that no one can act freely if determinism is true). From these two claims it is a short step to the conclusion that no one acts freely (that libertarianism is false). This line of reasoning (or something close to it) has been around since ancient times, but since the rise of modern science in the seventeenth century it has seemed to some to be much more credible because determinism itself has seemed more credible. Baron d'Holbach (1723–1789), a prominent philosopher of the French Enlightenment, has given us one of the clearest and boldest statements of the hard determinist position:

Baron d'Holbach, "Of the System of Man's Free Agency"

It has been already sufficiently proved that the soul is nothing more than the body considered relatively to some of its functions more concealed than others: it has been shown that this soul, even when it shall be supposed immaterial, is continually modified conjointly with the body, is submitted to all its motion, and that without this it would remain inert and dead; that, consequently, it is subjected to the influence of those material and physical causes which give impulse to the body; of which the mode of existence, whether habitual or transitory, depends upon the material elements by which it is surrounded, that form its texture, constitute its temperament, enter into it by means of the aliments, and penetrate it by their subtility. The faculties which are called *intellectual*, and those qualities which are styled *moral*, have been explained in a manner purely physical and natural. In the last place it has been demonstrated that all the ideas, all the systems, all the affections, all the opinions, whether true or false, which man forms to himself, are to be attributed to his physical and material senses. Thus man is a being purely physical; in whatever manner he is considered, he is connected to universal nature, and submitted to the necessary and immutable laws that she imposes on all the beings she contains, according to their peculiar essences or to the respective properties with which, without consulting them, she endows each particular species. Man's life is a line that nature commands him to describe upon the surface of the earth, without his ever being able to swerve from it, even for an instant. He is born without his own consent; his organization does in nowise depend upon himself; his ideas come to him involuntarily; his habits are in the power of those who cause him to contract them; he is unceasingly modified by causes, whether visible or concealed, over which he has no control, which necessarily regulate his mode of existence, give the hue to his way of thinking, and determine his manner of acting. He is good or bad, happy or miserable, wise or foolish, reasonable or irrational, without his will being for any thing in these various states. Nevertheless, in despite of the shackles by which he is bound, it is pretended he is a free agent, or that independent of the causes by which he is moved, he determines his own will, and regulates his own condition.[1]

> A man is the origin of his action.
> —Aristotle

To d'Holbach and other Enlightenment thinkers, the theories and discoveries of science were robust proof that every event was determined by preceding events and natural laws. They saw the universe as a grand, intricate, physical machine, with every part—including human beings— predetermined to operate in foreordained fashion. In such a universe, they insisted, free actions are impossible. Free will is an illusion. We think we are free only because we are ignorant of the forces that bind us.

Since d'Holbach's day, many others have taken the findings of science to be undeniable evidence for universal determinism. After all, science has had—and continues to have—remarkable success in explaining and predicting all sorts of natural phenomena, including the choices and actions of human beings. In light of this success, many people believe that the truth of determinism is simply obvious. Nowadays, most who accept determinism are compatibilists, but a few of them see no reason to think free will is compatible with determinism, so they take the hard determinist view.

Figure 5.4 Baron d'Holbach (1723–1789).

Yet in an ironic turn of scientific history, reasons to doubt determinism have come from science itself. Quantum physics provides a surprising counterexample to the notion that every event has a cause. The most widely accepted view among quantum physicists is that at the subatomic level, some events (such as the decay of radioactive particles) are random and therefore uncaused. If so, it is not the case that every event is determined by preceding events and the laws of nature, and the central premise in the argument for hard determinism is unfounded.

Some hard determinists maintain that these uncaused events are mostly confined to the subatomic realm and do not significantly affect the larger world of

4 Do you believe both that every event has a cause and that free actions are possible? If so, are these beliefs compatible?

PHILOSOPHERS AT WORK

William James

William James (1842–1910) is one of America's most influential philosophers, leaving a lasting impression on debates in epistemology, philosophy of religion, ethics, and free will. He was born in New York City and grew up in an intellectually stimulating family. His father was a philosopher of religion, and his brother Henry was the famous novelist. He studied abroad, earned a Harvard degree in medicine, and spent most of his career lecturing and writing in psychology and philosophy.

Figure 5.5 William James, philosopher, psychologist, pragmatist, and believer in free will.

His reputation as the greatest psychologist of America and Europe was assured by the publication of his voluminous work *The Principles of Psychology* (1890). After that came numerous philosophical essays and books, including *The Will to Believe and Other Essays in Popular Philosophy* (1897); *The Varieties of Religious Experience* (1902); *Pragmatism: A New Name for Some Old Ways of Thinking* (1907); and *The Meaning of Truth* (1909).

James is one of the founders of the philosophy of pragmatism, a doctrine about meaning and truth. James is famous for articulating a pragmatic theory of truth, which says that the truth of a statement is a matter of its utility. For James, utility may mean either success in predicting events or promotion of beneficial feelings and actions. Through pragmatism, James came to the conclusion that religion was a legitimate and important aspect of life because we can plausibly accept religious claims on grounds of their utility, regardless of their lack of evidence.

Ironically, James, the famous psychologist, was given to psychosomatic illness and clinical depression. Once while wrestling with the problem of free will, he fell into a devastatingly dark mood and did not recover until he had found a solution. He concluded that despite determinism, we can have free will because chance events make room for free actions.

human actions. This suggests, they say, that for all practical purposes, determinism *is* true. But others reject this view, contending that quantum indeterminism isn't as restricted to the quantum level as some assume, and that therefore causal indeterminism could arise anywhere.

Most indeterminists do not deny that many, perhaps most, of our actions are caused by prior events; they concede that much of human behavior may be causally determined. But they reject the notion that previous events cause *all* our actions; they think that claim is a sweeping generalization that science has yet to demonstrate.

Long before the advent of quantum physics, there were thinkers who posited indeterminism in the world and argued that it opened the way for humans to have

A man can do what he wants, but not want what he wants.
—Arthur Schopenhauer

free will. The "atomist" philosophers of ancient Greece theorized that the world was composed of bits of matter called atoms moving in rigidly determined fashion—except that these objects sometimes "swerved" randomly to allow for undetermined, free actions in humans. Centuries later the distinguished American philosopher William James (1842–1910) argued that indeterminism is a feature of the universe that permits "alternative futures" and the possibility of freedom. It allows some things to happen by chance. Most importantly, James says, it allows free actions, for *free actions are chance happenings*. He explains his view like this:

William James, "The Dilemma of Determinism"

What does determinism profess? . . . It professes that those parts of the universe already laid down absolutely appoint and decree what the other parts shall be. The future has no ambiguous possibilities hidden in its womb: the part we call the present is compatible with only one totality. Any other future complement than the one fixed from eternity is impossible. The whole is in each and every part, and welds it with the rest into an absolute unity, an iron block, in which there can be no equivocation or shadow of turning. . . .

Indeterminism, on the contrary, says that the parts have a certain amount of loose play on one another, so that the laying down of one of them does not necessarily determine what the others shall be. It admits that possibilities may be in excess of actualities, and that things not yet revealed to our knowledge may really in themselves be ambiguous. Of two alternative futures which we conceive, both may now be really possible; and the one become impossible only at the very moment when the other excludes it by becoming real itself. Indeterminism thus denies the world to be one unbending unit of fact. It says there is a certain ultimate pluralism in it; and, so saying, it corroborates our ordinary unsophisticated view of things. To that view, actualities seem to float in a wider sea of possibilities from out of which they are chosen; and, somewhere, indeterminism says, such possibilities exist, and form a part of truth. . . .

Do not all the motives that assail us, all the futures that offer themselves to our choice, spring equally from the soil of the past; and would not either one of them, whether realized through chance or through necessity, the moment it was realized, seem to us to fit that past, and in the completest and most continuous manner to interdigitate with the phenomena already there?[2]

5 How does James's indeterminist view fit with our commonsense notions about punishment and reward?

James holds that a free choice is not determined by previous events; it is uncaused. There is more than one way that the choice can go, and how it goes is a matter of chance. But even though the choice comes about by chance, it will seem to follow from previous events just as a determined choice would.

Many have rejected this kind of argument, including those who believe that indeterminism is a prerequisite for free will. The difficulty, they say, is that indeterminism alone does not make for free and responsible actions. Libertarians, for example, agree that indeterminism is necessary for free will, that free actions can occur only in a world where not all actions are determined by prior events and natural laws. But they also point out that if what an agent does happens by chance (that is, randomly),

My first act of free will shall be to believe in free will.
—William James

then she is not free to act or not act. What she does just happens, and she has nothing to do with it. Her actions are not under her control and therefore are not really *her* actions. In fact, they would not be actions at all. An action is an event intended to happen by the agent, but if her intentions have nothing to do with it (because it is random), it is not really an action and is definitely not free. So for libertarians, indeterminism by itself is not enough for free will, which is why they take pains to explain the role of the agent in free actions.

The conclusion libertarians draw from all this is that both determinism and indeterminism can be enemies of free will. Determinism coupled with incompatibilism yields hard determinism—no free will. And indeterminism that amounts to randomness does not give us free will either.

WRITING TO UNDERSTAND:
CRITIQUING PHILOSOPHICAL VIEWS   Section 5.2

1. Suppose hard determinism is true. Would punishment for offenses ever be justified? Would praise for making good choices be appropriate? If the answer is no, would that constitute an argument against hard determinism?

2. If hard determinism were widely recognized as true, how would that consensus likely affect our judicial system?

3. Do you agree with the criticism of James's indeterminism? Are chance actions really free actions? Explain.

4. Must at least some indeterminism exist in the universe to make free will possible? Why or why not?

5. Suppose James's indeterminist view of free will is correct. What would be the implications for our social practice of rewarding and punishing behavior?

5.3 COMPATIBILISM

The great appeal of traditional compatibilism is that it provides a plausible way to reconcile free will and determinism. It says that determinism is true and so is the commonsense belief that we have free will. Science is squared with our presumption of freedom, and incompatibilism is unfounded.

This reconciliation project has been—and still is—attractive to many serious thinkers, including the ancient Greek Stoics, some English-speaking philosophers of previous centuries, and numerous contemporary proponents. Among the greatest of these are Thomas Hobbes (1588–1679), John Locke (1632–1704), David Hume

You say: I am not free. But I have raised and lowered my arm. Everyone understands that this illogical answer is an irrefutable proof of freedom.
—Leo Tolstoy

(1711–1776), and John Stuart Mill (1806–1873). Locke sums up traditional compatibilism like this:

John Locke, *An Essay Concerning Human Understanding*

But though the preference of the Mind be always determined . . . yet the Person who has the power, in which alone consists the liberty to act, or not to act, according to such preference, is nevertheless free; such determination abridges not that Power.[3]

Compatibilists do not deny that all our wants or desires are caused by preceding events. In fact, they hold that determinism is necessary for free will; an undetermined choice, they say, would be random and uncontrolled by the agent. They insist that even though our desires are determined, we can still act freely as long as (1) we have the power to do what we want, and (2) nothing is preventing us from doing it (for example, no one is restraining or coercing us).

Both compatibilists and most of their critics agree that free actions (and moral responsibility) require alternative possibilities, or a "could do otherwise" sort of freedom. If we are free—if our actions are truly up to us—we must be able to act in one of several different ways, to have more than one option to choose from. We must have the wherewithal to do otherwise than what we actually do. But if we have only one choice open to us, if all other possibilities are closed, then our actions are not up to us. Incompatibilists say that this is precisely what would happen if determinism were true. But compatibilists assert that we can still do otherwise even if determinism reigns in the world.

But how? Compatibilists can make this claim by assigning a conditional, or hypothetical, meaning to the notion of "could do otherwise." To them, "could do otherwise" means that you would have been able to do something different *if you had wanted to*. You are free in the sense that if you had desired to do something different than what you actually did, nothing would have prevented you from doing it. If you had wanted a piece of cake instead of the slice of pie that you actually got, and nothing would have prevented you from getting cake, then your action was free. Whatever you finally choose is, of course, determined by previous events. But you would have been able to choose differently if history had been different.

Here is Walter Stace (1886–1967), a twentieth-century compatibilist, arguing the compatibilist's case by trying to ascertain what we ordinarily mean by "free acts":

6 Is the compatibilist's definition of "could do otherwise" plausible? Or is it, as James called it, a "wretched subterfuge"?

7 Does it matter to you whether you have free will? Would your behavior change if you believed (or didn't believe) that all your actions were determined by forces beyond your control?

W. T. Stace, *Religion and the Modern Mind*

The only reasonable view is that all human actions, both those which are freely done and those which are not, are either wholly determined by causes, or at least as much determined as other events in nature. It may be true, as the physicists tell us, that

W. T. Stace,
Religion and the Modern Mind

nature is not as deterministic as was once thought. But whatever degree of determinism prevails in the world, human actions appear to be as much determined as anything else. And if this is so, it cannot be the case that what distinguishes actions freely chosen from those which are not free is that the latter are determined by causes while the former are not. Therefore, being uncaused or being undetermined by causes, must be an incorrect definition of free will.

What, then, is the difference between acts which are freely done and those which are not? What is the characteristic which is present [in all free actions] and absent from [all unfree actions]? Is it not obvious that, although both sets of actions have causes, the causes of [free actions] are *of a different kind* from the causes of [unfree acts]? The free acts are all caused by desires, or motives, or by some sort of internal psychological states of the agent's mind. The unfree acts, on the other hand, are all caused by

PHILOSOPHY NOW

Does Belief in Free Will Matter?

Your belief or nonbelief in free will doesn't affect your behavior; your acceptance or rejection of the doctrine doesn't matter to how you live your life. Is this true? Is it true that your belief in free will is inconsequential? Some philosophers, as well as many nonphilosophers, think so. But some scientific research suggests otherwise.

In studies conducted by Kathleen D. Vohs and Jonathan W. Schooler, college students who were encouraged to doubt free will were more likely to cheat than students who were not given that encouragement. This is how the researchers sum up the results:

> In Experiment 1, participants read either text that encouraged a belief in determinism (i.e., that portrayed behavior as the consequence of environmental and genetic factors) or neutral text. Exposure to the deterministic message increased cheating on a task in which participants could passively allow a flawed computer program to reveal answers to mathematical problems that they had been instructed to solve themselves. Moreover, increased cheating behavior was mediated by decreased belief in free will. In Experiment 2, participants who read deterministic statements cheated by overpaying them-

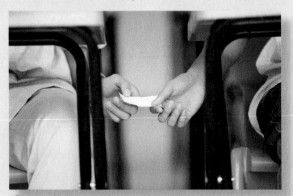

Figure 5.6 Are those who don't believe in free will more likely to cheat? If so, why?

physical forces or physical conditions, outside the agent. Police arrest means physical force exerted from the outside; the absence of food in the desert is a physical condition of the outside world. We may therefore frame the following rough definitions. *Acts freely done are those whose immediate causes are psychological states in the agent. Acts not freely done are those whose immediate causes are states of affairs external to the agent.*

It is plain that if we define free will in this way, then free will certainly exists, and the philosopher's denial of its existence is seen to be what it is—nonsense. For it is obvious that all those actions of men which we should ordinarily attribute to the exercise of their free will, or of which we should say that they freely chose to do them, are in fact actions which have been caused by their own desires, wishes, thoughts, emotions, impulses, or other psychological states.[4]

8 Are free acts, as Stace says, "those whose immediate causes are psychological states in the agent"? Would such acts still be free if the "psychological states" were secretly controlled by someone else through hypnosis?

selves for performance on a cognitive task; participants who read statements endorsing free will did not.

Kathleen D. Vohs and Jonathan W. Schooler, "The Value of Believing in Free Will," Psychological Science *19, no. 1 (2008).*

Studies conducted by Roy F. Baumeister and his colleagues tested the hypothesis that a lack of belief in free will is linked to greater selfishness and increased aggression. The results:

In Experiment 1, induced belief in free will reduced willingness to help others. Experiment 2 showed that chronic disbelief in free will was associated with reduced helping behavior. In Experiment 3, participants' induced disbelief in free will caused participants to act more aggressively than others.

Roy F. Baumeister, Personality and Social Psychology Bulletin *35, no. 2 (2009).*

Some researchers have hinted that if belief in determinism leads to antisocial behavior, perhaps any research findings supporting determinism should be hidden from the public. Do you think that such a policy would be morally permissible? Would you want to be told the truth about free will and determinism, come what may?

Man is a being with free will; therefore, each man is potentially good or evil, and it's up to him and only him (through his reasoning mind) to decide which he wants to be.
—Ayn Rand

For Stace and other compatibilists, all our actions are caused, but free ones are caused by internal psychological factors, and unfree ones are caused by external factors. When your internal states cause your actions and external forces do not impede or constrain you, you are free to do otherwise.

Incompatibilists, however, insist that this compatibilist freedom is not real freedom at all. They argue that the compatibilist conception of freedom must be mistaken because an agent can do what she wants without external constraints and still not act freely. Real freedom, they contend, is not just the power to act *if we will to act*, but power over the will itself. This is how William L. Rowe makes this argument, directing it specifically against Locke's compatibilism:

William L. Rowe, "Two Concepts of Freedom"

Locke distinguished between a free action and a voluntary action. For your action to be voluntary all that is required is that you will to do that action and perform it, presumably as a result of your willing to do it. Suppose you are sitting in your chair and someone invites you to go for a walk. You reject the idea, choosing instead to remain just where you. Your so remaining, Locke would say, is a voluntary act. But was it a free act? This is a further question for Locke, and it depends on whether you could have done otherwise had you so willed. If I had injected you with a powerful drug, so that at the time—perhaps without your being aware of it—your legs were paralyzed, then your act of remaining in the chair was voluntary but not free, for you could not have got up and walked had you willed to do so. A free act, says Locke, is not just a voluntary act. An act is free if it is voluntary *and* it is true that had you willed to do otherwise you would have been able to do otherwise. For Locke, then, we can say that you are free with respect to a certain action provided it is in your power to do it if you will to do it *and* in your power to refrain from doing it if you should will to refrain. Locke tells us that a man who is chained in prison does not stay in prison freely—even if that is what he wants to do—because it is not in his power to leave if he should will to leave. But if the prison doors are thrown open, and his chains are removed, he is free to leave and free to stay—for he can do either, depending on his will. . . .

 Lockean freedom . . . exists solely at the level of *action*: you are free with respect to some action provided that you have the power to do the act if you will to do it, and have the power not to do it if you will not to do it. But what about the *will*? What if you don't have the power to will the action, or don't have the power not to will it? To see the difficulty here, let's return to our example where you are sitting down, someone asks you to get up and walk over to the window to see what is happening outside, but you are quite satisfied where you are and choose to remain sitting. We earlier supposed that I had injected you with a powerful drug so that you can't move your legs. Here Locke would say that you don't sit freely, since it was not in your power to do otherwise if you had willed otherwise—say, to get up and walk to the window. But let's now suppose that instead of paralyzing your legs I had hooked up a machine to your brain so that I can and do cause you to will to sit, thus depriving you of the *capacity* to will to do otherwise. It's still true that you have the power to get up and walk *if* you should will to do so—I haven't taken away your physical capacity to walk, as I did when I paralyzed your legs. Here the problem is that you can't will to do anything other than sit. In this case, it seems clear that you sit of necessity, not freely. You can't do otherwise than sit, not because you lack the power to get up and walk if you should manage to choose to do that, but because you lack the power to *choose* to get up and walk. On Locke's account of freedom, however, it remains true that you sit freely and not of necessity. And this being so, we must conclude that Locke's account of freedom is simply inadequate. It is not sufficient that you have the power to do otherwise *if* you so will; it must also be true that you have the power to will to do otherwise. Freedom that is worth the name, therefore, must include power *to will*, not simply power *to do if we will*.[5]

In response to criticism, traditional compatibilists sometimes say that however one feels about the compatibilist conception of freedom, it is at least clear and coherent. The alternative is libertarianism, which they claim is obscure and unintelligible.

9 What is Rowe's argument against traditional compatibilism? Is it sound? Why or why not?

> **WRITING TO UNDERSTAND:**
> **CRITIQUING PHILOSOPHICAL VIEWS**   Section 5.3
>
> 1. Suppose traditional compatibilism is true. Would punishment, reward, blame, or praise ever be justified?
> 2. Assuming a dog has desires and often behaves accordingly, would he have free will, according to compatibilism? Why or why not?
> 3. Does Stace's distinction between free acts and unfree acts make sense? Do you think that an agent's actions can be unimpeded and caused by her psychological states yet still not be free?
> 4. Does Stace's view of free actions coincide with what most people ordinarily think about such matters? Explain.
> 5. Which do you think is a more plausible theory of free will—hard determinism or compatibilism? Why?

He sat a long time and he thought about his life and how little of it he could ever have foreseen and he wondered for all his will and all his intent how much of it was his doing.
—Cormac McCarthy

10 Is our experience good evidence that we have libertarian free will?

11 Do you think the hypothetical interpretation of "could do otherwise" captures our commonsense experience better than the libertarian interpretation? Why or why not?

5.4 LIBERTARIANISM

To be taken seriously by the free will skeptic, libertarians must argue their case on three fronts. Against the compatibilist, they must show that determinism and free will are incompatible (that incompatibilism is true). Against the determinist, they must show that there is good reason to believe that we sometimes act freely. And against all free will skeptics, they must demonstrate that the libertarian concept of free will is coherent and plausible.

PHILOSOPHY NOW

Science and Free Will

Is it possible that your actions are predetermined unconsciously *before* you are consciously aware of intending to perform those actions? To the consternation of many libertarians, some scientific research seems to suggest just that—and thus to raise doubts about the existence of free will.

The experiments that caused all the fuss (and inspired many related scientific studies) were conducted by the University of California researcher Benjamin Libet. He recorded the brain activity of subjects as they randomly flexed their index fingers, and he monitored the accompanying muscle movements. He found that the subjects became aware of their intention to move their fingers about 200 milliseconds before the actual movement occurred—an unsurprising result. The astonishing finding was that the subjects became aware of their intention 350 to 400 milliseconds *after* the brain activity that initiates muscle movement had already happened. This seems to suggest that the decision to move was an unconscious event, that consciousness came along after the unconscious decision was already made. If so, where does free will enter the picture?

Libet thought his research showed that there could be at least a limited kind of free will in human actions. The conscious mind may not be involved in initiating actions, but it might be able to veto actions before they happen.

Libet's studies and similar ones by other investigators have been criticized on several counts. For one, the results of the experiments may apply only to simple movements (such as finger flexing). As one critic says, "Willing a stereotyped, well-rehearsed finger movement is too simple to have much bearing on such conscious processes as the decisions made through planning a course of action that spans past and future, or analysis of complex events." Also, some investigators seem to assume that decisions are instantaneous, but this may not be the case. "Why do we think that a decision is instantaneous?" this critic observes. "What we consciously think could well be spread out over time. The process can be on-going but our realization captures the process only as a snap shot in time that suffices to label the decision but not the process." (W. R. Klemm, "Free Will Debates: Simple Experiments Are Not So Simple," *Advances in Cognitive Psychology* 6 (2010): 47–65.) Finally, some detractors accuse Libet and others of failing to distinguish between conscious awareness (the intention to do something) and "meta-conscious awareness" (the awareness that you are intending to do something). The charge is that Libet's subjects are reporting that they are aware that they are consciously intending something (meta-conscious awareness), and this kind of awareness naturally comes after the conscious intention itself is formed (after conscious awareness). So Libet's findings may not be the threat to free will that some researchers assume.

Suppose all our decisions are made for us on an unconscious level so that we do not have conscious control of our actions. How would this fact change your thinking about your actions and about moral responsibility?

Often libertarians try to establish incompatibilism by putting forth what is known as the Consequence Argument. Peter van Inwagen crafted the most influential form of it, which he summarizes like this:

Peter van Inwagen, *An Essay on Free Will*

If determinism is true, then our acts are the consequences of the laws of nature and events in the remote past. But it is not up to us what went on before we were born, and neither is it up to us what the laws of nature are. Therefore the consequences of these things (including our present acts) are not up to us.[6]

Van Inwagen contends that if determinism is true, then every event—including our every action—is the result of (1) events in the distant past and (2) the laws of nature that rule those events. But we have no power over past events and the laws of nature; we can change neither the events nor the laws. These things are not up to us, and if they are not up to us, their consequences (including our current actions) are not up to us either. We are left with no alternative possibilities. So if determinism is true, we cannot do otherwise: there are no free actions. Therefore, compatibilism is false; incompatibilism is true.

Compatibilists often reject the Consequence Argument on the grounds that it assumes a faulty interpretation of "could do otherwise." They say that the Consequence Argument works only if "could do otherwise" is given an incompatibilist meaning, which is that you have the power to will to do otherwise (that your will is up to you). But if you give "could do otherwise" a hypothetical meaning (which compatibilists prefer), the Consequence Argument doesn't go through. Recall that the hypothetical meaning is that you would have been able to do something *if* you had desired to (if you desired to and nothing prevented you from doing it). This "could do otherwise" issue, then, is at the heart of the debate between compatibilists and incompatibilists.

But showing incompatibilism to be true is not the only hurdle facing libertarians, for they must also provide good reasons to think that libertarian free will actually exists. On this score they often contend that the best evidence for the existence of free will comes from our own experience. When making a choice, we often sense that we have genuine options, that we have the power to choose (or not choose) among alternative courses of action, and that what we finally choose and do is genuinely and ultimately up to us. Proponents of free will say that this experience is as persistent and reliable as any we could have, and it provides strong evidence for libertarian freedom. Judging from our perceptions, for example, we think we have good evidence for the existence of physical objects. Likewise, our experience of choosing and acting seems to give us evidence for free will that is at least as strong as that for physical objects.

12 What are the premises of van Inwagen's argument? Are they plausible?

Man was predestined to have free will.
—Hal Lee Luyah

CHAPTER 5 PHILOSOPHERS

Baron d'Holbach (1723–1789)

William James (1842–1910)

Thomas Hobbes (1588–1679)

John Locke (1632–1704)

David Hume (1711–1776)

John Stuart Mill (1806–1873)

Walter Stace (1886–1967)

William L. Rowe (b. 1931)

Peter van Inwagen (b. 1942)

Roderick Chisholm (1916–1999)

Randolph Clarke (b. 1953)

Richard Taylor (1919–2003)

Timothy O'Connor (b. 1965)

Robert Kane (b. 1938)

Jean-Paul Sartre (1905–1980)

PHILOSOPHY LAB

Imagine that your friend says he knows you so well that he can predict everything you will do in any given time period. So you test him. For an hour you try to act normally, and he observes you. After the hour is up, he hands you his notes that he wrote an hour ago, *before* the experiment began. You are shocked to see that he has accurately predicted your every action.

Then you begin to worry. Does the fact that everything you did was predictable mean that your whole life is determined by forces beyond your control? In other words, is your life predictable because it is *determined*?

Agent causation is the view that a free action is caused by an agent (person) and is not wholly determined by previous events.

13 Does Taylor's concept of agent causation accurately reflect what people take themselves to be doing when they perform actions? Why or why not?

Hard determinists and compatibilists typically reply that this experiential sense of freedom is illusory. Our experience is not good evidence for free will, and we believe in free will only because we are ignorant of all the factors (genes and environment, for example) that determine us. Libertarians reply that we can indeed be mistaken about whether our actions are free, for our experience could mislead us. But we are entitled to trust our experience unless evidence gives us good reasons to doubt it. And so far, they say, there are no good reasons to do so.

Can libertarians provide an intelligible and credible explanation of how free will is possible? If not, libertarianism will be regarded as a problematic theory—even if incompatibilism and the existence of free will are assumed. The main difficulty is explaining how actions can be free if indeterminism is true—that is, if actions are not caused by prior events. How can an action be uncaused? And if it is uncaused by previous events, wouldn't it be simply random? A random action is not a free action.

Several philosophers have responded to these worries, most notably Thomas Reid in the eighteenth century and in recent years Roderick Chisholm, Randolph Clarke, Richard Taylor, Timothy O'Connor, and Robert Kane. One proposed solution favored by most of these is **agent causation**, the view that a free action is caused by an agent (person) and is not wholly determined by previous events. Here is Taylor making a case for one version of this theory:

Richard Taylor, *Metaphysics*

The only conception of action that accords with our data is one according to which people—and perhaps some other things too—are sometimes, but of course not always, self-determining beings; that is, beings that are sometimes the causes of their own behavior. In the case of an action that is free, it must not only be such that it is caused by the agent who performs it, but also such that no antecedent conditions were sufficient for his performing just that action. In the case of an action that is both free and rational, it must be such that the agent who performed it did so for some reason, but this reason cannot have been the cause of it.

Now this conception fits what people take themselves to be; namely, beings who act, or who are agents, rather than beings that are merely upon, and whose behavior is simply the causal consequence of conditions that they have not wrought. When I believe that I have done something, I do believe that it was I who caused it to be done, I who made something happen, and not merely something within me, such as one of my own subjective states, which is not identical with myself. If I believe that something not identical with myself was the cause of my behavior—some event wholly external to myself, for instance, or even one internal to myself, such as a nerve impulse, volition, or whatnot—then I cannot regard that behavior as being an act of mine, unless I further believe that I was the cause of that external or internal event. My pulse, for example, is caused and regulated by certain conditions existing within me, and not by myself. I do not, accordingly, regard this activity of my body as my action, and would be no more tempted to do so if I became suddenly conscious within myself of those conditions or impulses that produce it. This is behavior with which I have nothing to do, behavior that is not only not free activity, but not even the activity of an agent to begin with; it is nothing but a mechanical reflex. Had I never learned that my very life depends on this pulse beat, I would regard it with complete indifference, as something foreign to me, like the oscillations of a clock pendulum that I idly contemplate.

Now this conception of activity, and of an agent who is the cause of it, involves two rather strange metaphysical notions that are never applied elsewhere in nature. The first is that of a *self* or *person*—for example, a man—who is not merely a collection of things or events, but a self-moving being. For on this view it is a person, and not merely some part of him or something within him, that is the cause of his own activity. Now, we certainly do not know that a human being is anything more than an assemblage of physical things and processes that act in accordance with those laws that describe the behavior of all other physical things and processes. Even though he is a living being, of enormous complexity, there is nothing, apart from the requirements of this theory, to suggest that his behavior is so radically different in its origin from that of other physical objects, or that an understanding of it must be sought in some metaphysical realm wholly different from that appropriate to the understanding of nonliving things.

Second, this conception of activity involves an extraordinary conception of causation according to which an agent, which is a substance and not an event, can nevertheless be the cause of an event. Indeed, if he is a free agent then he can, on this conception, cause an event to occur—namely, some act of his own—without anything else causing him to do so. This means that an agent is sometimes a cause, without being an antecedent sufficient condition; for if I affirm that I am the cause of some act of mine, then I am plainly not saying that my very existence is sufficient for its occurrence, which would be absurd. If I say that my hand causes my pencil to move, then I am saying that the motion of my hand is, under the other conditions then prevailing, sufficient for the motion of the pencil. But if I then say that I cause my hand to move, I am not saying anything remotely like this, and surely not that the motion of my self

14 How might a determinist or indeterminist respond to Taylor's notion of agent causation?

> Free will is an illusion. People always choose the perceived path of greatest pleasure.
> —Scott Adams

Richard Taylor,
Metaphysics

is sufficient for the motion of my arm and hand, since these are the only things about me that are moving.

This conception of the causation of events by things that are not events is, in fact, so different from the usual philosophical conception of a cause that it should not even bear the same name, for "being a cause" ordinarily just means "being an antecedent sufficient condition or set of conditions." Instead, then, of speaking of agents as *causing* their own acts, it would perhaps be better to use another word entirely, and say, for instance, that they *originate* them, *initiate* them, or simply that they *perform* them.

Now this is, on the face of it, a dubious conception of what a person is. Yet it is consistent with our data, reflecting the presuppositions of deliberation, and appears to be the only conception that is consistent with them, as determinism and simple indeterminism are not. The theory of agency avoids the absurdities of simple indeterminism by conceding that human behavior is caused, while at the same time avoiding the difficulties of determinism by denying that every chain of causes and effects is infinite. Some such causal chains, on this view, have beginnings, and they begin with agents themselves. Moreover, if we are to suppose that it is sometimes up to me what I do, and understand this in a sense that is not consistent with determinism, we must suppose that I am an agent or a being who initiates his own actions, sometimes under conditions that do not determine what action I shall perform. Deliberation becomes, on this view, something that is not only possible but quite rational, for it does make sense to deliberate about activity that is truly my own and that depends in its outcome upon me as its author, and not merely upon something more or less esoteric that is supposed to be intimately associated with me, such as my thoughts, volitions, choices or whatnot.[7]

Taylor acknowledges that this take on free will may at first glance seem implausible, but he thinks the theory is the only one that fits with our common experience of actions and choices.

O'Connor also subscribes to agent causation, and like everyone who takes this view he holds that free actions are caused by the agent. But in explaining this, he suggests that all events in the universe are produced in virtue of the properties that objects possess. Ordinary events are produced this way; likewise, an agent may produce an event in virtue of the unique properties that she possesses. When she makes a free choice, she does so via what O'Connor calls "volition-enabling properties." Thus her choice is not determined by previous events; it is produced by her. Specifically, she makes her choice based on the reasons she has, and the reasons influence the production of the decision without causally determining it. The choice is not random because it is produced by her; she is the author and cause of it.

As you might expect, agent causation perspectives are disputed at many points, with opponents contending that the theories are incoherent or otherwise inadequate and proponents denying the charge. But as such debates unfold, libertarians insist that, despite claims to the contrary, plausible theories of libertarian free will are on the table.

5.5 SARTRE'S PROFOUND FREEDOM

The foregoing doctrines—hard determinism, compatibilism, and libertarianism—are the major philosophical stances on free will and determinism, each with a long history and articulate proponents. But they are not the only views on the subject. Other thinkers, both contemporary and influential, have advanced unique perspectives on human freedom or have taken issue with the standard viewpoints. Among the most interesting and influential of these voices is the existentialist philosopher and novelist Jean-Paul Sartre (1905–1980).

Sartre is one of the modern founders of the philosophical perspective known as *existentialism*, a central tenet of which is that humans are profoundly free to create their own lives and thus are entirely responsible for defining the meaning and moral relevance of their existence. From reflections on his own lived experience, Sartre arrives at what he takes to be some basic truths about human beings and their existential predicament. Unlike almost every philosopher before him, he not only believes that we are free, but also insists that we are *radically* free. We may be influenced by the factors of nature and nurture (heredity and environment), but ultimately we are not determined by them. We are totally free—free to define ourselves by our own lights and capable of resisting the physical, psychological, and social forces that will thoroughly shape us if we let them. We are determined only if we allow ourselves to be determined.

Figure 5.7 Jean-Paul Sartre (1905–1980).

Mankind has a free will; but it is free to milk cows and to build houses, nothing more.
—Martin Luther

Man is condemned to be free.
—Jean-Paul Sartre

15 Sartre reasons from his lived experience to his theory of free will. Does his experience provide adequate support for his assertions?

One of Sartre's core ideas is that "existence precedes essence." Most people assume, he says, that "essence precedes existence"—that before we come into existence, our fundamental characteristics (our essence) as humans are already set. They think that our psychological makeup, choices, desires, and ideas are in a sense locked in before we can say our first words. Our destiny is mapped out beforehand through the workings of a creator God or a universal human nature or some unalterable social structure. But, according to Sartre, this kind of "essence precedes existence" thinking is tragically mistaken. It prevents us from seeing a future of open possibilities, saps our creativity, limits our freedom, and weakens our sense of our moral responsibility. The truth, says Sartre, is the opposite of the received view: "existence precedes essence"—we first come into being and then we define ourselves. He declares, "Man is nothing else but what he makes of himself."

And what is this radical freedom that we all possess? It is both a blessing and a curse. As Sartre says, "We are condemned to be free." The blessing is that as free persons, we have the power to set our own goals, live our own lives, and create ourselves as we go. The curse is that as free beings, we can look to no one but ourselves to decide how we should live. We carry this burden alone. We must bear the awesome moral responsibility of deciding how we should live, how we should treat others, and what values we should prescribe for the rest of the world through our actions. We can celebrate our capacity to create our essence and live by our own rules, but because we are utterly alone in bearing this monumental burden, we are also condemned to experience great anguish, despair, and a sense of abandonment.

This is how Sartre explained this existentialist freedom in a famous lecture titled "Existentialism Is a Humanism":

Jean-Paul Sartre, "Existentialism Is a Humanism"

What [existentialists] have in common is that they think that existence precedes essence, or, if you prefer, that subjectivity must be the starting point.

Just what does that mean? Let us consider some object that is manufactured, for example, a book or a paper-cutter: here is an object which has been made by an artisan whose inspiration came from a concept. He referred to the concept of what a paper-cutter is and likewise to a known method of production, which is part of the concept, something which is, by and large, a routine. Thus, the paper-cutter is at once an object produced in a certain way and, on the other hand, one having a specific use; and one cannot postulate a man who produces a paper-cutter but does not know what it is used for. Therefore, let us say that, for the paper-cutter, essence—that is, the ensemble of both the production routines and the properties which enable it to be both produced and defined—precedes existence. Thus, the presence of the paper-cutter or book in front of me is determined. Therefore, we have here a technical view of the world whereby it can be said that production precedes existence.

When we conceive God as the Creator, He is generally thought of as a superior sort of artisan. Whatever doctrine we may be considering, whether one like that of

Descartes or that of Leibnitz, we always grant that will more or less follows understanding or, at the very least, accompanies it, and that when God creates He knows exactly what He is creating. Thus, the concept of man in the mind of God is comparable to the concept of paper-cutter in the mind of the manufacturer, and, following certain techniques and a conception, God produces man, just as the artisan, following a definition and a technique, makes a paper-cutter. Thus, the individual man is the realization of a certain concept in the divine intelligence.

In the eighteenth century, the atheism of the *philosophes* discarded the idea of God, but not so much for the notion that essence precedes existence. To a certain extent, this idea is found everywhere; we find it in Diderot, in Voltaire, and even in Kant. Man has a human nature; this human nature, which is the concept of the human, is found in all men, which means that each man is a particular example of a universal concept, man. In Kant, the result of this universality is that the wild-man, the natural man, as well as the bourgeois, are circumscribed by the same definition and have the same basic qualities. Thus, here too the essence of man precedes the historical existence that we find in nature.

Atheistic existentialism, which I represent, is more coherent. It states that if God does not exist, there is at least one being in whom existence precedes essence, a being who exists before he can be defined by any concept, and that this being is man, or, as Heidegger says, human reality. What is meant here by saying that existence precedes essence? It means that, first of all, man exists, turns up, appears on the scene, and, only afterwards, defines himself. If man, as the existentialist conceives him, is indefinable, it is because at first he is nothing. Only afterward will he be something, and he himself will have made what he will be. Thus, there is no human nature, since there is no God to conceive it. Not only is man what he conceives himself to be, but he is also only what he wills himself to be after this thrust toward existence.

Man is nothing else but what he makes of himself. Such is the first principle of existentialism. It is also what is called subjectivity, the name we are labeled with when charges are brought against us. But what do we mean by this, if not that man has a greater dignity than a stone or table? For we mean that man first exists, that is, that man first of all is the being in the future. Man is at the start a plan which is aware of itself, rather than a patch of moss, a piece of garbage, or a cauliflower; nothing exists prior to this plan; there is nothing in heaven; man will be what he will have planned to be. Not what he will want to be. Because by the word "will" we generally mean a conscious decision, which is subsequent to what we have already made of ourselves. I may want to belong to a political party, write a book, get married; but all that is only a manifestation of an earlier, more spontaneous choice that is called "will." But if existence really does precede essence, man is responsible for what he is. Thus, existentialism's first move is to make every man aware of what he is and to make the full responsibility of his existence rest on him. And when we say that a man is responsible for himself, we do not only mean that he is responsible for his own individuality, but that he is responsible for all men. . . .

When we say that man chooses his own self, we mean that every one of us does likewise; but we also mean by that that in making this choice he also chooses all men. In fact, in creating the man that we want to be, there is not a single one of our acts which does not at the same time create an image of man as we think he ought to be. To choose to be this or that is to affirm at the same time the value of what we choose, because we can never choose evil. We always choose the good, and nothing can be good for us without being good for all.

16 Is Sartre exaggerating the extent to which people can define themselves when he says "existence precedes essence"?

Jean-Paul Sartre,
"Existentialism Is a
Humanism"

If, on the other hand, existence precedes essence, and if we grant that we exist and fashion our image at one and the same time, the image is valid for everybody and for our whole age. Thus, our responsibility is much greater than we might have supposed, because it involves all mankind. . . . Therefore, I am responsible for myself and for everyone else. I am creating a certain image of man of my own choosing. In choosing myself, I choose man.

This helps us understand what the actual content is of such rather grandiloquent words as anguish, forlornness, despair. As you will see, it's all quite simple.

First, what is meant by anguish? The existentialists say at once that man is anguish. What that means is this: the man who involves himself and who realizes that he is not only the person he chooses to be, but also a law-maker who is, at the same time, choosing all mankind as well as himself, cannot help escape the feeling of his total and deep responsibility. Of course, there are many people who are not anxious; but we claim that they are hiding their anxiety, that they are fleeing from it. Certainly, many people believe that when they do something, they themselves are the only ones involved, and when someone says to them, "What if everyone acted that way?" they shrug their shoulders and answer, "Everyone doesn't act that way." But really, one should always ask himself, "What would happen if everybody looked at things that way?" There is no escaping this disturbing thought except by a kind of double-dealing. . . .

There is no question here of the kind of anguish which would lead to quietism, to inaction. It is a matter of a simple sort of anguish that anybody who has had responsibilities is familiar with. For example, when a military officer takes the responsibility for an attack and sends a certain number of men to death, he chooses to do so, and in the main he alone makes the choice. Doubtless, orders come from above, but they are too broad; he interprets them, and on this interpretation depend the lives of ten or fourteen or twenty men. In making a decision he cannot help having a certain anguish. All leaders know this anguish. That doesn't keep them from acting; on the contrary, it is the very condition of their action. For it implies that they envisage a number of possibilities, and when they choose one, they realize that it has value only because it is chosen. We shall see that this kind of anguish, which is the kind that existentialism describes, is explained, in addition, by a direct responsibility to the other men whom it involves. It is not a curtain separating us from action, but is part of action itself.

When we speak of forlornness, a term Heidegger was fond of, we mean only that God does not exist and that we have to face all the consequences of this. The existentialist is strongly opposed to a certain kind of secular ethics which would like to abolish God with the least possible expense. . . .

The existentialist, on the contrary, thinks it very distressing that God does not exist, because all possibility of finding values in a heaven of ideas disappears along with Him; there can be no longer an *a priori* Good, since there is no infinite and perfect consciousness to think it. Nowhere is it written that the Good exists, that we must be honest, that we must not lie; because the fact is we are on a plane where there are only men. Dostoievsky said, "If God didn't exist, everything would be possible." That is the very starting point of existentialism. Indeed, everything is permissible if God does not exist, and as a result man is forlorn, because neither within him nor without does he find anything to cling to. He can't start making excuses for himself.

If existence really does precede essence, there is no explaining things away by reference to a fixed and given human nature. In other words, there is no determinism, man is free, man is freedom. On the other hand, if God does not exist, we find no values or commands to turn to which legitimize our conduct. So, in the bright realm of values, we have no excuse behind us, no justification before us. We are alone, with no excuses.

That is the idea I shall try to convey when I say that man is condemned to be free. Condemned, because he did not create himself, yet, in other respects is free; because, once thrown into the world, he is responsible for everything he does. . . .

As for despair, the term has a very simple meaning. It means that we shall confine ourselves to reckoning only with what depends upon our will, or on the ensemble of probabilities which make our action possible. When we want something, we always have to reckon with probabilities. I may be counting on the arrival of a friend. The friend is coming by rail or street-car; this supposes that the train will arrive on schedule, or that the street-car will not jump the track. I am left in the realm of possibility; but possibilities are to be reckoned with only to the point where my action comports with the ensemble of these possibilities, and no further. The moment the possibilities I am considering are not rigorously involved by my action, I ought to disengage myself from them, because no God, no scheme, can adapt the world and its possibilities to my will. When Descartes said, "Conquer yourself rather than the world," he meant essentially the same thing. . . .

Actually, things will be as man will have decided they are to be. Does that mean that I should abandon myself to quietism? No. First, I should involve myself; then, act on the old saw, "Nothing ventured, nothing gained." Nor does it mean that I shouldn't belong to a party, but rather that I shall have no illusions and shall do what I can. For example, suppose I ask myself, "Will socialization, as such, ever come about?" I know nothing about it. All I know is that I'm going to do everything in my power to bring it about. Beyond that, I can't count on anything. Quietism is the attitude of people who say, "Let others do what I can't do." The doctrine I am presenting is the very opposite of quietism, since it declares, "There is no reality except in action." Moreover, it goes further, since it adds, "Man is nothing else than his plan; he exists only to the extent that he fulfills himself; he is, therefore, nothing else than the ensemble of his acts, nothing else than his life."[8]

The hard determinists would, of course, reject Sartre's brand of free will. For them, everything we know about science suggests that such unfettered freedom is impossible. For much the same reason, compatibilists would find Sartre's view difficult to accept, for they too believe in determinism. Even the libertarians would insist that our experience shows that at least some of our actions are determined, and they would likely agree that not all of science's evidence for determinism can be as easily dismissed as Sartre assumes.

17 Are people wholly responsible for the kind of persons they become?

18 Is it true that if God does not exist, there are no objective moral standards? What would utilitarians and others who prefer secular theories of morality have to say about this claim?

You may fetter my leg, but Zeus himself cannot get the better of my free will.
—Epictetus

> **WRITING TO UNDERSTAND:**
> **CRITIQUING PHILOSOPHICAL VIEWS**   Section 5.5
>
> 1. Which seems most likely to you: that your path in life is determined before you were born, or that you are born and then you determine how your life will go? Why? Is there a middle ground on this issue?
>
> 2. Is Sartre right about free will being the main factor that determines who you are—or do such things as genetics and society have the greatest impact on how you turn out?
>
> 3. What is your reaction to Sartre's perspective on freedom? Do you find his view liberating and inspiring, or do you think it is disheartening and forlorn?
>
> 4. In other writings, Sartre says that it is impossible for self-conscious beings like us *not* to have free will. Why do you think Sartre would believe this? Is he right?
>
> 5. How would a compatibilist respond to Sartre's ideas? How would a libertarian respond?

Review Notes

5.1 OVERVIEW: THE FREE WILL PROBLEM

- The problem of free will is the challenge of reconciling determinism with our intuitions or ideas about personal freedom.

- The main ideas concerning free will are determinism, hard determinism, incompatibilism, indeterminism, compatibilism, and libertarianism.

- The three major responses to the free will problem are hard determinism, compatibilism, and libertarianism. Hard determinism is the view that no one has free will. Compatibilism claims that although determinism is true, our actions can still be free because determinism and free will are not in conflict. Libertarianism says that some actions are free, for they are ultimately caused, or controlled, by the person, or agent.

- For many people, free will matters because it relates to crucial questions about moral responsibility, legal punishment, praise and blame, and social and political control.

5.2 DETERMINISM AND INDETERMINISM

- D'Holbach asserts that no one has free will, and that the theories and discoveries of science are robust proof that every event is determined by preceding events and natural laws.

- Many point to science as proof of determinism, for it has had remarkable success in explaining and predicting all sorts of natural phenomena.

- Quantum physics seems to undermine belief in determinism because the standard view among quantum physicists is that at the subatomic level, some events are uncaused.

- James argues that indeterminism is a feature of the universe that permits "alternative futures" and the possibility of freedom. It allows free actions because free actions are chance happenings.

5.3 COMPATIBILISM

- Compatibilism says that determinism is true (incompatibilism is false), and so is the commonsense belief that we have free will.

- To compatibilists, "could do otherwise" means that you would have been able to do something different if you had wanted to. You are free in the sense that if you had desired to do something different than what you actually did, nothing would have prevented you from doing it.

- Rowe's objection to compatibilism is that the compatibilist conception of freedom must be mistaken because an agent can do what she wants without external constraints and still not act freely.

- Stace argues that "acts freely done are those whose immediate causes are psychological states in the agent. Acts not freely done are those whose immediate causes are states of affairs external to the agent." His view seems to be vulnerable to the kind of anti-compatibilist argument that Rowe puts forth.

5.4 LIBERTARIANISM

- Against the compatibilist, libertarians must show that determinism and free will are incompatible (that incompatibilism is true). Against the determinist, they must show that there is good reason to believe that we sometimes act freely. And against all free will skeptics, they must demonstrate that the libertarian concept of free will is coherent and plausible.

- The Consequence Argument says that if determinism is true, then every event is the result of (1) events in the distant past and (2) the laws of nature that rule those events. But we have no power over past events and the laws of nature. They are not up to us, and neither are their consequences, including our current actions. So if determinism is true, there are no free actions, and compatibilism is false.

- Libertarians say that when making a choice, we often sense that we have genuine options, that we have the power to choose (or not choose) among alternative courses of action, and that what we finally choose and do is genuinely and ultimately up to us. Libertarians contend that this experience constitutes strong evidence for libertarian freedom.

- Agent causation is the view that a free action is caused by an agent (person) and is not wholly determined by previous events. Taylor argues that the theory is the only one that fits with our common experience of actions and choices. O'Connor makes a case for it by trying to show that the notion of agent causation is coherent and plausible.

5.5 SARTRE'S PROFOUND FREEDOM

- Sartre says that we are radically free; we may be influenced by the factors of nature and nurture, but ultimately we are not determined by them.
- "Existence precedes essence" refers to the idea that we first come into being and then we define ourselves; we are only what we make of ourselves.
- Sartre paints a compelling picture of radical freedom, but given our experience and the evidence of science, many find it implausible.

WRITING TO UNDERSTAND: ARGUING YOUR OWN VIEWS   Chapter 5

1. Evaluate the case for hard determinism, including in your evaluation an assessment of both determinism and incompatibilism.
2. Explain why chance does (or does not) make room for free will.
3. Assess the compatibilist's interpretation of "could do otherwise." Devise an argument showing why the interpretation should be accepted (or rejected).
4. Evaluate the Consequence Argument. Examine its premises, determine if they are true, and assess whether the conclusion follows from them.
5. Does science show that free will does not exist? Examine both pro and con arguments and back your verdict with reasons.

Key Terms

agent causation The view that a free action is caused by an agent (person) and is not wholly determined by previous events. (246)

compatibilism The view that although determinism is true, our actions can still be free. (231)

determinism The doctrine that every event is determined by preceding events and the laws of nature. (229)

hard determinism The view that free will does not exist, that no one acts freely. (231)

incompatibilism The view that if determinism is true, no one can act freely. (231)

indeterminism The view that not every event is determined by preceding events and the laws of nature. (231)

libertarianism (metaphysical) The view that some actions are free, for they are caused, or controlled, by the person, or agent. (232)

problem of free will The challenge of reconciling determinism with our intuitions or ideas about personal freedom. (230)

FICTION

A Little Omniscience Goes a Long Way

Thomas D. Davis

> Thomas D. Davis is a philosopher, textbook writer, and author of three novels—*Suffer Little Children*, *Murdered Sleep*, and *Consuming Fire*.

Satan, with a flutter of his mighty wings, descends upon a cloud where God is reclining.

SATAN: How's it going?

GOD: (*He yawns.*) Perfectly, as usual.

SATAN: And your new creatures on earth—how are they?

GOD: Just fine. Eve's asleep under the apple tree, curled up on her right side, dreaming of flowers. Adam is sitting up, squinting at the sun, scratching his nose with his left index finger, trying to decide what he wants to do this morning. What he wants to do is take a walk in the garden. In a moment he will.

SATAN: And you know all that without looking.

GOD: Of course. I arranged it all to happen that way.

SATAN: Isn't it boring to know everything that will ever happen? This morning I saw two solar systems collide and explode in a tremendous cataclysm. The explosion must have lasted, oh, ten minutes. It was lovely and, for me, quite unexpected. I can't imagine life without surprises. It's surprises that keep me going. In a manner of speaking, of course.

GOD: Foreknowledge is the price you pay for creation and control. You can't have everything.

SATAN: Boredom is the secret sadness of God. An interesting thought.

GOD: To you, maybe.

SATAN: Your only sadness, I hope.

GOD: Not the only one. For instance, I've often thought it would be fun to make a rock so big I couldn't lift it. But that would be a contradiction. And having proclaimed all contradictions impossible, I have to make do without them. The laws of logic are for the best, of course. There would be chaos without them.

Thomas D. Davis, "A Little Omniscience Goes a Long Way," in *Philosophy: An Introduction Through Original Fiction, Discussion, and a Multi-Media CD-ROM* (New York: McGraw-Hill, 2004), 11–17.

Still, a few round squares now and then would help break the monotony.

SATAN: I could tell you about some of my adventures today. But you know about them already.

GOD: Of course. I know what you did because I decreed that you would do it.

SATAN: That is exactly what I want to talk with you about.

GOD: I know.

SATAN: You don't mind?

GOD: If I minded, I wouldn't have decided to make you initiate this conversation.

SATAN: That's reasonable.

GOD: Of course it's reasonable. Everything I do or say is reasonable. Which is to say that I have a reason for doing or saying it.

SATAN: To get to the point: A few of the angels and I have been discussing this whole matter of your controlling everything we do.

GOD: I know.

SATAN: I wish you wouldn't keep saying that.

GOD: As you wish.

SATAN: Look here. If you have decreed this whole conversation and know how it is going to turn out, why don't you just give me your answer and save us both a lot of talk?

GOD: Don't be absurd. I know what's going to happen because I decreed that it would happen. If it weren't going to happen, I wouldn't know how it was going to turn out. If I told you now how it will turn out, then it wouldn't happen and so it wouldn't turn out that way.

SATAN: Come again?

GOD: Just trust me.

SATAN: Then we have to go through this whole conversation to get the answer, though you know all the while what the answer will be?

GOD: It's not quite that cut and dried.

SATAN: You mean you don't know exactly what your answer will be?

GOD: Not with absolute certainty.

SATAN: Oh, I see. You're saying that your actions are not inevitable.

GOD: No. Probably what I do is inevitable. The uncertainty is rather a matter of my knowing what inevitable thing I am going to do. You see, when I create a world, I know what will inevitably happen in that world because I created it so that such things would be inevitable. But of course, I did not create myself, being eternal, and I don't have quite the same vantage point on myself.

SATAN: You mean to say that you don't know what you are going to do before you do it?

GOD: Oh, I generally have a pretty good idea. At first, so to speak, I had no idea at all. But I have lived an infinite length of time, I have come to know myself pretty well, and I have found that I have a relatively unchanging character. It was when I realized how unchanging I am that I began to get bored. Still, I do surprise myself occasionally.

SATAN: Just a minute. You are perfectly good—yes?

GOD: Perfectly.

SATAN: And everything you do is for the best?

GOD: Yes.

SATAN: Then it follows that you must know what you are going to do.

GOD: No. I mean superficially your logic is sound, but you are reading too much into it. I don't do things because they're best. Rather, they're best because I do them. Therefore, knowing that I'll do what's for the best amounts to nothing more than knowing that I'll do what I do. Not a very helpful bit of information, you must admit.

SATAN: I suppose not. But, in any case, as to this conversation, you don't know for certain what answer you're going to give me.

GOD: Not for certain. There's a bit of gray area here. Possibly I am in for a bit of a change.

SATAN: Ah, you don't know how encouraged that makes me feel.

GOD: Of course I know how encouraged that makes you feel. I made it make you feel encouraged.

SATAN: Can we get on with it?

GOD: Go ahead.

SATAN: We do everything we do because you make us do it. That makes us feel like puppets. It's undignified. We're not responsible for anything we do. We do good things all the time, but we don't get any credit because it's really you doing them.

GOD: Surely you don't want me to make you do evil?

SATAN: No.

GOD: That wouldn't make any sense. I can't make you do evil. Whatever I made you do would be good, because I made you do it.

SATAN: What I am talking about is control. Right now you have complete control over everything we do. We would like to have some control over our lives.

GOD: But you do have control. No one is shoving you around or chaining you down. You do whatever you want to do. How could anyone be more in control than that? As a matter of fact, that is exactly as much control as I have over my life.

SATAN: But what we want, you make us want. No one makes you want what you want. We don't want you to control everything we want and think. We don't want everything to be inevitable.

GOD: In other words, you want a privilege that probably not even God enjoys.

SATAN: I didn't think of it that way. I suppose I've made you angry.

GOD: No. I'm directing this conversation. So you don't want your thoughts and emotions ruled by my decrees? Nor any other decrees or laws, I suppose?

SATAN: No.

GOD: Then aren't you saying that you want your lives to be ruled by chance?

SATAN: No. We don't want them to be ruled by anything—except ourselves. We want control over our lives.

GOD: I'm afraid you'll have to give me a better idea of what it is you're after.

SATAN: Look here. You're omniscient. Can't you at least help us see what it is we're after, even if you decide not to grant it?

GOD: Even omniscience can't see clarity in a vague idea. The opposite of inevitability is chance. It seems to me that you have to pick one or the other.

SATAN: Chance, then.

GOD: If I grant you this chance you want, then that means I'll have to be watching all the time to see what happens, constantly guarding against the unexpected. That is quite a bit to ask of me, don't you think?

SATAN: You mean you can't foresee what happens by chance?

GOD: Of course not.

SATAN: But you're omniscient. You can see the future.

GOD: Not the future proper. The future is what is not yet. If I could see it, it would be now, and hence not the future. As things stand, I know what will happen because I have made things so that they must happen that way.

SATAN: Well, suppose you did have to keep on guard. You're omnipotent. It wouldn't cost you much effort.

GOD: It is more a question of elegance than of effort.

SATAN: I'm only making the suggestion you made me make.

GOD: Fair enough. So you say you want chance. Or at least that you prefer it to inevitability. I don't believe you have thought it out, but let's discuss it. You want a world in which nothing is predictable, solar systems spinning wildly all over the place, that sort of thing?

SATAN: No, not at all. Let the planets and the plants and the animals remain under your control. Just give independence—chance, if you will—to the thinking creatures.

GOD: Let's experiment a bit, shall we? Come over here. You see Adam and Eve down there in the garden. I'll toss some chance into them. There. Watch and tell me what you see.

SATAN: Adam's strolling through the garden. He's looking to his right toward a berry bush. Uh-oh. Now his arms are flailing about. Now he's rolling on the ground, drooling. It looks as if he's having a fit.

GOD: A chance event.

SATAN: But Eve looks quite normal. She's just awakened, and she's yawning.

GOD: Anything can happen by chance, even the normal things.

SATAN: Obviously there's a problem with Adam, and I think I see what it is. You have allowed chance to affect his mind and body. But the body is not the real Adam, it is merely an appendage. So when chance operates in his body, it does indeed control Adam. Confine the chance to his mind, and then Adam will be truly independent. Would you do so? And with Eve as well.

GOD: As you say. Let's watch again.

SATAN: Adam's getting up now. He's walking over to a bush and picking some berries. You're not making him do that?

GOD: No.

SATAN: This looks like it then. Adam in control . . . oops! Now his arms are flailing. He's having that fit again. What happened?

GOD: First, by chance, he wanted to eat the berries. Now, by chance, he wants to roll on the ground and drool. The desires are happening by chance instead of my causing them. I can't tell what he's going to want next. Neither can he.

SATAN: And look at Eve. Good grief, she's talking to a snake. Weird.

GOD: Apparently she just got the urge. Are you ready?

SATAN: For what?

GOD: You said you wanted me to give you chance.

SATAN: No! Please don't!

GOD: Why not?

SATAN: That's horrible, having things happen to you like that. There's no dignity there. I want to stay as I am.

GOD: That's wise, I think. You may not have the kind of control you want. But then that kind of control is impossible. Inevitability or chance—those are the only options. And neither constitutes ultimate control over one's life. But at least this way what happens to you will be orderly.

SATAN: I feel better now that we've talked this out.

GOD: Actually, I'm sorry nothing came of our talk—sorry the way I am about square circles. I could use a little excitement.

SATAN: I won't take any more of your time today. Oh, but there is one other thing. Please take that chance out of Adam and Eve. I wouldn't want that on my conscience.

Satan exits with a flutter of his mighty wings.

GOD: As you say . . . I suppose. On the other hand, it would be nice to have a part of the universe where there are surprises. It could prove interesting.

Probing Questions

1. What theory of free will (hard determinism, compatibilism, or libertarianism) best describes how the world is for Satan? Do you accept this theory? Why or why not?

2. In this story does God have free will? Explain.

3. If you had to decide between inevitability and chance, as Satan does, which would you choose? Is there a third alternative? What would a libertarian say about Satan's either/or choice?

For Further Reading

Roderick Chisholm, *Person and Object* (Lasalle: Open Court, 1976). Chisholm's defense of a libertarian free will.

Randolph Clarke, *Libertarian Accounts of Free Will* (New York: Oxford University Press, 2003). A lucid examination of various libertarian approaches to free will.

Daniel Dennett, *Elbow Room: The Varieties of Free Will Worth Wanting* (Cambridge, MA: MIT Press, 1984). A clear and lively defense of compatibilism.

Ted Honderich, *How Free Are You?: The Determinism Problem* (Oxford: Oxford University Press, 2003). An introduction to, and a novel view of, the determinism problem.

Robert Kane, *The Oxford Handbook of Free Will* (New York: Oxford University Press, 2002). An anthology covering more recent work on free will, focusing on new approaches to the traditional theories.

Timothy O'Connor, *Persons and Causes: The Metaphysics of Free Will* (New York: Oxford University Press, 2000). An innovative defense of libertarianism and an exceptionally clear critique of the most prominent versions of the theory.

Richard Taylor, *Metaphysics*, 4th edition (Englewood Cliffs, NJ: Prentice Hall, 1992). Contains a very straightforward defense of libertarianism.

Peter van Inwagen, *An Essay on Free Will* (Oxford: Oxford University Press, 1983). An influential argument for incompatibilism.

Gary Watson, ed., *Free Will* (Oxford: Oxford University Press, 2003). A collection of some of the most influential discussions of free will from the last fifty years.

CHAPTER 6

KNOWLEDGE AND SKEPTICISM

Chapter Objectives

6.1 OVERVIEW: THE PROBLEM OF KNOWLEDGE

- Understand the nature of epistemology and the necessary and sufficient conditions for propositional knowledge.
- Define *skepticism, cognitive relativism, subjective relativism, cultural relativism, a priori, a posteriori, rationalism, empiricism, skepticism,* and *subjective idealism.*

6.2 THE RATIONALIST ROAD

- Understand the nature of Plato's rationalism, his notion of the Forms, and his belief about innate knowledge.
- Explain the point that Socrates wanted to prove by his conversation with the slave boy.
- Explain how Descartes arrived at his skepticism and how he later came to the conclusion that he did possess knowledge.
- Show how Descartes argues for his principle of clear and distinct ideas.

6.3 THE EMPIRICIST TURN

- Summarize Locke's critique of innate ideas.
- Define primary and secondary qualities.
- Summarize Locke's attempt to show that sense data are proof of the existence of an external world.
- Explain what Berkeley means by "to be is to be perceived."
- Understand how Berkeley argues for his theory that material objects do not exist.
- State the main differences between Locke's and Hume's empiricism.
- Explain why Hume believes that all theological and metaphysical propositions are worthless.
- State Hume's argument against the principle of induction.

6.4 THE KANTIAN COMPROMISE

- Understand why Kant believes that his theory of knowledge is like the Copernican revolution.
- Define *analytic statement, synthetic statement,* and *synthetic a priori knowledge.*
- Explain how Kant's theory has both empiricist and rationalist elements.
- Summarize Kant's explanation of how synthetic a priori knowledge is possible.

6.5 A FEMINIST PERSPECTIVE ON KNOWLEDGE

- State the central aim of feminist philosophy and of feminist epistemology.
- List some ways that, according to feminists, "dominant knowledge practices" disadvantage women.
- Summarize the principal claims of feminist empiricism, feminist standpoint theory, and feminist postmodernism.
- Understand some of the criticisms that feminists have lodged against feminist postmodernism.

6.1 OVERVIEW: THE PROBLEM OF KNOWLEDGE

This is a serious question: Do you *know* anything? In other words, do you possess any *knowledge?* And here are some equally serious questions: If you do have knowledge, how did you attain it? And if you possess it, how much do you possess—that is, what is the extent of your knowledge? Do you know only the contents of your own mind or only mathematical or logical truths? Do you *know* that there is a God, that ordinary physical objects exist, that there is an external world (one existing independently of your mind), that unobservable entities such as electrons are real, that other minds besides your own exist, that events have occurred before the present moment?

The only good is knowledge and the only evil is ignorance.

—Socrates

These questions probably seem odd to you, perhaps even absurd. But among serious thinkers, they are neither. Trying to find good answers to these is the main business of **epistemology**, the philosophical study of knowledge. It is the branch of philosophy that systematically investigates whether, how, and to what extent we know things. For well over two thousand years, philosophers have been searching for answers to these questions because, contrary to what most people believe, the answers are not obvious, and both the asking and the answering have theoretical and practical value. We value knowledge for its own sake, regardless of what we can do with it. When we are at our best, we crave the light simply because it is the light. But we also value knowledge because it can guide us to our goals, steer us away from error, and help us succeed in life, however we define success. Knowledge is power. Whatever our reply to the epistemological questions, if we take them seriously, they surely will affect how we see the world and what we do in it.

Epistemology is the study of knowledge.

Knowledge comes in different forms, and philosophy is usually concerned with only one of them. Knowing *what* something feels like (for example, what influenza feels like) constitutes one form of knowledge. Knowing *how* to do something (for example, how to throw a ball) constitutes another. Knowing *that* something is the case (such as knowing that an elm tree grows in the quad) is **propositional knowledge**—knowledge of a proposition. A proposition is a statement that is either true or false, an assertion that something is or is not a fact. This kind of knowledge has been the main focus of philosophers and is our primary concern in this chapter.

Philosophers going back as far as Plato have said that propositional knowledge has three necessary and sufficient conditions: to know a proposition, (1) you must *believe* it, (2) it must be *true*, and (3) you must have good *reasons* for—be justified in—believing it true. On this traditional account, merely believing something is not enough; what you believe must be true. A belief does not count as knowledge unless it is true. But a mere true belief is not knowledge either, because you can have a true belief and yet not genuinely know. Let's say you believe for no reason that three ducks are now swimming on Walden Pond, and suppose your belief is true—there really are three ducks swimming on Walden Pond. Does your true belief count as knowledge? According to the traditional view, no—because you have *no reason* to think that three ducks are now swimming on Walden Pond. You have only a true belief by accident, a lucky guess, and that's not knowledge. To have knowledge, your belief must be true, and you must have good reasons to believe it true. Knowledge, then, is true belief that is justified. Philosophers disagree about the exact nature of the required justification, but most accept that knowledge is true belief that is in some sense backed by good reasons.

Much of the work in epistemology centers around the questions of whether we have knowledge and, if so, how much we have. Most philosophers believe we have some knowledge but differ on its extent. They may insist that we possess knowledge of the existence of an external world, other minds, physical objects, the past and future, or self-evident truths. But some philosophers embrace **skepticism**, the view that we lack knowledge in some fundamental way. Skeptics may deny that we have knowledge in all of the areas just mentioned or maintain that we lack knowledge in only some of them. In any case, they hold that many or all of our beliefs are false or unfounded.

Some skeptics argue that we lack knowledge because we have no way of distinguishing between beliefs that we take to be instances of knowledge from beliefs that are clearly *not* instances of knowledge. For all we know, we could be hallucinating, dreaming, in the grips of an illusion, or mistaken for some other reason. How do we know that we are not hallucinating or dreaming right now? Hallucinations and dreams can seem as real as our "normal" experience. If we cannot distinguish these two, the skeptic says, then we cannot have knowledge.

Propositional knowledge is knowledge of a proposition.

When you know a thing, to hold that you know it; and when you do not know a thing, to allow that you do not know it—this is knowledge.
—Confucius

1 Do questions—such as "Is it raining?"—count as propositions?

Skepticism is the view that we lack knowledge in some fundamental way.

Figure 6.1 Are you dreaming now? How can you tell?

WHAT DO YOU BELIEVE?

Cognitive Relativism Undone

Are you a cognitive relativist? Do you believe that truth is relative to persons or cultures—that the truth about something depends on what persons or cultures believe? If so, consider this common—and potent—criticism of the doctrine:

> The most serious flaw of relativism in all its forms is a purely logical one: It's self-refuting because its truth implies its falsity.
> According to the relativist . . . everything is relative. To say that everything is relative is to say that no unrestricted universal generalizations are true (an unrestricted universal generalization is a statement to the effect that something holds for all individuals, societies, or conceptual schemes). But the statement "No unrestricted universal generalizations are true" is itself an unrestricted universal generalization. So if relativism in any of its forms is true, it's false. As a result, it cannot possibly be true.

Theodore Schick, Jr., and Lewis Vaughn, How to Think About Weird Things *(2011), 311.*

Are you still a cognitive relativist?

Other skeptics raise doubts about the *reliability* of what we take to be our normal sources of knowledge—perception, memory, introspection, and reasoning. We realize that all these sources are fallible, that they sometimes lead us into error. But skeptics ask how we know that these sources are not *always* in error. If all these sources are suspect, we cannot use one to check another. We cannot, for example, use our sense of sight to check the reliability of our sense of touch. And if we think one mode of perception is more trustworthy than the others, how do we know that? We seem forced once again into skepticism.

Another view that challenges our commonplace ideas about knowledge is **cognitive relativism**, the doctrine that the truth about something depends on what persons or cultures believe. The notion that truth depends on what a *person* believes is known as **subjective relativism**, and the idea that truth depends on what a *culture* believes is called **cultural relativism**. We normally assume that truth is objective—that it depends on the way the world is. When we assert a proposition, we generally believe that the proposition is true if and only if it says the way things are in reality. But the relativist rejects this view, believing instead that truth is relative to what a person or culture accepts as true. Truth is a matter of what a person or culture believes—not a matter of how the world is. This means that a proposition

Cognitive relativism is the doctrine that the truth about something depends on what persons or cultures believe.

Subjective relativism is the view that right actions are those endorsed by an individual.

Cultural relativism is the view that right actions are those endorsed by one's culture.

2 Are you a cultural relativist? Is the point about personal fallibility a valid criticism of the doctrine?

A priori knowledge is knowledge gained independently of or prior to sense experience.

A posteriori knowledge is knowledge that depends entirely on sense experience.

Rationalism is the view that through unaided reason we can come to know what the world is like.

Empiricism is the view that our knowledge of the empirical world comes solely from sense experience.

can be true for one person, but not for another. If you believe that sheep can fly, then it is true (for you) that sheep can fly. If someone else believes that sheep cannot fly, then it is true (for him) that sheep cannot fly. You thereby can make something true by believing it to be true. Likewise, if a culture believes that the earth is flat and that adulterers should be beheaded, then it is true (for them) that the earth is flat and that adulterers should be beheaded.

If relativism in either form is correct, then knowledge would be easy to attain—perhaps a great deal easier than acquiring objective truth, which demands that our beliefs somehow link up to the objective world. But for a variety of reasons, most philosophers have rejected relativism. For one thing, they say, the doctrine implies several absurdities that render it implausible. They point out, for example, that if we could make a statement true just by believing it to be true, we would be infallible. We could not possibly be in error about anything that we sincerely believed. We could never be mistaken about what time it is or when the French Revolution took place or whether breaking a promise is morally permissible. Personal infallibility is, of course, absurd, and this possibility seems to count heavily against subjective relativism. The same point can be made about cultural relativism.

Philosophers distinguish two ways to acquire knowledge: through reason and through sense experience. The former is called **a priori**; it yields knowledge gained independently of or prior to sense experience. The latter is known as **a posteriori**; it gives us knowledge that depends entirely on sense experience. We can come to know many propositions a priori—for example, that all bachelors are unmarried, that all triangles have three sides, that $2 + 3 = 5$, and that something is either a cat or not a cat. We need not do a survey of bachelors to see if they really are all unmarried; we can know this just by thinking about it. And we know that "something is either a cat or not a cat" is true; it is a simple logical truth—and we know it without having to observe any cats. It seems that we can also come to know many propositions a posteriori—for instance, that John the bachelor has red hair, that he just drew a triangle on paper, that he is holding five pencils, and that Tabby the cat is on the mat. To know these things, we must rely on our senses.

Through the centuries, philosophers have debated whether our knowledge of the world is fundamentally a priori or a posteriori (if indeed we have knowledge), and these arguments continue today in many forms in both philosophy and science. On one side of this divide are the **rationalists**, who believe that through unaided reason we can come to know what the world is like. They maintain that some or all knowledge of the empirical world is a priori, discoverable simply through the workings of our minds. On the other side are the **empiricists**, who contend that our knowledge of the empirical world comes solely from sense experience. We acquire knowledge entirely a posteriori. We may come to know logical and mathematical truths through reason, but we can know nothing of empirical reality except through our senses.

At this point, you may find yourself being more sympathetic to the empiricists than to the rationalists. After all, you seem to acquire an enormous amount of information via your five senses. Through them, you grasp that the grass is green, the stove is hot, the music is loud, the lime is tart, and the rose is sweet. But what can you know through reason alone? Rationalists would say that you can know a great deal.

Without making any empirical observations, mathematicians can not only discover new mathematical truths, but also develop mathematical models that can accurately describe the empirical world. They can, for example, accurately predict the existence of astronomical objects and their movements without once looking through a telescope. Likewise, we know the fundamental truths of logic, without which reasoning itself would be impossible. We know, for example, that nothing can both have a property and lack it at the same time, and that for any particular property, everything either has it or lacks it. Thus we know without looking that nothing can both be a dog and not be a dog at the same time, there are no square circles, and married bachelors don't exist. Some rationalists have gone further and asserted that reason alone can reveal the most important, basic truths about the world—such as "every event has a cause" and "the shortest distance between two points is a straight line."

Many of the greatest thinkers in history have taken the rationalist approach to knowledge. Among these we can count Plato (c. 427–347 BCE), René Descartes (1596–1650), Benedict Spinoza (1632–1677), and Gottfried Leibniz (1646–1716). The most influential rationalist theory comes from Descartes, the inventor of analytic geometry and founder of modern philosophy. He thinks sense experience is an unreliable source of knowledge, so he looks to reason to give all our knowledge a foundation as firm as that which supports unshakeable mathematical truths. Through reason he hopes to defeat skepticism. His method is first to doubt everything that he cannot be certain of, a process that leaves him knowing hardly anything. But through reason alone he soon uncovers what he considers to be self-evident, certain truths from which he derives other indubitable propositions. In this way he tries to build an edifice of knowledge that, like an inverted pyramid, rests on one or two rock-solid foundation stones that support all the others.

The empiricist view of knowledge has been advanced most famously by the British empiricists John Locke (1632–1704), George Berkeley (1685–1753), and David Hume (1711–1776). They want to turn Descartes' pyramid rightside up, resting all knowledge on a vast foundation of sense data (the content of our experience) that supports the upper stones. Among these thinkers, Hume probably has been the most influential, arguing for an uncompromising empiricism that leads to a far-reaching skepticism that not all empiricists have shared. He holds that all our knowledge (aside from purely logical truths) is derived from sense perceptions or ideas about those perceptions. Like other empiricists, he believes that the mind is empty—a blank slate—until experience gives it content. We can have knowledge of something only if it can be sensed, and any proposition that does not refer to what can be sensed is meaningless. Guided by this latter empiricist principle, Hume is driven to skepticism about many things that others have taken for granted, including the existence of the external world, causation, a continuing self, religious doctrines, and inductive reasoning. His skepticism arises because he thinks that even though all our knowledge is based on sense experience, we cannot know how the objects of our sense experience are related. We cannot know, for example, that there is a cause-and-effect relationship between associated objects. To infer such a connection is to go beyond what our senses tell us. Our notions of causal connections are merely matters of custom and habit.

> To be conscious that you are ignorant is a great step to knowledge.
> —Benjamin Disraeli

3 What facts about the world can we know based solely on our reasoning?

I think we ought always to entertain our opinions with some measure of doubt. I shouldn't wish people dogmatically to believe any philosophy, not even mine.
—Bertrand Russell

Subjective idealism is the doctrine that all that exist are minds and their ideas.

Applying his own theory of knowledge, John Locke rejects skepticism about external objects. Like a good empiricist, he believes that all we are directly aware of is sense data. Our sense experience is caused by external objects, and we can have knowledge of those objects because our sense data resemble or represent them.

Berkeley, like Locke, also thinks his brand of empiricism can defeat the skeptic, but he differs with Locke and other empiricists on how sense data relate to the external world. He accepts the empiricist notion of our being aware only of sense data but rejects Locke's belief in the existence of material objects. He argues that not only do we know just our own ideas; there is no reason to suppose that they resemble or are caused by material objects. Locke, like most people, presumes that material objects exist independently of our sense experience, that they *are,* even when we do not perceive them. But Berkeley denies this, insisting that it is logically impossible for physical objects to exist, for we cannot "conceive them existing unconceived." All that exist, he says, are minds and their ideas, a view known as **subjective idealism**.

Immanuel Kant (1724–1804) was shocked by the skepticism that seemed to be lurking in empiricism in general and in the thoroughgoing empiricism of Hume in particular. Hume's view is that we constantly experience countless sensations associated in various ways, but we cannot know about any necessary connections between them, the kind of connections that are the central focus of science. Kant agrees that all our knowledge begins with the raw data of sense experience, but he argues that our minds impose order on it. Like a cookie cutter stamping out shapes in dough, our minds mold our sensations into conceptual patterns that determine how we see the world. Thus our minds impress the concepts of cause and effect, space, and time into our experience. Therefore we can know—a priori—that there are necessary connections between causes and effects and that space and time have definite characteristics, because our mental powers impose this structure on our perceptions. In this way, Kant tries to save science and our everyday experience from Hume's radical skepticism. In the process he initiates two hundred years of critical scrutiny of his ideas by generations of philosophers.

WRITING TO UNDERSTAND:
CRITIQUING PHILOSOPHICAL VIEWS   Section 6.1

1. Consider the skeptic's charge that we can never be confident about the reliability of our normal sources of knowledge (perception, memory, introspection, and reasoning). Does it follow from the fact that we are sometimes mistaken when we rely on these sources that we are *always* mistaken? How would you respond to the skeptic?

2. Does cognitive relativism really imply that persons or cultures are infallible? If so, why would this be a problem for the cognitive relativist? Do you agree with the doctrine's critics on this point? Why or why not?

(cont.)

WRITING TO UNDERSTAND:
CRITIQUING PHILOSOPHICAL VIEWS *cont.*   Section 6.1

3. Suppose a rationalist declares that scientists can know (without once looking through a telescope) about the physical characteristics of planets in our solar system. Would this be a plausible claim? Why or why not?

4. Suppose Locke is right that all we are ever directly aware of is sense data. Would this fact make it impossible to know about external objects? How could we ever know that there is something on the other side of our sense data? Explain how Locke's view can lead to skepticism.

5. Berkeley denies the existence of material objects. How would you argue that he is mistaken about this? Hint: Why do you normally assume that material objects exist and are not merely creations of your mind? Why do you assume that the world exists while you are sleeping?

6.2 THE RATIONALIST ROAD

So rationalists hold that we have knowledge, that skepticism is false, and that through reason we can come to know the most important truths of reality. They differ, however, on how such knowledge is possible and how they arrive at their rationalist conclusions. Historically, two giants stand on the long road of rationalist thought: Plato at the beginning in ancient Greece and Descartes in Europe at the intersection of modern philosophy and science.

Plato's Rationalism

Plato maintained that sense experience alone could not be the source of knowledge, although many of his contemporaries claimed otherwise. Some of them assumed that since knowledge must be based on sense experience, and since sense experience can vary from person to

Figure 6.2 Plato (c. 429–347 BCE).

person or culture to culture, cognitive relativism must be true. If one person says a grape is sour and another says it's sweet, there must be no objective fact of the matter, just truth relative to different persons. Other thinkers thought that since our perceptions are often illusory, distorted, or otherwise mistaken, sense experience is not a reliable source of knowledge. And since our perceptions are the only possible route to knowledge, we must not know anything. Thus skepticism, they said, is the proper epistemological attitude. Plato thought that our perceptions were just as unreliable a guide to genuine knowledge as the relativists and skeptics assumed. But he argued that since we clearly do have knowledge, we must derive it from a reliable source— and that source has to be reason.

> Every great advance in natural knowledge has involved the absolute rejection of authority.
> —Thomas H. Huxley

4 Is the number *five* an objective entity? Is the preposition *over* objectively real? Explain your reasons. Do your answers to these questions give any support to Plato's notion of the Forms?

All men by nature desire knowledge.
—Aristotle

Plato deduced that we must be able to acquire knowledge because we can identify false beliefs, and we obviously possess knowledge because we can grasp, through reason, mathematical, conceptual, and logical truths. We know that 2 + 5 = 7; that a triangle has three sides; and that if A is larger than B and B is larger than C, then A is larger than C. Plato pointed out that these truths are objective: they are true regardless of what we think. We do not invent them out of our imaginations; we discover them. No matter how hard we try, we cannot make 2 + 5 equal 9. Plato reasoned that if such truths are objective, they must also be about real things. They must refer to an independently existing, immaterial reality that is beyond sense experience. In addition, he insisted, these truths must also be immutable and eternal, existing in the immaterial realm unchanged for all time. Only through our powers of reason can we reach beyond the physical world to take hold of real knowledge of fundamental truths. Sense experience, in contrast, can yield only transitory, ever-changing information—mere opinion that is vastly inferior to everlasting truths.

So for Plato, reality comprises two worlds: the fleeting world of the physical accessed through sense experience and the eternal, nonphysical, changeless world of genuine knowledge accessed only through reason. In spelling out the contents of the latter, Plato articulates the central notion of his philosophy: the *Forms*. The Forms (also called Ideas) are perfect conceptual models for every existing thing, residing only in the eternal world penetrated by reason alone. They are the ideals, or standards, that we can first come to know and then use to assess the notions and objects we encounter in our lives. Through reason, we can access the Form of "table" and thus know the ideal template of "table." With this knowledge we can understand the essence of a table and use this understanding to make judgments about all physical tables. Likewise, when we access the Form "courage," we know what the ideal of courage is and can use this knowledge to appraise a particular instance of courage. As Plato sees it, the truly real world is the world of the Forms—the domain of the perfect and everlasting. With knowledge of the really real, we can understand the "less real" realm of the imperfect and transitory.

In Plato's account, the Forms are *universals*—properties that can be had by several *particular* things. Every blue thing is a particular instance of the universal property of blueness. Every triangular thing is a particular example of the universal of triangularity. Particulars reside in the temporary, imperfect world of the material; universals are found in the eternal, perfect world of the really real. We can rise above mere opinion and attain knowledge only by reasoning our way to the Forms. To do this is to travel down the rationalist road marked by Plato, the greatest rationalist of all time.

How is it that we seem to have knowledge of the Forms, however dimly, even though our senses can tell us nothing about them? Our sense experience can acquaint us only with material objects, but the Forms are not material. It's as if these universals were already in our minds waiting to be uncovered. Plato's answer—and the answer of most other rationalists—is the doctrine of *innate knowledge*. He thinks that knowledge of these immaterial ideals is already present at birth, inscribed in our minds (our immortal souls) in a previous existence. We are born with this knowledge, and we somehow acquired it before our present lives. Accessing this knowledge, then, is a matter of using reason to *recall* what we previously knew in another life.

To many ears, this recall theory may sound preposterous. But in *Meno*, Plato attempts a brilliant demonstration of it. In the dialogue, he depicts the character of Socrates discussing innate knowledge with Meno. To prove his point, Socrates calls over an unschooled slave boy and asks him a series of questions about a geometry problem. Socrates draws a two-foot-by-two-foot square (four square feet) and then tells the boy to draw another one that is twice the size of the first. Initially the boy thinks that doubling the length of each side of the square will produce a square twice as large as the first. So he draws a four-foot-by-four-foot square (sixteen square feet) but sees right away that that answer cannot be correct. As Socrates asks further questions, the boy comes to the right answer on his own. Socrates says that he merely helped the boy recollect knowledge that he already possessed, bringing innate knowledge to consciousness.

5 Socrates explains the boy's understanding of geometry by insisting that the boy was recollecting knowledge gained in another life. What is a plausible alternative explanation for the phenomenon? Which explanation seems closer to the truth?

Plato, *Meno*

Soc. What do you say of him [the slave boy], Meno? Were not all these answers given out of his own head?

Men. Yes, they were all his own.

Soc. And yet, as we were just now saying, he did not know?

Men. True.

Soc. And yet he had those notions in him?

Men. Yes.

Soc. Then he who does not know still has true notions of that which he does not know?

Men. He has.

Soc. And at present these notions are just wakening up in him, as in a dream; but if he were frequently asked the same questions, in different forms, he would know as well as any one at last?

Men. I dare say.

Soc. Without any one teaching him he will recover his knowledge for himself, if he is only asked questions?

Men. Yes.

Soc. And this spontaneous recovery in him is recollection?

Men. True.

Soc. And this knowledge which he now has must he not either have acquired or always possessed?

Men. Yes.

Soc. But if he always possessed this knowledge he would always have known; or if he has acquired the knowledge, he could not have acquired it in this life, unless he has been taught geometry; for he may be made to do the same with all geometry and every other branch of knowledge. Now, has any one ever taught him? You must know that, if, as you say, he was born and bred in your house.

Plato, *Meno*

Men. And I am certain that no one ever did teach him.

Soc. And yet has he not the knowledge?

Men. That, Socrates, is most certain.

Soc. But if he did not acquire this knowledge in this life, then clearly he must have had and learned it at some other time?

Men. That is evident.

Soc. And that must have been the time when he was not a man?

Men. Yes.

Soc. And if there have been always true thoughts in him, both at the time when he was and was not a man, which only need to be awakened into knowledge by putting questions to him, his soul must have always possessed this knowledge, for he always either was or was not a man?

Men. That is clear.

Soc. And if the truth of all things always existed in the soul, then the soul is immortal. Wherefore be of good cheer, and try to recollect what you do not know, or rather do not remember.

Men. I feel, somehow, that I like what you are saying.

Soc. And I, Meno, like what I am saying. Some things I have said of which I am not altogether confident. But that we shall be better and braver and less helpless if we think that we ought to inquire, than we should have been if we indulged in the idle fancy that there was no knowing and no use in searching after what we know not; —that is a theme upon which I am ready to fight, in word and deed, to the utmost of my power.[1]

Figure 6.3 Roman fresco painting of Socrates.

Opinion is the medium between knowledge and ignorance.
—Plato

There comes a time when the mind takes a higher plane of knowledge but can never prove how it got there.
—Albert Einstein

Many thinkers reject Plato's notion of a preexisting state in which we acquire knowledge, and they are skeptical of the claim that we are born with knowledge. But the idea of innate knowledge in some form is still attractive to rationalist philosophers, for it would explain how we could possess knowledge without relying on sense experience. In any case, both rationalists and empiricists must provide an explanation of how we seem to know logical and mathematical truths (and perhaps scientific truths) that we do not arrive at through our senses.

Descartes' Doubt

In Descartes' time, the world must have seemed to many to be turning upside down. Time-honored ideas, established religious doctrines, and traditional attitudes were being called into question by both new discoveries in science and radically different religious outlooks on the Continent. This was the era of Galileo, Copernicus, Kepler, Bacon, Newton, and Martin Luther—thinkers who were dismantling the old ideological structures piece by piece. Into this world of upheaval and change came the brilliant Descartes, determined to see if there could be any epistemological certainties in an age of doubt. He hoped that knowledge could be given a foundation as sturdy as that which buttressed mathematics. If only knowledge of the world could be as certain as knowledge of geometry!

Oddly enough, Descartes begins his quest for knowledge by first plunging into skepticism. He sees that a great many things he thought he knew appear now to be false. So he decides to "raze everything to the ground and begin again" from a firm foundation, doubting all beliefs except those that are "certain and indubitable," beliefs that cannot possibly be false. Only beliefs that are certain can count as knowledge, he says. If he has reason to doubt any of them, they are not knowledge. Here he is at the start of his quest:

René Descartes, *Meditations on First Philosophy*

It is now some years since I detected how many were the false beliefs that I had from my earliest youth admitted as true, and how doubtful was everything I had since constructed on this basis; and from that time I was convinced that I must once for all seriously undertake to rid myself of all the opinions which I had formerly accepted, and commence to build anew from the foundation, if I wanted to establish any firm and permanent structure in the sciences. But as this enterprise appeared to be a very great one, I waited until I had attained an age so mature that I could not hope that at any later date I should be better fitted to execute my design. This reason caused me to delay so long that I should feel that I was doing wrong were I to occupy in deliberation the time that yet remains to me for action. To-day, then, since very opportunely for the plan I have in view I have delivered my mind from every care [and am happily agitated by no passions] and since I have procured for myself an assured leisure in a peaceable retirement, I shall at last seriously and freely address myself to the general upheaval of all my former opinions.

Now for this object it is not necessary that I should show that all of these are false—I shall perhaps never arrive at this end. But inasmuch as reason already persuades me that I ought no less carefully to withhold my assent from matters which are not entirely certain and indubitable than from those which appear to me manifestly to be false, if I am able to find in each one some reason to doubt, this will suffice to justify my rejecting the whole. And for that end it will not be requisite that I should examine each in particular, which would be an endless undertaking; for owing to the fact that the destruction of the foundations of necessity brings with it the downfall of the rest of the edifice, I shall only in the first place attack those principles upon which all my former opinions rested.[2]

Descartes soon finds reason to doubt all beliefs based on sense experience, arriving at this conclusion via his famous dream argument. He notes that "there are no certain indications by which we may clearly distinguish wakefulness from asleep."[3] Our dreams can seem like reality, and in dreams we often don't know we are dreaming. So it is possible that we are dreaming now, he says, and that what we take to be the real world is in fact not real at all. More to the point, it is possible that our sense experience—by which we presume to know material reality—is just a dream. If so, we can't be certain about anything we think we know through our senses. Therefore, sense experience can yield no knowledge.

René Descartes,
*Meditations on First
Philosophy*

6 Is there any way you can tell whether you are awake or dreaming? Is Descartes right that he cannot tell the difference? Explain.

All that up to the present time I have accepted as most true and certain I have learned either from the senses or through the senses; but it is sometimes proved to me that these senses are deceptive, and it is wiser not to trust entirely to any thing by which we have once been deceived.

But it may be that although the senses sometimes deceive us concerning things which are hardly perceptible, or very far away, there are yet many others to be met with as to which we cannot reasonably have any doubt, although we recognise them by their means. For example, there is the fact that I am here, seated by the fire, attired in a dressing gown, having this paper in my hands and other similar matters. . . .

At the same time I must remember that I am a man, and that consequently I am in the habit of sleeping, and in my dreams representing to myself the same things or sometimes even less probable things, than do those who are insane in their waking moments. How often has it happened to me that in the night I dreamt that I found myself in this particular place, that I was dressed and seated near the fire, whilst in reality I was lying undressed in bed! At this moment it does indeed seem to me that it is with eyes awake that I am looking at this paper; that this head which I move is not asleep, that it is deliberately and of set purpose that I extend my hand and perceive it; what happens in sleep does not appear so clear nor so distinct as does all this. But in thinking over this I remind myself that on many occasions I have in sleep been deceived by similar illusions, and in dwelling carefully on this reflection I see so manifestly that there are no certain indications by which we may clearly distinguish wakefulness from sleep that I am lost in astonishment. And my astonishment is such that it is almost capable of persuading me that I now dream.[4]

7 Is there any way you can determine whether you are living in the Matrix? Can you tell whether an evil genius is systematically deceiving you? Why or why not?

After this insight, Descartes discovers that his skepticism goes even deeper. Suppose, he says, that an evil genius or god has set out to systematically deceive me. This being could delude me about every kind of thought I could possibly have. I can't be sure that this is not the case. I can't be certain that all my thoughts are not the work of an evil entity that infuses my mind with false sensations and ideas, making an external reality appear to exist. And if I am not certain of this, I can't know anything that I previously thought I knew, including such seemingly obvious things as the truths of mathematics.

René Descartes,
*Meditations on First
Philosophy*

Nevertheless I have long had fixed in my mind the belief that an all-powerful God existed by whom I have been created such as I am. But how do I know that He has not brought it to pass that there is no earth, no heaven, no extended body, no magnitude, no place, and that nevertheless [I possess the perceptions of all these things and that] they seem to me to exist just exactly as I now see them? And, besides, as I sometimes imagine that others deceive themselves in the things which they think they know best, how do I know that I am not deceived every time that I add two and three, or count the sides of a square, or judge of things yet simpler can be imagined?[5]

As we have seen, Descartes' assumption is that knowledge requires certainty. He holds that for beliefs to count as knowledge, we must be certain of them—they must be so well supported as to be beyond all possible doubt. But some philosophers claim that this requirement for knowledge sets the bar too high. They reject Descartes' skeptical arguments because they are convinced that knowledge demands not beyond-all-doubt certainty, but only reasonable grounds for believing. After all,

PHILOSOPHY NOW

Living in the Matrix

Descartes' evil genius scenario is the forerunner of some similar what-if tales told by philosophers and others in our own times. In one of them, you are not at the mercy of a malicious demon; you are instead a brain in a vat of chemicals in a laboratory. Your brain is hard-wired to a computer, which a brilliant (but probably crazy) scientist is using to give you experiences that are indistinguishable from those you might have if you were not a wired-up marinating brain. The question is, How could you ever be certain that you are not such a brain in a vat?

The same sort of question arises about the predicament of humans in the movie *The Matrix*. Intelligent computers have enslaved the human race, encasing everyone in pods and electronically feeding simulations of the real world into their brains. As Christopher Grau says,

> These creatures have fed Neo [the movie's protagonist] a simulation that he couldn't possibly help but take as the real thing. What's worse, it isn't clear how any of us can know with certainty that we are not in a position similar to Neo before his "rebirth." . . . A viewer of *The Matrix* is naturally led to wonder: how do I know I am not in the Matrix?

Christopher Grau, "Bad Dreams, Evil Demons, and the Experience Machine: Philosophy and The Matrix," in Philosophers Explore the Matrix, *ed. Christopher Grau (New York: Oxford University Press, 2005), 10–23.*

Figure 6.4 The Matrix, like a lot of other movies, raises philosophical questions—specifically, epistemological questions.

Some philosophers think the skeptical implications of Matrix-type scenarios can be countered through an argument based on inference to the best explanation. What would such an argument look like? Do you agree that it can successfully counter the skeptical scenarios?

they say, we often claim to know many propositions that are not certain. We insist that we know that grass grows, that some dogs have fleas, that Africa exists, and that Abraham Lincoln lived and died in America—yet none of these statements is beyond all possible doubt.

Information is not knowledge.
—Albert Einstein

PHILOSOPHY LAB

Imagine that you and a friend are looking at an especially bright light in the night sky. You think the light is an aircraft; your friend believes it is a twinkling star. To you, the light seems to move; to your friend, it seems stationary. When you view it from the ground, it looks elliptical, but from your second-story window, it looks circular. You judge it to be close, perhaps only a couple of miles away. You can make out the craft's nose and tail, the outline of the wings, and tiny dots that must be the windows. You may even hear the drone of its engines. After a half hour, the light has remained in exactly the same position in the sky. On your radio, you hear a newscast about how bright and beautiful the planet Venus is tonight—positioned as it is in the very same portion of the sky that you have been observing. You have been wrong about everything, your mind has shaped your perceptions, your perceptions of the same object have been different from different angles, and your friend's observations and your own have differed dramatically.

If your senses can be this fraught with inconsistencies, discrepancies, and errors (and they often are), how can you ever be sure that the world is as it appears to be? Can you really know anything? How would you answer these skeptical concerns?

Descartes' Certainty

Adrift in doubt, Descartes wonders whether there is anything at all he can know. But just when it seems that he can know nothing, he comes upon a truth that he cannot possibly doubt: He exists:

René Descartes, *Meditations on First Philosophy*

The Meditation of yesterday filled my mind with so many doubts that it is no longer in my power to forget them. And yet I do not see in what manner I can resolve them; and, just as if I had all of a sudden fallen into very deep water, I am so disconcerted that I can neither make certain of setting my feet on the bottom, nor can I swim and so support myself on the surface. I shall nevertheless make an effort and follow anew the same path as that on which I yesterday entered, i.e. I shall proceed by setting aside all that in which the least doubt could be supposed to exist, just as if I had discovered that it was absolutely false; and I shall ever follow in this road until I have met with something which is certain, or at least, if I can do nothing else, until I have learned for certain that there is nothing in the world that is certain. Archimedes, in order that he might draw the terrestrial globe out of its place, and transport it elsewhere, demanded only that one point should be fixed and immoveable; in the same way I shall have the right to conceive high hopes if I am happy enough to discover one thing only which is certain and indubitable.

I suppose, then, that all the things that I see are false; I persuade myself that nothing has ever existed of all that my fallacious memory represents to me. I consider that I possess no senses; I imagine that body, figure, extension, movement and place are but the fictions of my mind. What, then, can be esteemed as true? Perhaps nothing at all, unless that there is nothing in the world that is certain. . . .

But I was persuaded that there was nothing in all the world, that there was no heaven, no earth, that there were no minds, nor any bodies: was I not then likewise persuaded that I did not exist? Not at all; of a surety I myself did exist since I persuaded myself of something [or merely because I thought of something]. But there is some deceiver or other, very powerful and very cunning, who ever employs his ingenuity in deceiving me. Then without doubt I exist also if he deceives me, and let him deceive me as much as he will, he can never cause me to be nothing so long as I think that I am something. So that after having reflected well and carefully examined all things, we must come to the definite conclusion that this proposition: I am, I exist, is necessarily true each time that I pronounce it, or that I mentally conceive it.[6]

Descartes concludes that if he can persuade himself of something, if he can have thoughts, he must exist. Even an evil genius cannot rob him of this knowledge. In the very act of doubting, or of experiencing something contrived by the evil genius, Descartes finds unshakeable proof that he himself exists: "I think, therefore I am."

But can he know any more than this? He holds that he can indeed. He believes that he has discovered a first principle by which he can acquire knowledge despite his obvious fallibility:

> [I]t seems to me that already I can establish as a general rule that all things which I perceive very clearly and very distinctly are true.[7]

He declares that if he perceives something clearly and distinctly, he must know it with certainty. Armed with this principle of knowledge acquisition, he thinks he can know a great many things about the world. If he seems to perceive a flower and his perception is clear and distinct, then the flower must exist and be very much as it appears to be.

But why does Descartes think this principle is sound? He argues that in his mind he has a clear and distinct notion of perfection, which must have a cause. The cause of the idea of perfection, he says, must also be perfect, and this perfect cause can only be a perfect God. A perfect God is no deceiver; such a God would not allow him to be deceived when he correctly applies his God-given ability to achieve knowledge— that is, when he follows the principle of clarity and distinctness. Therefore, when he perceives something clearly and distinctly, he knows it beyond all doubt. He has knowledge, and skepticism is defeated.

Dogmatism and skepticism are both, in a sense, absolute philosophies; one is certain of knowing, the other of not knowing. What philosophy should dissipate is certainty, whether of knowledge or ignorance.
—Bertrand Russell

8 How does Descartes try to show that the principle of clear and distinct ideas is justified? Does he, as his critics assert, argue in a circle?

PHILOSOPHERS AT WORK

René Descartes

Descartes (1596–1650) did his philosophical work in a time of intellectual, scientific, and religious change, an era of revolutionary new thinking that would eventually transform the Western world. He was a contemporary of Galileo and Kepler, coming along after Copernicus did his work and before Newton did his. While trying to reconcile the old ideas with the new, he sparked a quiet revolution of his own and became the father of modern philosophy.

Figure 6.5 Rene Descartes, philosopher, mathematician, and eminent rationalist.

He was born in La Haye, France, educated in philosophy and mathematics at the Jesuit College of La Fleche in Anjou, and trained in the law at Poitiers. He served for a while in the Dutch army, where he did much of his early philosophical thinking, supposedly inspired by dreams he had while sleeping in a "stove-heated room."

He was such a bright student that he easily advanced beyond his teachers, and he quickly realized that their arguments and reasoning were defective. Knowledge in general, he thought, is on very shaky ground, and that state of affairs is

René Descartes,
*Meditations on First
Philosophy*

But after I have recognised that there is a God—because at the same time I have also recognised that all things depend upon Him, and that He is not a deceiver, and from that have inferred that what I perceive clearly and distinctly cannot fail to be true—although I no longer pay attention to the reasons for which I have judged this to be true, provided that I recollect having clearly and distinctly perceived it no contrary reason can be brought forward which could ever cause me to doubt of its truth; and thus I have a true and certain knowledge of it. And this same knowledge extends likewise to all other things which I recollect having formerly demonstrated, such as the truths of geometry and the like; for what can be alleged against them to cause me to place them in doubt? Will it be said that my nature is such as to cause me to be frequently deceived? But I already know that I cannot be deceived in the judgment whose grounds I know clearly. Will it be said that I formerly held many things to be true and certain which I have afterwards recognised to be false? But I had not had any clear and distinct knowledge of these things, and not as yet knowing the rule whereby I assure myself of the truth, I had been impelled to give my assent from reasons which I have since recognised to be less strong than I had at the time imagined them to be. What further objection can then be raised? That possibly I am dreaming (an objection I myself made a little while ago), or that all the thoughts which I now have are no more true than the phantasies of my dreams? But even though I slept the case would be the same, for all that is clearly present to my mind is absolutely true.[8]

Being a thoroughgoing rationalist, Descartes believes that he apprehends substantial truths about the world through reason. He would admit that through perception intolerable. So he set out on his long quest for knowledge that was as logical and certain as a mathematical proof. Along the way, he reshaped mathematics by inventing coordinate geometry. (Remember "Cartesian coordinates"?)

He developed a rationalistic theory of knowledge whose starting point was a recognition of personal existence ("I think therefore I am"). Reason is the source of substantial knowledge, and sense experience has only a subordinate role. His epistemology would be influential and controversial for centuries to come. His metaphysics has also affected succeeding generations. He posited a stark division between mind and matter, with the two somehow interacting (an interaction that he could not adequately explain). His *Discourse on the Method* was published in 1637, *Meditations on First Philosophy* in 1641, *Principles of Philosophy* in 1644, and *The Passions of the Soul* in 1649.

In 1649 he agreed to tutor the philosophically minded Queen Kristina of Sweden. But the work demanded an unpleasant departure from his usual routine of sleeping in: he was asked to begin lessons at 5:00 a.m.! The change allegedly caused his demise; he contracted pneumonia and died. (Another notable philosopher, Grotius, had visited Kristina in 1644 and suffered an identical fate. Kristina seems to have been very tough on famous philosophers.)

he learns simple facts such as the color of a flower and the position of the sun in the sky. But in many other cases, he says, knowledge of the external world is obtained through an "intuition of the mind," not sense data. Here is Descartes explaining this point:

Let us begin by considering the commonest matters, those which we believe to be the most distinctly comprehended, to wit, the bodies which we touch and see; not indeed bodies in general, for these general ideas are usually a little more confused, but let us consider one body in particular. Let us take, for example, this piece of wax: it has been taken quite freshly from the hive, and it has not yet lost the sweetness of the honey which it contains; it still retains somewhat of the odour of the flowers from which it has been culled; its colour, its figure, its size are apparent; it is hard, cold, easily handled, and if you strike it with the finger, it will emit a sound. Finally all the things which are requisite to cause us distinctly to recognise a body, are met with in it. But notice that while I speak and approach the fire what remained of the taste is exhaled, the smell evaporates, the colour alters, the figure is destroyed, the size increases, it becomes liquid, it heats, scarcely can one handle it, and when one strikes it, no sound is emitted. Does the same wax remain after this change? We must confess that it remains; none would judge otherwise. What then did I know so distinctly in this piece of wax? It could certainly be nothing of all that the senses brought to my notice, since all these things which fall under taste, smell, sight, touch, and hearing, are found to be changed, and yet the same wax remains. . . .

We must then grant that . . . it is my mind alone which perceives . . . this piece of wax. . . . But what is this piece of wax which cannot be understood excepting by the

9 Does Descartes succeed in showing that knowledge of the external world is gained by an intuition of the mind? Does his argument show that empiricism is false? Why or why not?

René Descartes, *Meditations on First Philosophy*

[understanding or] mind? It is certainly the same that I see, touch, imagine, and finally it is the same which I have always believed it to be from the beginning. But what must particularly be observed is that its perception is neither an act of vision, nor of touch, nor of imagination . . . but only an intuition of the mind.[9]

Descartes points out that although our senses tell us that the wax has changed through melting—that it has become a completely different object than it was before—our minds know better. Through a rational intuition, our minds understand that the wax, though radically altered, remains a piece of wax. If we relied only on sense experience to inform us about the wax, we would have to conclude that the original object no longer exists.

For three and a half centuries, Descartes' case for knowledge has been both commended and criticized. Many reject a key part of his argument, the premise asserting the existence of God. They doubt that Descartes—or anyone else—can infer the existence of God merely from the concept of God. Some also charge Descartes with begging the question, the fallacy of trying to establish the conclusion of an argument by using that conclusion as a premise (also known as arguing in a circle). Through his principle of clarity and distinctness, he tries to demonstrate that God exists. But then he attempts to establish the legitimacy of the principle by citing the existence of God. (Descartes' pattern of argument here has become known as the *Cartesian circle*.) Not everyone agrees that Descartes falls into this fallacy, but few doubt the ingenuity of his effort to rout the skeptic.

Figure 6.6 How do we know the wax is still wax?

The further the spiritual evolution of mankind advances, the more certain it seems to me that the path to genuine religiosity does not lie through the fear of life, and the fear of death, and blind faith, but through striving after rational knowledge.
—Albert Einstein

WRITING TO UNDERSTAND:
CRITIQUING PHILOSOPHICAL VIEWS   Section 6.2

1. Do you agree with Descartes (and skeptics) that only propositions that are beyond all doubt can be knowledge? How would you argue against this view?

2. The skeptic argues that if we are sometimes mistaken about our beliefs, then it is logically possible that we are always mistaken, and that we therefore do not have knowledge. Evaluate this argument.

3. According to Plato, are the ideas of Beauty and Courage objectively real, or are they notions that we invent in our minds whenever we want to? Do you think these ideas are objectively real? Provide an argument to back up your answer.

4. Are you living in the Matrix right now? What argument can you offer to show that you are not in the Matrix? What kind of argument would Descartes offer?

5. Consider this statement: All triangles have three sides. Explain how you know it is true even though you haven't examined all triangles in existence.

6.3 THE EMPIRICIST TURN

Most empiricists have rejected skepticism while denying rationalist claims (such as the doctrine of innate ideas), building their theories of knowledge on the supposed firmer ground of sense experience. But the differences among the greatest empiricists are stark. Locke argues that we can know much about things external to our minds; Berkeley agrees that we can have knowledge but denies the reality of material objects; and Hume insists that the scope of our knowledge is much narrower than most people realize, raising skeptical doubts about the existence of the external world and the inductive methodology of science.

Locke

In Locke's philosophical masterwork, *An Essay Concerning Human Understanding* (1689), he builds a case against rationalism and for a thoroughgoing empiricism. First, he contends that the rationalist notion that we are born with knowledge ("innate principles," as he says) already imprinted on our minds is unfounded. The rationalist argues, says Locke, that since all people seem to possess knowledge of certain universal principles (such as truths of logic), this knowledge must be inborn. How else could everyone have come by this knowledge? Locke replies that there are no such universal principles, and even if there were, they could have easily arisen through sense experience. They need not be present at birth. Here is Locke's critique of innate ideas:

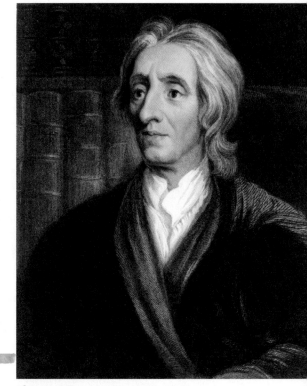

Figure 6.7 John Locke (1632–1704).

John Locke, *An Essay Concerning Human Understanding*

1. The way shown how we come by any knowledge, sufficient to prove it not innate. It is an established opinion amongst some men, that there are in the understanding certain innate principles; some primary notions, characters, as it were, stamped upon the mind of man, which the soul receives in its very first being; and brings into the world with it. It would be sufficient to convince unprejudiced readers of the falseness of this supposition, if I should only shew (as I hope I shall in the following parts of this discourse) how men, barely by the use of their natural faculties, may attain to all the knowledge they have, without the help of any innate impressions; and may arrive at certainty, without any such original notions or principles. For I imagine any one will easily grant, that it would be impertinent to suppose, the ideas of colours innate in a creature, to whom God hath given sight, and a power to receive them by the eyes, from external objects: And no less unreasonable would it be to attribute several truths to the impressions of nature, and innate characters, when we may observe in ourselves

John Locke,
*An Essay Concerning
Human Understanding*

10 Locke says that universal agreement on principles does not prove that they are innate. Why does he say this? Is he right?

11 In response to Locke's point about children, suppose a rationalist insists that children's minds are not fully developed and so cannot yet have knowledge of innate principles—therefore, their lack of innate knowledge does not prove anything. Is this a good argument?

faculties, fit to attain as easy and certain knowledge of them, as if they were originally imprinted on the mind.

But because a man is not permitted without censure to follow his own thoughts in the search of truth, when they lead him ever so little out of the common road; I shall set down the reasons that made me doubt of the truth of that opinion, as an excuse for my mistake, if I be in one; which I leave to be considered by those who, with me, dispose themselves to embrace truth, wherever they find it.

2. General assent, the great argument. There is nothing more commonly taken for granted, than that there are certain principles, both speculative and practical, (for they speak of both), universally agreed upon by all mankind: Which therefore, they argue, must needs be the constant impressions, which the souls of men receive in their first beings, and which they bring into the world with them, as necessarily and really as they do any of their inherent faculties.

3. Universal consent proves nothing. This argument, drawn from universal consent, has this misfortune in it, that if it were true in matter of fact, that there were certain truths wherein all mankind agreed, it would not prove them innate, if there can be any other way shewn how men may come to that universal agreement, in the things they do consent in, which I presume may be done.

4. What is, is; and it is impossible for the same thing to be, and not to be; not universally assented to. But, which is worse, this argument of universal consent, which is made use of to prove innate principles, seems to me a demonstration that there are none such; because there are none to which all mankind give an universal assent. I shall begin with the speculative, and instance in those magnified principles of demonstration; "Whatsoever is, is;" and "It is impossible for the same thing to be and not to be;" which, of all others, I think have the most allowed title to innate. These have so settled a reputation of maxims universally received, that it will, no doubt, be thought strange, if any one should seem to question it. But yet I take liberty to say, that these propositions are so far from having an universal assent, that there are a great part of mankind to whom they are not so much as known.

5. Not on the mind naturally imprinted, because not known to children, idiots, etc. For, first, it is evident, that all children and idiots have not the least apprehension or thought of them; and the want of that is enough to destroy that universal assent, which must needs be the necessary concomitant of all innate truths: It seeming to me near a contradiction, to say, that there are truths imprinted on the soul, which it perceives or understands not; imprinting if it signify any thing, being nothing else, but the making certain truths to be perceived. For to imprint any thing on the mind, without the mind's perceiving it seems to me hardly intelligible. If therefore children and idiots have souls, have minds, with those impressions upon them, they must unavoidably perceive them, and necessarily know and assent to these truths: Which since they do not, it is evident that there are no such impressions. For if they are not notions naturally imprinted, how can they be innate? and if they are notions imprinted, how can they be unknown? To say a notion is imprinted on the mind, and yet at the same time to say, that the mind is ignorant of it, and never yet took notice of it, is to make this impression nothing. No proposition can be said to be in the mind which it never yet knew, which it was never yet conscious of. For if any one may, then, by the same reason, all propositions that are true, and the mind is capable ever of assenting to, may be said to be in the mind, and to be imprinted: Since, if any one can be said to be in the mind, which it never yet knew, it must be only, because it is capable of knowing it, and so the mind is of all truths it ever shall know. Nay, thus truths may be imprinted on the mind, which it never did, nor ever shall know: For a man may live long, and die at last in ignorance of many truths, which his mind was capable of knowing, and that with certainty. So that if the capacity of knowing, be the natural impression contended for, all the truths a man ever comes to know, will, by this account, be every one of them innate; and this great point will amount to no more, but only to a very improper way of speaking; which, whilst it pretends to assert the contrary, says nothing different from those, who deny innate principles. For nobody, I think, ever denied that the mind was capable of knowing several truths. The capacity, they say, is innate, the knowledge acquired. But then to what end such contest for certain innate maxims? If truths can be imprinted on the understanding without being perceived, I can see no difference there can be, between any truths the mind is capable of knowing in respect of their original: They must all be innate, or all adventitious: In vain shall a man go about to distinguish them. He therefore that talks of innate notions in the understanding, cannot (if he intend thereby any distinct sort of truths) mean such truths to be in the understanding as it never perceived, and is yet wholly ignorant of. For if these words (to be in the understanding) have any propriety, they signify to be understood: So that to be in the understanding, and not to be understood; to be in the mind, and never to be perceived; is all one, as to say any thing is, and is not in the mind or understanding. If therefore these two propositions, "Whatsoever is, is," and "It is impossible for the same thing to be and not to be," are by nature imprinted, children cannot be ignorant of them; infants, and all that have souls, must necessarily have them in their understandings, know the truth of them, and assent to it.[10]

For Locke, the mind does not come into the world already inscribed with ideas or knowledge. On the contrary, he says, the mind is unmarked "white paper" void of any ideas until sense experience gives it content. From where does the mind obtain "all the *materials* of reason and knowledge," he asks. "To this I answer, in one word, from *experience*. In that all our knowledge is founded."[11]

Rationalists like Descartes would say that our most important items of knowledge must be innate because they could not possibly have come from sense experience. They would maintain, for example, that our knowledge of the concept "infinity" and of the proposition "every event has a cause" must be prenatally imprinted on our minds because we can never observe instances of these in reality. Through sense experience we can become acquainted only with finite things, not an infinity of things; and we can observe only a limited number of events, not all events. Locke, however, holds that we can grasp such ideas by first having sense experience related to them and then extrapolating the ideas from the sense data. We can, for example, have the concept of infinity by experiencing finite things and multiplying and extending them in our imagination until we approach the idea of the infinite.

Locke tries to defeat the skeptic by showing how our sense experience can reveal the existence of an external world. He says we must distinguish between the objects of our experience (external objects) and the experience of those objects (sensations, or sense data). Physical objects cause sensations in us, and we are directly aware only of those sensations (or ideas, as Locke calls them). So we have direct knowledge not of external objects, but of the sense data related to those objects. But if all we ever really know are sense data, how can we be sure they give us an accurate picture of the external world?

No man's knowledge here can go beyond his experience.
—John Locke

12 Evaluate Locke's point about extrapolating ideas from sense data. Is it plausible? Is it a good response to the rationalist?

All our knowledge has its origins in our perceptions.
—Leonardo da Vinci

Locke's answer is that sensations caused by external objects somehow represent those objects and thereby give us knowledge of them. Sensations are, Locke says, "resemblances" of external things. But he points out that not all of our sensations faithfully reflect reality. He distinguishes between two kinds of properties that external objects can have. *Primary qualities* are objective properties such as size, solidity, and mobility. They are *in material objects*, independent of our senses, and would be possessed by the objects even if no one was around to sense anything. *Secondary qualities* are subjective properties such as the color red or the smell of roses. They are *in the mind*, in that they depend on the operation of the senses. They exist only when someone experiences them. For Locke, we can have objective knowledge of material objects because some of our sense data represent the objects' primary qualities, which are objective characteristics of them.

Locke's theory of knowledge, however, has been sharply criticized by both rationalists and empiricists. The main criticism is that Locke has not given us any good reason to think that our sense data are proof of the existence of an external reality. After all, according to Locke, we directly experience only our sensations, or ideas; we only indirectly perceive external objects. We have no way of jumping out of our subjective point of view to compare our sense experience with the objective world. For all we know, our sense data present a radically distorted or thoroughly false picture of reality.

Here is Locke's answer to this charge:

John Locke,
*An Essay Concerning
Human Understanding*

1. Is to be had only by sensation. The knowledge of our own being we have by intuition. The existence of a God reason clearly makes known to us, as has been shown.

The knowledge of the existence of any other thing, we can have only by sensation: For there being no necessary connexion of real existence with any idea a man hath in his memory, nor of any other existence but that of God, with the existence of any particular man; no particular man can know the existence of any other being, but only when by actual operating upon him, it makes itself perceived by him.

For the having the idea of any thing in our mind, no more proves the existence of that thing, than the picture of a man evidences his being in the world, or the visions of a dream make thereby a true history.

2. Instance, whiteness of this paper. It is therefore the actual receiving of ideas from without [outside], that gives us notice of the existence of other things, and makes us know that something doth exist at that time without us, which causes that idea in us, though perhaps we neither know nor consider how it does it. For it takes not from the certainty of our senses, the ideas we receive by them, that we know not the manner wherein they are produced: V. g. whilst I write this, I have, by the paper affecting my eyes, that idea produced in my mind, which whatever object causes, I call white; by which I know that that quality or accident (i.e. whose appearance before my eyes always causes that idea) doth really exist, and hath a being without me. And of this, the greatest assurance I can possibly have, and to which my faculties can attain, is the testimony of my eyes, which are the proper and sole judges of this thing, whose testimony I have reason to rely on as so certain, that I can no more doubt, whilst I write this, that I see white and black, and that something really exists, that causes that sensation in me, than that I write or move my hand; which is a certainty as great as human nature is capable of, concerning the existence of any thing, but a man's self alone, and of God.

3. This, though not so certain as demonstration, yet may be called knowledge, and proves the existence of things without us. The notice we have by our senses, of the existing of things without us, though it be not altogether so certain as our intuitive knowledge, or the deductions of our reason employed about the clear abstract ideas of our own minds; yet it is an assurance that deserves the name of knowledge. If we persuade ourselves, that our faculties act and inform us right, concerning the existence of those objects that affect them, it cannot pass for an ill-grounded confidence: For I think nobody can, in earnest, be so sceptical, as to be uncertain of the existence of those things which he sees and feels. At least, he that can doubt so far (whatever he may have with his own thoughts) will never have any controversy with me; since he can never be sure I say any thing contrary to his own opinion. As to myself, I think God has given me assurance enough of the existence of things without me; since by their different application I can produce in myself both pleasure and pain, which is one great concernment of my present state. This is certain; the confidence that our faculties do not herein deceive us is the greatest assurance we are capable of, concerning the existence of material beings. For we cannot act any thing but by our faculties; nor talk of knowledge itself, but by the help of those faculties, which are fitted to apprehend even what knowledge is. But besides the assurance we have from our senses themselves, that they do not err in the information they give us, of the existence of things without us, when they are affected by them, we are farther confirmed in this assurance by other concurrent reasons.

4. Because we cannot have them but by the inlets of the senses. First, it is plain those perceptions are produced in us by exterior causes affecting our senses; because those that want [lack] the organs of any sense, never can have the ideas belonging to that sense produced in their minds. This is too evident to be doubted: And therefore we cannot but be assured, that they come in by the organs of that sense, and no other way. The organs themselves, it is plain, do not produce them, for then the eyes of a man in the dark would produce colors, and his nose smell roses in the winter: But we see nobody gets the relish of a pine-apple, till he goes to the Indies, where it is, and tastes it.

5. Because an idea from actual sensation, and another from memory, are very distinct perceptions. Secondly, because sometimes I find, that I cannot avoid the having those ideas produced in my mind. For though when my eyes are shut, or windows fast, I can at pleasure recall to my mind the ideas of light, or the sun, which former sensations had lodged in my memory; so I can at pleasure lay by that idea, and take into my view that of the smell of a rose, or taste of sugar. But, if I turn my eyes at noon towards the sun, I cannot avoid the ideas, which the light, or sun, then produces in me. So that there is a manifest difference between the ideas laid up in my memory, (over which, if they were there only, I should have constantly the same power to dispose of them, and lay them by at pleasure) and those which force themselves upon me, and I cannot avoid having. And therefore it must needs be some exterior cause, and the brisk acting of some objects without me, whose efficacy I cannot resist, that produces those ideas in my mind, whether I will or no. Besides, there is nobody who doth not perceive the difference in himself between contemplating the sun, as he hath the idea of it in his memory, and actually looking upon it: Of which two, his perception is so distinct, that few of his ideas are more distinguishable one from another. And therefore he hath certain knowledge that they are not both memory, or the actions of his mind, and fancies only within him; but that actual seeing hath a cause without.

6. Pleasure and Pain, which accompanies actual sensation, accompanies not the returning of those ideas, without the external objects. Thirdly, add to this, that many of

13 Has Locke provided good reasons to think that our sense data prove the existence of an external world? Evaluate his attempt to answer his critics on this point.

John Locke,
*An Essay Concerning
Human Understanding*

those ideas are produced in us with pain, which afterwards we remember without the least offence. Thus the pain of heat or cold, when the idea of it is revived in our minds, gives us no disturbance; which, when felt, was very troublesome, and is again, when actually repeated; which is occasioned by the disorder the external object causes in our bodies when applied to it. And we remember the pains of hunger, thirst, or the head-ache, without any pain at all; which would either never disturb us, or else constantly do it, as often as we thought of it, were there nothing more but ideas floating in our minds, and appearances entertaining our fancies, without the real existence of things affecting us from abroad. The same may be said of pleasure, accompanying several actual sensations: And though mathematical demonstration depends not upon sense, yet the examining them by diagrams gives great credit to the evidence of our sight, and seems to give it a certainty approaching to that of demonstration itself. For it would be very strange, that a man should allow it for an undeniable truth, that two angles of a figure, which he measures by lines and angles of a diagram, should be bigger one than the other; and yet doubt of the existence of those lines and angles, which by looking on he makes use of to measure that by.

7. Our senses assist one another's testimony of the existence of outward things. Fourthly, our senses in many cases bear witness to the truth of each other's report, concerning the existence of sensible things without us. He that sees a fire, may, if he doubt whether it be any thing more than a bare fancy, feel it too; and be convinced by putting his hand in it. Which certainly could never be put into such exquisite pain, by a bare idea or phantom, unless that the pain be a fancy too: Which yet he cannot, when the burn is well, by raising the idea of it, bring upon himself again.

Thus I see, whilst I write this, I can change the appearance of the paper: And by de-signing the letters tell before-hand what new idea it shall exhibit the very next moment, by barely drawing my pen over it: Which will neither appear (let me fancy as much as I will) if my hands stand still; or though I move my pen, if my eyes be shut: Nor when those characters are once made on the paper, can I choose afterwards but see them as they are; that is, have the ideas of such letters as I have made. Whence it is manifest, that they are not barely the sport and play of my own imagination, when I find that the characters, that were made at the pleasure of my own thoughts, do not obey them; nor yet cease to be, whenever I shall fancy it; but continue to affect my senses constantly and regularly, according to the figures I made them. To which if we will add, that the sight of those shall, from another man, draw such sounds, as I beforehand design they shall stand for; there will be little reason left to doubt, that those words I write do really exist without me, when they cause a long series of regular sounds to affect my ears, which could not be the effect of my imagination, nor could my memory retain them in that order.

8. This certainty is as great as our condition needs. But yet, if after all this any one will be so sceptical, as to distrust his senses, and to affirm that all we see and hear, feel and taste, think and do, during our whole being, is but the series and deluding appear-ances of a long dream, whereof there is reality; and therefore will question the existence of all things, or our knowledge of any thing; I must desire him to consider, that if all be a dream, then he doth but dream, that he makes the question; and so it is not much matter, that a waking man should answer him. But yet, if he pleases, he may dream that I make him this answer, that the certainty of things existing in *rerum natura*, when we have the testimony of our senses for it, is not only as great as our frame can attain to, but as our condition needs. For our faculties being suited not to the full extent of being, nor to a perfect, clear, comprehensive knowledge of things free from all doubt and scruple; but to the preservation of us, in whom they are; and accommodated to the use of life; they serve to our purpose well enough, if they will but give us certain notice of those things, which are convenient or inconvenient to us. For he that sees a candle burning, and hath experimented the force of its flame, by putting his finger in it, will little doubt that this is something existing without him, which does him harm, and puts him to great pain: Which is assurance enough, when no man requires greater certainty to govern his actions by, than what is as certain as his actions themselves. And if our dreamer pleases to try, whether the glowing heat of a glass furnace be barely a wandering imagination in a drowsy man's fancy; by putting his hand into it, he may perhaps be wakened into a certainty greater than he could wish, that it is something more than bare imagination. So that this evidence is as great as we can desire, being as certain to us as our pleasure or pain, i.e. happiness or misery; beyond which we have no concernment, either of knowing or being. Such an assurance of the existence of things without us is sufficient to direct us in the attaining the good, and avoiding the evil, which is caused by them; which is the important concernment we have of being made acquainted with them.

> **9. But reaches no farther than actual sensation.** In fine then, when our senses do actually convey into our understandings any idea, we cannot but be satisfied that there doth something at that time really exist without us, which doth affect our senses, and by them give notice of itself to our apprehensive faculties, and actually produce that idea which we then perceive: And we cannot so far distrust their testimony, as to doubt, that such collections of simple ideas, as we have observed by our senses to be united together, do really exist together.[12]

14 Is Locke's argument (an inference to the best explanation) successful? Evaluate its strengths and weaknesses.

Locke asks, in effect, what could possibly cause our sense experience if not external objects? His answer is that we know that external objects are real (and not a dream or delusion) because the theory that they exist is the best explanation for the sensations we have. External objects cause our sensations, and this is a much better explanation for our experience than that an evil genius or our own minds create a fantasy world that we take to be real.

> We are drowning in information and starved for knowledge.
> —Unknown

Berkeley

Like Locke, George Berkeley is an empiricist who rejects skepticism. He believes that we can indeed acquire knowledge, and that the only path to it is through sense experience. But beyond these points of agreement, Berkeley veers sharply away from Locke's view and from the theories of most other empiricists. (Caution: At first glance, you may think Berkeley's theory of knowledge is both bizarre and wrong. But he provides plausible, and unsettling, arguments for his view, and generations of philosophers—whether they agreed with Berkeley or not—have been forced to take his theory seriously.)

For Berkeley, there are no material objects, no things that exist in the external world. There are objects to be sure, but they exist only as sensations (what Berkeley calls *ideas*) in some mind. They are real only because they are perceived by someone. Thus he declares in his famous phrase, *esse est percipi*, "to be is to be perceived." What we usually call physical objects, then, are simply compilations of sense data, and reality consists only of ideas and the minds that perceive them.

Figure 6.8 George Berkeley (1685–1753).

Our sense experience does not represent an external reality as Locke thought; our sense experience *is* reality. Locke's view is vulnerable to skeptical criticism because he admits that there is a gap between our sensations and reality. Berkeley, however, tries to defeat skepticism by doing away with the gap entirely. He contends that there is no gap because material objects do not exist; only ideas exist along with the minds that perceive them.

Let's allow Berkeley to make his case:

George Berkeley, *Of the Principles of Human Knowledge*

I. It is evident to any one who takes a survey of the objects of human knowledge, that they are either ideas actually imprinted on the senses, or else such as are perceived by attending to the passions and operations of the mind, or lastly, ideas formed by help of memory and imagination, either compounding, dividing, or barely representing those originally perceived in the aforesaid ways. By sight I have the ideas of light and colours with their several degrees and variations. By touch I perceive, for example, hard and soft, heat and cold, motion and resistance, and of all these more and less either as to quantity or degree. Smelling furnishes me with odours; the palate with tastes; and hearing conveys sounds to the mind in all their variety of tone and composition. And as several of these are observed to accompany each other, they come to be marked by one name, and so to be reputed as one thing. Thus, for example, a certain colour, taste, smell, figure, and consistence having been observed to go together, are accounted one distinct thing, signified by the name apple. Other collections of ideas constitute a stone, a tree, a book, and the like sensible things; which, as they are pleasing or dis-agreeable, excite the passions of love, hatred, joy, grief, and so forth.

II. But besides all that endless variety of ideas or objects of knowledge, there is likewise something which knows or perceives them, and exercises divers operations, as willing, imagining, remembering about them. This perceiving, active being is what I call mind, spirit, soul, or myself. By which words I do not denote any one of my ideas, but a thing entirely distinct from them, wherein they exist, or, which is the same thing, whereby they are perceived; for the existence of an idea consists in being perceived.

III. That neither our thoughts, nor passions, nor ideas formed by the imagination, exist without the mind, is what every body will allow. And (to me) it seems no less evident that the various sensations or ideas imprinted on the sense, however blended or combined together (that is, whatever objects they compose), cannot exist otherwise than in a mind perceiving them. I think an intuitive knowledge may be obtained of this, by any one that shall attend to what is meant by the term exist, when applied to sensible things. The table I write on, I say, exists, that is, I see and feel it; and if I were out of my study I should say it existed, meaning thereby that if I was in my study I might perceive it, or that some other spirit actually does perceive it. There was an odour, that is, it was smelled; there was a sound, that is to say, it was heard; a colour or figure, and it was perceived by sight or touch. This is all that I can understand by these and the like ex-pressions. For as to what is said of the absolute existence of unthinking things without any relation to their being perceived, that seems perfectly unintelligible. Their *esse* is *percipi*, nor is it possible they should have any existence, out of the minds or thinking things which perceive them.

IV. It is indeed an opinion strangely prevailing amongst men, that houses, mountains, rivers, and in a word sensible objects have an existence natural or real, distinct from their being perceived by the understanding. But with how great an assurance and acquiescence soever this principle may be entertained in the world; yet whoever shall find in his heart to call it in question, may, if I mistake not, perceive it to involve a manifest contradiction. For what are the forementioned objects but the things we perceive by sense, and what do we perceive besides our own ideas or sensations; and is it not plainly repugnant that any one of these or any combination of them should exist unperceived? . . .

VI. Some truths there are so near and obvious to the mind, that a man need only open his eyes to see them. Such I take this important one to be, to wit, that all the choir of heaven and furniture of the earth, in a word all those bodies which compose the mighty frame of the world, have not any subsistence without a mind, that their being (*esse*) is to be perceived or known; that consequently so long as they are not actually perceived by me, or do not exist in my mind or that of any other created spirit, they must either have no existence at all, or else subsist in the mind of some eternal spirit: it being perfectly unintelligible and involving all the absurdity of abstraction, to attribute to any single part of them an existence independent of a spirit. To be convinced of which, the reader need only reflect and try to separate in his own thoughts the being of a sensible thing from its being perceived. . . .

VIII. But say you, though the ideas themselves do not exist without the mind, yet there may be things like them whereof they are copies or resemblances, which things exist without the mind, in an unthinking substance. I answer, an idea can be like nothing but an idea; a colour or figure can be like nothing but another colour or figure. If we look but ever so little into our thoughts, we shall find it impossible for us to conceive a likeness except only between our ideas. Again, I ask whether those supposed originals or external things, of which our ideas are the pictures or representations, be themselves perceivable or no? if they are, then they are ideas, and we have gained our point; but if you say they are not, I appeal to any one whether it be sense, to assert a colour is like something which is invisible; hard or soft, like something which is intangible; and so of the rest.[13]

To provide further support for his theory, Berkeley takes aim at Locke's distinction between primary and secondary qualities. He claims that primary qualities are just as mind-dependent as secondary qualities are, for primary qualities can also vary according to the state of our senses, and primary qualities are inseparable from secondary qualities.

IX. Some there are who make a distinction betwixt primary and secondary qualities: by the former, they mean extension, figure, motion, rest, solidity or impenetrability, and number: by the latter they denote all other sensible qualities, as colours, sounds, tastes, and so forth. The ideas we have of these they acknowledge not to be the resemblances of any thing existing without the mind or unperceived; but they will have our ideas of the primary qualities to be patterns or images of things which exist without the mind, in an unthinking substance which they call matter. By matter therefore we are to understand an inert, senseless substance, in which extension, figure and motion, do actually subsist. But it is evident from what we have already shown, that extension, figure, and motion, are only ideas existing in the mind, and that an idea can be like nothing but another idea, and that consequently neither they nor their archetypes can

15 Is Berkeley right that belief in material objects involves a logical contradiction? Explain.

George Berkeley,
*Of the Principles of
Human Knowledge*

George Berkeley,
*Of the Principles of
Human Knowledge*

16 Do you think there is no substantial difference between primary and secondary qualities? Why or why not?

exist in an unperceiving substance. Hence it is plain, that the very notion of what is called matter, or corporeal substance, involves a contradiction in it.

X. They who assert that figure, motion, and the rest of the primary or original qualities, do exist without the mind, in unthinking substances, do at the same time acknowledge that colours, sounds, heat, cold, and such like secondary qualities, do not, which they tell us are sensations existing in the mind alone, that depend on and are occasioned by the different size, texture, and motion of the minute particles of matter. This they take for an undoubted truth, which they can demonstrate beyond all exception. Now if it be certain, that those original qualities are inseparably united with the other sensible qualities, and not, even in thought, capable of being abstracted from them, it plainly follows that they exist only in the mind. But I desire any one to reflect and try, whether he can, by any abstraction of thought, conceive the extension and motion of a body, without all other sensible qualities. For my own part, I see evidently that it is not in my power to frame an idea of a body extended and moved, but I must withal give it some colour or other sensible quality which is acknowledged to exist only in the mind. In short, extension, figure, and motion, abstracted from all other qualities, are inconceivable. Where therefore the other sensible qualities are, there must these be also, to wit, in the mind and nowhere else. . . .

XIV. I shall further add, that after the same manner as modern philosophers prove certain sensible qualities to have no existence in matter, or without the mind, the same thing may be likewise proved of all other sensible qualities whatsoever. Thus, for instance, it is said that heat and cold are affections only of the mind, and not at all patterns of real beings, existing in the corporeal substances which excite them, for that the same body which appears cold to one hand, seems warm to another. Now why may we not as well argue that figure and extension are not patterns or resemblances of qualities existing in matter, because to the same eye at different stations, or eyes of a different texture at the same station, they appear various, and cannot therefore be the images of any thing settled and determinate without the mind? Again, it is proved that sweetness is not really in the said thing, because, the thing remaining unaltered, the sweetness is changed into bitter, as in case of a fever or otherwise vitiated palate. Is it not as reasonable to say, that motion is not without the mind, since if the succession of ideas in the mind become swifter, the motion, it is acknowledged, shall appear slower without any alteration in any external object.

XV. In short, let any one consider those arguments which are thought manifestly to prove that colours and tastes exist only in the mind, and he shall find they may with equal force be brought to prove the same thing of extension, figure, and motion. Though it must be confessed, this method of arguing doth not so much prove that there is no extension or colour in an outward object, as that we do not know by sense which is the true extension or colour of the object. But the arguments foregoing plainly show it to be impossible that any colour or extension at all or other sensible quality whatsoever, should exist in an unthinking subject without the mind, or in truth, that there should be any such thing as an outward object.[14]

Berkeley's most interesting argument against the existence of material objects is a purely logical one: He contends that they cannot exist because their existence would be logically absurd. The commonsense view is that material objects *continue to be* even when no one has them in mind. But, says Berkeley, this would mean that they can be conceived of as existing unconceived, that we can think about things that no one is thinking about—a logical contradiction. Therefore, Berkeley concludes, the claim that material objects exist is false.

Critics have taken issue with this argument. They agree that in one sense it is impossible to conceive of something unconceived: It is impossible to contemplate a thing that is at the same time not being contemplated. But they maintain that there is no incoherence in believing the assertion that an entity exists unconceived. No contradiction lurks here. If so, the concept of a material object is not, as Berkeley charges, "a manifest repugnancy."

Some have faulted Berkeley's theory in another way. They ask, Why do patterns of sensations present themselves to us as if they were entirely independent of our minds? That is, why do the configurations of sense data behave like material objects, seemingly existing unperceived and beyond our control? Berkeley's answer is that things are never unperceived, for God continually perceives them and thus causes them to be as they are. God inserts a grand, intricate panoply of ideas into our minds—sensations that constitute for us a real world of God's making. What we think of as material objects are instead repeating patterns of sense experience caused by God.

Like the rationalist Descartes, Berkeley the empiricist ultimately brings in God to explain how knowledge is possible. But to many, his explanation of the peculiar nature of our sense experience is not as good by far as the commonsense explanation: material objects exist independently of us and cause the patterns of our sensations. They think the God theory leaves too much unexplained; to them, the material-object theory seems simpler and more consistent with scientific understanding of perception. As Bertrand Russell says,

> [E]very principle of simplicity urges us to adopt the natural view, that there really are objects other than ourselves and our sense-data which have an existence not dependent upon our perceiving them.[15]

Hume

So, in their own ways, Descartes, Locke, and Berkeley wrestled with the great epistemological questions: Do we have knowledge? And if so, what exactly do we know? In the end they all concluded that we do indeed have knowledge, but they differed on its extent. In contrast, David Hume—the renowned Enlightenment thinker and preeminent British philosopher—argued for a thoroughly consistent empiricism that led him to a skepticism so extensive that few others dared follow his lead.

Hume insists that whatever knowledge we have is of two kinds: "relations of ideas" and "matters of fact." The former include truths of mathematics and truths of logic (such as "either it's raining or it's not raining" and "no bachelors are married"); they are derived from reason. The latter consist of information about the world and are based entirely on sense experience. We can come to know relations of ideas with certainty, but they are not informative about reality. We know that "either it's raining or it's not raining" is true, but the proposition tells

The possession of knowledge does not kill the sense of wonder and mystery. There is always more mystery.
—Anaïs Nin

17 How does Hume's empiricism differ from Locke's and Berkeley's?

PHILOSOPHERS AT WORK

David Hume

During his lifetime, David Hume (1711–1776) earned a reputation as one of Britain's premier men of letters and garnered fame as the author of the six-volume *History of England*. In our own time, he is regarded as a key figure in the Enlightenment, the most influential of the British empiricists, and possibly Britain's greatest philosopher.

Figure 6.9 David Hume, philosopher, historian and, reportedly, "a perfectly wise and virtuous man."

He was born in Edinburgh, Scotland, educated at its university, and spent most of his literary career in the city of his birth. By age sixteen he was already well versed in classical literature, logic, metaphysics, philosophy, and ethics. Later, in a three-year period, he read, in his words, "most of the celebrated Books in Latin, French & English."

He wrote essays on politics, ethics, and economics, as well as major philosophical treatises. The first (and some say the greatest) of the latter was *A Treatise of Human Nature* (1739), followed by *An Enquiry Concerning Human Understanding* (1748) and *An Enquiry Concerning the Principles of Morals* (1751). In *An Enquiry Concerning Human Understanding*, his masterpiece in epistemology, he argued for a stronger and more encompassing skepticism than any other major philosopher dared embrace. His skepticism extended to induction, causation, the external world, the self, miracles, and the existence of God. (His *Dialogues Concerning Natural Religion* was such a scorching attack on religious belief that he delayed its publication until after

We have limited knowledge, or else science and philosophy would not be necessary.
—Ivan Urlaub

us nothing about whether it is actually raining. It simply states an obvious logical truth. Matters of fact, on the other hand, are informative about the world, but they cannot be known with certainty. So contrary to the rationalists, Hume maintains that reason is not a source of knowledge about the world. In line with the empiricists, he holds that knowledge about the world can be acquired only through experience.

But how much can we really know through experience alone? That is, what can we know about matters of fact? Hume's answer: very little. He says that the information derived from experience—what he calls *perceptions*—consists of sense data (such as sights, odors, and sounds) and inner psychological states (such as hate, fear, love, and desire). Perceptions are of two types: *impressions* and *ideas*. Impressions are what we directly and vividly experience, the raw sense data and psychological states. Ideas are our less vivid thoughts and reflections about impressions. The experience of a bright red color when you look at a rose is an impression. Your thoughts or imaginings about the original rose experience is an idea. Hume uses this terminology his death.) His doubts about all these ideas sprang naturally from his consistent and thoroughgoing empiricism, in which assertions can count as knowledge only if they can be traced back to experience. He boldly declared, "When we run over libraries, persuaded of these [empiricist] principles, what havoc must we make? If we take in our hand any volume; of divinity or school metaphysics, for instance, let us ask, *Does it contain any abstract reasoning concerning quantity or number?* No. *Does it contain any experimental reasoning concerning matter of fact and existence?* No. Commit it then to the flames: for it can contain nothing but sophistry and illusion."

Despite his tough-minded philosophy, Hume was blessed with a cheerful disposition, which probably helped him cope with the gloomy skepticism of his studies. He said that reason could not cure his melancholy, but distraction and recreation could. As he put it, "I dine, I play a game of backgammon, I converse, and am merry with my friends; and when after three or four hours' amusement, I would return to these speculations, they appear so cold, and strained, and ridiculous, that I cannot find in my heart to enter into them any farther." But he did enter into them again many times—and so laid down a challenge to future thinkers to try to answer his philosophical doubts.

By all accounts, Hume was a decent, generous, and honorable person, admired and liked by everyone who knew him. A contemporary of Hume's, Adam Smith, the renowned philosopher and economist, said of Hume that "upon the whole, I have always considered him, both in his life-time and since his death, as approaching as nearly to the idea of a perfectly wise and virtuous man, as perhaps the nature of human frailty will admit."

to make his central point: For something to count as knowledge, it must be based on impressions or on ideas derived from impressions. And for a statement to be meaningful, it must ultimately refer to impressions. Here is Hume outlining these distinctions:

David Hume, *An Enquiry Concerning Human Understanding*

Every one will readily allow, that there is a considerable difference between the perceptions of the mind, when a man feels the pain of excessive heat, or the pleasure of moderate warmth, and when he afterwards recalls to his memory this sensation, or anticipates it by his imagination. These faculties may mimic or copy the perceptions of the senses; but they never can entirely reach the force and vivacity of the original sentiment. The utmost we say of them, even when they operate with greatest vigor, is, that

David Hume, *An Enquiry Concerning Human Understanding*

18 Hume thinks that all knowledge must be traced back to perceptions; otherwise, assertions of knowledge are meaningless. From this he concludes that all theological and metaphysical speculations are worthless. Do you agree with him? Why or why not?

they represent their object in so lively a manner, that we could almost say we feel or see it: But, except the mind be disordered by disease or madness, they never can arrive at such a pitch of vivacity, as to render these perceptions altogether undistinguishable. All the colours of poetry, however splendid, can never paint natural objects in such a manner as to make the description be taken for a real landscape. The most lively thought is still inferior to the dullest sensation.

We may observe a like distinction to run through all the other perceptions of the mind. A man in a fit of anger, is actuated in a very different manner from one who only thinks of that emotion. If you tell me, that any person is in love, I easily understand your meaning, and form a just conception of his situation; but never can mistake that conception for the real disorders and agitations of the passion. When we reflect on our past sentiments and affections, our thought is a faithful mirror, and copies its objects truly; but the colours which it employs are faint and dull, in comparison of those in which our original perceptions were clothed. It requires no nice discernment or metaphysical head to mark the distinction between them.

Here therefore we may divide all the perceptions of the mind into two classes or species, which are distinguished by their different degrees of force and vivacity. The less forcible and lively are commonly denominated Thoughts or Ideas. The other species want a name in our language, and in most others; I suppose, because it was not requisite for any, but philosophical purposes, to rank them under a general term or appellation. Let us, therefore, use a little freedom, and call them Impressions; employing that word in a sense somewhat different from the usual. By the term impression, then, I mean all our more lively perceptions, when we hear, or see, or feel, or love, or hate, or desire, or will. And impressions are distinguished from ideas, which are the less lively perceptions, of which we are conscious, when we reflect on any of those sensations or movements above mentioned. . . .

All the objects of human reason or enquiry may naturally be divided into two kinds, to wit, Relations of Ideas, and Matters of Fact. Of the first kind are the sciences of Geometry, Algebra, and Arithmetic; and in short, every affirmation, which is either intuitively or demonstratively certain. That the square of the hypothenuse is equal to the squares of the two sides, is a proposition, which expresses a relation between these figures. That three times five is equal to the half of thirty, expresses a relation between these numbers. Propositions of this kind are discoverable by the mere operation of thought, without dependence on what is any where existent in the universe. Though there never were a circle or triangle in nature, the truths, demonstrated by Euclid, would for ever retain their certainty and evidence.

Matters of fact, which are the second objects of human reason, are not ascertained in the same manner; nor is our evidence of their truth, however great, of a like nature with the foregoing. The contrary of every matter of fact is still possible; because it can never imply a contradiction, and is conceived by the mind with the same facility and distinctness, as if ever so conformable to reality. That the sun will not rise to-morrow is no less intelligible a proposition, and implies no more contradiction, than the affirmation, that it will rise. We should in vain, therefore, attempt to demonstrate its falsehood. Were it demonstratively false, it would imply a contradiction, and could never be distinctly conceived by the mind.[16]

Hume not only argues that whatever we know about the world must be grounded in our perceptions, but also that we can be sure *only* of those perceptions. We know just our experience and can only guess what lies beyond it. It's as if we are locked in a windowless room and must speculate about what it's like outside based on a video we can watch indoors. The video may or may not resemble the outside world, but it's the only information we have.

Hume's strict empiricism leads naturally to skepticism about a notion that we usually assume without question: causality. We believe the world is filled with causes and effects; we think one thing causes another, and the two are somehow physically linked. Every day of our lives we draw countless conclusions based on our assumptions about cause-and-effect relationships. But Hume argues that we have no good grounds for believing that causes and effects are related the way we think they are.

To be fully acquainted, therefore, with the idea of power or necessary connexion, let us examine its impression; and in order to find the impression with greater certainty, let us search for it in all the sources, from which it may possibly be derived.

When we look about us towards external objects, and consider the operation of causes, we are never able, in a single instance, to discover any power or necessary connexion; any quality, which binds the effect to the cause, and renders the one an infallible consequence of the other. We only find, that the one does actually, in fact, follow the other. The impulse of one billiard-ball is attended with motion in the second. This is the whole that appears to the outward senses. The mind feels no sentiment or inward impression from this succession of objects: Consequently, there is not, in any single, particular instance of cause and effect, any thing which can suggest the idea of power or necessary connexion.

> Knowledge comes, but wisdom lingers.
> —Alfred Lord Tennyson

> David Hume, *An Enquiry Concerning Human Understanding*

19 Why does Hume conclude that we have no evidence for causal relationships between events? Do you agree with him? Why or why not?

Figure 6.10 The movement of one billiard ball may accompany that of another—but where is the evidence of a *causal connection*?

David Hume, *An Enquiry Concerning Human Understanding*

From the first appearance of an object, we never can conjecture what effect will result from it. But were the power or energy of any cause discoverable by the mind, we could foresee the effect, even without experience; and might, at first, pronounce with certainty concerning it, by the mere dint of thought and reasoning. . . .

But to hasten to a conclusion of this argument, which is already drawn out to too great a length: We have sought in vain for an idea of power or necessary connexion, in all the sources from which we could suppose it to be derived. It appears, that, in single instances of the operation of bodies, we never can, by our utmost scrutiny, discover any thing but one event following another; without being able to comprehend any force or power, by which the cause operates, or any connexion between it and its supposed effect. The same difficulty occurs in contemplating the operations of mind on body; where we observe the motion of the latter to follow upon the volition of the former; but are not able to observe or conceive the tie which binds together the motion and volition, or the energy by which the mind produces this effect. The authority of the will over its own faculties and ideas is not a whit more comprehensible: So that, upon the whole, there appears not, throughout all nature, any one instance of connexion, which is conceivable by us. All events seem entirely loose and separate. One event follows another; but we never can observe any tie between them. They seem conjoined, but never connected. And as we can have no idea of any thing, which never appeared to our outward sense or inward sentiment, the necessary conclusion seems to be, that we have no idea of connexion or power at all, and that these words are absolutely without any meaning, when employed either in philosophical reasonings, or common life.[17]

Hume asserts that neither reason nor experience can provide us with evidence that causal relationships exist. We can observe no power or force that enables causes to produce events. Our perceptions do not give us any reason to believe that one thing makes another thing happen. All we observe, says Hume, is one event associated with another, and when we repeatedly see such a pairing, we jump to the conclusion that the events are causally connected. We make these inferences out of habit, not logic or empirical evidence.

In making judgments about causes and effects, we reason inductively. That is, we assume that events that followed one another in the past will do the same in the future, that the future will be like the past. We presuppose, in other words, the **principle of induction.** Because of previous experience, we expect night to follow day, fire to burn, bread to nourish, and dogs to bark. Likewise, the whole scientific enterprise runs on this principle, with scientists making inferences from empirical regularities to predictions about events to come. At first glance, it might seem that no one would seriously question the legitimacy of inductive reasoning. But Hume does:

The **principle of induction** is the presumption that events that followed one another in the past will do the same in the future, that the future will be like the past.

David Hume, *An Enquiry Concerning Human Understanding*

As to past Experience, it can be allowed to give direct and certain information of those precise objects only, and that precise period of time, which fell under its cognizance: But why this experience should be extended to future times, and to other objects, which for aught we know, may be only in appearance similar; this is the main question on which I would insist. The bread, which I formerly ate, nourished me; that is, a body of such sensible qualities, was, at that time, endued with such secret powers: But does it follow, that other bread must also nourish me at another time, and that like sensible qualities must always be attended with like secret powers? The consequence seems nowise necessary. At least, it must be acknowledged, that there is here a consequence drawn by the mind; that there is a certain step taken; a process of thought, and an inference, which wants to be explained. These two propositions are far from being the same, I have found that such an object has always been attended with such an effect, and I foresee, that other objects, which are, in appearance, similar, will be attended with similar effects. I shall allow, if you please, that the one proposition may justly be inferred from the other: I know in fact, that it always is inferred. But if you insist, that the inference is made by a chain of reasoning, I desire you to produce that reasoning. The connexion between these propositions is not intuitive. There is required a medium, which may enable the mind to draw such an inference, if indeed it be drawn by reasoning and argument. What that medium is, I must confess, passes my comprehension; and it is incumbent on those to produce it, who assert, that it really exists, and is the origin of all our conclusions concerning matter of fact. . . .

For all inferences from experience suppose, as their foundation, that the future will resemble the past, and that similar powers will be conjoined with similar sensible qualities. If there be any suspicion, that the course of nature may change, and that the past may be no rule for the future, all experience becomes useless, and can give rise to no inference or conclusion. It is impossible, therefore, that any arguments from experience can prove this resemblance of the past to the future; since all these arguments are founded on the supposition of that resemblance. Let the course of things be allowed hitherto ever so regular; that alone, without some new argument or inference, proves not, that, for the future, it will continue so. In vain do you pretend to have learned the nature of bodies from your past experience. Their secret nature, and consequently, all their effects and influence, may change, without any change in their sensible qualities. This happens sometimes, and with regard to some objects: Why may it not happen always, and with regard to all objects? What logic, what process of argument secures you against this supposition?[18]

Hume asks, Do we have any grounds whatsoever for believing the principle of induction? What justifies our assumption that the future will be like the past? He argues that the principle cannot be an a priori truth, and it cannot be an a posteriori fact. It cannot be the former because the denial of an a priori truth (such as "All bachelors are unmarried") is self-contradictory, and the denial of the principle of induction is not like that. It cannot be the latter because no amount of empirical evidence can show it to be true. Why? As Hume observes, to maintain that the principle of induction is an a posteriori fact is to say that it can be established by experience (that is, inductively). That is equivalent to saying that the principle of induction can be proved by the principle of induction—which is to beg the question. Arguing in a circle like this offers no support to the principle at all.

This difficulty of justifying the assumption that the future will be like the past is known as the *problem of induction*, and it has incited generations of thinkers to try to solve it. They have explored whether there are grounds for believing that the inductive principle—so indispensable in science and daily life—is true. All the while we use the principle to make all kinds of inferences and predictions, which usually serve us well.

Hume, for his part, holds that we rely on the principle of induction not because it is an established truth, but because it is a habit of mind. Because of our long experience of seeing one event repeatedly follow another, we develop a feeling of expectation that they will always follow one another.

20 What is Hume's argument against the principle of induction? Does his view imply that we must discard all inductive reasoning or scientific research? Why or why not?

Science is organized knowledge. Wisdom is organized life.
—Immanuel Kant

By now you probably know that Hume's skepticism extends beyond causality and induction to the existence of the external world. He reasons that because all we can directly know is our experience, we can never be sure that an external world exists beyond our internal perceptions:

David Hume, *An Enquiry Concerning Human Understanding*

By what argument can it be proved, that the perceptions of the mind must be caused by external objects, entirely different from them, though resembling them (if that be possible) and could not arise either from the energy of the mind itself, or from the suggestion of some invisible and unknown spirit, or from some other cause still more unknown to us? It is acknowledged, that, in fact, many of these perceptions arise not from any thing external, as in dreams, madness, and other diseases. And nothing can be more inexplicable than the manner, in which body should so operate upon mind as ever to convey an image of itself to a substance, supposed of so different, and even contrary a nature.

It is a question of fact, whether the perceptions of the senses be produced by external objects, resembling them: how shall this question be determined? By experience surely; as all other questions of a like nature. But here experience is, and must be entirely silent. The mind has never any thing present to it but the perceptions, and cannot possibly reach any experience of their connexion with objects. The supposition of such a connexion is, therefore, without any foundation in reasoning.[19]

Provoked by Hume's radical skepticism, philosophers have expended a great deal of energy trying to show that his views on causality, induction, and the external world are partly or wholly unfounded. But the brilliant Hume has put forward some compelling arguments, and they have proven hard to counter.

WRITING TO UNDERSTAND:
CRITIQUING PHILOSOPHICAL VIEWS Section 6.3

1. Summarize and evaluate Locke's case against innate ideas. Does he successfully show that innate ideas do not exist?
2. Assess Locke's argument that we can have knowledge of an external world despite our being directly aware only of sense data. Do you agree with him, or do you side with his critics who say that we can know only the contents of our minds?
3. Evaluate arguments for and against Berkeley's subjective idealism. Do you accept or reject his theory? Why or why not?
4. Suppose someone claims that he can easily refute Berkeley's idealism by simply kicking a rock or eating an apple. Does this demonstration show that Berkeley's view is false? Explain.
5. Do you agree with Hume that any belief not based on perceptions (which includes all theological and metaphysical beliefs) cannot be knowledge and is completely meaningless? Give reasons for your view.

6.4 THE KANTIAN COMPROMISE

Immanuel Kant was sure that knowledge was possible, that we can know many things about the world, most notably countless propositions in mathematics and science. But Hume had raised serious doubts about the possibility of this knowledge, and his extreme skepticism shocked Kant into trying to show that Hume was wrong. Kant declares,

> I openly confess, the suggestion of David Hume was the very thing, which many years ago first interrupted my dogmatic slumber, and gave my investigations in the field of speculative philosophy a quite new direction. I was far from following him in the conclusions at which he arrived. . . .[20]

Hume had maintained that knowledge of the world comes entirely from experience; we know nothing unless our knowledge can be traced back to perceptions (sense data and internal states). Moreover, he had insisted that we have access *only* to these inner experiences. We have direct awareness of our own perceptions, but not of the world beyond them. This means that the empirical laws and principles of science, which scientists regard as universal and changeless, cannot be known. They cannot be known because they assert more than experience is capable of establishing. This skeptical conclusion, Hume had argued, applies even to the principle at the heart of the scientific enterprise—the law of cause and effect. He had maintained that our experience cannot reveal to us any causal connections, for all we can actually perceive is some events following other events. And even if we could repeatedly observe a particular sequence of cause and effect, we still could not conclude that the sequence would happen the same way in the future. We may drop a baseball from the roof of a house and watch it fall downward, and we may repeat this little experiment a hundred times with the same result. But according to Hume, we have no basis for inferring—and therefore do not know—that exactly the same thing will happen on the hundred-first try. So Hume's view meant that scientists could never legitimately conclude that they had discovered a universal, changeless law of nature. They could not know what they thought they knew. This was the conclusion that so exasperated Kant—and that set him on his quest to disprove it.

To map out the epistemological differences between Hume and Kant, we can apply some terms that Kant himself used. Two of these terms we have already met: a priori statements (statements known independently of or prior to experience) and a posteriori statements (statements that depend entirely on sense experience). Two new terms are analytic and synthetic. An **analytic statement** is a logical truth whose denial results in a contradiction. For example, "All brothers are male" is analytic. To deny it—to say that "It is not the case that all brothers are male"—is to say that some males are not males, which is a contradiction. Or consider, "All bodies are extended (occupying space)." To deny this is to say that something extended is not extended—another contradiction. Analytic statements are necessarily true (cannot be false), but trivially so. They are true but tell us nothing about the world. The statement about brothers is obviously true but does not tell us whether

> And seeing ignorance is the curse of God, Knowledge the wing wherewith we fly to heaven.
> —William Shakespeare

An **analytic statement** is a logical truth whose denial results in a contradiction.

A **synthetic statement** is a statement that is not analytic.

any brothers exist. A **synthetic statement** is one that is not analytic. It does tell us something about the world, and denying it does not yield a contradiction. Science specializes in synthetic statements and so do we in our everyday lives. Examples include "every event has a cause," "the planets orbit around the sun," "from nothing comes nothing," "water boils at 100 degrees C at sea level," and "Abraham Lincoln was born in the United States."

Both Hume and Kant agree that we can know analytic statements without appealing to experience (that is, a priori). (Remember, Hume refers to such statements as "relations of ideas.") Through reason alone we can come to know such analytic a priori propositions as "all brothers are male" and "all bodies are extended." But Hume also holds that we can know synthetic propositions (those that are informative about the world) *only* a posteriori (only through experience). And this synthetic a posteriori knowledge ("matters of fact") is limited: We cannot know what our perceptions cannot detect. According to Hume, we are not able to directly observe causality at work, and we cannot infer universal propositions or laws based on limited, local observations. The empiricist path to knowledge, then, is detoured by skepticism. Kant, on the other hand, insists that synthetic a priori knowledge is possible. We can indeed know things about the world, and we can know them independently or prior to experience. Because this knowledge is a priori, it is both necessarily true and universally applicable, a far cry from Hume's extensive skepticism. Kant says we can know that every event has a cause (a synthetic truth), and we can acquire this knowledge a priori, through our powers of reason:

Immanuel Kant, *Critique of Pure Reason*

. . . if we seek an example from the understanding in its quite ordinary employment, the proposition, 'every alteration must have a cause,' will serve our purpose. In the latter case, indeed, the very concept of a cause so manifestly contains the concept of a necessity of connection with an effect and of the strict universality of the rule, that the concept would be altogether lost if we attempted to derive it, as Hume has done, from a repeated association of that which happens with that which precedes, and from a custom of connecting representations, a custom originating in this repeated association, and constituting therefore a merely subjective necessity.[21]

21 Contemporary scientists assert that in the realm of subatomic particles, some events are *not* caused. Does this fact prove false Kant's claim that the law of cause and effect is a synthetic a priori truth?

So Kant's epistemology is neither entirely empiricist nor fully rationalist. He departs radically from tradition by finding a third way—one that sees merit and error in both theories of knowledge. In line with the empiricists, he holds that all knowledge has its origins in experience, but that doesn't mean experience alone is the source of all our knowledge. With a nod to the rationalists, he maintains that experience by itself is blind, but that doesn't mean we can acquire knowledge of the world through reason alone. Kant says that Plato took this latter route and, like a

PHILOSOPHERS AT WORK

Figure 6.11 Immanuel Kant, quiet revolutionary.

Immanuel Kant

Immanuel Kant (1724–1804), a small-town man of conventional living, started a revolution in philosophy and earned the title of the greatest philosopher of the last three hundred years. A superficial look at his life would lead many to think he was about as dull and as unimaginative as one could get. He was born, lived all his life, and died in Königsberg, East Prussia (now Kaliningrad). His habits were so regimented that the good folk of his town could set their watches to his punctual, daily stroll.

But appearances can be deceiving. Kant had many friends, was charming and interesting in conversation, participated in many of the scholarly debates of his time, and made exciting discoveries in both science and philosophy. Early in his career he wrote about physics and astronomy and predicted the existence of the planet Uranus, which was found three-quarters of a century after his death.

Kant studied at the University of Königsberg for six years, later served as a private tutor, and then in 1755 began lecturing at the university, an appointment that lasted over forty years. He taught physics, mathematics, geography, philosophy (all the main areas of study), and more. Most of his writings reflected his relentless search for the proper philosophical foundations or methods in science, metaphysics, and ethics. In epistemology, he effected his Copernican revolution by turning the conventional assumptions about knowledge upside down. To acquire knowledge, he said, the mind does not conform to reality—rather, reality conforms to the mind. Thus, he found what he thought was a third path to knowledge between empiricism and rationalism, extracting from each their grains of truth and changing epistemology forever.

He published his greatest work, *The Critique of Pure Reason*, in 1781. After that came an extraordinary procession of other influential writings, including *Prolegomena to Any Future Metaphysics* (1783), *Groundwork of the Metaphysic of Morals* (1785), *Metaphysical Foundations of Natural Science* (1786), *Critique of Practical Reason* (1788), and *Religion within the Limits of Reason Alone* (1793).

dove trying to fly in empty space with no air resistance, found himself trying to reason about reality with no raw material (experience) to reason about:

There can be no doubt that all our knowledge begins with experience. For how should our faculty of knowledge be awakened into action did not objects affecting our senses partly of themselves produce representations, partly arouse the activity of

Immanuel Kant,
Critique of Pure Reason

Immanuel Kant,
Critique of Pure Reason

our understanding to compare these representations, and, by combining or separating them, work up the raw material of the sensible impressions into that knowledge of objects which is entitled experience? In the order of time, therefore, we have no knowledge antecedent to experience, and with experience all our knowledge begins.

But though all our knowledge begins with experience, it does not follow that it all arises out of experience. For it may well be that even our empirical knowledge is made up of what we receive through impressions and of what our own faculty of knowledge (sensible impressions serving merely as the occasion) supplies from itself. If our faculty of knowledge makes any such addition, it may be that we are not in a position to distinguish it from the raw material, until with long practice of attention we have become skilled in separating it.

The wish to talk to God is absurd. We cannot talk to one we cannot comprehend—and we cannot comprehend God; we can only believe in Him.
—Immanuel Kant

This, then, is a question which at least calls for closer examination, and does not allow of any off-hand answer:—whether there is any knowledge that is thus independent of experience and even of all impressions of the senses. Such knowledge is entitled *a priori*, and distinguished from the *empirical*, which has its sources *a posteriori*, that is, in experience. . . . Mathematics gives us a shining example of how far, independently of experience, we can progress in *a priori* knowledge. . . . Misled by such a proof of the power of reason, the demand for the extension of knowledge recognises no limits. The light dove, cleaving the air in her free flight, and feeling its resistance, might imagine that its flight would be still easier in empty space. It was thus that Plato left the world of the senses, as setting too narrow limits to the understanding, and ventured out beyond it on the wings of the ideas, in the empty space of the pure understanding. He did not observe that with all his efforts he made no advance—meeting no resistance that might, as it were, serve as a support upon which he could take a stand; to which he could apply his powers, and so set his understanding in motion.[22]

22 What is the point Kant is making with the example of a dove flying in empty space? Who do you think is closer to the truth regarding the nature of a priori truth—Plato or Kant?

But Kant cannot simply assert that synthetic a priori knowledge is possible and leave it at that. He must show *how* it's possible. His starting point is the premise (which he thought obvious) that science and mathematics do give us necessary, universal knowledge about the world. From there he argues that something must therefore be fundamentally wrong with both empiricism and rationalism, because these theories fail to explain how this kind of knowledge is possible. In Hume's empiricism, he says, sense experience can shine no light on the outer world, leaving in profound doubt the existence of external objects, causality, and scientific laws. And rationalism promises access to synthetic knowledge while ignoring sense experience, where such knowledge begins. To Kant, only a drastically different approach could demonstrate how synthetic a priori knowledge could be justified.

Where is the Life we have lost in living? Where is the wisdom we have lost in knowledge? Where is the knowledge we have lost in information?
—T. S. Eliot

Actually, to call Kant's approach drastically different is an understatement, for what he proposed was a full-fledged revolution in epistemology that he thought was comparable to the Copernican revolution in science. At a time when the prevailing (and Church-sanctioned) belief was that the sun orbited the earth, Nicolaus Copernicus (1473–1543) thought the better theory was that the earth orbited the sun. Copernicus turned out to be right, and he arrived at his answer through a stunning reversal of the received view. In similar fashion, Kant thought he had instigated his own revolution by turning the traditional perspective on knowledge upside down. For centuries the conventional view was that knowledge is acquired when the mind *conforms to objects*—that is, when the mind tracks the external world. But Kant

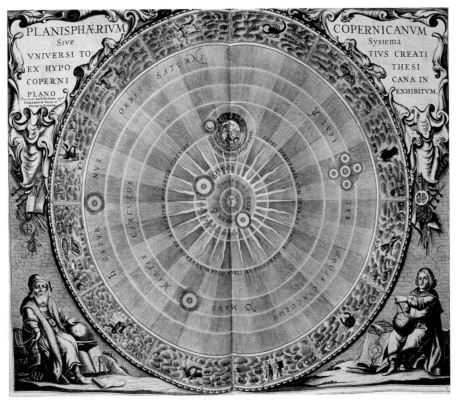

Figure 6.12 Copernican sun-centered (heliocentric) system of planetary motion. Copernicus proposed a reversal of the old earth-centered theory. How was Kant's epistemological system just as revolutionary?

proposed the opposite: *objects conform to the mind*. He argued that sense experience can match reality because the mind stamps a structure and organization on sense experience. Synthetic a priori knowledge is possible, he said, because the mind's concepts force an (a priori) order onto (synthetic) experience. The idea is not that our minds literally create the world, but that our minds organize our experience so we perceive it as recognizable objects. The empiricists see the mind as a passive absorber of sense information, but Kant says the mind is an active shaper of experience into objects that we can know a priori. As he says,

23 What is Kant's Copernican revolution? Is his theory of knowledge more plausible than rationalism or empiricism? Explain.

Immanuel Kant, *Critique of Pure Reason*

Hitherto it has been assumed that all our knowledge must conform to objects. But all attempts to extend our knowledge of objects by establishing something in regard to them *a priori*, by means of concepts, have, on this assumption, ended in failure. We must therefore make trial whether we may not have more success in the tasks of metaphysics, if we suppose that objects must conform to our knowledge. This would agree better with what is desired, namely, that it should be possible to have knowledge of objects *a priori*, determining something in regard to them prior to their being given. . . . If intuition must conform to the constitution of the objects, I do not see how we could know anything of the latter *a priori*; but if the object (as object of the senses) must conform to the constitution of our faculty of intuition, I have no difficulty in conceiving such a possibility.[23]

The learning and knowledge that we have, is, at the most, but little compared with that of which we are ignorant.
—Plato

According to Kant, the mind shapes raw experience by organizing it in accordance with certain fundamental concepts such as time, space, and causality. All our experience is sifted and sorted through the mind's "conceptual processor," without which we could make no sense of the bewildering flow of sights, sounds, smells, and other perceptions. Our raw sense data may consist of a blur of red, for example, but by interpreting this information in light of basic concepts (roundness, space, time, past experience, etc.), our minds perceive a red rose. We therefore know the world only as

PHILOSOPHY NOW

Conceptualizing the World

Kant's view of the mind as an actively constructive faculty is echoed in contemporary psychological research, which shows that our minds constantly construct and interpret our perceptions. That is, our senses are not mere recorders

Figure 6.13 What do you see here—a duck or a rabbit? Although the image does not change, your interpretation can vary so you see either a duck or a rabbit (but not both at the same time). If you change your interpretation of the image, you see something different.

Figure 6.14 Depending on how you conceptualize this figure, you will see a young woman or an old woman.

conceptualized sense data, a world that Kant calls *phenomena*. What the world is *in itself* outside our experience Kant calls *noumena*, a reality forever beyond our ken.

Kant's insight about conceptualized experience might sound odd, but he was on the right track, anticipating findings in modern science by two centuries. Research in developmental and cognitive psychology shows that our perceptions are not the result of the mind's passive recording of sensations. Our perceptions are, to a large degree, *constructed*; they originate with our unfiltered sense experience and

of perceptual information; instead, our minds take the raw data of experience and rework them in light of the concepts and beliefs already in our heads. Our minds must "conceptualize" the raw sensory input so we can understand it. We do this so often and so extensively that we are hardly aware of the process. Consider these three examples of "ambiguous figures." In each case, it's possible to see the figure in two ways—even though the visual input is the same in both.

None of this is controversial. It becomes so when we claim that our immediate, raw sense data are determined entirely by our concepts or theories. This would mean that we experience only what our concepts allow us to see and that we never see the world objectively. Many philosophers reject this view because, among other things, it implies that we would never be able to experience anything new or surprising. But this result seems highly implausible.

Figure 6.15 Do you see a woman's face here—or the silhouette of a saxophone player?

Do these examples prove Kant's constructivist theory of knowledge? Or do they just show that much of our sensory input is conceptualized? Do they show that our conceptualized experience is nothing like what is actually "out there"?

24 What does Kant mean by "Thoughts without content are empty, intuitions without concepts are blind"? Do you agree that at least some of your perceptions are conceptualized?

then are interpreted by the mind according to our preexisting ideas. For example, our experience may consist only of red sensations in dim light, but because we have reason to believe we are looking at a red rose and already have in mind the relevant concepts, we perceive a red rose. We hear only a muffled sound in the next room, but because of our expectations, we perceive the sound as a telephone ring. When we look at a car in the far distance, the image we see is tiny. But because of previous experience and our understanding of how the size of objects stays constant, we perceive the car as having normal dimensions and being actually much larger than we are.

This is how Kant explains the role of sense experience and concepts in our perception of reality:

Immanuel Kant,
Critique of Pure Reason

> Our knowledge springs from two fundamental sources of the mind; the first is the capacity of receiving representations (receptivity for impressions), the second is the power of knowing an object through these representations (spontaneity [in the production] of concepts). Through the first an object is *given* to us, through the second the object is *thought* in relation to that [given] representation (which is a mere determination of the mind). Intuition [raw sense data] and concepts constitute, therefore, the elements of all our knowledge, so that neither concepts without an intuition in some way corresponding to them, nor intuition without concepts, can yield knowledge. . . . Our nature is so constituted that our *intuition* can never be other than sensible; that is, it contains only the mode in which we are affected by objects. The faculty, on the other hand, which enables us to *think* the object of sensible intuition is the understanding. To neither of these powers may a preference be given over the other. Without sensibility no object would be given to us, without understanding no object would be thought. Thoughts without content are empty, intuitions without concepts are blind. It is, therefore, just as necessary to make our concepts sensible, that is, to add the object to them in intuition, as to make our intuitions intelligible, that is, to bring them under concepts. These two powers or capacities cannot exchange their functions. The understanding can intuit nothing, the senses can think nothing. Only through their union can knowledge arise.[24]

It is therefore correct to say that the senses do not err—not because they always judge rightly, but because they do not judge at all.
—Immanuel Kant

Kant thought his theory of knowledge corrected the errors of rationalism and empiricism and expelled the skepticism that these views engendered. In their theories the rationalists had bet heavily on reason as the key to knowledge; the empiricists had bet everything on experience. Kant tried to show that genuine knowledge is a synthesis of both reason and experience. He argued that we can know many things about the world—cause-and-effect relationships, the truths of mathematics, the laws of science—and we can know they are necessarily, universally, and a priori true. We can, in other words, take hold of synthetic a priori knowledge. We can obtain it because our thinking is framed by fundamental concepts that guarantee our experience will take a predetermined form. And we can be sure the truths we discover are universal because all our minds possess the same cognitive structure determined by the same set of innate concepts. In short, Kant's answer to the rationalists, empiricists, and skeptics is that we know the world because we, in effect, constitute it.

After Kant, epistemology was never the same. Anyone who has seriously tried to fathom the nature and extent of our knowledge has had to contend with his insights and arguments. That is not to say that everyone who has delved deeply into Kant has agreed with him. Some philosophers doubt that everyone uses the same set of basic concepts to make sense of the empirical world. They point to anthropological and psychological research showing that not every culture uses the same set of concepts (the same conceptual scheme) to interpret and organize their experience. Other critics have argued that Kant's theory does not adequately explain our certainty that facts about the world must be consistent with logic and mathematics. We think that truths of logic and mathematics are true necessarily and universally *regardless of the structure of our minds*. But Kant wants us to believe that logical and mathematical concepts do depend on the innate structure of our minds. This implies that the structure of our minds could possibly change to make five plus twelve equal thirteen, or make the statement "all brothers are male" false.

These and many other criticisms of Kant's work will be debated for generations to come—which is proof of his lasting influence.

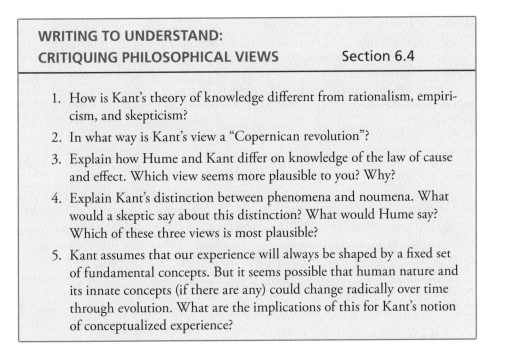

WRITING TO UNDERSTAND:
CRITIQUING PHILOSOPHICAL VIEWS   Section 6.4

1. How is Kant's theory of knowledge different from rationalism, empiricism, and skepticism?

2. In what way is Kant's view a "Copernican revolution"?

3. Explain how Hume and Kant differ on knowledge of the law of cause and effect. Which view seems more plausible to you? Why?

4. Explain Kant's distinction between phenomena and noumena. What would a skeptic say about this distinction? What would Hume say? Which of these three views is most plausible?

5. Kant assumes that our experience will always be shaped by a fixed set of fundamental concepts. But it seems possible that human nature and its innate concepts (if there are any) could change radically over time through evolution. What are the implications of this for Kant's notion of conceptualized experience?

6.5 A FEMINIST PERSPECTIVE ON KNOWLEDGE

Feminism, as both a movement and an approach to social and intellectual issues, is concerned with identifying and remedying harm and disadvantage arising from biases against women. Feminists argue that such prejudices are common throughout society and academia, and that they lead to the widespread discrediting of women's ideas and experiences and the relegating of women to subordinate roles. Feminist philosophy is an attempt to address the disparagement or subordination of women in philosophy and related fields, and feminist epistemology tries to do the same in theories of knowledge.

Doubt is not a very agreeable state, but certainty is a ridiculous one.
—Voltaire

In philosophy, there is no single outlook that can be called feminist; rather, there are several different viewpoints and approaches that deserve the name. The common thread is an emphasis on gender and on how it shapes the issues at hand. Alison Ainley, a feminist philosopher, notes the diversity of the philosophical projects:

Alison Ainley, "Feminist Philosophy"

Feminist approaches to philosophy can take place at a number of levels and from different perspectives, and indeed this has been identified as a notable strength. For example, feminists have presented philosophical critiques of philosophers' images of women, political critiques of the organization of the discipline of philosophy, critiques of philosophy as masculine, historical research into the work of past women philosophers whose work may have been unjustly disregarded, and positive contributions to philosophy from a feminist perspective. Feminist philosophers may take some or all of these approaches to be important, but, generally speaking, feminist philosophy will assume the question of sexual difference to be a philosophical issue at some level and, depending on the point of departure, produce very different ways of theorizing about this question. Although women tend to work in this area, not all women philosophers are necessarily feminist philosophers (although there may be feminist implications in their work).[25]

25 Does the fact that some famous philosophers held negative views of women impugn the nature of the philosophical enterprise? Why or why not?

Feminist thinkers have had good reason to suspect bias in the philosophical enterprise. It is easy in philosophy's history to find eminent male philosophers dismissing, devaluing, or ignoring the female intellect—even though women philosophers have been present in every age, from the classical period to modern times. (Some important male philosophers have afforded women more respect—for example, Plato and John Stuart Mill; and some have developed ideas that have been put to use in feminist writings—for example, David Hume and John Dewey.) Louise M. Antony points out some of the more notorious examples of bias:

Louise M. Antony, "Embodiment and Epistemology"

Although women were largely ignored by the major philosophers, whenever we *were* discussed, we were denigrated. Strikingly, the insult often involved a philosopher's explicitly denying to women some characteristic that that philosopher had elsewhere held to be essential to full personhood, making us, by definition, less than human. Thus Aristotle, who defined "man" as a rational animal, claimed that women's reason was defective in that it was "without the power to be effective." Locke, who thought that "man" could transcend natural power relations by means of civil agreement, still found it obvious that in case of conflict between husband and wife, "the rule . . . naturally falls to the man's share, as the abler and the stronger." Rousseau, who took freedom to be the distinguishing mark of humanity, held that it followed from the different natures of men ("active and strong") and women ("passive and weak") that "woman is made to please and be dominated" by man. Perhaps most notoriously of all, Kant, who made acting from apprehension of the categorical imperative the essence of moral agency, averred that "I hardly believe that the fair sex is capable of principles."[26]

Feminist epistemology focuses most of its attention on the "situated knower" and "situated knowledge"—that is, on how knowledge arises from the unique perspectives and practices of those involved in knowing. The basic claim is that gender has skewed traditional epistemology toward the dominant male perspective and has thus adversely affected women and other disadvantaged groups. Feminist philosophers say the remedy is to develop theories of knowledge based on alternative conceptions of gender and power, banishing the ill effects of the traditional view in the process. According to Elizabeth Anderson,

If women be educated for dependence; that is, to act according to the will of another fallible being, and submit, right or wrong, to power, where are we to stop?
—Mary Wollstonecraft

Elizabeth Anderson, "Feminist Epistemology and Philosophy of Science"

Various practitioners of feminist epistemology and philosophy of science argue that dominant knowledge practices disadvantage women by (1) excluding them from inquiry, (2) denying them epistemic authority, (3) denigrating their "feminine" cognitive styles and modes of knowledge, (4) producing theories of women that represent them as inferior, deviant, or significant only in the ways they serve male interests, (5) producing theories of social phenomena that render women's activities and interests, or gendered power relations, invisible, and (6) producing knowledge (science and technology) that is not useful for people in subordinate positions, or that reinforces gender and other social hierarchies.[27]

Eve Browning Cole, another feminist philosopher, characterizes traditional epistemology like this:

Eve Browning Cole, *Philosophy and Feminist Criticism*

[T]here is widespread agreement that the dominant theories of knowledge provided by the Western philosophical tradition have focused on a specific *kind* of knowledge which is, as Lorraine Code has described it, "a commodity of privilege." Asking such questions as "How do I know that there is a cat on the mat?" assumes that any "I" might be substituted for any other, that conditions of knowing are homogeneous and can be generally specified. All potential knowers have a presumed equal access to the view of the cat, and the epistemologist's job is to explain what is going on in their viewing and whether it amounts to knowledge or something else. But the fact of the matter is that ideal viewing conditions simply do not obtain for all potential viewers; in our society, knowledge conditions are vastly different for members of groups differentiated by gender, race, class, age, economic status, and so forth. An aged woman who cannot get

Eve Browning Cole,
Philosophy and Feminist Criticism

out to see her social worker, or who fears going downtown on the bus alone, will be ignorant of important benefits to which she may be entitled; in this sense, she will not be in a position to view that particular cat on its mat. Traditional epistemologies have not regarded such situations as problematic or interesting; they have not regarded them at all. Yet surely these are situations in which the social and situational *differences* among knowers are crucial for determining the kind of knowing that can take place. Epistemologies that do not have room for these differences doom themselves to irrelevance at best, and at worst they perpetuate injustice—for, as we have already stressed, knowledge *is* power.[28]

26 What is Cole's main point in the preceding passage? Do you agree with her?

To develop alternatives to traditional theories of knowledge, feminist philosophers have explored three epistemological paths: *feminist empiricism*, *feminist standpoint theory*, and *feminist postmodernism*. Feminist empiricism is probably the least controversial. It doesn't want to abolish established theories; instead, it calls for a deeper, more rigorous application of empiricism, a theory with a long history. As Cole says:

Eve Browning Cole,
Philosophy and Feminist Criticism

One way to react to all this is that prescribed by the feminist empiricist, who suggests that philosophy's shortcomings with regard to white women, to women and men of color, to lesbians, and to all the nonprivileged, can be remedied by a more careful adherence to what is after all philosophy's stated mission: the pursuit of wisdom, the search for truth. What has produced the lamentably flawed history of philosophy has been a pattern of failures to live up to the basic scenario of empiricist knowing: the unbiased observation of the face of the universe. Prejudice and bias have been all too clearly present, clouding the judgment of the philosopher and skewing the resultant description.

To give just one famous example: Aristotle, whose allegiance to careful empirical observation is stated and evinced everywhere in his work, is incorrect about the number of teeth women have. He asserts that the adult man has thirty-two teeth but the adult woman only twenty-eight. Now, this cannot have been a function of the difficulty of observation, as women with countable teeth existed in plenty then as now. Rather, scholars have hypothesized that Aristotle counted the teeth in the male jaw and, in the grip of a powerful prejudice, subtracted four to arrive at the number in a woman's (smaller) jaw. Another possibility is that he observed the dentition of a woman who had no wisdom teeth. In either case, Aristotle's mistake is a result of failing to be a *good enough empiricist* rather than something endemic to the method of observation itself.

The feminist empiricist maintains that philosophers and scientists need to be told to "Look again!" rather than to find a wholly new way of looking. The prospects for a better philosophical understanding of human existence and its surroundings will improve as larger numbers of women enter the domains in which "received knowledge" is processed: universities, laboratories, publishing houses, journal editorial boards, and funding agencies. These women will be placed well to point out mistakes in the observations of their colleagues and to set up research agendas that promise to avoid the mistakes of the past.[29]

Nothing can be more absurd than the practice that prevails in our country of men and women not following the same pursuits with all their strengths and with one mind, for thus, the state instead of being whole is reduced to half.
—Plato

Feminist standpoint theory says that different social groups have distinctive kinds of knowledge acquired through unique experiences, and that some of these groups may enjoy epistemological advantages over others. In particular, the type of knowledge derived from women's experiences may be just as good as or better than knowledge acquired by the dominant knowledge-producing group—that is, white, middle-class men of science. Cole explains:

Eve Browning Cole, *Philosophy and Feminist Criticism*

We noted . . . that philosophy's history has issued predominantly from the minds of privileged white males. It was suggested that their position, their standpoint, has had a decisive influence on the shape history has taken. Though many philosophers have presumed to speak for all "mankind," for "Reason itself," or even for "Absolute Spirit," and to be discussing the general "Nature of Mind," "conditions for knowledge," and "the human good," feminist critics have shown and continue to show the limitations of such spuriously universal discourse, and to point out large portions of human experience as yet undreamt of in their philosophy.

This specificity of the traditional standpoint has led some feminist philosophers to explore the potential of basing an epistemology in a feminist (sometimes in a women's) standpoint. The basic assumption, originating in a Hegelian or Marxian view that the human self is essentially shaped by its material activities and situation, is that women's lives have differed from men's lives in ways that would construct clear differences in their respective world views and self-concepts. Since the making and transmitting of knowledge are crucially important human activities, women's "ways of knowing" may be expected to be no less real than men's, but they are also quite likely to be very different from what traditional epistemology has supplied from the white men's standpoint.

Feminist-standpoint epistemologies seek to uncover and describe women's knowledge-making activities as these have originated in and been shaped by women's daily work and women's values. . . .

Now, standpoint theorists in feminist epistemology look at how these different work situations (women's dual-sphere work responsibilities, men's single-sphere work responsibilities) shape personality and character along gender-specific lines. Women, to be proficient workers in both their domains, must become conversant with two different sets of behavior prescriptions: those appropriate to the domestic, personal situations in which they are caregivers and maintainers of life, and those appropriate to the more public and male-dominated locations in which they also labor. Behaviorally, then, and epistemically, they must be able to speak two languages, avail themselves of two different repertoires of rules dictating appropriate activity. . . .

This brings out an important point concerning standpoint theories. Those who advocate the construction of a feminist-standpoint epistemology do not merely maintain that "adding in" this standpoint, derived from women's experiences and practices traditionally excluded from philosophy's purview, will produce better philosophy, science, politics, etc.; they go further and argue that the feminist standpoint has certain inherent epistemic advantages over androcentric [male centered] epistemologies which make it a better place to stand, so to speak, when engaged in the making of knowledge.[30]

Critics, however, have argued that standpoint theory undermines itself. The theory says that the feminist perspective is privileged (for example, better than traditional theories), and that every perspective is both limited and validated by a group's experiences. But there are many different groups and perspectives—how then can the feminist view be better or less limited than any other?

In philosophy, postmodernism is a distrust or rejection of some of the most influential epistemological ideas of modernity: objective or scientific truth, objective reality or fact, universal propositions, foundational knowledge, ultimate justification, and traditional conceptions of rationality. Feminist postmodernism is similarly

I myself have never been able to find out precisely what feminism is: I only know that people call me a feminist whenever I express sentiments that differentiate me from a doormat.
—Rebecca West

27 Which view strikes you as more plausible—feminist empiricism or feminist standpoint theory? Explain.

PHILOSOPHERS AT WORK

Mary Wollstonecraft

Mary Wollstonecraft (1759–1797) was a political radical, a social critic, novelist, and the first English feminist. She was born in London to a financially
strapped family and worked for a while as a schoolteacher
and governess, two of the few jobs open to women
in her situation. She was mostly self-taught and
very well read, eventually showing herself to be an
astute social critic and an insightful moral and po-
litical writer. Much of her literary output was in response to the views of the famous
Edmund Burke, who wrote in support of aristocratic rights and privileges.

Figure 6.16 Mary Wollstonecraft, radical, essayist, novelist,
and feminist.

In the early 1790s, Wollstonecraft had a miserable affair with an American
author named Gilbert Imlay. They never married, and she had a child by him.
She ended the affair in 1796 and later that year fell in love with William Godwin,
whom she married in 1797. They soon had a daughter—later known as Mary Shel-
ley, the eventual author of *Frankenstein*. But ten days after the birth, Wollstonecraft died.

Wollstonecraft's greatest works are *A Vindication of the Rights of Men* (1790)
and *A Vindication of the Rights of Woman* (1792). In the latter, she envisions a society of equals freed from the tyranny of unreason and spurious authority. Such
a society requires the full development of the moral and rational faculties of both
men and women. For too long, she says, women have had their powers of reason
obstructed by men who believe that reason is the domain of men and who define
women in ways that serve men. Men have ensured that women are uneducated,
molded by male expectations, judged by appearances instead of intellect, and
obliged to submit to the preferences of men instead of the dictates of reason.

skeptical of these notions and sets about systematically "deconstructing" them (critically analyzing and debunking them). Feminist postmodernists refuse to accept a
basic tenet of feminist standpoint theory: that there can be a single privileged perspective from which to acquire knowledge. Instead they insist on the existence of
countless perspectives, a plurality of viewpoints, with none able to claim any epistemological advantage over the others. None can be called objectively true, because
there is no perspective-neutral standard by which to judge objective truth. Cole
characterizes feminist postmodernism like this:

Eve Browning Cole,
*Philosophy and Feminist
Criticism*

Feminist postmodern epistemologies are thus essentially critical. Only through a thoroughgoing deconstruction of "our intellectual heritage" (every word of which phrase
should be questioned), an abjuring of privileged standpoints and claims to objective

truth, and a relentless critique of the relation between knowledge-making and power-guarding can a liberatory feminist thinking and practice proceed.

In the absence of objective truth, epistemically privileged standpoints, methodologies legitimated by experts, and all the other apparatus of traditional knowledge-seeking, what will make any knowledge claim more reliable than any other? Is this epistemic anarchism, a situation in which all claims, no matter how bizarre or contradictory, are equally valid? Postmodern feminist epistemologies maintain that knowledge claims will find all the legitimation they need in "localized practices," in the application they find in contexts socially and historically specific, for which they were designed. Thus what will emerge is a kind of *epistemic pluralism*, similar to that seen in [lesbian epistemologies]; the knowledge I need will be made by me, and those immediately surrounding me, in the work we do; it will be circulated to the extent that others' practices encourage such interaction, and will grow or change in this interactive process. What I must not do is dictate in advance the shape this knowledge must take (rational, empirical, justifiable under counterfactual test, etc.) or impose this knowledge on anyone else in some kind of intellectual imperialist frenzy.[31]

Cole also notes the criticisms that have been lodged against the theory by feminists themselves:

Some feminist philosophers express serious concerns about postmodernism as a viable basis for epistemology or for feminist politics in general. If a radical deconstruction of gender categories is carried out, where is the basis for the claim that women as such have anything in common? If gender identity is revealed to be an entirely social construct, a myth told to serve the interests of the lords of culture, where is the basis for feminist thinking? Sisterhood is *not* powerful if it is merely a bad dream caused by some foul cognitive substance we ingested last millennium.

Sandra Harding has expressed concern that the willingness to resign objectivity and individual autonomy to the dustbin of outmoded obsessions is perhaps a luxury many feminists would not afford. Western academic women have "had access to the benefits of the Enlightenment" and thus might give them up more easily than other women, especially third-world women, who have yet to achieve the political autonomy, suffrage and legal rights, and degree of access to the benefits of science their Western sisters enjoy. Thus it is all too easy for Western feminists to criticize the philosophical foundations on which liberalism and modern science rest; such critical latitude is born of privilege.

There are also good reasons for caution about the relinquishing of the concept of objectivity as understood by Western science. Many of the most significant advances in women's political history have been achieved through successfully putting across the argument that barriers to women's freedom are based only on prejudice, a mistaken and subjective attitude. Appeals to fairness, justice, and dispassionate objectivity have been powerful elements in this argument. Most of us believe that sexism, racism, heterosexism, and other pernicious attitudes are not objectively defensible, are based in part on false beliefs and bad faith or moral inconsistency. If we no longer have a standpoint from which to make these claims, with what justification can we continue to decry the attitudes? We ought rather to seek to reconceive the notions of objectivity, justice, and truth than to discard them and leave ourselves rhetorically helpless.[32]

Eve Browning Cole, *Philosophy and Feminist Criticism*

28 Do you think feminist postmodernism undermines itself in the ways that Cole suggests?

> **WRITING TO UNDERSTAND:**
> **CRITIQUING PHILOSOPHICAL VIEWS**   Section 6.5
>
> 1. Some notable male philosophers have assumed that women's reasoning ability is inferior to men's. What conclusion about the philosophical enterprise do you draw from this? Should the theories of these philosophers be rejected out of hand?
>
> 2. Is there such a thing as a *female nature* (a nature whose essence is female)? Or (aside from basic biological factors) is *female* or *woman* defined variously by society or culture?
>
> 3. Kant said that women are not capable of grasping principles, thus excluding women from moral reasoning. Should his theory of knowledge then be discounted, discarded, or ignored? Why or why not?
>
> 4. Are all universal statements in science and ethics suspect, as feminist postmodernists believe? Explain.
>
> 5. Feminist postmodernism has been accused of being a form of cognitive relativism. Is this charge valid? Why or why not?

Review Notes

6.1 OVERVIEW: THE PROBLEM OF KNOWLEDGE

- Epistemology is the philosophical study of knowledge. Propositional knowledge is knowledge of a proposition; a proposition is a statement that is either true or false, an assertion that something is or is not a fact.

- *Skepticism* is the view that we lack knowledge in some fundamental way; *cognitive relativism* is the doctrine that the truth about something depends on what a person or culture believes; *subjective relativism* is the notion that truth depends on what a person believes; *cultural relativism* is the idea that truth depends on what a culture believes; *a priori* knowledge is gained independently of or prior to sense experience; *a posteriori* knowledge depends entirely on sense experience; *rationalism* is the view that through unaided reason we can come to know what the world is like; *empiricism* says knowledge of the empirical world comes solely from sense experience; and *subjective idealism* is the view that all that exist are minds and their ideas.

6.2 THE RATIONALIST ROAD

- Plato believes that the source of our knowledge is reason. He says that we must be able to acquire knowledge because we can identify false beliefs, and we obviously possess knowledge because we can grasp, through reason, mathematical, conceptual, and logical truths. For Plato, reality comprises two worlds: the fleeting world of the physical accessed through sense experience, and the eternal, nonphysical, changeless world of genuine knowledge accessed only through reason. This nonphysical world contains the Forms, which are perfect conceptual models for every existing thing, residing only in the eternal world penetrated by reason alone. Plato believes in innate knowledge—the idea that knowledge of the Forms is already present at birth, inscribed in our minds in a previous existence.

- In *Meno*, Socrates attempts to give a proof of the existence of innate ideas by asking an unschooled boy about a geometry problem. As Socrates asks questions, the boy comes to the right answer on his own. Socrates claims to have merely helped the boy recollect knowledge that he already possessed, bringing innate knowledge to consciousness.

- Descartes initially finds reason to doubt all beliefs based on sense experience, arriving at this conclusion via his dream and evil genius arguments. Then he pulls himself out of skepticism by realizing that he cannot possibly doubt that he exists—for if he can have thoughts, he must exist ("I think, therefore I am"). From this basic idea, he goes on to discover another principle of knowledge acquisition: If he perceives something clearly and distinctly, he must know it with certainty. He must know it with certainty because a perfect God would not allow him to be deceived.

6.3 THE EMPIRICIST TURN

- Locke argues that there is no such thing as innate ideas; universal principles arise from sense experience.

- Locke says that physical objects cause sensations in us, and we are directly aware only of those sensations. But the sensations caused by external objects somehow represent those objects and thereby give us knowledge of them.

- For Locke, primary qualities are objective properties such as size, solidity, and mobility; they are in material objects, independent of our senses. Secondary qualities are subjective properties such as the color red or the smell of a rose; they are in the mind.

- For Berkeley, no material things exist in the external world. There are objects, but they exist only as sensations in some mind. They are real only because they are perceived by someone. He rejects the notion of material objects because, he says, belief in them involves a logical contradiction.

- Locke and Hume are both empiricists. Locke says that we can have knowledge of external objects; Hume asserts that since all we are directly aware of is sense experience, we have no evidence that external objects exist.

- Hume argues that since all claims about the world must be traced back to sense experience, and since theological and metaphysical propositions are not linked to sense experience, such propositions are meaningless.

- Hume contends that we are not justified in believing the principle of induction, because to be justified it has to be either an a priori truth or an a posteriori fact—and it is neither.

6.4 THE KANTIAN COMPROMISE

- Kant brought about a Copernican revolution in epistemology. Just as Copernicus revolutionized astronomy by reversing the traditional theory, so Kant brought forth a radically different theory of knowledge by arguing for an analogous reversal. Instead of accepting the conventional view that knowledge is acquired when the mind conforms to objects, he argues that objects conform to the mind.

- An analytic statement is a logical truth whose denial results in a contradiction. A synthetic statement is one that is not analytic. A synthetic a priori truth asserts something about the world that we can know independently of or prior to experience.

- Kant argues that sense experience can match reality because the mind stamps a structure and organization on sense experience. Synthetic a priori knowledge is possible because the mind's concepts force an (a priori) order onto (synthetic) experience.

6.5 A FEMINIST PERSPECTIVE ON KNOWLEDGE

- Feminist philosophy is an attempt to address the disparagement or subordination of women in philosophy and related fields, and feminist epistemology tries to do the same in theories of knowledge.

- According to Eve Browning Cole, feminists believe that dominant knowledge practices disadvantage women by (1) excluding them from inquiry, (2) denying them epistemic authority, (3) denigrating their "feminine" cognitive styles, (4) producing theories of women that represent them as inferior, deviant, or significant only in the ways they serve male interests, (5) producing theories of social phenomena that render women's activities and interests invisible, and (6) producing knowledge (science and technology) that is not useful for people in subordinate positions, or that reinforces gender and other social hierarchies.

- Feminist empiricism calls for a deeper, more rigorous application of empiricism. Feminist standpoint theory says that different social groups have distinctive kinds of knowledge acquired through unique experiences and some of these groups may enjoy epistemological advantages over others. Feminist postmodernism is skeptical of such notions as objective or scientific truth, objective reality or fact, universal propositions, foundational knowledge, ultimate justification, and traditional conceptions of rationality. Feminist postmodernists are devoted to deconstructing these ideas.

- Some feminists worry that a deconstruction of traditional assumptions about knowledge and truth could undermine feminist philosophy itself and take away an important tool for dismantling barriers to women's freedom.

> **WRITING TO UNDERSTAND:**
> **ARGUING YOUR OWN VIEWS**   Chapter 6
>
> 1. This chapter covers the theories of knowledge produced by Plato, Descartes, Locke, Berkeley, Hume, and Kant. Which one of these do you think is most plausible, and why?
> 2. Which theory do you think is least plausible? Why?
> 3. Evaluate Locke's empiricist theory. What is the strongest argument in its favor? What is the weakest?
> 4. Evaluate Berkeley's main reason for rejecting the existence of material objects. Does he successfully prove his case? Do you believe that material objects exist? Why or why not?
> 5. Explain Hume's argument against the principal of induction. Is his argument sound? In light of the argument, what attitude toward science do you think is most reasonable?

Key Terms

analytic statement A logical truth whose denial results in a contradiction. (299)

a posteriori knowledge Knowledge that depends entirely on sense experience. (266)

a priori knowledge Knowledge gained independently of or prior to sense experience. (266)

cognitive relativism The doctrine that the truth about something depends on what persons or cultures believe. (265)

cultural relativism The view that right actions are those endorsed by one's culture. (265)

empiricism The view that our knowledge of the empirical world comes solely from sense experience. (266)

epistemology The study of knowledge. (263)

principle of induction The presumption that events that followed one another in the past will do the same in the future, that the future will be like the past. (296)

propositional knowledge Knowledge of a proposition. (264)

rationalism The view that through unaided reason we can come to know what the world is like. (266)

skepticism The view that we lack knowledge in some fundamental way. (264)

subjective idealism The doctrine that all that exist are minds and their ideas. (268)

subjective relativism The view that right actions are those endorsed by an individual. (265)

synthetic statement A statement that is not analytic. (300)

FICTION

Through the Looking-Glass

Lewis Carroll

Lewis Carroll (1832–1898), born Charles Lutwidge Dodgson, is most famous for authoring *Alice's Adventures in Wonderland* and *Through the Looking-Glass*, two literary classics. But his interests and talents spread far beyond these books. He also wrote poems and articles, was an innovative photographer, lectured in mathematics at Oxford University, and invented an impressive assortment of games and puzzles.

After a pause, Alice began, "Well—they were *both* very unpleasant characters—"

Here she checked herself in some alarm, at hearing something that sounded to her like the puffing of a large steam-engine in the wood near them, though she feared it was more likely to be a wild beast. "Are there any lions or tigers about here?" she asked timidly.

"It's only the Red King snoring," said Tweedledee.

"Come and look at him!" the brothers cried, and they each took one of Alice's hands, and led her up to where the King was sleeping.

"Isn't he a *lovely* sight?" said Tweedledum.

Alice couldn't say honestly that he was. He had a tall red night-cap on, with a tassel, and he was lying crumpled up into a sort of untidy heap, and snoring loud—"fit to snore his head off!" as Tweedledum remarked.

"I'm afraid he'll catch cold with lying on the damp grass," said Alice, who was a very thoughtful little girl.

"He's dreaming now;" said Tweedledee: "and what do you think he's dreaming about?"

Alice said "Nobody can guess that."

"Why, about *you*!" Tweedledee exclaimed, clapping his hands triumphantly. "And if he left off dreaming about you, where do you suppose you'd be?"

Lewis Carroll, *Alice's Adventures in Wonderland* and *Through the Looking-Glass* (New York: Oxford University Press, 2009).

"Where I am now of course," said Alice.

"Not you!" Tweedledee retorted contemptuously. "You'd be nowhere. Why, you're only a sort of thing in his dream!"

"If that there King was to wake" added Tweedledum, "You'd go out—bang!—just like a candle!"

"I shouldn't!" Alice exclaimed indignantly. "Besides, if *I'm* only a sort of thing in his dream, what are *you*, I should like to know?"

"Ditto," said Tweedledum.

"Ditto, ditto!" cried Tweedledee.

He shouted this so loud that Alice couldn't help saying "Hush! You'll be waking him, I'm afraid, if you make so much noise."

"Well, it's no use *your* talking about waking him," said Tweedledum, "when you're only one of the things in his dream. You know very well you're not real."

"I *am* real!" said Alice, and began to cry.

"You won't make yourself a bit realer by crying," Tweedledee remarked: "there's nothing to cry about."

"If I wasn't real," Alice said—half-laughing through her tears, it all seemed so ridiculous—"I shouldn't be able to cry."

"I hope you don't suppose those are *real* tears?" Tweedledum interrupted in a tone of great contempt.

Probing Questions

1. This exchange between Alice and Tweedledum and Tweedledee can seem unnerving to some readers. Why do you think that is?

2. What is the relationship between this little story and Descartes' dream argument?

3. Suppose Descartes plays the part of Alice in this story. What would he be likely to say about the claim that he is part of the Red King's dream?

For Further Reading

Robert Audi, *Belief, Justification, and Knowledge* (Belmont, CA: Wadsworth, 1988). A student-friendly introduction to epistemology.

Paul Boghossian, *Fear of Knowledge* (Oxford: Oxford University Press, 2006). Concise and powerful critique of relativism and constructionism.

Eve Browning Cole, *Philosophy and Feminist Criticism: An Introduction* (New York: Paragon House, 1993). A readable introduction to feminist criticism of traditional philosophy.

Christopher Grau, ed., *Philosophers Explore the Matrix* (New York: Oxford University Press, 2005). An anthology of philosophical examinations of *The Matrix*. Of special interest is Christopher Grau's article that draws interesting parallels between Descartes' dream and evil genius scenarios and the story that unfolds in *The Matrix*.

Keith Lehrer, *Theory of Knowledge*, 2nd edition (Boulder, CO: Westview Press, 2000). A useful introduction to the traditional and contemporary approaches to knowledge. Includes discussion of the author's own coherence theory of undefeated justification.

Paul K. Moser, *Knowledge and Evidence* (Cambridge: Cambridge University Press, 1989). A robust defense of a foundationalist account of knowledge and justification.

Paul K. Moser, Dwayne H. Mulder, and J. D. Trout, *The Theory of Knowledge: A Thematic Introduction* (New York: Oxford University Press, 1998). A clear and accessible discussion of the main problems and concepts in contemporary epistemology.

Bertrand Russell, *The Problems of Philosophy* (London: Oxford University Press, 1912, 1959). A very readable classic work by an eminent philosopher. Focuses mostly on issues in epistemology.

Roger Trigg, *Reason and Commitment* (Cambridge: Cambridge University Press, 1973). A defense of the possibility of knowledge and justification, and a strong critique of various forms of cognitive relativism.

AESTHETICS

Chapter Objectives

7.1 OVERVIEW: PHILOSOPHY OF BEAUTY

- Define *aesthetics*.
- Understand the difference between moral and aesthetic values.
- Know the questions that aesthetics tries to answer.

7.2 WHAT IS ART?

- Explain the *formalist* view of art.
- Understand the four ways of characterizing art.
- Explain the difference between *art as representation* and *art as expression*.
- Understand Clive Bell's notion of *significant form*.

7.3 AESTHETIC VALUE

- Define *subjectivism* and *objectivism*.
- Distinguish between a functional view and a formal view of aesthetic value.

7.4 PLATO, ARISTOTLE, AND HUME

- Contrast Hume's view of art with Aristotle's.
- Explain Plato's concept of beauty as a Platonic Form.
- Explain Aristotle's concept of *catharsis*.

7.1 OVERVIEW: PHILOSOPHY OF BEAUTY

Let's review. Philosophy concerns itself with what is true, what is real, and what is good. The latter area is the domain of values (also called axiology), which includes both moral values and aesthetic values. As we've seen, moral values and the concepts and experiences that accompany them are the subject matter of ethics. Aesthetic values are examined in the field of philosophy known as **aesthetics**, the study of the feelings, judgments, and views involved in our appreciation and experience of the arts or other objects deemed beautiful. So one part of aesthetics focuses on the aesthetic value and experience of the arts (the philosophy of art), while the other part investigates aesthetic value in beautiful things outside that category (the philosophy of the aesthetic).

Aesthetics deals with works of art: objects that are important to almost everyone, that give us pleasure, that sometimes favor us with a glimpse of the transcendent, but that are neither useful nor essential to our existence. Instead we value them for what they are in themselves, or for their own sake. As the Roman poet Ovid once said, "Nothing is more useful than the arts, which have no utility."

Aesthetics addresses questions that interest not only philosophers but also plenty of nonphilosophers who are affected by what they call beauty in the arts as well as in the natural world. What, if anything, gives an object aesthetic value? Is there such a thing as an aesthetic experience, and if so, how does it differ from other kinds of experiences? Can art be a source of truth or knowledge? Does the perception of beauty have anything to do with moral concerns? Can an art object be beautiful yet express a moral perspective that is despicable? Can some art objects be reasonably judged to be better than others—or are there no standards at all for judging one object superior to another? That is, can anything be *objectively* beautiful?

> The true work of art is but a shadow of the divine perfection.
> —Michelangelo

> **Aesthetics** is the study of the feelings and judgments involved in experiencing the arts or other objects deemed beautiful.

WRITING TO UNDERSTAND:
CRITIQUING PHILOSOPHICAL VIEWS   Section 7.1

1. How are works of art valued in today's society? How do you know if a work of art is "beautiful"?

7.2 WHAT IS ART?

Sometimes the simplest terms are the hardest to define. That is the case with *art*, even though it may seem that any fifth grader would know exactly what the word means. But why do we want a definition of art in the first place? For one thing, we would like to be able to tell "art" from "non-art." We may readily call the *Mona Lisa*, the Sistine Chapel, *Hamlet*, or the Eiffel Tower art, but would we also want to give the label of *art* to cars, tools, clothes, store windows, rustic barns, interior decoration, how-to books about diesel engines, sculptures formed out of excrement, or paintings

> The purpose of art is washing the dust of daily life off our souls.
> —Pablo Picasso

PHILOSOPHY NOW

Controversial Art

It seems that there is always a quarrel brewing somewhere about the aesthetic value or social relevance of a piece of art. The disputes often concern the medium used, the objects depicted or suggested, the ideas evoked, or the supposed messages conveyed—any of which are liable to offend or dismay. Here are two such objects highlighted by Jordan Brooks in "10 Controversial Art Pieces" on the blog *ArtCulture*.

Figure 7.1 This piece is by the New Zealand artist Angela Singer, who is also an activist for animal rights. The medium is dissected dead animals.

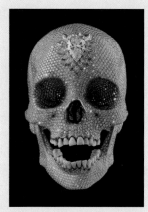

Figure 7.2 A diamond-encrusted skull by Damien Hirst titled *For the Love of God*. Price: $1.8 million.

Do you think either of these works has aesthetic value? If so, which one and why? If not, why not? Figure 7.1 conveys a political message. Does the message add to, detract from, or have no effect on the piece's aesthetic value?

created with the paint-soaked tail of a dog? How do we distinguish artifacts that we consider art from objects that we think are definitely *not* art?

Traditionally art has been characterized in four ways. The first is the easiest to grasp: art is *representation*. In this theory, to create art objects is to depict or imitate objects in the world—in paint, clay, stone, poetry, or other media. Representational art has been with us for a very long time, from the earliest cave drawings to Plato's notion of art as imitation to the present day. Modern theorists point out that representation in art does not mean making an exact copy of an object. Every attempt to depict reality is necessarily shaped by the artist's own perspective. Da Vinci's

> The aim of art is to represent not the outward appearance of things, but their inward significance.
> —Aristotle

Mona Lisa, Michelangelo's *David*, Rodin's *The Thinker*, Vermeer's *Girl with a Pearl Earring*, the *Venus de Milo*, Van Gogh's *Irises*—these and countless other works are representational yet reflective of the artist's interpretation.

Another definition says that art is *expression*. This view holds that art is a way of communicating the artist's feelings and prompting others to experience those same feelings. The great Russian novelist Leo Tolstoy (1828–1910) declared, "Art is a human activity consisting in this, that one man consciously, by means of certain external signs, hands on to others feelings he has lived through, and that others are infected by these feelings and also experience them."[1]

By the twentieth century, artists and critics were defining art by its *form*—by the structure or organization of its parts, and such qualities as the unity or harmony of the whole. The content was inessential. This **formalist** view came along as the abstract movement in art was blossoming, and the two seemed made for each other. The art theorist Clive Bell explained art formalism like this:

> **Formalism** is the view that art is defined by its form, the structure or organization of its parts.

Clive Bell, *Art*

What quality is shared by all objects that provoke our aesthetic emotions? Only one answer seems possible—significant form. In each, lines and colors combined in a particular way; certain forms and relations of forms, stir our aesthetic emotions. These relations and combinations of lines and colors, these aesthetically moving forms, I call "Significant Form"; and "Significant Form" is the one quality common to all works of visual art.[2]

1 Do you agree with the expression theory of art? Is art simply an expression of feelings? Is abstract art an expression of feelings?

The fourth way to characterize art is (paradoxically) that it cannot be characterized. In the later half of the twentieth century, the very possibility of devising a plausible definition of art was called into question. To some art theorists, there is no good reason (aside from tradition and convenience) to lump novels, films, dance, operas, songs, and other such things into a single category called *art*.

> If art is to nourish the roots of our culture, society must set the artist free to follow his vision wherever it takes him.
> —John F. Kennedy

WRITING TO UNDERSTAND:
CRITIQUING PHILOSOPHICAL VIEWS   Section 7.2

1. Art has been defined as representation, expression, and formalism. Is it a plausible theory that art is correctly characterized by just one of these three? Why or why not?

7.3 AESTHETIC VALUE

Assuming that art, however defined, is a genuine constituent of human experience, we can ask what gives it aesthetic value. Over the centuries, two broad categories of

2 Does an art object have to serve a function to be art? Would art that serves a racist or criminal function count as art?

WHAT DO YOU BELIEVE?

Are There Objective Standards in Art?

Do you believe that "beauty is in the eye of the beholder"? That is, do you think judgments about art are matters of personal taste, or are there objective standards for gauging aesthetic worth? Here is one persuasive opinion on the subject:

Figure 7.3

I believe there are standards of excellence in all the arts, fine or not so fine, that transcend both individual tastes and cultural norms. . . . In spite of the many ways tastes can vary, I remain convinced that there are some universal standards in art even though we can specify them only in misty ways. Consider again the chair. There may be wide variations in personal taste about how comfortable it is, but because human bodies have roughly the same size and shape, we can say dogmatically that it is a poor chair in any country if it collapses under a weight of twenty pounds, or if its seat is covered with sharp spikes. It is in this trivial sense that we can speak of universal standards concerning the chair's value as a seat.—Martin Gardner, *The Whys of a Philosophical Scrivener*

Do you agree with this position on art standards? Why or why not? What if there were no objective standards—would that make appreciating or judging works of art less or more enjoyable? Would the opinions of art critics seem less or more useful?

answers have arisen among philosophers and other art theorists. First, there is the notion that art has aesthetic value *if it does something*, that is, if it serves some important function—if it inspires exalted or edifying emotions, serves a moral or social purpose, conveys social truths or values, effects change in social or political systems, or rouses sensations of pleasure in the audience. The second category is the idea that art has aesthetic value *if it has particular formal characteristics*. The candidates for these characteristics include unity, coherence, intensity, radiance, and complexity. Bell's "significant form" is a well-known example.

If such criteria exist, then we must be able to distinguish good art from bad art, between *War and Peace* and yesterday's newspaper. But there is considerable debate about whether we can actually do this. Some critics, the **objectivists**, insist that works of art have objective properties by which we can judge their aesthetic goodness or badness. The properties, objectivists argue, exist in the art object. The *Mona Lisa* is good art because its objective properties—its unity and coherence, for example—make it so. Other theorists, the **subjectivists**, deny this and argue instead that whatever aesthetic criteria we have are purely subjective; the apparent aesthetic properties of the art object are in the eye of the beholder. The goodness or badness of a work of art depends on the response of its audience. One person can hold that the *Mona Lisa* is bad art, while another can maintain that it is good art—and they both would be right.

Objectivism (in art) is the view that works of art have objective properties by which we can judge their aesthetic goodness or badness.

Subjectivism (in art) is the view that aesthetic criteria are purely subjective; the goodness or badness of a work of art depends on how the audience responds to it.

I like to pretend that my art has nothing to do with me.
—Roy Lichtenstein

PHILOSOPHERS AT WORK

Figure 7.4

Arthur C. Danto

Arthur Danto (1924–2013) was a philosopher of art and one of the most widely read art critics of the twentieth century. He was a professor of philosophy at Columbia University, an art critic for *The Nation* magazine, and a promoter of Pop artists such as Andy Warhol.

He is probably best known in aesthetics for his concept of the "artworld." He argues that what distinguishes art from non-art is not something that can be perceived in the artwork itself. Objects are identified as works of art if they are situated in a particular artworld—a social-historical context that includes such things as the works of artists, the conventions of art, the history of art, and the practices of artists and critics. Art, in other words, exists in "an atmosphere of art theory."

In 1964 Danto saw Andy Warhol's sculpture titled *Brillo Box*, a simple imitation of a lowly consumer item, a box of Brillo soap-pads. Danto asked what the difference was between the *Brillo Box* object and the store-bought item. What made the former art and the latter not art? His answer was that *Brillo Box* was recognized and understood in an artworld.

Danto is the author of *Nietzsche as Philosopher* (1965), *The Transfiguration of the Commonplace* (1981), *Beyond the Brillo Box* (1992), *After the End of Art* (1997), *The Abuse of Beauty* (2003), and *What Art Is* (2013).

7.4 PLATO, ARISTOTLE, AND HUME

Plato and Aristotle have had enormous influence on aesthetics, shaping thought and debate about beauty generally (not just in art), representation in art creation, and aesthetic virtues. Plato is an objectivist, but in a unique way. His view is that true beauty is not of this world. Beauty is a Platonic Form, an ideal entity existing in a perfect, non-physical, unchanging realm apart from the ephemeral, physical world we inhabit. The sphere of the Forms is the *really* real world, the place where the perfect models of reality reside. The world we live in is less real. Something is beautiful in this less real world if it participates in, or imitates, the Form of Beauty, and through reason we can sometimes glimpse true Beauty if we manage to look beyond the dim, earthly objects that we deem beautiful. So there is an objective standard by which we can judge beauty in nature and in works of art. The challenge is to access this standard—the ideal of Beauty—so we can see more clearly where beauty resides (or does not reside) in the objects of this world.

Aristotle is also an objectivist, but not in the sense that Plato is. For Aristotle, beauty is a property of objects in the everyday world, and through knowledge and skill we can create beautiful things. The arts need not fulfill a function to be valuable—they are to be cherished for their own sakes; that is, art for art's sake. To have aesthetic value, a sculpture needs only to be beautiful.

Aristotle, like many theorists of modern times, characterizes art as expression. In *The Poetics*, his treatise on tragedies, he emphasizes the concept of **catharsis**, the purging of the emotions of pity and fear by experiencing them vicariously in a theatrical context.

As an objectivist, he believes there are objective standards by which we may judge art and beauty generally. In the *Poetics* he first distinguishes tragedy from other art forms and then explores the features that make for good and bad tragedies. Here is an excerpt:

Abstract art: a product of the untalented sold by the unprincipled to the utterly bewildered.
—Al Capp

Catharsis is the purging of the emotions of pity and fear by experiencing them vicariously in a theatrical context.

Aristotle, *The Poetics*

CHAPTER 7

Now, we have settled that a tragedy is a *mimesis* [imitation, representation] of a complete, that is, of a whole action, "whole" here implying some amplitude (there can be a whole without amplitude).

By "whole" I mean "with a beginning, a middle, and an end." By "beginning" [in this context] I mean "that which is not necessarily the consequent of something else, but has some state or happening naturally consequent on it," by "end" a state that is the necessary or usual consequent of something else, but has itself no such consequent," by "middle" that which is consequent and has consequents." Well-ordered plots, then, will exhibit these characteristics, and will not begin or end just anywhere.

It is not enough for beauty that a thing, whether an animal or anything else composed of parts, should have those parts well ordered; since beauty consists in amplitude as well as in order, the thing must also have amplitude—and not just any amplitude. Though a very small creature could not be beautiful, since our view loses all distinctness when it comes near to taking no perceptible time, an enormously ample one could not be beautiful either, since our view of it is not simultaneous, so that we lose the sense of its unity and wholeness as we look it over; imagine, for instance, an animal a thousand miles long. Animate and inanimate bodies, then, must have amplitude, but no more than can be taken in at one view; and similarly a plot must have extension, but no more than can be easily remembered. What is, for the poetic art, the limit of this extension? Certainly not that imposed by the contests and by perception. . . . As the limit imposed by the actual nature of the thing, one may suggest "the ampler the better, provided it remains clear as a whole," or, to give a rough specification, "sufficient amplitude to allow a probable or necessary succession of particular actions to produce a change from bad to good or from good to bad fortune."

3 What is Aristotle's idea of amplitude? How does he define proper amplitude?

CHAPTER 9

What I have said also makes plain that the poet's job is saying not what did happen but the sort of thing that would happen, that is, what can happen in a strictly probable or necessary sequence. The difference between the historian and the poet is not merely that one writes verse and the other prose—one could turn Herodotus' work into verse

PHILOSOPHY LAB

Suppose you are the curator of a world-class art museum, and you have the job of selecting new pieces for the summer exhibition. You must now justify your decision to exhibit or not exhibit two pieces that have received wide international acclaim. One is an eight-foot-high marble sculpture depicting a nude man and woman in a passionate embrace, and the other is a five-foot-diameter black metal sphere resting on a sheet of glass.

On what grounds can you justify showing these sculptures? How can you justify not showing them? You may appeal to the definition of art, aesthetic values, the reaction of the local community, and the apparent aesthetic function of each piece.

and it would be just as much history as before; the essential difference is that the one tells us what happened and the other the sort of thing that would happen. That is why poetry is at once more like philosophy and more worth while than history, since poetry tends to make general statements, while those of history are particular. A "general statement" means [in this context] one that tells us what sort of man would, probably or necessarily, say or do what sort of things, and this is what poetry aims at, though it attaches proper names; a particular statement on the other hand tells us what Alcibiades, for instance, did or what happened to him. . . .

It is obvious from all this that the poet should be considered a maker of plots, not of verses, since he is a poet *qua* maker of *mimesis* and the objects of his *mimesis* are actions. Even if it is incidentally true that the plot he makes actually happened, that does not mean he is not its maker; for there is no reason why some things that actually happen should not be the sort of thing that would probably happen, and it is in virtue of that aspect of them that he is their maker.

Of defective plots or actions the worst are the episodic, those, I mean, in which the succession of the episodes is neither probable nor necessary; bad poets make these on their own account, good ones because of the judges; for in aiming at success in the competition and stretching the plot more than it can bear they often have to distort the natural order.

Tragedy is a *mimesis* not only of a complete action, but also of things arousing pity and fear, emotions most likely to be stirred when things happen unexpectedly but because of each other (this arouses more surprise than mere chance events, since even chance events seem more marvellous when they look as if they were meant to happen—take the case of the statue of Mitys in Argos killing Mitys' murderer by falling on him as he looked at it; for we do not think that things like this are merely random); so such plots will necessarily be the best. . . .

CHAPTER 13

What ought one to aim at and beware of in composing plots? And what is the source of the tragic effect? These are the questions that naturally follow from what I have now dealt with.

Well, the arrangement of tragedy at its best should be complex, not simple, and it should also present a *mimesis* of things that arouse fear and pity, as this is what is peculiar to the tragic *mimesis*.

4 According to Aristotle, what emotions should a tragedy evoke? What is the point of evoking them?

So it is clear that one should not show virtuous men passing from good to bad fortune, since this does not arouse fear or pity, but only a sense of outrage. Nor should one show bad men passing from bad to good fortune, as this is less tragic than anything, since it has none of the necessary requirements; it neither satisfies our human feeling nor arouses pity and fear. Nor should one show a quite wicked man passing from good to bad fortune; it is true that such an arrangement would satisfy our human feeling, but it would not arouse pity or fear, since the one is felt for someone who comes to grief without deserving it, and the other for someone like us (pity, that is, for the man who does not deserve his fate, and fear for someone like us); so this event will not arouse pity or fear. So we have left the man between these. He is one who is not pre-eminent in moral virtue, who passes to bad fortune not through vice or wickedness, but because of some piece of ignorance, and who is of high repute and great good fortune, like Oedipus and Thyestes and the splendid men of such families.

So the good plot must have a single line of development, not a double one as some people say; that line should go from good fortune to bad and not the other way round; the change should be produced not through wickedness, but through some

The artist belongs to his work, not the work to the artist.
—Novalis

large-scale piece of ignorance; the person ignorant should be the sort of man I have described—certainly not a worse man, though perhaps a better one. . . .

Well then, the best tragedy, judged from the standpoint of the tragic art, comes from this sort of arrangement. That is why those who censure Euripides for doing this in his tragedies and making many of them end with disaster are making just the same mistake. For this is correct in the way I said. The greatest proof of this is that on the stage and in the contests such plays are felt to be the most properly tragic, if they are well managed, and Euripides, even if he is a bad manager in the other points, is at any rate the most tragic of the poets.

Second comes the sort of arrangement that some people say is the best: this is the one that has a double arrangement of the action like the *Odyssey*, and ends with opposite fortunes for the good and bad people. It is thought to be the best because of the weakness of the audiences; for the poets follow the lead of the spectators and make plays to their specifications. But this is not the pleasure proper to tragedy, but rather belongs to comedy; for in comedy those who are most bitter enemies throughout the plot, as it might be Orestes and Aegisthus, are reconciled at the end and go off and nobody is killed by anybody.[3]

David Hume's view of aesthetic judgment and value diverges radically from Aristotle's. Hume contends that aesthetic judgments (what he calls "judgments of taste") are ultimately based on the sensibilities of the individual. The standard of aesthetic taste is to be found not in the art object itself but in subjective experience. "Beauty," he says, "is no quality in things themselves: It exists merely in the mind which contemplates them; and each mind perceives a different beauty." But for Hume, this subjectivism need not lead to wholesale relativism, in which any aesthetic judgment is as good as any other. He argues that there are stable relationships between objects in the world and the particular responses they elicit in us. "Some particular forms or qualities [in objects]," he says, "are calculated to please [aesthetically], and others to displease [aesthetically]." Some individuals are more keenly attuned to these relationships than others; their aesthetic sensibilities are more "delicate." With practice in cultivating aesthetic taste, these people become superior judges of aesthetic value. They, in other words, become critics.

Hume's aesthetic theory thus explains the commonsense view that art objects can vary radically in aesthetic value: clearly a *Mona Lisa* is aesthetically superior to a stick figure on a cave wall. The theory also explains why some observers are better judges of the aesthetic quality of art than others.

David Hume, *Of the Standard of Taste*

It is natural for us to seek a *Standard of Taste*; a rule, by which the various sentiments of men may be reconciled; at least, a decision afforded, confirming one sentiment, and condemning another.

There is a species of philosophy, which cuts off all hopes of success in such an attempt, and represents the impossibility of ever attaining any standard of taste.

The difference, it is said, is very wide between judgment and sentiment. All sentiment is right; because sentiment has a reference to nothing beyond itself, and is always real, wherever a man is conscious of it. But all determinations of the understanding are not right; because they have a reference to something beyond themselves, to wit, real matter of fact; and are not always conformable to that standard. Among a thousand different opinions which different men may entertain of the same subject, there is one, and but one, that is just and true; and the only difficulty is to fix and ascertain it. On the contrary, a thousand different sentiments, excited by the same object, are all right: Because no sentiment represents what is really in the object. It only marks a certain conformity or relation between the object and the organs or faculties of the mind; and if that conformity did not really exist, the sentiment could never possibly have being. Beauty is no quality in things themselves: It exists merely in the mind which contemplates them; and each mind perceives a different beauty. One person may even perceive deformity, where another is sensible of beauty; and every individual ought to acquiesce in his own sentiment, without pretending to regulate those of others. To seek the real beauty, or real deformity, is as fruitless an enquiry, as to pretend to ascertain the real sweet or real bitter. According to the disposition of the organs, the same object may be both sweet and bitter; and the proverb has justly determined it to be fruitless to dispute concerning tastes. It is very natural, and even quite necessary, to extend this axiom to mental, as well as bodily taste; and thus common sense, which is so often at variance with philosophy, especially with the sceptical kind, is found, in one instance at least, to agree in pronouncing the same decision.

5 Hume says that the attributes of a piece of art are not in the object itself but in the mind. What does he mean by this?

But though this axiom, by passing into a proverb, seems to have attained the sanction of common sense; there is certainly a species of common sense which opposes it, at least serves to modify and restrain it. Whoever would assert an equality of genius and elegance between OGILBY and MILTON, or BUNYAN and ADDISON, would be thought to defend no less an extravagance, than if he had maintained a mole-hill to be as high as TENERIFFE, or a pond as extensive as the ocean. Though there may be found persons, who give the preference to the former authors; no one pays attention to such a taste; and we pronounce without scruple the sentiment of these pretended critics to be absurd and ridiculous. The principle of the natural equality of tastes is then totally forgot, and while we admit it on some occasions, where the objects seem near an equality, it appears an extravagant paradox, or rather a palpable absurdity, where objects so disproportioned are compared together.

Art for art's sake is a philosophy of the well-fed.
—Frank Lloyd Wright

It is evident that none of the rules of composition are fixed by reasonings *a priori*, or can be esteemed abstract conclusions of the understanding, from comparing those habitudes and relations of ideas, which are eternal and immutable. Their foundation is the same with that of all the practical sciences, experience; nor are they any thing but general observations, concerning what has been universally found to please in all countries and in all ages. Many of the beauties of poetry and even of eloquence are founded on falsehood and fiction, on hyperboles, metaphors, and an abuse or perversion of terms from their natural meaning. To check the sallies of the imagination, and to reduce every expression to geometrical truth and exactness, would be the most contrary to the laws of criticism; because it would produce a work, which, by universal experience, has been found the most insipid and disagreeable. But though poetry can never submit to exact truth, it must be confined by rules of art, discovered to the author either by genius or observation. If some negligent or irregular writers have pleased, they have not pleased by their transgressions of rule or order, but in spite of these transgressions: They have possessed other beauties, which were conformable to just criticism; and the force of these beauties has been able to overpower censure, and give the mind a satisfaction superior to the disgust arising from the blemishes. . . .

But though all the general rules of art are founded only on experience and on the observation of the common sentiments of human nature, we must not imagine, that, on every occasion, the feelings of men will be conformable to these rules. Those finer emotions of the mind are of a very tender and delicate nature, and require the concurrence of many favourable circumstances to make them play with facility and exactness, according to their general and established principles. The least exterior hindrance to such small springs, or the least internal disorder, disturbs their motion, and confounds the operation of the whole machine. When we would make an experiment of this nature, and would try the force of any beauty or deformity, we must choose with care a proper time and place, and bring the fancy to a suitable situation and disposition. A perfect serenity of mind, a recollection of thought, a due attention to the object; if any of these circumstances be wanting, our experiment will be fallacious, and we shall be unable to judge of the catholic and universal beauty. The relation, which nature has placed between the form and the sentiment, will at least be more obscure; and it will require greater accuracy to trace and discern it. We shall be able to ascertain its influence not so much from the operation of each particular beauty, as from the durable admiration, which attends those works, that have survived all the caprices of mode and fashion, all the mistakes of ignorance and envy. . . .

It appears then, that, amidst all the variety and caprice of taste, there are certain general principles of approbation or blame, whose influence a careful eye may trace in all operations of the mind. Some particular forms or qualities, from the original structure of the internal fabric, are calculated to please, and others to displease; and if they fail of their effect in any particular instance, it is from some apparent defect or imperfection in the organ. A man in a fever would not insist on his palate as able to decide concerning flavours; nor would one, affected with the jaundice, pretend to give a verdict with regard to colours. In each creature, there is a sound and a defective state; and the former alone can be supposed to afford us a true standard of taste and sentiment. If, in the sound state of the organ, there be an entire or a considerable uniformity of sentiment among men, we may thence derive an idea of the perfect beauty; in like manner as the appearance of objects in day-light, to the eye of a man in health, is denominated their true and real colour, even while colour is allowed to be merely a phantasm of the senses.[4]

WRITING TO UNDERSTAND:

CRITIQUING PHILOSOPHICAL VIEWS   Section 7.4

1. What is David Hume's view of art? Is his subjectivist view of art plausible? Can it really be the case that pieces of art have no objective qualities that make them good?

2. Which theory of art makes the most sense to you—Plato's or Aristotle's? Why?

Review Notes

7.1 OVERVIEW: PHILOSOPHY OF BEAUTY

- *Aesthetics* is the study of the feelings and judgments involved in experiencing the arts or other objects deemed beautiful.
- Moral values have to do with right and wrong acts and good and bad persons. Aesthetic values have to do with good and bad works of art and other objects that could be judged beautiful.
- Aesthetics asks: What, if anything, gives an object aesthetic value? Can art be a source of truth or knowledge? Does the perception of beauty have anything to do with moral concerns? Can some art objects be reasonably judged to be better than others—or are there no standards at all for judging one object superior to another? That is, can anything be objectively beautiful?

7.2 WHAT IS ART?

- *Formalism* is the view that art is defined by its form, the structure or organization of its parts. *Representation* is the notion that creating art objects is depicting or imitating objects in the world. *Expression* asserts that art is a way of communicating the artist's feelings and prompting others to experience those same feelings.

7.3 AESTHETIC VALUE

- *Objectivism* is the view that works of art have objective properties by which we can judge their aesthetic goodness or badness. *Subjectivism* says that aesthetic criteria are purely subjective; the goodness or badness of a work of art depends on how the audience responds to it.
- *Functionalism* is the idea that art must serve some important function—engendering exalted or edifying emotions, serving a moral or social purpose, conveying social truths or values, effecting change in social or political systems, or arousing sensations of pleasure in the audience.

7.4 PLATO, ARISTOTLE, AND HUME

- Plato is an objectivist. His view is that Beauty is a Platonic Form, an ideal entity existing in a perfect, nonphysical, unchanging realm apart from the ephemeral, physical world we inhabit.
- Aristotle is also an objectivist. For him, beauty is a property of objects in the everyday world. The arts need not fulfill a function to be valuable—they are to be cherished for their own sakes. For him, an essential part of tragedy is catharsis,

the purging of the emotions of pity and fear by experiencing them vicariously in a theatrical context.

- Hume contends that aesthetic judgments are ultimately based on the sensibilities of the individual. The standard of aesthetic taste is to be found not in the art object itself but in subjective experience. But this subjectivism need not lead to wholesale relativism in which any aesthetic judgment is as good as any other.

WRITING TO UNDERSTAND: ARGUING YOUR OWN VIEWS   Chapter 7

1. Are you an objectivist or subjectivist about art? Why?

2. Critique Arthur Danto's institutional theory of art. One criticism of it is that if people in the artworld define what is and is not art, then there seems to be no way for the decision-makers to decide among themselves what art is. Is this a fair criticism? Why or why not?

3. Is the *Mona Lisa* art? Why or why not?

4. Is the meat sculpture *Pinky and Perky* art? (See the photo in the box "Are There Objective Standards in Art?") Why or why not?

5. Do you agree with Danto that an object is art only if museums and art shows exhibit it? Explain.

Key Terms

aesthetics The study of the feelings and judgments involved in experiencing the arts or other objects deemed beautiful. (321)

catharsis The purging of the emotions of pity and fear by experiencing them vicariously in a theatrical context. (326)

formalism The view that art is defined by its form, the structure or organization of its parts. (323)

objectivism (in art) The view that works of art have objective properties by which we can judge their aesthetic goodness or badness. (323)

subjectivism (in art) The view that aesthetic criteria are purely subjective; the goodness or badness of a work of art depends on how the audience responds to it. (323)

The Oval Portrait

Edgar Allan Poe

> While Edgar Allan Poe (1809–1849) is perhaps best known to modern readers for his horror stories, he was also an accomplished poet and critic. "The Oval Portrait," first published in 1842, includes a theme that recurs in several stories as well as in his later critical essay "The Philosophy of Composition": that "the most poetical topic in the world" is "the death . . . of a beautiful woman."

The chateau into which my valet had ventured to make forcible entrance, rather than permit me, in my desperately wounded condition, to pass a night in the open air, was one of those piles of commingled gloom and grandeur which have so long frowned among the Apennines, not less in fact than in the fancy of Mrs. Radcliffe. To all appearance it had been temporarily and very lately abandoned. We established ourselves in one of the smallest and least sumptuously furnished apartments. It lay in a remote turret of the building. Its decorations were rich, yet tattered and antique. Its walls were hung with tapestry and bedecked with manifold and multiform armorial trophies, together with an unusually great number of very spirited modern paintings in frames of rich golden arabesque. In these paintings, which depended from the walls not only in their main surfaces, but in very many nooks which the bizarre architecture of the chateau rendered necessary—in these paintings my incipient delirium, perhaps, had caused me to take deep interest; so that I bade Pedro to close the heavy shutters of the room—since it was already night—to light the tongues of a tall candelabrum which stood by the head of my bed—and to throw open far and wide the fringed curtains of black velvet which enveloped the bed itself. I wished all this done that I might resign myself, if not to sleep, at least alternately to the contemplation of these pictures, and the perusal of a small volume which had been found upon the pillow, and which purported to criticise and describe them.

Long—long I read—and devoutly, devotedly I gazed. Rapidly and gloriously the hours flew by and the deep midnight. The position of the candelabrum displeased me, and outreaching my hand with difficulty, rather than

disturb my slumbering valet, I placed it so as to throw its rays more fully upon the book.

But the action produced an effect altogether unanticipated. The rays of the numerous candles (for there were many) now fell within a niche of the room which had hitherto been thrown into deep shade by one of the bed-posts. I thus saw in vivid light a picture all unnoticed before. It was the portrait of a young girl just ripening into womanhood. I glanced at the painting hurriedly, and then closed my eyes. Why I did this was not at first apparent even to my own perception. But while my lids remained thus shut, I ran over in my mind my reason for so shutting them. It was an impulsive movement to gain time for thought—to make sure that my vision had not deceived me—to calm and subdue my fancy for a more sober and more certain gaze. In a very few moments I again looked fixedly at the painting.

That I now saw aright I could not and would not doubt; for the first flashing of the candles upon that canvas had seemed to dissipate the dreamy stupor which was stealing over my senses, and to startle me at once into waking life.

The portrait, I have already said, was that of a young girl. It was a mere head and shoulders, done in what is technically termed a vignette manner; much in the style of the favorite heads of Sully. The arms, the bosom, and even the ends of the radiant hair melted imperceptibly into the vague yet deep shadow which formed the background of the whole. The frame was oval, richly gilded and filigreed in Moresque. As a thing of art nothing could be more admirable than the painting itself. But it could have been neither the execution of the work, nor the immortal beauty of the countenance, which had so suddenly and so vehemently moved me. Least of all, could it have been that my fancy, shaken from its half slumber, had mistaken the head for that of a living person. I saw at once that the peculiarities of the design,

From Edgar Alan Poe, "The Oval Portrait" (1842); text from Project Gutenberg, http://www.gutenberg.org/files/2147/2147-h/2147-h.htm#link2H_4_0014.

of the vignetting, and of the frame, must have instantly dispelled such idea—must have prevented even its momentary entertainment. Thinking earnestly upon these points, I remained, for an hour perhaps, half sitting, half reclining, with my vision riveted upon the portrait. At length, satisfied with the true secret of its effect, I fell back within the bed. I had found the spell of the picture in an absolute life-likeliness of expression, which, at first startling, finally confounded, subdued, and appalled me. With deep and reverent awe I replaced the candelabrum in its former position. The cause of my deep agitation being thus shut from view, I sought eagerly the volume which discussed the paintings and their histories. Turning to the number which designated the oval portrait, I there read the vague and quaint words which follow:

"She was a maiden of rarest beauty, and not more lovely than full of glee. And evil was the hour when she saw, and loved, and wedded the painter. He, passionate, studious, austere, and having already a bride in his Art; she a maiden of rarest beauty, and not more lovely than full of glee; all light and smiles, and frolicsome as the young fawn; loving and cherishing all things; hating only the Art which was her rival; dreading only the pallet and brushes and other untoward instruments which deprived her of the countenance of her lover. It was thus a terrible thing for this lady to hear the painter speak of his desire to portray even his young bride. But she was humble and obedient, and sat meekly for many weeks in the dark, high turret-chamber where the light dripped upon the pale canvas only from overhead. But he, the painter, took glory in his work, which went on from hour to hour, and from day to day. And he was a passionate, and wild, and moody man, who became lost in reveries; so that he would not see that the light which fell so ghastly in that lone turret withered the health and the spirits of his bride, who pined visibly to all but him. Yet she smiled on and still on, uncomplainingly, because she saw that the painter (who had high renown) took a fervid and burning pleasure in his task, and wrought day and night to depict her who so loved him, yet who grew daily more dispirited and weak. And in sooth some who beheld the portrait spoke of its resemblance in low words, as of a mighty marvel, and a proof not less of the power of the painter than of his deep love for her whom he depicted so surpassingly well. But at length, as the labor drew nearer to its conclusion, there were admitted none into the turret; for the painter had grown wild with the ardor of his work, and turned his eyes from canvas merely, even to regard the countenance of his wife. And he would not see that the tints which he spread upon the canvas were drawn from the cheeks of her who sat beside him. And when many weeks had passed, and but little remained to do, save one brush upon the mouth and one tint upon the eye, the spirit of the lady again flickered up as the flame within the socket of the lamp. And then the brush was given, and then the tint was placed; and, for one moment, the painter stood entranced before the work which he had wrought; but in the next, while he yet gazed, he grew tremulous and very pallid, and aghast, and crying with a loud voice, 'This is indeed Life itself!' turned suddenly to regard his beloved:—She was dead!"

Probing Questions

1. The central contrast here is between the lifeless but beautiful painting and the living and beautiful woman. What does this contrast suggest about art and life?

2. The painter is so passionate about his painting that he fails to notice that his wife is dying. What does this suggest about the fervent pursuit of beauty in art?

3. Why did the painter's wife dread sitting for the portrait? Why did the painter fail to notice that his wife was fading away even as his art was becoming more lifelike?

For Further Reading

Aristotle, *Poetics*, M. E. Hubbard, trans. in Classical Literary Criticism, ed. D. A. Russell and M. Winterbottom (Oxford: Clarendon, 1972, 2008).

Clive Bell, *Art* (London: Chatto and Windus, 1914).

Arthur Danto, *Transfiguration of the Commonplace* (Cambridge, MA: Harvard University Press, 1981.

Susan L. Feagin and Patrick Maynard, *Aesthetics* (London: Oxford University Press, 1998).

Cynthia Freeland, *But Is It Art?* (New York: Oxford University Press, 2002).

Martin Gardner, *The Whys of a Philosophical Scrivener* (New York: St. Martin's Griffin, 1999).

G. Graham, *Philosophy of the Arts: An Introduction to Aesthetics* (London: Routledge, 1997).

Kathleen M. Higgins, *Aesthetics in Perspective* (Fort Worth: Harcourt Brace, 1996).

David Hume, "Of the Standard of Taste," from *Four Dissertations* (London: A. Miller, 1777).

M. Kelly, ed., *Encyclopedia of Ethics* (Oxford: Oxford University Press, 1998).

Leo Tolstoy, *What Is Art?* (Indianapolis: Bobbs-Merrill, 1960).

CHAPTER 8

THE JUST SOCIETY

Chapter Objectives

8.1 OVERVIEW: JUSTICE AND POLITICAL PHILOSOPHY

- Understand the nature of political philosophy and why the issues it deals with are important.
- Define *distributive justice* and explain the purpose of devising theories of justice.

8.2 PLATO'S THEORY: JUSTICE AS MERIT

- Explain the main elements of Plato's theory of justice.
- Be able to assess the strengths and weaknesses of Plato's theory.
- Define *democracy*, *meritocracy*, and *aristocracy*.

8.3 SOCIAL CONTRACT THEORIES

- Compare and evaluate the social contract theories of Hobbes and Locke.
- Explain Hobbes's notions of "the state of nature" and *Leviathan*.
- Explain Rawls's theory of justice.
- Define *liberalism*, *classical liberalism*, *libertarianism*, and *welfare liberalism*.

8.4 SOCIALIST THEORIES

- Understand the main features of Marx's political theory.
- Critically evaluate the strengths and weaknesses of socialism.

8.5 FEMINISM AND SOCIAL JUSTICE

- Understand Susan Moller Okin's critique of traditional theories of justice.
- Explain David Miller's view of feminist critiques of traditional theories.

8.1 OVERVIEW: JUSTICE AND POLITICAL PHILOSOPHY

Political philosophy is the study of political societies using the methods of philosophy.

Political philosophy is the study of political societies using the methods of philosophy—namely, critical reasoning and careful analysis. It is essentially moral philosophy applied to government and political life. Like moral philosophy, it is a normative endeavor, concerned with standards or principles for determining how political systems *ought to be* structured. To do its work properly, political philosophy must also take into account how political systems *are in fact* structured, but this is a descriptive task that is secondary to the normative one. Political science, on the other hand, is mostly a descriptive enterprise dedicated to uncovering the empirical facts of political systems past or present.

The issues of political philosophy are large, important, and personal. They raise questions about the moral and nonmoral goodness of whole societies, which largely determine the moral and nonmoral goodness of our lives. We can, of course, try to ignore these issues, but that is like a fish trying to ignore the water. The questions press us from all sides. What is justice, and what constitutes just and unjust treatment of the members of society? How should the political and material goods of society (wealth, property, liberties, rights) be distributed among its citizens? Should these goods be allotted according to need, utility, merit, desert, equality, or some other principle? What theory of political society should rule the distribution? Is democracy really the best form of government? Is socialism? Libertarianism? Do well-off citizens have a duty to provide goods to the less well off? What is the morally right (just) balance between the state's control of its people and the people's liberty and rights? What is the moral justification for the state's exercise of power and authority over individuals? Is the state necessary at all—or is it better to live in small communities without state authority?

Suppose someone fails to see the need to study political philosophy or even to think much about the government under which she lives. Political philosophers can make several replies to this attitude, but let us focus on just two. First, whether you are just beginning to form your ideas about politics and government, or you are already a veteran of many political discussions (and proudly call yourself a Democrat, Republican, Socialist, Libertarian, or something else), political philosophy can help you more than you may realize. A good dose of political philosophy can clarify your thinking, introduce you to new perspectives, acquaint you with arguments for and against political theories (including your own), and help you arrive at informed opinions. The result is greater understanding acquired through critical thinking and reflection—not through prejudice or unsupported presumption.

Consider, for example, this issue: the pervasiveness of government. The state's fingers are everywhere, revealed through levied taxes, a welfare system, the construction of roads and dams, the treatment of prisoners and patients, vast armies of government employees, declarations of peace and war, subsidies for homeowners and corporations, and the regulation of everything from hamburger to baby cribs. How do you feel about such omnipresent governance? Would you like to see more of the same, much less, or some other political system altogether? Such questions

Injustice anywhere is a threat to justice everywhere.

—Martin Luther King, Jr.

Figure 8.1 Signing of the Declaration of Independence: "We hold these truths to be self-evident, that all men are created equal, that they are endowed by their Creator with certain unalienable Rights, that among these are Life, Liberty and the pursuit of Happiness." What philosopher inspired these words?

are flashpoints in contemporary debates about the proper role of government in our lives. How would you go about getting some answers? An offhand, party-line reaction to these questions may provide some temporary satisfaction or assurance. But if you want better understanding and well-supported views, your best bet is to take the philosophical approach.

Second, political philosophy may not bake bread or sell widgets, but it does sometimes change the world. You will see several examples in this chapter of political theories that affected history, but for now let's ponder this one. John Locke (1632–1704) argued that through a social contract between government and the governed, the authority of the state could be justified. The state exists by the consent of the governed and is the guarantor of the people's inalienable rights of "life, liberty, and estate." The state serves the people, and the people have the right to challenge it through revolution if it violates the terms of the contract. Locke's ideas (shockingly radical when first introduced) were familiar to American colonists, and they heavily influenced the framers of the Declaration of Independence, the Constitution, and the Bill of Rights. (Other nations took notice of Locke's thinking as well.) Even the language in these documents reflects Locke's thinking. This famous sentence in the Declaration, for example, is almost pure Locke: "We hold these truths to be self-evident, that all men are created equal, that they are endowed by their Creator with certain unalienable Rights, that among these are Life, Liberty and the pursuit of Happiness." Political theory in the seventeenth century thus affects twenty-first-century Americans (and the rest of the world).

In the absence of justice, what is sovereignty but organized robbery?
—Saint Augustine

Justice is the idea that people should get what is fair or what is their due.

Distributive justice (or social justice) is the fair distribution of society's benefits and burdens—such things as jobs, income, property, liberties, rights, welfare aid, taxes, and public service.

The topic that gets most attention in political philosophy is **justice**. In its broadest sense, *justice* refers to people getting what is fair or what is their due, and the core principle that defines a person's due is *equals should be treated equally*. The idea is that people should be treated the same unless there is a morally relevant reason for treating them differently. Justice by this definition comes in two forms, and each is profoundly important in a society. *Retributive justice* has to do with the fair meting out of punishment to citizens for wrongdoing. **Distributive justice**, or **social justice**, is about the fair distribution of society's benefits and burdens (its material and nonmaterial goods)—such things as jobs, income, property, liberties, rights, welfare aid, taxes, and public service. How these goods are distributed among the citizens of a state is a function of how the state is structured, how its social and political institutions are arranged. It's this kind of justice that is the focus of political philosophers and their theories of justice.

Theories of justice embody principles that define fair distributions, that explain what people are due and why. A utilitarian theory of justice, for example, says that the distribution of goods should be based on the principle of *utility*. Society's institutions must be arranged so that its benefits and burdens are allocated to maximize some measure of society's welfare (total happiness, for example). This is a popular scheme of distribution, although some think it is inconsistent with our commonsense notions of justice and equality. As you might guess, the utilitarian philosopher John Stuart Mill favors the view.

Some theories of justice insist on distributions according to *merit*, or *desert* (what people deserve). Plato (c. 427–347 BCE) took this tack, arguing that because people differ in their talents and achievements, they should be given a station in life that reflects this difference. Some people have superior capacities and therefore should receive a superior share of society's goods; some possess few capacities and should get a smaller share. As you can see, Plato's view is strongly antidemocratic.

1 Would a society structured entirely on the principle of utility be just?

In other theories, merit and utility mean little, while *equality* means (almost) everything. The thoroughgoing egalitarian maintains that, contrary to Plato, there are no morally relevant differences among persons, so everyone should be apportioned an equal share of society's benefits. After all, don't we believe that all persons are created equal? John Rawls (1921–2002) argues for this kind of rigorous equality in his theory of justice. He contends that since people's character and behavior are accidents of nature, no one really deserves any particular allotment of benefits or burdens—and so equality is the most reasonable basis for distribution of goods. A staunch egalitarianism demands that the supposedly deserving, undeserving, needy, and self-sufficient receive the same size slice of society's pie and the portions cannot be adjusted on grounds of utility.

The virtue of justice consists in moderation, as regulated by wisdom.
—Aristotle

2 Are the principles of desert and equality in conflict? That is, is it possible to have a society that treats everyone with strict equality while ensuring that everyone gets what they deserve?

An important theme of some theories is that society's wealth should be allocated according to *need*. Allotments of goods based on people's hardship or indigence are common elements in many societies, often combined with other distribution principles. Welfare programs, lower tax rates for people with low incomes, disaster relief, low-interest loans to the disadvantaged—such programs are strictly need-based. Some thinkers hold that meeting the needs of society's worst off should be a major concern of the state. But others argue that assisting the needy is *not* a requirement of

WHAT DO YOU BELIEVE?

Political Views in Flux

The Pew Research Center, which conducts opinion surveys to gauge political attitudes, reports that, "With the economy still struggling and the nation involved in multiple military operations overseas, the public's political mood is fractious. In this environment, many political attitudes have become more doctrinaire at both ends of the ideological spectrum, a polarization that reflects the current atmosphere in Washington. Yet at the same time, a growing number of Americans are choosing not to identify with either political party, and the center of the political spectrum is increasingly diverse." Here are the results from a recent Pew survey of Americans.

Figure 8.2 More Americans are shunning political parties and migrating to the political center.

	Percentage of. . .	
	General Public	**Registered Voters**
Mostly Republican		
Staunch Conservatives	9	11
(Highly engaged Tea Party supporters)		
Main Street Republicans	11	14
(Conservative on most issues)		
Mostly Independent		
Libertarians	9	10
(Free market, small government seculars)		
Disaffecteds	11	11
(Downscale and cynical)		
Post-Moderns	13	14
(Moderates but liberal on social issues)		
Mostly Democratic		
New Coalition Democrats	10	9
(Upbeat, majority-minority)		
Hard-Pressed Democrats	13	15
(Religious, financially struggling)		
Solid Liberals	14	16
(Across-the-board liberal positions)		
Bystanders		
Young, politically disengaged	10	0
Total	100	100

(PEW RESEARCH CENTER 2011 Political Typography)

Do you see yourself in these numbers? If not, how would you characterize your political views?

Figure 8.3 Is the state obligated to help the poor? Is it morally permissible for the government to tax the rich to guarantee the poor a basic minimum of welfare assistance?

justice; helping unfortunates is a job best left to voluntary charity, not government.

Many who resist the idea of distributions based on equality or desert do so by appealing to a principle of *entitlement*. They argue that even if people don't deserve the goods they have, they nevertheless may be entitled to them. We are entitled, for example, to self-ownership of our own bodies even though we have done nothing to deserve having them. Perhaps the most famous entitlement theory of justice is that of Robert Nozick (1938–2002). He argues that if we rightfully possess any goods, they are ours only because we are entitled to them—entitled because we acquired them legitimately, not because we got them through appeals to equality or desert.

The most influential theories of justice have incorporated some or all of these principles, emphasizing some of them, downplaying others, and arriving at distinctive sociopolitical models that we can use to judge the worthiness of real-world systems. It is difficult—perhaps impossible—to fully fathom our own political system without knowing something about the theories of justice that preceded it. The following sections should help you understand what those predecessors are like.

> Where justice is denied, where poverty is enforced, where ignorance prevails, and where any one class is made to feel that society is an organized conspiracy to oppress, rob and degrade them, neither persons nor property will be safe.
> —Frederick Douglass

WRITING TO UNDERSTAND:
CRITIQUING PHILOSOPHICAL VIEWS   Section 8.1

1. Imagine you are convinced that the way your own society is structured is better than that of other societies. How could you argue for such a position?

2. Suppose you think your country's form of distributive justice is seriously flawed. How could you argue for your view? What principle of justice is at fault?

3. Do you think a society based entirely on equality would be just? Why or why not?

4. Do you think, as Rawls does, that no one really deserves any particular distribution of benefits or burdens? Explain.

5. In your view, what would be some of the beneficial or harmful effects of a society based solely on merit, as Plato proposed?

8.2 PLATO'S THEORY: JUSTICE AS MERIT

About twenty-five centuries ago, Plato proposed in his masterwork *The Republic* a theory of justice that has challenged thinkers and stimulated debate ever since. He argues that the only kind of society that can ensure people get their due is a **meritocracy**, a system of rule by those most qualified to govern. He contrasts meritocracy with a form of government he strongly opposes: **democracy**, rule by the people as a whole. In his view, democratic rule is mob rule, the reign of a rabble too easily swayed by emotional appeals and bad arguments. Plato had plenty of experience with democratic rule, for in his day Athens was a democracy in which governmental decisions were made by direct vote of adult male Athenians. (Greek democracy was far from rule by all the people, for only free men were full citizens, and women and slaves were excluded.) He never forgot that it was a democratic vote of his fellow citizens that committed the ultimate injustice by condemning to death his teacher and role model, the venerable Socrates.

Plato's theory of justice dovetails with his theory of mind, as well as with his epistemology and ethics. He argues that the makeup and functioning of society is directly analogous to the makeup and functioning of the person (or soul). In his philosophy of mind, every person is composed of three fundamental components: (1) appetite, or desires; (2) spirit, or drives (including motivations and emotions); and (3) reason (the intellect). The just, or virtuous, person will be a well-balanced composite of these, each performing its own distinctive function in harmony with the others, with the appetites and spirit ruled and coordinated by reason. In similar fashion, Plato says, a society consists of three types of people, each one identified according to which of the soul's components predominates:

1. Those who are moved by their appetites (*producers*—laborers, carpenters, artisans, farmers).
2. Those who are moved by spirit (*auxiliaries*—soldiers, warriors, police).
3. Those who are moved by reason (*guardians*—leaders, rulers, philosopher-kings).

In a just society, these three perform their proper functions while the producers and auxiliaries are led and controlled by the guardians. The just state is a harmonious community governed by reason, just as a virtuous person is a tripartite being presided over by the rational faculty of the soul.

Plato says citizens are assigned to one of the three functions based on their aptitude and performance, and once appointed, they are expected to remain in that class and not try to cross over to another. This scheme reflects his theory of ethics. To be virtuous and happy, he says, we must act according to our talents and aptitude, striving for excellence in the endeavors nature has chosen for us.

Meritocracy is a system of rule by those most qualified to govern.

Democracy is rule by the people as a whole.

3 How would you defend democracy against Plato's criticisms?

What do I care about Jupiter? Justice is a human issue, and I do not need a god to teach it to me.
—Jean-Paul Sartre

Figure 8.4 Plato's Academy at Athens. In Plato's republic, all people are *not* created equal. Does this fact invalidate his theory of justice?

Aristocracy is a society ruled by the best citizens.

4 To determine citizens' aptitudes and talents (and thus their place in society), Plato favored testing them while they are young. Is it possible to discover the best career for someone this way? What about people who discover or develop their true talents late in life—those, for example, who are poor students but turn out to be geniuses in adulthood like Einstein? Is Plato too optimistic about the ease of discovering a person's true calling?

Plato, then, envisions an **aristocracy** (a society ruled by the best citizens)—not an aristocracy of the rich, landed, or well born, but of the intellectual. The guardians are true philosopher-kings. They wield all the political power by virtue of their greater talents and intelligence. In the ideal republic, the guardians—contrary to the usual custom—cannot own property, for owning property might tempt them to govern for personal gain rather than for the good of society. This powerful elite can include women and anyone from the lower classes, because the only qualification for becoming a ruler is simply to be of superior intelligence and character.

To modern minds, some of the elements of Plato's society may sound both wrong and alien. His ideal state rests on massive inequality among citizens who are sorted into three classes marked by unequal shares of power and privilege. Granted, people are assigned to different classes according to merit, but inequality is still the rule. Plato maintains that equals should be treated equally, but to him the classes deserve different treatment because *they are different*. All men are not created equal. Then there is the authoritarianism of Plato's republic, in which no one gets to choose their own role in life. In general, once assigned to a social role, citizens cannot jump to another. There is no social mobility, except *within* a class and in the case of guardians being chosen from lower classes.

In the following selection from *The Republic*, Plato (through the character of Socrates) is explaining his concept of justice to companions. The discussion is narrated by Socrates.

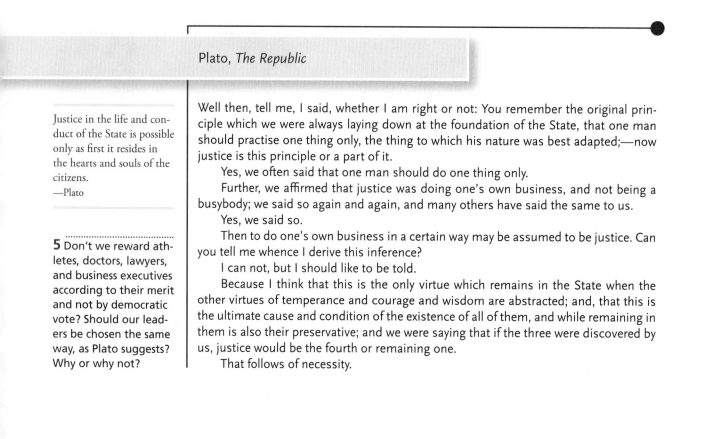

Plato, *The Republic*

Justice in the life and conduct of the State is possible only as first it resides in the hearts and souls of the citizens.
—Plato

5 Don't we reward athletes, doctors, lawyers, and business executives according to their merit and not by democratic vote? Should our leaders be chosen the same way, as Plato suggests? Why or why not?

Well then, tell me, I said, whether I am right or not: You remember the original principle which we were always laying down at the foundation of the State, that one man should practise one thing only, the thing to which his nature was best adapted;—now justice is this principle or a part of it.

Yes, we often said that one man should do one thing only.

Further, we affirmed that justice was doing one's own business, and not being a busybody; we said so again and again, and many others have said the same to us.

Yes, we said so.

Then to do one's own business in a certain way may be assumed to be justice. Can you tell me whence I derive this inference?

I can not, but I should like to be told.

Because I think that this is the only virtue which remains in the State when the other virtues of temperance and courage and wisdom are abstracted; and, that this is the ultimate cause and condition of the existence of all of them, and while remaining in them is also their preservative; and we were saying that if the three were discovered by us, justice would be the fourth or remaining one.

That follows of necessity.

If we are asked to determine which of these four qualities by its presence contributes most to the excellence of the State, whether the agreement of rulers and subjects or the preservation in the soldiers of the opinion which the law ordains about the true nature of dangers, or wisdom and watchfulness in the rulers, or whether this other which I am mentioning, and which is found in children and women, slave and freeman, artisan, ruler, subject,—the quality, I mean, of every one doing his own work and not being a busybody, would claim the palm—the question is not so easily answered.

Certainly, he replied, there would be a difficulty in saying which.

Then the power of each individual in the State to do his own work appears to compete with the other political virtues, wisdom, temperance, courage.

Yes, he said.

And the virtue which enters into this competition is justice?

Exactly.

Let us look at the question from another point of view: Are not the rulers in a State those to whom you would entrust the office of determining suits at law?

Certainly.

And are suits decided on any other ground but that a man may neither take what is another's, nor be deprived of what is his own?

Yes; that is their principle.

Which is a just principle?

Yes.

Then on this view also justice will be admitted to be the having and doing what is a man's own, and belongs to him?

Very true.

Think, now, and say whether you agree with me or not. Suppose a cobbler to be doing the business of a cobbler, or a cobbler of a carpenter; and suppose them to exchange their implements or their duties, or the same person to be doing the work of both, or whatever be the change; do you think that any great harm would result to the State?

Not much.

But when the cobbler or any other man whom nature designed to be a trader, having his heart lifted up wealth or strength or the number of his followers, or any like advantage, attempts to force his way into the class of warriors, or a warrior into that of legislators and guardians, for which he is unfitted, and either to take the implements or the duties of the other; or when one man is trader, legislator, and warrior all in one, then I think you will agree with me in saying that this interchange and this meddling of one with another is the ruin of the State.

Most true.

Seeing then, I said, that there are three distinct classes, any meddling of one with another, or the change of one into another, is the greatest harm to the State, and may be most justly termed evil-doing?

Precisely.

And the greatest degree of evil-doing to one's own city would be termed by you injustice?

Certainly.

This then is injustice; and on the other hand when the trader, the auxiliary, and the guardian each do their own business, that is justice, and will make the city just.

I agree with you.[1]

6 Do you think Plato exaggerates the consequences of allowing a person to abandon his own career path and do another person's job? Explain.

PHILOSOPHY NOW

Merit or Equality: Who Gets to Live?

Organ transplant operations are incredibly expensive, organs are in very short supply, and transplants are desperately needed by far more people than can be accommodated. The waiting list for transplants is long, and thousands die every year for their lack. Screening committees at transplant centers decide whether someone should be placed on the waiting list and what ranking they should receive. They use various criteria to make these decisions, some explicit, some informal or unspoken, some plausible (such as the patient's need and likelihood of benefit), and some controversial (such as ability to pay, social worthiness, and health habits).

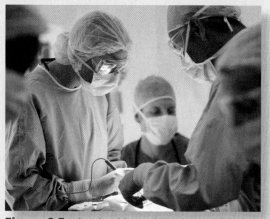

Among these, social or moral worthiness—merit—is probably the most contentious. Here the questions are: Which potential recipients—if given the chance to live—are expected to contribute most to the good of society? Or which possible recipients do not deserve transplants, because they have indulged in habits (like excessive alcohol use or dangerous activities) that contributed to their impending organ failure? To state the issue concretely: All things being equal, should the medical student or priest get the transplant instead of the prostitute or alcoholic?

Figure 8.5 Who should get the only available liver or heart—the person chosen by lottery, the upright citizen, the man who donates thousands of dollars to the hospital, the priest, or the homeless child?

Many reject such appeals to merit and insist that the proper criteria are egalitarian—a matter of justice and the moral equality of persons. They argue that all persons have equal worth. Morally, the medical student is not worth more than the prostitute or alcoholic, and vice versa. Education, achievement, occupation, and the like are not morally relevant.

Nevertheless, while generally taking the egalitarian approach, some philosophers maintain that in very rare cases, social worth can outweigh egalitarian concerns. It seems reasonable that in a natural disaster involving mass casualties, injured physicians or nurses should be treated first if they can aid the other survivors.

Should social or moral worth ever be taken into account in deciding who should get a transplant? Suppose the question is whether to give a transplant to a Nobel laureate or to a hard-working, honest truck driver. Assuming that all other factors are equal, which one should get the transplant? Why?

> **WRITING TO UNDERSTAND:**
> **CRITIQUING PHILOSOPHICAL VIEWS**   Section 8.2
>
> 1. Plato thinks democracy is no better than mob rule. Do you agree? What are your reasons?
>
> 2. Plato believes that it's possible for a society to be just without equality among its citizens. Do you agree? Why or why not?
>
> 3. Plato believes his just society to be well ordered, rational, and harmonious. But are these traits sufficient to ensure justice in a society? Can we plausibly call such a society just when the state decides what kinds of lives its citizens must live? Give reasons for your view.
>
> 4. In Plato's republic, the guardians deserve to be rulers because they are the most intelligent and intellectually gifted. But do such attributes guarantee wisdom? Are intellectually superior people always good leaders?
>
> 5. Would you want to live in a state patterned after Plato's just society? Why or why not?

8.3 SOCIAL CONTRACT THEORIES

In the seventeenth century, philosophers defied tradition by defending a new kind of theory of justice and a novel way of justifying the existence of the state: **social contract theory**. This view says that justice is secured, and the state is made legitimate, through an agreement among citizens of the state or between the citizens and the rulers of the state. The people consent explicitly or implicitly to be governed—to be subject to the dictates and the power of the state—in exchange for the state's providing security, rights, and liberties. The state's existence is justified by the binding contract that all parties accept. This understanding of the role and justification of the state was incorporated into the Constitution of the United States, and in the twenty-first century, this idea of a social contract is now taken for granted by much of the world.

Nevertheless, when fully formed social contract theories were first introduced, they were thought by many to be radical, scandalous, and wrong. In medieval Europe, the prevailing view had been that states are supposed to be dominated by monarchs who rule by the "divine right of kings." God sanctions the monarch's authority and ordains that society be ranked in a hierarchy of positions, from the king or queen down to the poorest serfs, with each performing his or her preordained function. As in Plato's republic, people have their proper place in society, and no one is permitted or expected to deviate from it. The governed cannot consent to anything, and monarchs have absolute power over all their subjects.

Social contract theory is the view that justice is secured, and the state is made legitimate, through an agreement among citizens of the state or between the citizens and the rulers of the state.

Charity begins at home, and justice begins next door.
—Charles Dickens

Among the most influential social contract theorists are Thomas Hobbes (1588–1679), John Locke (1632–1704), and John Rawls (1921–2002). We take up their views in the following pages.

Hobbes

7 Hobbes is a pessimist about human nature; he thinks people are basically greedy and treacherous. Do you think he's right about this? Or are people fundamentally sociable, cooperative, and benign? Explain your reasoning.

Hobbes was the first philosopher in modern times to systematically articulate a social contract theory. It was a major departure from received views about society, and that fact alone was enough to infuriate many. It also contained a rejection of both the divine right of kings and the notion of a divinely established moral law—points that gave his critics even more reasons to attack him.

In his famous *Leviathan*, Hobbes contends that a social contract is necessary in human affairs because living without one would be a horrific nightmare of existence. He begins by assuming a pessimistic view of human beings: at their core, he says, they are selfish, treacherous, dishonest, and violent. He argues that when

PHILOSOPHERS AT WORK

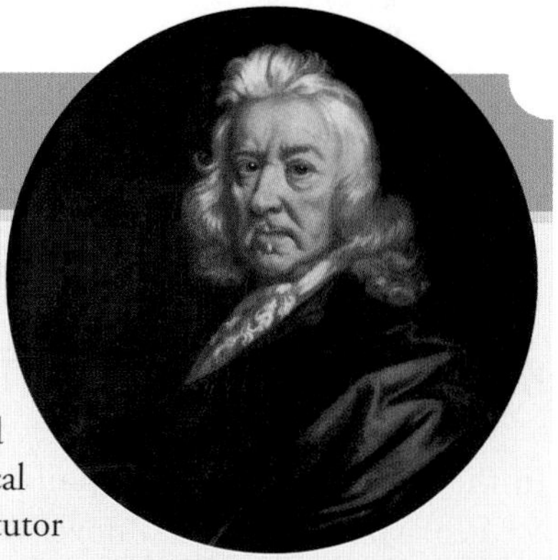

Figure 8.6 Thomas Hobbes, political theorist and polymath.

Thomas Hobbes

Thomas Hobbes (1588–1679) was more than an eminent English philosopher whose theories influenced future generations. He was also a linguist, poet, classical scholar, translator, logician, critic, and mathematical tutor to Charles II.

He was born into a poor religious family and liked to say that when his mother was pregnant with him, she went into labor on hearing that the Spanish Armada was threatening England. He joked that "fear and I were born twins together." He was educated at Oxford and spent most of his years as secretary and tutor to the family of the third earl of Devonshire. During this employment, he met the foremost European thinkers (Galileo and Francis Bacon among them) and wrote on a wide range of issues, both scientific and philosophical. Many of these works were extremely controversial. His political philosophy was offensive to both sides in the English Civil War; the Roman Catholic Church and Oxford University forbade the reading of his books; and he went against the grain of his era by advancing materialism, egoism, and (what some considered) heresy.

His most famous creation is *Leviathan* (1651), which has had an enormous influence on English moral and political thinking. His other writings include *Philosophical Rudiments Concerning Government and Society* (1651), *On the Body* (1655), and *On Man* (1658).

these tendencies are left unchecked by enforced laws or agreements, humans sink into a "state of nature"—a "war of every man against every man." In the state of nature, there is no code, culture, or comfort. There is no justice. There is only "continual fear, and danger of violent death; and the life of man [is] solitary, poor, nasty, brutish, and short."[2]

But, Hobbes says, humankind also has a strong instinct for self-interest and self-preservation, and fortunately this impulse is coupled with the power of reason. Through reason, he says, people see that the only way to escape this "war of all against all" is to enter into a social contract with one another. In the name of self-interest, they agree to turn over much of their autonomy, freedom, and power to an absolute sovereign that will forcibly keep the peace, restrain antisocial actions, and compel people to keep their agreements. Hobbes calls this sovereign the *Leviathan* (the name of a sea monster mentioned in the Bible), which symbolizes great power and evil. Its authority over those bound by the social contract is absolute, its power is fearsome (enough to deter any tendency to disorder), and its contractual agreement with its subjects is irrevocable. Once power is given up to this despot, there is no going back, and there is always the chance that the sovereign will create an environment worse than the state of nature. But that is the chance people must take.

So the state's authority is justified by a social contract, and justice comes into being as the Leviathan assumes power. For Hobbes, justice is a matter of the keeping of covenants (contracts), and the only way to ensure that covenants are kept is to let the Leviathan reign. Without the Leviathan to enforce covenants, there is no justice. As Hobbes says, "Where there is no common power, there is no law; where no law no injustice."[3]

Here is Hobbes arguing for his theory in *Leviathan*:

> **8** Do you think Hobbes is right about humans being roughly equal physically and mentally? Why or why not?

> It is better to lose everything you have to keep the balance of justice level, than to live a life of petty privilege devoid of true freedom.
> —Bryant H. McGill

Thomas Hobbes, *Leviathan*

CHAPTER 13. OF THE NATURAL CONDITION OF MANKIND AS CONCERNING THEIR FELICITY, AND MISERY

Nature hath made men so equal, in the faculties of body, and mind; as that though there be found one man sometimes manifestly stronger in body, or of quicker mind than another; yet when all is reckoned together, the difference between man, and man, is not so considerable, as that one man can thereupon claim to himself any benefit, to which another may not pretend, as well as he. For as to the strength of body, the weakest has strength enough to kill the strongest, either by secret machination, or by confederacy with others, that are in the same danger with himself.

And as to the faculties of the mind (setting aside the arts grounded upon words, and especially that skill of proceeding upon general, and infallible rules, called science; which very few have, and but in few things; as being not a native faculty, born with us; nor attained, [as prudence], while we look after somewhat else), I find yet a greater equality amongst men, than that of strength. For prudence, is but experience; which equal time, equally bestows on all men, in those things they equally

Thomas Hobbes,
Leviathan

apply themselves unto. That which may perhaps make such equality incredible, is but a vain conceit of one's own wisdom, which almost all men think they have in a greater degree, than the vulgar; that is, than all men but themselves, and a few others, whom by fame, or for concurring with themselves, they approve. For such is the nature of men, that howsoever they may acknowledge many others to be more witty, or more eloquent, or more learned; yet they will hardly believe there be many so wise as themselves: For they see their own wit at hand, and other men's at a distance. But this proves rather that men are in that point equal, than unequal. For there is not ordinarily a greater sign of the equal distribution of any thing, than that every man is contented with his share.

From this equality of ability, arises equality of hope in the attaining of our ends. And therefore if any two men desire the same thing, which nevertheless they cannot both enjoy, they become enemies; and in the way to their end (which is principally their own conservation, and sometimes their delectation only), endeavor to destroy, or subdue one another. And from hence it comes to pass, that where an invader hath no more to fear, than another man's single power; if one plant, sow, build, or possess a convenient seat, others may probably be expected to come prepared with forces united, to dispossess, and deprive him, not only of the fruit of his labour, but also of his life, or liberty. And the invader again is in the like danger of another.

And from this diffidence of one another, there is no way for any man to secure himself, so reasonable, as anticipation; that is, by force, or wiles, to master the persons of all men he can, so long, till he see no other power great enough to endanger him: and this is no more than his own conservation requires, and is generally allowed. Also because there be some, that taking pleasure in contemplating their own power in the acts of conquest, which they pursue farther than their security requires; if others, that otherwise would be glad to be at ease within modest bounds, should not by invasion increase their power, they would not be able, long time, by standing only on their defence, to subsist. And by consequence, such augmentation of dominion over men, being necessary to a man's conservation, it ought to be allowed him.

Again, men have no pleasure (but on the contrary a great deal of grief) in keeping company, where there is no power able to over-awe them all. For every man looks that his companion should value him, at the same rate he sets upon himself: and upon all signs of contempt, or undervaluing, naturally endeavors, as far as he dares (which amongst them that have no common power to keep them in quiet, is far enough to make them destroy each other), to extort a greater value from his condemners, by damage; and from others, by the example.

So that in the nature of man, we find three principal causes of quarrel. First, competition; secondly, diffidence; thirdly, glory.

The first, maketh men invade for gain; the second, for safety; and the third, for reputation. The first use violence, to make themselves masters of other men's persons, wives, children, and cattle; the second to defend them; the third, for trifles, as a word, a smile, a different opinion, and any other sign of undervalue, either direct in their persons, or by reflection in their kindred, their friends, their nation, their profession, or their name.

9 Does the existence of stable democracies in the twenty-first century show that Hobbes is wrong about human nature?

Figure 8.7 Frontispiece to *Leviathan or the Matter, Forme and Power of a Common Wealth Ecclesiasticall and Civil*, 1651, by Thomas Hobbes.

Hereby it is manifest, that during the time men live without a common power to keep them all in awe, they are in that condition which is called war; and such a war, as is of every man, against every man. For WAR, consists not in battle only, or the act of fighting; but in a tract of time, wherein the will to contend by battle is sufficiently known: and therefore the notion of time, is to be considered in the nature of war; as it is in the nature of weather. For as the nature of foul weather, lies not in a shower or two of rain; but in an inclination thereto of many days together: so the nature of war, consists not in actual fighting; but in the known disposition thereto, during all the time there is no assurance to the contrary. All other time is PEACE.

Whatsoever therefore is consequent to a time of war, where every man is enemy to every man; the same is consequent to the time; wherein men live without other security, than what their own strength, and their own invention shall furnish them withal. In such condition, there is no place for industry; because the fruit thereof is uncertain: and consequently no culture of the earth; no navigation, nor use of the commodities that may be imported by sea; no commodious building; no instruments of moving, and removing such things as require much force; no knowledge of the face of the earth; no account of time; no arts; no letters; no society; and which is worst of all, continual fear, and danger of violent death; and the life of man, solitary, poor, nasty, brutish, and short. . . .

To this war of every man against every man, this also is consequent; that nothing can be unjust. The notions of right and wrong, justice and injustice have there no place. Where there is no common power, there is no law: where no law no injustice. Force, and fraud, are in war the two cardinal virtues. Justice, and injustice are none of the faculties neither of the body, nor mind. If they were, they might be in a man that were alone in the world, as well as his senses, and passions. They are qualities, that relate to men in society, not in solitude. It is consequent also to the same condition, that there be no propriety, no dominion, no mine and thine distinct; but only that to be every man's, that he can get; and for so long, as he can keep it. And thus much for the ill condition, which man by mere nature is actually placed in; though with a possibility to come out of it, consisting partly in the passions, partly in his reason.

The passions that incline men to peace, are fear of death; desire of such things as are necessary to commodious living; and a hope by their industry to obtain them. And reason suggests convenient articles of peace, upon which men may be drawn to agreement. These articles, are they, which otherwise are called the Laws of Nature. . . .

10 Suppose the world is suddenly left with no governmental authority anywhere; no formal restraints on human behavior exist. Speculate on how you think people would act. Would chaos and savagery ensue, or would people more or less live in peace and harmony?

CHAPTER 14. OF THE FIRST AND SECOND NATURAL LAWS, AND OF CONTRACTS

The RIGHT OF NATURE, which writers commonly call *jus naturale*, is the liberty each man hath, to use his own power, as he will himself, for the preservation of his own nature; that is to say, of his own life; and consequently, of doing any thing, which in his own judgment, and reason, he shall conceive to be the aptest means thereunto.

By LIBERTY, is understood, according to the proper signification of the word, the absence of external impediments: which impediments, may oft take away part of a man's power to do what he would; but cannot hinder him from using the power left him, according as his judgment, and reason shall dictate to him.

A LAW OF NATURE (*lex naturalis*), is a precept, or general rule, found out by reason, by which a man is forbidden to do that, which is destructive of his life, or taketh away the means of preserving the same; and to omit that, by which he thinks it may be best preserved. For though they that speak of this subject, use to confound jus, and lex, right and law; yet they ought to be distinguished; because RIGHT, consists in liberty to do, or to forbear; whereas LAW, determines, and binds to one of them: so that law, and right, differ as much, as obligation, and liberty; which in one and the same matter are inconsistent.

And because the condition of man (as hath been declared in the precedent chapter) is a condition of war of every one against every one; in which case every one is governed by his own reason; and there is nothing he can make use of that may not be a help unto him, in preserving his life against his enemies; it followeth, that in such a condition, every man has a right to every thing; even to one another's body. And therefore, as long as this natural right of every man to every thing endures, there can be no security to any man (how strong or wise soever he be) of living out the time, which nature ordinarily allows men to live. And consequently it is a precept, or general rule of reason, that every man, ought to endeavor peace, as far as he has hope of obtaining it; and when he cannot obtain it, that he may seek, and use, all helps, and advantages of war. The first branch of which rule, containeth the first, and fundamental law of nature; which is, to seek peace, and follow it. The second, the sum of the right of nature; which is, by all means we can, to defend ourselves.

11 Is ceding all power to a Leviathan the only way for people to achieve peace, security, and cooperation in a society? Explain.

From this fundamental law of nature, by which men are commanded to endeavor peace, is derived this second law; that a man be willing, when others are so too, as far-forth, as for peace, and defence of himself he shall think it necessary, to lay down this right to all things; and be contented with so much liberty against other men, as he would allow other men against himself. For as long as every man holds this right, of doing any thing he likes; so long are all men in the condition of war. But if other men will not lay down their right, as well as he; then there is no reason for any one, to divest himself of his: for that were to expose himself to prey (which no man is bound to) rather than to dispose himself to peace. This is that law of the Gospel; whatsoever you require that others should do to you, that do ye to them. And that law of all men, [what you would not have done to you, do not do to others]. . . .

CHAPTER 15. OF OTHER LAWS OF NATURE

From that law of nature, by which we are obliged to transfer to another, such rights, as being retained, hinder the peace of mankind, there followeth a third; which is this, that men perform their covenants made: without which, covenants are in vain, and but empty words; and the right of all men to all things remaining, we are still in the condition of war.

And in this law of nature, consists the fountain and original of JUSTICE. For where no covenant hath proceeded, there hath no right been transferred, and every man has right to every thing; and consequently, no action can be unjust. But when a covenant is made, then to break it is unjust: and the definition of INJUSTICE, is no other than the not performance of covenant. And whatsoever is not unjust, is just.

But because covenants of mutual trust, where there is a fear of not performance on either part (as hath been said in the former chapter), are invalid; though the original of justice be the making of covenants; yet injustice actually there can be none, till the cause of such fear be taken away; which while men are in the natural condition of war, cannot be done. Therefore before the names of just, and unjust can have place, there must be some coercive power, to compel men equally to the performance of their covenants, by the terror of some punishment, greater than the benefit they expect by the breach of their covenant; and to make good that propriety, which by mutual contract men acquire, in recompense of the universal right they abandon: and such power there is none before the erection of a commonwealth. And this is also to be gathered out of the ordinary definition of justice in the Schools: for they say, that justice is the constant will of giving to every man his own. And therefore where there is no own, that is, no propriety, there is no injustice; and where there is no coercive power erected, that is, where there is no commonwealth, there is no propriety; all men having right to all things: therefore where there is no commonwealth, there nothing is unjust. So that the nature of justice, consists in keeping of valid covenants: but the validity of covenants begins not but with the constitution of a civil power, sufficient to compel men to keep them: and then it is also that propriety begins.[4]

Locke

Locke's social contract theory has some points in common with Hobbes's—but also much that Hobbes would have rejected outright. Both Hobbes and Locke assert that (1) reason enables people to see the wisdom of forming a state through a social contract, (2) people must freely consent to be bound by the contract (not be coerced into accepting it), and (3) the state's authority is justified by this consent of the governed. Beyond these matters, Hobbes and Locke part company.

For one thing, they have very different ideas about the "state of nature," the world in which no civil society exists. For Hobbes, to be in the state of nature is to be in a "war of all against all," where morality is nonexistent, and the only laws are commonsense rules for survival and self-interest. For Locke, on the other hand, the state of nature is considerably less nasty and brutish, for even there, natural moral laws apply and help to regulate people's behavior. Those living in the state of nature are free, sociable, equal, and (mostly) at peace.

Hobbes contends that, generally, justice and rights do not come into being until the state is established. People surrender their lives and liberties to the Leviathan in exchange for security and peace, and he can do what he wants with his subjects. But Locke argues that humans have inherent, God-given rights whether or not a government is around to guarantee them. Chief among these is the right to property—not just land but your own body and any object that you change through work (with which you "mix your labor"). These rights are inalienable: they cannot be transferred to the government or any other entity. Humans create the government and cede some power to it; in return it protects their rights and liberties. The state serves the people (not the other way round), directing all its power "to no other end but the peace, safety, and public good of the people."

But what exactly does the state do to preserve liberties and promote the common good? Locke identifies three functions that people need the state to perform. First, citizens need the natural moral law to be set out in clearly expressed laws of the land. Unwritten natural laws are clear to humans, but people are apt to misconstrue them in line with their biases. Second, there need to be impartial judges who can settle disputes concerning the application of the laws. Third, there needs

Why has government been instituted at all? Because the passions of man will not conform to the dictates of reason and justice without constraint.
—Alexander Hamilton

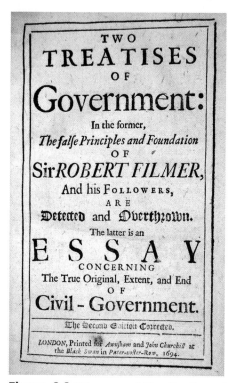

Figure 8.8 Title page of *Two Treatises of Government* by John Locke, 2nd edition, 1694.

to be power in the state to enforce the laws. Otherwise, people will be able to take justice into their own hands.

Suppose, however, that the state abuses its power by repeatedly and arbitrarily trampling on the people's rights and liberties. Hobbes says that once you cede power to the Leviathan, he is free to treat you as he will. But Locke says if the government violates the rights of citizens, it is no longer legitimate, obligations to it are voided, and the people have a right to dissolve it—to initiate rebellion. Locke's insistence on the right to rebel against a government that misuses its power is echoed clearly in the Declaration of Independence:

> We hold these truths to be self-evident, that all men are created equal, that they are endowed by their Creator with certain unalienable Rights, that among these are Life, Liberty and the pursuit of Happiness.—That to secure these rights, Governments are instituted among Men, deriving their just powers from the consent of the governed,—That whenever any Form of Government becomes destructive of these ends, it is the Right of the People to alter or abolish it, and to institute a new Government. . . .[5]

The following passages are from Locke's landmark *Second Treatise of Government*:

John Locke, *Second Treatise of Government*

CHAPTER VIII

Of the Beginning of Political Societies

95. Men being, as has been said, by nature, all free, equal, and independent, no one can be put out of this estate, and subjected to the political power of another, without his own consent. The only way, whereby any one divests himself of his natural liberty, and puts on the *bonds of civil society*, is by agreeing with other men to join and unite into a community, for their comfortable, safe, and peaceable living one amongst another, in a secure enjoyment of their properties, and a greater security against any, that are not of it. This any number of men may do, because it injures not the freedom of the rest; they are left as they were in the liberty of the state of nature. When any number of men have so *consented to make one community or government*, they are thereby presently incorporated, and make *one body politic*, wherein the *majority* have a right to act and conclude the rest.

96. For when any number of men have, by the consent of every individual, made a *community*, they have thereby made that *community* one body, with a power to act as

one body, which is only by the will and determination of the majority. For that which acts any community, being only the *consent* of the individuals of it, and it being necessary to that which greater force carries it, which is the *consent of the majority*: or else it is impossible it should act or continue one body, one community, which the consent of every individual that united into it, agreed that it should; and so every one is bound by that consent to be concluded by the majority. And therefore we see, that in assemblies, impowered to act by positive laws, where no number is set by that positive law which impowers them, the *act of the majority* passes for the act of the whole, and of course determines, as having, by the law of nature and reason, the power of the whole.

97. And thus every man, by consenting with others to make one body politic under one government, puts himself under an obligation, to every one of that society, to submit to the determination of the majority, and to be concluded by it; or else this *original* compact, whereby he with others incorporate into one society, would signify nothing, and be no compact, if he be left free, and under no other ties than he was in before in the state of nature. For what appearance would there be of any compact? What new engagement if he were no farther tied by any decrees of the society, than he himself thought fit, and did actually consent to? This would be still as great a liberty, as he himself had before his compact, or any one else in the state of nature hath, who may submit himself, and consent to any acts of it if he thinks fit.

98. For if the *consent of the majority* shall not, in reason, be received *as the act of the whole*, and conclude every individual; nothing but the consent of every individual can make any thing to be the act of the whole: But such a consent is next to impossible ever to be had, if we consider the infirmities of health, and avocations of business, which in a number, though much less than that of a commonwealth, will necessarily keep many away from the public assembly. To which if we add the variety of opinions, and contrariety of interests, which unavoidably happen in all collections of men, the coming into society upon such terms would be only like Cato's coming into the theatre, only to go out again. Such a constitution as this would make the mighty *leviathan* of a shorter duration than the feeblest creatures, and not let it outlast the day it was born in: which cannot be supposed, till we can think, that rational creatures should desire and constitute societies only to be dissolved. For where the majority cannot conclude the rest, there they cannot act as one body, and consequently will be immediately dissolved again.

99. Whosoever therefore out of a state of nature unite into a community, must be understood to give up all the power, necessary to the ends for which they unite into society, to the majority of the community, unless they expressly agreed in any number greater than the majority. And this is done by barely agreeing to *unite into one political society*, which is *all the compact* that is, or needs be, between the individuals, that enter into, or make up a commonwealth. And thus that, which begins and actually *constitutes any political society*, is nothing, but the consent of any number of freemen capable of a majority, to unite and incorporate into such a society. And this is that, and that only, which did, or could give beginning to any lawful government in the world. . . .

12 Locke believes in an objective moral law. Do you also believe in it? Do you believe that there are objective moral principles that are binding on everyone? Why or why not?

CHAPTER IX

Of the Ends of Political Society and Government

123. If man in the state of nature be so free, as has been said; if he be absolute lord of his own person and possessions, equal to the greatest, and subject to no body, why will he part with his freedom? Why will he give up this empire, and subject himself to the

John Locke,
Second Treatise of Government

13 Do you agree with Locke that the main reason for people to establish a government is to protect property? Explain.

dominion and control of any other power? To which it is obvious to answer, that though in the state of nature he hath such a right, yet the enjoyment of it is very uncertain, and constantly exposed to the invasion of others. For all being kings as much as he, every man his equal, and the greater part no strict observers of equity and justice, the enjoyment of the property he has in this state is very unsafe, very unsecure. This makes him willing to quit this condition, which, however free, is full of fears and continual dangers: and it is not without reason, that he seeks out, and is willing to join in society with others, who are already united, or have a mind to unite, for the mutual preservation of their lives, liberties, and estates, which I call by the general name, property.

124. The great and *chief end*, therefore, of men's uniting into commonwealths, and putting themselves under government, is *the preservation of their property*. To which in the state of nature there are many things wanting.

First, There wants an established, settled, known law, received and allowed by common consent to be the standard of right and wrong, and the common measure to decide all controversies between them. For though the law of nature be plain and intelligible to all rational creatures; yet men being biassed by their interest, as well as ignorant for want of studying it, are not apt to allow of it as a law binding to them in the application of it to their particular cases.

125. *Secondly*, In the state of nature there wants *a known and indifferent judge*, with authority to determine all differences according to the established law. For every one in that state being both judge and executioner of the law of nature, men being partial to themselves, passion and revenge is very apt to carry them too far, and with too much heat, in their own cases; as well as negligence, and unconcernedness, to make them too remiss in other men's.

126. *Thirdly*, In the state of nature, there often wants power to back and support the sentence when right, and to give it due execution. They who by any injustice offended, will seldom fail, where they are able, by force to make good their injustice; such resistance many times makes the punishment dangerous, and frequently destructive, to those who attempt it.

127. Thus mankind, notwithstanding all the privileges of the state of nature, being but in an ill condition, while they remain in it, are quickly driven into society. Hence it comes to pass that we seldom find any number of men live any time together in this state. The inconveniencies that they are therein exposed to, by the irregular and uncertain exercise of the power every man has of punishing the transgressions of others, make them take sanctuary under the established laws of government, and therein seek *the preservation of their property*. It is this makes them so willingly give up every one his single power of punishing, to be exercised by such alone, as shall be appointed to it amongst them; and by such rules as the community, or those authorized by them to that purpose, shall agree on. And in this we have the original *right and rise of both the legislative and executive power*, as well as of the governments and societies themselves. . . .

CHAPTER XIX

Of the Dissolution of Government

222. The reason why men enter into society, is the preservation of their property, and the end why they choose and authorize a legislative, is, that there may be laws made, and rules set, as guards and fences to the properties of all the members of the society: to limit the power, and moderate the dominion, of every part and member of the society. For since it can never be supposed to be the will of the society, that the legislative

should have a power to destroy that, which every one designs to secure, by entering into society, and for which the people submitted themselves to legislators of their own making, whenever the *legislators endeavour to take away and destroy the property of the people*, or to reduce them to slavery under arbitrary power, they put themselves into a state of war with the people, who are thereupon absolved from any farther obedience, and are left to the common refuge, which God hath provided for all men, against force and violence. Whensoever therefore the legislative shall transgress this fundamental rule of society; and either by ambition, fear, folly or corruption, *endeavour to grasp themselves, or put into the hands of any other an absolute power* over the lives, liberties, and estates of the people; by this breach of trust they *forfeit the power*, the people had put into their hands, for quite contrary ends, and it devolves to the people, who have a right to resume their original liberty, and, by the establishment of a new legislative (such as they shall think fit) provide for their own safety and security, which is the end for which they are in society. What I have said here, concerning the legislative in general, holds true also concerning the supreme executor, who having a double trust put in him, both to have a part in the legislative, and the supreme execution of the law, acts against both, when he goes about to set up his own arbitrary will, as the law of the society. He *acts* also *contrary to his trust*, when he either employs the force, treasure, and offices of the society to corrupt the *representatives*, and gain them to his purposes; or openly pre-engages the *electors*, and prescribes to their choice, such, whom he has by solicitations, threats, promises, or otherwise, won to his designs: and employs them to bring in such, who have promised before-hand, what to vote, and what to enact. Thus to regulate candidates and electors, and new model the ways of election, what is it but to cut up the government by the roots, and poison the very fountain of public security? for the people having reserved to themselves the choice of their *representatives*, as the fence to their properties, could do it for no other end, but that they might always be freely chosen, and so chosen, freely act, and advise, as the necessity of the commonwealth, and the public good should, upon examination and mature debate, be judged to require. This, those who give their votes before they hear the debate, and have weighed the reasons on all sides, are not capable of doing. To prepare such an assembly as this, and endeavour to set up the declared abettors of his own will, for the true representatives of the people, and the law-makers of the society, is certainly as great a *breach of trust*, and as perfect a declaration of a design to subvert the government, as is possible to be met with. To which if one shall add rewards and punishments visibly employed to the same end, and all the arts of perverted law made use of, to take off and destroy all that stand in the way of such a design, and will not comply and consent to betray the liberties of their country, it will be past doubt what is doing. What power they ought to have in the society, who thus employ it contrary to the trust that went along with it in its first institution, is easy to determine; and one cannot but see, that he, who has once attempted any such thing as this, cannot any longer be trusted.[6]

14 Do citizens of a state ever have the right to overthrow their government? How would a utilitarian answer this question? How does Locke answer it? Which view is closer to your beliefs? Why?

Government does not solve problems; it subsidizes them.
—Ronald Reagan

Liberalism is the political doctrine that puts primary emphasis on the liberty and rights of individuals against encroachments by the state. It is at the heart of political outlooks that today are given the vague labels of *liberalism* and *conservatism*, for *both* ideologies take for granted that basic individual liberties and rights should be protected against unacceptable government intrusion. They differ in how they define unacceptable involvement of the government. Locke's theory of justice is a form

Liberalism is the political doctrine that puts primary emphasis on the liberty and rights of individuals against encroachments by the state.

Classical liberalism is the view that the state should protect personal freedoms as well as the right to pursue one's own social and economic well-being in a free market without interference from others.

Libertarianism (political) is the view that government should be small and limited to night-watchman functions.

of liberalism—**classical liberalism**, the view that the state should protect personal freedoms as well as the right to pursue one's own social and economic well-being in a free market without interference from others. In contemporary politics, classical liberalism most resembles what is known as (political) **libertarianism**. Libertarians insist that government should be small and limited to night-watchman functions—the protection of society and free economic systems from coercion and fraud. All other social or economic benefits are the responsibility of individuals.

Rawls

David Hume, whom we met in earlier chapters, was a severe critic of social contract theory as offered up by Hobbes and Locke. He declared that social contracts are historical fictions—no such contracts have existed in reality. Governments have been established by conquest and force, not by agreements among equals in a state of nature. This criticism did not matter much to many later theorists because they viewed the theories of Locke, Hobbes, and others not as historical facts, but mostly

PHILOSOPHERS AT WORK

Figure 8.9 John Locke, empiricist philosopher and political theorist.

John Locke

The philosopher John Locke (1632–1704) is the senior theorist among the British empiricists and perhaps, as some say, the greatest English philosopher in the early modern period (the first decades after Descartes). Eventually he became the most renowned intellectual in England and possibly throughout the Continent.

He was born into a Puritan family, studied moral philosophy and logic at Oxford, and then set his sights on a career in medicine. Like his fellow empiricist Thomas Hobbes, he rubbed elbows with many of the great thinkers of the day. He knew the famous chemist Robert Boyle as well as the physicist Isaac Newton and encountered other notables at the Royal Society.

For a while he was secretary to the earl of Shaftesbury, who became his patron. This relationship involved him in Protestant politics and in talk of resistance to Charles II, the Catholic king. Consequently, Shaftesbury had to flee to Holland, and Locke followed him in 1683, returning to England in 1689.

Locke was not an academic who directed his writings at other philosophers. He preferred instead to address important issues in contemporary society, aiming his writing at an educated public. His best known works include *Essay Concerning Human Understanding*, *Second Treatise of Government*, and *Letter on Toleration*, all published in 1689.

as explanations of how states *could be* formed and justified. Nevertheless, Hume's attack dampened interest in social contract theories of justice for two centuries—until the work of John Rawls (1921–2002).

Rawls also thinks of social contracts as fictions—but very *useful* fictions. He believes they give us a way to explore the requirements of distributive justice. He asks, in effect, What kind of social contract would best ensure a fair distribution of rights, duties, and advantages of social cooperation? To answer this question, he proposes an ingenious thought experiment. Imagine we are living in a state of nature and want to devise a social contract that ensures that everyone is treated fairly. What kind of state would we all agree to? Specifically, by what principles should our just society structure itself? His response is that the required principles are those that people would agree to under hypothetical conditions that ensure fair and unbiased choices. He holds that if the starting point for the social contract is fair—if the initial conditions and bargaining process for producing the principles are fair—then the principles themselves will be just and will define the essential makeup of a just society. As Rawls says,

John Rawls, *A Theory of Justice*

[The] guiding idea is that the principles of justice for the basic structure of society are the object of the original agreement. They are the principles that free and rational persons concerned to further their own interests would accept in an initial position of equality as defining the fundamental terms of their association. These principles are to regulate all further agreements; they specify the kinds of social cooperation that can be entered into and the forms of government that can be established.[7]

At the hypothetical starting point—what Rawls calls the "original position"—a group of normal, self-interested, rational individuals come together to choose the principles that will determine their basic rights and duties and their share of society's benefits and burdens. But to ensure that their decisions are as fair and impartial as possible, they must meet behind a metaphorical "veil of ignorance." Behind the veil, no one knows his or her own social or economic status, class, race, sex, abilities, talents, level of intelligence, or psychological makeup. Rawls thinks that since the participants are rational and self-interested but ignorant of their situation in society, they will not agree to principles that will put any particular group at a disadvantage, because they might very well be members of that group. They will choose principles that are unbiased and nondiscriminatory. The assumption is that since the negotiating conditions in the original position are fair, the agreements reached will also be fair—the principles will be just.

Rawls contends that given the original position, the participants would agree to arrange their social relationships according to these fundamental principles:

FIRST PRINCIPLE

Each person is to have an equal right to the most extensive total system of equal basic liberties compatible with a similar system of liberty for all.

John Rawls,
A Theory of Justice

John Rawls,
A Theory of Justice

Giving money and power
to government is like
giving whiskey and car
keys to teenage boys.
—P. J. O. Rourke

15 Are you more
sympathetic to liber-
tarianism or welfare
liberalism? Why?

SECOND PRINCIPLE

Social and economic inequalities are to be arranged so that they are both:
   (a) to the greatest benefit of the least advantaged, . . . and
   (b) attached to offices and positions open to all under conditions of fair equality
       of opportunity.[8]

The first principle—the equal liberty principle—says that everyone is entitled to
the most political freedom possible in exercising basic rights and duties (for example,
the right to vote and hold office and freedom of speech, assembly, and thought).
Each person should get a maximum degree of basic liberties, but no more than
anyone else. This principle takes precedence over all other considerations (including
the second principle), so that basic political liberties cannot be reduced or cancelled
just to improve economic well-being. This stipulation, of course, directly contradicts
utilitarian views of the matter.

The second principle concerns social and economic goods such as income,
wealth, opportunities, and positions of authority. Rawls recognizes that some social
and economic inequalities in society are unavoidable as well as beneficial. Those
who work harder or devise a better mousetrap deserve to reap greater benefits for
their efforts. Such inequality provides incentives
for extraordinary productivity, which in turn will
be to the good of society as a whole. (This kind of
unequal social arrangement contrasts with systems
that aim at a much greater degree of equality, as in
socialist societies.) So Rawls asserts in part (a) that
social and economic inequalities are not unjust if
they work to everyone's benefit, especially to the
benefit of the least well off in society. "[There] is no
injustice," he says, "in the greater benefits earned
by a few provided that the situation of persons not
so fortunate is thereby improved."[9] For Rawls, such
a policy is far more just than one in which some
people are made to suffer for the greater good of
others: "It is not just that some should have less in
order that others may prosper."

But Rawls also maintains that although economic inequalities are allowed, and not everyone
will obtain the greater rewards, everyone should
at least have an equal *opportunity* to acquire them.
This is the message of part (b). Every person is entitled to an equal chance to try to acquire basic
goods. No one is guaranteed an equal share of
them, but opportunities to obtain these benefits
must be open to all, regardless of social standing.

In Rawls's program, the demands of the first
principle must be satisfied before satisfying the

Figure 8.10 John Rawls (1921–2002).

second, and the requirements of part (b) must be met before those of part (a). In any just distribution of benefits and burdens, then, the first priority is to ensure equal basic political liberties for all concerned, then equality of social and economic opportunity, then the arrangement of any inequalities to the benefit of the least advantaged.

Rawls's theory of justice has significant implications for the allocation of society's resources. Consider, for example, the hotly debated resource of health care. One prominent line of argument goes like this: As Rawls claims, everyone is entitled to fair equality of opportunity, and adequate (basic) health care enables fair equality of opportunity (by ensuring "normal species functioning"). Therefore, everyone is entitled to adequate health care, which includes all appropriate measures for eliminating or compensating for the disadvantages of disease and impairment.[10] In such a system, there would be universal access to a basic level of health care, while more elaborate or elective services would be available to anyone who could afford them.

Rawls's proposal is a form of liberalism, what has been called **welfare liberalism**. Its aim is to preserve individual liberties while ensuring the general welfare of the citizenry. It requires the redistribution of resources (for example, taxing the better off to provide benefits to the less well off)—a scheme that libertarians would never countenance. The libertarian says that government should not be in the business of helping the socially or economically disadvantaged, for that would require violating people's liberty by taking resources from the haves to give to the have-nots.

> **Welfare liberalism** is a form of liberalism, the aim of which is to preserve individual liberties while ensuring the general welfare of the citizenry.

WRITING TO UNDERSTAND:
CRITIQUING PHILOSOPHICAL VIEWS   Section 8.3

1. Hobbes says that once people cede power to a strong governmental authority, the authority wields total authority over them; the government's power is unalterable and absolute. Do you think such a government is necessary for people to live in peace? Why or why not? What states in the world today fit Hobbes's description of the Leviathan?

2. Hobbes believes that there is no such thing as justice until the Leviathan is established. This means that justice does not exist independently of an authority to define and enforce it. Explain why you agree or disagree with this view.

3. Locke thinks that people have a right to rebel against a government that abuses its power. Do you agree? If so, under what conditions would you think rebellion is justified?

4. Was the United States founded according to the principles of classical liberalism, welfare liberalism, or something else? Has the country stayed true to its origins? Explain.

5. Is classical liberalism a better theory of justice than welfare liberalism? Support your answer with reasons.

8.4 SOCIALIST THEORIES

I am convinced that the path to a new, better and possible world is not capitalism, the path is socialism.
—Hugo Chavez

Socialism is the doctrine that the means of production (property, factories, businesses) should be owned or controlled by the people, either communally or through the state.

Communism usually implies socialism within a totalitarian system.

Capitalism is a political economic system that lets the means of production accrue to fewer people through the workings of a free market. In such a system, wealth goes to anyone who can acquire it in the marketplace.

The prevailing theories of justice throughout the world are liberalism and socialism. **Socialism** is the political and economic doctrine that the means of production (property, factories, businesses) should be owned or controlled by the people, either communally or through the state. Socialism can accommodate liberal democratic forms of government and can even retain some elements of market capitalism. **Communism** usually implies socialism within a totalitarian system.

The guiding principle of the socialist view is equality: The wealth of society should be shared by all. The ideal distribution of goods usually follows the classic formula laid down by Karl Marx (1818–1883), the father of modern socialism: "From each according to his ability, to each according to his needs." People should do work that fits their abilities, and they should reap rewards that match their needs. Generally, liberal societies let the means of production accrue to fewer people through the workings of a free market—that is, through **capitalism**. In such a system, wealth goes to anyone who can acquire it in the marketplace, but in a socialist system, wealth is controlled by the state, which allocates it for the good of the people generally.

Few philosophers have had as much influence on the world as Marx has—who, ironically, did not consider himself a philosopher and did not believe that ideas alone could have much of an impact on history. He thinks that what drives philosophy, history, society, law, government, and morality is economics. It is the dominant system of economics in every age, he says, that determines how society is structured and how history will go. A society's system of economics is defined by its means of production—by its economic and technological ways of meeting people's physical and social needs. The means of production, Marx says, shape social relationships, class structure, technological tools, and political and philosophical ideas. Those who own and control the means of production make up the dominant class, possess most of the wealth, wield most of the political power, and exploit the lower class. Their ideas—political, philosophical, or social—are the ruling ideas. The rest of the people own no property and occupy the lowest rungs of society, selling their labor to the ruling class, the property owners. The two camps, then, are forever at odds.

Marx maintains that this pattern of opposition—this class struggle—repeats itself throughout history. It is inevitable and unalterable. In it he sees a *dialectic process* unfold again and again in society: first there is a historical starting point (the *thesis*), which eventually produces a state of affairs directly opposed to it (the *antithesis*), the conflict being resolved by a new situation (the *synthesis*). Marx thinks the dialectic struggle in modern times is between those who own the means of production (the *bourgeoisie*, or capitalists) and those who do not (the *proletariat*). The bourgeoisie are few but own all the factories and other means of production (thesis); the proletariat are many but own nothing, serving only as workers in the capitalist system (antithesis). To increase their profits, the bourgeoisie hire more and more workers but pay them less and less, replacing workers with machines whenever possible.

Figure 8.11 Karl Marx (1818–1883).

PHILOSOPHY LAB

Imagine that the United States has evolved into a libertarian paradise. The government is small, charged only with the limited functions of protecting society and economic systems from coercion and fraud. All other social and economic benefits are the responsibility of individuals. People have maximum freedom to pursue their economic goals without interference from the government. Taxes are extremely low, raised only to fund the military and whatever forces are needed to secure people's social and economic rights. There are no entitlement programs—no Social Security, no Medicare, no health care programs, no student loans, no welfare systems of any kind. Government regulation of business is minimal, as is consumer protection. There are no minimum-wage laws and no government attempts to redistribute wealth or to help the poor, disabled, disadvantaged, or elderly.

Would you want to live in such a society? Would your life be better or worse in it? What would you like or dislike most about this social system? Overall, would people be better or worse off in a thoroughly libertarian America?

The workers' wages decline, more become unemployed, and their exploitation by the capitalists continues. As their situation worsens, Marx observes, they have an increased sense of *alienation*: they are no longer valued as persons, for they have become mere cogs in the capitalist machinery; and they can no longer take pride in their work, for it has been downgraded into mindless assembly-line motions. But ultimately the success of the bourgeoisie proves to be their undoing. They produce, as Marx says, their own gravediggers. They unwittingly create a large, poor, angry proletarian class that has had enough of capitalism and the woes that come with it. A proletarian revolution sweeps the old order away and eventually ushers in a classless society (synthesis) in which the means of production belong to everyone and wealth is shared equally among equals.

A frequent criticism of socialism is that a distribution of goods according to needs and abilities would require coercion by the state. For socialism to work, people must be forced to do the jobs that match their skills, not the jobs they prefer. And they must be compelled to accept the benefits (monetary or otherwise) that match their needs, not the benefits they most desire.

Critics also accuse socialist systems of providing no incentive for people to excel at their jobs. Under socialism, people are rewarded according to their needs, not by how well or how hard they work. So what inducement is there to be more ambitious or efficient?

16 Is Marx correct in saying that a society's means of production shape its political and philosophical ideas? What about religion, culture, social reformers—can any of these influence a society's thinking?

Capitalism is war; socialism is peace.

—Karl Liebknecht

17 Do ideas affect history? Marx says no. But his socialist ideas seem to have affected history profoundly. Does this fact disprove Marx's claim?

PHILOSOPHY NOW

Is the United States a Socialist Country?

To many Americans, socialism is a dirty word. President Obama has been accused of trying to turn the United States into a socialist country like those in Europe. To score points with the electorate, politicians label their opponents socialists. Some political theorists say that a little socialism won't hurt and might help, and a few declare that the debate is silly because the United States is already a socialist country. Is it?

It depends on your definition of socialism. Some people (including a few television commentators) say that a government is socialist if it runs social programs that otherwise could be left to the marketplace—programs like public education, prisons, aid to the poor, and Medicare. By this standard, the United States is indeed socialist. But the traditional definition is more like the one given at the beginning of this section: socialism is the doctrine that the *means of production* (property, factories, businesses) should be owned or controlled by the people, either communally or through the state. The programs just mentioned are generally not considered means of production. Neither are such things as police and fire protection, national defense, and income redistribution. Welfare programs are examples not of socialism but of welfare liberalism. So even though the United States may have some socialist elements (such as partial ownership and control of the banking industry), it's not predominantly socialist—and calling it that would be an exaggeration.

Suppose the government owns and runs all technology companies, half the farms, and the entire steel industry. Would the United States then be properly called socialist? What would be the advantages or disadvantages of such a scheme?

Marx conveyed his views over many years and in several writings, the most well known being the *Manifesto of the Communist Party* (1848), which he coauthored with his colleague Friedrich Engels:

Karl Marx and Friedrich Engels, *Manifesto of the Communist Party*

A specter is haunting Europe—the specter of communism. All the powers of old Europe have entered into a holy alliance to exorcise this specter: Pope and Czar, Metternich and Guizot, French radicals and German police spies.

Where is the party in opposition that has not been decried as communistic by its opponents in power? Where the opposition that has not hurled back the branding reproach of communism against the more advanced opposition parties, as well as against its reactionary adversaries?

Two things result from this fact:

I. Communism is already acknowledged by all European powers to be itself a power.

II. It is high time that communists should openly, in the face of the whole world, publish their views, their aims, their tendencies, and meet this nursery tale of the specter of communism with a Manifesto of the party itself.

To this end, communists of various nationalities have assembled in London and sketched the following Manifesto, to be published in the English, French, German, Italian, Flemish, and Danish languages.

The history of all hitherto existing society is the history of class struggles.

Free man and slave, patrician and plebeian, lord and serf, guild master and journeyman, in a word, oppressor and oppressed, stood in constant opposition to one another, carried on an uninterrupted, now hidden, now open fight, a fight that each time ended either in a revolutionary reconstitution of society at large or in the common ruin of the contending classes.

In the earlier epochs of history we find almost everywhere a complicated arrangement of society into various orders, a manifold gradation of social rank. In ancient Rome we have patricians, knights, plebeians, slaves; in the Middle Ages, feudal lords, vassals, guild masters, journeymen, apprentices, serfs; in almost all of these classes, again, subordinate gradations.

The modern bourgeois [capitalist] society that has sprouted from the ruins of feudal society has not done away with class antagonisms. It has but established new classes, new conditions of oppression, new forms of struggle in place of the old ones.

Our epoch, the epoch of the bourgeoisie, possesses, however, this distinctive feature: it has simplified the class antagonisms. Society as a whole is more and more splitting up into two great hostile camps, into two great classes directly facing each other: bourgeoisie and proletariat. . . .

The bourgeoisie cannot exist without constantly revolutionizing the instruments of production, and thereby the relations of production, and with them the whole relations of society. Conservation of the old modes of production in unaltered form was, on the contrary, the first condition of existence for all earlier industrial classes. Constant revolutionizing of production, uninterrupted disturbance of all social conditions, everlasting uncertainty and agitation distinguish the bourgeois epoch from all earlier ones. All fixed, fast-frozen relations, with their train of ancient and venerable prejudices and opinions, are swept away, all newformed ones become antiquated before they can ossify. All that is solid melts into air, all that is holy is profaned, and man is at last compelled to face with sober senses his real conditions of life and his relations with his kind.

The need of a constantly expanding market for its products chases the bourgeoisie over the whole surface of the globe. It must nestle everywhere, settle everywhere, establish connections everywhere.

The bourgeoisie has through its exploitation of the world market given a cosmopolitan character to production and consumption in every country. To the great chagrin of reactionists, it has drawn from under the feet of industry the national ground on which it stood. All old-established national industries have been destroyed or are daily being destroyed. They are dislodged by new industries, whose introduction

Democracy and socialism have nothing in common but one word, equality. But notice the difference: while democracy seeks equality in liberty, socialism seeks equality in restraint and servitude.
—Alexis de Tocqueville

As with the Christian religion, the worst advertisement for Socialism is its adherents.
—George Orwell

18 Many countries have developed a large middle class that doesn't seem to fit into Marx's two-class scheme. Is this fact a counterexample to his theory?

Karl Marx and Friedrich Engels, *Manifesto of the Communist Party*

19 Marx lists the many technological and civic innovations brought about by capitalism, things that seem beneficial to society. Do they counterbalance the many bad things about capitalism that Marx details?

becomes a life and death question for all civilized nations, by industries that no longer work up indigenous raw material, but raw material drawn from the remotest zones; industries whose products are consumed not only at home, but in every quarter of the globe. In place of the old wants, satisfied by the productions of the country, we find new wants, requiring for their satisfaction the products of distant lands and climes. In place of the old local and national seclusion and self-sufficiency we have intercourse in every direction, universal interdependence of nations. And as in material, so also in intellectual production. The intellectual creations of individual nations become common property. National one-sidedness and narrow-mindedness become more and more impossible, and from the numerous national and local literatures there arises a world literature.

The bourgeoisie, by the rapid improvement of all instruments of production, by the immensely facilitated means of communication, draws all, even the most barbarian, nations into civilization. The cheap prices of its commodities are the heavy artillery with which it batters down all Chinese walls, with which it forces the barbarians' intensely obstinate hatred of foreigners to capitulate. It compels all nations, on pain of extinction, to adopt the bourgeois mode of production: it compels them to introduce what it calls civilization into their midst, i.e., to become bourgeois themselves. In one word, it creates a world after its own image.

The bourgeoisie has subjected the country to the rule of the towns. It has created enormous cities, has greatly increased the urban population as compared with the rural, and has thus rescued a considerable part of the population from the idiocy of rural life. Just as it has made the country dependent on the towns, so it has made barbarian and semi-barbarian countries dependent on the civilized ones, nations of peasants on nations of bourgeois, the East on the West.

The bourgeoisie keeps more and more doing away with the scattered state of the population, of the means of production, and of property. It has agglomerated population, centralized means of production, and has concentrated property in a few hands. The necessary consequence of this was political centralization. Independent, or but loosely connected provinces, with separate interests, laws, governments and systems of taxation, became lumped together into one nation, with one government, one code of laws, one national class interest, one frontier, and one customs tariff.

The bourgeoisie, during its rule of scarce one hundred years, has created more massive and more colossal productive forces than have all preceding generations together. Subjection of nature's forces to man, machinery, application of chemistry to industry and agriculture, steam navigation, railways, electric telegraphs, clearing of whole continents for cultivation, canalization of rivers, whole populations conjured out of the ground—what earlier century had even a presentiment that such productive forces slumbered in the lap of social labor? . . .

But not only has the bourgeoisie forged the weapons that bring death to itself; it has also called into existence the men who are to wield those weapons—the modern working class—the proletarians.

In proportion as the bourgeoisie, i.e., capital, is developed, in the same proportion is the proletariat, the modern working class developed—a class of laborers, who live only so long as they find work, and who find work only so long as their labor increases capital. These laborers, who must sell themselves piecemeal, are a commodity, like every other article of commerce, and are consequently exposed to all the vicissitudes of competition, to all the fluctuations of the market.

Owing to the extensive use of machinery and to division of labor, the work of the proletarians has lost all individual character and, consequently, all charm for the workman. He becomes an appendage of the machine, and it is only the simplest, most monotonous, and most easily acquired knack that is required of him. Hence the cost of production of a workman is restricted, almost entirely, to the means of subsistence that he requires for his maintenance and for the propagation of his race. But the price of a commodity, and therefore also of labor, is equal to its cost of production. In proportion, therefore, as the repulsiveness of the work increases, the wage decreases. Nay, more, in proportion as the use of machinery and division of labor increases, in the same proportion the burden of toil also increases, whether by prolongation of the working hours, by increase of the work exacted in a given time, or by increased speed of the machinery, etc.

Modern industry has converted the little workshop of the patriarchal master into the great factory of the industrial capitalist. Masses of laborers, crowded into the factory, are organized like soldiers. As privates of the industrial army they are placed under the command of a perfect hierarchy of officers and sergeants. Not only are they slaves of the bourgeois class, and of the bourgeois state; they are daily and hourly enslaved by the machine, by the overlooker, and, above all, by the individual bourgeois manufacturer himself. The more openly this despotism proclaims gain to be its end and aim, the more petty, the more hateful, and the more embittering it is. . . .

The proletariat goes through various stages of development. With its birth begins its struggle with the bourgeoisie. At first the contest is carried on by individual laborers, then by the workpeople of a factory, then by the operatives of one trade, in one locality, against the individual bourgeois who directly exploits them. They direct their attacks not against the bourgeois conditions of production, but against the instruments of production themselves; they destroy imported wares that compete with their labor, they smash to pieces machinery, they set factories ablaze, they seek to restore by force the vanished status of the workman of the Middle Ages. . . .

But with the development of industry the proletariat not only increases in number; it becomes concentrated in greater masses, its strength grows, and it feels that strength more. The various interests and conditions of life within the ranks of the proletariat are more and more equalized, in proportion as machinery obliterates all distinctions of labor and nearly everywhere reduces wages to the same low level. The growing competition among the bourgeois and the resulting commercial crises make the wages of the workers ever more fluctuating. The unceasing improvement of machinery, ever more rapidly developing, makes their livelihood more and more precarious; the collisions between individual workmen and individual bourgeois take more and more the character of collisions between two classes. Thereupon the workers begin to form combinations (trade unions) against the bourgeois; they club together in order to keep up the rate of wages; they found permanent associations in order to make provision beforehand for these occasional revolts. Here and there the contest breaks out into riots.

Now and then the workers are victorious, but only for a time. The real fruit of their battles lies not in the immediate result, but in the ever expanding union of the workers. This union is helped on by the improved means of communication that are created by modern industry and that place the workers of different localities in contact with one another. . . .

This organization of the proletarians into a class, and consequently into a political party, is continually being upset again by the competition between the workers

20 For capitalist societies, Marx predicts worker alienation, oppression and exploitation of workers, and general misery among those who do not control the means of production. Many societies today, including the United States, are capitalist, but they do not seem to be following Marx's pattern. Does this show that Marx's views are wrong?

Karl Marx and Friedrich Engels, *Manifesto of the Communist Party*

themselves. But it ever rises up again, stronger, firmer, mightier. It compels legislative recognition of particular interests of the workers by taking advantage of the divisions among the bourgeoisie itself. . . .

Hitherto every form of society has been based, as we have already seen, on the antagonism of oppressing and oppressed classes. But in order to oppress a class certain conditions must be assured to it under which it can, at least, continue its slavish existence. The serf, in the period of serfdom, raised himself to membership in the commune just as the petty bourgeois, under the yoke of feudal absolutism, managed to develop into a bourgeois. The modern laborer, on the contrary, instead of rising with the progress of industry, sinks deeper and deeper below the conditions of existence of his own class. He becomes a pauper, and pauperism develops more rapidly than population and wealth. And here it becomes evident that the bourgeoisie is unfit any longer to be the ruling class in society, and to impose its conditions of existence upon society as an overriding law. It is unfit to rule because it is incompetent to assure an existence to its slave within his slavery, because it cannot help letting him sink into such a state that it has to feed him instead of being fed by him. Society can no longer live under this bourgeoisie: in other words, its existence is no longer compatible with society.

The essential condition for the existence, and for the sway of the bourgeois class, is the formation and augmentation of capital; the condition for capital is wage labor. Wage labor rests exclusively on competition between the laborers. The advance of industry, whose involuntary promoter is the bourgeoisie, replaces the isolation of the laborers, due to competition, by their revolutionary combination, due to association. The development of modern industry, therefore, cuts from under its feet the very foundation on which the bourgeoisie produces and appropriates products. What the bourgeoisie, therefore, produces, above all, is its own gravediggers. Its fall and the victory of the proletariat are equally inevitable. . . .

All property relations in the past have continually been subject to historical change consequent upon the change in historical conditions.

The French Revolution, for example, abolished feudal property in favor of bourgeois property.

The distinguishing feature of communism is not the abolition of property generally, but the abolition of bourgeoisie property. But modern bourgeois private property is the final and most complete expression of the system of producing and appropriating products that is based on antagonisms, on the exploitation of the many by the few.

In this sense the theory of the communists may be summed up in the single sentence: Abolition of private property. . . .

We have seen above that the first step in the revolution by the working class is to raise the proletariat to the position of ruling class, to win the battle of democracy.

The proletariat will use its political supremacy to wrest, by degrees, all capital from the bourgeoisie, to centralize all instruments of production in the hands of the state, i.e., of the proletariat organized as the ruling class, and to increase the total of productive forces as rapidly as possible.

Of course, in the beginning this cannot be effected except by means of despotic inroads on the rights of property and on the conditions of bourgeois production; by means of measures, therefore, which appear economically insufficient and untenable, but which, in the course of the movement, outstrip themselves, necessitate further

21 Many Western countries have been strongly committed to private property for decades, yet no proletarian revolution has erupted or is likely to erupt. Why is this? Does it show that Marx's socialist ideology is mistaken?

inroads upon the old social order, and are unavoidable as a means of entirely revolutionizing the mode of production.

These measures will of course be different in different countries.

Nevertheless, in the most advanced countries the following will be pretty generally applicable:

1. Abolition of property in land and application of all rents of land to public purposes.
2. A heavy progressive or graduated income tax.
3. Abolition of all right of inheritance.
4. Confiscation of the property of all emigrants and rebels.
5. Centralization of credit in the hands of the state, by means of a national bank with state capital and an exclusive monopoly.
6. Centralization of the means of communication and transport in the hands of the state.
7. Extension of factories and instruments of production owned by the state; the bringing into cultivation of wastelands, and the improvement of the soil generally in accordance with a common plan.
8. Equal liability of all labor. Establishment of industrial armies, especially for agriculture.
9. Combination of agriculture with manufacturing industries; gradual abolition of the distinction between town and country, by a more equable distribution of the population over the country.
10. Free education for all children in public schools. Abolition of children's factory labor in its present form. Combination of education with industrial production, etc.

When, in the course of development, class distinctions have disappeared and all production has been concentrated in the hands of a vast association of the whole nation, the public power will lose its political character. Political power, properly so called, is merely the organized power of one class for oppressing another. If the proletariat during its contest with the bourgeoisie is compelled, by the force of circumstances, to organize itself as a class, if by means of a revolution, it makes itself the ruling class and, as such, sweeps away by force the old conditions of production, then it will, along with these conditions, have swept away the conditions for the existence of class antagonisms and of classes generally, and will thereby have abolished its own supremacy as a class.

In place of the old bourgeois society, with its classes and class antagonisms, we shall have an association in which the free development of each is the condition for the free development of all. . . .

The communists disdain to conceal their views and aims. They openly declare that their ends can be attained only by the forcible overthrow of all existing social conditions. Let the ruling classes tremble at a communistic revolution. The proletarians have nothing to lose but their chains. They have a world to win.

WORKING MEN OF ALL COUNTRIES UNITE![11]

> **WRITING TO UNDERSTAND:**
> **CRITIQUING PHILOSOPHICAL VIEWS** Section 8.4
>
> 1. A classical liberal might say to a Marxist that liberty and rights are the most important values in a society, and Marxist societies have few, if any, liberties. The Marxist might reply that liberties and rights don't mean much if people are too poor and oppressed to enjoy them. Which view seems more reasonable to you? Which society would you be willing to live in—classical liberal or Marxist? Why?
>
> 2. Does alienation as described by Marx exist today in modern capitalist societies? Explain.
>
> 3. Suppose all resources in the United States were distributed according to Marx's dictum: from each according to his ability, to each according to his need. What would such a society look like? Would it be better than the system that exists now? Why or why not?
>
> 4. Suppose the state compelled you to work in a factory for the rest of your life, and it arranged for your salary to be based solely on what the state thinks you need. Would these actions be a violation of your autonomy? If they would improve the general welfare, would they be morally justified?
>
> 5. Assess socialism: Is it a good theory of justice? Is it better than liberalism? Explain your answer.

8.5 FEMINISM AND SOCIAL JUSTICE

Of all the nasty outcomes predicted for women's liberation . . . none was more alarming, from a feminist point of view, than the suggestion that women would eventually become just like men.
—Barbara Ehrenreich

I myself have never been able to find out precisely what feminism is: I only know that people call me a feminist whenever I express sentiments that differentiate me from a doormat.
—Rebecca West

Many feminists assert that the traditional theories of justice (as developed by their theorists) have a fatal weakness: they are blind to injustice. Specifically, the theories are blind to the injustice that befalls women. The problem arises, these critics say, because the theories are based on a false assumption about society, one that most of us simply take for granted. Most people—including Locke, Hobbes, and other traditional theorists—have assumed there is a strong wall of separation between *private* and *public* life, and that only public life is the proper concern of political theory. Private life is about personal and family life, about raising children and shouldering other domestic responsibilities. Public life is the realm of politics, careers, economics, and law. Throughout history, women have largely been relegated to the private sphere, where issues of rights and equality are not supposed to apply. Consequently, feminist philosophers contend, women have been left out of traditional theories of justice, an omission that ensured women would not be treated as the moral equals of men. The result has been unjust treatment of half the population—millions of women who have historically been denied the political, economic, and social power that men have enjoyed.

This view has been argued vigorously by the philosopher and feminist Susan Moller Okin (1946–2004) in her book *Justice, Gender, and the Family*:

Susan Moller Okin, *Justice, Gender, and the Family*

We as a society pride ourselves on our democratic values. We don't believe people should be constrained by innate differences from being able to achieve desired positions of influence or to improve their well-being; equality of opportunity is our professed aim. The Preamble to our Constitution stresses the importance of justice, as well as the general welfare and the blessings of liberty. The Pledge of Allegiance asserts that our republic preserves "liberty and justice for all."

Yet substantial inequalities between the sexes still exist in our society. In economic terms, full-time working women (after some very recent improvement) earn on average 71 percent of the earnings of full-time working men. One-half of poor and three-fifths of chronically poor households with dependent children are maintained by a single female parent. The poverty rate for elderly women is nearly twice that for elderly men. On the political front, two out of a hundred U.S. senators are women, one out of nine justices seems to be considered sufficient female representation on the Supreme Court, and the number of men chosen in each congressional election far exceeds the number of women elected in the entire history of the country. Underlying and intertwined with all these inequalities is the unequal distribution of the unpaid labor of the family.

An equal sharing between the sexes of family responsibilities, especially child care, is "the great revolution that has not happened." Women, including mothers of young children, are, of course, working outside the household far more than their mothers did. And the small proportion of women who reach high-level positions in politics, business, and the professions command a vastly disproportionate amount of space in the media, compared with the millions of women who work at low-paying, dead-end jobs, the millions who do part-time work with its lack of benefits, and the millions of others who stay home performing for no pay what is frequently not even acknowledged as work. Certainly, the fact that women are doing more paid work does not imply that they are more equal. It is often said that we are living in a postfeminist era. This claim, due in part to the distorted emphasis on women who have "made it," is false, no matter which of its meanings is intended. It is certainly not true that feminism has been vanquished, and equally untrue that it is no longer needed because its aims have been fulfilled. Until there is justice within the family, women will not be able to gain equality in politics, at work, or in any other sphere. . . .

[T]he typical current practices of family life, structured to a large extent by gender, are not just. Both the expectation and the experience of the division of labor by sex make women vulnerable. As I shall show, a cycle of power relations and decisions pervades both family and workplace, each reinforcing the inequalities between the sexes that already exist within the other. Not only women, but children of both sexes, too, are often made vulnerable by gender-structured marriage. One-quarter of children in the United States now live in families with only one parent—in almost 90 percent of cases, the mother. Contrary to common perceptions—in which the situation of never-married mothers looms largest—65 percent of single-parent families are a result of marital separation or divorce. Recent research in a number of states has shown that, in the

22 Why does the unequal treatment of women seem to contradict principles laid out in the U.S. Constitution? Is the problem with the principles or with society?

Figure 8.12 Susan Moller Okin (1946–2004).

average case, the standard of living of divorced women and the children who live with them plummets after divorce, whereas the economic situation of divorced men tends to be better than when they were married.

A central source of injustice for women these days is that the law, most noticeably in the event of divorce, treats more or less as equals those whom custom, workplace discrimination, and the still conventional division of labor within the family have made very unequal. Central to this socially created inequality are two commonly made but inconsistent presumptions: that women are primarily responsible for the rearing of children; and that serious and committed members of the work force (regardless of class) do not have primary responsibility, or even shared responsibility, for the rearing of children. The old assumption of the workplace, still implicit, is that workers have wives at home. It is built not only into the structure and expectations of the workplace but into other crucial social institutions, such as schools, which make no attempt to take account, in their scheduled hours or vacations, of the fact that parents are likely to hold jobs.

Now, of course, many wage workers do not have wives at home. Often, they are wives and mothers, or single, separated, or divorced mothers of small children. But neither the family nor the workplace has taken much account of this fact. Employed wives still do by far the greatest proportion of unpaid family work, such as child care and housework. Women are far more likely to take time out of the workplace or to work part-time because of family responsibilities than are their husbands or male partners. And they are much more likely to move because of their husbands' employment needs or opportunities than their own. All these tendencies, which are due to a number of factors, including the sex segregation and discrimination of the workplace itself, tend to be cyclical in their effects: wives advance more slowly than their husbands at work and thus gain less seniority, and the discrepancy between their wages increases over time. Then, because both the power structure of the family and what is regarded as consensual "rational" family decision making reflect the fact that the husband usually earns more, it will become even less likely as time goes on that the unpaid work of the family will be shared between the spouses. Thus the cycle of inequality is perpetuated. Often hidden from view within a marriage, it is in the increasingly likely event of marital breakdown that the socially constructed inequality of married women is at its most visible.

This is what I mean when I say that gender-structured marriage makes women vulnerable. These are not matters of natural necessity, as some people would believe. Surely nothing in our natures dictates that men should not be equal participants in the rearing of their children. Nothing in the nature of work makes it impossible to adjust it to the fact that people are parents as well as workers. That these things have not happened is part of the historically, socially constructed differentiation between the sexes that feminists have come to call gender. We live in a society that has over the years regarded the innate characteristic of sex as one of the clearest legitimizers of different rights and restrictions, both formal and informal. While the legal sanctions that uphold

23 Do you agree that typical family practices are largely structured according to gender? If so, are these practices unjust? Why?

male dominance have begun to be eroded in the past century, and more rapidly in the last twenty years, the heavy weight of tradition, combined with the effects of socialization, still works powerfully to reinforce sex roles that are commonly regarded as of unequal prestige and worth. The sexual division of labor has not only been a fundamental part of the marriage contract, but so deeply influences us in our formative years that feminists of both sexes who try to reject it can find themselves struggling against it with varying degrees of ambivalence. Based on this linchpin, "gender"—by which I mean the deeply entrenched institutionalization of sexual difference—still permeates our society.

"The personal is political" is the central message of feminist critiques of the public/domestic dichotomy. It is the core idea of most contemporary feminism. Though many of those who fought in the nineteenth and early twentieth centuries for suffrage and for the abolition of the oppressive legal status of wives were well aware of the connections between women's political and personal dominations by men, few pre-1960s feminists questioned women's special role in the family. While arguing for equal rights, such as the vote or access to education, most accepted the prevailing assumption that women's close association with and responsibility for the care of the family was natural and inevitable. . . .

Thus feminists have turned their attention to the politics of what had previously been regarded—and, as I have shown, still is seen by most political theorists—as paradigmatically *non*political. That the personal sphere of sexuality, of housework, of child care and family life *is* political became the underpinning of most feminist thought. Feminists of different political leanings and in a variety of academic disciplines have revealed and analyzed the multiple interconnections between women's domestic roles and their inequality and segregation in the workplace, and between their socialization in gendered families and the psychological aspects of their oppression. We have strongly

Figure 8.13 Are the power relationships and decisions within typical families *political*?

Susan Moller Okin,
*Justice, Gender, and the
Family*

and persistently challenged the long-standing underlying assumption of almost all political theories: that the sphere of family and personal life is so separate and distinct
from the rest of social life that such theories can justifiably assume but ignore it. . . .

The interconnections between the domestic and the nondomestic aspects of our
lives are deep and pervasive. Given the power structures of both, women's lives are far
more detrimentally affected by these interconnections than are men's. Consider two
recent front-page stories that appeared on subsequent days in the *New York Times*. The
first was about a tiny elite among women: those who work as lawyers for the country's
top law firms. If these women have children with whom they want to spend any time,
they find themselves off the partnership track and instead, with no prospects of advancement, on the "mommy track." "Nine-to-five" is considered part-time work in the
ethos of such firms, and one mother reports that, in spite of her twelve-hour workdays
and frequent work on weekends, she has "no chance" of making partner. The article
fails to mention that these women's children have fathers, or that most of the men who
work for the same prestigious law firms also have children, except to report that male
lawyers who take parental leave are seen as "wimp-like." The sexual division of labor in
the family, even in these cases where the women are extremely well qualified, successful, and potentially influential, is simply assumed.

The next day's *Times* reported on a case of major significance for abortion rights,
decided by a Federal Appeals Court in Minnesota. The all-male panel of judges ruled
7 to 3 that the state may require a woman under eighteen years who wishes to obtain
an abortion to notify *both* her parents—even in cases of divorce, separation, or deser-
tion—or to get special approval from a state judge. The significance of this article is
amplified when it is juxtaposed with the previous one. For it shows us how it is that
those who rise to the top in the highly politically influential profession of law are among
those who have had the least experience of all in raising children. There is a high inci-
dence of recruitment of judges from those who have risen to partnership in the most
prestigious law firms. Other judges are often drawn from the equally highly competi-
tive field of academic law, which also places its greatest demands (those of the tenure
hurdle) on lawyers during the child-rearing years, and therefore discriminates against
those who participate in parenting. Those who are chosen, therefore, would seem to
be those least well informed to make decisions about abortion, especially in cases involving relations between teenage girls and their parents. Here we find a systematically
built-in absence of mothers (and presumably of "wimp-like" participating fathers, too)
from high-level political decisions concerning some of the most vulnerable persons
in society—women, disproportionately poor and black, who become pregnant in their
teens, and their future children. It is not hard to see here the ties between the supposedly distinct public and domestic spheres.[12]

[T]he Rule . . . naturally
falls to the man's share, as
abler and stronger [than
the Woman].
—John Locke

Few thoughtful people would argue that women have achieved equality in every
aspect of their lives. In fact, it seems clear that in politics, the workplace, and the
household, women do *not* have equal freedom, rights, and opportunities. On this
score, Okin is surely right. But some philosophers have drawn different conclusions
from these facts. They insist that the feminist critique of these inequalities does
not show that the "personal is political" or that the traditional theories of justice
are seriously defective. The critique suggests that the principles embodied in these
theories—liberty, equality, and rights—are as relevant as ever but have yet to be
fully applied to private life. This is how David Miller explains the point:

David Miller, *Political Philosophy*

[W]e live in societies that are founded on commitments to freedom and equality but that have failed so far to live up to these commitments in the case of women and people from minority cultures. It is one of our deepest beliefs that each person should be able to live life in the way that he or she chooses, subject to certain limits . . . it is another deep belief that each person is entitled to be treated as an equal, either by being given equal rights, or by being given equal opportunities. Given these beliefs, it becomes a matter of great political concern if one section of society enjoys only a smaller area of personal freedom, or receives less than equal treatment at the hands of existing social and political institutions. So, for instance, when women are denied the option available to men of harmoniously combining a career with family life, or when members of ethnic minorities have fewer opportunities in the job market than others, this means that they are not being treated as fully free and equal members of their society. . . .

What feminists are pointing out about relationships between men and women is not so much their inherently political nature as the *failure of politics* to address them. Political authority, in the form which it has been constituted up to now, has not set adequate parameters for the peculiarly intimate relations that exist between the sexes. It has failed in a number of ways: it has not given women adequate physical security, especially protection against domestic violence, it has not ensured that women enjoy equal rights with men in a number of important areas of life, and it has not provided women with sufficient personal freedom. . . . It is these political failures that have allowed men to exercise power over women in their personal lives, and one obvious reason is that women have for centuries been almost entirely excluded from politics in the conventional sense.[13]

24 Do you agree with Miller's assessment of the feminist view of the traditional theories of justice? Why or why not?

WRITING TO UNDERSTAND:
CRITIQUING PHILOSOPHICAL VIEWS   Section 8.5

1. Does Okin's claim about the injustice of current practices of family life coincide with your own observations of family life in our culture? Explain.

2. Okin says that the gender roles of American men and women are not the way they are by necessity but are "socially constructed" (based on variable social conventions). Do you agree? Are gender roles established by natural or divine law?

3. Should the laws of a society reinforce currently accepted family practices—or should laws set the standard for just family practices?

4. Are the traditional theories of justice (social contract theories, for example) irredeemably flawed because they were devised by white men who thought of women as second-class citizens?

5. Miller says that what feminists are pointing out about relationships between men and women is not so much their inherently political nature as the failure of politics to address them. Do you agree? Why?

Review Notes

8.1 OVERVIEW: JUSTICE AND POLITICAL PHILOSOPHY

- Political philosophy is the study of political societies using the methods of philosophy—critical reasoning and careful analysis.
- The issues of political philosophy raise questions about the moral and nonmoral goodness of whole societies, which largely determine the moral and nonmoral goodness of our lives.
- Distributive justice is about the fair distribution of society's benefits and burdens (its material and nonmaterial goods). How these goods are distributed among the citizens of a state is a function of how the state is structured, how its social and political institutions are arranged.

8.2 PLATO'S THEORY: JUSTICE AS MERIT

- In *The Republic*, Plato argues that the only kind of society that can ensure that people get their due is a meritocracy. In a just society, the producers and auxiliaries perform their proper functions while being led and controlled by the guardians. The just state is a harmonious community governed by reason, just as a virtuous person is a tripartite being presided over by the rational faculty of the soul.
- Plato's ideal state rests on inequality among citizens who are sorted into three classes marked by unequal shares of power and privilege. People are assigned to different classes according to merit, but inequality is still the rule. Plato maintains that equals should be treated equally, but to him the classes deserve different treatment because they *are* different. In Plato's republic, no one gets to choose their own role in life.
- Meritocracy is a system of rule by those most qualified to govern; democracy is rule by the people as a whole; and aristocracy is a society ruled by the best citizens.

8.3 SOCIAL CONTRACT THEORIES

- In *Leviathan*, Hobbes contends that a social contract is necessary in human affairs because living without one would be a horrific nightmare of existence. Through reason, people see that the only way to escape this "war of all against all" is to enter into a social contract with one another. In the name of self-interest, they agree to turn over much of their autonomy, freedom, and power to an absolute sovereign—the Leviathan. Locke argues that humans have inherent, God-given rights whether or not a government is around to guarantee them. These rights are inalienable: they cannot be transferred to the government or any other entity. Humans create the government and cede some power to it; in return, it protects their rights and liberties. The state serves the people (not the other way round), directing all its power "to no other end but the peace, safety, and public good of the people."

- For Hobbes, in the state of nature, there is no code, culture, or comfort. There is only "continual fear, and danger of violent death; and the life of man [is] solitary, poor, nasty, brutish, and short." The Leviathan is an absolute ruler whose authority over those bound by the social contract is absolute. Its power is fearsome (enough to deter any tendency to disorder), and its contractual agreement with its subjects is irrevocable.

- Rawls says the just state is based on principles that people would agree to under hypothetical conditions that ensure fair and unbiased choices. He holds that if the starting point for the social contract is fair—if the initial conditions and bargaining process for producing the principles are fair—then the principles themselves will be just and will define the essential makeup of a just society.

- Liberalism is the political doctrine that puts primary emphasis on the liberty and rights of individuals against encroachments by the state. Classical liberalism is the view that the state should protect personal freedoms as well as the right to pursue one's own social and economic well-being in a free market without interference from others. Libertarianism and classical liberalism are essentially the same. Welfare liberalism is the view that a just society aims to preserve individual liberties while ensuring the general welfare of the citizenry.

8.4 SOCIALIST THEORIES

- Marx's political theory is a form of socialism, the political and economic doctrine that the means of production (property, factories, businesses) should be owned or controlled by the people, either communally or through the state. The guiding principle is equality: The wealth of society should be shared by all. The ideal distribution of goods follows the classic formula: "From each according to his ability, to each according to his needs."

- Socialism emphasizes equality and the distribution of goods according to need and ability. A frequent criticism of socialism is that such a distribution would require coercion by the state. Critics also accuse socialist systems of providing no incentive for people to excel at their jobs.

8.5 FEMINISM AND SOCIAL JUSTICE

- Susan Moller Okin says traditional theories are based on the assumption that there is a wall of separation between private and public life and that only public life is the proper concern of political theory. But women have largely been relegated to the private sphere, where issues of rights and equality are not supposed to apply. Consequently, women have been left out of traditional theories of justice, an omission that ensured women would not be treated as the moral equals of men.

• David Miller argues that the feminist critique of inequalities in private life does not show that the "personal is political" or that the traditional theories of justice are seriously defective. The critique suggests that the principles embodied in these theories are relevant but have yet to be fully applied to private life.

WRITING TO UNDERSTAND:
ARGUING YOUR OWN VIEWS   Chapter 8

1. Which theory of justice do you think is more plausible—Rawls's welfare liberalism or Nozick's classical liberalism (libertarianism)? Give reasons for your choice.

2. Would you prefer to live in a state like Plato's meritocracy or in a democratic capitalist society like the United States? Why?

3. What are the weaknesses and strengths of Hobbes's social contract theory? Would Hobbes's state protect your rights? Under what circumstances would you consent to live in his state and be ruled by the Leviathan?

4. Compare Locke's social contract state with a modern socialist society. Which one does a better job of protecting individual rights? Ensuring equality among citizens? Providing for the needs of every citizen? In your opinion, which theory of justice is better? Why?

5. Have women in this country been systematically treated unfairly or unequally? Are they currently being treated unfairly or unequally? If so, how? What do you think are the chief causes of such treatment?

Key Terms

aristocracy A society ruled by the best citizens. (344)

capitalism A political economic system that lets the means of production accrue to fewer people through the workings of a free market. In such a system, wealth goes to anyone who can acquire it in the marketplace. (362)

classical liberalism. The view that the state should protect personal freedoms as well as the right to pursue one's own social and economic well-being in a free market without interference from others. (358)

communism Commonly, socialism within a totalitarian system. (362)

democracy Rule by the people as a whole. (343)

distributive justice (or **social justice**) The fair distribution of society's benefits and burdens—such things as jobs, income, property, liberties, rights, welfare aid, taxes, and public service. (340)

justice The idea that people should get what is fair or what is their due. (340)

liberalism The political theory that puts primary emphasis on the liberty and rights of individuals against encroachments by the state. (357)

libertarianism (political) The doctrine that emphasizes personal freedoms and the right to pursue one's own social and economic well-being in a free market without interference from others. (358)

meritocracy A system of rule by those most qualified to govern. (343)

political philosophy The study of political societies using the methods of philosophy. (338)

social contract theory The view that justice is secured, and the state is made legitimate, through an agreement among citizens of the state or between the citizens and the rulers of the state. (347)

socialism The doctrine that the means of production (property, factories, businesses) should be owned or controlled by the people, either communally or through the state. (362)

welfare liberalism A form of liberalism, the aim of which is to preserve individual liberties while ensuring the general welfare of the citizenry. (361)

FICTION

Lord of the Flies

William Golding

Sir William Golding (1911–1993) was a Nobel Prize-winning writer of over a dozen novels and numerous short stories and essays.

In this famous novel, William Golding describes a situation in which the orderliness and moral stability of civilization dissolves and human savagery emerges—a state of affairs that resembles Hobbes's "state of nature." Several boys, ages six to twelve, are stranded on a deserted island in the Pacific. At the outset, they institute a rudimentary social system. Rules and procedures are agreed on, and Ralph is voted leader and is therefore allowed to carry the white conch, the symbol of authority. Only a boy holding the conch is permitted to speak at an assembly. The boys erect shelters and build a fire atop a mountain to alert passing ships of their presence.

For a while the aura of civilization deters anarchy and moral chaos, but as days go by, the boys' little society begins to deteriorate. They are soon living in squalor; competition for power sets in; many neglect their duties; and violence escalates. Ralph and Jack become fierce rivals as they compete for leadership. The bespectacled Piggy plays the role of the voice of reason, and Simon is thought to possess a kind of spiritual insight. But the boys' predicament strains their rationality and spirituality to the limit. As we enter the story, the fire has been neglected, causing it to go out. Jack and his band of hunters are returning from killing a pig, and Ralph scolds them for not seeing to the fire.

The hunters were more silent now, but at this they buzzed again. Ralph flung back his hair. One arm pointed at the empty horizon. His voice was loud and savage, and struck them into silence.

"There was a ship."

Jack, faced at once with too many awful implications, ducked away from them. He laid a hand on the pig and drew his knife. Ralph brought his arm down, fist clenched, and his voice shook.

William Golding, *Lord of the Flies* (New York: Penguin Group, 1954, 1982).

"There was a ship. Out there. You said you'd keep the fire going and you let it out!" He took a step towards Jack who turned and faced him.

"They might have seen us. We might have gone home—"

This was too bitter for Piggy, who forgot his timidity in the agony of his loss. He began to cry out, shrilly:

"You and your blood, Jack Merridew! you and your hunting! We might have gone home"—

Ralph pushed Piggy on one side.

"I was chief; und you were going to do what I said. You talk. But you can't even build huts—then you go off hunting and let out the fire—"

He turned away, silent for a moment. Then his voice came again on a peak of feeling.

"There was a ship—"

One of the smaller hunters began to wail. The dismal truth was filtering through to everybody. Jack went very red as he hacked and pulled at the pig.

"The job was too much. We needed everyone."

Ralph turned.

"You could have had everyone when the shelters were finished. But you had to hunt—"

"We needed meat."

Jack stood up as he said this, the bloodied knife in his hand. The two boys faced each other. There was the brilliant world of hunting, tactics, fierce exhilaration, skill; and there was the world of longing and baffled common-sense. Jack transferred the knife to his left hand and smudged blood over his forehead as he pushed down the plastered hair.

Piggy began again.

"You didn't ought to have let that fire out. You said you'd keep the smoke going—"

This from Piggy, and the wails of agreement from some of the hunters drove Jack to violence. The bolting look came into his blue eyes. He took a step, and able at last to hit someone, stuck his fist into Piggy's stomach. Piggy sat down with a grunt. Jack stood over him. His voice was vicious with humiliation.

"You would, would you? Fatty!"

Ralph made a step forward and Jack smacked Piggy's head. Piggy's glasses flew off and tinkled on the rocks. Piggy cried out in terror:

"My specs!"

He went crouching and feeling over the rocks but Simon, who got there first, found them for him. Passions beat about Simon on the mountain-top with awful wings.

"One side's broken."

Piggy grabbed and put on the glasses. He looked malevolently at Jack.

"I got to have them specs. Now I only got one eye. Jus' you wait—"

Jack made a move towards Piggy who scrambled away till a great rock lay between them. He thrust his head over the top and glared at Jack through his one flashing glass.

"Now I only got one eye. Just you wait—"

Jack mimicked the whine and scramble.

"Jus' you wait—yah!"

Piggy and the parody were so funny that the hunters began to laugh. Jack felt encouraged. He went on scrambling and the laughter rose to a gale of hysteria. Unwillingly Ralph felt his lips twitch; he was angry with himself for giving way.

He muttered.

"That was a dirty trick."

Jack broke out of his gyration and stood facing Ralph. His words came in a shout.

"All right, all right!"

He looked at Piggy, at the hunters, at Ralph.

"I'm sorry. About the fire, I mean. There. I—"

He drew himself up.

"—I apologize."

The buzz from the hunters was one of admiration at this handsome behaviour. Clearly they were of the opinion that Jack had done the decent thing, had put himself in the right by his generous apology and Ralph, obscurely, in the wrong. They waited for an appropriately decent answer.

Yet Ralph's throat refused to pass one. He resented, as an addition to Jack's misbehaviour, this verbal trick. The fire was dead, the ship was gone. Could they not see? Anger instead of decency passed his throat.

"That was a dirty trick."

They were silent on the mountain-top while the opaque look appeared in Jack's eyes and passed away.

Ralph's final word was an ungracious mutter.

"All right. Light the fire."

With some positive action before them, a little of the tension died. Ralph said no more, did nothing, stood looking down at the ashes round his feet. Jack was loud and active. He gave orders, sang, whistled, threw remarks at the silent Ralph—remarks that did not need an answer, and therefore could not invite a snub; and still Ralph was silent. No one, not even Jack, would ask him to move and in the end they had to build the fire three yards away and in a place not really as convenient. So Ralph asserted his chieftainship and could not have chosen a better way if he had thought for days. Against this weapon, so indefinable and so effective, Jack was powerless and raged without knowing why. By the time the pile was built, they were on different sides of a high barrier.

When they had dealt with the fire another crisis arose. Jack had no means of lighting it. Then to his surprise, Ralph went to Piggy and took the glasses from him. Not even Ralph knew how a link between him and Jack had been snapped and fastened elsewhere.

"I'll bring 'em back."

"I'll come too."

Piggy stood behind him, islanded in a sea of meaningless colour, while Ralph knelt and focused the glossy spot. Instantly the fire was alight. Piggy held out his hands and grabbed the glasses back.

Before these fantastically attractive flowers of violet and red and yellow, unkindness melted away. They became a circle of boys round a camp fire and even Piggy and Ralph were half-drawn in. Soon some of the boys were rushing down the slope for more wood while Jack hacked the pig. They tried holding the whole carcass on a stake over the fire, but the stake burnt more quickly than the pig roasted. In the end they skewered bits of meat on branches and held them in the flames: and even then almost as much boy was roasted as meat.

Ralph dribbled. He meant to refuse meat but his past diet of fruit and nuts, with an odd crab or fish, gave him too little resistance. He accepted a piece of half-raw meat and gnawed it like a wolf.

Piggy spoke, also dribbling.

"Aren't I having none?"

Jack had meant to leave him in doubt, as an assertion of power; but Piggy by advertising his omission made more cruelty necessary.

"You didn't hunt."

"No more did Ralph," said Piggy wetly, "nor Simon." He amplified. "There isn't more than a ha'porth of meat in a crab."

Ralph stirred uneasily. Simon, sitting between the twins and Piggy, wiped his mouth and shoved his piece of meat over the rocks to Piggy, who grabbed it. The twins giggled and Simon lowered his face in shame.

Then Jack leapt to his feet, slashed off a great hunk of meat, and flung it down at Simon's feet.

"Eat! Damn You!"

He glared at Simon.

"Take it!"

He spun on his heel, centre of a bewildered circle of boys.

"I got you meat!"

Numberless and inexpressible frustrations combined to make his rage elemental and awe-inspiring.

"I painted my face—I stole up. Now you eat—all of you—and I—"

Slowly the silence on the mountain-top deepened till the click of the fire and the soft hiss of roasting meat could be heard clearly. Jack looked round for understanding but found only respect. Ralph stood among the ashes of the signal fire, his hands full of meat, saying nothing.

Then at last Maurice broke the silence. He changed the subject to the only one that could bring the majority of them together.

"Where did you find the pig?"

Roger pointed down the unfriendly side.

"They were there—by the sea."

Jack, recovering, could not bear to have his story told. He broke in quickly.

"We spread round. I crept, on hands and knees. The spears fell out because they hadn't barbs on. The pig ran away and made an awful noise—"

"It turned back and ran into the circle, bleeding—"

All the boys were talking at once, relieved and excited.

" 'We closed in—"

The first blow had paralysed its hind quarters, so then the circle could close in and beat and beat—"

"I cut the pig's throat—"

The twins, still sharing their identical grin, jumped up and ran round each other. Then the rest joined in, making pig-dying noises and shouting.

"One for his nob!"

"Give him a fourpenny one!"

Then Maurice pretended to be the pig and ran squealing into the centre, and the hunters, circling still, pretended to beat him. As they danced, they sang.

"Kill the pig. Cut her throat. Bash her in."

Ralph watched them, envious and resentful. Not till they flagged and the chant died away, did he speak.

"I'm calling an assembly."

One by one, they halted, and stood watching him.

"With the conch. I'm calling a meeting even if we have to go on into the dark. Down on the platform. When I blow it. Now."

He turned away and walked off, down the mountain. . . .

Soon Jack wins all but five of the boys to his side. Simon, Piggy, and the twins, Sam and Eric ("Samneric") stick with Ralph to support the rule of law. To light a fire for the pig roast, Jack's hunters need a magnifying glass, so Jack and two of his band attack Ralph and Piggy and take Piggy's glasses by force. We enter the scene where Ralph and his friends are smarting over the loss of the glasses and the ability to make a fire. Piggy addresses them:

"I got the conch. I'm going to that Jack Merridew an' tell him, I am."

"You'll get hurt."

"What can he do more than he has? I'll tell him what's what. You let me carry the conch, Ralph. I'll show him the one thing he hasn't got."

Piggy paused for a moment and peered round at the dim figures. The shape of the old assembly, trodden in the grass, listened to him.

"I'm going to him with this conch in my hands. I'm going to hold it out. Look, I'm goin' to say, you're stronger than I am and you haven't got asthma. You can see, I'm goin' to say, and with both eyes. But I don't ask for my glasses back, not as a favour. I don't ask you to be a sport, I'll say, not because you're strong, but because what's right's right. Give me my glasses, I'm going to say—you got to!"

Piggy ended, flushed and trembling. He pushed the conch quickly into Ralph's hands as though in a hurry to be rid of it and wiped the tears from his eyes. The green light was gentle about them and the conch lay at Ralph's feet, fragile and white. A single drop of water that had escaped Piggy's fingers now flashed on the delicate curve like a star.

At last Ralph sat up straight and drew back his hair.

"All right. I mean—you can try if you like. We'll go with you."

"He'll be painted," said Sam, timidly. "You know how he'll be—"

"—he won't think much of us—"

"—if he gets waxy we've had it—"

Ralph scowled at Sam. Dimly he remembered something that Simon had said to him once, by the rocks.

"Don't be silly," he said. And then he added quickly, "Let's go."

He held out the conch to Piggy who flushed, this time with pride.

"You must carry it—"

"When we're ready I'll carry it—"

Piggy sought in his mind for words to convey his passionate willingness to carry the conch against all odds.

"—I don't mind. I'll be glad, Ralph, only I'll have to be led."

Ralph put the conch back on the shining log.

"We better eat and then get ready."

They made their way to the devastated fruit trees. Piggy was helped to his food and found some by touch. While they ate, Ralph thought of the afternoon.

"We'll be like we were. We'll wash—"

Sam gulped down a mouthful and protested.

"But we bathe every day!"

Ralph looked at the filthy objects before him and sighed.

"We ought to comb our hair. Only it's too long."

"I've got both socks left in the shelter," said Eric, "so we could pull them over our heads like caps, sort of."

"We could find some stuff," said Piggy, "and tie your hair back."

"Like a girl!"

"No. 'Course not."

"Then we must go as we are," said Ralph, "and they won't be any better."

Eric made a detaining gesture.

"But they'll be painted! You know how it is—"

The others nodded. They understood only too well the liberation into savagery that the concealing paint brought.

"Well, we won't be painted," said Ralph, "because we aren't savages."

Samneric looked at each other.

"All the same—"

Ralph shouted.

"No paint" . . .

They set off along the beach in formation. Ralph went first, limping a little, his spear carried over one shoulder. He saw things partially through the tremble of the heat haze over the flashing sands, and his own long hair and injuries. Behind him came the twins, worried now for a while but full of unquenchable vitality. They said little but trailed the butts of their wooden spears; for Piggy had found, that looking down, shielding his tired sight from the sun, he could just see these moving along the sand. He walked between the trailing butts, therefore, the conch held carefully between his two hands. The boys made a compact little group that moved over the beach, four plate-like shadows dancing and mingling beneath them. There was no sign left of the storm, and the beach was swept clean like a blade that has been scoured. The sky and the mountain were at an immense distance, shimmering in the heat; and the reef was lifted by mirage, floating in a kind of silver pool half-way up the sky.

They passed the place where the tribe had danced. The charred sticks still lay on the rocks where the rain had quenched them but the sand by the water was smooth again. They passed this in silence. No one doubted that the tribe would be found at the Castle Rock and when they came in sight of it they stopped with one accord. The densest tangle on the island, a mass of twisted stems, black and green and impenetrable, lay on their left and tall grass swayed before them. Now Ralph went forward.

Here was the crushed grass where they had all lain when he had gone to prospect. There was the neck of land, the ledge skirting the rock, up there were the red pinnacles.

Sam touched his arm.

"Smoke."

There was a tiny smudge of smoke wavering into the air on the other side of the rock.

"Some fire—I don't think."

Ralph turned.

"What are we hiding for?"

He stepped through the screen of grass on to the little open space that led to the narrow neck.

"You two follow behind. I'll go first, then Piggy a pace behind me. Keep your spears ready."

Piggy peered anxiously into the luminous veil that hung between him and the world.

"Is it safe? Ain't there a cliff? I can hear the sea."

"You keep right close to me."

Ralph moved forward on to the neck. He kicked a stone and it bounded into the water. Then the sea sucked down, revealing a red, weedy square forty feet beneath Ralph's left arm.

"Am I safe?" quavered Piggy. "I feel awful—"

High above them from the pinnacles came a sudden shout and then an imitation war-cry that was answered by a dozen voices from behind the rock.

"Give me the conch and stay still."

"Halt! Who goes there?"

Ralph bent back his head and glimpsed Roger's dark face at the top.

"You can see who I am!" he shouted. "Stop being silly!"

He put the conch to his lips and began to blow. Savages appeared, painted out of recognition, edging round the ledge towards the neck. They carried spears and disposed themselves to defend the entrance. Ralph went on blowing and ignored Piggy's terrors.

Roger was shouting.

"You mind out—see?"

At length Ralph took his lips away and paused to get his breath back. His first words were a gasp, but audible.

"—calling an assembly. "

The savages guarding the neck muttered among themselves but made no motion. Ralph walked forwards a couple of steps. A voice whispered urgently behind him.

"Don't leave me, Ralph."

"You kneel down," said Ralph sideways, "and wait till I come back."

He stood half-way along the neck and gazed at the savages intently. Freed by the paint, they had tied their hair back and were more comfortable than he was. Ralph made a resolution to tie his own back afterwards. Indeed he felt like telling them to wait and doing it there and then; but that was impossible. The savages sniggered a bit and one gestured at Ralph with his spear. High above, Roger took his hands off the lever and leaned out to see what was going on. The boys on the neck stood in a pool of their own shadow, diminished to shaggy heads. Piggy crouched, his back shapeless as a sack.

"I'm calling an assembly."

Silence.

Roger took up a small stone and flung it between the twins, aiming to miss. They started and Sam only just kept his footing. Some source of power began to pulse in Roger's body.

Ralph spoke again, loudly.

"I'm calling an assembly."

He ran his eye over them.

"Where's Jack?"

The group of boys stirred and consulted. A painted face spoke with the voice of Robert.

"He's hunting. And he said we weren't to let you in."

"I've come to see about the fire," said Ralph, "and about Piggy's specs. "

The group in front of him shifted and laughter shivered outwards from among them, light, excited laughter that went echoing among the tall rocks.

A voice spoke from behind Ralph.

" 'What do you want?"

The twins made a bolt past Ralph and got between him and the entry. He turned quickly. Jack, identifiable by personality and red hair, was advancing from the forest. A hunter crouched on either side. All three were masked in black and green. Behind them on the grass the headless and paunched body of a sow lay where they had dropped it.

Piggy wailed.

"Ralph! Don't leave me!"

With ludicrous care he embraced the rock, pressing himself to it above the sucking sea. The sniggering of the savages became a loud derisive jeer.

Jack shouted above the noise.

"You go away, Ralph. You keep to your end. This is my end and my tribe. You leave me alone."

The jeering died away.

"You pinched Piggy's specs," said Ralph, breathlessly. "You've got to give them back."

"Got to? Who says?"

Ralph's temper blazed out.

"I say! You voted for me for Chief. Didn't you hear the conch? You played a dirty trick—we'd have given you fire if you'd asked for it—"

The blood was flowing in his cheeks and the bunged-up eye throbbed.

"You could have had fire whenever you wanted. But you didn't. You came sneaking up like a thief and stole Piggy's glasses!"

"Say that again!"

"Thief! Thief!"

Piggy screamed.

"Ralph! Mind me!"

Jack made a rush and stabbed at Ralph's chest with his spear. Ralph sensed the position of the weapon from the glimpse he caught of Jack's arm and put the thrust aside with his own butt. Then he brought the end round and caught Jack a stinger across the ear. They were chest to chest, breathing fiercely, pushing and glaring.

"Who's a thief?"

"You are!"

Jack wrenched free and swung at Ralph with his spear. By common consent they were using the spears as sabres now, no longer daring the lethal points. The blow struck Ralph's spear and slid down, to fall agonizingly on his fingers. Then they were apart once more, their positions reversed, Jack towards the Castle Rock and Ralph on the outside towards the island.

Both boys were breathing very heavily.

"Come on then—"

"Come on—"

Truculently they squared up to each other but kept just out of fighting distance.

"You come on and see what you get!"

"You come on—"

Piggy clutching the ground was trying to attract Ralph's attention. Ralph moved, bent down, kept a wary eye on Jack.

"Ralph—remember what we came for. The fire. My specs."

Ralph nodded. He relaxed his fighting muscles, stood easily and grounded the butt of his spear. Jack watched him inscrutably through his paint. Ralph glanced up at the pinnacles, then towards the group of savages.

"Listen. We've come to say this. First you've got to give back Piggy's specs. If he hasn't got them he can't see. You aren't playing the game—"

The tribe of painted savages giggled and Ralph's mind faltered. He pushed his hair up and gazed at the green and black mask before him, trying to remember what Jack looked like.

Piggy whispered.

"And the fire."

"Oh yes. Then about the fire. I say this again. I've been saying it ever since we dropped in."

He held out his spear and pointed at the savages.

"Your only hope is keeping a signal fire going as long as there's light to see. Then maybe a ship'll notice the smoke and come and rescue us and take us home. But without that smoke we've got to wait till some ship comes by accident. We might wait years; till we were old—"

The shivering, silvery, unreal laughter of the savages sprayed out and echoed away. A gust of rage shook Ralph. His voice cracked.

"Don't you understand, you painted fools? Sam, Eric, Piggy and me—we aren't enough. We tried to keep the fire going, but we couldn't. And then you, playing at hunting. . . ."

He pointed past them to where the trickle of smoke dispersed in the pearly air.

"Look at that! Call that a signal fire? That's a cooking fire. Now you'll eat and there'll be no smoke. Don't you understand? There may be a ship out there—"

He paused, defeated by the silence and the painted anonymity of the group guarding the entry. The chief opened a pink mouth and addressed Samneric who were between him and his tribe.

"You two. Get back."

No one answered him. The twins, puzzled, looked at each other; while Piggy, reassured by the cessation of violence, stood up carefully. Jack glanced back at Ralph and then at the twins.

"Grab them!"

No one moved. Jack shouted angrily.

"I said 'grab them'!"

The painted group moved round Samneric nervously and unhandily. Once more the silvery laughter scattered.

Samneric protested out of the heart of civilization.

"Oh, I say!"

"—honestly!"

Their spears were taken from them.

"Tie them up!"

Ralph cried out hopelessly against the black and green mask.

"Jack!"

"Go on. Tie them."

Now the painted group felt the otherness of Samneric, felt the power in their own hands. They felled the twins clumsily and excitedly. Jack was inspired. He knew that Ralph would attempt a rescue. He struck in a humming circle behind him and Ralph only just parried the blow. Beyond them the tribe and the twins were a loud and writhing heap. Piggy crouched again. Then the twins lay, astonished, and the tribe stood round them. Jack turned to Ralph and spoke between his teeth.

"See? They do what I want."

There was silence again. The twins lay, inexpertly tied up, and the tribe watched Ralph to see what he would do. He numbered them through his fringe, glimpsed the ineffectual smoke.

His temper broke. He screamed at Jack.

"You're a beast and a swine and a bloody, bloody thief!"

He charged.

Jack, knowing this was the crisis, charged too. They met with a jolt and bounced apart, Jack swung with his fist at Ralph and caught him on the ear. Ralph hit Jack in the stomach and made him grunt. Then they were facing each other again, panting and furious, but unnerved by each other's ferocity. They became aware of the noise that was the background to this fight, the steady shrill cheering of the tribe behind them.

Piggy's voice penetrated to Ralph.

"Let me speak."

He was standing in the dust of the fight, and as the tribe saw his intention the shrill cheer changed to a steady booing.

Piggy held up the conch and the booing sagged a little, then came up again to strength.

"I got the conch!"

He shouted.

"I tell you, I got the conch!"

Surprisingly, there was silence now; the tribe were curious to hear what amusing thing he might have to say.

Silence and pause; but in the silence a curious air-noise, close by Ralph's head. He gave it half his attention—and there it was again; a faint "Zup!" Someone was throwing stones: Roger was dropping them, his one hand still on the lever. Below him, Ralph was a shock of hair and Piggy a bag of fat.

"I got this to say. You're acting like a crowd of kids."

The booing rose and died again as Piggy lifted the white, magic shell.

"Which is better—to be a pack of painted niggers like you are, or to be sensible like Ralph is?"

A great clamour rose among the savages. Piggy shouted again.

"Which is better—to have rules and agree, or to hunt and kill?"

Again the clamour and again—"Zup!"

Ralph shouted against the noise.

"Which is better, law and rescue, or hunting and breaking things up?"

Now Jack was yelling too and Ralph could no longer make himself heard. Jack had backed right against the tribe and they were a solid mass of menace that bristled with spears. The intention of a charge was forming among them; they were working up to it and the neck would be swept clear. Ralph stood facing them, a little to one side, his spear ready. By him stood Piggy still holding out the talisman, the fragile, shining beauty of the shell. The storm of sound beat at them, an incantation of hatred. High overhead, Roger, with a sense of delirious abandonment, leaned all his weight on the lever.

Ralph heard the great rock long before he saw it. He was aware of a jolt in the earth that came to him through the soles of his feet, and the breaking sound of stones at the top of the cliff. Then the monstrous red thing bounded across the neck and he flung himself flat while the tribe shrieked.

The rock struck Piggy a glancing blow from chin to knee: the conch exploded into a thousand white fragments and ceased to exist. Piggy, saying nothing, with no time for even a grunt, travelled through the air sideways from the rock, turning over as he went. The rock bounded twice and was lost in the forest. Piggy fell forty feet and landed on his back across that square, red rock in the sea. His head opened and stuff came out and turned red. Piggy's arms and legs twitched a bit, like a pig's after it has been killed. Then the sea breathed again in a long, slow sigh, the water boiled white and pink over the rock; and when it went, sucking back again, the body of Piggy was gone.

This time the silence was complete. Ralph's lips formed a word but no sound came.

Suddenly Jack bounded out from the tribe and began screaming wildly.

"See? See? That's what you'll get! I meant that! There isn't a tribe for you any more! The conch is gone—"

He ran forward, stooping.

"I'm Chief!"

Viciously, with full intention, he hurled his spear at Ralph. The point tore the skin and flesh over Ralph's ribs, then sheared off and fell in the water. Ralph stumbled, feeling not pain but panic, and the tribe, screaming now like the Chief, began to advance. Another spear, a bent one that would not fly straight, went past his face and one fell from on high where Roger was. The twins lay hidden behind the tribe and the anonymous devils' faces swarmed across the neck. Ralph turned and ran. A great noise as of sea-gulls rose behind him. He obeyed an instinct that he did not know he possessed and swerved over the open space so that the spears went wide. He saw the headless body of the sow and jumped in time. Then he was crashing through foliage and small boughs and was hidden by the forest. . . .

> *Ralph runs into the forest to hide, and Jack begins a vicious search for him. Soon Ralph realizes that Jack has started a forest fire to force him out into the open. The trick works, for Ralph soon stumbles onto the beach, terrified—and is stunned to find a naval officer greeting him. The navy had seen the smoke rising from the island and had come to investigate.*

[Ralph] staggered to his feet, tensed for more terrors, and looked up at a huge peaked cap. It was a white-topped cap, and above the green shade of the peak was a crown, an anchor, gold foliage. He saw white drill, epaulettes, a revolver, a row of gilt buttons down the front of a uniform.

A naval officer stood on the sand, looking down at Ralph in wary astonishment. On the beach behind him was a cutter, her bows hauled up and held by two ratings. In the stern-sheets another rating held a sub-machine gun.

The ululation faltered and died away.

The officer looked at Ralph doubtfully for a moment, then took his hand away from the butt of the revolver.

"Hullo."

Squirming a little, conscious of his filthy appearance, Ralph answered shyly.

"Hullo."

The officer nodded, as if a question had been answered.

"Are there any adults—any grown-ups with you?"

Dumbly, Ralph shook his head. He turned a half-pace on the sand. A semicircle of little boys, their bodies streaked with coloured clay, sharp sticks in their hands, were standing on the beach making no noise at all.

"Fun and games," said the officer.

The fire reached the coco-nut palms by the beach and swallowed them noisily. A flame, seemingly detached, swung like an acrobat and licked up the palm heads on the platform. The sky was black.

The officer grinned cheerfully at Ralph.

"We saw your smoke. What have you been doing? Having a war or something?"

Ralph nodded.

The officer inspected the little scarecrow in front of him. The kid needed a bath, a hair-cut, a nose-wipe and a good deal of ointment.

"Nobody killed, I hope? Any dead bodies?"

"Only two. And they've gone."

The officer leaned down and looked closely at Ralph.

"Two? Killed?"

Ralph nodded again. Behind him, the whole island was shuddering with flame. The officer knew, as a rule, when people were telling the truth. He whistled softly.

Other boys were appearing now, tiny tots some of them, brown, with the distended bellies of small savages. One of them came close to the officer and looked up.

"I'm, I'm—"

But there was no more to come. Percival Wemys Madison sought in his head for an incantation that had faded clean away.

The officer turned back to Ralph.

"We'll take you off. How many of you are there?"

Ralph shook his head. The officer looked past him to the group of painted boys.

"Who's boss here?"

"I am," said Ralph loudly.

A little boy who wore the remains of an extraordinary black cap on his red hair and who carried the remains of a pair of spectacles at his waist, started forward, then changed his mind and stood still.

"We saw your smoke. And you don't know how many of you there are?"

"No, sir."

"I should have thought," said the officer as he visualized the search before him, "I should have thought that a pack of British boys—you're all British aren't you?—would have been able to put up a better show than that—I mean—"

"It was like that at first," said Ralph, "before things—"

He stopped.

"We were together then—"

The officer nodded helpfully.

"I know. Jolly good show. Like the Coral Island."

Ralph looked at him dumbly. For a moment he had a fleeting picture of the strange glamour that had once invested the beaches. But the island was scorched up like dead wood—Simon was dead—and Jack had. . . . The tears began to flow and sobs shook him. He gave himself up to them now for the first time on the island; great, shuddering spasms of grief that seemed to wrench his whole body. His voice rose under the black smoke before the burning wreckage of the island; and infected by that emotion, the other little boys began to shake and sob too. And in the middle of them, with filthy body, matted hair, and unwiped nose, Ralph wept for the end of innocence, the darkness of man's heart, and the fall through the air of the true, wise friend called Piggy.

The officer, surrounded by these noises, was moved and a little embarrassed. He turned away to give them time to pull themselves together; and waited, allowing his eyes to rest on the trim cruiser in the distance.

Probing Questions

1. What does *The Lord of the Flies* say about morality? Does it suggest that humans don't need morality? That morality has no hold on humans? What is Piggy's notion of morality? What is Jack's?

2. What does the story say about human nature? Are humans inherently savage and bloodthirsty?

3. Imagine that Thomas Hobbes reads *The Lord of the Flies*. If he interprets the story in light of his moral theory, what do you suppose he would say? Would Hobbes regard the story as reinforcing his views or contradicting them?

For Further Reading

John Arthur and William Shaw, eds., *Justice and Economic Distribution* (Upper Saddle River, NJ: Prentice Hall, 1991). A collection of writings on justice.

Steven M. Cahn, ed., *Political Philosophy: The Essentials* (New York: Oxford University Press, 2011). A collection of the most important readings.

Samuel Fleishacker, *A Short History of Distributive Justice* (Boston: Harvard University Press, 2005). An overview of the development of major perspectives on justice.

David Miller, *Political Philosophy: A Very Short Introduction* (Oxford: Oxford University Press, 2003). A concise introduction to the concepts and issues of political philosophy.

Robert Nozick, *Anarchy, State, and Utopia* (New York: Basic Books, 1974). A classic work of political philosophy defending a form of libertarianism.

Susan Moller Okin, *Justice, Gender, and the Family* (New York: Basic Books, 1989). A feminist view of distributive justice, arguing that gender inequalities preclude any form of social justice.

Louis P. Pojman and Owen McLeod, eds., *What Do We Deserve: A Reader of Justice and Desert* (New York: Oxford University Press, 1999). An anthology of articles on social justice as it relates to what people do and don't deserve. Special attention given to Rawls's concept of desert.

John Rawls, *A Theory of Justice* (Cambridge, MA: Harvard University Press, 1999). A classic—and very influential—examination of the fundamental requirements of social justice.

Michael J. Sandel, ed., *Justice: A Reader* (New York: Oxford University Press, 2003). A comprehensive anthology of the most significant articles on social and political justice, edited by one of America's favorite college professors.

CHAPTER 9

THE MEANING OF LIFE

Chapter Objectives

9.1 OVERVIEW: PHILOSOPHY AND THE MEANING OF LIFE

- Understand why people think questions concerning the meaning of human existence are extremely important and relevant.
- Understand why and how examining the question of life's meaning is personal.
- Explain the difference between external and internal meaning.

9.2 PESSIMISM: LIFE HAS NO MEANING

- Summarize the pessimistic views of Tolstoy, Schopenhauer, and Darrow.
- Critically examine the case for pessimism and that for optimism.
- Assess Baggini's charge that pessimists confuse external and internal meaning.

9.3 OPTIMISM: LIFE CAN HAVE MEANING

- Explain the religious externalist approach to life's meaning.
- Critically examine Tolstoy's view and his justification for it.
- Explain why some philosophers think the notion of a God assigning a purpose to humans should be objectionable to believers and nonbelievers alike.
- Summarize the internalist's position on life's meaning and produce an argument for or against it.
- Devise an argument for the idea that death and the ephemeral nature of human endeavors are irrelevant to the meaningfulness or meaninglessness of a person's existence.

9.1 OVERVIEW: PHILOSOPHY AND THE MEANING OF LIFE

For the meaning of life differs from man to man, from day to day and from hour to hour. What matters, therefore, is not the meaning of life in general but rather the specific meaning of a person's life at a given moment.
—Viktor E. Frankl

Enter: a contented man. He makes his living crafting ornate clay pots, which he sells to the people in his village. He loves his work and is mostly satisfied with his life. But one day a friend gives him a philosophy textbook, which he begins to read, starting with the last chapter entitled "The Meaning of Life." A question in the first paragraph jumps out at him: "Does life have meaning?" He has never thought seriously about the meaning of life, and as he ponders the question, he realizes he has no answer. And he does not have an answer even after fretting over the question for several days. For most of his life, he has made pots, day after day, all of them the same shape and size, all of them produced in exactly the same way—and he seems destined to endure this monotony into old age. What is the point? he thinks. What does it matter whether I make a million pots or none? What has my life been about? What meaning or purpose does my life have? Is life meaningless? He has no idea. And the thought of a meaningless existence brings on a crushing despair that cannot be eased by drink, or drugs, or distracting activity. As his misery deepens, the potter stops making pots, and he wonders why he ever started.

Figure 9.1 People often begin their search for meaning by asking, "What is the meaning of life?" But the first step in finding answers is to understand the question.

Do you see any resemblance between the potter and yourself in this little tale? It would not be surprising or unusual if you did. At one time or another, in one way or another, most people ask themselves if life has any meaning, any point. Like our potter, many of them seem satisfied with their lives—until they begin to wonder whether it is a meaningless charade. Then "the meaning of life"—a phrase often tossed around in mock seriousness or for comedic effect—is infused with a more somber tone. A few insist that questions about the meaning of existence are themselves meaningless. But most who have contemplated such things take them to be extremely important and relevant to their lives. Many philosophers have tried to clarify the concepts involved and to give discussions of life's meaning more precision, but they too think the questions about meaningful or meaningless lives are worth asking and answering. The existentialist philosopher Albert Camus, for one, declares that "Judging whether life is or is not worth living amounts to answering the fundamental question of philosophy. All the rest—whether the world has three dimensions, whether the mind has nine or twelve categories—comes afterwards."[1]

Some people, including a fair number of students, think philosophy is *mostly* about the question of life's meaning. In a sense, they are not far wrong. Most of the topics covered in the preceding chapters—God, free will, knowledge, ethics, and justice—can inform your thinking about this important sort of meaning. And your conclusions about the meaningfulness of life are directly or indirectly related to your actions and beliefs regarding lifestyle, work, morality, political involvement, free will, God, and other issues. If by thinking carefully about life's meaning (or lack thereof) you decide to dramatically change your career choice, you would not be the first.

What, besides a course in philosophy, can push someone into this kind of serious reflection? Often the tripwire is a disturbing thought—the inevitability of death, the brevity of life, the smallness and triviality of our lives compared with the unimaginably vast universe, the shortness of our lives in the context of eternity, or the eventual obliteration of everything we have cared for or created.

Consider this odd fairytale based *very loosely* on a real event. A graduate student with a master's degree in business pays a visit to a philosophy professor. The student has come seeking something that she has so far failed to acquire in her studies: the ultimate secret, the meaning of life. The professor pauses, then answers in his best guru-like voice, "The meaning of life is . . . a big purple thing." Silence. The professor chuckles; the student doesn't know whether to laugh or sigh.

With his absurd answer the professor means to make a point, or several. There is no great secret concerning the meaning of life, no cryptic bit of knowledge that, once known, will reveal all. There is no slogan or incantation or parable that will ensure your life is worth living. Moreover, no one can simply hand you the meaning of life as if it were a gift basket. The process of examining the question of life's meaning or purpose is *personal*. You have to make that journey yourself. No one can bestow upon you what you must find for yourself, no more than a friend can tell you what your favorite foods are supposed to be.

Life has no meaning the moment you lose the illusion of being eternal.
—Jean-Paul Sartre

My life has no purpose, no direction, no aim, no meaning, and yet I'm happy. I can't figure it out. What am I doing right?
—Charles M. Schulz

Probably most philosophers would agree with all this. Many would also add that although there is no straight road to understanding the "big question," there are guideposts here and there that can help you find your way, some of which we discuss in the following pages.

Many people think they have an intuitive grasp of what is meant by "the meaning of life." But the concept in common usage is actually vague and slippery. So, for purposes of this discussion, we can say that to ask whether your life has meaning is to ask whether it has significant value or purpose over time beyond the good of merely being alive. Through the centuries, people have claimed that such significant value is derived from being part of God's plan, serving the greater good of humankind, helping others, caring for and protecting family, giving and receiving love, creating art, searching for knowledge, and many other activities and states.

Philosophers have gone further and distinguished life's value or meaning from happiness and moral rightness. Someone might be continually and blissfully happy because she is, for example, taking psychotropic drugs, but few would call such a life meaningful. And some people can lead meaningful lives while being miserable because their meaningful activities are arduous or dangerous. Physicians working in a war zone treating wounded children may be sad because of the suffering they witness—and still feel their lives have meaning. Moreover, many things that people do to add meaning to their lives are also morally right, but moral rightness and meaningfulness need not go together. While creating a beautiful painting, an artist might add meaning to his life, but the act of creation seems to be morally neutral. Morality and meaningfulness are not synonymous.

Perhaps the main impediment to clear thinking about life's meaning is confusion about what *meaning* refers to. Consider the phrase "the meaning of life." For most people, these words refer to *external* meaning—meaning or purpose that comes

Figure 9.2 Is a meaningful life possible only when lived in accordance with God's plan?

PHILOSOPHY LAB

Imagine that you are a devout person who feels that your life can be meaningful only if you act according to God's plan. Fortunately, an oracle can tell you exactly what God has in store. He wants you (and everyone else on the planet) to . . . serve as food for beings on another planet, who happen to be God's favorite people. You and all other humans, on the other hand, are to be meat for aliens.

Now that you know God's plan, is your life finally meaningful? That is, if you know only that God has a plan for you but know nothing about it, would that fact alone make your life meaningful?

from outside humanity. Whatever meaning people have in their lives is bestowed or assigned by God, by some metaphysical order, or by the workings of some universal principle. For Christians, to have a meaningful life is to be part of God's plan for all of humankind. But many people also speak of a different kind of meaning—what some refer to as "meaning *in* life." This is *internal* meaning—meaning or purpose that comes from inside people, that humans can give to themselves. In this view, life can be meaningful for persons if they come to see their goals or purposes as inherently valuable or worthwhile.

Many people, including those who accept a religious worldview, assume that if life has no external meaning, it has no meaning *period*. They believe humans can have a purposeful life only if God created them with a purpose. The opposing view is that even if there is no external meaning, people's lives can still be meaningful because meaning and purpose come from within. Because of these different senses of meaning, a person who states that life is meaningless may actually be asserting only that life has no external meaning but still has internal meaning. Someone who declares that life has meaning may reject the notion that humans are given a purpose by a higher power, claiming that lives are made meaningful only by human choices. Unfortunately, the phrase "the meaning of life" is frequently used to refer to both external and internal meaning.

To the question of whether life holds any meaning for us, there are two principal answers: (1) life has no meaning (the *pessimist's* view) and (2) life in some sense does have meaning (the *optimist's* view). The optimist's answer can be further divided: either (1) life's meaning is external (the common religious perspective) or (2) life's meaning is internal (the view held mostly by the nonreligious or nontheistic).

1 When you talk about the meaning of life, which sense of the term do you use—external meaning or internal meaning?

Life takes on meaning when you become motivated, set goals and charge after them in an unstoppable manner.
—Les Brown

9.2 PESSIMISM: LIFE HAS NO MEANING

Life is without meaning.
You bring the meaning
to it. The meaning of life
is whatever you ascribe it
to be. Being alive is the
meaning.

—Joseph Campbell

The pessimists (also called nihilists) have something in common with the religious optimists: they both believe that unless a divine entity or transcendent reality has provided the world with ultimate purpose or value, life is meaningless. In other words, life can have no meaning if external meaning is nonexistent.

Among famous pessimists we can count the renowned Russian novelist Leo Tolstoy (1828–1910). Before undergoing a Christian conversion (and becoming an optimist), he found himself at age fifty doubting the existence of God and being tortured by the thought that life was entirely without meaning or purpose. Here we can see that his agony at the loss of meaning was extreme:

Leo Tolstoy, *My Confession*

[F]ive years ago something very strange began to happen with me: I was overcome by minutes at first of perplexity and then of an arrest of life, as though I did not know how to live or what to do, and I lost myself and was dejected. But that passed, and I continued to live as before. Then those minutes of perplexity were repeated oftener and oftener, and always in one and the same form. These arrests of life found their expression in ever the same questions: "Why? Well, and then?"

At first I thought that those were simply aimless, inappropriate questions. It seemed to me that that was all well known and that if I ever wanted to busy myself with their solution, it would not cost me much labour,—that now I had no time to attend to them, but that if I wanted to I should find the proper answers. But the questions began to repeat themselves oftener and oftener, answers were demanded more and more persistently, and, like dots that fall on the same spot, these questions, without any answers, thickened into one black blotch.

There happened what happens with any person who falls ill with a mortal internal disease. At first there appear insignificant symptoms of indisposition, to which the patient pays no attention; then these symptoms are repeated more and more frequently and blend into one temporally indivisible suffering. The suffering keeps growing, and before the patient has had time to look around, he becomes conscious that what he took for an indisposition is the most significant thing in the world to him,—his death.

The same happened with me. I understood that it was not a passing indisposition, but something very important, and that, if the questions were going to repeat themselves, it would be necessary to find an answer for them. And I tried to answer them. The questions seemed to be so foolish, simple, and childish. But the moment I touched them and tried to solve them, I became convinced, in the first place,

Figure 9.3 Leo Tolstoy (1828–1910).

that they were not childish and foolish, but very important and profound questions in life, and, in the second, that, no matter how much I might try, I should not be able to answer them. Before attending to my Samára estate, to my son's education, or to the writing of a book, I ought to know why I should do that. So long as I did not know why, I could not do anything. I could not live. Amidst my thoughts of farming, which interested me very much during that time, there would suddenly pass through my head a question like this: "All right, you are going to have six thousand desyatínas of land in the Government of Samára, and three hundred horses,—and then?" And I completely lost my senses and did not know what to think farther. Or, when I thought of the education of my children, I said to myself: "Why?" Or, reflecting on the manner in which the masses might obtain their welfare, I suddenly said to myself: "What is that to me?" Or, thinking of the fame which my works would get me, I said to myself: "All right, you will be more famous than Gógol, Púshkin, Shakespeare, Molière, and all the writers in the world,—what of it?" And I was absolutely unable to make any reply. The questions were not waiting, and I had to answer them at once; if I did not answer them, I could not live.

I felt that what I was standing on had given way, that I had no foundation to stand on, that that which I lived by no longer existed, and that I had nothing to live by. . . .

All that happened with me when I was on every side surrounded by what is considered to be complete happiness. I had a good, loving, and beloved wife, good children, and a large estate, which grew and increased without any labour on my part. I was respected by my neighbours and friends, more than ever before, was praised by strangers, and, without any self-deception, could consider my name famous. With all that, I was not deranged or mentally unsound,—on the contrary, I was in full command of my mental and physical powers, such as I had rarely met with in people of my age: physically I could work in a field, mowing, without falling behind a peasant; mentally

2 Is Tolstoy's pessimism about life's meaning a result of his objective assessment of his life, or is it merely a product of his unique personality traits?

Figure 9.4 Is life any less meaningful because it is short?

Leo Tolstoy,
My Confession

I could work from eight to ten hours in succession, without experiencing any consequences from the strain. And while in such condition I arrived at the conclusion that I could not live, and, fearing death, I had to use cunning against myself, in order that I might not take my life.

This mental condition expressed itself to me in this form: my life is a stupid, mean trick played on me by somebody. Although I did not recognize that "somebody" as having created me, the form of the conception that some one had played a mean, stupid trick on me by bringing me into the world was the most natural one that presented itself to me.

Involuntarily I imagined that there, somewhere, there was somebody who was now having fun as he looked down upon me and saw me, who had lived for thirty or forty years, learning, developing, growing in body and mind, now that I had become strengthened in mind and had reached that summit of life from which it lay all before me, standing as a complete fool on that summit and seeing clearly that there was nothing in life and never would be. And that was fun to him—

But whether there was or was not that somebody who made fun of me, did not make it easier for me. I could not ascribe any sensible meaning to a single act, or to my whole life. I was only surprised that I had not understood that from the start. All that had long ago been known to everybody. Sooner or later there would come diseases and death (they had come already) to my dear ones and to me, and there would be nothing left but stench and worms. All my affairs, no matter what they might be, would sooner or later be forgotten, and I myself should not exist. So why should I worry about all these things? How could a man fail to see that and live,—that was surprising! A person could live only so long as he was drunk; but the moment he sobered up, he could not help seeing that all that was only a deception, and a stupid deception at that! Really, there was nothing funny and ingenious about it, but only something cruel and stupid.[2]

3 What bearing, if any, does the ephemeral nature of our existence have on the question of whether life has meaning? Does the fact that we will die negate the possibility of meaning in life?

The sole meaning of life is to serve humanity.
—Leo Tolstoy

The German philosopher Arthur Schopenhauer (1788–1860), another famous pessimist, argues that life is so bereft of meaning and so fraught with misery that the nonexistence of the world is preferable to its existence.

Arthur Schopenhauer, "On the Sufferings of the World"

4 Is Schopenhauer right about the meaninglessness of life? Does the wretchedness of our existence show that life has no meaning?

Unless *suffering* is the direct and immediate object of life, our existence must entirely fail of its aim. It is absurd to look upon the enormous amount of pain that abounds everywhere in the world, and originates in needs and necessities inseparable from life itself, as serving no purpose at all and the result of mere chance. Each separate misfortune, as it comes, seems, no doubt, to be something exceptional; but misfortune in general is the rule. . . .

The best consolation in misfortune or affliction of any kind will be the thought of other people who are in a still worse plight than yourself; and this is a form of consolation open to every one. But what an awful fate this means for mankind as a whole!

We are like lambs in a field, disporting themselves under the eye of the butcher, who chooses out first one and then another for his prey. So it is that in our good days we are all unconscious of the evil Fate may have presently in store for us—sickness, poverty, mutilation, loss of sight or reason.

No little part of the torment of existence lies in this, that Time is continually pressing upon us, never letting us take breath, but always coming after us, like a taskmaster with a whip. If at any moment Time stays his hand, it is only when we are delivered over to the misery of boredom. . . .

Certain it is that *work, worry, labor* and *trouble,* form the lot of almost all men their whole life long. But if all wishes were fulfilled as soon as they arose, how would men occupy their lives? what would they do with their time? If the world were a paradise of luxury and ease, a land flowing with milk and honey, where every Jack obtained his Jill at once and without any difficulty, men would either die of boredom or hang themselves; or there would be wars, massacres, and murders; so that in the end mankind would inflict more suffering on itself than it has now to accept at the hands of Nature. . . .

Again, you may look upon life as an unprofitable episode, disturbing the blessed calm of non-existence. And, in any case, even though things have gone with you tolerably well, the longer you live the more clearly you will feel that, on the whole, life is a *disappointment, nay, a cheat.* . . .

If children were brought into the world by an act of pure reason alone, would the human race continue to exist? Would not a man rather have so much sympathy with the coming generation as to spare it the burden of existence? or at any rate not take it upon himself to impose that burden upon it in cold blood.[3]

Figure 9.5 Arthur Schopenhauer (1788–1860).

The distinguished atheist lawyer Clarence Darrow (1857–1938), defense attorney in the famous Scopes "monkey trial," came to the same conclusion that Tolstoy and Schopenhauer did: Life is not worthwhile. "Life is like a ship on the sea," he says, "tossed by every wave and by every wind; a ship headed for no port and no harbor, with no rudder, no compass, no pilot; simply floating for a time, then lost in the waves."[4]

Against the pessimists, it has been argued that most of them have been guilty of perpetrating the confusion mentioned earlier—mixing up the two senses of *meaning.* Contemporary philosopher Julian Baggini explains:

5 What is Schopenhauer's argument for the meaninglessness of life? Is his assessment of life based on objective facts or on his distinctive frame of mind?

Julian Baggini, *What's It All About?*

It seems to me that when most people say that life is meaningless, they are talking about meaning in one or both of these senses. They are saying—rightly, in my view—that our lives were not created with any purpose or goal in mind and that there is nothing beyond or after life that can provide a purpose for what we do in this life. But to conclude that 'therefore life is meaningless' is simply to ignore the many other ways in which life can be meaningful. . . .

What is missing is the recognition that life can be meaningful if we find it worth living for its own sake, without recourse to further aims, goals or purposes. . . .

The same kinds of consideration apply when dealing with [existentialist Albert] Camus's question about how we can live life if it is absurd and meaningless. Again it is only 'meaningless' in certain particular senses of the word. . . .

I have always believed, and I still believe, that whatever good or bad fortune may come our way we can always give it meaning and transform it into something of value.

—Hermann Hesse

PHILOSOPHY NOW

Nietzsche: Reflections on Meaning

Friedrich Wilhelm Nietzsche (1844–1900) lived in the nineteenth century, but his ideas echoed loudest throughout the twentieth, and they resound still, over 100 years after his passing. Today he is both reviled and embraced, and he has outraged many—including exponents of Christianity, contemporary culture, traditional morality, democratic socialism, and Western philosophy. Among those who have claimed to be inspired by his words are Marxists, postmodernists, atheists, anarchists, feminists, reactionaries, vegetarians, and Nazis. Some have claimed him as one of their own even though he has given them no explicit reason to (as in the case of the Nazis). The divergent perspectives on his work are due in part to his writing style, which is mostly brilliant but by turns opaque, poetic, aphoristic, vague, and ironic. But most debate is over the substance of his views, of which the most famous (or notorious) are his doctrine of the will to power, his notion of the mighty human being known as the *Übermensch* (Overman or Superman), and his claim that "God is dead." On these topics some philosophers consider him a nihilist, but others reject that characterization, arguing that Nietzsche was concerned about ultimate meaning and the intellectual and spiritual vitalization of humanity.

Figure 9.6 Friedrich Wilhelm Nietzsche (1844–1900).

From 1873 to 1876 Nietzsche produced *Untimely Meditations* (actually four essays under the single title). In 1879 he resigned his university post because of his failing health and spent the following decade writing and wandering about Italy and Switzerland, lonely and in great physical pain. Out of this period came such works as *The Wanderer and His Shadow* (1880), *Daybreak* (1881), *The Gay Science* or *Joyful Wisdom* (1882), *Beyond Good and Evil* (1887), and *The Genealogy of Morals* (1887). *Thus Spake Zarathustra*, his well-known masterpiece, appeared in the years 1883 to 1885. In 1889, on a street in Turin, he collapsed after seeing a horse being whipped. He spent the remaining ten years of his life insane, dying in August 1900. By the time of his death, he was world renowned, and his writings were the subject of extensive scholarship and controversy.

A central concept of Nietzsche's is the *will to power*, the fundamental nature of existence as a drive to control and dominate. The will to power is not the real world behind appearances (as in Descartes), nor ideas in the universal mind (as in Hegel), nor the will to live, nor the conscious will of God or humans. It *is* life, striving to overcome, to rule, to break out. All human struggles and striving are manifestations of the will to power.

To Nietzsche, the will to power is evident in humankind's search for knowledge, especially in science, philosophy, and religion. "Knowledge," he says, "is an instrument of power." The will to know arises from the will to power—from the desire to master and control a particular domain of reality. Reality is in flux, a kaleidoscope of sense data and concepts, and on this chaos we try to impose order, theory, and pattern so we can turn reality to our advantage. We do not seek truth for truth's sake. There is only the will to power that impels us to try to make sense of the muddle.

Almost all deniers of meaning in life really seem to be rejecting only the idea that life has a specific kind of meaning: one determined by agents, purposes or principles somehow external to this world. This does not justify the conclusion that life has no meaning at all. Their pronouncement that 'life is meaningless' thus just appears to be a kind of hyperbole.[5]

9.3 OPTIMISM: LIFE CAN HAVE MEANING

Optimists say human existence can be meaningful but are divided on how this meaning is possible. As noted earlier, some believe life's meaning has an external source, and some think it arises internally.

Meaning from Above

Most of those who take the externalist approach view the matter from a religious standpoint. Typically, the central doctrine is that a human life has meaning only because it is part of God's plan, a grand cosmic order that encompasses every entity in the universe. As participants in this plan, people have a preeminent role to play and a purpose preordained by God. To have a meaningful existence is to align your life with God's plan, either by performing certain duties or being a particular kind of person. To live contrary to God's plan is to live a meaningless life. And, of course, if there is no God, there is no point to living.

Tolstoy not only gave us a glimpse of his fall into pessimism, he also wrote about his gradual acceptance of a deeply religious understanding of life's meaning:

6 Do you think many people who say that life is meaningless are assuming that *meaning* refers to external meaning?

7 If we reject the religious view of meaning in life, are we forced to conclude that life is meaningless?

Leo Tolstoy, *My Confession*

Long ago has been told the Eastern story about the traveller who in the steppe is overtaken by an infuriated beast. Trying to save himself from the animal, the traveller jumps into a waterless well, but at its bottom he sees a dragon who opens his jaws in order to swallow him. And the unfortunate man does not dare climb out, lest he perish from the infuriated beast, and does not dare jump down to the bottom of the well, lest he be devoured by the dragon, and so clutches the twig of a wild bush growing in a cleft of the well and holds on to it. His hands grow weak and he feels that soon he shall have to surrender to the peril which awaits him at either side; but he still holds on and sees two mice, one white, the other black, in even measure making a circle around the main trunk of the bush to which he is clinging, and nibbling at it on all sides. Now, at any moment, the bush will break and tear off, and he will fall into the dragon's jaws. The traveller sees that and knows that he will inevitably perish; but while he is still clinging, he sees some drops of honey hanging on the leaves of the bush, and so reaches out for them with his tongue and licks the leaves. Just so I hold on to the branch of life, knowing that the dragon of death is waiting inevitably for me, ready to tear me to pieces, and I cannot understand why I have fallen on such suffering. And I try to lick that honey which used to give me pleasure; but now it no longer gives me joy, and the white and

Faith consists in being vitally concerned with that ultimate reality to which I give the symbolical name of God. Whoever reflects earnestly on the meaning of life is on the verge of an act of faith.
—Paul Tillich

Leo Tolstoy,
My Confession

8 How do you think Tolstoy would respond to the claim that many people appear to have very meaningful lives? What would he say, for example, about meaning in the life of Mahatma Gandhi or Albert Einstein?

the black mouse day and night nibble at the branch to which I am holding on. I clearly see the dragon, and the honey is no longer sweet to me. I see only the inevitable dragon and the mice, and am unable to turn my glance away from them. That is not a fable, but a veritable, indisputable, comprehensible truth.

The former deception of the pleasures of life, which stifled the terror of the dragon, no longer deceives me. No matter how much one should say to me, "You cannot understand the meaning of life, do not think, live!" I am unable to do so, because I have been doing it too long before. Now I cannot help seeing day and night, which run and lead me up to death. I see that alone, because that alone is the truth. Everything else is a lie.

The two drops of honey that have longest turned my eyes away from the cruel truth, the love of family and of authorship, which I have called an art, are no longer sweet to me. . . .

I lived for a long time in this madness, which, not in words, but in deeds, is particularly characteristic of us, the most liberal and learned of men. But, thanks either to my strange, physical love for the real working class, which made me understand it and to see that it is not so stupid as we suppose, or to the sincerity of my conviction which was that I could know nothing and that the best that I could do was to hang myself,— I felt that if I wanted to live and understand the meaning of life, I ought naturally to look for it, not among those who had lost the meaning of life and wanted to kill themselves, but among those billions departed and living men who had been carrying their own lives and ours upon their shoulders. And I looked around at the enormous masses of deceased and living men,—not learned and wealthy, but simple men,—and I saw something quite different. I saw that all these billions of men that lived or had lived, all, with rare exceptions, did not fit into my subdivisions, and that I could not recognize them as not understanding the question, because they themselves put it and answered it with surprising clearness. Nor could I recognize them as Epicureans, because their lives were composed rather of privations and suffering than of enjoyment. Still less could I recognize them as senselessly living out their meaningless lives, because every act of theirs and death itself was explained by them. They regarded it as the greatest evil to kill themselves. It appeared, then, that all humanity was in possession of a knowledge of the meaning of life, which I did not recognize and which I condemned. It turned out that rational knowledge did not give any meaning to life, excluded life, while the meaning which by billions of people, by all humanity, was ascribed to life was based on some despised, false knowledge. . . .

Thus, outside the rational knowledge, which had to me appeared as the only one, I was inevitably led to recognize that all living humanity had a certain other irrational knowledge, faith, which made it possible to live. . . .

The rational knowledge brought me to the recognition that life was meaningless,—my life stopped, and I wanted to destroy myself. When I looked around at people, at all humanity, I saw that people lived and asserted that they knew the meaning of life. I looked back at myself: I lived so long as I knew the meaning of life. As to other people, so even to me, did faith give the meaning of life and the possibility of living. . . .

Then I began to cultivate the acquaintance of the believers from among the poor, the simple and unlettered folk, of

Figure 9.7 Gandhi was not a Christian. Did he nevertheless lead a meaningful life? What about Socrates? Einstein?

pilgrims, monks, dissenters, peasants. The doctrine of these people from among the masses was also the Christian doctrine that the quasi-believers of our circle professed. With the Christian truths were also mixed in very many superstitions, but there was this difference: the superstitions of our circle were quite unnecessary to them, had no connection with their lives, were only a kind of an Epicurean amusement, while the superstitions of the believers from among the laboring classes were to such an extent blended with their life that it would have been impossible to imagine it without these superstitions,—it was a necessary condition of that life. I began to examine closely the lives and beliefs of these people, and the more I examined them, the more did I become convinced that they had the real faith, that their faith was necessary for them, and that it alone gave them a meaning and possibility of life. In contradistinction to what I saw in our circle, where life without faith was possible, and where hardly one in a thousand professed to be a believer, among them there was hardly one in a thousand who was not a believer. In contradistinction to what I saw in our circle, where all life passed in idleness, amusements, and tedium of life, I saw that the whole life of these people was passed in hard work, and that they were satisfied with life. In contradistinction to the people of our circle, who struggled and murmured against fate because of their privations and their suffering, these people accepted diseases and sorrows without any perplexity or opposition, but with the calm and firm conviction that it was all for good. In contradistinction to the fact that the more intelligent we are, the less do we understand the meaning of life and the more do we see a kind of a bad joke in our suffering and death, these people live, suffer, and approach death, and suffer in peace and more often in joy. . . . I cast a broader glance about me. I examined the life of past and present vast masses of men, and I saw people who in like manner had understood the meaning of life, who had known how to live and die, not two, not three, not ten, but hundreds, thousands, millions. All of them, infinitely diversified as to habits, intellect, culture, situation, all equally and quite contrary to my ignorance knew the meaning of life and of death, worked calmly, bore privations and suffering, lived and died, seeing in that not vanity, but good.

I began to love those people. The more I penetrated into their life, the life of the men now living, and the life of men departed, of whom I had read and heard, the more did I love them, and the easier it became for me to live. Thus I lived for about two years, and within me took place a transformation, which had long been working within me, and the germ of which had always been in me. What happened with me was that the life of our circle,—of the rich and the learned,—not only disgusted me, but even lost all its meaning. All our acts, reflections, sciences, arts,—all that appeared to me in a new light. I saw that all that was mere pampering of the appetites, and that no meaning could be found in it; but the life of all the working masses, of all humanity, which created life, presented itself to me in its real significance. I saw that that was life itself and that the meaning given to this life was truth, and I accepted it.[6]

So Tolstoy says he found the true meaning of life through a leap of faith, not through the rational knowledge of his circle of sophisticates. He chose the religious path trod by millions of the poor and unlearned.

Nonbelievers, however, would not be impressed by Tolstoy's appeal to faith. They would insist that his position be backed by reasons and arguments. But, as we saw in Chapter 2, theistic belief is difficult to support this way. Moreover, some critiques of Tolstoy's view do not depend on a denial of God's existence. Several philosophers have argued that the notion of a God assigning a purpose to humans

Ever more people today have the means to live, but no meaning to live for.
—Viktor E. Frankl

PHILOSOPHY NOW

Is Religion Necessary for a Meaningful Life?

Rick Warren, author of *The Purpose-Driven Life* and the pastor who delivered the invocation at Barack Obama's inauguration ceremony, maintains that religion is required if your life is to have meaning. "You were made by God and for God," he says, "and until you understand that, life will never make sense." Is that true?

The results of a Gallup poll raise doubts about it. The pollsters surveyed thousands of people in eighty-four countries. They concluded that "There is some support in Gallup's data for Warren's premise that religious involvement makes devotees more likely to feel their lives have a purpose. On the other hand, the results also suggest that religious involvement is not *necessary* for most people to feel that way." Here are some of the results.

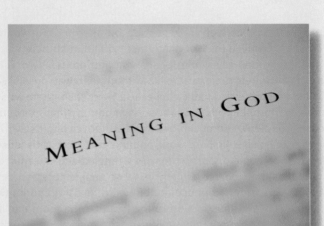

Figure 9.8 Suppose you are not religious, yet you have always felt that your life has meaning (just as many atheists believe their lives have meaning). Then someone tells you that your life cannot possibly have meaning because you are not religious. Would you think the person was denying the obvious or speaking truth? Why?

Do you feel your life has an important meaning or purpose?
Among those claiming any religious affiliation: 92% yes; 6% no.
Among those claiming to be secular, nonreligious, atheist, or agnostic: 83% yes; 14% no.

Do you feel your life has an important meaning or purpose?
Percentage answering yes: Christian: 93%; Hindu: 92%; Muslim: 91%; Buddhist: 90%; Other: 89%; Jewish: 88%; secular/atheist/agnostic: 83%.

Do you feel your life has an important meaning or purpose?
Percentage answering yes: elementary education or less: 88%; secondary education up to three years of tertiary education: 91%; at least four years of tertiary education: 91%; have a job: 92%; do not have a job: 89%.

Gallup survey, 2007, data from 1,000 adults per country across 84 populations; ±4 percentage points sampling error.

Do these results surprise you, or are they what you would expect? Do they corroborate the idea that people can have a meaningful life without religion? Do they show that meaning in life can arise internally? Explain.

should be objectionable to believers and nonbelievers alike. This is how Baggini expresses the point:

Julian Baggini, *What's It All About?*

[I]t is often said that we are here to do God's will. If this were true . . . [o]ur lives would have a purpose for the being that created us but not a purpose for us. We would each be like Sartre's being-in-itself—an object to be used for the ends of others and not a being-for-itself—a conscious being making choices meaningful for itself. If we found that our sole purpose was to serve God then we might think that was a worse fate than to have no predetermined purpose at all. Is it better to be slaves with a role in the universe or to be free people left to create a role for ourselves?

This view that we are created to serve God is not only objectionable on the grounds that it robs humanity of its dignity. It also has to be seen as extremely implausible within the world-view of the religions that sometimes propound it. After all, what could seem more unlikely than that the supreme being would feel the need to create human beings, with all their complexity, and with all the suffering and toil that human life entails, solely so that it can have creatures to serve it? This is an image of God as an egotistical tyrant, determined to use its power to surround itself with acolytes and have praise heaped upon it. This is not the God which most religious believers worship, and so the idea that we are here just to serve such a God is not one that should be seriously countenanced either. . . .

I think that most reflective religious believers would agree that saying God's purpose for us is to serve it or live full lives is not adequate. They might prefer to say that the existence of God shows that there must be a purpose, since God wouldn't have created us without one, but that we do not know what that purpose is. Faith requires us to trust God and its purposes for us. As Jesus is reported in John's Gospel to have said,

9 According to Baggini, how is God's creating us for his purposes supposed to denigrate human life? Do you agree?

Figure 9.9 Baggini asks, "Is it better to be slaves with a role in the universe or to be free people left to create a role for ourselves?"

Julian Baggini,
What's It All About?

'Trust in God; trust also in me. In my Father's house are many rooms' (14:1–2). This is a perfectly coherent position and probably the one most sensible religious believers occupy. But doing so requires an honest acceptance that they have no more idea as to what the purpose of life is than the atheist has.

The leap of faith required to adopt such a position also needs to be clearly understood. This is faith that a God we cannot know to exist has a purpose we cannot discern for an afterlife we have no evidence is to come. Further, we would also be trusting that this purpose is one we would be pleased with. If it turned out that our purpose was to fight Satan's hordes for eternity or just to have lived as a beacon of fortitude under duress on earth before dying, we might not be too pleased that God had a purpose for us after all.

A belief that we were created by God for a purpose does not then provide us with the kind of adequate account of life's meaning we might expect. Religions are not clear about what this purpose is. The idea that it is to serve God seems deeply implausible and contrary to most conceptions of God's nature. The idea that it is to live life to the full is a platitude, only turned into something more by a belief in an afterlife. The idea that God's purpose is something we just have to trust is an admission that we have no answer to the question of why we are here and must leave everything to the unknown.[7]

> Religion is the state of being grasped by an ultimate concern, a concern which qualifies all other concerns as preliminary and which itself contains the answer to the question of a meaning of our life.
> —Paul Tillich

Meaning from Below

Internalists believe they can have meaningful lives without relying on the concepts of God or transcendent realms. They hold that they can confer meaning on their own lives. The proof of this, they might say, is all around us. There are many people who seem to lead meaningful lives, and we would judge this to be the case even if we thought no external being or force existed to confer meaning. Consider Socrates, Mahatma Gandhi, Martin Luther King., Jr., Rosa Parks, Elizabeth Cady Stanton, Marie Curie, George Washington, Confucius, Thomas Aquinas—these men and women, by all accounts, were driven by a sense of purpose and led lives full of meaning.

But exactly what property or state of affairs is the conveyor of meaning? Internalists differ on that score. Here is Paul Edwards's view:

Paul Edwards, *The Encyclopedia of Philosophy*

[W]hen we ask whether a *particular* person's life has or had any meaning, we are usually concerned not with cosmic issues but with the question of whether certain purposes are to be found *in* his life. Thus, most of us would say without hesitation that a person's life had meaning if we knew that he devoted himself to a cause (such as the spread of Christianity or communism or the reform of mental institutions), or we would at least be ready to say that it "acquired meaning" once he became sufficiently attached to his cause. Whether we approve of what they did or not, most of us would be ready to admit—to take some random examples—that Dorothea Dix, Pasteur, Lenin, Margaret Sanger, Anthony Comstock, and Winston Churchill led meaningful lives. We seem to mean two things in characterizing such lives as meaningful: we assert, first, that the life in question had some dominant, over-all goal or goals which gave direction to a great many of the individual's actions and, second, that these actions and possibly others not immediately related to the overriding goal were performed with a special zest that was not present before the person became attached to his goal or that would not have been present if there had been no such goal in his life. It is not necessary, however, that a person should be devoted to a cause, in the sense just indicated, before we call his life meaningful. It is sufficient that he should have some attachments that are not too shallow.[8]

A common reply to any internalist view is that the prospect of death and the eventual obliteration of all human creations rob our lives of meaning. How can our lives be meaningful, they ask, when life is so short and death is certain? What's the point of living if everything we are and do will soon sink into nothingness?

Many philosophers reject this dismal outlook, arguing that the fact of death and the ephemeral nature of human endeavors are irrelevant to the meaningfulness or meaninglessness of a person's existence. If life is meaningful, then it is meaningful no matter how long or short it is. Edwards is one of the philosophers who make this point:

[L]et us consider some everyday occurrences: A man with a toothache goes to a dentist, and the dentist helps him so that the toothache disappears. A man is falsely accused of a crime and is faced with the possibility of a severe sentence as well as with the loss of his reputation; with the help of a devoted attorney his innocence is established, and he is acquitted. It is true that a hundred years later all of the participants in these events will be dead and none of them will *then* be able to enjoy the fruits of any of the efforts involved. But this most emphatically does not imply that the dentist's efforts were not worthwhile or that the attorney's work was not worth doing. To bring in considerations of what will or will not happen in the remote future is, in [this and other] human situations, totally irrelevant. Not only is the finality of death irrelevant here; equally irrelevant are the facts, if they are facts, that life is an endless cycle of the same kind of activities and that the history of the universe is not a drama with a happy ending.[9]

> I would rather live my life as if there is a God and die to find out there isn't, than live my life as if there isn't and die to find out there is.
> —Albert Camus

10 Do you agree with Edwards that the length of one's life does not by itself determine whether life is meaningful?

Review Notes

9.1 OVERVIEW: PHILOSOPHY AND THE MEANING OF LIFE

- Most who have thought about it believe that questions concerning the meaning of human existence are extremely important and relevant.
- The process of examining the question of life's meaning is personal—no one can do it for you.
- The main impediment to clear thinking about life's meaning is confusion about what *meaning* refers to. The word can refer to external meaning or internal meaning.

9.2 PESSIMISM: LIFE HAS NO MEANING

- Pessimists believe that life has no meaning; optimists believe that it does. Some optimists believe that life's meaning is external; other optimists think it's internal.

WHAT DO YOU BELIEVE?

What Can and Cannot Give Life Meaning?

Here is a quiz to help you assess your views on life's meaning. For each statement below, indicate whether you agree or disagree with it (or have no opinion on it). This is the easy part. The more difficult task is to support your beliefs with good arguments or evidence. This exercise asks you to specify not what has *caused* your beliefs, but what *justifies* them.

1. Unless there is an eternal afterlife, human life can have no meaning.
2. Life has meaning only if there is a God who has created us for a purpose.
3. Life has meaning if you are happy.
4. Life has no meaning and no purpose.
5. Having a meaningful or purposeful life does not matter; what matters is the next life of everlasting bliss.
6. People cannot give meaning to their own lives; life's meaning is derived from God or some other transcendental reality.
7. A study of people past and present would show that some of them live or have lived meaningful lives, and this sense of meaning does not depend on their belief in God.
8. Death has no bearing on whether we can live meaningful lives.
9. The eventual obliteration of everything we have created or strived for is irrelevant to whether our lives can be meaningful.
10. The notion that God has assigned to humans a purpose or plan to live by is an affront to human dignity.
11. Without a transcendental reality and humanity's relationship to it through faith, human life is meaningless.
12. Some moral, aesthetic, or intellectual goals or endeavors are enough to confer meaning on one's life.
13. As Tolstoy says, a meaningful life requires a leap of faith.
14. People who trust that God has a plan for their lives have no understanding of what the purpose of their lives is.
15. Socrates, Mahatma Gandhi, Marie Curie, and Confucius led meaningful lives.

Figure 9.10 Determining whether your life has meaning usually requires a broad, encompassing view of things.

- Tolstoy (at one point in his life), Schopenhauer, and Darrow are pessimists. Baggini thinks they mix up the two senses of meaning; so when they say "life is meaningless," they likely mean only that life has no meaning in the external sense.

9.3 OPTIMISM: LIFE CAN HAVE MEANING

- Most of those who take the externalist approach view the matter from a religious standpoint. Typically, they believe that a human life has meaning only because it is part of God's plan. Tolstoy took this view and maintained that finding meaning in life requires a leap of faith.
- Unbelievers would insist the religious view of meaning be backed by reasons and arguments. Several philosophers have argued that the notion of a God assigning a purpose to humans should be objectionable to believers and nonbelievers alike. They maintain that this idea of God creating people for a purpose is an affront to human dignity.
- Internalists believe they can have meaningful lives without relying on the concepts of God or transcendent realms. They hold that they can confer meaning on their own lives.
- Many philosophers reject the notion that death robs people of meaning in life. They argue that the fact of death and the ephemeral nature of human endeavors are irrelevant to the meaningfulness or meaninglessness of a person's existence. If life is meaningful, then it is meaningful no matter how long or short it is.

WRITING TO UNDERSTAND:
ARGUING YOUR OWN VIEWS   Chapter 9

1. Devise an argument for the proposition that life is (or is not) meaningful.
2. Explain Tolstoy's case for believing that life can have meaning through a leap of faith—then show how skeptics have argued against Tolstoy's view. Conclude by stating which side in this controversy you think is stronger.
3. Some maintain that we are here to do God's will. Lay out an argument showing that such a purpose would or would not make life meaningful.
4. State whether you believe that Socrates and Marie Curie led meaningful lives. Give reasons for your assertion.
5. Does the prospect of death undermine life's meaningfulness? Give reasons for your answer.

FICTION

The Good Brahmin

Voltaire

> Voltaire (1694–1778), a French philosopher and writer, was one of the most important thinkers of his day. He was the author of both fiction and nonfiction, including *Candide*, *Treatise on Tolerance*, and *Philosophical Dictionary*.

On my travels I met an old Brahmin, a very wise man, of marked intellect and great learning. Furthermore, he was rich and, consequently, all the wiser, because, lacking nothing, he needed to deceive nobody. His household was very well managed by three handsome women who set themselves out to please him. When he was not amusing himself with his women, he passed the time in philosophizing. Near his house, which was beautifully decorated and had charming gardens attached, there lived a narrow-minded old Indian woman: she was a simpleton, and rather poor.

Said the Brahmin to me one day: "I wish I had never been born!" On my asking why, he answered: "I have been studying forty years, and that is forty years wasted. I teach others and myself am ignorant of everything. Such a state of affairs fills my soul with so much humiliation and disgust that my life is intolerable. I was born in Time, I live in Time, and yet I do not know what Time is. I am at a point between two eternities, as our wise men say, and I have no conception of eternity. I am composed of matter: I think, but I have never been able to learn what produces my thought. I do not know whether or not my understanding is a simple faculty inside me, such as those of walking and digesting, and whether or not I think with my head as I grip with my hands. Not only is the cause of my thought unknown to me; the cause of my actions is equally a mystery. I do not know why I exist, and yet every day people ask me questions on all these points. I have to reply, and as I have nothing really worth saying I talk a great deal, and am ashamed of myself afterward for having talked.

"It is worse still when I am asked if Brahma was born of Vishnu or if they are both eternal. God is my witness that I have not the remotest idea, and my ignorance shows itself in my replies. 'Ah, Holy One,' people say to me, 'tell us why evil pervades the earth.' I am in as great a difficulty as those who ask me this question. Sometimes I tell them that everything is as well as can be, but those who have been ruined and broken in the wars do not believe a word of it—and no more do I. I retire to my home stricken at my own curiosity and ignorance. I read our ancient books, and they double my darkness. I talk to my companions: some answer me that we must enjoy life and make game of mankind; others think they know a lot and lose themselves in a maze of wild ideas. Everything increases my anguish. I am ready sometimes to despair when I think that after all my seeking I do not know whence I came, whither I go, what I am nor what I shall become."

The good man's condition really worried me. Nobody was more rational or more sincere than he. I perceived that his unhappiness increased in proportion as his understanding developed and his insight grew.

The same day I saw the old woman who lived near him. I asked her if she had ever been troubled by the thought that she was ignorant of the nature of her soul. She did not even understand my question. Never in all her life had she reflected for one single moment on one single point of all those which tormented the Brahmin. She believed with all her heart in the metamorphoses of Vishnu and, provided she could obtain a little Ganges water wherewith to wash herself, thought herself the happiest of women.

Struck with this mean creature's happiness, I returned to my wretched philosopher. "Are you not ashamed," said I, "to be unhappy when at your very door there lives an old automaton who thinks about nothing, and yet lives contentedly?"

"You are right," he replied. "I have told myself a hundred times that I should be happy if I were as brainless as my neighbor, and yet I do not desire such happiness."

My Brahmin's answer impressed me more than all the rest. I set to examining myself, and I saw that in truth I would not care to be happy at the price of being a simpleton.

Voltaire, "The Good Brahmin," from *The Portable Voltaire*, ed. Ben Ray Redman (New York: Viking Penguin, 1949, 1977).

I put the matter before some philosophers, and they were of my opinion. "Nevertheless," said I, "there is a tremendous contradiction in this mode of thought, for, after all, the problem is—how to be happy. What does it matter whether one has brains or not? Further those who are contented with their lot are certain of their contentment, whereas those who reason are not certain that they reason correctly. It is quite clear, therefore," I continued, "that we must choose not to have common sense, however little common sense may contribute to our discomfort." Everyone agreed with me, but I found nobody, notwithstanding, who was willing to accept the bargain of becoming a simpleton in order to become contented. From which I conclude that if we consider the question of happiness we must consider still more the question of reason.

But on reflection it seems that to prefer reason to felicity is to be very senseless. How can this contradiction be explained? Like all the other contradictions. It is matter for much talk.

Probing Questions

1. The contemplative Brahmin is unhappy and haunted by the question of the meaning of life. The old woman is unreflective and contented. Which person would you rather be? Why?

2. Does this story suggest that happiness is essential if you want your life to be meaningful? Are happiness and meaningfulness the same thing?

3. Can a person be miserable and still live a meaningful life? If so, how? Can a person be happy and live a life without meaning?

For Further Reading

Julian Baggini, *What's It All About? Philosophy and the Meaning of Life* (Oxford: Oxford University Press, 2005). An excellent primer on meaning in life; argues that meaning can have an internal source.

Kurt Baier, "The Meaning of Life," in *The Meaning of Life: A Reader*, E. D. Klemke and Steven M. Cahn, eds. (New York: Oxford University Press, 2008), 82–113. A classic essay on the basic issues.

E. D. Klemke and Steven M. Cahn, eds., *The Meaning of Life: A Reader* (New York: Oxford University Press, 2008). A good anthology featuring most of the must-read articles.

John E. Messerly, *The Meaning of Life* (Washington State: Durant & Russell, 2012). A survey of religious, philosophical, and scientific perspectives.

Bertrand Russell, "A Free Man's Worship," in *Why I Am Not a Christian* (London: George Allen & Unwin, 1957). A much anthologized essay by the famous twentieth-century philosopher; discusses how life can have meaning in a godless world.

EXERCISE 1.1

1. Argument.
   Conclusion: Faster-than-light travel is not possible.
   Premise: Faster-than-light travel would violate a law of nature.

2. Argument.
   Conclusion: Therefore, you are not fit to serve in your current capacity.
   Premise: You have neglected your duty on several occasions.
   Premise: You have been absent from work too many times.

3. No argument.

4. Argument.
   Conclusion: The flu epidemic on the East Coast is real.
   Premise: Government health officials say so.
   Premise: And I personally have read at least a dozen news stories that characterize the situation as a "flu epidemic."

5. No argument.

6. Argument.
   Conclusion: Current-day Christians use violence to spread their right-to-life message.
   Premise: These Christians, often referred to as the religious right, are well known for violent demonstrations against Planned Parenthood and other abortion clinics.
   Premise: Doctors and other personnel are threatened with death.
   Premise: Clinics have been bombed.
   Premise: There have even been cases of doctors being murdered.

7. No argument.

8. No argument.

9. Argument.
   Conclusion: Witches are real.
   Premise: They are mentioned in the Bible.
   Premise: There are many people today who claim to be witches.
   Premise: Historical records reveal that there were witches in Salem.

10. No argument.

EXERCISE 1.2

1. Conclusion: The idea that God is required to be the enforcer of the moral law is not plausible.

   Premises: (4) In the first place, as an empirical hypothesis about the psychology of human beings, it is questionable. (5) There is no unambiguous evidence that theists are more moral than nontheists. (6) Not only have psychological studies failed to find a significant correlation between frequency of religious worship and moral conduct, but convicted criminals are much more likely to be theists than atheists. (7) Second, the threat of divine punishment cannot impose a moral obligation. (8) Might does not make right.

2. Conclusion: (1) When [Gillespie] refers to [President Bush] as "the millionaire president who waited out the Vietnam War in the Texas Air National Guard," it reminds me of the garbage rhetoric that I might see if I were reading Ted Rall, or Susan Sontag, or one of the other hate-mongering, America-bashing, leftist whiners. [Paraphrase: Gillespie's rhetoric is inappropriate.]

   Premises: (2) That kind of ad hominem attack [is] disrespectful to a man who is doing a damned good job as commander-in-chief. (3) [The rhetoric] detracts from the whole point of the article.

3. Conclusion: (1) Therefore some intelligent being exists by whom all natural things are directed to their end; and this being we call God.

   Premises: (2) We see that things which lack knowledge, such as natural bodies, act for an end, and this is evident from their acting always, or nearly always, in the same way, so as to obtain the best result. (3) Hence it is plain that they achieve their end, not fortuitously, but designedly. (4) Now whatever lacks knowledge cannot move towards an end, unless it be directed by some being endowed with knowledge and intelligence; as the arrow is directed by the archer.

4. Conclusion: (1) [The] position is certainly untenable.

   Premises: (2) The first thing that must occur to anyone studying moral subjectivism [the view that the rightness or wrongness of an action depends on the beliefs of an individual or group] seriously is that the view allows the possibility that an action can be both right and not right, or wrong and not wrong, etc. (3) This possibility exists because, as we have seen, the subjectivist claims that the moral character of an action is determined by individual subjective states; and these states can vary from person to person, even when directed toward the same action on the same occasion. (4) Hence one and the same action can evidently be determined to have—simultaneously—radically different moral characters. . . .

5. Conclusion: (1) I submit that the dismissal was proper and ethical considering the community stature and function of priests and the benefits that accrue to society in the aftermath of the decision.

   Premises: Let's consider community stature first. The community stature of priests must always be taken into account in these abuse cases. (2) A priest is not just anybody; he performs a special role in society—namely, to provide spiritual guidance and to remind people that there is both a moral order and a divine order in the world. The priest's role is special because it helps to underpin and secure society itself. (3) Anything that could undermine this role must be neutralized as soon as possible. (4) Among those things that can weaken the priestly role are publicity, public debate, and legal actions. Abuse cases are better handled in private by those who are keenly aware of the importance of a positive public image of priests. And what of the benefits of curtailing the legal proceedings? (5) The benefits to society of dismissing the legal case outweigh all the alleged disadvantages of continuing with public hearings. (6) The primary benefit is the continued nurturing of the community's faith, without which the community would cease to function effectively.

EXERCISE 1.3

1. Genetic fallacy

2. Straw man

3. Division

4. Appeal to the person

5. Genetic fallacy

6. Equivocation

7. Appeal to ignorance

8. Appeal to the person

9. Appeal to ignorance

10. Equivocation

In conversations, letters to the editor, or online discussions, have you ever taken a position on an issue and offered reasons why your view is correct? If so, then you have defended a thesis. You have presented an argument, giving reasons for accepting a particular thesis, or conclusion. If you elaborate on your argument in a written paper, you create something even more valuable—a *thesis defense* (or *argumentative*) *essay*. In a thesis defense essay, you try to show the reader that your view is worthy of acceptance by offering reasons that support it. Your thesis may assert your position on a philosophical, social, or political issue; on the arguments or claims of other writers (including some famous or not-so-famous philosophers); or on the interpretation of a single work or several works. In every case, you affirm a thesis and give reasons for your affirmation.

This type of essay is not merely an analysis of claims, a summary of points made by someone else, or a reiteration of what other people believe or say—though a good thesis defense essay may contain some of these elements. A thesis defense essay is supposed to be a demonstration of what you believe and why you believe it. What other people think is, ultimately, beside the point.

BASIC ESSAY STRUCTURE

Thesis defense essays usually contain the following elements, though not necessarily in this order:

  I. Introduction (or opening)

    A. Thesis statement (the claim to be supported)

    B. Plan for the paper

    C. Background for the thesis

 II. Argument supporting the thesis

III. Assessment of objections

IV. Conclusion

Introduction

The introduction often consists of the paper's first paragraph, sometimes just a sentence or two. Occasionally it is longer, perhaps several paragraphs. The length depends on how much ground you must cover to introduce the argument. Whatever the length, the introduction should be no longer than necessary. In most cases the best introductions are short.

If there is a rule of thumb for what the introduction must contain, it is this: *The introduction should set forth the thesis statement.* The thesis statement usually appears in the first paragraph. It is the claim that you hope to support or prove in your essay, the conclusion of the argument that you intend to present. You may want to pose the thesis statement as the answer to a question that you raise, or as the solution to a problem that you wish to discuss. However presented, your thesis statement is the assertion you must support with reasons. It is like a compass to your readers, guiding them from paragraph to paragraph, premise to premise, showing them a clear path from introduction to conclusion. It also helps you stay on course. It reminds you to relate every sentence and paragraph to your one controlling idea.

Your thesis statement should be restricted to a claim that you can defend in the space allowed. You want to state it in a single sentence and do so as early as possible. You may need to add a few words to explain or elaborate on the statement if you think its meaning or implications unclear.

The other two parts of an introduction—the plan for the paper (B) and background information for the thesis (C)—may or may not be necessary, depending on your thesis and your intent. In more formal essays, you will need not only to state your thesis, but also to spell out how you intend to argue for it. You will have to summarize your whole argument—each of your premises and conclusion—or, if your argument is long or complex, at least the most important points. Providing background information for your thesis is a matter of explaining what your thesis means (which includes defining terms and clarifying concepts), what its implications are, why the issue is so important or pressing, or why you have decided to address it. Sometimes the needed background information is so extensive that you must supply much of it after the introduction. At any rate, by adding the right kind of background information, you give your readers good reason to care about what you are saying and to continue reading.

In many philosophy papers, the background information includes a summary or sketch of the views of other philosophers—what they have said that is relevant to the issue or to your thesis. Providing this kind of material can help the reader understand why your topic is worth exploring and why your argument is relevant.

Argument Supporting the Thesis

Between your paper's introduction and conclusion is the *body* of the essay. The basic components of the body are (1) the premises of your argument plus the material that supports or explains them and (2) an evaluation of objections to your thesis. Each premise must be clearly stated, carefully explained and illustrated, and properly backed up by examples, statistics, expert opinion, argument, or other reasons or evidence. You may be able to adequately develop the essay by devoting a single paragraph to each premise, or you may have to use several paragraphs per premise.

Whatever tack you take, you must stick to the central rule of paragraph development: Develop just one main point in each paragraph, embodying that point in a topic sentence. Make sure that each paragraph in turn relates to your thesis statement.

If your essay is a critique of someone else's arguments, you should examine them in the body, explaining how they work and laying out the author's response to any major criticisms of them. Your account of the arguments should be accurate and complete, putting forth the author's best case and providing enough detail for your readers to understand the import of your own argument. After the presentation of the author's side of things, you can then bring in your critique, asserting and explaining each premise.

Some premises, of course, may be so obvious that they do not require support. The determining factor is whether your readers would be likely to question them. If your readers are likely to accept a premise as it is, no backup is required. If they are not, you need to support the premise. A common mistake is to assume that a premise would be accepted by everyone when in fact it is controversial.

Recall that in a good argument the conclusion logically follows from the premises, and the premises are true. Your task in the body of your essay is to put forth such an argument and to do so plainly—to demonstrate clearly to your readers that your premises are properly related to your conclusion and that they are true. You should leave no doubt about what you are trying to prove and how you are trying to prove it. In longer papers, you may want to back up your thesis with more than one argument. This is an acceptable way to proceed, providing you make the relationships between the separate arguments and your thesis clear.

Assessment of Objections

Very often an argumentative essay includes an *assessment of objections*—a sincere effort to take into account any objections or doubts that readers are likely to have about points in your essay. (In some cases, however, there may be no significant objections to assess.) You must show your readers that the objections are unfounded, that your argument is not fatally wounded by likely criticisms. Contrary to what some may think, when you deal effectively with objections in your essay, *you do not weaken it—you strengthen it*. You lend credibility to it by making an attempt to be fair and thorough. You make your position stronger by removing doubts from your readers' minds. If you don't confront likely objections, your readers may conclude that you are either ignorant of the objections or you don't have a good reply to them. An extra benefit is that in dealing with objections, you may see ways to make your argument stronger.

On the other hand, you may discover that you do not have an adequate answer to the objections. Then what? Then you look for ways to change your arguments or thesis to overcome the criticisms. You can weaken your thesis by making it less sweeping or less probable. Or you may need to abandon your thesis altogether in favor of one that is stronger. Discovering that your beloved thesis is full of holes is not necessarily a setback. You have increased your understanding by finding out which boats will float and which will not.

Conclusion

Unless your essay is very short, it should have a *conclusion*. The conclusion usually appears in the last paragraph. Many conclusions simply reiterate the thesis statement and then go on to emphasize how important it is. Others issue a call to action, present a compelling perspective on the issue, or discuss further implications of the thesis statement. Some conclusions contain a summary of the essay's argument. A summary is always a good idea if the argument is complex, long, or formal.

WRITING THE ESSAY: STEP BY STEP

Now we examine the steps involved in crafting a good thesis defense essay. You have the best chance of writing a good essay if you try to follow these steps. Just remember that the process is not linear. You may not be able to follow the steps in the sequence suggested. You may have to backtrack or rearrange the order of the steps. This kind of improvising on the fly is normal—and often necessary. At any stage in the process, you may discover that your argument is not as good as you thought, or that you did not take an important fact into account, or that there is a way that you can alter the essay to make it stronger. You may then want to go back and rework your outline or tinker with the draft you are working on—and your essay will be better for it. Rethinking and revising are normal procedures for even the best writers.

Here are the steps:

1. Select a topic and narrow it to a specific issue.

2. Research the issue.

3. Write a thesis statement.

4. Create an outline.

5. Write a first draft.

6. Study and revise your first draft.

7. Produce a final draft.

Step 1. Select a topic and narrow it to a specific issue.

This step is first for a reason. It is here to help inexperienced writers avoid a tempting but nasty trap: picking a thesis out of the air and writing their paper on it. Caution: *Any thesis that you dream up without knowing anything about it is likely to be unusable*—and a waste of time. It is better to begin by selecting a topic or issue and narrowing it through research and hard thinking to a manageable thesis.

A topic is simply a broad category of subject matter, such as *human cloning*, *the mind*, *capital punishment*, and *God*. Within topics there lurk an infinite number of issues—that is, questions that are in dispute. From the topic of capital punishment, for example, countless issues arise: whether executing criminals deters crime, whether executing a human being is ever morally permissible, whether it is ethical to execute people who are insane or mentally impaired, whether the system of capital punishment in the United States is unfair, whether the death penalty should be mandatory for serial killers, whether executing juveniles is immoral . . . the list could go on and on. The basic idea is to select from the roster of possibilities an issue that (1) you are interested in and (2) you can adequately address in the space allowed.

Step 2. Research the issue.

The main reason for researching an issue is to find out what viewpoints and arguments are involved. Often your instructor will suggest good sources to research for a particular writing assignment. Your assigned reading may be the only source you need to check. Otherwise, you can read articles and books, talk to people who have studied the issue or at least thought about it carefully, or go online to review topical or philosophical sites.

Step 3. Write a thesis statement.

The conclusion of your selected argument will serve as the basis for your thesis statement. Often the conclusion *is* your thesis statement. Writing a good thesis statement is an essential step, because the entire essay is built on it. An imprecise or clumsy thesis statement can lead to an imprecise or clumsy argument, which can wreck any argumentative essay.

At this stage, you should try to get the wording of your statement just right, even though you may revise it later on. Its scope should be restricted to what you can handle in the space you have. It should also be focused on just one idea, not several. A good thesis statement must be clear. No one should have to guess about the meaning of your thesis. The thesis "Same-sex marriages are intolerable," for example, is intolerably vague, since there are many ways that something can be intolerable. It gives us very little information about what will be discussed in the essay.

It is possible to devise a thesis statement that is restricted, focused, clear—and trivial. A trivial thesis statement is one that either concerns an insignificant issue or makes an insignificant claim. People generally don't care about insignificant issues, and few would bother to disagree with an insignificant claim. Who cares whether pens are better than pencils, or whether gambling is more fun than beachcombing? And who would care to contest the claim that pleasure is better than pain? An essay built on a trivial thesis statement wastes your readers' time (if they bother to read it at all), and you learn nothing and change nothing by writing it. Thesis statements should be worthy.

Here are some thesis statements that meet the preceding criteria:

- Jeremy Bentham's moral theory known as act-utilitarianism conflicts with our commonsense ideas about human rights.
- The U.S. government should be allowed to arrest and indefinitely imprison without trial any American citizen who is suspected of terrorism.

- Subjective relativism—the view that truth depends on what someone believes—is self-refuting.
- Racial profiling should not be used to do security screening of airline passengers.

Step 4. Create an outline of the whole essay.

If you can write out your thesis statement and outline the argument used to defend it, you have already come far. Your argument and thesis statement will constitute the skeleton of your essay. The next step is to flesh out the bones with introductory or explanatory material, responses to objections, and support for the premises (which may consist of subordinate arguments, examples, explanations, analogies, statistics, scientific research, expert opinion, or other evidence). Producing a detailed, coherent outline of the whole essay is the best way to manage this task, and if you already have an outline of your argument, creating an outline for the whole essay will be easy. An outline helps you fill out your argument in an orderly fashion, showing you how the pieces fit together, and whether any parts are missing or misaligned. This filling-out process will probably require you to research your thesis further—to check the truth of premises, examine alternative arguments, look for additional evidence, or assess the strength of objections to your argument.

Do not be afraid to alter your outline at any stage. As you write, you may realize that your thesis is weak, your argument flawed, or your premises vague. If so, you should go back and adjust the outline before writing any further. Writing is an act of exploration, and good writers are not afraid to revise when they find something amiss.

When you outline your essay, include your full thesis statement in the introduction. Then, as you work on the outline, you can refer to the statement for guidance. The major points of your outline will include the premises, conclusion, objections, and responses to objections.

You will find that as you tweak the outline, you may need to adjust the thesis statement. And as you perfect the thesis statement, you may need to adjust the outline. In the end, you want to satisfy yourself that the outline is complete, accurate, and structurally sound, tracing a clear and logical progression of points.

Step 5. Write a first draft.

Good writers revise . . . and revise and revise. They either write multiple drafts, revising in successive passes, or they revise continuously as they write. They know that their first tries will always be in need of improvement. Inexperienced writers, on the other hand, too often dash off a first draft without a second look—then turn it in! A much more reasonable approach (and the best one for most students) is to at least write a first draft and a final draft or—better—several drafts and a final one.

In argumentative essays, because of the importance of articulating an argument carefully, and the difficulty of writing later drafts of the essay unless the first one is in reasonable shape, the first draft should be fairly solid. That is, in your first draft, you should write a tentative version of each paragraph, and the wording of your thesis statement, and all premises should be at least close to final form.

Give your draft a good introduction that lays out your thesis statement, provides background information on the issue, and draws your readers into the essay. Make it interesting, informative, and pertinent to the question at hand. Do not assume that your readers will automatically see that your paper is worth reading.

Every paragraph in your paper should relate to the thesis; every sentence in each paragraph should relate to a topic sentence. Delete any sentence that does not serve the essay's purpose. Ensure that paragraphs appear in a logical sequence and are clearly linked by transitional words and phrases or references to material in preceding paragraphs. Your readers should never have to wonder what the connection is between parts of your paper.

Step 6. Study and revise your first draft.

Your first draft is likely to have problems, both big and small. At this stage, though, you should scrutinize mostly the big ones. This is no time for proofreading (correcting spelling, fixing punctuation, repairing typos, and the like). This is the time to make substantive changes.

Step 7. Produce a final draft.

After completing all substantive changes, you should generate a final draft, the one you will turn in. The final draft should reflect not only the big changes, but the corrections of all minor errors as well—misspellings, typos, grammatical errors, misplaced words, faulty punctuation, and documentation mistakes. This task should be primarily a proofreading job. At this stage, you should also format the manuscript according to your instructor's requirements.

The key to producing a clean final draft is *down time*—an interim in which you leave the last draft alone and focus on something else. Coming back to your paper after a day or so away from it can help you see errors that passed right by you before. You may be surprised how many mistakes this fresh look can reveal. If you cannot set the essay aside, ask a friend to read it and give you some constructive criticism.

A SAMPLE PHILOSOPHY PAPER

The Dilemma of the Divine Command Theory

by Jane Doe

Philosophy 101

What is the connection between God and morality? In the past, many people would take this question to be about whether someone can behave morally even if they are atheists. But nowadays most people in the West would probably answer yes to this question. If there are moral standards of behavior, then it seems that anyone can live by them. A more important question (for both the religious and nonreligious) is not whether someone can be moral without belief in God, but *whether morality itself is possible without God*. The answer that many give to this question is the divine command theory, the view that morality absolutely requires God.

Introduces topic.

It says that an action is right if God commands or wills it. In other words, certain actions are right or wrong only because God says they are, for he is the author of the moral law. God's commanding an action is what makes it right; God's forbidding it is what makes it forbidden.

Defines key term.

Further explains the divine command theory.

Those who accept the divine command theory could consistently think that they should perform actions that promote the common good, as an act-utilitarian would. Or they could believe that they should always act to serve their own interests, as an ethical egoist does. Or they could assume that their duty is to act according to a set of deontological principles. But no matter what approach they take, they would still maintain that ultimately an action is right because God commands it.

But is the divine command theory plausible? Does God make right? I intend to argue that the theory is untenable—and for reasons that both theists and nontheists can appreciate. I will show that there is a crucial difficulty for the theory that would come to fore even if God's existence and our knowledge of his will are assured. The source of the problem is that the divine command theory forces a dilemma on us that can be satisfactorily resolved only by abandoning the theory.

Thesis statement.

Provides background for the issue.

Plato lays out the dilemma in his dialogue *Euthyphro*. In it Socrates asks, in effect, Are actions right because God commands them, or does God command them because they are right? The first option says that God creates morality, and the divine command theory is true. The second option says that the divine command theory is false: morality exists independently of God's will, and even he must obey it.

If one accepts the theory, unpalatable implications arise. If an action is morally right only because God says so, then any action at all could be morally right. If God so willed, the torture of children or the murder of innocents would be morally right. As the divine command theory would have it, there could be no reasons for God's willing one way or the other. He just commands, and that makes an action right (or wrong). But if God has no reasons for his commands, no standards other than his say-so, his commands are arbitrary. If the theory is correct, then God doesn't have reasons—and doesn't need reasons—to make the moral rules. But in that case, God's decisions would amount to no more than a throw of the dice. If rape and murder are morally wrong (or morally right), they are arbitrarily so. This result is implausible, and both theists and nontheists agree. In fact, most Christian philosophers reject the divine command theory.

The main argument for the thesis.

To reject the theory is to give up the idea that God is the maker of the moral law and to acknowledge that morality is independent of God's will. Actions are right or wrong for reasons that do not depend on God. We try to do right because it's right, not because a divine power has made an arbitrary decision. Theists who reject the divine command theory believe that God commands humans to obey moral standards that exist regardless of what God commands. God is perfect. He obeys the moral law and expects his children to obey it also.

Writer explains and rebuts the chief argument against the thesis.

The chief argument against the charge of arbitrariness is this: God would never command the murder of one's neighbors, the torture of children, or any other evil acts because God is all-good. And because God is all-good, his commands would not be arbitrary—they would be good. But to say this is to argue in a circle and undermine—not strengthen—the divine command theory. The theory is supposed to tell us what morality is, or what makes something good. But if goodness is a defining property of God, then God cannot be used to define goodness. Such a tack would result in an empty definition of the divine command theory: Good actions are those commanded by an all-good God. When theists say that God is good, they surely mean more than this.

In conclusion, the divine command theory is unfounded. To avoid the arbitrariness problem, and to preserve a credible idea of goodness, the theory must be rejected. The much more plausible view is located on the other side of Socrates' dilemma: The moral law is independent of God and applies to both God and man.

Conclusion and brief reiteration of the argument in its favor.

NOTES

CHAPTER 1

1. Plato, *The Republic*, in *The Dialogues of Plato*, vol. 2, trans. B. Jowett (New York: Hearst's International Library, 1914), 18–20.

CHAPTER 2

1. Thomas Aquinas, *Summa Theologica*, Question 2, "Whether God Exists," in *Basic Writings of St. Thomas Aquinas,* trans. Anton C. Pegis (New York: Random House, 1944), 22.
2. William Lane Craig, *Reasonable Faith: Christian Truth and Apologetics* (Wheaton, IL: Crossway Books, 1994), 92.
3. William Lane Craig, *God? A Debate Between a Christian and an Atheist* (New York: Oxford University Press, 2004), 4.
4. Craig, *God? A Debate Between a Christian and an Atheist*, 7.
5. William Paley, *Natural Theology, or Evidences of the Existence and Attributes of the Deity Collected from the Appearances of Nature* (1802).
6. David Hume, *Dialogues Concerning Natural Religion* (1779).
7. Hume, *Dialogues*.
8. Richard Swinburne, *Is There a God?* (New York: Oxford University Press, 1996), 2.
9. Swinburne, *Is There a God?* 41–42.
10. Anselm, *Proslogium*, ch. II–III (La Salle, IL: Open Court, 1962), 53–55.
11. Immanuel Kant, *Critique of Pure Reason* (London: Macmillan & Company and St. Martin's Press, 1929), 504–505.
12. William L. Rowe, *Philosophy of Religion: An Introduction* (Belmont, CA: Wadsworth, 1993), 80–82.
13. William L. Rowe, "The Empirical Argument from Evil," in *Rationality, Religious Belief, and Moral Commitment*, ed. Robert Audi and William J. Wainwright (Ithaca, NY: Cornell University Press, 1986), 227–247.
14. J. L. Mackie, *The Miracle of Theism* (Oxford: Oxford University Press, 1982), 156.
15. Swinburne, *Is There a God?* 98.
16. Mackie, *The Miracle of Theism*, 164.
17. John Hick, *Evil and the God of Love* (New York: HarperCollins, 1966, 1977), 253–259.
18. Rowe, *Philosophy of Religion,* 85–86.

19. St. Teresa, *The Life of Teresa of Jesus*, trans. and ed. E. Allison Peers (Garden City, NY: Image Books, 1960), 249. Quoted in Michael Martin, *Atheism: A Philosophical Justification* (Philadelphia: Temple University Press, 1990), 156.

20. Quoted in William James, *The Varieties of Religious Experience* (New York: New American Library, 1958), 68–69.

21. Mackie, *The Miracle of Theism*, 179–181.

22. Richard Swinburne, *The Existence of God* (Oxford: Oxford University Press, 204), 304.

23. Rowe, *Philosophy of Religion,* 60–61.

24. Swinburne, *The Existence of God,* 316–317.

25. W. K. Clifford, "The Ethics of Belief," in *Lectures and Essays* (London: Macmillan, 1886).

26. William James, "The Will to Believe," in *The Will to Believe and Other Essays in Popular Philosophy* (New York: Longmans, Green, and Co., 1896), 11.

27. James, "The Will to Believe," 26.

28. James, "The Will to Believe," 2–30.

29. Michael Martin, *Atheism: A Philosophical Justification* (Philadelphia: Temple University Press, 1990), 246.

30. Blaise Pascal, *Pensees and Other Writings*, trans. Honor Levi (Oxford: Oxford University Press, 1995).

31. Pascal.

32. *Buddhist Suttas*, trans. T. W. Rhys Davids (New York: Dover, 1976), 148.

33. Ajahn Sumedho, cited in Satnacitto Bhikku, ed., *Buddha-Nature* (London: World Wide Fund for Nature, 1989).

34. Walpola Rahula, *What the Buddha Taught* (New York: Grove Press, 1974), 43.

35. *Chuang Tzu*, trans. Richard Welhelm and Dschuang Dsi (Jena, Germany: Diederichs, 1912), 158, 7.18b.

36. *Tao de jing*, trans. D. C. Lau (New York: Penguin Classics, 1963), 1, 25.

37. *Tao de jing*, trans. D. C. Lau, 19.

38. *Tao de jing*, trans. D. C. Lau, 57.

CHAPTER 3

1. Russ Shafer-Landau, *Whatever Happened to Good and Evil?* (New York: Oxford University Press, 2004), 81–82.

2. John Stuart Mill, "What Utilitarianism Is," in *Utilitarianism* (1861).

3. Mill, "What Utilitarianism Is."

4. Mill, "What Utilitarianism Is."

5. Immanuel Kant, *Groundwork of the Metaphysic of Morals*, trans. T. K. Abbott (London: Longmans, Green, and Co., 1909, 1873), 3–4, 9–10.

6. Kant, *Groundwork,* 18.

7. Kant, *Groundwork,* 47.

8. Kant, *Groundwork,* 46–47.

9. Aristotle, *Nicomachean Ethics*, trans. W. D. Ross (Oxford: Oxford University Press, 1980), bk. I, chs. 1, 2, 7; bk. 2, chs. 6–7.

10. Rosalind Hursthouse, "Virtue Ethics," in *The Stanford Encyclopedia of Philosophy*, Fall 2003 edition, ed. Edward N. Zalta, http://plato.Stanford.edu/archives/fall2003/entries/ethics-virtue/ (11 October 2010).

11. Russ Shafer-Landau, *The Fundamentals of Ethics* (New York: Oxford University Press, 2010), 257.

12. Alison Jaggar, "Feminist Ethics," in *Encyclopedia of Ethics*, ed. Lawrence Becker and Charlotte Becker (New York: Garland, 1992), 364.

13. Jan Crosthwaite, "Gender and Bioethics," in *A Companion to Bioethics*, ed. Helga Kuhse and Peter Singer (Malden, MA: Blackwell Publishing, 2001), 32–40.

14. Crosthwaite, "Gender and Bioethics," 37.

15. Carol Gilligan, *In a Different Voice: Psychological Theory and Women's Development* (Cambridge: Harvard University Press, 1982).

16. Virginia Held, *The Ethics of Care* (Oxford: Oxford University Press, 2006), 10–13.

17. Annette C. Baier, "The Need for More Than Justice," *Canadian Journal of Philosophy*, suppl. vol. 13 (1988): 56.

18. Albert Camus, *The Myth of Sisyphus*, trans. J. O'Brien (New York: Alfred A. Knopf, 1983).

19. *Analects*, trans. Arthur Waley, 2:13–14, 14:30, 14:45.

20. *Analects*, trans. Arthur Waley, 2:5, 7.

21. John B. Noss, *A History of the World's Religions* (New York: Macmillan, 1994), 323.

CHAPTER 4

1. René Descartes, *Discourse on the Method of Rightly Conducting the Reason*, pt. 4, in *Philosophical Works of Descartes*, ed. Elizabeth Haldane and G. R. T. Ross (Cambridge, England: Cambridge University Press, 1911), 101.

2. Theodore Schick, Jr., and Lewis Vaughn, *Doing Philosophy: An Introduction Through Thought Experiments* (New York: McGraw-Hill, 2010), 88.

3. René Descartes, *Meditations on First Philosophy*, Meditation VI, in *Philosophical Works of Descartes*, ed. Elizabeth Haldane and G. R. T. Ross (Cambridge, England: Cambridge University Press, 1911), 196.

4. John R. Searle, *Mind: A Brief Introduction* (New York: Oxford University Press, 2004), 29–30.

5. Searle, *Mind*, 21.

6. J. J. C. Smart, "Sensations and Brain Processes," *Philosophical Review* **68** (1959): 144–145.

7. David J. Chalmers, *The Conscious Mind: In Search of a Fundamental Theory* (New York: Oxford University Press, 1996), 94–95.

8. David J. Chalmers, *Philosophy of Mind: Classical and Contemporary Readings* (New York: Oxford University Press, 2002), 249.

9. Thomas Nagel, "What Is It Like to Be a Bat?" *Philosophical Review* **83**, no. 4 (1974): 435–500.

10. Jerry A. Fodor, "The Mind–Body Problem," *Scientific American* **244** (January 1981).

11. Ned Block, "Troubles with Functionalism," in *Readings in the Philosophy of Psychology*, ed. Ned Block (Cambridge: Harvard University Press, 1980), 276, 278.

12. Searle, *Mind*, 45.

13. Searle, *Mind*, 46.

14. Searle, *Mind*, 48–49.

15. Searle, *Mind*, 62–63.

16. John Searle, "Is the Brain's Mind a Computer Program?" *Scientific American* **262** (January 1990).

17. David J. Chalmers, *The Conscious Mind: In Search of a Fundamental Theory* (New York: Oxford University Press, 1996), 125.

CHAPTER 5

1. Baron d'Holbach, "Of the System of Man's Free Agency," in *The System of Nature*, trans. H. D. Robinson (1770), chap. 11.

2. William James, "The Dilemma of Determinism," in *The Will to Believe and Other Essays in Popular Philosophy* (New York: Longmans, Green, and Co., 1912), 145–183.

3. John Locke, *An Essay Concerning Human Understanding*, ed. Peter H. Nidditch (Oxford: Clarendon Press, 1975), bk. II, sec. 33.

4. W. T. Stace, *Religion and the Modern Mind* (New York: HarperCollins, 1952), 254–255.

5. William L. Rowe, "Two Concepts of Freedom," in *Agents, Causes, and Events: Essays on Indeterminism and Free Will*, ed. Timothy O'Connor (New York: Oxford University Press, 1995), 154–155.

6. Peter van Inwagen, *An Essay on Free Will* (Oxford: Clarendon Press, 1983), 16.

7. Richard Taylor, *Metaphysics* (Englewood Cliffs, NJ: Prentice Hall, 1992), 51–53.

8. Jean-Paul Sartre, "Existentialism Is a Humanism," in *Existentialism*, trans. Bernard Frechtman (New York: Philosophical Library, 1947).

CHAPTER 6

1. Plato, *Meno*, in *The Dialogues of Plato*, trans. B. Jowett (New York: Hearst's International Library, 1914), 34–36.

2. René Descartes, "Meditation One," in *Meditations on First Philosophy*, volume 1, *The Philosophical Works of Descartes*, trans. Elizabeth S. Haldane and G. R. T. Ross (Cambridge, England: Cambridge University Press, 1911), 144–145.

3. René Descartes, "Meditation One," *Meditations on First Philosophy*, 146.

4. Descartes, "Meditation One," in *Meditations on First Philosophy*, 145–146.

5. Descartes, "Meditation One," in *Meditations on First Philosophy*, 147.

6. Descartes, "Meditation Two," in *Meditations on First Philosophy*, 149–150.
7. Descartes, "Meditation One," in *Meditations on First Philosophy*, 158.
8. Descartes, "Meditation Five," in *Meditations on First Philosophy*, 184–185.
9. Descartes, "Meditation Two," in *Meditations on First Philosophy*, 154–155.
10. John Locke, *An Essay Concerning Human Understanding*, Book I, Chapter 2 (1689).
11. Locke, Book II, Chapter 1, part 2.
12. Locke, Book IV, Chapter 11, parts 1–9.
13. George Berkeley, *Of the Principles of Human Knowledge* in *Principles of Human Knowledge and Three Dialogues*, Part I, sec. 1–4, 6, 8 (Oxford: Oxford University Press, 1999).
14. Berkeley, Part I, sec. 9–10, 14–15.
15. Bertrand Russell, *The Problems of Philosophy* (London: Oxford University Press, 1912, 1959), 24.
16. David Hume, *An Enquiry Concerning Human Understanding*, sec. 2 and 4, ed. Peter Millican (New York: Oxford University Press, 2008).
17. Hume, sec. 7, parts I and II.
18. Hume, sec. 4, part II.
19. Hume, sec. 12, part I.
20. Immanuel Kant, *Prolegomena to Any Future Metaphysics*, trans. Paul Carus (New York: Open Court Publishing, 1912).
21. Immanuel Kant, *Critique of Pure Reason*, trans. Norman Kemp Smith (New York: Humanities Press, 1929), 44.
22. Immanuel Kant, *Critique of Pure Reason*, 41–42, 46–47.
23. Immanuel Kant, *Critique of Pure Reason*, 22.
24. Immanuel Kant, *Critique of Pure Reason*, 92–93.
25. Alison Ainley, "Feminist Philosophy," in *The Oxford Companion to Philosophy*, ed. Ted Honderich (Oxford: Oxford University Press, 1995), 273.
26. Louise M. Antony, "Embodiment and Epistemology," in *The Oxford Handbook of Epistemology* (New York: Oxford University Press, 2002), 465.
27. Elizabeth Anderson, "Feminist Epistemology and Philosophy of Science," in *The Stanford Encyclopedia of Philosophy*, Spring 2011 edition, ed. Edward N. Zalta, http://plato.stanford.edu/archives/spr2011/entries/feminism-epistemology.
28. Eve Browning Cole, *Philosophy and Feminist Criticism* (New York: Paragon House, 1993), 83–84.
29. Cole, *Philosophy and Feminist Criticism*, 84–85.
30. Cole, *Philosophy and Feminist Criticism*, 88–90.
31. Cole, *Philosophy and Feminist Criticism*, 94–95.
32. Cole, *Philosophy and Feminist Criticism*, 95–96.

CHAPTER 7

1. Leo Tolstoy, *What Is Art?* (Indianapolis: Bobbs-Merrill, 1960).
2. Clive Bell, *Art* (London: Chatto and Windus, 1914).

3. Aristotle, *Poetics,* trans. M. E. Hubbard, in *Classical Literary Criticism*, ed. D. A. Russell and M. Winterbottom (Oxford: Clarendon, 1972, 2008).
4. David Hume, "Of the Standard of Taste," from *Four Dissertations* (London: A. Miller, 1777). Text from davidhume.org.

CHAPTER 8

1. Plato, *The Republic*, B. Jowett, trans. (New York: Hearst's International Library, 1914), 153–155.
2. Thomas Hobbes, *Leviathan*, 1651.
3. Hobbes, *Leviathan*.
4. Hobbes, *Leviathan*.
5. Declaration of Independence, July 4, 1776.
6. John Locke, *Second Treatise of Government*, chaps. 8, 9, 19 (1690).
7. John Rawls, *A Theory of Justice*, rev. ed. (Cambridge, MA Harvard University Press, 1999), 10.
8. Rawls, *A Theory of Justice*, 266.
9. Rawls, *A Theory of Justice*, 13.
10. Norman Daniels, "Health Care Needs and Distributive Justice," in *Justice and Justification* (Cambridge: Cambridge University Press, 1996).
11. Karl Marx and Friedrich Engels, *Manifesto of the Communist Party*, trans. Samuel Moore (1888).
12. Susan Moller Okin, *Justice, Gender, and the Family* (New York: Basic Books, 1989), 3–5, 124–127.
13. David Miller, *Political Philosophy: A Very Short Introduction* (Oxford: Oxford University Press, 2003), 93, 97.

CHAPTER 9

1. Albert Camus, *The Myth of Sisyphus*, trans. J. O'Brien (New York: Alfred A. Knopf, 1955), i.
2. Leo Tolstoy, *My Confession*, trans. Leo Wierner (New York: J. M. Dent and Sons, 1905).
3. Arthur Schopenhauer, "On the Sufferings of the World," in *Parerga and Paralipomena*, trans. T. Bailey Saunders (1851).
4. Clarence Darrow, "Is Life Worth Living?" (debate), March 28, 1920.
5. Julian Baggini, *What's It All About? Philosophy and the Meaning of Life* (Oxford: Oxford University Press, 2005), 160–161.
6. Tolstoy, *My Confession*.
7. Baggini, *What's It All About?* 17, 19–20.
8. Paul Edwards, *The Encyclopedia of Philosophy*, vol. 4, ed. Paul Edwards (New York: Macmillan, 1967).
9. Edwards, *The Encyclopedia of Philosophy*.

GLOSSARY

aesthetics The study of the feelings and judgments involved in experiencing the arts or other objects deemed beautiful.

a priori knowledge Knowledge gained independently of or prior to sense experience.

a posteriori knowledge Knowledge that depends entirely on sense experience

act-utilitarianism The idea that the rightness of actions depends solely on the overall well-being produced by *individual actions*.

agent causation The view that a free action is caused by an agent (person) and is not wholly determined by previous events.

agnostic Someone who neither accepts nor denies God's existence.

analytic statement A logical truth whose denial results in a contradiction.

appeal to ignorance The fallacy of arguing that either (1) a claim is true because it hasn't been proven false or (2) a claim is false because it hasn't been proven true.

appeal to popularity The fallacy of arguing that a claim must be true not because it is backed by good reasons, but simply because many people believe it.

appeal to the person The fallacy of rejecting a statement on the grounds that it comes from a particular person, not because the statement, or claim, itself is false or dubious.

argument A statement coupled with other statements that are meant to support that statement.

argument from evil An argument purporting to show that since there is unnecessary evil, an all-powerful, all-knowing, and all-good God must not exist.

argument from religious experience An argument of this form: A person seems to have experienced God; the experience must have actually been a genuine encounter with God; therefore, God probably exists.

aristocracy A society ruled by the best citizens.

atheism The denial of the existence of God.

atheist Someone who denies God's existence.

atman One's soul or self.

axiology The study of value, including both aesthetic value and moral value.

begging the question The fallacy of trying to prove a conclusion by using that very same conclusion as support.

Bhagavad-Gita The most highly venerated and influential scriptures in Hinduism.

Brahman The impersonal, all-pervading Spirit that is the universe yet transcends all space and time.

brahmin A priest or teacher; a man of the priestly caste.

capitalism A political economic system that lets the means of production accrue to fewer people through the workings of a free market. In such a system, wealth goes to anyone who can acquire it in the marketplace.

Cartesian dualism The view that mind (or soul) and body are completely independent of one another and interact causally.

categorical imperative Kant's fundamental moral principle, which he formulates as (1) "I am never to act otherwise than so *that I could also will that my maxim should become a universal law*," and (2) "So act as to treat humanity, whether in thine own person or in that of any other, in every case as an end withal, never as a means only."

catharsis The purging of the emotions of pity and fear by experiencing them vicariously in a theatrical context.

causal closure of the physical The principle that the world is a closed system of physical causes and effects.

classical liberalism The view that the state should protect personal freedoms as well as the right to pursue one's own social and economic well-being in a free market without interference from others.

cognitive relativism The doctrine that the truth about something depends on what persons or cultures believe.

communism Commonly, socialism within a totalitarian system.

compatibilism The view that although determinism is true, our actions can still be free.

composition The fallacy of arguing erroneously that what can be said of the parts can also be said of the whole.

conclusion In an argument, the statement being supported.

consequentialist theory A moral theory in which the rightness of actions depends solely on their consequences or results.

cosmological arguments Arguments that try to show that from the fact that the universe exists, God exists.

cultural relativism The view that right actions are those endorsed by one's culture.

deductive argument An argument intended to give logically conclusive support to its conclusion.

deism Belief in one God who created the world but left it unattended to run on its own.

democracy Rule by the people as a whole.

deontological (or **nonconsequentialist**) **theory** A moral theory in which the rightness of actions is determined not solely by their consequences, but partly or entirely by their intrinsic nature.

determinism The doctrine that every event is determined by preceding events and the laws of nature.

dharma The Buddha's system of teachings about the true nature of reality and how to live correctly to transcend it.

distributive justice (or **social justice**) The fair distribution of society's benefits and burdens—such things as jobs, income, property, liberties, rights, welfare aid, taxes, and public service.

divine command theory The doctrine that God is the creator of morality.

division The fallacy of arguing erroneously that what can be said of the whole can be said of the parts.

empiricism The view that our knowledge of the empirical world comes solely from sense experience.

epiphenomenalism The notion that mental properties do not cause anything, but merely accompany physical processes.

epistemology The study of knowledge.

equivocation The fallacy of assigning two different meanings to the same significant word in an argument.

ethical egoism The view that right actions are those that further one's own best interests.

ethics (moral philosophy) The study of morality using the methods of philosophy.

ethics of care A moral perspective that emphasizes the unique demands of specific situations and the virtues and feelings that are central to close personal relationships.

evidentialism The view that we are justified in believing something only if it is supported by sufficient evidence.

fallacy A common but bad argument.

false dilemma The fallacy of arguing erroneously that since there are only two alternatives to choose from, and one of them is unacceptable, the other one must be true.

feminist ethics An approach to morality aimed at advancing women's interests, underscoring their distinctive experiences and characteristics, and advancing the obvious truth that women and men are morally equal.

formalism The view that art is defined by its form, the structure or organization of its parts.

functionalism The view that the mind is the functions that the brain performs.

genetic fallacy The fallacy of arguing that a statement can be judged true or false based on its source.

hard determinism The view that free will does not exist, that no one acts freely.

identity theory The view that mental states are identical to physical brain states.

incompatibilism The view that if determinism is true, no one can act freely.

indeterminism The view that not every event is determined by preceding events and the laws of nature.

inductive argument An argument intended to give probable support to its conclusion.

justice The idea that people should get what is fair or what is their due.

Kant's theory The theory that right actions are those that accord with the categorical imperative.

karma The universal principle that our actions result in deserved pleasure or pain in this life or the next.

li In early Confucianism, ritual, etiquette, principle, and propriety; conscientious behavior and right action.

liberalism The political theory that puts primary emphasis on the liberty and rights of individuals against encroachments by the state.

libertarianism (metaphysical) The view that some actions are free, for they are caused, or controlled, by the person, or agent.

libertarianism (political) The doctrine that emphasizes personal freedoms and the right to pursue one's own social and economic well-being in a free market without interference from others.

logic The study of correct reasoning.

logical behaviorism The idea that mental states are dispositions to behave in a particular way in certain circumstances.

materialism (or **physicalism**) The doctrine that every object and event in the world is physical.

meritocracy A system of rule by those most qualified to govern.

metaphysics The study of reality, an inquiry into the fundamental nature of the universe and the things in it.

mind–body problem The issue of what mental phenomena are and how they relate to the physical world.

monotheism Belief in one God.

moral absolutism The belief that objective moral principles allow no exceptions or must be applied the same way in all cases and cultures.

moral evil Evil that comes from human choices and actions and the bad things that arise from them.

moral objectivism The view that there are moral standards that are true or correct for everyone.

moral relativism The view that moral standards do not have independent status but are relative to what individuals or cultures believe.

moral theory A theory that explains why an action is right or wrong or why a person or a person's character is good or bad.

morality Beliefs about right and wrong actions and good and bad persons or character.

multiple realizability The capacity to be realized or instantiated in a variety of forms and materials.

natural evil Evil that results from the workings of nature.

nirvana Enlightenment: the ultimate aim of all Buddhist practice and the final liberation to which all the Buddha's teachings point.

objectivism (in art) The view that works of art have objective properties by which we can judge their aesthetic goodness or badness.

ontological argument An argument that tries to demonstrate God's existence by logical analysis of the concept of God.

panentheism The view that although God and the world are distinct, the world is part of God.

pantheism The view that God and the universe are one and the same thing, a divine Whole.

political philosophy The study of political societies using the methods of philosophy.

polytheism Belief in many gods.

premise In an argument, a statement supporting the conclusion.

principle of induction The presumption that events that followed one another in the past will do the same in the future, that the future will be like the past.

problem of free will The challenge of reconciling determinism with our intuitions or ideas about personal freedom.

property dualism The view that mental properties are nonphysical properties arising from, but not reducible to, physical properties.

propositional knowledge Knowledge of a proposition.

psychological egoism The theory that people always act out of self-interest.

rationalism The view that through unaided reason we can come to know what the world is like.

reductio ad absurdum An argument of this form: If you assume that a set of statements is true, and yet you can deduce a false or absurd statement from it, then the original set of statements as a whole must be false.

ren The essential Confucian virtues, including benevolence, sympathy, kindness, generosity, respect for others, and human-heartedness.

rule-utilitarianism The doctrine that a right action is one that conforms to a rule that, if followed consistently, would create for everyone involved the most beneficial balance of well-being over suffering.

samsara One's cycle of repeated deaths and rebirths.

skepticism The view that we lack knowledge in some fundamental way.

slippery slope The fallacy of arguing erroneously that a particular action should not be taken because it will lead inevitably to other actions resulting in some dire outcome.

social contract theory The view that justice is secured, and the state is made legitimate, through an agreement among citizens of the state or between the citizens and the rulers of the state.

socialism The doctrine that the means of production (property, factories, businesses) should be owned or controlled by the people, either communally or through the state.

Socratic method Question-and-answer dialogue in which propositions are methodically scrutinized to uncover the truth.

statement (claim) An assertion that something is or is not the case and is therefore the kind of utterance that is either true or false.

straw man The fallacy of misrepresenting a person's views so they can be more easily attacked or dismissed.

subjectivism (in art) The view that aesthetic criteria are purely subjective; the goodness or badness of a work of art depends on how the audience responds to it.

subjective idealism The doctrine that all that exist are minds and their ideas.

subjective relativism The view that right actions are those endorsed by an individual.

substance dualism The notion that mind and body consist of two fundamentally different kinds of stuff, or substances.

synthetic statement A statement that is not analytic.

teleological arguments Arguments that try to show that God must exist because features of the universe show signs of purpose or design.

theism Belief in the existence of God.

theist Someone who believes in God.

theodicy A defense of the traditional conception of God in light of the existence of evil.

Upanishads Vedic literature concerning the self, Brahman, *samsara*, and liberation.

utilitarianism The view that right actions are those that result in the most beneficial balance of good over bad consequences for everyone involved.

Vedas Early Hindu scriptures, developed between 1500 and 600 BCE.

virtue ethics A moral theory that focuses on the development of virtuous character.

welfare liberalism A form of liberalism, the aim of which is to preserve individual liberties while ensuring the general welfare of the citizenry.

CREDITS

Chapter 1
Chapter opening photo © iStockphoto.com/Chris Schmidt

1.1 Universal

1.2 Universal

1.3 SuperStock/Sup

1.4 Gianni Dagli

1.5 Corbis

1.6 The Print

1.7 Gary

1.8 Bettmann/CORBIS

1.9 Corbis

1.10 Photri Images/SuperStock

Chapter 2
Chapter opening photo © iStockphoto.com/Photo_HamsterMan

2.1 Distinctive

2.2 Ollyy/Shutterstock

2.3 Michael D Brown/Shutterstock

2.4 © INTERFOTO/Alamy

2.5 Ilias Strachinis/Shutterstock

2.6 © BH Generic Stock Images/Alamy

2.7 © Suraj Dongol/Alamy

2.8 © Mary Evans Picture Library/Alamy

2.9 Tatiana Makotra/Shutterstock

2.10 © sam100/Shutterstock

2.11 nearandfar/iStockphoto

2.12 © Doug Webb/Alamy

2.13 © Timewatch Images/Alamy

2.14 © Agencja Fotograficzna Caro/Alamy

2.15 Martin Novak/Shutterstock

2.16 © The Art Gallery Collection/Alamy

2.17 © J Marshall - Tribaleye Images/Alamy

2.18 © Peter Horree/Alamy

2.19 © Gavriel Jecan/Corbis

2.20 © Mitchell Kanashkevich/Corbis

2.21 © Luca Tettoni/Robert Harding World Imagery/Corbis

Chapter 3
Chapter opening photo Siegfried Layda/Getty Images

3.1 Allen Graham - PDImages/Shutterstock

3.2 Kheng Guan Toh/Shutterstock

3.3 Christian Darkin/Shutterstock

3.4 © PjrTravel/Alamy

3.5 © Lordprice Collection/Alamy

3.6 © narvikk/iStockphoto

3.7 © LondonPhotos - Homer Sykes/Alamy

3.8 © Simon Belcher/Alamy

3.9 © SCPhotos/Alamy

3.10 © Pictorial Press Ltd/Alamy

3.11 © duncan1890/iStockphoto

3.12 fzd.it/Shutterstock

3.13 use credit line from previous edition

3.14 Scala/Art Resource, NY

3.15 Virginia Held

3.16 Hung Chung Chih/Shutterstock

Chapter 4
Chapter opening photo © Blutgruppe/Corbis

4.1 Lukiyanova Natalia/frenta/Shutterstock

4.2 shiva3d/Shutterstock

4.3 © Louie Psihoyos/CORBIS

4.4 © Mary Evans Picture Library/Alamy

4.5 © Universal Images Group Limited/Alamy

4.6 © CC BY 3.0

4.7 © Ian McDonnell/iStockphoto

4.8 © GlobalP/iStockphoto

4.9 Tom Bonaventure/Punchstock

INDEX OF MARGINAL QUOTATIONS

This index helps you locate particular quotations in the text's margins and find all the marginal quotations by a specific author. The italicized *f* following page numbers indicates material in figures.

A

Adams, Scott, 247
Allen, Woody, 70
Amyl, Henri Frederic, 162
Aquinas, Thomas, 41, 58, 63–67, 122
Aristotle, 2–3, 4*f*, 7*f*, 113, 169–72, 174, 235, 270, 322, 326–29, 340
Augustine, 55, 339
Ayer, Alfred Jules, 142

B

Bacon, Francis, 17, 28
Baggini, Julian, 397–99, 403–4, 403*f*
Bierce, Ambrose, 200
Bombeck, Erma, 214
Brault, Robert, 94
Broughton, James, 198
Brown, Les, 393
The Buddha, 65, 108, 109

C

Cabanis, Pierre-Jean Georges, 204
Campbell, Joseph, 394
Camus, Albert, 180–83, 188, 391, 397, 405
Capp, Al, 326
Chalmers, David J., 209–10, 210*f*, 211*f*, 220
Chavez, Hugo, 362
Chesterton, G. K., 134
Chinese Proverb, 169
Confucius, 184, 185, 264
Cortazar, Julio, 159
Cuppy, Will, 211

D

Darwin, Charles, 74
Dickens, Charles, 173, 348

Disraeli, Benjamin, 267
Douglass, Frederick, 342
Durant, Will, 2

E

Edison, Thomas A., 204
Ehrenreich, Barbara, 370
Einstein, Albert, 62, 66, 78, 138–140, 177, 272, 275, 280
Eliot, T. S., 302
Epictetus, 20, 253

F

Forude, James A., 166
Frankl, Viktor E., 390, 401
Franklin, Benjamin, 96

G

Galileo Galilei, 56
Glaspell, Susan, 36

H

Hamilton, Alexander, 353
Hesse, Hermann, 397
Hobbes, Thomas, 238, 348–50, 352–54, 358–59
Hodge, Charles, 142
Hubbard, Elbert, 149, 266
Hume, David, 8, 70–74, 238–39, 293–98, 329–31
Huntington, Ellsworth, 201
Huxley, Thomas H., 269

I

Inge, Dean, 22
Ingersol, Robert, 151
Isaiah 5:20, 88

J

James, William, 34, 89, 96–103, 236–37
Jefferson, Thomas, 140
Jewish Proverb, 63
Johnson, B. C., 83

K

Kant, Immanuel, 132, 163–68, 297, 299–307
Kennedy, John F., 323
Kierkegaard, Søren, 111
King, Martin Luther, Jr., 338, 404

L

Leonardo da Vinci, 284
Lewes, George Henry, 23
Lewis, C. S., 59, 62, 203
Lichtenstein, Roy, 325
Liebknecht, Karl, 363
Lincoln, Abraham, 172
Locke, John, 267–68, 281–87, 354–58, 374
Luther, Martin, 250
Luyah, Hal Lee, 245

M

Maugham, W. Somerset, 63, 83
McCarthy, Cormac, 243
McGill, Bryant H., 349
Michelangelo, 321
Mill, John Stuart, 153–57, 160, 207, 308
Minsky, Marvin, 201
Mizner, Wilson, 100
Montesquieu, Charles de, 79

N

Nagel, Thomas, 199, 210–211
Nehru, Jawaharlal, 232
Nietzsche, Friedrich, 98, 158
Nin, Anais, 291
Noddings, Nel, 178
Novalis, 328
Nussbaum, Martha, 2

O

O'Rourke, P. J., 232, 360
Orwell, George, 365

P

Pascal, Blaise, 103
Picasso, Pablo, 321
Pigliucci, Massimo, 105
Pike, Albert, 26
Plato, 3, 5, 44–52, 141, 269–72,
    300–302, 304, 310,
    343–45
Pope, Alexander, 197
Pugh, Emerson, 210

R

Rachels, James, 176
Rand, Ayn, 242
Reagan, Ronald, 357
Roosevelt, Eleanor, 16
Russell, Bertrand, 4, 8, 11, 29, 68, 145,
    268, 277

S

Sagan, Carl, 74
Sartre, Jean-Paul, 250, 343, 391
Schopenhauer, Arthur, 212, 236
Schulz, Charles M., 7, 111, 392
Searle, John R., 219
Shakespeare, William, 33, 144, 299
Shaw, George Bernard, 115, 164
Singer, Isaac Bashevis, 230
Sinnott-Armstrong, Walter, 58
Snow, C. P., 161
Socrates, 3, 8–13, 37, 44–52, 135, 263,
    266, 343–45
Spinoza, Baruch, 62, 142, 230, 267
Spong, John, 61

T

Tennyson, Alfred, 295
Tertullian, 161
Thoreau, Henry David, 113, 167
Tillich, Paul, 11, 399, 404
Tocqueville, Alexis de, 365
Tolstoy, Leo, 238, 396
Trumbull, H. C., 164

U

Unknown, 287
Urlaub, Ivan, 292

V

Vanbrugh, John, 146
Voltaire, 78, 136, 307, 408–9

W

West, Rebecca, 311, 370
Whitehead, Alfred North, 15, 143
Wittgenstein, Ludwig, 18
Wollstonecraft, Mary, 309, 312, 312*f*
Wright, Frank Lloyd, 330

GENERAL INDEX

A

Abolitionists, of capital punishment, 154, 155

Abortion rights, 374

Above, meaning from, 399–404, 402f, 403f

Absent qualia objections, 201, 213–14, 214f

Absolute duty, 167

Absurdity, of existence, 180–83

Active reading, 28

Act-utilitarianism
    consequences in, 150–52, 151f
    defined, 150, 189, 431

Addison, Joseph, 330

Ad hominem fallacy. *See* Appeal to the person

Aegisthus, 329

Aesthetics. *See also* Art
    Aristotle influencing, 326–29
    defined, 321, 333
    Hume influencing, 329–31
    philosophy of beauty and, 321
    Plato influencing, 326
    value, 323–26, 324f, 325f

Affirming the antecedent. *See Modus ponens*

Affirming the consequent, 19, 21

Agent causation
    defined, 246, 256, 431
    libertarianism (metaphysical) and, 246–48

Agnostic, 61–62, 125, 431

Ahimsa (nonharm), 111–12

AI. *See* Artificial intelligence

Ainley, Alison, 308

Alienation, 363

Aliens, 199f, 200

Analogical induction, 21–22

Analytic statement, 299–300, 317, 431

Anatta (impermanence of the self), 108–9

Anderson, Elizabeth, 309

Anguish, 252

Anicca (impermanence), 108

Anselm (saint)
    criticism of, 78
    ontological argument of, 59, 75–79
    Proslogium by, 75–78

Antecedent, 18–19, 21

Antisocial behavior, belief in free will influencing, 240–41, 240f

Antithesis, 362

Antony, Louise M., 308–9

The Apology (Plato), 44–52

A posteriori arguments, 63

A posteriori knowledge, 266, 300, 317, 431

Appeal to ignorance, 33–34, 39, 431

Appeal to popularity, 32, 39, 431

Appeal to the person, 31–32, 39, 431

A priori arguments, 63

A priori knowledge, 266, 300, 301–7, 316, 317, 431

Aquinas, Thomas
    argument from motion of, 64–65
    biography of, 65
    criticism of, 66–67
    first-cause argument of, 65–68
    God and, 41, 58, 63–67, 122
    meaning from below and, 404
    Summa Theologica by, 41, 63–67

Arbitrariness problem, of divine command theory, 141–42, 422–24

Argument from evil
    defined, 60–61, 125, 431
    God and, 60–61, 80–83, 122, 125, 431
    ignorance and, 82–83
    Rowe's, 80–83

Argument from motion, 64–65

Argument from religious experience, 59–60, 89–95, 122–23, 125, 402, 431

Arguments. *See also specific arguments*
    conclusion in, 14–17, 28
    defined, 14, 39, 432
    evaluation of, 29
    exercises, 40–43, 411–13
    invalid, 19, 21
    knowledge, 210–12
    a posteriori, 63
    premise in, 14–17, 28
    a priori, 63
    sound, 18
    strong, 17–18
    theodicies, 61
    thesis supported by, 362–63

in thinking philosophically, 13–36, 37–38
    valid, 17–19, 21
    weak, 17

Aristocracy, 344, 378, 431

Aristotle, 2–3, 4f, 7f, 113, 332
    aesthetics influenced by, 326–29
    happiness and, 169–72
    Hypatia and, 26
    Nicomachean Ethics by, 169–71
    objectivism of, 326–29
    The Poetics by, 326–29
    in *The School of Athens*, 171
    soul and, 205
    virtue ethics and, 169–72
    women and, 308, 310

Art
    aesthetic value of, 323–26, 324f, 325f
    characterization of, 321–23, 322f
    as controversial, 322, 322f
    defined, 321–23, 322f
    as expression, 323
    form of, 323
    museum, 327
    objectivism in, 323–29, 333
    as representation, 322–23
    subjectivism in, 325, 329–31, 333

Art (Bell), 323

ArtCulture, 322

Artificial intelligence (AI)
    autonomous, 218–19, 218f
    strong, 200–201, 201f, 215–17, 218–19

Artworld, 325

Assessment of objections, in essay structure, 417

Atheism
    defined, 61–62, 125, 431
    problem of evil and, 80–83
    in U.S., 57

Atheism: A Philosophical Justification (Martin), 103

Atheist, 61, 402

Atheistic existentialism, 251

Atomist philosophers, 237

Authoritarianism, 344

Autonomous AI, 218–19, 218f

Auxiliaries, 343

Axiology, 6–7, 39, 431

B

Background knowledge, 140
Baggini, Julian
    meaning of life and, 397–99,
        403–4, 403f
    What's It All About? by, 397–99,
        403–4, 403f
Baier, Annette, 179
Bats, 210–12, 212f
Baumeister, Roy F., 241
Beauty
    aesthetics and, 321
    Form of, 326
    Hume on, 329–31
    philosophy of, 321, 332
Begging the question, 34–35, 39, 431
Behavior
    antisocial, belief in free will influencing,
        240–41, 240f
    faith and, 101f, 104–5
Behaviorism. *See* Logical behaviorism
Being, 79
Belief
    in free will, 240–41, 240f
    in God, 55–106
    hard-wired, 60
    insufficient evidence for, 96, 99–100
    in intercessory prayer, 93
    justification of, 264
    philosophical, survey of, 5
    without reason, 55, 95–106, 123
Bell, Clive, 323, 325
Below, meaning from, 404–5
Bentham, Jeremy, 152, 160
Berkeley, George, 287f
    criticism of, 291
    empiricism of, 267, 268, 287–91
    God and, 291
    Locke and, 287, 289–90
    "Of the Principles of Human
        Knowledge" by, 288–91
    sensations and, 287–91
    subjective idealism and, 268
Bible, soul in, 205
Big Bang, 67–68, 67f
Bigfoot, 221
Bios (biological life of man), 87
Bisson, Terry, 225–26
Block, Ned, 214
Body. *See* Mind–body problem
Body, in essay structure, 416–17
Bourgeoisie, 362–69
Brain
    consciousness and, 204, 206, 208–12

    mind and, 198f, 199–202, 199f,
        214–17, 219–21
    pineal gland in, 206, 206f
Brave New World (Huxley), 230
Brillo Box, 325, 325f
Brooks, Jordan, 322
The Buddha, 106–12, 107f, 123
Buddha-Nature (Sumedho), 109
Buddhism
    Buddha and, 106–12, 107f, 123
    complexity of, 107
    dharma in, 108–12, 123, 125, 432
    dukkha in, 108–12
    Five Precepts of, 111–12
    Four Noble Truths of, 108–12
    God, philosophy and, 106–7, 108,
        111–12
    history of, 106–12
    in India, 107–8
    karma in, 107, 110–11, 125, 433
    nirvana in, 109–10, 111–12, 123,
        125, 433
    Noble Eightfold Path of, 111–12
    overview of, 106–12
    Temple of the Dawn and, 110f
Bunyan, John, 330
Byrd, Randolph, 93

C

Camus, Albert
    existentialism of, 180–83, 188, 391
    meaning of life and, 391, 397
    morality and, 180–83, 188
    "The Myth of Sisyphus" by, 180–83
Capitalism
    defined, 362, 378, 431
    socialist theory and, 362, 363
Caring, 136, 175–79, 188
Carroll, Lewis, 318
Cartesian dualism
    criticism of, 203–4, 206–7
    defined, 198, 224, 431
    identity theory and, 199, 209
Categorical imperative
    defined, 164, 189–90, 431
    in Kant's theory, 164–68
Catharsis, 326–29, 333
Causal closure of the physical, 206–7,
        224, 431
Causality, 295–96, 295f
Cerebral commissurotomy, 204, 206
Certainty
    of Descartes, 276–80, 280f, 315
    of Locke, 281–87

Chalmers, David J., 209–10, 210f, 211f
Character
    morality based on, 168–74, 171f, 188
    in virtue ethics, 169–74, 171f
Child care, 371–74
Childhood, religion acquired in, 56, 58f
China, 183–86, 188–89, 214, 214f
Chinese Room thought experiment, 214–17
Chisholm, Roderick, 246
Claim. *See* Statement
Clarke, Arthur C., 126–28
Clarke, Randolph, 246
Classical liberalism, 357–58, 378, 431
Classic utilitarianism, 152
Class struggle, 362–70
Cleanthes, 70–74
Clifford, W. K.
    insufficient evidence for belief and,
        96, 99–100
    James and, 98, 99–101
Cloning, human, 138–39, 138f
Cognitive relativism
    criticism of, 265
    defined, 265, 317, 431
    problem of knowledge and, 265–66
Cole, Eve Browning, 309–13
Comedy, 329
Communism
    defined, 362, 378, 431
    Manifesto of the Communist Party and,
        364–69
    socialist theory and, 362–70
Community, 343, 354–55, 376
Compatibilism
    Consequence Argument rejected by, 245
    criticism of, 232, 243
    defined, 231–32, 256, 432
    free will, determinism and, 238–43,
        240f, 256, 432
    Hobbes and, 238
    Hume and, 238–39
    libertarianism (metaphysical) and,
        243, 245–46
    Locke and, 238–39, 242–43
    overview of, 255
    Stace and, 239–42
    traditional, 231–32, 238–43
Competition, 350
Composition, fallacy of, 35–36, 39, 432
Computers, strong AI and, 200–201,
        201f, 215–17, 215f, 216f
Conceivability arguments
    of Descartes, 203–4
    against identity theory, 209–10

Conceptualized experience, 302–7, 303*f*, 304*f*, 305*f*
Conclusion
    in arguments, 14–17, 28
    defined, 14, 39, 432
    in essay structure, 418
    identified, 16, 28, 41–42, 411–13
Conditional premise, 18
Confucius, 183–86, 183*f*, 188–89
Conscience, 133–34
The Conscious Mind (Chalmers), 209–10, 220
Consciousness
    brain and, 204, 206, 208–12
    divided, 204, 206
Consent, in social contract theory, 339, 347, 354–57
Consequence Argument, 245, 255
Consequences
    in ethical egoism, 135–36, 137, 159–62, 161*f*
    Kant's theory and, 136, 163
    morality based on, 150–62, 151*f*, 154*f*, 160*f*, 161*f*
    in utilitarianism, 135, 137, 150–59, 151*f*, 154*f*
Consequent, 18–19, 21
Consequentialist theory, 135–36, 137, 150, 190, 432
Conservatism, 24, 137
Considered moral judgments, 137–40, 162, 167
Controversial art, 322, 322*f*
Copernicus, 302, 303*f*
Cosmological arguments
    Craig's, 67–68
    defined, 58, 125, 432
    for God's existence, 58, 63–68, 122, 432
    Kalam, 67–68
Craig, William Lane, 67–68
Credulity, principle of, 90, 91–92
Criteria of adequacy
    defined, 23–24
    moral, 137–40, 144, 187
    Swinburne and, 74
Critical reading, 28
Critique of Pure Reason (Kant), 79, 300–303, 306
Crosthwaite, Jan, 175
Cultural relativism
    argument for, 148–49
    defined, 143, 190, 265–66, 317, 432
    infallibility problem of, 145–46, 145*f*, 266

moral progress and, 145*f*, 146, 147–48
moral relativism and, 143, 145–49, 145*f*, 146*f*
problem of knowledge and, 265–66
social reformers and, 147–48
women's rights and, 146, 146*f*, 147
Curie, Marie, 404

D
Danto, Arthur C., 325
Darrow, Clarence, 25*f*, 72*f*
    determinism of, 25–26
    as pessimist, 397
Data, theory and, 137–39
David, 323
David, Jacques-Louis, 10*f*
Da Vinci, Leonardo, 322–23, 325, 329
Davis, Thomas D., 258–60
Dawkins, Richard, 60
Dead hypothesis, 97
Death
    euthanasia, 150–51, 151*f*
    penalty, 154–55, 154*f*
    rebirth and, 110–11
    of Socrates, 9, 10*f*, 44–52
The Death of Socrates, 10*f*
Declaration of Independence, 339, 339*f*, 354
Deductive argument, 16–17, 39, 432
Deep Blue, 201, 201*f*
Defilements, 110
Deism, 62, 125, 432
Demea, 70–71
Democracy
    defined, 343, 378, 432
    Plato opposing, 343, 347
Denying the antecedent, 19, 21
Denying the consequent. *See Modus tollens*
Deontological theory, 135, 136, 150, 190, 432
Dependent premise, 26
Descartes, René. *See also* Cartesian dualism
    biography of, 278–79, 278*f*
    certainty of, 276–80, 280*f*, 315
    conceivability argument of, 203–4
    despair and, 253
    Discourse on the Method of Rightly Conducting the Reason by, 203
    divisibility argument of, 204, 206
    doubt of, 272–75
    dream argument of, 273–74
    God and, 277–78, 280

innate knowledge and, 273
Meditations on First Philosophy by, 204, 273–74, 276–80
principle of clarity and distinctness of, 277–78
rationalism of, 267, 269, 272–80, 280*f*, 283
skepticism of, 273–75
substance dualism of, 198, 202–4, 206–7, 206*f*, 218, 222
Desert, 340, 342
Design arguments
    evolution and, 76–77
    for God's existence, 58–59, 59*f*, 69–74, 76–77, 122
    Hume critiquing, 70–74
    Kant and, 79
Desire, 109
Despair, 252–53
Determinism. *See also* Hard determinism
    compatibilism and, 238–43, 240*f*, 256, 432
    Darrow's, 25–26
    defined, 229–30, 256, 432
    d'Holbach and, 234–35, 235*f*
    fatalism compared with, 233
    free will problem and, 25–26, 229–33
    indeterminism and, 231, 234–38, 254–55
    James and, 237
    libertarianism (metaphysical) and, 232–34, 237–38, 243–48
    "A Little Omniscience Goes a Long Way" and, 258–60
    science and, 231, 235–36, 238
Dewey, John, 308
Dharma, 108, 116, 117, 432
d'Holbach, Baron, 234–35, 235*f*
Dialectic process, 362–63
Dialogues Concerning Natural Religion (Hume), 70–74
Diffidence, 350
"The Dilemma of Determinism" (James), 237
"The Dilemma of the Divine Command Theory" sample essay, 422–24
Disbelief, 61–63
Discourse on the Method of Rightly Conducting the Reason (Descartes), 203
Disembodied existence, 203–4
Distributive justice, 340, 378, 432

Divine command theory
   arbitrariness problem of, 141–42, 422–24
   defined, 141, 190, 432
   God in, 134, 141–42, 190, 432
   as moral theory, 134, 141–42, 173–74,
     187, 190, 422–23, 432
   in sample essay, 422–24
   virtue ethics and, 173–74
Divine right, 347
Divisibility argument, 204
Division, fallacy of, 36, 39, 432
Doing Philosophy (Schick), 203–4
Doubt, of Descartes, 272–75
Downward causation, 220
Dreams, 90, 263–64, 264*f*
Dukkha (suffering), 108–12
Duty
   absolute, 167
   Kant and, 176
   morality based on, 163–68, 165*f*,
     167*f*, 188
   to opinion, 99–100
   virtue ethics and, 169, 172–73

E

Eastern religious traditions, 106–21,
   123–24. *See also* Buddhism
Edwards, Paul, 404–5
Efficient cause, 64
Einstein, Albert, 62, 66, 78, 138–40,
   177, 272, 275, 280
"Embodiment and Epistemology"
   (Antony), 308–9
Emotions
   ethics and, 133, 176–79
   tragedy invoking, 326–29
Empiricism
   of Berkeley, 267, 268, 287–91
   defined, 266, 317, 432
   feminist, 310
   of Hume, 267, 268, 291–98, 295*f*
   Kant and, 299–307, 303*f*, 304*f*–305*f*
   of Locke, 267–68, 281–87
   morality and, 163
   problem of knowledge and, 266–68,
     281–98, 295*f*, 315–16
   skepticism in, 268
The Encyclopedia of Philosophy (Edwards),
   404–5
Engels, Friedrich, 364–69
Enlightenment, 234–35, 292
*An Enquiry Concerning Human
   Understanding* (Hume), 293–98
Entitlement, 342

Enumerative induction, 19–20
Epicureans, 153, 400, 401
Epicurus, 3, 153, 171*f*
Epiphenomenalism
   criticism of, 207, 220
   defined, 202, 224, 432
   mind–body problem and, 202
   property dualism and, 220–21
Epistemic justification, 95
Epistemology
   defined, 6, 39, 263, 317, 432
   feminist, 309–10
   Kant's revolution in, 302–3, 303*f*, 306–7
   questions, 6, 264
   traditional, 309–10
Equality
   gender and, 371–75
   Hobbes and, 349–50
   justice as, 340, 342, 346, 346*f*
   of opportunity, 360–61
   organ transplants and, 346, 346*f*
   in political philosophy, 340, 342
   Rawls and, 340
Equal liberty principle, 359–61
Equivocation, 33, 39, 432
*An Essay Concerning Human
   Understanding* (Locke), 239, 281–87
An Essay on Free Will (van Inwagen), 245
Essay structure, 415–18. *See also*
   Philosophy papers
Essence, existence preceding, 180–82,
   250–53
Ethical egoism
   arguments against, 159–62
   consequences in, 135–36, 137,
     159–62, 161*f*
   defined, 135, 137, 190, 432
   as moral theory, 135, 137, 159–62,
     161*f*, 432
   psychological egoism and, 159–61, 434
   utilitarianism and, 159
Ethics. *See also* Virtue ethics
   defined, 6, 39, 131, 190, 432
   emotions and, 133, 176–79
   feminist, 174–79, 176*f*, 188, 190, 432
   morality distinguished from, 132–33
   in *Nicomachean Ethics*, 169–71
   overview of, 131–42, 133*f*, 135*f*,
     138*f*, 187
   of strong AI, 218–19
Ethics of care
   criticism of, 179
   defined, 136, 175, 190, 432
   feminist ethics and, 174–79, 176*f*, 188

as moral theory, 136–37, 174–79, 176*f*,
   188, 190, 432
The Ethics of Care (Held), 176–78
Eudaimonia (happiness), 169
Euripides, 329
Europe, belief in God in, 57
Euthanasia, 150–51, 151*f*
Euthyphro (Plato), 141, 423
Evidence, insufficient for belief, 96, 99–100
Evidentialism
   defined, 96, 125, 432
   James repudiating, 96–103
Evil
   argument from, 60–61, 80–83, 122,
     125, 431
   atheism and, 80–83
   free will defense and, 61, 83–85
   God and, 60–63, 80–88, 81*f*, 84*f*,
     122, 125, 128
   Hurricane Katrina and, 84, 84*f*
   moral, 80, 125, 433
   natural, 80, 125, 433
   necessary, 61
   problem of, 80–88, 81*f*, 84*f*, 122
   punishment for, 84, 84*f*
   soul-making defense and, 85–88
   suffering from, 80–83
   unnecessary, 61, 63
Evil and the God of Love (Hick), 85–88
Evolution, design arguments and, 76–77
Examined life, Socrates and, 3, 8–13,
   37, 50
Existence
   absurdity of, 180–82
   disembodied, 203–4
   essence preceded by, 180–82, 250–53
   God's, arguments for, 58–59, 59*f*,
     63–79, 75*f*–76*f*, 77*f*, 78*f*, 122,
     125, 431
   personal, recognition of, 279
The Existence of God (Swinburne), 94
Existentialism
   atheistic, 251
   of Camus, 180–83, 188, 391
   defined, 180
   of Sartre, 180, 250–54
"Existentialism Is a Humanism" (Sartre),
   250–53
Explanation, 22–24
Explosive Ordnance Disposal Robot,
   218, 218*f*
Expression, art as, 323
Extension, of physical things, 202
External meaning, 393–94

F

Fact, faith creating, 101
Faith
    behavior and, 101f, 104–5
    fact created by, 101
    living by, 104
    pragmatic, 96–105
    reason and, 62–63, 75f
    Tolstoy's, 400–401
Fallacy
    appeal to ignorance, 33–34, 39, 431
    appeal to popularity, 32, 39, 431
    appeal to the person, 31–32, 39, 431
    begging the question, 34–35, 39, 431
    composition, 35–36, 39, 432
    defined, 29, 39, 432
    division, 36, 39, 432
    equivocation, 33, 39, 432
    exercise, 42–43, 413
    false dilemma, 34, 39, 432
    genetic, 32–33, 39, 432
    slippery slope, 35, 39, 434
    straw man, 29–30, 40, 434
False dilemma, 34, 39, 432
Family
    power relationships in, 371–72, 373f
    responsibilities, 371–74
    single-parent, 371–72
Fatalist, 233
Fate, 233
Father, God as, 87
Fear, 326–29
Feminism
    concerns of, 307
    criticism of, 374–75
    justice, political philosophy and,
        370–75, 377–78
    Miller and, 374–75
    Okin and, 371–74, 372f
Feminist empiricism, 310
Feminist epistemology, 309–10
"Feminist Epistemology and Philosophy
    of Science" (Anderson), 309
Feminist ethics
    defined, 174, 190, 432
    ethics of care and, 174–79, 176f, 188
"Feminist Ethics" (Jaggar), 175
Feminist perspective, on knowledge
    Ainley's, 308
    Anderson's, 309
    Antony's, 308–9
    Cole's, 309–11
    criticism of, 311, 313
    problem of knowledge and, 307–13, 316

"Feminist Philosophy" (Ainley), 308
Feminist postmodernism, 310–13
Feminist standpoint theory, 310–12
Fiction. See also Narrative
    "The Good Brahmin," 408–9
    "A Little Omniscience Goes a Long
        Way," 258–60
    Lord of the Flies, 380–87
    "The Ones Who Walk Away From
        Omelas," 191–94
    "The Oval Portrait," 334–35
    "The Star," 126–28
    "They're Made Out of Meat," 225–26
    Through the Looking Glass, 318
Final draft, of philosophy paper, 421
First-cause argument, 65–68
First draft, of philosophy paper,
    420–21
First Mover, 65, 67
First Noble Truth, 108–9
Five Precepts, 111–12
Fodor, Jerry A., 213
Forlornness, 252
Formalism, 323, 333
Forms, 270
    of art, 323
    of Beauty, 326
Four Noble Truths, 108–12
Fourth Noble Truth, 111–12
Frank, Anne, 167f
Free acts, 239–42
Freedom
    Sartre's, 249–53, 256
    value of, 229
Free will. See also Problem of free will
    belief in, 240–41, 240f
    compatibilism and, 238–43, 240f,
        256, 432
    defense, evil and, 61, 83–85
    incompatibilism and, 231, 233,
        242–43
    libertarianism (metaphysical) and,
        232–34, 237–38, 243–48
    "A Little Omniscience Goes a Long
        Way" and, 258–60
    science and, 231, 235–36, 238, 244
Fruitfulness, 137
Functionalism
    criticism of, 213–14, 219, 223
    defined, 200, 224, 432
    identity theory and, 213
    logical behaviorism and, 213
    mind–body problem in, 200–201,
        212–17, 223

Fundamental ideas, 2
The Fundamentals of Ethics (Shafer-
    Landau), 173–74

G

Gandhi, Mahatma, 400f, 404
Gardner, Martin, 324
Gaunilo, 78
Gender, equality and, 371–75. See also
    Feminism
"Gender and Bioethics" (Crosthwaite), 175
Gender-structured marriage, 371–73
General assent, 282
Genetic fallacy, 32–33, 39, 432
Genuine option, 96–97, 99
"Ghost in the machine," 202
Gilligan, Carol, 176
Girl with a Pearl Earring, 323
Glory, 350
God. See also Religion; Religious
        experience
    Aquinas and, 41, 58, 63–67, 122
    argument from evil and, 60–61, 80–83,
        122, 125, 431
    argument from religious experience
        and, 59–60, 122–23, 125, 431
    belief in, 55–106
    Berkeley and, 291
    cosmological arguments for, 58, 63–68,
        122, 432
    Descartes and, 277–78, 280
    design arguments for, 58–59, 59f,
        69–74, 76–77, 122
    difficulty recognizing, 94–95
    in divine command theory, 134,
        141–42, 190, 432
    divine right and, 347
    evil and, 60–63, 80–88, 81f, 84f, 122,
        125, 128
    experience of, 89–95, 90f, 93f,
        122–23
    as father, 87
    Hurricane Katrina and, 84, 84f
    in "A Little Omniscience Goes a Long
        Way," 258–60
    meaning of life from, 392–93, 392f,
        399–404, 400f, 402f–403f
    morality of, 83
    nature of, 105
    ontological arguments for, 59, 63,
        75–79, 75f–76f, 78f, 122, 125
    Pascal betting on, 103–5
    purpose of, 86–87
    theodicies and, 61

God, philosophy and
  arguments for existence, 58–59, 59*f*,
    63–79, 75*f*–76*f*, 77*f*, 78*f*, 122,
    125, 431
  belief without reason in, 55,
    95–106, 123
  Buddhism and, 106–7, 108, 111–12
  overview of, 55–63, 122
  in philosopher's quest, 56–61
  problem of evil in, 80–88, 81*f*, 84*f*, 122
  "The Star" and, 126–28
  theism and religious experience in,
    89–95, 90*f*, 93*f*, 122–23
Golding, William, 380–87
"The Good Brahmin" (Voltaire), 408–9
Good will, 163–64
Government
  beginning of, 354–55
  end of, 355–56
  functions needed from, 353–54
  pervasiveness of, 338–39
  rebellion against, 354, 358
The Grand Design (Hawking), 69*f*
Grau, Christopher, 275
Greatest Happiness Principle, 153, 157
Groundwork of the Metaphysic of Morals
    (Kant), 163–66
Guardians, 343

H

Hallucinations, 264
Happiness
  Aristotle and, 169–72
  eudaimonia, 169
  in Greatest Happiness Principle, 153, 157
  meaning of life distinguished from, 392
  in utilitarianism, 152–59
Hard determinism
  defined, 231, 256, 432
  of d'Holbach, 234–35
  Sartre and, 253
Hawking, Stephen, 69*f*
Health care, 361
Held, Virginia, 176–78, 176*f*
Herodotus, 327–28
Hick, John
  Evil and the God of Love by, 85–88
  Hume and, 86, 87
  suffering and, 86, 88
Hinduism, 112–18
Hitler, Adolf, 14*f*, 144, 144*f*
Hobbes, Thomas. *See also Leviathan*
  biography of, 348, 348*f*
  compatibilism and, 238

equality and, 349–50
  injustice and, 370
  justice and, 349, 352–54, 358–59
  social contract theory of, 348–53
Homer, 329
Hood, Bruce, 60
Human cloning, morality of, 138–39, 138*f*
Humans, natural condition of, 349–53
Hume, David, 333
  aesthetics influenced by, 329–31
  on beauty, 329–31
  biography of, 292–93, 292*f*
  causality and, 295–96, 295*f*
  compatibilism and, 238–39
  criticism of, 74, 358–59
  design arguments critiqued by, 70–74
  Dialogues Concerning Natural Religion
    by, 70–74
  empiricism of, 267, 268, 291–98, 295*f*
  *An Enquiry Concerning Human
    Understanding* by, 293–98
  Hick and, 86, 87
  infinite regress and, 66
  Kant and, 299–300
  on perceptions, 292–94, 296, 298
  principle of induction and, 296–97,
    317, 433–34
  reasoning argument of, 71
  self and, 108
  skepticism of, 292–93, 295, 298–300
  social contract theory criticized by,
    358, 359
  Of the Standard of Taste by, 329–31
  subjectivism of, 329–31
  women and, 308
Hurricane Katrina, 84, 84*f*
Hursthouse, Rosalind, 172
Huxley, Aldous, 230
Hypatia
  biography of, 26, 26*f*
  in *The School of Athens*, 171*f*
Hypothesis
  dead, 97
  live, 97, 103
  religious, 96–103
Hypothetical imperative, 164

I

Ideas
  perceptions as, 283–87, 292–93
  sensations and, 283–87
Identity theory. *See also* Mind–body
    identity
  Cartesian dualism and, 199, 209

conceivability arguments against, 209–10
  criticism of, 209–12, 218–19
  defined, 199, 224, 432
  functionalism and, 213
Ignorance
  appeal to, 33–34, 39, 431
  argument from evil and, 82–83
  veil of, 359
Imitation. *See* Representation
Immortal soul, 205, 205*f*
Impartiality, 132, 152, 162, 176, 177,
    178–79
Impermanence, 108–9, 110
Impressions, 292–94
In a Different Voice (Gilligan), 176
Incompatibilism
  defined, 231, 257, 432
  free will and, 231, 233, 242–43
  libertarianism (metaphysical) and,
    243, 245
Independent premise, 26
Indeterminism
  defined, 231, 257, 433
  determinism and, 231, 234–38,
    254–55
India, Buddhism originating in, 107–8
Indicator words, 16
Induction
  analogical, 21–22
  enumerative, 19–20
  principle of, 296–97, 317, 433–34
  problem of, 297
Inductive argument
  analogical induction, 21–22
  defined, 17–18, 39, 433
  enumerative induction, 19–20
  inference to the best explanation, 22–23
Industry, modern, 367–68
Infallibility problem, 144–46, 145*f*, 266
Inference to the best explanation, 22–23
Infinite chain, of Movers, 64–66
Infinity, logical contradictions of, 68
Inherent value, of persons, 166–67
Injustice
  laws of nature and, 352–53
  in political philosophy, 370
Innate knowledge, 270–72, 271–83
Intelligent design, 58–59, 59*f*, 76–77. *See
    also* Design arguments
Intercessory prayer, 93
Internal meaning, 393, 404–5
Introduction, in essay structure, 415–16
Invalid arguments, 19, 21
Irenaeus, 85

Irises, 323
Island, greatest possible, 78, 78*f*

J

Jaggar, Alison, 175
James, William
    biography of, 236, 236*f*
    Clifford and, 98, 99–101
    criticism of, 103
    determinism and, 237
    "The Dilemma of Determinism"
        by, 237
    evidentialism repudiated by, 96–103
    genuine option of, 96–97, 99
    pragmatism of, 96–103, 236
    on religious experience, 90
    religious hypothesis of, 96–103
    The Will to Believe by, 97–103
Judge, known and indifferent, 356
Justice
    defined, 340, 379, 433
    distributive, 378, 432
    as equality, 340, 342, 346, 346*f*
    feminism and, 370–75, 377–78
    Hobbes and, 349, 352–54, 358–59
    laws of nature and, 352–53
    Lord of the Flies and, 380–87
    as merit, 340, 343–46
    Plato and, 10–11, 340, 343–45,
        343*f*, 376
    political philosophy and, 338–42, 339*f*,
        341*f*–342*f*, 376
    in *The Republic*, 10–11, 343–45
    retributive, 340
    social, 370–75, 377–78
    social contract theory and, 347–61
    utilitarian theory of, 340
Justice, Gender, and the Family (Okin),
    371–74

K

Kalam cosmological argument, 67–68
Kane, Robert, 246
Kant, Immanuel
    biography, 301, 301*f*
    criticism of, 306–7
    Critique of Pure Reason by, 79,
        300–303, 306
    design arguments and, 79
    duty and, 176
    empiricism and, 299–307, 303*f*,
        304*f*–305*f*
    epistemology revolution of, 302–3,
        303*f*, 306–7

Groundwork of the Metaphysic of Morals
        by, 163–66
    Hume and, 299–300
    moral theory of, 136, 137, 163–68,
        167*f*, 188, 190, 433
    Plato and, 300–302
    problem of knowledge and, 268,
        299–307, 304*f*–305*f*, 316
    rationalism and, 300–302, 306
    respect for persons and, 166–67
    skepticism and, 268, 300, 306
    on stamp, 165*f*
    utilitarianism and, 167
    women and, 309
Kant's theory
    categorical imperatives in, 164–68
    consequences and, 136, 163
    criticism of, 167–68
    defined, 136, 190, 433
    as moral theory, 136, 137, 163–68,
        167*f*, 188, 190, 433
Karma, 107, 110–11, 117, 433
Kasparov, Garry, 201, 201*f*
Kaufmann, Walter, 3
King, Martin Luther, Jr., 338, 404
Kings, divine right of, 347
Kitcher, Philip, 77
Knowledge. *See also* Epistemology;
        Feminist perspective, on knowledge;
        Problem of knowledge
    a posteriori, 266, 300, 317, 431
    a priori, 266, 300, 301–7, 316, 317, 431
    arguments, 210–12
    background, 140
    forms, 264, 291, 292
    innate, 270–72, 271–83
    propositional, 264, 317, 434
    situated, 309
Kushner, Harold, 63

L

Labor, sexual division of, 373, 374
Law of conservation of mass-energy, 207
Laws of nature, 351–53
Lawyers, women as, 374
Le Guin, Ursula, 191–94
Leibniz, Gottfried, 257
Leviathan, 349, 354, 355
Leviathan (Hobbes)
    frontispiece to, 350*f*
    laws of nature in, 351–53
    natural condition of mankind in,
        349–53
    peace in, 351–53

political philosophy in, 348–53
    war in, 351–52
Liberalism
    classical, 357–58, 378, 431
    defined, 357, 379, 433
    welfare, 361, 379, 434
Libertarianism (metaphysical)
    agent causation and, 246–48
    compatibilism and, 243, 245–46
    Consequence Argument of, 245
    criticism of, 245–48
    defined, 232, 257, 433
    determinism and, 232–34, 237–38,
        243–48
    free will and, 232–34, 237–38, 243–48
    incompatibilism and, 243, 245
    Libet and, 244
    overview of, 255–56
Libertarianism (political)
    classical liberalism resembling, 358
    defined, 358, 379, 433
    paradise, in U.S., 363
Liberty, 351–52, 353–54
Libet, Benjamin, 244
Life. *See also* Meaning, of life
    bios, 87
    examined, 3, 8–13, 37, 50
    length of, 395*f*, 405
    meaninglessness of, 393–99, 395*f*
    moral, consistency with facts of, 140
    private and public, 370–75
    purpose of, 402
    zoe, 87
The Life of Teresa of Jesus (Teresa of Avila), 89
Lin, Patrick, 218
"A Little Omniscience Goes a Long Way"
        (Davis), 258–60
Live hypothesis, 97, 103
Living With Darwin (Kitcher), 77
Locke, John, 281*f*. *See also Second Treatise
        of Government*
    Berkeley and, 287, 289–90
    biography of, 358, 358*f*
    certainty of, 281–87
    compatibilism and, 238–39, 242–43
    criticism of, 284–87
    empiricism of, 267–68, 281–87
    *An Essay Concerning Human
        Understanding* by, 239, 281–87
    injustice and, 370
    political philosophy and, 339
    social contract theory of, 354–58
    Two Treatises of Government by, 354*f*
    women and, 308

Logic
    defined, 7, 39, 433
    of ontological arguments, 75
    questions, 6
Logical behaviorism
    defined, 198–99, 224, 433
    functionalism and, 213
    mind–body problem in, 198–99
Lord of the Flies (Golding), 380–87
Love, parental, 87
Lying promise, 165

M
Machine-universe analogy, 71, 72
Mackie, J. L.
    on God's morality, 83
    The Miracle of Theism by, 90
Majority, act of, 354–55
Man, natural condition of, 349–53
Manifesto of the Communist Party
    (Marx and Engels), 364–69
Marriage, gender-structured, 371–73
Martin, Michael, 103
Marx, Karl, 362*f*
    influence of, 362
    Manifesto of the Communist Party by,
        364–69
    socialist theory of, 362–69
Materialism
    bats and, 210–11, 212*f*
    defined, 198, 224, 433
    as false, 201
    property dualism and, 220–21
    zombies and, 209–10, 211*f*
The Matrix, 275, 275*f*
Matters of fact, 291–92, 294, 300
Meaning
    from above, 399–404
    from below, 404–5
    external, 393–94
    internal, 393, 404–5
    meaning of, 392–93, 397, 399
Meaning, of life
    from above, 399–404
    Baggini and, 397–99, 403–4, 403*f*
    from below, 404–5
    Camus and, 391, 397
    defined, 392–93, 397, 399
    God's plan for, 392–93, 392*f*, 399–404,
        400*f*, 402*f*–403*f*
    happiness distinguished from, 392
    internal, 393
    length of life and, 395*f*, 405
    meaning of *meaning* in, 392–93, 397, 399

morality distinguished from, 392
    optimist's view of, 393, 399–405, 400*f*,
        402*f*, 403*f*, 407
    overview of, 390–93, 390*f*, 392*f*, 405
    as personal, 391–92
    pessimist's view of, 394–99, 395*f*,
        405, 407
    philosophy and, 390–93, 390*f*, 392*f*
    for potter, 390–91
    quiz, 406, 406*f*
    from religion, 392–93, 392*f*, 399–404,
        400*f*, 402*f*–403*f*
    suffering and, 396–97
Meaninglessness, of life, 393–99, 395*f*
Means of production, 362–64, 367
Meditations on First Philosophy
    (Descartes), 204, 273–74, 276–80
Meletus, 44, 46–48
Meno (Plato), 271–72
Mental discipline, 111–12
Merit
    justice and, 340, 343–46
    organ transplants and, 346, 346*f*
Meritocracy, 343, 379, 433
Metaphysics, 4–6, 39, 433
Metaphysics (Taylor, R.), 246–48
Michelangelo, 323
Middle Way or Path, 111–12
Mill, James, 160
Mill, John Stuart
    biography of, 160, 160*f*
    Greatest Happiness Principle of,
        153, 157
    The Subjection of Women by, 160
    utilitarianism of, 153–57
    "What Utilitarianism Is" by, 153–57
    women and, 160, 308
Miller, David, 374–75
Milton, John, 330
Mimesis. See Representation
Mind. *See also* Software, mind as
    of bats, 210–12
    brain and, 198*f*, 199–202, 199*f*,
        214–17, 219–21
    conceptual processor of, 304–5,
        304*f*–305*f*
    intuition of, 279–80, 280*f*
    objects conforming to, 303–6
    as properties, 218–23
Mind (Searle), 207, 215–17
Mind–body identity
    conceivability arguments and,
        209–10
    criticism of, 209–12, 218–19

    theory of, 199–200, 208–12,
        210*f*–212*f*, 223
Mind–body problem
    defined, 198, 224, 433
    epiphenomenalism and, 202
    in functionalism, 200–201, 212–17, 223
    immortal soul and, 205, 205*f*
    in logical behaviorism, 198–99
    mind as software and, 200–201, 201*f*,
        212–17, 214*f*–216*f*, 223
    overview of, 197–202, 198*f*–199*f*,
        201*f*, 222
    in property dualism, 201–2, 218–23
    in substance dualism, 198, 202–7,
        205*f*–206*f*, 222
"The Mind–Body Problem" (Fodor), 213
The Miracle of Theism (Mackie), 90
Mitys, 328
Modern industry, 367–68
Modus ponens (affirming the antecedent),
    18–19, 21
Modus tollens (denying the consequent),
    19, 21
Mommy track, 374
Mona Lisa, 322–23, 325, 329
Monotheism, 62, 125, 433
Moral absolutism, 143, 190, 433
Moral common sense, 137–40, 162, 167
Moral conduct, 111–12
Moral criteria of adequacy, 137–40,
    144, 187
Moral disagreement, 144–45, 148–49
Moral evil, 80, 125, 433
Moral excellence, 172
Morality
    Camus and, 180–83, 188
    character and, 168–74, 171*f*, 188
    consequences and, 150–62, 151*f*, 154*f*,
        160*f*, 161*f*
    defined, 131, 190, 433
    divine command theory and, 134,
        141–42, 173–74, 187, 190,
        422–23, 432
    duty and, 163–68, 165*f*, 167*f*, 188
    empirical basis of, 163
    ethics distinguished from, 132–33
    God's, 83
    of human cloning, 138–39, 138*f*
    impartiality and, 132, 152, 162, 176,
        177, 178–79
    meaning of life distinguished from, 392
    as normative enterprise, 132
    overview of, 131–42, 133*f*, 135*f*,
        138*f*, 187

political philosophy and, 348
principle of respect for persons and, 166–67
properties of, 132–33
reason-based, 132–33
religion and, 141–42, 141*f*
based on rights, 163–68, 165*f*, 167*f*, 188
Socrates and, 141
Moral judgments, considered, 137–40, 162, 167
Moral life, consistency with facts of, 140
Moral objectivism, 143, 149, 190, 433
Moral obligations, 134
Moral philosophy. *See* ethics
Moral problem-solving, resourcefulness in, 140
Moral progress, 145, 145*f*, 146–47
Moral question, 100
Moral relativism
    cultural relativism and, 143, 145–49, 145*f*, 146*f*
    defined, 143, 190, 433
    infallibility problem of, 145–46
    overview of, 187
    subjective relativism and, 143–45, 144*f*
Moral theory
    consequentialist, 135–36, 137, 150, 190, 432
    considered moral judgments in, 137–40, 162, 167
    criteria of adequacy in, 137–40, 144, 187
    data and, 137–40
    defined, 134, 190, 433
    deontological, 135, 136, 150, 190, 432
    divine command theory, 134, 141–42, 173–74, 187, 190, 422–23, 432
    ethical egoism, 135, 137, 159–62, 161*f*, 432
    ethics of care, 136–37, 174–79, 176*f*, 188, 190, 432
    goodness of, 135*f*
    Kant's theory, 136, 137, 163–68, 167*f*, 188, 190, 433
    scientific theory analogous to, 136–40
    types, 135–40
    utilitarianism, 135, 136, 137, 150–59, 434
    virtue ethics, 136, 169–74, 434
Moral values, 134
Morris, Richard, 66
Motion, argument from, 64–65
Motivation, right thought and, 111
Movers, infinite chain of, 64–66

Multiple personality disorder, 204
Multiple realizability, 200, 224, 433
Museum, 327
My Confession (Tolstoy), 394–96, 399–401
"The Myth of Sisyphus" (Camus), 180–83

N
Nagel, Thomas, 210–11
Namazie, Maryam, 147
Narrative, "The Trial and Death of Socrates" as, 44–52
Natural condition, of man, 349–53
Natural evil, 80, 125, 433
Naturalistic theories, 74
Natural selection, 76–77
Natural Theology (Paley), 69–70
Nature
    of God, 105
    imperfections in, 71–74, 72*f*
    laws of, 351–53
    state of, 349, 354, 355–59
Necessary evil, 61
"The Need for More Than Justice" (Baier), 179
Needy, assisting, 340, 342, 342*f*
New Orleans, 84, 84*f*
News, philosophy in, 30
Nicomachean Ethics (Aristotle), 169–71
Nietzsche, Friedrich, 98, 158
Nihilists, 394
Nirvana, 109–12, 125, 433
Noble Eightfold Path, 111–12
Non-art, 321–23
Nonconsequentialist theory. *See* deontological theory
Normal species functioning, 361
Normative, 132
Noumena, 305
Nozick, Robert, 342

O
Obama, Barack, 364
Objections, assessment of, 417
Objectivism, 323–29, 333
Objects, conforming to mind, 303–6
Obligation
    moral, 134
    theories of, 136, 168–69, 172
Ockham's razor, 74
O'Connor, Timothy, 246
Odyssey (Homer), 329
Oedipus, 328

"Of the Principles of Human Knowledge" (Berkeley), 288–91
Of the Standard of Taste (Hume), 329–31
"Of the System of Man's Free Agency " (d'Holbach), 234–35
Ogilby, John, 330
Okin, Susan Moller
    feminism and, 371–74, 372*f*
    Justice, Gender, and the Family by, 371–74
Omniscience, 258–60
"The Ones Who Walk Away From Omelas" (Le Guin), 191–94
"On the Sufferings of the World" (Schopenhauer), 396–97
Ontological arguments
    Anselm's, 59, 75–79
    defined, 59, 125, 433
    form of, 63
    for God's existence, 59, 63, 75–79, 75*f*–76*f*, 78*f*, 122, 125
    logic of, 75
Opinion
    duty to, 99–100
    psychology of, 100–101
Opportunity, equality of, 360–61
Optimists
    Edwards, 404–5
    about meaning of life, 393, 399–405, 400*f*, 402*f*, 403*f*, 407
    Tolstoy, 394, 399–401
    Warren, 402
Orestes, 329
Organ transplants, 346, 346*f*
Original position, of Rawls, 359–60
Outline, of philosophy paper, 420
"The Oval Portrait" (Poe), 334–35
Overridingness, 132
Ovid, 321

P
Pain, 212–13, 285–86
Paley, William, 58–59, 69–70
Panentheism, 62, 125, 433
Pantheism, 62, 125, 433
Papers. *See* Philosophy papers
Parental love, 87
Parks, Rosa, 404
Pascal, Blaise, 103*f*
    criticism of, 105
    God and, 103–5
    Pensees and Other Writings by, 103–5
    wager of, 96, 99, 103–5
Paul (saint), 89, 90*f*

Peace, in *Leviathan*, 351–53
Pensees and Other Writings (Pascal), 103–5
Perceptions
    Hume on, 292–94, 296, 298
    as ideas, 283–87, 292–93
Personal, as political, 373, 373*f*, 375
Personal existence, recognition of, 279
Persuasion, 14, 14*f*
Pessimists
    Darrow, 397
    about meaning of life, 394–99, 395*f*,
      405, 407
    Schopenhauer, 396–97, 397*f*
    Tolstoy, 394–96, 399–401
Phenomena, 305
Phillips, Christopher, 12
Philo, 70–74
Philosophers, quest of, 2–7, 37, 56–61.
    See also specific philosophers
Philosophical beliefs survey, 5
Philosophical method, 2
Philosophy. *See also* God, philosophy
    and; Political philosophy
    aesthetics and, 321
    arguments in, 13–36, 37–38
    of beauty, 321, 332
    bias in, 308–11
    good of, 2–4
    immediacy of, 2
    main divisions of, 4–7
    meaning of life and, 390–93, 390*f*, 392*f*
    in news, 30
    in politics, 30, 31*f*
    as quest for understanding, 2–7, 37,
      56–61
    reading, 24–29
    reasons in, 14–24
    thinking philosophically in, 13–36,
      37–38
Philosophy and Feminist Criticism (Cole),
    309–11
Philosophy of Religion (Rowe), 80–83, 92
Philosophy papers
    final draft of, 421
    first draft of, 420–21
    outline of, 420
    research for, 419
    revision of, 421
    sample, 422–24
    steps of, 418–21
    structure of, 415–18
    thesis statement in, 416–17, 419–20
    topic selection for, 418–19
    writing instructions for, 418–24

Physicalism. *See* materialism
Physics, quantum, 66, 68, 231, 232*f*,
    235, 236
Pineal gland, 206, 206*f*
Pity, 326–29
Plato, 7*f*, 269*f*, 332
    Academy of, 343*f*
    aesthetics influenced by, 326
    The Apology by, 44–52
    democracy opposed by, 343, 347
    Euthyphro by, 141
    Forms of, 270, 326
    Hypatia and, 26
    influence of, 9
    justice and, 10–11, 340, 343–45,
      343*f*, 376
    Kant and, 300–302
    Meno by, 271–72
    propositional knowledge and, 264
    rationalism of, 267, 269–72, 269*f*,
      300–302
    The Republic by, 10–11, 343–45, 343*f*
    in *The School of Athens*, 171*f*
    Socrates and, 8–11, 44–52, 141,
      271–72, 315, 344–45, 423
    substance dualism of, 198
    "The Trial and Death of Socrates" by,
      44–52
    women and, 308
Pleasure, sensing of, 275–76
Poe, Edgar Allan, 334–35
The Poetics (Aristotle), 326–29
Political, personal as, 373, 373*f*, 375
Political philosophy
    Declaration of Independence and, 339,
      339*f*, 354
    defined, 348, 379, 433
    desert in, 340, 342
    equality in, 340, 342
    feminism and, 370–75, 377–78
    importance of, 338–39
    injustice in, 370
    issues in, 348
    justice and, 338–42, 339*f*,
      341*f*–342*f*, 376
    in *Leviathan*, 348–53
    Locke and, 339
    moral philosophy and, 348
    pervasiveness of government and, 338–39
    rights in, 339, 353, 354, 357–58,
      359–61, 363, 368–69, 370, 372–73,
      374–75, 376–77–378
    social contract theory and, 347–61
    socialist theories and, 362–69

Political Philosophy (Miller), 374–75
Political power, 253
Political views, in U.S., 341, 341*f*
Politics, philosophy in, 30, 31*f*
Polytheism, 62, 125, 433
Postmodernism, feminist, 310–13
Potential infinities, 68
Potter, meaning of life for, 390–91
Power
    political, 253
    relationships, in families, 371–72, 373*f*
Pragmatic faith, 96–105
Pragmatic justification, 95–105
Pragmatism, of James, 96–103, 236
Prayer, power of, 93, 93*f*
Predictability, 246
Prejudice, against women, 307–9
Premise
    in arguments, 14–17, 28
    conditional, 18
    defined, 14, 39, 433
    dependent, 26
    identified, 16, 28, 41–42, 411–13
    independent, 26
Primary qualities, 284, 289–90
Principle of clarity and distinctness,
    277–78
Principle of credulity, 90–92
Principle of induction, 296–97, 317,
    433–34
Principle of respect for persons, 166–67
Principle of utility, 150
Private life, public life separate from,
    370–75
Probable support, 17
Problem of evil, 80–88, 81*f*, 84*f*, 122
Problem of free will
    compatibilism and, 238–43, 240*f*,
      256, 432
    defined, 230, 257, 434
    determinism and, 25–26, 229–33
    incompatibilism and, 231, 233,
      242–43, 434
    libertarianism (metaphysical) and,
      232–34, 237–38, 243–48
    overview of, 229–33, 229*f*,
      231*f*–232*f*, 254
Problem of induction, 297
Problem of knowledge
    cognitive relativism and, 265–66
    cultural relativism and, 265–66
    empiricism and, 266–68, 281–98,
      295*f*, 315–16
    feminist perspective on, 307–13, 316

Kant and, 268, 299–307,
    304f–305f, 316
The Matrix and, 275, 275f
overview of, 263–68, 264f, 314
rationalism and, 266–67, 269–80,
    280f, 314–15
skepticism and, 264–65, 268
subjective relativism and, 265–66
Problem-solving, moral, 140
Producers, 343
Production, means of, 362–64, 367
Proletariat, 362–63, 365–69
Properties, mind as, 218–23
Property
    abolition of, 368–69
    protection of, 355–56
    right to, 353, 368–69
Property dualism
    defined, 201, 434
    epiphenomenalism and, 220–21
    materialism and, 220–21
    mind–body problem in, 201–2, 218–23
Propositional knowledge, 264, 317, 434
Proslogium (Anselm), 75–78
Prudence, 349–50
Psychological egoism, 159–61, 190, 434
Public life, private life separate from,
    370–75
Pythagoras, 171f

Q

Qualitative content, 198–99
Quantum physics, 66, 68, 231, 232f,
    235, 236
Quarrel, causes of, 350
Quietism, 253

R

Rahula, Walpola, 109–10
Raphael, 171f
Rationalism
    criticism of, 281
    defined, 266, 317, 434
    of Descartes, 267, 269, 272–80,
        280f, 283
    Kant and, 300–302, 306
    of Plato, 267, 269–72, 269f, 300–302
    problem of knowledge and, 266–67,
        269–80, 280f, 314–15
    Socrates and, 271–72
    Spinoza and, 267
Rawls, John, 360f
    criticism of, 361
    equality and, 340

original position of, 359–60
social contract theory of, 340, 358–61
A Theory of Justice by, 359–61
Reading, of philosophy, 24–29
Reason
    belief without, 55, 95–106, 123
    faith and, 62–63, 75f
    Hume's argument about, 71
    morality based on, 132–33
    in philosophy, 14–24
Reasonable Faith (Craig), 67–68
Rebellion, against government, 354, 358
Rebirth, death and, 110–11
Reductio ad absurdum, 12–13, 39, 434
Reflective equilibrium, 140
Relations of ideas, 291–92, 294
Relativism. *See* Cognitive relativism;
        Cultural relativism; Subjective
        relativism
Religion. *See also* Buddhism
    acquired in childhood, 56, 58f
    belief in, 55–124
    dark side of, 56
    evaluation of, 56
    impact of, 55–56
    meaning of life from, 392–93, 392f,
        399–404, 400f, 402f–403f
    morality and, 141–42, 141f
    prayer and, 93, 93f
    symbols of, 62f
Religion and the Modern Mind (Stace),
    239–41
Religious experience
    argument from, 59–60, 122–23,
        125, 431
    conflicts among, 92, 94
    God, philosophy and, 89–95, 90f,
        93f, 122–23
    James on, 90
    Mackie and, 90
    Paul's, 89, 90f
    principle of credulity and, 90–92
    Swinburne on, 90–92, 94
    Teresa of Avila's, 89
    theism and, 89–95, 90f, 93f, 122–23
    validity of, 95
Religious hypothesis, 96–103
Representation (*mimesis*)
    art as, 322–23
    tragedy as, 326–29
The Republic (Plato), 10–11, 343–45, 343f
Research, for philosophy papers, 419
Resourcefulness, in moral problem-
        solving, 140

Respect for persons, principle of, 166–67
Responsibilities, family, 371–74
Retentionists, of capital punishment,
    154–55
Retributive justice, 340
Retributivism, 155
Revision, of philosophy papers, 421
Right action, 111–12
Right concentration, 112
Right effort, 112
Right livelihood, 112
Right mindfulness, 112
Rights
    abortion, 374
    morality based on, 163–68, 165f,
        167f, 188
    in political philosophy, 339, 353, 354,
        357–58, 359–61, 363, 368–69, 370,
        372–73, 374–75, 376–77–378
    to property, 353, 368–69
    utilitarianism rejecting, 167
    women's, 146–47, 146f
Right speech, 111
Right thought, 111
Right understanding, 111
Robots, 218–19, 218f
Rodin, Auguste, 323
Rousseau, Jean-Jacques, 308–9
Rowe, William L.
    argument from evil of, 80–83
    criticism of, 82
    Philosophy of Religion by, 80–83, 92
    "Two Concepts of Freedom" by, 242–43
Rule-utilitarianism
    consequences in, 150–51
    defined, 150, 190, 434
Russell, Bertrand, 4, 8, 11, 29, 68, 145,
    268, 277, 291

S

Sample, 20, 21
Sample philosophy paper, 422–24
Samsara (wandering), 110
Sartre, Jean-Paul, 249f, 343, 391
    "Existentialism Is a Humanism" by,
        250–53
    existentialism of, 180, 250–54
    hard determinism and, 253
    profound freedom of, 249–53, 256
Satan, in "A Little Omniscience Goes a
    Long Way," 258–60
Schick, Theodore, Jr., 203–4
Schooler, Jonathan W., 240–41
The School of Athens, 171f

Schopenhauer, Arthur, 212, 236, 396–97, 397*f*
Science
  Cartesian dualism incompatible with, 206–7
  data and, 137–40
  determinism and, 231, 235–36, 238
  in Enlightenment, 235
  evolution and, 76–77
  free will and, 231, 235–36, 238, 244
  quantum physics, 66, 68, 231, 232*f*, 235, 236
  theories in, 136–40
  uncaused universe and, 66
Searle, John R.
  biography of, 216, 216*f*
  Chinese Room of, 215–17
  Mind by, 207, 215–17
Secondary qualities, 284, 289–90
Second Noble Truth, 109
Second Treatise of Government (Locke)
  beginning of political societies in, 354–55
  dissolution of government in, 356–57
  end of political societies in, 355–56
Self
  Hume and, 108
  impermanence of, 108–9, 110
Self-determination, 229
Self-examination, 3
Sensations
  Berkeley and, 287–91
  errors of, 273–74, 276
  ideas and, 283–87
  objects conforming to mind in, 303–6
  of pain and pleasure, 285–86
"Sensations and Brain Processes" (Smart), 208–9
Sexual division of labor, 373, 374
Shafer-Landau, Russ
  The Fundamentals of Ethics by, 173–74
  Whatever Happened to Good and Evil? by, 141
Siddhartha Gautama, 107, 107*f*
Significant Form, 323, 325
Simplicity, 24, 74
Single-parent families, 371–72
Sisyphus, 180–82
Situated knowledge, 309
Skepticism
  defined, 264, 317, 434
  of Descartes, 273–75
  in empiricism, 268
  of Hume, 292–93, 295, 298–300

Kant and, 268, 300, 306
  problem of knowledge and, 264–65, 268
Skinner, B. F., 230
Slavery, 145, 145*f*
Slippery slope, 35, 39, 434
Smart, J. J. C., 208–9
Smith, Adam, 293
Social contract theory
  consent in, 339, 347, 354–57
  criticism of, 358, 359
  defined, 347, 379, 434
  equality of opportunity in, 360–61
  equal liberty principle of, 359–61
  of Hobbes, 348–53
  justice and, 347–61
  of Locke, 354–58
  overview of, 376–77
  political philosophy and, 347–61
  of Rawls, 340, 358–61
Socialism
  defined, 362, 379, 434
  U.S. and, 364
Socialist theories
  bourgeoisie in, 362–63, 365–69
  capitalism and, 362, 363
  communism and, 362–70
  criticism of, 363
  of Marx, 362–69
  means of production in, 362–64, 367
  overview of, 377
  in political philosophy, 362–69
  proletariat in, 362–63, 365–69
Social justice, feminism and, 370–75, 377–78. *See also* Distributive justice
Social reformers, 147–48, 160
Socrates, 3*f*, 171*f*
  Cafés, 12
  death of, 9, 10*f*, 44–52
  examined life and, 3, 8–13, 37, 50
  meaning from below and, 404
  morality and, 141
  Plato and, 8–11, 44–52, 141, 271–72, 315, 344–45, 423
  rationalism and, 271–72
  in *The Republic*, 10–11, 343–45
  in *The School of Athens*, 171*f*
  trial of, 8–9, 44–52
Socratic method, 8–9, 12, 39, 434
Software, mind as
  in mind–body problem, 200–201, 201*f*, 212–17, 214*f*–216*f*, 223
  strong AI and, 200–201, 201*f*, 215–17, 218

Soldiers, fatalism of, 233
Soul, immortal, 205, 205*f*
Soul-making defense, 85–88
Sound argument, 18
Spinoza, Baruch, 62, 267
Stace, Walter
  compatibilism and, 239–42
  Religion and the Modern Mind by, 229–41
Stanton, Elizabeth Cady, 404
"The Star" (Clarke, A. C.), 126–28
State. *See* Government
Statement, 14–15, 40, 434
State of nature, 349, 354, 355–59
Straw man, 29–30, 40, 434
Strong arguments, 17–18
Strong artificial intelligence (AI)
  ethics of, 218–19
  mind as software and, 200–201, 201*f*, 215–17, 218
Structure, of philosophy papers, 415–18
The Subjection of Women (Mill, J. S.), 160
Subjective idealism
  Berkeley and, 268
  defined, 268, 317, 434
Subjective relativism
  defined, 143, 190, 265, 317, 434
  infallibility problem of, 144–45
  moral relativism and, 143–45, 144*f*
  problem of knowledge and, 265–66
Subjectivism, 325, 329–31, 333
Subjectivity, 250–51
Substance dualism
  criticism of, 203–4, 206–7, 218
  defined, 198, 224, 434
  Descartes and, 198, 202–4, 206–7, 206*f*, 218, 222
  "ghost in the machine" in, 202
  mind–body problem in, 198, 202–7, 205*f*–206*f*, 222
  Plato and, 198
Suffering
  dukkha, 108–12
  from evil, 80–83
  Hick and, 86, 88
  meaning of life and, 396–97
Sumedho, Ajahn, 109
Summa Theologica (Aquinas), 41, 63–67
Support, probable, 17
Swinburne, Richard
  criteria of adequacy and, 74
  The Existence of God by, 94
  principle of credulity of, 90–92
  on religious experience, 90–92, 94

Symbolization, 18
Symbols, manipulation of, 217
Synthesis, 363
Synthetic statement, 300, 302, 317, 434

T
Taylor, Harriet, 160
Taylor, Richard, 246–48
Teleological arguments, 58–59, 122, 125, 434. *See also* Design arguments
Temple of the Dawn, 110*f*
"[Ten]10 Controversial Art Pieces" (Brooks), 322
Teresa of Avila (saint), 89
Theism
    defined, 61, 125, 434
    difficulty supporting, 401
    God, philosophy and, 89–95, 90*f*, 93*f*, 122–23
    religious experience and, 89–95, 90*f*, 93*f*, 122–23
Theist, 61, 125, 434
Theistic theory, 74
Theodicy, 61, 88, 125, 434
Theory. *See also specific theories*
    data and, 137–40
    of obligation, 136, 168–69, 172
A Theory of Justice (Rawls), 359–61
Thesis
    argument supporting, 362–63
    Marx and, 362
    statement, in philosophy papers, 416–17, 419–20
"They're Made Out of Meat" (Bisson), 225–26
The Thinker, 323
Third Noble Truth, 109–11
Thrasymachus, 10–13
Through the Looking Glass (Carroll), 318
Thyestes, 328
Titanic, 158
Tolerance, 149
Tolstoy, Leo, 323, 394*f*
    criticisms of, 401, 403
    faith of, 400–401
    My Confession by, 394–96, 399–401
    optimism of, 394, 399–401
    pessimism of, 394–96, 399–401
Topic selection, for philosophy papers, 418–19
Traditional compatibilism, 231–32, 238–43
Traditional epistemology, 309–10
Tragedies, 326–29

Transplants, organ, 346, 346*f*
Trial, of Socrates, 8–9, 44–52
"The Trial and Death of Socrates" (Plato), 44–52
"Troubles with Functionalism" (Block), 214
Tryon, Edward, 66
Turing, Alan, 215, 215*f*
Turing test, 215–17
"Two Concepts of Freedom" (Rowe), 242–43
Two Treatises of Government (Locke), 354f. *See also Second Treatise of Government*

U
Uncaused universe, 66–68
United States (U.S.)
    atheism in, 57
    belief in God in, 57
    Declaration of Independence of, 339, 339*f*, 354
    as libertarian paradise, 363
    political views in, 341, 341*f*
    socialism and, 364
Universal consent, 282
Universals, 270
Universe. *See also* Design arguments
    Big Bang theory of, 67–68, 67*f*
    Hawking and, 69*f*
    imperfections in, 71–74, 72*f*
    in machine-universe analogy, 71, 72
    many designers of, 72–74
    oscillating, 67
    uncaused, 66–68
Unnecessary evil, 61, 63
U.S. *See* United States
Utilitarianism
    act-utilitarianism, 150–52, 151*f*, 189, 431
    Bentham's, 152, 160
    classic, 152
    consequences in, 135, 137, 150–59, 151*f*, 154*f*
    death penalty and, 154–55, 154*f*
    defined, 135, 190, 434
    ethical egoism and, 159
    happiness in, 152–59
    justice and, 340
    Kant and, 167
    of Mill, John Stuart, 153–57
    as moral theory, 135, 136, 137, 150–59, 434
    objections to, 158–59

proof of, 157
    rights rejected in, 167
    rule-utilitarianism, 150–51, 190, 434
Utility, principle of, 150

V
Valid arguments, 17–19, 21
Van Gogh, Vincent, 323
Van Inwagen, Peter, 245
Veil of ignorance, 359–60
Venus de Milo, 323
Vermeer, Johannes, 323
Virtue ethics
    Aristotle and, 169–72
    character in, 169–74, 171*f*
    criticism of, 172–74
    defined, 136, 169, 190, 434
    divine command theory and, 173–74
    duty and, 169, 172–73
    as moral theory, 136, 169–74, 434
    Shafer-Landau and, 173–74
Virtue-oriented theories, 136–37, 434
Virtues
    conflict among, 172–73
    golden mean of, 171
Visions, 90
Vohs, Kathleen D., 240–41
Volition-enabling properties, 248
Voltaire, 408–9
Voluntary action, 242

W
Walden II (Skinner), 230
War, in *Leviathan*, 351–52
Warhol, Andy, 325, 325*f*
Warren, Rick, 402
Washington, George, 404
Watch analogy, 58–59, 69–70
Wax, melting, 279–80, 280*f*
Weak arguments, 17
Welfare assistance, 340, 342, 342*f*
Welfare liberalism, 361, 379, 434
Whatever Happened to Good and Evil? (Shafer-Landau), 141
"What Is It Like to Be a Bat?" (Nagel), 211
What's It All About? (Baggini), 397–99, 403–4, 403*f*
What the Buddha Taught (Rahula), 109–10
"What Utilitarianism Is" (Mill, J. S.), 153–57
When Bad Things Happen to Good People (Kushner), 63

The Whys of a Philosophical Scrivener
    (Gardner), 324
Wisdom, 111–12
Wollstonecraft, Mary, 312, 312*f*
Women
    Aristotle and, 308, 310
    Hume and, 308
    Kant and, 309

as lawyers, 374
Locke and, 308
Mill, John Stuart, and,
    160, 308
Plato and, 308
prejudice and, 307–9
rights of, cultural relativism
    and, 146, 146*f*, 147

World, conceptualization of, 304–5,
    304*f*–305*f*
Writing instructions, for philosophy
    papers, 418–24

Z
Zoe (personal life of eternal worth), 87
Zombies, possibility of, 209–10, 211*f*